THE UNBOUND PROMETHEUS

*Technological change and industrial
development in Western Europe
from 1750 to the present*

DAVID S. LANDES

Professor of History, Harvard University

*The right of the
University of Cambridge
to print and sell
all manner of books
was granted by
Henry VIII in 1534.
The University has printed
and published continuously
since 1584.*

CAMBRIDGE UNIVERSITY PRESS

CAMBRIDGE

NEW YORK   NEW ROCHELLE   MELBOURNE   SYDNEY

Published by the Press Syndicate of the University of Cambridge
The Pitt Building, Trumpington Street, Cambridge CB2 1RP
32 East 57th Street, New York, N.Y. 10022
10 Stamford Road, Oakleigh, Melbourne 3166, Australia

First published 1969
Reprinted 1970, 1972, 1975, 1976,
1977, 1978, 1979, 1980, 1981, 1982,
1985, 1986, 1987 (twice), 1988

Printed in the United States of America

Library of Congress Catalogue Card Number: 68-21194

ISBN 0 521 07200 X hard covers
ISBN 0 521 09418 6 Paperback

Chapters 2-5 and the Conclusions are revised versions of material first published
in chapter 5 of *The Cambridge Economic History of Europe,* volume 6, part I

To my Parents

CONTENTS

PREFACE

This study has a long history. It goes back to 1954, when Professor M. M. Postan asked me to write a chapter on technological change and industrial development in western Europe for the Cambridge Economic History. The subject was vast and I was soon caught up in the seamless web of the historian's history; so that by the time I had reached what seemed to me to be a convenient stopping place—that point, around 1870, when the leading industrial nations of continental Europe had effected their own breakthroughs to a modern economic system and were prepared to compete with Britain on even terms—I had far exceeded the space originally allotted to me. Even so, the editors of the Cambridge Economic History felt that it was not a good idea for my chapter to deviate in this manner from the general pattern of the larger volume, which was to take the story into the twentieth century; and they asked me to add a section on the period from 1870 to World War I. This was in 1958. I submitted a draft of the additional material in 1960, revised it somewhat in 1961-2, and the entire essay finally appeared in Volume VI of the Cambridge Economic History in 1965. Publication is a long and painful parturition.

By this time, what had begun as a chapter was as long as a book, and I thought, as did a number of readers, that it ought to appear as such. For one thing, the story was one that could stand on its own, even though certain aspects of European development—in particular, agriculture, transportation, population—had been reserved by the editors for treatment in other chapters; hence the deliberate use of 'Industrial Development' in the title. For another, there was a manifest need for a general, truly comparative survey of the course of the European industrial revolution. The nearest thing to this in English has been the textbooks in economic history currently used in American colleges and universities, but a textbook has very different objectives from an interpretive essay, and these in any case go back to before World War II. Since Volume VI of the Cambridge Economic History (a double volume) is too costly for all but the most affluent students, it seemed desirable to bring the essay out separately in a less expensive format. The officers of the Cambridge University Press were good enough to accept this reasoning and encourage me in this project.

The prospect of a new edition of the essay immediately posed a difficult choice. On the one hand, the officers of the Press felt that the book would have considerably more usefulness if the story could be brought up to date, and this entailed a substantial research and writing commitment at a time when new university and personal obligations left me even less free time than usual. On the other, here was an opportunity to revise the original text to take into account the new work in European economic history that had appeared since the first writing; and given the time that had elapsed and the rapid pace of research in this field, this too was a large task. It was clear, however, that any effort to do both would delay publication considerably.

I chose to do the former, that is, bring the story up to the present, on the ground that this would do more to meet the specific needs of the constituency to which the book is directed. It remains my intention to bring out a fully revised version of the original essay. What I should like to do is not only add and modify as required by the latest findings, but broaden the geographical perspective and give more attention to the countries on the periphery of the western European industrial heartland: Scandinavia, Holland, the Mediterranean countries, the area once comprised in the Austrian empire. This, I fear, will be an even bigger job than the preparation of the chapters on the period since 1914. In the meantime, I have made a few changes in that part of the text that deals with the Industrial Revolution in Britain. This was the oldest part (the first draft goes back to 1957); also it deals with the area where research has been most active and productive. These changes, however, are not the equivalent of a systematic revision. Rather they reflect some of my own special interests and are unevenly dispersed through the chapter. The other sections remain as before, save for some corrections of errors of fact or print.

Given the format of the Cambridge Economic History, I was not able, at the time of publication of the original essay, to thank the many institutions and persons who had assisted me in its preparation and writing. The list of obligations has since grown much longer, and I am delighted to have this opportunity to express my gratitude. I shall not try to list by name the individuals who helped me with their criticism and counsel. The list would be far too long, and in view of the history of this project, I would inevitably commit the injustice of omitting some. Suffice it to say that I have profited from the knowledge and wisdom of some of the best men in history, economics, economic history, and related disciplines; and that whatever the merits or defects of this essay, it is far better than it would have been had I been confined to my own resources. To all of these friends and colleagues, I am grateful.

I should also like to express my gratitude to those institutions and foundations that made it possible for me to do this research and live and consult with other scholars; the Center for Advanced Study in the Behavioral Sciences in Stanford, California (I was a fellow of the class of 1957-8, which brought together one of the most brilliant groups of economists ever assembled in one place for a protracted period of dialogue and interaction); the Institute of Industrial Relations of the University of California, Berkeley; the Rockefeller Foundation; the Social Science Research Council; the Program for Technology and Society of Harvard University (I have had the good fortune to participate in an interdisciplinary Study Group that has done much to clarify for me the course and character of contemporary technological change); and two informal dinner groups of economists and economic historians—the first a Berkeley–Stanford partnership, the second a union of interested persons from Harvard and M.I.T. In all of these contexts I have never failed to receive the kind of keen, candid criticism that is the hallmark of true friendship and disinterested scholarship.

Finally, I want to express special thanks to two friends who have been engaged with me in the preparation of another work, a history of the Berlin banking house of S. Bleichröder: Prof. Fritz Stern of Columbia University and Mr F. H. Brunner of Arnhold and S. Bleichröder, New York. They have stood by patiently and understandingly while I devoted a large share of my free time to a project that has proved far bigger than I had originally anticipated. I only hope I can repay them.

D.S.L.

Harvard University
April 1968

CHAPTER I

Introduction

When dealing with ambiguous terms, the first duty of a writer is definition. The words 'industrial revolution'—in small letters—usually refer to that complex of technological innovations which, by substituting machines for human skill and inanimate power for human and animal force, brings about a shift from handicraft to manufacture and, so doing, gives birth to a modern economy. In this sense, the industrial revolution has already transformed a number of countries, though in unequal degree; other societies are in the throes of change; the turn of still others is yet to come.

The words sometimes have another meaning. They are used to denote any rapid significant technological change, and historians have spoken of an 'industrial revolution of the thirteenth century', an 'early industrial revolution', the 'second industrial revolution', an 'industrial revolution in the cotton south'. In this sense, we shall eventually have as many 'revolutions' as there are historically demarcated sequences of industrial innovation, plus all such sequences as will occur in the future; there are those who say, for example, that we are already in the midst of the third industrial revolution, that of automation, air transport, and atomic power.

Finally, the words, when capitalized, have still another meaning. They denote the first historical instance of the breakthrough from an agrarian, handicraft economy to one dominated by industry and machine manufacture. The Industrial Revolution began in England in the eighteenth century, spread therefrom in unequal fashion to the countries of Continental Europe and a few areas overseas, and transformed in the span of scarce two lifetimes the life of Western man, the nature of his society, and his relationship to the other peoples of the world. The Industrial Revolution, as it took place in western Europe, is the subject of this book.

The heart of the Industrial Revolution was an interrelated succession of technological changes. The material advances took place in three areas: (1) there was a substitution of mechanical devices for human skills; (2) inanimate power—in particular, steam—took the place of human and animal strength; (3) there was a marked improvement in the getting and working of raw materials, especially in what are now known as the metallurgical and chemical industries.

Concomitant with these changes in equipment and process went new forms of industrial organization. The size of the productive unit grew: machines and power both required and made possible the concentration of manufacture, and shop and home workroom gave way to mill and factory. At the same time, the factory was more than just a larger work unit. It was a system of production, resting on a characteristic definition of the functions and responsibilities of the different participants in the productive process. On the one side was the employer, who not only hired the labour and marketed the finished product, but supplied the capital equipment and oversaw its use. On the other side there stood the worker, no longer capable of owning and furnishing the means of production and reduced to the status of a hand (the word is significant and symbolizes well this transformation from producer to pure labourer). Binding them were the economic relationship—the 'wage nexus'—and the functional one of supervision and discipline.

Discipline, of course, was not entirely new. Certain kinds of work—large construction projects, for example—had always required the direction and co-ordination of the efforts of many people; and well before the Industrial Revolution there were a number of large workshops or 'manufactories' in which traditional unmechanized labour operated under supervision. Yet discipline under such circumstances was comparatively loose (there is no overseer so demanding as the steady click-clack of the machine); and such as it was, it affected only a small portion of the industrial population.

Factory discipline was another matter. It required and eventually created a new breed of worker, broken to the inexorable demands of the clock. It also held within itself the seeds of further technological advance, for control of labour implies the possibility of the rationalization of labour. From the start, the specialization of productive functions was pushed farther in the factory than it had been in shops and cottages; at the same time, the difficulties of manipulating men and materials within a limited area gave rise to improvements in layout and organization. There is a direct chain of innovation from the efforts to arrange the manufacturing process so that the raw material would move downwards in the plant as it was treated, to the assembly line and transmission belts of today.

In all of this diversity of technological improvement, the unity of the movement is apparent: change begat change. For one thing, many technical improvements were feasible only after advances in associated fields. The steam engine is a classic example of this technological interrelatedness: it was impossible to produce an effective condensing engine until better methods of metal working could turn out accurate cylinders. For another, the gains in productivity and output of a given innovation inevitably exerted pressure on related industrial operations. The demand for coal pushed mines deeper until water seepage became a serious hazard; the answer was the creation of a more efficient pump, the atmospheric steam engine. A cheap supply of coal proved a godsend to the iron industry, which was stifling for lack of fuel. In the meantime, the invention and diffusion of machinery in the textile manufacture and other industries created a new demand for energy, hence for coal and steam engines; and these engines, and the machines themselves, had a voracious appetite for iron, which called for further coal and power. Steam also made possible the factory city, which used unheard-of quantities of iron (hence coal) in its many-storied mills and its water and sewage systems. At the same time, the processing of the flow of manufactured commodities required great amounts of chemical substances: alkalis, acids, and dyes, many of them consuming mountains of fuel in the making. And all of these products—iron, textiles, chemicals—depended on large-scale movements of goods on land and on sea, from the sources of the raw materials into the factories and out again to near and distant markets. The opportunity thus created and the possibilities of the new technology combined to produce the railroad and steamship, which of course added to the demand for iron and fuel while expanding the market for factory products. And so on, in ever-widening circles.

In this sense, the Industrial Revolution marked a major turning point in man's history. To that point, the advances of commerce and industry, however gratifying and impressive, had been essentially superficial: more wealth, more goods, prosperous cities, merchant nabobs. The world had seen other periods of industrial prosperity—in medieval Italy and Flanders, for example—and had seen the line of economic advance recede in each case; in the absence of qualitative changes, of improvements in productivity, there could be no guarantee that mere quantitative gains would be consolidated. It was the Industrial Revolution that initiated a cumulative, self-sustaining advance in technology whose repercussions would be felt in all aspects of economic life.

To be sure, opportunity is not necessarily achievement. Economic progress has been uneven, marked by spurts and recessions, and there is no reason to be complacent about the prospect of an indefinite climb. For one thing, technological advance is not a smooth, balanced process. Each innovation seems to have a life span of its own, comprising periods of tentative youth, vigorous maturity, and declining old age. As its technological possibilities are realized, its marginal yield diminishes and it gives way to newer, more advantageous techniques. By the same token, the divers branches of production that embody these techniques follow their own logistic curve of growth toward a kind of asymptote.

Thus the climb of those industries that were at the heart of the Industrial Revolution—textiles, iron and steel, heavy chemicals, steam engineering, railway transport—began to slow toward the end of the nineteenth century in the most advanced west European countries, so much so that some observers feared that the whole system was running down. (At this point, the Industrial Revolution in these countries was substantially complete.) Similar dire prognoses accompanied the world depression of the 1930's, particularly by those Marxist critics who saw the capitalist economy as incapable of sustained creativity. In fact, however, the advanced industrial economies have given proof of considerable technological vitality. The declining momentum of the early-modernizing branches in the late nineteenth century was more than compensated by the rise of new industries based on spectacular advances in chemical and electrical science and on a new, mobile source of power—the internal combusion engine. This is the cluster of innovations that is often designated as the second industrial revolution. Similarly, the contraction of the 1930's has been followed by decades of unusual creativity, consisting once again primarily in innovations in the application of chemical and electrical science, plus advances in the generation and delivery of power —the abovementioned third industrial revolution.

A more serious cause of concern lies outside the productive system proper—in the area of political economy and politics *tout court*. Even assuming that the ingenuity of scientists and engineers will always generate new ideas to relay the old and that they will find ways to overcome such shortages as may develop (whether of food, water, or industrial raw materials), there is no assurance that those men charged with utilizing these ideas will do so intelligently—intelligently, that is, not only in the sense of effective exploitation of their productive possibilities but in the larger sense of effective adaptation to the material and human environment so as to minimize waste, pollution, social friction, and other 'external' costs. Similarly, there is no assurance that noneconomic exogenous factors—above all, man's incompetence in dealing with his fellow-man—will not reduce the whole magnificent structure to dust.

In the meantime, however, the climb has been spectacular. Improvements in productivity of the order of several thousand to one have been achieved in certain sectors—prime movers and spinning for example. In other areas, gains have been less impressive only by comparison: of the order of hundreds to one in weaving, or iron smelting, or shoemaking. Some areas, to be sure, have seen relatively little change: it still takes about as much time to shave a man as it did in the eighteenth century.

Quantitative gains in productivity are, of course, only part of the picture. Modern technology produces not only more, faster; it turns out objects that could not have been produced under any circumstances by the craft methods of yesterday. The best Indian hand spinner could not turn out yarn so fine and regular as that of the mule; all the forges in eighteenth-century Christendom could not have produced steel sheets so large, smooth, and homogeneous as those of a modern strip mill. Most important, modern technology has created things that could scarcely have been conceived in the pre-industrial era: the camera, the motor car, the aeroplane, the whole array of electronic devices from the radio to the high-speed computer, the nuclear power plant, and so on almost *ad infinitum*. Indeed, one of the primary stimuli of modern technology is free-ranging imagination; the increasing autonomy of pure science and the accumulation of a pool of untapped knowledge, in combination with the ramifying stock of established technique, have given ever wider scope to the inventive vision. Finally, to this array of new and better products—introduced, to be sure, at the expense of some of the more artistic results of hand craftsmanship—should be added that great range of exotic commodities, once rarities or luxuries, that are now available at reasonable prices thanks to improved transportation. It took the Industrial Revolution to make tea and coffee, the banana of Central America and the pineapple of Hawaii everyday foods. The result has been an enormous increase in the output and variety of goods and services, and this alone has changed man's way of life more than anything since the discovery of fire: the Englishman of 1750 was closer in material things to Caesar's legionnaires than to his own great-grand-children.

These material advances in turn have provoked and promoted a large complex of economic, social, political, and cultural changes, which have reciprocally influenced the rate and course of technological development. There is, first, the transformation that we know as *industrialization*. This is the industrial revolution, in the specifically technological sense, plus its economic consequences, in particular the movement of labour and resources from agriculture to industry. The shift reflects the interaction of enduring characteristics of demand with the changing conditions of supply engendered by the industrial revolution. On the demand side, the nature of human wants is such that rises in income increase the appetite for food less than for manufactures. This is not true of people who have been living on the borderline of subsistence; they may use any extra money to eat better. But most Europeans were living above this level on the eve of industrialization; and although they did spend more for food as income went up, their expenditures on manufactures increased even faster. On the supply side, this shift in demand was reinforced by the relatively larger gains in industrial as against

agricultural productivity, with a consequent fall in the price of manufactures relative to that of primary products.

Whether this disparity is inherent in the character of the industrial
process, in other words, whether manufacture is intrinsically more susceptible of technological improvement than cultivation and husbandry,
is an interesting but moot question. The fact remains that in the period
of the Industrial Revolution and subsequently, industry moved ahead
faster, increased its share of national wealth and product, and drained
away the labour of the countryside. The shift varied from one country
to another, depending on comparative advantage and institutional resistance. It was most extreme in Britain, where free trade stripped the
farmer of protection against overseas competition; by 1912, only 12
per cent of Britain's labour force was employed in agriculture; by 1951,
the proportion had fallen to an almost irreducible 5 per cent. And it
was slowest in France, a country of small landholders, where a more
gradual introduction of the new industrial technology combined with
high tariffs on food imports to retard the contraction of the primary
sector. Over half the French labour force was in agriculture in 1789
(perhaps 55 per cent or more), and this was still true in 1866, after three
quarters of a century of technological change; as recently as 1950, the
proportion was still a third.[1]

Industrialization in turn is at the heart of a larger, more complex
process often designated as *modernization*. This is that combination of
changes—in the mode of production and government, in the social and
institutional order, in the corpus of knowledge and in attitudes and
values—that makes it possible for a society to hold its own in the twentieth century; that is, to compete on even terms in the generation of
material and cultural wealth, to sustain its independence, and to promote and accommodate to further change. Modernization comprises
such developments as urbanization (the concentration of the population
in cities that serve as nodes of industrial production, administration, and
intellectual and artistic activity); a sharp reduction in both death rates
and birth rates from traditional levels (the so-called demographic transition); the establishment of an effective, fairly centralized bureaucratic
government; the creation of an educational system capable of training
and socializing the children of the society to a level compatible with
their capacities and best contemporary knowledge; and of course, the
acquisition of the ability and means to use an up-to-date technology.

All of these elements are interdependent, as will become apparent in

[1] Simon Kuznets, *Six Lectures on Economic Growth* (Glencoe, Ill. 1959), pp. 50–1;
J. C. Toutain, *La population de la France de 1700 à 1959* [J. Marczewski, ed., *Histoire
quantitative de l'économie française*, vol. III], in *Cahiers de l'Institut de Sciences Economiques
Appliquées*, Series AF, no. 3, Suppl. no. 133 (January, 1963), p. 127.

the discussion that follows, but each is to some degree autonomous, and it is quite possible to move ahead in some areas while lagging in others—witness some of the so-called developing or emerging nations of today. The one ingredient of modernization that is just about indispensable is technological maturity and the industrialization that goes with it; otherwise one has the trappings without the substance, the pretence without the reality.

It was Europe's good fortune that technological change and industrialization preceded or accompanied *pari passu* the other components of modernization, so that on the whole she was spared the material and psychic penalties of unbalanced maturation. The instances of marked discrepancy that come to mind—the effort of Peter to force the westernization of a servile society in Russia, the explosion of population in Ireland in a primitive and poor agricultural environment, the urbanization of Mediterranean Europe in the context of a pre-industrial economy—yielded a harvest of death, misery, and enduring resentment.

Even so, industrial Europe had its own growing pains, which were moderate only by comparison with extreme cases of accelerated modernization or with the deep poverty and suffering of that outer world (the so-called Third World) of technologically backward, non-industrializing societies in Asia, Africa, and Latin America. For one thing, if mechanization opened new vistas of comfort and prosperity for all men, it also destroyed the livelihood of some and left others to vegetate in the backwaters of the stream of progress. Change is demonic; it creates, but it also destroys, and the victims of the Industrial Revolution were numbered in the hundreds of thousands or even millions. (On the other hand, many of these would have been even worse off without industrialization.) By the same token, the Industrial Revolution tended, especially in its earlier stages, to widen the gap between rich and poor and sharpen the cleavage between employer and employed, thereby opening the door to class conflicts of unprecedented bitterness. It did not create the first true industrial proletariat: the blue-nails of medieval Flanders and the Ciompi of the Florence of the *quattrocento* are earlier examples of landless workers with nothing to sell but their labour. Indeed, as we shall see, the putting-out system was in its day as productive of class hostility as the factory. But the eighteenth and nineteenth centuries did see the growth of a working class more numerous and concentrated than ever before. And with size and concentration came slums and class consciousness, workers' parties and radical panaceas.

In similar fashion, the Industrial Revolution generated painful changes in the structure of power. It did not create the first capitalists, but it did produce a business class of unprecedented numbers and strength. The hegemony of landed wealth, long threatened by the mobile fortunes of commerce but never overturned, yielded to the assaults of the new chimney aristocrats. Largely as the result of a series of revolutions, domestic government policy came to be determined in most of western Europe by the manufacturing interest and its allies in trade and finance, with or without the co-operation of the older landed establishment. In central Europe—Germany and Austria–Hungary—the picture was different: the attempt at revolution failed, and the aristocracy continued to hold the reins of government; business ambitions were subordinated to, rather than identified with, the goals of unity and power. Even there, however, the growing wealth and influence of the industrial and commercial bourgeoisie was apparent in the course of legislation and in the penetration by parvenus of the social and occupational strongholds of the old elites. In the course of the nineteenth century, much of the privileged knights' land (*Rittergüter*) of east-Elbian Prussia came into the hands of commoners; while from 1870 to 1913, the proportion of aristocrats in the officer corps of the Prussian army fell from 70 to 30 per cent.[1]

To be sure, this kind of victory often spelled a kind of defeat: the rising bourgeois could be more snobbish than the blooded nobleman, stiffer and more arrogant than a Junker guardsman. Whereas in Britain and France, the new business elite competed for power, in Germany they acquiesced in the status quo and sold their liberal birthright for a mess of chauvinistic pottage seasoned by commercial legislation and administration favourable to business enterprise. The fact remains that they did have to be bought off; and indeed everywhere the balance of status and power shifted, in greater or lesser degree, from the older landed elite toward the new rich of industry and trade.

Two of the factors conducing in this direction were the separation of the aristocracy from the mass of the country population and the general decline of rural forces in national life. Partly (though only partly) owing to industrialization, the traditional system of land tenure, with its vestiges of feudal privileges and its tenacious communal rights, was replaced by one of unlimited ownership of enclosed parcels. A certain amount of the traditional paternalistic authority of the 'lord of the manor' was lost in the process, especially in those regions where the changed was forced. Even more important, however, was a progressive anaemia of rural life: on the one hand, a massive exodus to the cities at the expense of marginal lands; on the other, an invasion of agricultural areas by industry—how green was my valley!

The growth of a factory proletariat, the rise of the industrial bour-

[1] Hans Rosenberg, 'Die Pseudodemokratisierung der Rittergutsbesitzerklasse', in H. U. Wehler, ed., *Moderne deutsche Sozialgeschichte* (Cologne and Berlin, 1966), pp. 287–308; Karl Demeter, *Das deutsche Offizierkorps in Gesellschaft und Staat 1650–1945* (Frankfurt-am-Main, 1962), p. 26.

geoisie and its progressive merger with the old elite, the ebbing resistance of the peasantry to the lure of the city and to the competition of new ways and a new scale of cultivation—all of these trends encouraged some observers to predict a polarization of society between a large mass of exploited wage earners and a small group of exploiting owners of the means of production. The trend to size and concentration seemed inexorable and pervasive. Every advance in technology seemed to hurt the ability of the small, independent operator to survive in the impersonally competitive market place.

Yet this was a serious misreading of the course of change. Mass production and urbanization stimulated, indeed required, wider facilities for distribution, a larger credit structure, an expansion of the educational system, the assumption of new functions by government. At the same time, the increase in the standard of living due to higher productivity created new wants and made possible new satisfactions, which led to a spectacular flowering of those businesses that cater to human pleasure and leisure: entertainment, travel, hotels, restaurants, and so on. Thus the growth of a factory labour force was matched by a proliferation of service and professional people, white-collar workers, functionaries, engineers, and similar servants of the industrial system and society. Indeed, as productivity rose and the standard of living with it, this administrative and service sector of the economy—what some economists have called the tertiary sector—grew more rapidly than industry itself.

In sum, the Industrial Revolution created a society of greater richness and complexity. Instead of polarizing it into bourgeois minority and an almost all-embracing proletariat, it produced a heterogeneous bourgeoisie whose multitudinous shadings of income, origin, education, and way of life are overridden by a common resistance to inclusion in, or confusion with, the working classes, and by an unquenchable social ambition.

For the essence of the bourgeois is that he is what the sociologists call upwardly mobile; and nothing has ever furnished so many opportunities to rise in the social scale as the Industrial Revolution. Not everyone seized these opportunities. For many, the shift from country to city, from farm to industry or trade, marked simply the exchange of one labouring status for another. The factory worker could be, and usually was, as tradition-bound in his expectations for himself and his children as the peasant. But for thousands, the move to town, or often to another region or country, marked a decisive break with the past; the migrant found himself afloat in a fluid society. Some rose and founded unexampled fortunes in their own lifetimes; others climbed slowly, generation by generation. For many, education was the open-sesame to higher status, and this channel was in itself evidence of the more explicit functional requirements of a technologically advanced society. More and more, it became important to choose someone for a job or place on universalistic rather than particularistic grounds, on the basis of what he could do rather than who he was or whom he knew.

But universalism cuts both ways. While some rise on merit, others must fall; some succeed, but others fail. It has been said of political revolutions that they devour their children. So do economic revolutions. Thus the small machines of the early Industrial Revolution were succeeded by big ones; the little mills became giant factories; the modest partnerships were converted to large public companies; the victims and laggards of the early decades were succeeded by new victims and laggards. The resulting concentration of enterprise in certain sectors of the economy did not displace the small firm or make it obsolete. The very forces that promoted industrial and commercial giantism opened new possibilities for small ventures: service enterprises, distribution agencies, subcontractors, and so on. The fact remains, however, that smaller firms in traditional lines were pressed hard by bigger and more efficient competitors; many collapsed in spite of all the resistance, ingenuity, and sacrifice that old-style family enterprises are capable of. Both casualties and survivors proved easy converts for the preachers of discontent and reaction: in some countries they turned the government into the instrument of vested interests; in others, they became the troops of right-wing revolution.

For if the first effect of the Industrial Revolution was to shift drastically the balance of political power in favour of the commercial and industrial classes, subsequent economic development raised up new enemies of the liberal, parliamentary system that was the symbol and instrument of bourgeois government. On the one hand, there was concentrated, class-conscious industrial labour; on the other, the bourgeois victims of economic and social change: the marginal entrepreneurs, the discontented, the *déclassés*. Between the two extremes the gulf widened, as each reacted to the other. The World War brought the latent conflict to a head by stimulating the demands of labour while ravaging the savings of the bourgeoisie. In all countries, the postwar years saw a flow of political power outward from the centre to the extremes. In a nation like England, the result was a new party alignment and gradual movement to a new position of compromise. In countries like Germany and Italy, the resolution was more radical. In France, the centrifugal trend was countered by the distraction of logrolling; the heterogeneous special interests of the bourgeoisie found a *modus vivendi* in the manipulation of government on behalf of the status quo and at the expense of a divided labour movement.

In each case, of course, the nature of the political adaptation to the economic changes wrought by the Industrial Revolution was a function of the existing political structure and traditions, social attitudes, the particular effects of the war, and the differential character of economic development. For the Industrial Revolution, as we shall see, was not a uniform wave of change; nor did it roll up on like shores. On the contrary, it came to a great variety of places, with differing resources, economic traditions, social values, entrepreneurial aptitudes, and technological skills.

This unevenness of timing and distribution in turn has had the most serious consequences. Politically it has meant a complete revision of the balance of power. The basis of military strength has shifted from sheer numbers—and tactical inspiration—to industrial capacity, particularly the ability to turn out guns and munitions and move them to combat. Money was once the sinews of war because it could buy men; now it must produce fire power as well. As a result, the nineteenth century saw a unified Germany rise to Continental hegemony on the strength of the Ruhr and Silesia; while France, slower to industrialize, was never again to enjoy the pre-eminence to which the *levée en masse* and the genius of Napoleon had raised her on the eve of economic revolution. With the spread of the new techniques, moreover, new powers arose: the twentieth century saw the millennial predominance of Europe dwindle before the unprecedented might of the United States and Soviet Russia.

At the same time, the technological gap has made possible and economic interest has called forth a spectacular expansion of Western power in the preindustrial areas of the world; in this respect, the Industrial Revolution consummated the process begun by the voyages and overseas conquests of the fifteenth and sixteenth centuries. And while in recent decades the tide of imperial dominion has receded, it has left its indelible imprint wherever its waters have rolled: all of the undeveloped countries of the globe are converted to the religions of industry and wealth with a faith that surpasses that of their teachers. Never in the thousands of years of contact between civilizations has one of them enjoyed such universal success.

Yet up to now, at least, faith has not been enough. The nations of the Third World have yet to effect their industrial revolution, and the gulf in wealth and standard of living between them and the economically advanced countries has increased to the point of scandal and danger. The disparity has been aggravated by the partial character of their modernization. The West has brought them lower death rates, but not lower birth rates; so that population growth has eaten up, and in some instances outstripped, their gains in income. The West has provided them with some education—enough to know their dependence and to dream of freedom, but not enough to create and operate a modern economy. It has given them a distorted underview, the view from the kitchen, the mine, and the labour camp, of the potentialities and rewards of an industrial technology—a tantalizing taste of what seems to be a material paradise; but it has not given them the means to satisfy the appetite thus engendered. It has also left them a memory of brutality and humiliation, a stain that some have argued can be erased only in blood.[1]

This is not to imply that the conduct of colonial powers has always been reprehensible or the consequences of their rule invariably bad. On the contrary, one could argue that many of the colonial peoples were better off under European rule than they have been since independence. But as we all know, the evil that men do lives after them; besides, most of the peoples in the world (with the possible exception of Puerto Rico) have opted for freedom even in mediocrity as against prosperity in subordination.

The explosive implications of this legacy of jealousy, frustration, hatred and alienation need not be laboured here.

In sum, the Industrial Revolution has been like in effect to Eve's tasting of the fruit of the tree of knowledge: the world has never been the same. (There is no point in arguing here whether the change is for the better or the worse. The question is one of ends more than means and has its place in moral philosophy, not economic history.)

★   ★   ★   ★

So much for the wider historical implications of the Industrial Revolution. For the economic historian *qua* economist, the problem has another side. His concern is with the processes of industrial change as such: how did they occur? why did they move faster in some places than others? why did they take different forms in different economies? In short, he is interested in the causes and process of growth.

From this point of view, the Industrial Revolution poses two problems: (1) why did this first breakthrough to a modern industrial system take place in western Europe? and (2) why, within this European experience, did change occur when and where it did?

The essay that follows is concerned with the second of these questions; but it will not be amiss to consider the first by way of introduction.

The first point that needs to be made is that Europe on the eve of the Industrial Revolution was a society that had already advanced a long

[1] The most powerful and popular expression of this thesis is the late Frantz Fanon's *Les damnés de la terre* (English translation: *The Wretched of the Earth* [London, 1965]).

way economically beyond the level of minimal subsistence. The significance of this advance is apparent from a comparison of such estimates as we can make of income per head in eighteenth-century England, say, and pre-industrial economies of the twentieth century. Phyllis Deane, who bases her calculations on the estimates of contemporary observers, tells us that the average for England and Wales at the end of the seventeenth century was about £9 per year;[1] in the 1750's, between £12 and £13. Given the revolution in consumption that has taken place since then, it is hazardous to convert these sums into their twentieth-century equivalents; but on the reasonable assumption that money was worth at least eight times as much 200 and 250 years ago (Miss Deane's multiplier of six is far too low), we are talking of incomes of about £70 in 1700, £100 a half-century later. Comparable figures for the France of the eighteenth century have to be inferred from even more precarious 'guesstimates'; but it seems reasonable to suppose that income per head was moderately lower than in Britain at the beginning and that it kept pace fairly well until the last quarter of the century.[2] By comparison, average annual income in Nigeria, one of the richer African countries, was about £30 per head in the early 1960's, while that of India was even lower—about £25. To find something comparable to the western European level of two centuries ago, one has to look at the already semi-industrialized countries of Latin America: Brazilian income *per capita* was some £95 per annum in 1961; Mexican income, about £105.[3]

Western Europe, in other words, was already rich before the Industrial Revolution—rich by comparison with other parts of the world of that day and with the pre-industrial world of today. This wealth was the product of centuries of slow accumulation, based in turn on investment, the appropriation of extra-European resources and labour, and

[1] Deane, *The First Industrial Revolution* (Cambridge, 1965), p. 6; cf. her earlier article, 'The Implications of Early National Income Estimates for the Measurement of Long-Term Economic Growth in the United Kingdom', *Econ. Devel. and Cult. Change*, IV, no. 1 (1955).
[2] In 1688, Gregory King estimated that income per head in Britain was higher than anywhere else in Europe except Holland; and that it was 20 per cent above that of France. On the course of French and British economic growth in the eighteenth century, see François Crouzet, 'Angleterre et France au XVIIIᵉ siècle: essai d'analyse comparée de deux croissances économiques', *Annales; économies, sociétés, civilisations,* XXI (1966), 270. J. Marczewski, 'Le produit physique de l'économie française de 1789 à 1913', *Histoire quantitative de l'économie française (Cahiers de l'I.S.E.A.,* AF, 4, no. 163 [July 1965]), p. lxxix, Table 30, shows English and French physical products per head as approximately equal at the start of the nineteenth century. From what is known of comparative productivities in the two economies and the effect of the Revolution on French industry, this comparison would seem to be too favourable to France.
[3] Deane, *The First Industrial Revolution*, p. 7.

substantial technological progress, not only in the production of material goods, but in the organization and financing of their exchange and distribution.

Economic growth in this period of preparation, as it were, was by no means continuous: there was a major setback in the late fourteenth and fifteenth centuries, in the aftermath of the Black Death; and certain parts of Europe suffered grievously and long in the following period from the effects of war and pestilence. Nor was the rate of growth at best anything like so rapid as it was to become during and after the Industrial Revolution. (We have no true statistical estimates of pre-modern growth; but one has only to extrapolate the levels of income prevalent on the eve of industrialization backward at the rates of growth prevailing after 1700, and one arrives very quickly at levels of income too low for human survival.) Indeed, there is good reason to believe that much of such economic growth as did take place was translated into population growth: increased income meant lower death rates, in some instances higher birth rates; and larger numbers either ate up the gain or, outstripping it, set the stage for Malthusian disaster. Even so, it seems clear that over the near-millennium from the year 1000 to the eighteenth century, income per head rose appreciably—perhaps tripled—and that this rise accelerated sharply in the eighteenth century, even before the introduction of the new industrial technology.

In a sense, this preparation alone is sufficient explanation of the European achievement: Europe industrialized because she was ready to; and she was the first to industrialize because she alone was ready to. But this kind of statement is merely an evasion of the issue; the question still remains, why Europe alone effected this advance.

A definitive answer is impossible. We are dealing here with the most complex kind of problem, one that involves numerous factors of variable weights working in changing combinations. This sort of thing is hard to deal with even if one has precise data that lend themselves to refined techniques of analysis. But we have almost no evidence of this kind for the pre-modern period (say, before the eighteenth century), so that any judgment must be based on an impressionistic examination of the record. Such a judgment is necessarily personal: it would be hard, I think, to find two historians who would agree across the board on the 'causes' of the European economic advance. Still, one man's interpretation can serve to guide or sharpen the appreciation of others, if only on an adversary basis. The analysis that follows, therefore, is my own—though it rests heavily on the work of those specialists whose arguments on particular points I have found persuasive. The method of inquiry is to seek out these factors of European development that seem to be both significant and different; that set Europe apart, in other words, from the rest of the world. By holding Europe up against the mirror of the most advanced non-European societies, we should be able to discern some—surely not all—of the critical elements in her economic and technological precedence.

From this point of view two particularities seem to me to be salient: the scope and effectiveness of private enterprise; and the high value placed on the rational manipulation of the human and material environment.

The role of private economic enterprise in the West is perhaps unique: more than any other factor, it made the modern world. It was primarily the rise of trade that dissolved the subsistence economy of the medieval manor and generated the cities and towns that became the political and cultural, as well as economic, nodes of the new society. And it was the new men of commerce, banking, and industry who provided the increment of resources that financed the ambitions of the rulers and statesmen who invented the polity of the nation-state. Business, in other words, made kings—figuratively; and literally in the case of the Medici, who ruled Florence and whose children sat on the throne of France.

To be sure, kings could, and did, make or break the men of business; but the power of the sovereign was constrained by the requirements of state (money was the sinews of war) and international competition. Capitalists could take their wealth and enterprise elsewhere; and even if they could not leave, the capitalists of other realms would not be slow to profit from their discomfiture.

Because of this crucial role as midwife and instrument of power *in a context of multiple, competing polities* (the contrast is with the all-encompassing empires of the Orient or of the Ancient World), private enterprise in the West possessed a social and political vitality without precedent or counterpart. This varied, needless to say, from one part of Europe to another, depending on comparative economic advantage, historical experience, and the circumstances of the moment. Some countries were better endowed by nature for industry and trade than others. Some—especially those on the turbulent frontier of European civilization—came to accord inordinate place and prestige to the military and its values. And sometimes, adventitious events like war or a change of sovereign produced a major alteration in the circumstances of the business classes. On balance, however, the place of private enterprise was secure and improving with time; and this is apparent in the institutional arrangements that governed the getting and spending of wealth.

Take the idea and nature of property. This was often hedged around in the pre-industrial period by restrictions on use and disposition and by complications of title. Land especially was caught up in a thicket of conflicting rights of alienation and usufruct, formal and customary, which were a powerful obstacle to productive exploitation. Over time, however, the nations of western Europe saw an increasing proportion of the national wealth take the form of full property—full in the sense that the various components of ownership were united in the person or persons of the possessor, who could use the object of ownership and dispose of it as he saw fit.

Concomitant with this development and, indeed, implicit in it was the growing assurance of security in one's property—an indispensable condition of productive investment and the accumulation of wealth. This security had two dimensions: the relationship of the individual owner of property to the ruler; and the relationship of the members of the society to one another.

With respect to the first, the ruler abandoned, voluntarily or involuntarily, the right or practice of arbitary or indefinite disposition of the wealth of his subjects. The issue was joined very early, and its outcome was clearly linked to the larger question of the political as well as economic status of the business classes. Lambert of Hersfeld, an ecclesiastical chronicler of the eleventh century, tells the story of a confrontation on this score between the Archbishop of Cologne and the merchant community. The Archbishop wanted a boat for his friend and guest, the Bishop of Münster, and sent his men to commandeer a suitable vessel. The Archbishop may have been acting within his traditional rights; that is, the residents of Cologne may well have been obliged to furnish such facilities as a *corvée*. But in this instance, the son of the owner of the boat refused to submit and, calling some friends together, drove off the Archbishop's men-at-arms. The conflict quickly burgeoned into a riot, which the Archbishop finally succeeded in repressing by a show of force and threats of reprisal. Yet this was not the end of the matter:[1]

...the young man, who was filled with anger and drunk with his initial success, did not stop making all the trouble he could. He went about the town making speeches to the people about the bad government of the Archbishop, accusing him of imposing unjust charges on the people, of depriving innocent men of their property, and of insulting honorable citizens...It was not hard for him to arouse the populace...

This was surely not the last such incident at Cologne or elsewhere; but eventually the ruler learned that it was easier and in the long run more profitable to expropriate with indemnification rather than con-

[1] From the French of Jacques Le Goff, *La civilisation de l'Occident médiéval* (Paris, 1965), p. 368. I am indebted to my colleague Giles Constable for advice on the significance and credibility of this account.

fiscate, to take by law or judicial proceedings rather than by seizure. Above all, he came to rely on regular taxes at stipulated rates rather than on emergency exactions of indefinite amount. The revenue raised by the older method was almost surely less than that yielded by the new; over time, therefore, it constituted a smaller burden on the subject. But the effect of this uncertainty was to encourage concealment of wealth (hence discourage spending and promote hoarding) and to divert investment into those activities that lent themselves to this concealment. This seems to have been a particularly serious handicap to the economies of the great Asian empires and the Muslim states of the Middle East, where fines and extortions were not only a source of quick revenue but a means of social control—a device for curbing the pretensions of *nouveaux riches* and foreigners and blunting their challenge to the established power structure; and it was the experience of European traders in those countries that gave us from the Arabic the word 'avania' (French *avanie;* Italian *avania*), meaning both insult and exaction.[1]

At the same time—this is the second of our two dimensions—Europeans learned to deal with one another in matters of property on the basis of agreement rather than of force; and of contract between nominal equals rather than of personal bonds between superior and inferior. Jerome Blum, in his valuable study of Russian agrarian society, tells of one among many instances of violent seizure of land by a local lord from a nominally free peasant: the people in the area called the piece in question the 'cudgel field', because the servants of the rich man had beaten the poor farmer in public to exact his consent to the transfer.[2] (In most cases, of course, no beating would have been required; little men knew their place.) Predatory behaviour of this kind was easiest and most persistent in societies divided by wide barriers of power and status. Anywhere east of the Elbe, for example—in Prussia, Poland, Russia—the local lord enjoyed so much authority over the population that abusive treatment even of those residents who were nominally free,

[1] In these 'Oriental despotisms' one response to the threat of arbitrary levies was the investment of business profits in land, which had two major virtues in this respect: it was a fixed form of wealth, hence less tempting to covetous officials than liquid assets; and it sometimes conferred on its possessor political power, that is, a certain immunity from despoilment. Thus we find the richest business community of Safavid Persia, the Armenian silk merchants of Julfa, ready to risk their money in trading ventures as far afield as Poland and the Baltic, but hoarding it at home or using it to buy country estates. Amin Banani, 'The Social and Economic Structure of the Persian Empire in Its Heyday' (paper presented to the Colloquium in Middle Eastern Studies, Harvard University, 5 January 1968).

[2] Jerome Blum, *Lord and Peasant in Russia from the Ninth to the Nineteenth Century* (Princeton, 1961), p. 535.

let alone the unfree serfs, was widespread and unrestrainable. In these areas of seigneurial autonomy, moreover, conditions actually grew worse from the sixteenth to the eighteenth centuries, as the spread of commercial agriculture enhanced the incentive to exploit the weak.

In western Europe, however, the abuse of private power and recourse to violence were rarer and tended to diminish over time. (La Fontaine's *raison du plus fort* was reserved increasingly to international relations.) Here, too, the trend went back to the Middle Ages, when the ambitious rulers of inchoate nation-states succeeded in substituting their writ for that of their vassals; and in developing, as an instrument of royal power, a judicial apparatus operating in a context of established rules. They were helped in this effort by the bourgeoisie (in the strict sense of the citizens of the towns), who needed the protection of the law to flourish and, flourishing, provided the crown with a counterweight to the common feudal enemy.

The shift from diffuse obligations to explicit contract was part of the same development. Medieval society had been held together by loosely defined, open-ended personal bonds between lord and vassal, seigneur and serf; but business could not operate in this realm of indeterminacy and needed a measure for all things. The new law provided the measure, and the new nation-state enforced it.

These political and legal changes combined with economic and social developments to undermine seigneurial authority and enhance the personal status of the peasantry. Without attempting to examine this process in detail, one may point to a few major influences: the Black Death and subsequent epidemics, which altered sharply the ratio of land to labour and compelled the propertied classes to offer substantial inducements to attract and hold the manpower needed to work their estates; the long inflation of the sixteenth century, which found many peasants holding long-term leases whose burden diminished with the value of the currency; above all, the rise throughout western Europe of prosperous cities and towns, which offered refuge, employment and freedom to the serf who left the land and which thus acted as a constant source of upward pressure on the conditions of rural life. As a result, the opportunities created by a growing market for cash crops conduced not, as in the East, to the aggravation of labour services and a tightening of control, but to the solution of personal bonds and the substitution of free peasant enterprise for managed domains. This in turn laid the basis for what was to prove a crucial element in the rise of industrial capitalism: the spread of commercial manufacture from the towns to the countryside. It was this that enabled European industry to draw on an almost unlimited supply of cheap labour and to produce at a price that opened to it the markets of the world.

The rise of rural manufacture was the most striking and significant expression of freedom of enterprise; but one should not infer from the fact of this rise a state of generalized freedom. On the contrary, the very unevenness of this development—cottage production for market came far earlier in England than elsewhere—is testimony to the fierce and successful opposition it encountered from privileged interests in the towns; and these privileges are only one example of the many fetters on trade and industry. Thus essential commodities like food were subject to formal and customary restrictions designed to insure the nourishment and tranquillity of the population. Land, as noted above, was *sui generis:* because of its tie to social status and power, rights of purchase and alienation were often severely limited. Entrance into numerous occupations was subject to official authorization or to the permission of guilds that had every incentive to minimize competition by excluding newcomers. By the same token, the authorities often tried to confine business activity to fixed channels, to prohibit as unfair a wide range of what we would consider perfectly permissible behaviour, to discourage innovation that might harm vested interests. Much of this reflected the values of the medieval village or town community, which saw wealth as more or less fixed and assumed that the only way one got rich was at the expense of one's neighbour. Yet these constraints made little sense in a context of increasing wealth and rising productivity.

For all that, the scope of private economic activity was far larger in western Europe that in other parts of the world and grew as the economy itself grew and opened new areas of enterprise untrammelled by rule or custom. The trend was self-reinforcing: those economies grew fastest that were freest. This is not to imply that state enterprise or control is intrinsically inferior to private enterprise; simply that, given the state of knowledge in pre-industrial Europe, the private sector was in a better position to judge economic opportunity and allocate resources efficiently. Even more important, perhaps, was the impulse given thereby to innovation: in an age when the nature and direction of technological opportunity were far less obvious than now, the multiplication of points of creativity was a great advantage. The more persons who sought new and better ways of doing things, the greater the likelihood of finding them. Again the process was self-reinforcing: those economies that were freest seem to have been most creative; creativity promoted growth; and growth provided opportunities for further innovation, intended or accidental.

Why the rest of the world failed to develop a business class of comparable vitality and influence is still more a matter for speculation than analysis. The explanations offered by the specialists are not fully persuasive; often they take the form of bald assertions of cause-and-effect without specification of the intervening mechanism of change. Thus Prof. Wu Ta-k'un tells us that the establishment in China of a state monopoly of salt and metals (Han dynasty, 206 B.C. to A.D. 220) 'effectively checked the development of a mercantile class separate from the land-owning interest'. Perhaps; though one is more impressed by his reference to the congruency of the administrative and landowning elites and the assimilation of successful merchants into this group. 'For this reason,' he writes, 'the development of merchant capital led, not to the formation of a capitalist class, but to the continuous reinforcement of the landowning ruling class.'[1]

These and similar explanations are the ones usually offered for the abortion of economic development in non-European societies. Sometimes the historian stresses the subordination of trade and traders to an all-powerful central authority; sometimes the social inferiority and disabilities of the merchant class; sometimes the precarious character of private property and the heavy burden of arbitrary exactions; sometimes all of these. None of these was wholly absent in Europe; but the usual argument is that the differences in degree were so great as to be differences in kind. Where, for example, in Europe does one find anything comparable to the Egyptian principle that all wealth is the property of the ruler, lent by him to his subjects and taxable or confiscable at will?

In any event, it was surely one of Europe's great advantages that its first capitalist entrepreneurs worked and flourished in autonomous city-states, hence political units where the influence of landed wealth was necessarily limited; and that even in the larger embryonic nation-states, the special juridical status of the urban commune made it possible for its inhabitants to develop and sustain their own distinct political interest, while it isolated them culturally and socially from the great agrarian world around them. In this way the cities were not only foci of economic activity but schools of political and social association—

[1] Wu Ta-k'un, 'An Interpretation of Chinese Economic History', *Past and Present*, no. 1 (1952), pp. 6, 9. Cf. Frederic Wakeman, Jr., *Strangers at the Gate: Social Disorder in South China, 1839–1861* (Berkeley and Los Angeles, 1966), p. 45: 'But Chinese society was bureaucratic, state-centered. Tax-farming or monopoly capitalism was the only sure road to wealth. Instead of being an independent, vigorous class that challenged a ruling aristocracy, the Cantonese merchants lived in symbiosis with the state and its mandarinate. Status honor being what it was, wealth invariably led to the purchase of office, or conspicuous consumption in the scholar-gentry manner, both of which dissipated capital. Thus the merchants of China were perpetually servile to the honored symbols of that society, the gentry.' For similar tendencies in the Mameluke Empire of Egypt and Syria during the fifteenth century, see Ira M. Lapidus, *Muslim Cities in the Later Middle Ages* (Cambridge, Mass., 1967), p. 126.

incubators of the bourgeoisie as a self-conscious, assertive interest group. They were also crucibles for the refinement of values that, although profoundly rooted in European culture, were still deviant and limited to a minority—values ultimately subversive of the feudal order.

This brings us to what I suggested was the second of Europe's salient particularities: the high value placed on the rational manipulation of the environment. This in turn may be decomposed into two elements: rationality, and what we may call the Faustian sense of mastery over man and nature. (Such decomposition does violence to the historical reality, for the two are intertwined; but it is useful for purposes of analysis.)

Rationality may be defined as the adaptation of means to ends. It is the antithesis of superstition and magic. For this history, the relevant ends are the production and acquisition of material wealth. It goes without saying that these are not man's highest ends; and that rationality is not confined to the economic sphere. But whatever the area of activity, the means-end criterion holds; besides, there is good reason to believe that rationality is a homogeneous character trait, that is, that he who is rational in one area is more likely to be rational in others.[1]

The story of rationality as value and way of life has yet to be written, although a number of social scientists, notably Max Weber, have expatiated on its significance for the course of Western development. It shows up earliest perhaps in the sphere of religion, where one finds a strong tendency in the Judaic tradition to eliminate magic and superstition as a senseless degradation of faith. To be sure, this catharsis was never complete, and the rise of Christianity introduced a new emphasis on the instinctual and emotional aspects of faith and action. Yet the rational tradition remained powerful and found expression in the invention of a calculus of salvation and in the elaboration of codes and techniques for the management of the material possessions of the Church.

To what extent the Church was motivated here by internal values and to what extent by the values of secular society, is hard to say. Clearly the place of magic and superstition in Christian worship has always varied markedly from one part of Europe to another; and indeed much of the Church's effectiveness in proselytization has stemmed from its readiness to find compromises between an austere orthodoxy and

[1] Rationality in this sense should be distinguished from rationalism, which is the doctrine or principle that the universe of perception and experience can be understood in terms of thought or reason, as against emotion, intuition, or extra-sensory modes of apprehension. Rationality is thus a way of doing things, the application of the principles of rationalism to action. It is quite possible to behave rationally, however, in the sense of adapting means to ends, without explicit or conscious adherence to the doctrines of rationalism; that is, one does not have to be a philosopher to act rationally.

the ways of indigenous paganism. Yet there is good reason to believe that already in the Middle Ages, Europe was freer of superstition and more rational in behaviour than other parts of the world.

How does one know this? We have no measures. But there is one indicator that may be a valid surrogate, and that is population control. European birth rates before industrialization were well below the biological maximum—significantly lower, for example, than the rates of today's pre-industrial societies before and even after the introduction of programmes of family planning. Moreover, in so far as there were variations in birth rates—and they range from 55 to 60 per thousand in colonial America and French Canada to 15 per thousand in Iceland at the beginning of the eighteenth century—they seem to have been closely related to the ratio of resources to population.[1] This is evidence presumably of self-restraint—an effort to restrict commitments to means—and as such is an excellent example of rationality in a particularly crucial and sensitive area of life.[2]

It is against this background that one can best appreciate the significance of the so-called Protestant ethic for the development of European capitalism. The reference, of course, is to the work of Max Weber, who first advanced the hypothesis that the rise of Protestantism, particularly in its Calvinist version, was a major factor (not the only factor) in the creation of a modern industrial economy in western Europe. Weber was not the first to observe a link between Protestant belief and economic advance; already in the seventeenth century, observers were struck by the apparent congruency of the Reformed faith and business success. But Weber offered a new and coherent explanation for the link in terms, not of the content of Protestant doctrine, but of the pattern of behaviour inculcated by Protestantism on its adherents.

Hence the emphasis on ethics, that is, a set of values governing everyday conduct. In brief, Weber argued that the Calvinist doctrine of predestination instilled in its believers a deep anxiety about their salvation that could be appeased only by leading the kind of life that those

[1] John T. Krause, 'Some neglected factors in the English Industrial Revolution', *Journal of Economic History*, xix (1959), 528–40. Demographic research has shown, however, that the Asian peasant who has as many children as possible is following a rationality of his own: given the high mortality, numbers are a kind of guarantee against a childless old age; they are the equivalent of an insurance policy. Yet this merely displaces the question. Mortality rates were presumably just as high in western Europe in the pre-industrial period as in contemporary Asia. Why did the European peasant not feel this need? The answer may lie in better arrangements for mutual support in time of need—group insurance, as it were, instead of family insurance. The problem is much too complex and little known for us to explore here.

[2] Professor Henry Rosovsky tells me that there is good evidence of fertility control in pre-industrial Japan as well.

destined for salvation might be expected to lead; and that this life was one of in-the-world asceticism (as opposed to the monastic asceticism of the Catholic Church)—a life in which one's time and energies were devoted exclusively to those worthy activities (prayer and work) that conduced to the glory of God. Such a standard, argued Weber, was obviously also conducive to the accumulation of wealth: the good Calvinist was diligent, thrifty, honest, austere. Moreover this way of life, originally rooted in religious doctrine, came to have a force of its own: it became important to live this way, not because it provided assurance of probable salvation, but because this was the right way to live. In short, the means had become end. So that even after the first surge of Protestant zeal had subsided, the ethic remained; and such new Protestant sects as made their appearance in subsequent centuries— Pietism, Quakerism, Baptism, Methodism—incorporated these standards of behaviour in their moral codes.

Few historical arguments have aroused so much controversy as the so-called Weber thesis; there is a library on the subject, and the debate still rages. Most of the objections follow one or more of three lines: (1) It was not Protestantism that promoted capitalism, but the reverse: pushful, hard-working, successful businessmen sought moral sanction for their way of life and their gains and found it in Protestantism. (2) The superior performance of certain Protestant business communities may be explained, not by their religion, but by their status as persecuted minorities. Deprived of the opportunity to enter established universities or pursue respected careers in the liberal professions or state service, they turned to business, where they worked harder and better than their competitors, the more so as their cohesion and mutual support gave them an advantage over outsiders. (3) There is no empirical link between Protestantism and business success.

The last of these may be dismissed out of hand; it has been advanced by some reputable scholars, but it is simply erroneous, as any examination of the British, French, or German record makes clear. The other two objections are more serious, though they are not necessarily incompatible with the Weber thesis. It is quite reasonable to argue, for example, that the Protestant ethic constituted religious sanction for an already established pattern of behaviour and still attribute considerable influence to it as a support for and propagator of this pattern in the face of competitive value systems. And by the same token, positive religious or ethical standards may well have reinforced the negative stimulus to performance provided by minority status.

Still, this is much too complex and embroiled a question to resolve here. What is important for this analysis is the significance of the Calvinist ethic, whatever its source, as an extreme example of the application of rationality to life. The insistence on the value of time, the condemnation and abhorrence of pleasure and diversion—all those censorious prohibitions and internalized inhibitions that we denote as puritanism with a small *p*—were more than a new version of the appetite for wealth. They constituted in effect an imposition of the criterion of efficiency on every activity, whether or not directly connected with getting and spending.

The complement of this spirit of rationality was what we may call the Faustian ethic, the sense of mastery over nature and things. The one reinforced the other: mastery entailed an adaptation of means to ends; and attention to means and ends was the precondition of mastery. The theme is an old one in Western culture, going back to the myths of Daedalus and Prometheus, or even to the stories of the Tower of Babel and of Eve, the serpent, and the tree of knowledge (knowledge is mastery). The ancients were dreadfully afraid of this emulation of the gods, and not coincidentally the protagonists in each case were punished for their *hubris*. For similar reasons, the Christian Church, itself heir to both the Judaic and Greek traditions, repeatedly condemned as heresy those doctrines—Pelagian and pseudo-Pelagian—that magnified man's natural ability and, explicitly or implicitly, denied his dependence on God for grace and the Church for salvation. There remains a strong current in popular Christianity that condemns certain acts of techno- logical prowess as assaults on the divine order: if God had intended man to fly, he'd have given him wings.

On the other hand, the very reiteration of this theme is evidence of the persistence of the aspiration towards mastery of the environment; and indeed some would argue that the Church itself contributed un- wittingly to the heresy by its sanctification of work and its opposition to animism. So long as every tree had its dryad and every fountain or stream its naiad, man was intimidated and inhibited in his confrontation with nature. But when, writes Lynn White, 'saint replaced animistic sprite as the most frequent and intimate object of popular religious concern, our race's earthly monopoly on "spirit" was confirmed, and man was liberated to exploit nature as he wished. The cult of saints smashed animism and provided the cornerstone for the naturalistic (but not necessarily irreligious) view of the world which is essential to a highly developed technology.'[1]

Be that as it may, it is clear that the urge to mastery grew with time

[1] Lynn White, Jr., 'What Accelerated Technological Progress in the Western Middle Ages?', in A. C. Crombie, ed., *Scientific Change* (New York, 1963), p. 283. (I owe this reference to Prof. Nathan Rosenberg.) Cf. the observations of Jacques Le Goff on the desacralization of nature in Gothic art. *La Civilisation de l'Occident médiéval*, p. 435.

and fed on success, for every achievement was justification for the pre-
tension; while the moral force of the Church's opposition waned with
its temporal power and its own growing insecurity in the face of a
triumphant materialism. Even more important, perhaps, was the
scientific revolution of the early modern period, which not only upset
specific articles of religious faith but implicitly discredited all traditional
wisdom and authority. Science indeed was the perfect bridge between
rationality and mastery: it was the application of reason to the understanding of natural and, with time, human phenomena; and it made
possible a more effective response to or manipulation of the natural and
human environment.

More than that: it was precisely the applicability of scientific knowledge to the environment that was the test of its validity. The mode of
perception and thought that we know as science was not, and is not,
the only such mode. Certain Asian societies in particular have devoted
considerable effort to the exploration of a world that lies outside or
beyond the material universe accessible to ordinary sensory cognition.
This other world may lie within or without the observer, who enters it
usually with the assistance of drugs or through the medium of a deliberately induced trance-like state. Sometimes the claim is made that
this is a higher form of consciousness; sometimes, merely that this other
world is another, rich realm of a larger universe of experience. In
either case, the assumption is that this, too, is real.

Western societies have also had their exploration of other realms,
with or without drugs—their religious ecstasies, magical rites, super-
stitions, fairy tales, daydreams. But Western societies, and more particularly their intellectual and scientific leadership, established very early
the boundary line between fantasy and reality, drawing careful distinctions between spiritual and material, between the realm of emotion and
imagination on the one hand and that of observation and reason on the
other. The shibboleth has been the communicability of experience:
something is real if it can and will be perceived and described, perhaps
even measured, by any person with the requisite faculties and instruments in the same terms.[1] In other words, what you see, I see.

This communicability of experience is the basis of scientific and tech-

[1] To be sure, any such definition of reality would seem to exclude a whole world of
abstract phenomena, no less actual and significant for their abstractness and inscruta-
bility. One thinks of the common coin of the social sciences—concepts like nationalism,
imperialism, class consciousness, and the like. With these and most other ideational
constructs, it is hard to achieve agreement on specific instances, let alone on general
definitions. Nevertheless here too the criterion of reality remains communicability of
experience, and in so far as the social sciences have not satisfied this criterion, they have
lagged behind the natural sciences in understanding and control (for better or worse)
of their subject matter.

nological advance, because it makes possible the transmission and cumulation of knowledge. The stuff of a dream is evanescent; the perceptions of a 'religious experience' are highly personal. These transcendental impressions may leave a legacy of emotions, attitudes, values. What they do not yield is cognitive building blocks. By carefully distinguishing between these two forms of knowledge, Western culture saved itself from material impotence, at the cost perhaps of a certain psychic impoverishment. (I say 'perhaps' because those who have not enjoyed transcendental experiences must take those who have at their word.)

The same point can be made about the highly complex and abstract reasoning of certain 'primitive' societies—reasoning that anthropologists are currently much concerned with and that they find to be different from, but not necessarily inferior to, the rationalism of science. This ethnological literature is curiously defensive: by stressing the profundity and intimacy of these other systems of thought, by minimizing the differences, for example, between science and magic, the savant seeks to elevate the 'savage' to intellectual as well as spiritual and moral parity with the 'civilisé'.[1] The cause is a worthy one. The anthropologist here has assumed the mantle of the priest who preaches humility by depreciating the works of man; and the humility of the twentieth century is relativism.

Yet although modesty is good for the soul, it is not always true. The difference between science and magic is the difference between rational and irrational; that is, the one makes possible effective action and the other does not, except adventitiously. 'It may be objected,' writes Lévi-Strauss, 'that science of this kind [that is, primitive thought] can scarcely be of much practical effect. The answer to this is that its main purpose is not a practical one. It meets intellectual requirements rather than or instead of satisfying needs' (p. 9). The answer is valid on the level of humanistic appreciation; it is irrelevant on the level of performance.

And it was primarily performance that was the criterion of the interest and validity of scientific inquiry in these first crucial centuries of intellectual exploration (as opposed to the medieval mastication of traditional wisdom). The performance in question was the production of wealth—hence the alchemist's obsession with the conversion of base substances into gold; the achievement of eternal youth; or the enhancement of power—hence the preoccupation with the laws of motion and trajectory (needed for effective use of artillery), the principles of hydraulics (of interest to builders of ports and canals), the chemistry of explosives (useful in the production of armaments), and similar problems.

As the reader will have noted, some of the above goals were in fact unattainable; much of this early science was still tinged with magic.

[1] Thus Claude Lévi-Strauss, *The Savage Mind* (Chicago, 1966), pp. 8-11.

Even so brilliant a scientist as Isaac Newton, the heir of a century of intellectual revolution, was credulous on this score. In his famous letter of 1669 (he was then only 26) to Francis Aston, advising that young man how to make the most of his travels, he suggests that Aston inquire whether 'in Hungary...they change Iron into Copper by dissolving it into a Vitriolate water wch they find in cavitys of rocks in the mines & then melting the slymy solution in a strong fire...'[1]

Yet it would be a mistake to equate this credulity with superstition. Rather, this kind of alchemy represented in effect a transitional stage between magic and science, between the irrational and the rational, in the sense that the change sought was to be accomplished by a real agent, and not by patently immaterial incantations. Newton did not know enough chemistry to realize that the kind of mutation he envisaged was impossible. But he and his contemporaries knew enough about the nature of reality and were sufficiently pragmatic to insist on results; so that when all the alchemical ingenuity in the world failed to turn up the philosophers' stone or the elixir of life, they abandoned the search and turned their knowledge and skills to the rational accomplishment of feasible ends. And so alchemy became chemistry.

The significance of Newton's letter, however, lies not in its instance of cultural lag, but in its theme, which is one of pervasive curiosity. Don't waste a moment, it says; come back with all the knowledge you can acquire. And Newton actually offers his friend a set of rules that will enable him to maximize the intellectual return to travel—among others: 'let your discours bee more in Quaerys & doubtings yn peremptory assertions or disputings, it being ye designe of Travellers to learne not teach...' The Europeans of the Middle Ages, and even more their children, were inveterate learners—above all, in technology. To be sure, the history of cultural diffusion in the pre-modern period is obscure; the specialists in the field rely heavily on discrete, ambiguous iconographic materials and treacherous philological evidence. Even so, it seems clear that Europe imported from the East over a period of centuries a whole array of valuable and sometimes fundamental techniques: the stirrup, the wheelbarrow, the crank (to convert reciprocal to rotary motion), gunpowder, the compass, paper and, very likely, printing. Many of these came originally from China, which enjoyed at various times during the T'ang (618–907) and Sung (960–1279) dynasties the most advanced technology and economic organization in the world.[2]

[1] H. W. Turnbull, ed., *The Correspondence of Isaac Newton*, vol. 1: *1661–1675* (Cambridge, 1959), pp. 9–11.

[2] The students of the subject are not always in agreement which innovations Europe imported from the Orient, which ones it developed independently, which ones both

This readiness and even eagerness to learn from others, including other Europeans—industrial espionage is a theme running all through modern European history—was testimony to an already thriving indigenous technology; good innovators make good imitators. It was also a great advantage for the nascent capitalist economy, the more so as other societies were less enterprising in this regard. The Chinese, for example, were wont to look at the rest of the world as a barbarian waste-land, with nothing to offer but tribute; and even the obvious lead of Western technology in the modern period was insufficient to disabuse them of this crippling self-sufficiency.[1] On the contrary, their contacts with Europeans in the eighteenth and early nineteenth centuries only confirmed their belief in their own superiority and enhanced the xenophobic component: the foreigners were dangerous animals—lewd, greedy, ignorant; and the Chinese who dealt with them always ran the risk of being denounced, or worse, as a traitor.[2] So that where the Japanese responded with alacrity and success to the technological and political challenge of the West, the Chinese vacillated between disdainful rejection and reluctant, constrained imitation and fell between the two stools.

In the Muslim world, it was religious rather than national or ethnic pride that posed an obstacle to the importation of knowledge from outside. From the start, Islamic culture was at best anxiously tolerant of scientific or philosophical speculation—partly because it might divert the attention of the faithful from their obligatory concern with God, his revelation, and the prophetic tradition; partly because profane thought might shake belief. Certain fields of inquiry were legitimate because they obviously contributed to the well-being of the community: medicine, a modicum of mathematics and astronomy (needed to determine the religious calendar), geography (needed for administration), and the theory of administration itself. This is the way von Grunebaum sees the problem:

But anything that goes beyond these manifest (and religiously justifiable) needs can, and in fact ought to, be dispensed with. No matter how important the contribution Muslim scholars were able to make to the natural sciences,

derived from a common source, and so on; but this absence of consensus is not sur-prising in view of the character of the evidence. See on this subject, *inter alia*, Lynn White, Jr., *Medieval Technology and Social Change* (Oxford, 1962), and J. Needham, 'L'unité de la science: l'apport indispensable de l'Asie', *Archives internationales d'histoire des sciences*, no. 7 [*Archeion*, nouv. série, XXVIII] (April, 1949), pp. 563–82 (the latter inclined perhaps to overstress the Asian contribution).

[1] Cf. John K. Fairbank *et al.*, 'The Influence of Modern Western Science and Technology on Japan and China', in Comitato Internazionale di Scienze Storiche, X Congresso Internazionale di Scienze Storiche, Roma 4–11 Settembre 1955, *Relazioni*, vol. V: *Storia contemporanea* (Florence, n.d.), pp. 243–69, esp. pp. 254–6.

[2] Cf. Wakeman, *Strangers at the Gate*, ch. iv: 'Traitor in Our Midst'.

and no matter how great the interest with which, at certain periods, the leading classes and the government itself followed and supported their researches, those sciences (and their technological application) had no root in the fundamental needs and aspirations of their civilization. Those accomplishments of Islamic mathematical and medical science which continue to compel our admiration were developed in areas and in periods where the elites were willing to go beyond and possibly against the basic strains of orthodox thought and feeling. For the sciences never did shed the suspicion of bordering on the impious which, to the strict, would be near-identical with the religiously uncalled-for. This is why the pursuit of the natural sciences as that of philosophy tended to become located in relatively small and esoteric circles and why but few of their representatives would escape occasional uneasiness with regard to the moral implications of their endeavors—a mood which not infrequently did result in some kind of an apology for their work. It is not so much the constant struggle which their representatives found themselves involved in against the apprehensive skepticism of the orthodox which in the end smothered the progress of their work; rather it was the fact, which became more and more obvious, that their researches had nothing to give to their community which this community could accept as an essential enrichment of their lives. When in the later Middle Ages scientific endeavor in certain fields very nearly died down, the loss did indeed impoverish Muslim civilization as we view its total unfolding and measure its contribution against that of its companion civilizations, but it did not affect the livability of the correct life and thus did not impoverish or frustrate the objectives of the community's existence as traditionally experienced.[1]

As von Grunebaum's analysis makes clear, the effect of this suspicion and hostility was to isolate the scientific community, place its representatives in an apologetically defensive posture, and render difficult, if not impossible, the kind of triumphant cumulative advance that was to occur in the West some hundreds of years later. Even so, the achievements of Muslim science were substantial, and it was through Arabic translations that the classics of Greek science were transmitted to late medieval Europe. In those days, Europe was the backward country, and Islam, the advanced exporter of knowledge. What caused Muslim science to vegetate just at the time when Western science was re-awakening? And why did knowledge not flow the other way once the balance of achievement had shifted?

The answer seems to be that the latent anti-intellectual values of the culture triumphed, in large part owing to the same kind of physical disaster that had overwhelmed the Roman Empire and set European science back almost a thousand years. For Islam too, it was a series of invaders—the Banu-Hilāl in North Africa; the Crusaders in Syria,

[1] G. E. von Grunebaum, *Islam: Essays in the Nature and Growth of a Cultural Tradition* (2nd ed., London, 1961), p. 114.

Palestine, and Egypt; above all, the waves of nomads from the Asian steppe, culminating in the terrifying Mongol hordes of the thirteenth century—that brought the classical civilization down. The political fabric was rent; the urban centres were sacked; the indispensable capital base of the society, the irrigation works, left in ruins. The Dark Ages that followed saw a revival of know-nothing mysticism and a reversion to uncompromising religious fundamentalism. Islam turned in on itself and found its own kind of peace in spiritual self-sufficiency: 'The Muslim's world is at rest, and he is at rest within it, and what strikes us as decadence, is to him repose in the bosom of eternal truth.'[1]

The obscurantist influence of Islam was the stronger for two considerations that distinguished sharply East and West. The first was the all-pervasive role of the Muslim religion, which reigned sovereign even in those spheres that had long been reserved in the West to secular authorities. The dichotomy between Caesar and God was never established in Islam, perhaps because the Muslim people (the *'umma*) and their world were a creation of the faith, whereas Christianity had had to make a place for itself in the powerful Roman state. There was, in other words, no legitimate source of sanction and authority in Islam outside the teachings of the Prophet and the lessons derived therefrom.

Secondly, the unity of Islam in the matter of intellectual inquiry worked against the success of deviant patterns of thought or behaviour. Not that Islam did not have its schisms and heresies. Almost from the start the faith was split into Sunnite and Shi'ite camps, and these in turn generated their own subdivisions. These sectarian movements, however, almost invariably embodied deviations to the 'right', in the direction of mysticism, devotionalism, more rigorous observance. Throughout the doctrinal spectrum, therefore, there prevailed a spiritual orthodoxy at best unfavourable, at worst hostile to scientific endeavour.

The pragmatic creativity of European science, like the vitality of the European business community, was linked to the separation of spiritual and temporal and to the fragmentation of power within each of these realms. Thanks to the Protestant revolt, there could be no peremptory orthodoxy in Europe like the *Shari'a* of Islam. Not that Protestants could not be as dogmatic as Catholics. But they were sectarians, and what is more, sectarians in a world that had not known serious religious division. There had been, to be sure, conflicts over the papal succession; but these were political rather than religious. There had also been eccentric heresies like that of the Cathars; but these had been confined in space and time and had not inflicted lasting damage on the Catholic edifice. The Reformation, on the other hand, effected the first signifi-

[1] J. J. Saunders, 'The Problem of Islamic Decadence', *Journal of World History*, VII (1963), 719.

cant rupture of Western Christianity since the suppression of the Arian heresy almost a thousand years before. The very existence of unsubmissive and unsuppressable Protestant sects was implicit justification for disobedience and schism.

Even more important, perhaps, was the content of the protest: the stress on personal faith and the primacy of conscience carried with it the seeds of unlimited dissent. These seeds did not always flower: witness the authority that Luther accorded the temporal power; or the conservative bias of English Methodism. Still, the principle was there, potent even in quiescence; and it came to serve as cover not only for religious nonconformity but for secular speculation. It was not hard to make the jump from one sphere to the other: if people were to let their conscience be their guide in matters of faith, why not let their intelligence be their guide in matters of knowledge? The result was far greater opportunity for scientific inquiry. In addition, more positive stimuli may well have played a role: a generation ago Robert Merton argued in a seminal monograph on *Science, Technology, and Society in Seventeenth Century England* that it was the ethical content of early Protestantism that accounted for the disproportionate achievement of Dissenter scientists; and this argument has been extended by inference to explain the larger shift of the intellectual centre of gravity from Italy to northern Europe.[1] Yet surely the other side of the coin is equally important, namely, the stultifying effect of the counter-Reformation on freedom of thought and investigation in Catholic lands.[2]

By the same token, European science and technology derived considerable advantage from the fact that the continent was divided into nation-states, rather than united under the rule of an ecumenical empire. Fragmentation, as we have seen, entailed competition, specifically competition among equals. In this contest, science was an asset of state, not only because it furnished new tools and improved techniques of war, but because it contributed directly and indirectly to the general prosperity, and prosperity contributed to power. This was true not only of natural science, but also of what has since come to be known as social science: one of the principal incentives to the analysis of social action was the pursuit of power.

Hence mercantilism. The state acted, controlling and manipulating

[1] Published originally in *Osiris: Studies on the History and Philosophy of Science, and on the History of Learning and Culture*, IV, part II (Bruges, 1938). The Merton thesis has given rise to considerable debate, which is as lively today as ever, in spite of urgings from opponents that the argument be laid to rest. See especially the exchanges in *Past and Present*, in particular, nos. 28 and 31.

[2] Cf. H. R. Trevor-Roper, *Religion, the Reformation and Social Change* (London, 1967), p. 42, n. 1; John Elliott, 'The Decline of Spain', *Past and Present*, no. 20 (November, 1961), p. 68.

the economy for its own advantage, and theory hastened to follow. (In this respect too, mercantilist thought and natural science had much in common: throughout this period and indeed well into the nineteenth century, theoretical science was in large measure devoted to understanding the achievements of technology.) The theory in turn provided man with new tools for mastery of his environment. Admittedly, mercantilist doctrine was shapeless, inconsistent. It was inconsistent because it reflected policy as much as guided it, and each state did with its economy what circumstances warranted, knowledge (or ignorance) suggested, and means permitted. Mercantilism was, in short, pragmatism gilded by principle.

Yet mercantilism was more than mere rationalization. Precisely because it was pragmatic, because it aimed at results, it contained the seeds of the sciences of human behaviour. Its principles were modelled on those propounded for the natural sciences: the careful accumulation of data, the use of inductive reasoning, the pursuit of the economical explanation, the effort to find a surrogate for the replicated experiment by the use of explicit international comparisons. Moreover, in this early modern period it was quite common for the natural scientist to interest himself in this realm of social behaviour. In the above-quoted letter from Newton to Aston, the first suggestions Newton makes are the following:

1 to observe ye policys wealth & state affaires of nations so far as a solitary Traveller may conveniently doe. 2 Their impositions upon all sorts of People Trades or commoditys yt are remarkeable. 3 Their Laws & Customes how far they differ from ours. 4 Their Trades & Arts wherin they excell or come short of us in England.

The preceding discussion is not intended to imply that mercantilism was uniformly promotive of European economic development; or even that it was so on balance. On the contrary, we know that it was often misdirected (just as certain efforts in the domain of natural science and technology were misdirected), and we shall have to consider later the effects of this misdirection on the timing and character of industrialization within Europe. Our point here is simply that mercantilism was the expression in the sphere of political economy—a particularly striking expression—of the rationality principle and the Faustian spirit of mastery. This is why it could generate a continuing flow of knowledge and outgrow the political circumstances that gave it birth. Because it was built on the same cognitive basis as natural science, because it accepted the criterion of performance, it was the initial stimulus to the collection of economic and social statistics and the forerunner of the whole range of economic theory, from *laissez-faire* to socialism.

All of this gave Europe a tremendous advantage in the invention and adoption of new technology. The will to mastery, the rational approach to problems that we call the scientific method, the competition for wealth and power—together these broke down the resistance of inherited ways and made of change a positive good. Nothing—not pride, nor honour, nor authority, nor credulity—could stand in the face of these new values. Not pride nor honour: the important thing, Newton wrote Aston, is 'to learne not teach'. Do not be umbrageous, he warns. If you find yourself insulted, let it pass; no one will know about it in England. Lack of forbearance, even under provocation, may pass among friends; among strangers, it 'only argue[s] a Travellers weaknesse'. Nor authority: Descartes' first principle of method 'was never to accept anything for true which I did not clearly know to be such; that is to say, carefully to avoid precipitancy and prejudice'. Nor credulity: Newton's fourth rule of reasoning stated that once one has induced the truth from empirical evidence, one should stick by it and not imagine or accept contrary hypotheses until there is hard evidence to support them.

These, it seems to me, are the crucial values of that European culture and society that gave birth to the modern industrial world: rationality in means and activist, as against quietist, ends. But these alone will not account for the entire discrepancy between Western economic development and that of the leading centres of civilization elsewhere. There was also the element of differential violence—violence, first, in the sense of destructive incursions; and second, in the sense of dominion and exploitation of one society by another.

Western Europe had known more than its share of the first in the late Roman Empire and Middle Ages; indeed the central institutio.. of medieval society—the personal subordination, the striving for self-sufficiency, the decentralization of authority—were all primarily responses to physical danger and insecure communications. But from the eleventh century on, the pressure of invasion diminished: the Norsemen settled in their new homes and became domesticated; the Hungarians did the same; the Saracens withdrew and confined themselves to desultory raids. Instead, Europe began thrusting outward—into Slavic lands to the east and Muslim countries in the Levant and to the south. From this time on, it expanded almost without interruption or setback; and with the exception of eastern Europe, which suffered periodically from the incursions of nomads from the Eurasian steppe and lost the Balkan peninsula to the Ottoman Turk, the continent was spared the death and ruin of outside aggression. To be sure, Europe was not free of war: one thinks of the intermittent Hundred Years' War between England and France; the civil and religious conflicts of the fifteenth and sixteenth centuries; worst of all, the disastrous Thirty Years' War (1618–48), which laid waste large areas of central Europe by fire, the sword, and disease, to the point where some districts lost five-sixths of their population by death and flight and took a century to recover. But now the only enemy that Europeans had to fear was other Europeans; and as the conflicting ambitions of the different nation states worked themselves out in the form of a more stable balance of power, the virulence of the fighting diminished, particularly in that north-western corner of Europe that had taken the lead in economic development.

Other areas were perhaps less fortunate. Certainly the Muslim world suffered blows far heavier than those inflicted on western Europe: the Mongol invasions of the thirteenth century were followed in the late fourteenth by the conquests of Timur, who ranged from Anatolia in the West to India in the East and marked his victories with minarets and pyramids of skulls—a monument to his power and a warning to the survivors. Timur in turn was followed by lesser Turkoman warlords, some of whom fought their way briefly on to the stage of history and then disappeared, while others established dynasties of varying durability in the successor states of the once mighty Mongol empire. As a result of this dissolution, the Muslim world found a new, though far from stable equilibrium in a division between Persian and Mogul East and Turkish–Arabic West. For more than two hundred years, from the early sixteenth century on, the Ottomans and the Safavid Persians waged intermittent war, addressing themselves the while to occasional bouts with other adversaries: nomads from the steppe, Russians spreading southward and eastward, the Afghan tribes and Mogul emperors to the east, the nations of Christian Europe in the Danube valley and the Mediterranean. The land was forever crisscrossed with armies; siege followed siege, massacre followed massacre. Even the ghastliest carnages of the Thirty Years' War—the sack of Magdeburg for example—pale alongside the bloodbaths of Delhi. The record of shifting dynasties, palace plots, reigns of terror, and mad rulers reads like an Oriental version of the Merovingian snakepit.

Meanwhile the growing technological superiority of the West enabled the European nations to impose their dominion on the most distant lands, sometimes on the basis of formal annexation and colonization of territory, sometimes by means of an informal commercial tie with weaker peoples. The story of this overseas expansion is too well known to require review here; but it is of interest to us to inquire what contribution imperialism made to the economic development of Europe on the one hand, to the retardation of the rest of the world on the other.

The answer is not easy to come by. For one thing, the issue is much vexed by political commitment and coloured by intellectual bias. Those who are indignant or angry at the wrongs inflicted by the West on the colonial peoples of the world—the nationals of these countries in particular—are inclined to impute the whole Western achievement to exploitation: the Industrial Revolution, say some Indian historians, was accomplished on the backs of the Indian peasant. Marxist historians offer similar judgments, which serve among other things to increase the burden of sin to be laid at the door of capitalism. The effect—and sometimes the aim—is to legitimize such reprisals as the Third World today may be able to wreak on its former masters: in the light of the historical record, vengeance is ostensibly nothing more than retribution. On the other side, those who reject the indictment in whole or in part (and it is not easy on this issue to preserve the nuances), or who give their support to capitalism as against other economic systems, are prone to depreciate the advantages of the colonial relationship to the dominant power and the disadvantages to the dominated. The effort here is to deny or minimize the debt; and since the nature and extent of the obligation of the rich nations to the poor is one of the most sensitive and potentially explosive issues of international relations, the verdict of history is in this case of more than academic interest.

Under the circumstances, it seems clear that we have here the kind of problem on which consensus is impossible. History is not an exact science (many would say that it is not a science at all), and even if we had all the data desirable, there would be disagreement on their interpretation. But we do not have all the data, so that all that one can do in a rapid analysis of this kind is review what seem to be the relevant considerations and see where they lead.

To begin with, one must distinguish between two kinds of return to colonial domination. (Our context here is the so-called Old Imperialism of the 16th to 18th centuries.) The first is the quick, spectacular reward of conquest: the seizure as booty of the accumulated wealth of the conquered society. This was of little moment in most colonial areas, for these were generally poor by European standards. The only significant exceptions—and these, momentous—were the American Indian empires of Mexico and Peru and the Mogul Empire of India. The former yielded at the outset enormous treasures of gold and silver bullion; and then for a century and more supplied a large flow of precious metal from mines; so that much of the subsequent exploration of the New World was motivated by the vain hope of finding other El Dorados. The Indian tribute was smaller; but the adoption into English of such words as *nabob* and *Golconda* is testimony to the riches that the more enterprising and less scrupulous Europeans found there.

The significance of this booty for European economic development has long been a subject of controversy. Precious metals and jewels are not productive capital; neither are they edible. But in the right hands, they can be used to command and combine the factors of production for useful purposes. In the right hands... The silver of America did little for Spain, which re-exported most of it to pay for military operations in other parts of Europe and for imports of food and manufactures from 'less fortunate' countries. Indeed one might reasonably argue that the colonial windfall did Spain serious harm by encouraging her to rely on tribute rather than work. In similar fashion, the wealth of the nabob returning home from India to England was more likely to go into land and office than into trade, for experience in colonial exaction is poor training for risk-taking ventures in a competitive market.

On the other hand, the Spanish re-export of bullion and the land purchases of nabobs were transfer payments: the wealth did find its way into other hands and constituted a net addition to Europe's and England's money supplies. This in turn presumably eased credit, increased demand, and stimulated industry—in those places that were in a position to respond to this opportunity. Admittedly this was a one-time stimulus that lost force when the inflow of precious metals diminished; plunder, silver mining, and quick monopoly profits are not a solid basis for development at home or abroad. Yet while the inflationary expansion lasted, it promoted abiding changes in the structure of the European economy: new scope for commercial enterprise, greater specialization in agriculture and manufacture, larger concentrations of capital, an increased scale of production in certain branches.

More durable and more stimulating to European economic development was the systematic exploitation of colonial territories through settlement. Practice varied considerably. In some areas (notably Spanish America), the native was impressed into service; in others (the West Indies and the southern colonies of British North America), he proved unwilling or unable to do the work required, and the colonists killed him or drove him off and brought in black slaves from Africa to take his place. Farther north, the settlers did their own work, establishing in the New World societies that were in many respects replicas of what they had known at home. In some places the Europeans constituted a thin surface layer over a far larger mass of Indians and Negroes; in others they were the whole or a substantial part of the population. Whatever the social structure, however, the significance of these colonies for European economic development is that they produced an ever-larger volume of goods for export, primarily food and raw materials, and took in return a growing stream of European manufactures. This was not a once-for-all gain. It constituted an enduring increment to the pressure of demand on European industry and thus contributed, as we shall see, to the Industrial Revolution.

To say that colonial possessions contributed to the enrichment and development of certain European countries, however, is one thing; to say that they were a necessary or a sufficient condition of this development, is quite another. The necessity argument implies that if there had been no overseas expansion, there would have been no Industrial Revolution. It is hard to prove or disprove this kind of contrafactual hypothesis. But it is worth observing that a similar argument about the indispensability of imperialism to the sustenance of the European economies in a more advanced stage of development has been put to the test and been found wanting—even in the cases of those countries, Belgium and Holland, most dependent on colonial profits.

The sufficiency thesis is more complicated, yet may be somewhat easier to deal with. It asserts that once Europe achieved superior power, it could despoil and exploit the outside world at will, and the rest— enrichment and industrial development—followed as a matter of course. By implication, the argument imputes enormous rewards to dominion, and assumes that the possession of superior power necessarily entails the rational and effective use of that power for personal or national advantage. Yet the historian must not take anything for granted in this regard—not even the fact of empire, for the overseas expansion of Europe was itself made possible by previous political and technological advances and was not a windfall. Similarly, the shift from plunder to exploitation was not implicit in European dominion. The world, after all, had known (and still knew and would know) other conquering peoples, some of whom had held sway over richer lands than the forests of North America or the semitropical isles of the Caribbean. Yet aside from cases of outright annexation *cum* assimilation, none of these had succeeded in converting their conquests into an enduring source of wealth; rather they had always chosen to seize the quick returns—to loot, take slaves, exact tribute. The decision of certain European powers, therefore, to establish 'plantations', that is to treat their colonies as continuous enterprises was, whatever one may think of its morality, a momentous innovation.[1]

Given the innovation, however, the question then arises of the returns to what Hobsbawm calls the 'new colonialism'. What, after all, constitutes a 'sufficiency' of gain for purposes of industrial revolution?

[1] On the differences between the colonialisms of plunder and of exploitation and the significance of the shift from the one to the other, see especially the stimulating article of Eric Hobsbawm, 'The Crisis of the 17th Century', *Past and Present*, no. 5 (May, 1954), pp. 33-53; no. 6 (November, 1954), pp. 44-65.

We shall have occasion to examine this problem in detail later on, when we compare the contributions of home market and export market to the demand for British manufactures. Suffice it here to say that while the large and growing home market might conceivably have been enough to elicit and sustain a revolution in the mode of production, the export trade (of which the colonial trade formed only a part) could not by itself have done so.

There remains one last point: the effect of European expansion on the colonial areas. Here the record of the early modern period is one of almost unrelieved oppression and brutalization of the indigenous populations. The enormity of the crime is a matter of historical research and debate: Did the Indian population of central Mexico fall from 11 million to 2 million in the first century of Spanish rule?[1] Was the number of slaves shipped from Africa in the sixteenth and seventeenth centuries (to say nothing of later years) 2 million, 3 million, or 5 million?[2] How many died in African wars or captivity before they could be put in the holds of a slave ship? We shall never have precise data on these points. But the effect of European dominion is indisputable: the destruction, eviction, or emasculation of the indigenous civilization.

To say this, however, is not to say that these societies would have effected a significant technological transformation of their own economies had it not been for European colonialism. In spite of current efforts to enhance the achievements of the African and American peoples before the coming of the European, it is clear that none of them was ever in the running for world economic leadership. The only serious contenders, going back to the Middle Ages, were China, India, and the Islamic world. The first was not significantly affected by European imperialism before the late eighteenth century, and by that time, the contest was over. The Muslim world suffered earlier wounds: the Spanish *reconquista*, the Crusades, the endemic piracy of the Mediterranean (which cut both ways). But the sources of the economic backwardness of the Muslim world must be sought, as we have seen, in the cultural and political history of the Islamic heartland—Egypt, Syria, Iraq, Persia; and here the effect of European expansion was not the decisive consideration. The same was true of India. Whatever nefarious deeds one may acribe to imperialism, one can hardly argue

[1] See Sherburne F. Cook and Woodrow Borah, *The Indian Population of Central Mexico 1531–1610* [Ibero-Americana, no. 44] (Berkeley and Los Angeles, 1960).

[2] Daniel P. Mannix and Malcolm Cowley, *Black Cargoes: A History of the Atlantic Slave Trade 1518–1865* (New York, 1962), p. 32, gives the following estimates of slaves shipped from 'all parts of Guinea' to the New World: 900,000 in the sixteenth century; 2,750,000, in the seventeenth.

that the states of the subcontinent were on their way to an industrial revolution before the Europeans interrupted.

In all instances, indeed, the failure of the colonial society to stand up to European aggression was in itself testimony to severe internal weakness. Karl Marx saw it very well in the case of India:[1]

A country not only divided between Mohammedan and Hindoo, but between tribe and tribe, between caste and caste; a society whose framework was based on a sort of equilibrium, resulting from a general repulsion and constitutional exclusiveness between all its members. Such a country and such a society, were they not the predestined prey of conquest? If we knew nothing of the past history of Hindostan, would there not be the one great and incontestable fact, that even at this moment India is held in English thraldom by an Indian army maintained at the cost of India? India, then, could not escape the fate of being conquered, and the whole of her past history, if it be anything, is the history of the successive conquests she has undergone.

From the side of the victim, therefore, as well as from the side of the conqueror, one cannot take the fact of domination *cum* exploitation for granted. The case of Japan is there to show that an alert and self-disciplined society, though backward in technology and armament, could stand up to European pressure—first by self-imposed isolation and then, when that became impossible, by meeting and matching the Westerner on his own ground of industrialization.

★   ★   ★   ★   ★

So much for the priority of Europe's industrial revolution. We may now turn to our central concern: why some countries in Europe accomplished this transformation earlier than others; also how the pattern of development differed from one nation to another and why. These are important matters, for they throw light on the general problem of growth and, by implication, *mutatis mutandis*, on the character and difficulties of contemporary industrialization. For this purpose, indeed, western Europe offers an ideal subject of analysis. It offers the possibility of comparing a good many of what would seem to be the relevant variables: we have in Europe large countries and small, rich countries and poor, all forms of government, a rich mosaic of social traditions and organization, a great variety of political experience. Europe also presents for analysis the fundamental contrast between self-generated change—Britain—and emulative response. In sum, if history is the laboratory of the social sciences, the economic evolution of Europe should provide the data for some rewarding experiments.

[1] In an article in the New York *Daily Tribune* of 8 August 1853; reprinted in Karl Marx and Frederick Engels, *Selected Works in Two Volumes* (Moscow, 1958), I, 352.

On the other hand, the very wealth of the material imposes handicaps on the author of a short synthesis. Clearly it is impossible to treat so complex a phenomenon in detail within the compass of a single book. We shall therefore be obliged to concentrate our attention on what seem to be the main threads of the story. In particular, we shall focus to begin with on those industries that have played the decisive role in the general transition: the textile manufacture because it was the first to convert to modern techniques of production and long was far and away the most important in terms of capital invested, labour force, value of product, and the other traditional criteria; metallurgy and chemicals, because of their direct link to all other industries; machine-building, because the machine is the heart of the new economic civilization. Coal mining will be considered not so much for itself (it was not changed so much as the others by the new technique), but as a part of the general problem of energy. And all of these will be situated in the context of industrial organization, a comprehensive rubric that includes not only all aspects of co-ordination of the factors of production, but also the handling and movement of the objects of manufacture in the course of their transformation.

CHAPTER 2

The Industrial Revolution in Britain

In the eighteenth century, a series of inventions transformed the manufacture of cotton in England and gave rise to a new mode of production—the factory system. During these years, other branches of industry effected comparable advances, and all these together, mutually reinforcing one another, made possible further gains on an ever-widening front. The abundance and variety of these innovations almost defy compilation, but they may be subsumed under three principles: the substitution of machines—rapid, regular, precise, tireless—for human skill and effort; the substitution of inanimate for animate sources of power, in particular, the introduction of engines for converting heat into work, thereby opening to man a new and almost unlimited supply of energy; the use of new and far more abundant raw materials, in particular, the substitution of mineral for vegetable or animal substances.

These improvements constitute the Industrial Revolution. They yielded an unprecedented increase in man's productivity and, with it, a substantial rise in income per head. Moreover, this rapid growth was self-sustaining. Where previously, an amelioration of the conditions of existence, hence of survival, and an increase in economic opportunity had always been followed by a rise in population that eventually consumed the gains achieved, now for the first time in history, both the economy and knowledge were growing fast enough to generate a continuing flow of investment and technological innovation, a flow that lifted beyond visible limits the ceiling of Malthus's positive checks. The Industrial Revolution thereby opened a new age of promise. It also transformed the balance of political power, within nations, between nations, and between civilizations; revolutionized the social order; and as much changed man's way of thinking as his way of doing.

In 1760 Britain imported some $2\frac{1}{2}$ million pounds of raw cotton to feed an industry dispersed for the most part through the countryside of Lancashire and existing in conjunction with the linen manufacture, which supplied it with the tough warp yarn it had not yet learned to produce. All of its work was done by hand, usually (excluding dyeing and finishing) in the homes of the workers, occasionally in the small shops of the master weavers. A generation later, in 1787, the consumption of raw cotton was up to 22 million pounds; the cotton manufacture was second only to wool in numbers employed and value of product; most of the fibre consumed was being cleaned, carded, and spun on machines, some driven by water in large mills, some by hand in smaller shops or even in cottages. A half-century later, consumption had increased to 366 million pounds; the cotton manufacture was the most important in the kingdom in value of product, capital invested, and numbers employed; almost all of its employees, except for the still large number of hand-loom weavers, worked in mills under factory discipline. The price of yarn had fallen to perhaps one twentieth of what it had been, and the cheapest Hindu labour could not compete in either quality or quantity with Lancashire's mules and throstles. British cotton goods sold everywhere in the world: exports, a third larger than home consumption, were worth four times those of woollens and worsteds. The cotton mill was the symbol of Britain's industrial greatness; the cotton hand, of her greatest social problem—the rise of an industrial proletariat.

Why did this revolution in the techniques and organization of manufacture occur first in Britain? A few theoretical considerations may help us to organize the argument. Technological change is never automatic. It means the displacement of established methods, damage to vested interests, often serious human dislocations. Under the circumstances, there usually must be a combination of considerations to call forth such a departure and make it possible: (1) an opportunity for improvement due to inadequacy of prevailing techniques,[1] or a need for improvement created by autonomous increases in factor costs; and (2) a degree of superiority such that the new methods pay sufficiently to cover the costs of the change. Implicit in the latter is the assumption that, however much the users of older, less efficient methods may attempt to survive by compressing the costs of the human factors of production, entrepreneurial or labour, the new techniques are enough of an improvement to enable progressive producers to outprice them and displace them.

The technological changes that we denote as the 'Industrial Revolution' implied a far more drastic break with the past than anything since the invention of the wheel. On the entrepreneurial side, they necessitated a sharp redistribution of investment and a concomitant revision of the concept of risk. Where before, almost all the costs of manufacture had been variable—raw materials and labour primarily—more and more would now have to be sunk in fixed plant. The flexibility of the older system had been very advantageous to the entrepreneur: in

[1] The criterion of adequacy would, for my purposes, be marginal costs. Steeply rising costs per unit of one or more factors of production under conditions of growing demand would imply an opportunity for and incentive to technological improvement.

time of depression, he was able to halt production at little cost, resuming work only when and in so far as conditions made advisable. Now he was to be a prisoner of his investment, a situation that many of the traditional merchant-manufacturers found very hard, even impossible, to accept.

For the worker, the transformation was even more fundamental, for not only his occupational role, but his very way of life was at stake. For many—though by no means for all—the introduction of machinery implied for the first time a complete separation from the means of production; the worker became a 'hand'. On almost all, however, the machine imposed a new discipline. No longer could the spinner turn her wheel and the weaver throw his shuttle at home, free of supervision, both in their own good time. Now the work had to be done in a factory, at a pace set by tireless, inanimate equipment, as part of a large team that had to begin, pause, and stop in unison—all under the close eye of overseers, enforcing assiduity by moral, pecuniary, occasionally even physical means of compulsion. The factory was a new kind of prison; the clock a new kind of jailer.

In short, only the strongest incentives could have persuaded entrepreneurs to undertake and accept these changes; and only major advances could have overcome the dogged resistance of labour to the very principle of mechanization.

The origins of the entrepreneurial interest in machines and factory production must be sought in the growing inadequacy of the older modes of production, an inadequacy rooted in internal contradictions, themselves aggravated by external forces.

Of these pre-factory forms of organization, the oldest was the independent craft shop, with master often assisted by one or more journeymen or apprentices. Fairly early, however—as far back as the thirteenth century—this independence broke down in many areas, and the artisan found himself bound to the merchant who supplied his raw materials and sold his finished work. This subordination of the producer to the intermediary (or, less often, of weak producers to strong ones) was a consequence of the growth of the market. Where once the artisan worked for a local clientele, a small but fairly stable group that was bound to him personally as well as by pecuniary interest, he now came to depend on sales through a middleman in distant, competitive markets. He was ill-equipped to cope with the fluctuations inherent in this arrangement. In bad times he might be completely idle, with no one to sell to; and when business improved, he usually had to borrow from his merchant the materials needed to get started again. Once caught on a treadmill of debt—his finished work mortgaged in advance to his creditor—the craftsman rarely regained his independence; his work sufficed to support him—no more—and he was in fact if not in principle a proletarian, selling not a commodity, but labour.

Aside from his pecuniary difficulties, the local artisan was in no position to know and exploit the needs of distant consumers. Only the merchant could respond to the ebb and flow of demand, calling for changes in the nature of the final product to meet consumer tastes, recruiting additional labour when necessary, supplying tools as well as materials to potential artisans. It was largely in this way that the rural population was drawn into the productive circuit. Very early, urban merchants came to realize that the countryside was a reservoir of cheap labour: peasants eager to eke out the meagre income of the land by working in the off-season, wives and children with free time to prepare the man's work and assist him in his task. And though the country weaver, nail-maker, or cutler was less skilled than the guildsman or journeyman of the town, he was less expensive, for the marginal utility of his free time was, initially at least, low, and his agricultural resources, however modest, enabled him to get by on that much less additional income. Furthermore, rural putting-out was free of guild restrictions on the nature of the product, the techniques of manufacture, and the size of enterprise.

The above description of a long and complex historical process inevitably oversimplifies. If it seems reasonable to assert that, taking Europe as a whole, most putters-out came from the mercantile side, it is important to note the many exceptions: the weavers who became clothiers by hiring their less enterprising neighbours; the fullers and dyers who had accumulated capital in the finishing processes and integrated backwards by contracting directly for yarn and cloth. In some areas, most notably the region around Leeds in the West Riding of Yorkshire, rural artisans organized their own small weaving sheds, joined when necessary to create common facilities, and sold their pieces as independent clothiers in the weekly cloth halls. But even in Yorkshire, this fragmentation of enterprise was characteristic primarily of the woollen trade; in the worsted manufacture, where capital requirements were greater, the productive unit was larger and the merchant putter-out more important.[1]

The English textile industry built its fortune in the late medieval and

---

[1] In his discussion of the shift from urban to rural industry, P. Mantoux, *The Industrial Revolution in the Eighteenth Century* (London, 1928), pp. 64–6, conveys the impression that the putting-out system was the result of the decay of what he describes as 'domestic manufacture', that is, dispersed independent cottage industry of the kind found in Yorkshire. Often, as we noted, this was true, but even more often, probably, putting out was the product of mercantile initiative seeking new sources of labour and drawing the rural population into the commercial circuit.

early modern periods on rural manufacture. No centre of production, except perhaps Flanders, was so quick to turn from the towns to the countryside; it is estimated that as early as 1400 over half the output of wool cloth was accounted for in this manner.[1] The trend continued: by the mid-eighteenth century, the great preponderance of the British wool manufacture was cottage industry; of all the towns immemorially associated with the wool trade, only Norwich remained as an important urban centre, and it was rapidly declining in relative importance. Allowing for such regional variations, moreover, and for occasional pauses, the industry as a whole had prospered impressively. In the late seventeenth and early eighteenth centuries, at a time when the Italian manufacture was a shadow of its former self, when Dutch cloth output was shrinking steadily, and when France was in the throes of a prolonged depression, British consumption of raw wool was growing at the rate of about 8 per cent a decade; and from about 1740 to 1770, the decennial increase was 13 or 14 per cent.[2]

This growth merits detailed attention, for it was the principal precipitant of the changes we denote by the Industrial Revolution, and understanding it may help us understand the reasons for British precedence in technological and economic development. In part the wool industry grew because of favourable conditions of production. Thus no country had so abundant a supply of raw wool, particularly the long wool required for the lighter, harder, worsted fabrics. And rural manufacture, largely unhampered by guild restrictions or government regulation, was in a position to make the most of this resource advantage by suiting its product to demand and changes in demand. In particular, it was free to develop cheaper fabrics, perhaps less sturdy than the traditional broadcloths and stuffs, but usable and often more comfortable. This freedom to adjust and innovate is particularly important in light industry, where resources and similar material considerations often are less important as locational factors than entrepreneurship. A good example from within the British wool industry is the rapid growth of the Yorkshire worsted trade, to the point where it passed the

[1] H. L. Gray, 'The Production and Exportation of English Woollens in the Fourteenth Century', *English Historical Review*, XXXIX (1924), 32.

[2] P. Deane, 'The Output of the British Woollen Industry in the Eighteenth Century', *J. Econ. Hist.* XVII (1957), 220. These figures are derived from informed contemporary guesses and are therefore gross approximations. But it is the trend that interests us here. On this, compare the much slower growth of the Verviers-Hodimont area near Liège, one of the most enterprising centres of wool manufacture on the Continent. P. Lebrun, *L'industrie de la laine à Verviers pendant le XVIIIe et le début du XIXe siècle* (Liège, 1948), pp. 518–19. Note also the difference in size of output between Yorkshire alone (aulnage returns in T. S. Ashton, *An Economic History of England: the Eighteenth Century* (London, 1955), pp. 249–50) and the Verviers area.

older centre of East Anglia in the course of the eighteenth century; compare Clapham's explanation: 'the ordinary case of a pushing, hard-working locality with certain slight advantages, attacking the lower grades of an expanding industry'.[1] We shall have occasion to remark comparable examples of the advantages of entrepreneurial freedom when we turn to the continental countries. In the meantime, we may note that the British wool manufacture profited the more from its liberty because some of its most dangerous competitors across the Channel were being subjected in the seventeenth and early eighteenth centuries to increasing regulation and control.

Finally, one should cite the relative freedom of British industry from the disturbance and destruction of war, the uneven but long and often rich inflow of skilled foreign artisans, and the access of the producing centres to water transport, hence distant markets—all factors conducive to lower costs of manufacture and distribution.

On the demand side, the British wool manufacture was comparably favoured. The population of the kingdom was not large, but it was growing, faster probably by the middle of the eighteenth century than that of any of the countries across the Channel. From not quite 6 millions around 1700, it rose to almost 9 millions in 1800; 70–90 per cent of the gain came in the second half of the period.[2] What is more, the absence of internal customs barriers or feudal tolls created in Britain the largest coherent market in Europe. This political unity was confirmed by the geography of the island: the land mass was small; the topography, easy; the coastline, deeply indented. By contrast, a country like France, with more than three times as many people, was cut up by internal customs barriers into three major trade areas, and by informal custom, obsolete tolls and charges, and, above all, poor communications into a mosaic of semi-autarkic cells.

Moreover, what nature bestowed, man improved. From the mid-seventeenth century on, there was a continuous and growing investment of both public and private resources in the extension of the river system and the construction of new roads and bridges. By 1750 there were over a thousand miles of navigable streams in Britain; and Parliament

---

[1] J. H. Clapham, 'The Transference of the Worsted Industry from Norfolk to the West Riding', *Econ. J.* XX (1910), 203. Eric M. Sigsworth, *Black Dyke Mills: a History: with Introductory Chapters on the Development of the Worsted Industry in the Nineteenth Century* (Liverpool: University Press, 1958), p. 17, subscribes to this point of view.

[2] For different but roughly concordant estimates of this increase, see Phyllis Deane and W. A. Cole, *British Economic Growth 1688–1959: Trends and Structure* (Cambridge, 1962), p. 5, n. 3. In the same period, the population of France went from about 20 to 27½ millions. E. Levasseur, *La population française* (3 vols.; Paris, 1889), I, 201–6, 215–18.

had been passing turnpike acts at the rate of eight a year for half a century. Impressive as this development was, it was inadequate to the needs of the economy, and the pace of investment increased markedly in the fifties and sixties. These years saw the first canals (Sankey Navigation, 1755–9; Duke of Bridgewater's canal, 1759–61) and turnpike acts at the rate of forty a year. In two decades (1760–80), navigable water and solid roads linked the major industrial centres of the North to those of the Midlands, the Midlands to London, and London to the Severn basin and the Atlantic.

Within the market of Britain, purchasing power per head and standard of living were significantly higher than on the Continent. We have no precise measures of national income for the eighteenth century,[1] but there is an abundance of impressionistic testimony by travellers from both sides of the Channel to the greater equality of wealth, higher wages, and greater abundance to be found in Britain. Thus one of the best signs of comfort in Europe is the consumption of white bread; in the nineteenth century, one can almost follow the rise in *per capita* income and the diffusion of higher living standards among the poorer sections of the population, into rural areas, and into central and eastern Europe by the wheat frontier. In the eighteenth century England was known as the country of the wheaten loaf. This was an exaggeration: in large areas, particularly in the Midlands and North, rye and barley were the staple grains, especially in the early part of the century. Even there, however, the bread grew whiter over the years, and nowhere was there anything like the reliance one found across the Channel on coarser cereals like buckwheat and oats. Similarly, there was much myth in the image of John Bull, beefeater. Yet when Arthur Young sat down to soup in the Pays Basque—'what we should call the farmer's ordinary'— he received 'ample provision of cabbage, grease, and water, and about as much meat for some scores of people, as half a dozen English farmers would have eaten, and grumbled at their host for short commons'.[2] Even workhouse menus, hardly designed to make life agreeable for the residents, provided for meat daily or at least several times a week.[3]

The English labourer not only ate better; he spent less of his income on food than his continental counterpart, and in most areas this portion was shrinking, whereas across the Channel it may well have risen

[1] See, however, the article of P. Deane, 'The Implications of Early National Income Estimates for the Measurement of Long-Term Economic Growth in the United Kingdom', *Economic Development and Cultural Change*, IV (1955), 3–38.

[2] Young, *Travels during the Years 1787, 1788 and 1789* (2 vols.; Dublin, 1793), I, 87 f., 93.

[3] Cf. Dorothy Marshall, *The English Poor in the Eighteenth Century* (London, 1926), p. 268.

during much of the eighteenth century.[1] As a result, he had more to spare for other things, including manufactures. The Englishman was reputed for wearing leather shoes where the Fleming or Frenchman wore clogs. He was dressed in wool where the French or German peasant often shivered in linen, a noble fabric for table or bed, but a poor shield against the European winter. Defoe vividly and proudly described the importance of this demand for British manufactures in his *Plan of the English Commerce* in 1728:[2]

...for the rest, we see their Houses and Lodgings tolerably furnished, at least stuff'd well with useful and necessary household Goods: Even those we call poor People, Journey-men, working and Pains-taking People do thus; they lye warm, live in Plenty, work hard, and [need] know no Want.

These are the People that carry off the Gross of your Consumption; 'tis for these your Markets are kept open late on *Saturday* nights; because they usually receive their Week's Wages late...in a Word, these are the Life of our whole Commerce, and all by their Multitude: Their Numbers are not Hundreds or Thousands, or Hundreds of Thousands, but Millions; 'tis by their Multitude, I say, that all the Wheels of Trade are set on Foot, the Manufacture and Produce of the Land and Sea, finished, cur'd, and fitted for the Markets Abroad; 'tis by the Largeness of their Gettings, that they are supported, and by the Largeness of their Number the whole Country is supported; by their Wages they are able to live plentifully, and it is by their expensive, generous, free way of living, that the Home Consumption is rais'd to such a Bulk, as well of our own, as of foreign Production....

Defoe's reference to the Englishman's 'expensive, generous, free way of living' calls to mind a final aspect of the British domestic market: a consumption pattern favourable to the growth of manufactures. More than any other in Europe, probably, British society was open. Not only was income more evenly distributed than across the Channel, but the barriers to mobility were lower, the definitions of status looser. Nothing is more revealing in this regard than a comparison of contemporary images of society in the different countries of western Europe. For Britain, we have schemes like those of Gregory King or Joseph Massie—congeries of occupational groups ranked according to wealth and so intermingled as to preclude the drawing of horizontal status lines across the whole of the social pyramid. For France, we have a neater tripartite structure: aristocracy, bourgeoisie, *peuple*; within these, to be sure, there are fine distinctions, and it is not always easy to rank

---

[1] This is the position of C. E. Labrousse, *Origines et aspects économiques et sociaux de la Révolution française (1774–1791)* ['Les Cours de Sorbonne'] (Paris, n.d.), pp. 54–8.

[2] [Daniel Defoe], *A Plan of the English Commerce* (Oxford: Blackwell, 1928), pp. 76–7.

people of different occupations or to place borderline groups like artisans and retail shopkeepers; nevertheless, the arrangement is orderly, traditionally logical. For most of west Germany, we have the French system, but more rigid and carefully defined, to the point where status, even of sub-groups, is often written into law. And east of the Elbe, society was simpler yet: a small landholding aristocracy; the large mass of personally dependent peasants; in between, a thin layer of commercial bourgeois, spiritually and often ethnically alien to the body social within which they lived and moved encapsulated.

So far as the rate of consumption is concerned, the implications of greater equality of income are a matter of some debate.[1] Similarly, mobility is ambiguous in its effects: some people will save to climb; others will consume to announce their arrival. The net result will depend on circumstances.

Quality and direction of consumption, however, are something else again. In non-primitive societies, where skills are fairly advanced and there has been some accumulation of wealth, inequality fosters a taste for extravagant luxuries and services among the few, whereas equality encourages a demand for more sober, solid comforts among the many. Great riches amid a sea of poverty are generally the product of a low capital–labour ratio (or of misinvestment of capital). They give rise to a prodigal expenditure of labour on pleasure and elegance: an over-abundance of domestics—to the point where the mistress of the house spends more time supervising her staff than more modest wives spend doing their own chores; ornamental garments of great price; lavish decoration of residences; the production of exquisitely difficult works of art.

A more even diffusion of wealth, however, is the result of costly labour. This was indeed the case in Britain, where wages—allowing for the uncertainty and partial incomparability of the estimates—ran about twice as high as in France and higher yet than east of the Rhine. In such an economy, production functions are more capital-intensive, while the rich consumer caters less to whim and satisfies himself with a

---

[1] The traditional assumption is that inequality does increase the savings ratio. But there is some question whether this is justified for a pre-industrial society, especially one in which a small privileged group commands the levers of power and can draw a kind of tributary income from the rest of the nation. It seems quite probable, for example, that the court aristocracy of eighteenth-century France lived beyond its income, consuming freely in the knowledge that there would always be ways of obtaining more from the crown. Cf. Milton Friedman, *A Theory of the Consumption Function* (Princeton, 1957), pp. 235 f., who argues that inequality of 'permanent' (as against measured) income *per se* does not affect the consumption–savings ratio; that it is uncertainty about future income that promotes savings, against a rainy day as it were.

greater abundance of those goods that are available on a smaller scale and in lower quality to his poorer fellows. On the other hand, the relatively high purchasing power of the poorer elements of the population implies a correspondingly greater demand for the things they need and can afford—the cheaper, plainer articles most susceptible of mass production.[1]

Mobility in such a society is a force for standardization. For mobility implies emulation, and emulation promotes the diffusion of patterns of expenditure throughout the population. Where there is no movement between status groups, clear, inviolate distinctions of dress and way of life mark the gradations of hierarchy. Where there begins to be movement, as in the late Middle Ages, sumptuary laws are often needed to keep people in their place. And where mobility has become so commonplace as to seem to many a virtue, discriminatory controls over expenditure are unenforceable.

In England, sumptuary laws were dead letters by the end of the sixteenth century; they were repealed by James I in 1604. Over the next two centuries, the trend toward homogeneity of expenditure—the effacement of vertical regional differences as well as horizontal social distinctions—continued. Contemporaries complained of the luxury of the lower classes, who dressed so as to be indistinguishable from their betters. This was an exaggeration; social lament as a literary genre is invariably hyperbolic. Besides, much of the elegance of the populace was meretricious, the result of an active trade in second-hand clothes. Even so, the very demand for cast-offs was evidence of the absence or decay of customary distinctions: the poor man could and did wear the same kind of coat as the rich. Similarly, contemporaries complained of the farmer's imitation of city ways, his abandonment of the rustic simplicity of yore. Again an exaggeration—yet the truth was that in no economy was the countryside so closely integrated into the commercial circuit; nowhere were the local pockets of self-sufficiency so broken down.

---

[1] On the implication of inequality of income, or, more precisely, inequality of consumption, for the nature and composition of industrial output, see the suggestive article of W. Paul Strassman, 'Economic Growth and Income Distribution', *Quarterly J. of Economics*, LXX (1956), 425–40; also S. Kuznets, 'Economic Growth and Income Inequality', *Amer. Econ. Rev.* XLV (1955), 1–28, which is more concerned with the reverse relation.

The best single index to relative factor costs and the pattern of consumption is the extent and character of domestic service: the twentieth century, sometimes called the era of the common man, is also the age of the disappearing maid. And while the British merchant of the eighteenth century had less cause for frustration than his present-day descendants, he had his servant problem. Cf. Defoe, *Everybody's Business Is Nobody's Business*, in *The Novels and Miscellaneous Works of Daniel Defoe* ('Bohm's Standard Library'; 7 vols.; London, 1889), II, 499–500. See also J. Jean Hecht, *The Domestic Servant Class in Eighteenth-century England* (London, 1956), esp. chs. I and VI.

All of this was part of a general process of urbanization, itself a reflection of advanced commercialization and industrialization. London alone was a monster: Defoe estimated in 1725 that it contained a million and a half inhabitants, almost a quarter of the people in the kingdom. This figure is testimony, not to Defoe's accuracy, but to the impression the 'great wen' made on contemporaries; yet even conservative estimates put the population of the metropolitan area at about half that number. In the provinces, the cities and towns developed steadily after the Civil War; among the most rapidly expanding were unincorporated 'villages' like Manchester, which had perhaps 12,500 inhabitants in 1717 and 20,000 by 1758. An estimate of 15 per cent of the population in cities of 5000 and over by mid-century and 25 per cent by 1800 is probably close to the truth.[1] By contrast, the French figure on the eve of the Revolution was something over 10 per cent; and Germany was even more rural.

But it was not only that England had more people living in cities than any other European country except perhaps Holland;[2] it was the character of British urban life that made the pattern of settlement particularly significant. On the Continent, many of the cities were essentially administrative, judicial, ecclesiastical in function. Their populations consisted essentially of bureaucrats, professionals, soldiers, and the shopkeepers, artisans, and domestics to serve them. The city was not so much a node of economic activity, trading manufactures and mercantile services for the products of the countryside, as a political and cultural centre drawing tax revenues and rents from the rural population in return for government and by traditional right. Madrid is the classic example of this kind of agglomeration; but Paris was much like this, and perhaps a majority of the larger French provincial cities—including places like Arras, Douai, Caen, Versailles, Nancy, Tours, Poitiers, Aix, and Toulouse—were little else. In Germany, of course, the very fragmentation of political power was an incitement to the multiplication of semi-rural capitals, each with its court, bureaucracy, and garrison.

By contrast, the relatively smaller size of Britain's political apparatus and its concentration in London left the older provincial centres to somnolence and decay. Nothing is more striking about the map of Britain in the eighteenth century than the modernity of the urban pattern. The medieval county seats—Lancaster, York, Chester, Stafford

[1] Phyllis Deane and W. A. Cole, *British Economic Growth, 1688–1959: Trends and Structure* (Cambridge, 1962), p. 7.

[2] And Holland's urban population was declining sharply, both relatively and absolutely. Cf. William Petersen, *Planned Migration: the Social Determinants of the Dutch-Canadian Movement* [University of California Publications in Sociology and Social Institutions, vol. II] (Berkeley and Los Angeles, 1955), p. 20.

—were overshadowed by younger places like Liverpool, Manchester, Leeds, and Birmingham, and there was already a substantial shift of population in favour of the North and Midlands. Much of the increase, moreover, did not take place within the cities proper, but took the form of a thickening of the countryside. Numerous overgrown industrial villages sprang up—concentrations of hundreds of spinners and weavers in the manufacturing districts of Lancashire and Yorkshire, similar in many ways to the earlier rural agglomerations of East Anglia.

The pattern throughout was one of close contact and frequent exchange between city and land. Trade and shops went to the customers: the late A. P. Wadsworth noted the numerous advertisements of cottages-to-let for tradesmen in the villages around Manchester, reflecting on both sides the keen response to economic opportunity.[1] In spite of the sparseness of the data, it seems clear that British commerce of the eighteenth century was, by comparison with that of the Continent, impressively energetic, pushful, and open to innovation. Part of the explanation is institutional: British shopkeepers were relatively free of customary or legal restrictions on the objects or character of their activity. They could sell what and where they would; and could and did compete freely on the basis of price, advertising, and credit. If most shopkeepers continued to haggle, many followed the lead of the Quakers in selling at fixed, marked prices. In so far as such methods prevailed, they conduced to a more efficient allocation of economic resources and lower costs of distribution.

In sum, the home market for manufactures was growing, thanks to improving communication, increase in population, high and rising average income, a buying pattern favourable to solid, standardized, moderately priced products, and unhampered commercial enterprise. How much it grew, however, one cannot say precisely; we have no statistics on domestic consumption.

We are better informed about foreign trade, if only because most of the commodities that came in or went out of the country had to pass under the eyes of the customs officers. Admittedly, the trade statistics are incomplete, inaccurate, and biased by the use of fixed values in a world of fluctuating prices. But they do furnish an order of comparison, showing for example a three- or fourfold gain in British exports (including re-exports) in the century from 1660 to 1760.

We have seen that the growth of Britain's sales abroad, as at home, reflected in large part her natural endowment; to this should be added some institutional and historical advantages. She had a strong maritime tradition, and, unlike most of her continental rivals, did not divert her

---

[1] A. P. Wadsworth and Julia de L. Mann, *The Cotton Trade and Industrial Lancashire, 1600–1790* (Manchester, 1931), p. 276, n. 2.

energies into the maintenance of costly armies and territorial aggrandizement. Rather she concentrated her efforts on securing trading privileges and a colonial empire, in large part at the expense of her leading
continental rivals, France and Holland. This kind of thing cost less than
European territory and in the long run paid better. No state was more
responsive to the desires of its mercantile classes; no country more alert
to the commercial implications of war. Mr Ramsey perceptively notes
the role of London in promoting this harmony of trade and diplomacy,
contrasting in this regard the isolation of Bordeaux, Marseilles, and
Nantes from Paris and Versailles.[1]

At the same time, Britain developed a large, aggressive merchant
marine and the financial institutions to sustain it. Of all the Continental
countries, only Holland again could rival her in this regard, and the comparative advantage of Holland lay in trade, not industry. Between
Dutch mercantile power and Britain's combination of mercantile and
industrial strength, the issue was never in doubt; the greatest asset of a
port is a productive hinterland.

In the long run, this was Britain's forte: the ability to manufacture
cheaply precisely those articles for which foreign demand was most
elastic. The most promising markets for Britain in the seventeenth and
eighteenth centuries lay not in Europe, whose own industries were
growing and whose mercantilist rulers were increasingly hostile to the
importation of manufactures, but rather overseas: in the New World,
Africa, the Orient. These areas were very different in needs and tastes.
The tribesmen of Africa and the plantation hand of the Antilles
wanted thin, cool fabrics, bright colours, flashy metal—light woollens,
the cotton-linen checks of Manchester, the cheap stampings of Birmingham. The requirements of the Indian or Chinese peasant were similar
(excluding most cotton goods) though more sober. The New England
farmer or Philadelphia merchant, confronted by a harsher, more
variable climate and more sophisticated technologically, bought
heavier cloth and sturdier hardware. For all, however, there was one
common denominator, and that a negative one: they were not especially
interested in costly, highly finished luxuries.

The effect of increased export, then, was to reinforce the pressures
toward standardization as against differentiation, quantity as against
quality. The sacrifice of quality to quantity was an old story in English
manufacture. By this I do not mean adulteration or the sale of inferior
goods as first quality—this was an international evil, as the iteration of
government and guild regulations on the Continent evidences. Rather
I mean the adoption of new methods of production that save costs at

[1] G. D. Ramsay, *English Overseas Trade during the Centuries of Emergence* (London,
1957), pp. 247 f.

the expense of solidity or appearance; the use of coal in place of wood in glass-making or brewing is the best example.[1]

This readiness to abandon old ways for new, to place profit above craft pride and even the appearances of pride, implies a certain separation of the producer from production, an orientation to the market instead of to the shop. To some extent it reflected the early domination of British manufacture by mercantile interests and the reduction of the rural artisan to a mere employee of the putter-out. Clearly, however, this is not enough to account for the phenomenon; in the wool industry, for example, the most enterprising centre of manufacture was in Yorkshire, a stronghold of the small independent clothier; and in metallurgy, glass-making, brewing, and chemicals—the industries most affected by the introduction of mineral fuel—the organization of production had nothing to do with putting-out.

Instead, this cost-mindedness must be seen as part of a larger rationality, itself in some measure the result of material circumstances—above all, the greater cohesiveness of the British market and the effectiveness of competitive pressures—but also as an ideological force of its own, whose sources still remain to be explored. In no country in the eighteenth century, with the possible exception of Holland, was society so sophisticated commercially. Nowhere was the response to profit and loss so rapid; nowhere did entrepreneurial decisions less reflect non-rational considerations of prestige and habit. We shall have occasion to consider this again when we speak of investment and the supply of capital for industrialization. At the moment, my only concern is to explain where market pressures were pushing the producers and why the producers responded.

How much of the increase in demand and the trend toward mass production of cheaper articles is to be attributed to the expansion of home as against foreign markets is probably impossible to say. We have only the grossest, global estimates of the proportion of domestic to overseas sales, and these presumably comprise everything, including agricultural products. What interests us here, however, is the demand for manufactures, and only certain manufactures at that. One may perhaps attempt this kind of comparison for the wool industry: at the end of the seventeenth century English exports of wool cloth probably

---

[1] J. U. Nef has argued in a number of works that the adoption of mineral fuel itself gave strong impetus to the production of 'quantity and utility rather than quality and elegance'. See, inter alia, his *Cultural Foundations of Industrial Civilization* (Cambridge, 1958), pp. 52–3. Yet it is clear that the readiness to accept coal was itself indicative of a deeper rationality; such nations as France, confronted with the same choice, obdurately rejected coal—even where there were strong pecuniary incentives to switch over to the cheaper fuel.

accounted for upwards of 30 per cent of the output of the industry; by 1740, the proportion had apparently risen, possibly to over half, and in 1771-2, something under a half.[1] In this important branch, then, the major impetus seems to have come from the export trade, and the most active exporting area in the industry, Yorkshire, was also the most rapidly growing centre of manufacture. It has indeed been argued that not only was the minimum critical market required to induce a technological breakthrough too big for any one country to provide, but that only a large fraction of the growing world demand could supply the necessary push; and that it was that peculiar combination of economic and political circumstances that permitted Britain to win for herself in the eighteenth century so large a share of the trade in manufactures that accounts for the successful leap to the 'higher' mode of production.[2]

Yet the answer is not so simple. Such figures as we have on British exports (overwhelmingly manufactures) show a distinct levelling off in the third quarter of the century. The volume of woollen shipments falls from the late fifties; cottons falter in the late sixties and seventies; the break comes later in iron and steel—in the late sixties—but it is sharp and the drop persists until the nineties.[3] David Eversley argues cogently against the easy acceptance of exports as the leading sector of the economy in process of revolution: noting the weight and relative stability of home demand, he reasons that only the existence of this kind of dependable market justified and permitted the accumulation of capital in manufacture.[4] On the other hand (as in many historical questions, one can fairly shuttle back and forth between pros and cons), this very variability of exports was surely a stimulant to industrial change and growth. It is not only that the marginal increment of sales often spells the difference between profit and loss; the bursts of overseas demand placed abrupt and severe burdens on the productive system, pushed enterprise into a position of rapidly increasing costs, and enhanced the incentive for technological change. Certainly, from the late

[1] These figures are based on Phyllis Deane, 'The Output of the British Woollen Industry in the Eighteenth Century', *J. Econ. Hist.* XVII (1957), 209-10, 211-13, 215-16, 220. The article itself makes clear the limitations of these figures, which are essentially informed inferences from informed guesses.

[2] Cf. Kenneth Berrill, 'International Trade and the Rate of Economic Growth', *Econ. Hist. Rev.* 2nd ser. XII (1960), 351-9; also P.A., 'The Origins of the Industrial Revolution' [summary of a symposium], *Past and Present*, no. 17 (1960), pp. 71-81.

[3] Deane and Cole, *British Economic Growth*, pp. 46, 59.

[4] D. E. C. Eversley, 'The Home Market and Economic Growth in England, 1750-80', in *Land, Labour and Population in the Industrial Revolution* (London, 1967), pp. 206-59.

eighteenth century on, the waves of investment seem to follow on increases in sales abroad.[1]

In any event, this rising demand contained the seeds of difficulty. Every mode of industrial organization has, built into it, opportunities for conflict between employer and employed. These are particularly serious in putting-out because the system furnishes the arms as well as the causes of hostility: the worker has custody of the materials of the employer and transforms them in his own good time, in his own home, free of supervision. The only resource of the merchant is his limited control over the income of his employees: if he pays them little enough, they are compelled to work for fear of hunger; and if he abates their pay for any departure from standards of quality, they are compelled to maintain a minimum level of performance. To be sure, the exercise of such constraints is contingent on the establishment of some kind of monopsonistic bond between employer and worker; otherwise the employer can do no more than accept the prevailing market price for labour. That such a nexus did in fact often exist—because of actual monopsony in some areas, or personal ties, or debt—and that it led to abuses, seems incontrovertible.[2] There is a substantial body of folklore built around the figure of the grasping clothier and his even greedier minion, Jimmy Squeezum.

On the other hand, it is equally clear that these controls were at best spotty and limited in effect; that the worker early learned to eke out his income by setting aside for his own use or for resale some of the raw materials furnished by the merchant. Such embezzlement was usually effected at the expense of the finished product: the yarn was sized to give it false weight; the cloth was stretched up to and beyond the point of transparency. Nor was there any feeling of moral compunction about such abstraction; it was looked upon as a normal perquisite of the trade, more than justified by the exploitation of the manufacturer.

The employer's control over labour was strongest in a declining market. At such times, the menace of unemployment hung heavy over the domestic workers, and indeed, from the manufacturer's point of view, one of the greatest advantages of the putting-out system was the ease of laying off labour; overhead costs were minimal. (Later on,

---

[1] Cf. François Crouzet, 'La formation du capital en Grande-Bretagne pendant la Révolution Industrielle', *Deuxième Conférence Internationale d'Histoire Economique, Aix-en-Provence 1962*. [Ecole Pratique des Hautes Etudes, Sorbonne, Sixième Section: Sciences Economiques et Sociales, 'Congrès et colloques', VIII] (Paris, 1965), pp. 589–640.

[2] For one example of the role of debt in holding a worker to his employer, cf. T. S. Ashton, 'The Domestic System in the Early Lancashire Tool Trade', *Econ. Hist. Rev.* I (1926), 136.

when the alternative of concentrated factory production became available, many an entrepreneur, in the continental countries especially, delayed shifting over because of the flexibility of the older arrangements.) In the eighteenth century, however, the British putter-out was confronted with a secularly expanding market, which sapped industrial discipline while aggravating the conflicts endemic in the system. Thus the worker's predilection for embezzlement, sharpened in depression by the desire to compensate for increased abatements and lack of work, was nowise dulled in prosperity; on the contrary, the reward for theft was greater.

What is more, though the system was flexible downwards, expansion of output was difficult. Up to a point, rural manufacture expanded easily by opening new areas—moving from the environs of the manufacturing towns into nearby valleys, invading less accessible mountain regions, spreading like a liquid seeking its level, in this case the lowest possible wage level. It was in this way that the woollen industry filled the dales of Wiltshire and Somerset and came to thrive all along the Welsh marches by the end of the sixteenth century; on the Continent, the growing woollen *fabriques* of Verviers and Monschau were seeking their weavers in the Limburg by the mid-eighteenth century, while the cotton manufacture of Normandy, after covering the Pays de Caux, was spilling over into Picardy.

But in eighteenth-century Britain, the possibilities of geographical expansion had been largely exhausted. The most accessible areas had been explored and drawn into the system. The worsted weavers of the West Riding were buying yarn in the northern dales and as far afield as East Anglia. In Lancashire, by mid-century, weavers were walking miles to collect the weft needed to keep their looms busy the rest of the day and buying the spinsters with ribbons and other vanities. Much of the difficulty was due to the difference in labour requirements for spinning and weaving: it took at least five wheels to supply one loom, a proportion ordinarily at variance with the composition of the population. So long as it was merely a question of finding rural spinsters—whose husbands worked in the fields—to furnish yarn to urban weavers, there was no problem. But once weaving spread to the countryside and the men gave up cultivation for industry, the imbalance was bound to become an obstacle to expansion. There is evidence that some spinners had begun to specialize in particular types of yarn by the middle of the eighteenth century, that a division of labour had come about, in parts of Lancashire at least, in response to the pressure of demand. But this was hardly enough, given the state of technology, and the price of yarn rose sharply from the late seventeenth to the mid-eighteenth century.

Essentially the increase was due to the ever-wider dispersion of the labour force, for nominal spinning wages changed little. The cost of transport was high to begin with; even more serious, in a world of poor communications, the price of moving goods is not a smooth function of distance; costs jump sharply each time one has to cross a natural barrier or bridge gaps in the network of roads and waterways. Sooner or later, therefore, the expanding manufacturer was caught in a cost cage and compelled to seek higher output from within his zone of operations.[1]

In the long run, to be sure, he could expect immigration and natural increase to augment his labour force. Thus there was considerable movement of population in spite of restrictions due to the laws of settlement; Lancashire in particular was a kind of internal frontier, attracting thousands from the adjacent counties as well as from Ireland and Scotland well before the coming of machinery and the factory. And industrial activity, by providing new resources, made possible extensive division of the land, encouraged early marriage, and gave rise to densities of settlement that would otherwise have been inconceivable. Professor Habakkuk and others have called attention to the attraction of industry for overpopulated areas;[2] but here, as so often in history, the process is one of reciprocal reinforcement: rural industry frequently laid the basis of what was eventually to become overpopulation.[3]

Yet migration and natural increase are slow-acting palliatives. In the short run, the manufacturer who wanted to increase output had to get more work out of the labour already engaged. Here, however, he again ran into the internal contradictions of the system. He had no way of compelling his workers to do a given number of hours of labour; the domestic weaver or craftsman was master of his time, starting and stopping when he desired. And while the employer could raise the

[1] The above is not intended to imply that there was a profit squeeze (for which I have no evidence); simply that the costs of distribution and collection set spatial limits to the labour market, even under conditions of rising demand. But given the nature of putting-out, in particular the worker's temporary custody of the raw materials, one can conceive of the possibility that an increase in demand for and price of the finished article would so encourage pilferage (on which, see below), that labour cost per unit would rise sharply and profits diminish—at least until countermeasures could be taken.

[2] Cf. H. J. Habakkuk, 'Family Structure and Economic Change in Nineteenth-Century Europe', *J. Econ. Hist.* xv (1955), 1–12; Joan Thirsk, 'Industries in the Countryside', in F. J. Fisher, ed., *Essays in the Economic and Social History of Tudor and Stuart England in Honour of R. H. Tawney* (Cambridge, 1961), pp. 70–88.

[3] Perhaps the best study of the social and psychological, as well as economic, mechanisms by which the introduction of industry into the countryside promotes a higher rate of population growth is provided by Rudolf Braun's pioneering study of the Zurich highlands: *Industrialisierung and Volksleben: Die Veränderungen in einem ländlichen Industriegebiet vor 1800* (Erlenbach-Zurich and Stuttgart, 1960).

piece rates with a view to encouraging diligence, he usually found that this actually reduced output. The worker, who had a fairly rigid conception of what he felt to be a decent standard of living, preferred leisure to income after a certain point; and the higher his wages, the less he had to do to reach that point. In moments of affluence, the peasant lived for the day; gave no thought to the morrow; spent much of his meagre pittance in the local inn or alehouse; caroused the Saturday of pay, the sabbath Sunday, and 'Holy Monday' as well; dragged himself reluctantly back to work Tuesday, warmed to the task Wednesday, and laboured furiously Thursday and Friday to finish in time for another long weekend.[1]

Thus precisely at those times when profit opportunities were greatest, the manufacturer found himself frustrated by this unreasonable inversion of the laws of sensible economic behaviour: the supply of labour decreased as the price rose. Nor was the other tack more effective. Outright wage cuts were not feasible in the face of increasing demand, for there was a limit to the employer's hold over his workers. More common were surreptitious increases in the worker's task: he was given longer warps or less credit for waste; or procedures of measuring and weighing were altered in the employer's favour. This kind of cleverness, however, brought with it its own penalties. The resentful workers were incited thereby to embezzle the more, and frictions built into the system were correspondingly aggravated. The eighteenth century saw a persistent effort to halt the theft of materials by making embezzlement a criminal offence, providing employers and law officers with special rights of search and seizure, placing the burden of proof on any person holding materials he could not account for, and repeatedly increasing the penalties for violation. These last included corporal punishment, for fines were of no effect on penniless spinners and weavers. The very iteration of these acts is the best evidence of their ineffectiveness; by the last quarter of the century the black market in wool and yarn had become an organized business and many a cotton manufacturer was said to have begun his career by buying materials

---

[1] Adam Smith (*Wealth of Nations*, Book I, ch. VIII) perceptively noted the connection between intense application and prolonged relaxation, and argued that the former gave rise to the latter. Cf. T. S. Ashton, *An Economic History of England: the Eighteenth Century* (London, 1955), p. 205. This interpretation seems to put the cart before the horse. It was because the worker preferred this kind of leisure and could achieve it by working at full speed for two or three days that he adopted this sporadic pattern; not because he enjoyed working himself to the limit for a few days and needed a long weekend to rest. The latter position is equivalent to arguing that students rest the first three months of the term because of the heavy 'cramming' they do for final examinations.

from this source.[1] Similarly the laws to compel workers to finish their tasks promptly and to fulfil their obligations to one employer before hiring out to another—a problem that apparently grew with the demand for labour—were little more than admissions of difficulty and expressions of intent. The discipline of the industrial system was breaking down.

The shift in attitude toward the labouring poor in the late seventeenth and early eighteenth centuries reflects in part the employer's frustration and vexation. Where once poverty had been looked on as an unavoidable evil and the poor man as an object of pity and a responsibility to his neighbour, now poverty was a sin and the poor man a victim of his own iniquity. Defoe is only the clearest and most effective spokesman for this viewpoint, which castigated the worker for the sloth that made him waste his time in idleness and low diversion, and the vice that led him to squander his scanty resources on alcohol and debauchery. This virtuous indignation seems to have softened from the middle of the century; at least writers on economic matters were beginning to argue that labour was not incorrigibly lazy and would in fact respond to higher wages. Mr Coats has suggested that this shift owed much to the introduction of machinery and the promise of a definitive solution to the problem.[2] Perhaps; in the meantime, the businessman continued sceptical, and in places like Manchester people were still told in 1769 that the 'best friend' of the manufacturer was high provisions.[3] One can understand why the thoughts of employers turned to workshops where the men would be brought together to labour under watchful overseers, and to machines that would solve the shortage of manpower while curbing the insolence and dishonesty of the men.

Yet if the presence of this growing need for a change in the mode of production clarifies the demand side of technological innovation, it will not suffice to explain the supply side: the conditions that made possible the devising of new methods and their adoption by industry. One thing seems clear: if Britain was the country that felt most keenly the inadequacy of the prevailing system, she was not the only one. The major continental centres were also disturbed by shortages of labour and the abuses of domestic manufacture. As noted above, the weavers

[1] Travis, Notes...of Todmorden and District (1896), p. 56, cited by Wadsworth and Mann, Cotton Trade, p. 399.

[2] A. W. Coats, 'Changing Attitudes to Labour in the Mid-Eighteenth Century', Econ. Hist. Rev. 2nd ser. XI (1958), 46–8.

[3] Arthur Young's famous testimony, from his Six Months Tour Through the North of England (4 vols.; London, 1770), III, 248–9. Cf. Edgar S. Furniss, The Position of the Laborer in a System of Nationalism (New Haven, 1920), pp. 98–105.

and merchant-manufacturers of Normandy and Verviers, of the Rhine-land and Saxony, were obliged to find their yarn over an ever wider radius, often in the face of laws in the country of origin forbidding its export to competitors. Nor was this the first time in history that demand had pressed hard on the capacity of craft and domestic manu-facture: in medieval Italy and Flanders analogous difficulties arose without calling forth an industrial revolution.

The problem may be broken down into two aspects: the conditions governing the invention of labour-saving devices; and those determin-ing the adoption of these devices and their diffusion in industry.

On the first, it would seem clear, though by no means easy to demon-strate, that there existed in Britain in the eighteenth century a higher level of technical skill and a greater interest in machines and 'gym-cracks' than in any of the other countries of Europe. This should not be confused with scientific knowledge; in spite of some efforts to tie the Industrial Revolution to the Scientific Revolution of the sixteenth and seventeenth centuries, the link would seem to have been an extremely diffuse one: both reflected a heightened interest in natural and material phenomena and a more systematic application of empirical searching. Indeed, if anything, the growth of scientific knowledge owed much to the concerns and achievements of technology; there was far less flow of ideas or methods the other way; and this was to continue to be the case well into the nineteenth century.[1]

All of which makes the question of British mechanical skill the more mysterious. The testimony of contemporary observers on this point is mixed: some found the British creative as well as highly gifted crafts-men; others looked upon them as simply clever imitators; there is no evidence before the great innovations of the eighteenth century of any exceptional reservoir of talent in this sphere. To be sure, there were the millwrights, clock-makers, joiners, and other craftsmen whose experi-ence in construction and contriving trained them in effect to be the mechanics of a new age. But England was not the only country with such artisans, and nowhere else do we find this harvest of inventions.

Yet if there is no positive evidence of a superior level of technical skill in Britain, there is a strong indirect argument for this assumption: even after the introduction of the textile machines (and the new metal-lurgical and chemical techniques, as well), the continental countries were not prepared to imitate them. The most effective of the early copies were almost all the work of British emigrant mechanics, and it was a matter of decades before the rest of Europe freed itself from dependence on British skills. Nor was this long apprenticeship drawn

[1] This was true even of the steam-engine, which is often put forward as the prime example of science-spawned innovation. See below, p. 104.

out simply because of a desire to employ more productive workers. The English artisans who came to the Continent were costly, homesick, insubordinate. Their employers could hardly wait to be rid of them.

Why the British developed these skills earlier and faster than others is another matter. Was it because corporate controls of production and apprenticeship had largely broken down by the end of the seventeenth century, whereas the continued influence of guild organization and the active supervision of mercantilistic governments on the Continent tended to fix techniques in a mould and stifle imagination?[1] Is the *Encyclopédie*, with its careful descriptions of the proper way to do things, a symbol of this rigidity? Or was it because the avenues of social advancement were different in Britain than in the aristocratic monarchies of the Continent, that talent was readier to go into business, projecting, and invention than in more traditionalistic societies? One is struck by the middle-class origins of most of the creators of the first textile machines. John Kay was the son of a 'substantial yeoman'; Lewis Paul, the son of a physician. John Wyatt's background is vague, but he had attended grammar school and was presumably from the kind of family that felt schooling was desirable. Samuel Crompton's father was a farmer who produced cloth on the side and was apparently comfortably situated. Edmund Cartwright was the son of a gentleman and a graduate of Oxford. It was not discreditable in the eighteenth century for children of good families to be apprenticed out to weavers or joiners.[2] Manual labour and dexterity were not stigmata of the *peuple*, as opposed to the *bourgeoisie*.

[1] See Gabriel Jars's comparison of Sheffield, where industry was still fettered by the guild system in 1764–5 (though the growth of certain enterprises had burst these bonds), and Birmingham, where any man could engage in any business and at most 20 per cent of the workers had properly served their apprenticeships. 'The multiplicity of trades has given rise to emulation such that each manufacturer is ceaselessly occupied in inventing new means of cutting down labour costs and thereby increasing his profits. This has been pushed to such an extent that it seems unthinkable that ironmongery can be produced anywhere so cheaply as in Birmingham.' Chevalier, 'La mission de Gabriel Jars', *Trans. Newcomen Soc.* XXVI (1947/8 and 1948/9), 63.

[2] Thus Peter Ewart, son of a Scots clergyman, one of whose brothers became minister to the Prussian court, another a physician, a third, partner to John Gladstone in the Liverpool trade: because of his talent for mechanical matters, he was apprenticed as a millwright to John Rennie. W. C. Henry, 'A Biographical Notice of the Late Peter Ewart, Esq.', *Memoirs of the Literary and Philosophical Society of Manchester*, 2nd ser. VII (1846). Or James Watt, father of the famous inventor: son of a mathematics teacher who was an Elder of the presbytery and Kirk Treasurer at Cartsdyke (Scotland), he was apprenticed to a carpenter-shipwright. His brother was trained in mathematics and surveying. S. Smiles, *Lives of Boulton and Watt* (London, 1865), pp. 81–3. Or Charles Tennant, son of a farmer and 'factor to the Earl of Glencairn', who was apprenticed to a weaver. E. W. D. Tennant, 'The Early History of the

A further consideration suggests itself. Was it not only that the English atmosphere was more favourable to change, but also that special experience in certain areas provided unique facilities for training? What, for example, was the role of the Newcomen engine in shaping English metallurgy and machine construction? Or does the explanation lie simply in the *greater* need for innovation on the island (a matter of degree, to be sure, but questions of degree can often be decisive): need for labour-saving devices in a textile manufacture whose products lent themselves to mass production; for effective pumping equipment in mines; for ways to make use of mineral fuel in a country with the largest appetite for iron in the world?

The fresh and important researches of A. E. Musson and Eric Robinson offer an impressive picture of the energy with which Lancashire mobilized and trained technological skill in the second half of the eighteenth century—importing craftsmen from as far away as London and Scotland and capitalizing on its own strong traditions of skilled labour to turn joiners into millwrights and turners, smiths into foundrymen, clock-makers into tool and die cutters.[1] Even more striking is the theoretical knowledge of these men. They were not, on the whole, the unlettered tinkerers of historical mythology. Even the ordinary millwright, as Fairbairn notes, was usually 'a fair arithmetician, knew something of geometry, levelling, and mensuration, and in some cases possessed a very competent knowledge of practical mathematics. He could calculate the velocities, strength, and power of machines: could draw in plan and section....'[2] Much of these 'superior attainments and intellectual power' reflected the abundant facilities for technical education in 'villages' like Manchester during this period, ranging from Dissenters' academies and learned societies to local and visiting lecturers, 'mathematical and commercial' private schools with evening classes, and a wide circulation of practical manuals, periodicals, and encyclopaedias.

Whatever the reasons for British precocity in this domain, the results are clear; and equally clear is the relative ease with which inventors

St Rollox Chemical Works', *Chemistry and Industry*, 1 November 1947, p. 667. Similarly, there was no derogation in marrying a craftsman. See the pedigree of the Pilkington family in the eighteenth and early nineteenth centuries. T. C. Barker, *Pilkington Brothers and the Glass Industry* (London, 1960), pp. 20–30.

[1] A. E. Musson and Eric Robinson, 'The Origins of Engineering in Lancashire', *J. Econ. Hist.* XX (1960); 'Science and Industry in the Later Eighteenth Century', *Econ. Hist. Rev.* 2nd ser. XII (1960). Also G. H. Tupling, 'The Early Metal Trades and the Beginnings of Engineering in Lancashire', *Trans. Lancashire and Cheshire Antiquarian Soc.* LXI (1949), 25 f.

[2] Wm. Fairbairn, *Treatise on Mills and Millwork* (2nd ed.; 2 vols.; London, 1864), I, vi.

found financing for their projects and the rapidity with which the products of their ingenuity found favour with the manufacturing community—if anything, too much favour, for many of the earlier inventors spent more time enforcing their patent rights than earning them.[1] Some have accounted for this swift diffusion of change by the relatively greater accumulation of capital in Britain than anywhere else in Europe except Holland (which was kind enough to send some of its surplus funds to England, rather than invest them in its own industry). They argue that the greater supply of capital was reflected in lower interest rates, which tended to decline in the course of the eighteenth century, and that this in turn made change that much less costly and, *pari passu*, that much more profitable and attractive.[2]

The argument is persuasive, but the historical facts tend to modify it at a number of points, diminish its import at others. On the one hand, it is most unlikely that differences in the rate of interest of the order of two, three, even half-a-dozen points are a decisive consideration where the mechanical advantage of innovation is as great as it was for the early textile machines. One can understand that the timing of canal and road construction, or similar costly projects of slow gestation, was affected by shifts in the rate of interest, in part because the very possibility of flotation was frequently dependent on an easy money market. But for the prospective textile entrepreneur, the problem was not whether his profits would cover 6 per cent or 12 per cent on borrowed capital, but whether he could raise the capital at all.

In this regard, the cotton manufacturer of the eighteenth century was favoured by the very newness of the Industrial Revolution. The early machines, complicated though they were to contemporaries, were

---

[1] A number of writers have laid stress on the incentive effect of patent legislation. I am inclined to doubt its significance. This kind of protection was not new; the basis of the system was laid by the Statute of Monopolies of 1624. In our period, the cost and difficulty of obtaining a patent was rising steadily. Cf. Witt Bowden, *Industrial Society in England Towards the End of the Eighteenth Century* (New York), 1925, pp. 26–30. At the same time, there was good reason to doubt the efficacy of patents against determined competitors, as numerous inventors learned to their sorrow, and many an entrepreneur placed his reliance on secrecy, rather than the law.

[2] This was the position of Prof. T. S. Ashton in his *Industrial Revolution, 1760–1830* ('Home University Library', London, New York, and Toronto, 1949), pp. 9–11, 90–1, but he has since modified it considerably, emphasizing, not cost of capital but its availability. The rate of return on government securities was important, he argues, because of the 5 per cent ceiling on the rate of interest: when the funds fell and the return (including the prospect of capital gains) rose, capital would shift in that direction, diminishing the supply to industry and trade. *An Economic History of England: the Eighteenth Century*, pp. 26–9. There is an excellent discussion in L. S. Pressnell, 'The Rate of Interest in the Eighteenth Century', in Pressnell (ed.), *Studies in the Industrial Revolution* (London, 1960), pp. 190–7.

nevertheless modest, rudimentary, wooden contrivances, which could be built for surprisingly small sums. A forty-spindle jenny cost perhaps £6 in 1792; scribbling and carding machines cost £1 for each inch of roller width; a slubbing billy with thirty spindles cost £10. 10s.[1] And these were new. Similar equipment was frequently advertised in used condition at much lower prices. The only really costly items of fixed investment in this period were buildings and power, but here the historian must remember that the large, many-storeyed mill that awed contemporaries was the exception. Most so-called factories were no more than glorified workshops: a dozen workers or less; one or two jennies, perhaps, or mules; and a carding machine to prepare the rovings. These early devices were powered by the men and women who worked them.[2] Attics and cottages were reconverted for the purpose; later on a steam-engine might be added to this kind of impro-vised structure. Moreover, there were premises to rent—here we have another example of the responsiveness of English capital to economic opportunity. Not only were complete buildings offered to prospective tenants, but larger mills were subdivided and let in small units. So that an industrialist could in fact start with a minimal outlay—renting his plant, borrowing for equipment and raw materials, even raising funds for payment of wages by contracting in advance for the finished product. Some no doubt began with nothing more than the capital accumulated by petty local trading in yarn and cloth; others, as noted above, ap-parently built their fortunes in the black market for embezzled materials.

On the other hand, a good many of the early mill owners were men of substance—merchants whose experience in selling finished com-

[1] W. B. Crump (ed.), *The Leeds Woollen Industry, 1780–1820* (Leeds: The Thoresby Society, 1931), pp. 212–13, 293; also Herbert Heaton, 'Benjamin Gott and the Industrial Revolution in Yorkshire', *Econ. Hist. Rev.* III (1931), 52. For purposes of comparison, a cotton weaver earned perhaps 7s. 6d. a week in 1770, a hand spinner between 2s. and 3s. Thus the 40-spindle jenny cost about two weeks wages of the forty women it replaced. Wage figures from Wadsworth and Mann, *Cotton Trade*, pp. 402–3. A traditional hand-loom cost more than a jenny; anywhere from £7 to £10.

[2] The first application of water power to the mule was apparently in 1790 at the New Lanark mills. The increased drive made possible 'double mules' of 400 spindles; thus capital bred capital. George W. Daniels, *The Early English Cotton Industry* (Manchester, 1920), p. 125. It is not clear when the steam-engine was first so used—perhaps in the late 1780's, certainly in the early 1790's. A large proportion of these early engines were employed, not to drive the machinery directly, but to raise water upon a wheel; some of them, indeed, were Savery-type steam pumps (see below, p. 101), which were preferred to more efficient machines because of their lower initial cost. An engine delivering 2–4 h.p. could be had new for between £150 and £200. A larger Boulton and Watt rotative engine (15–20 h.p.) cost four or five times as much. Steam came earlier to frame spinning: Arkwright's atmospheric engine at Shudehill (Lancs.), to raise water for a wheel, was installed in 1783. A. E. Musson and E. Robin-son, 'The Early Growth of Steam Power', *Econ. Hist. Rev.* 2nd ser. XI (1959), 418–39.

modities had alerted them to the possibilities of large-scale, mechanized production; putters-out, who had had direct experience in manufacture; even independent small producers with enough set by to change their methods and expand. Thus of 110 cotton spinning mills established in the Midlands in the period 1769–1800, 62 were the creations of hosiers, drapers, mercers, and manufacturers from other districts or from other branches of the textile industry.[1] This previous accumulation of wealth and experience was a major factor in the rapid adoption of technological innovation—as it was in industries like iron and chemicals. We are now come full circle: the inventions came in part because the growth and prosperity of the industry made them imperative; and the growth and prosperity of the industry helped make their early and widespread utilization possible.

All of which serves to emphasize an important caution: it was not capital by itself that made possible Britain's swift advance. Money alone could have done nothing; indeed, in this regard, the entrepreneurs of the Continent, who could often count on direct subsidies or monopoly privileges from the state, were better off than their British counterparts. What distinguished the British economy, as we have already had several occasions to remark, was an exceptional sensitivity and responsiveness to pecuniary opportunity. This was a people fascinated by wealth and commerce, collectively and individually.

Why this was so is a question worthy of investigation. Certainly the phenomenon was closely related, as both cause and effect, to the already noted openness of society; and this was linked in turn to the peculiar position and character of the aristocracy.

Britain had no nobility in the sense of the other European countries. She had a peerage, composed of a small number of titled persons, whose essential and almost unique perquisite was the possibility of sitting in the House of Lords. Their children were commoners, who often received, to be sure, courtesy titles in token of their high birth, but were no different in civil status from other Britons. Even the peers had only the most modest privileges: trial by their fellow noblemen in criminal proceedings, for example, or the right of direct access to the sovereign. They did not enjoy fiscal immunities.

Below the nobility stood the gentry or so-called squirearchy, an amorphous group, without legal definition or status, that had no equivalent on the Continent. Its edges were blurred, its ranks loosely

[1] This figure of 62 actually understates the role of textile men in the new factory cotton manufacture, for it does not include some fifteen mills established by Arkwright, Strutt, and partners, most of whom were drawn from this milieu. Stanley D. Chapman, *The Early Factory Masters: The Transition to the Factory System in the Midlands Textile Industry* (Newton Abbot, 1967), p. 78.

and heterogeneously constituted. Some gentry were of noble antecedents; others had made their fortunes in trade or the professions or
government service and had purchased estates as much for their social
prestige as for their income; others were scions of old country families;
still others were farmers or yeomen grown wealthy. They had two
things in common: land ownership and a way of life that was a vestige
of medieval seignorialism. These were the local notabilities—lords of
the manor, justices of the peace, county sheriffs. With the peers, they
were the true rulers of provincial Britain.

Both nobility and gentry generally practised primogeniture: the
oldest male child inherited both title (where pertinent) and land. This
had two large consequences: it increased the economic burden of the
head of the family; and it compelled most of the children to earn their
living, in whole or part.

Thus it was no easy task to preserve and if possible increase the family
estate for transmission to one's heir while finding places for younger
sons and dowries for daughters. Daniel Finch, Earl of Nottingham, put
the point well in a letter of 1695 to his executors; he favoured primo-
genitary strict settlement, he wrote,

not so much out of a vain affectation of continuing a great estate in my
family, as because [my son] will thereby be under a necessity of observing
some good economy that he may be able to provide for his younger children,
and consequently will not run into that foolish or extravagant way of living
which debauches and corrupts the manners of many families, as well as ruins
their fortunes....[1]

To be sure, British society had provided careers for cadets of good
family: remunerative offices in government; Church livings; commissions in the armed forces; a growing number of potentially lucrative
situations in the colonies (not really important until the second half of
the eighteenth century). Yet excessive and otiose as many of these
places appeared to contemporary reformers, they were not enough to
satisfy the demand, as the competition for patronage testifies, and they
had to be shared with such other groups as the legal profession and the
mercantile interest. Sinecures and offices came high, and it was a rare
father who could place more than two or three sons well. To quote
Nottingham again: 'no estate can provide so fully for younger children,
but that they must in great degree help themselves'. The fourth and
fifth sons, of gentry and even noble families, would have to be apprenticed to trade—not the trade of the shop, to be sure, but the interna-

[1] Quoted by H. J. Habakkuk, 'Daniel Finch, 2nd Earl of Nottingham: His House
and Estate', in J. H. Plumb (ed.), *Studies in Social History: A Tribute to G. M. Trevelyan*
(London, New York, Toronto, 1955), p. 156.

tional commerce that was at once the pride of the English economy and the seed-bed of new houses.[1]

Admittedly, there were rarely as many as four or five sons that survived to manhood, and the flow of gentle talent into business was presumably small.[2] Certainly it was less important in the eighteenth century than it had been in earlier periods, partly perhaps because the royal house brought with it from Hanover strong German prejudices against this kind of mobility, partly because the proliferation of office and the extension of British dominion were opening up alternative opportunities that were more attractive and preferentially accessible.[3] Yet it was not so much the substantive contribution to enterprise that counted, as the symbolism of the example, the sanction that this legitimate participation, however small, conferred on trade as a respectable activity and on pecuniary rationality as a way of life.

In the meantime, the head of the family had to build the patrimony and make it work for him and his children. Not all landowners did well in the contest for fortune or even tried, but at their best they formed a class of 'spirited proprietors' that warmed the hearts of improvers like Arthur Young. Noble or gentle, they lived on their estates (and not at the court), rode their lands and noted their yield, sought improvements to enhance traditional revenues, conceived new ways to produce income. They rarely cultivated or operated directly—though one can cite contrary instances like Thomas Fitzmaurice, brother of the Earl of Shelburne, who, among other enterprises, bleached and sold the linens woven by his Irish tenants.[4] (Even if they

[1] Much depended, however, on necessity and opportunity. In Scotland, the gentry were poor and had few claims to preferment. The Established Church was closed to them; the prospect of fighting the battles of England, unattractive; foreign commerce and colonial enterprise offered few employments until the century was well advanced. The more intellectual could prepare for the Bar, but these were necessarily few. Many sought their livelihood, therefore, as shopkeepers, alias 'merchants'. As Henry G. Graham puts it in his classic study, '...in those days, a gentleman's son felt it as natural to fall into trade as for a rich tradesman to rise out of it'. *The Social Life of Scotland in the Eighteenth Century* (4th ed.; London, 1950), p. 33.

[2] We really do not know how important, absolutely or relatively, was the participation of these younger sons of noble or gentry families in business. A systematic survey of the entrepreneurs of the Industrial Revolution would be immensely valuable, though difficulties of definition (what is active participation?) would confuse the issue, especially as regards the aristocratic contribution. In the meantime, we are reduced to discrete impressions. Cf. Walter E. Minchinton, 'The Merchants in England in the Eighteenth Century', *Explorations in Entrepreneurial History* [henceforth *Explorations*], x (1957), 62.

[3] For the earlier period, see Lawrence Stone, 'The Nobility in Business', *ibid.* pp. 54–61.

[4] A. H. Dodd, *The Industrial Revolution in North Wales* (Cardiff, 1933), pp. 32–3.

had made their fortune in trade and continued in the firm, they inevitably gave less time to mercantile concerns.) Rather they leased their land to tenants—peasants, commercial farmers, or industrial contractors. When they financed business ventures, it was as creditors more than as partners; or they bought shares in joint-stock companies and trusts. Their interests were generally handled by stewards, agents, and solicitors, and this exposed them to abuses of confidence. Yet that was all the more reason to supervise their affairs closely, and many of them made the decisions that are the hallmark of active entrepreneurship. A significant few opened mines, built iron works and mills, dug canals, developed ports, and leased their urban properties for building. What is more, they anticipated demand, undertook investments on speculation, advertised if necessary for tenants, and stood ready to operate their installations through agents or partners if no lessees were forthcoming.

They also enclosed the land, concentrated their holdings, introduced or found tenants who would introduce better crop rotations and techniques of cultivation, helped spread new ideas about the country. This is not the place to discuss the so-called 'agricultural revolution' of the eighteenth century, or to assess the benefits or injustices that accompanied it. My aim here is to underline the generality of this spirit of innovation and its effects; and also to recall the well-known fact that this was a society that interposed relatively few institutional barriers to a fundamental change of this kind. The Tudor monarchy may have been concerned about enclosures; the parliamentary regime of the eighteenth century was less paternalistic. For good or evil, Britain's countryside was being kneaded like dough; and the improving landlords were a powerful leaven.

It is probable that such industrial ventures as people 'of name' undertook were on the whole less remunerative than competitive efforts by 'professional' businessmen; or for that matter, that the great estates could not bear comparison with the lands of the small proprietors in their neighbourhood.[1] It is also true that the nobility and gentry tended over time to change from active entrepreneurs into rentiers; this was the experience, for example, of areas like Wales and Northumberland, where large coal and ore deposits had initially provided a favourable base for industrial activity by landowners. Yet the significance of these efforts lay in the efforts themselves, not in their return. Once again it lay in the legitimacy conferred on innovation and the pursuit of wealth as a way of life.

A comparison will illuminate the argument. Thus far I have treated

[1] Cf. Adam Smith, *Wealth of Nations*, Book III, ch. II; Arthur Young, *Travels during the Years 1787, 1788 and 1789*, I, 90, 99, 108, and especially 198.

this permeation of country life by the spirit of enterprise and calculation as a consequence of social structure and the system of inheritance. There was undoubtedly more to it. In part, it reflected the quickening pace of the economy: new men kept moving up and the older families had to move faster to hold their own. In part, it was probably a response to new opportunities, in particular, to the increasing demand for resources that lay in the hands of the landed proprietors. Yet this response was neither necessary nor inevitable. It would have been just as easy for the nobility and gentry to turn their backs on their new rivals and break off competition by defining the means of their ascension as intrinsically ignoble. This is what the aristocracy of Europe had done in the Renaissance, when it had developed the very idea of the gentleman as a weapon against the pretensions of the bourgeoisie.[1] And this was to be the reaction of much of Europe's aristocracy in the nineteenth century in the face of industrial revolution and a corresponding shift in the balance of political power. The British nobility and gentry chose to meet the newcomers on middle ground: they affirmed their distinction of blood or breeding; but they buttressed it with an active and productive cultivation of gain.

This momentous decision was self-reinforcing. The concern of the British gentleman for the accretion of his fortune made him a participant in society rather than a parasite upon it—whatever judgement one may pass on the character of this participation. Business interests promoted a degree of intercourse between people of different stations and walks of life that had no parallel on the Continent. 'We used to sit down to dinner,' wrote Lord Hervey in 1731, 'a little snug party of about thirty odd, up to the chin in beef, venison, geese, turkeys, etc.; and generally over the chin in claret, strong beer and punch. We had Lords Spiritual and Temporal, besides commoners, parsons and freeholders innumerable.'[2] Compare Arthur Young's reflections on a visit with the Duc de la Rochefoucauld:[3]

At an English nobleman's, there would have been three or four farmers asked to meet me, who would have dined with the family amongst the ladies of the first rank. I do not exaggerate, when I say, that I have had this at least an hundred times in the first houses of our islands. It is however, a thing that in the present state of manners in France, would not be met with from Calais to Bayonne, except by chance in the house of some great lord that had been much in England, and then not unless it was asked for.

[1] See the article by Arthur Livingston on 'Gentleman, Theory of the' in the *Encyclopaedia of the Social Sciences* and the references given there.

[2] A. Goodwin (ed.), *The European Nobility in the Eighteenth Century* (London, 1953), p. 4.

[3] Young, *Travels*, I, 207.

Or, to return to Britain, consider the friendship of Robert Hewer, successful supercargo and trader turned landowner and lord of the manor of Manadon (near Plymouth), with the Duke and Duchess of Bedford: he spent weeks as their guest at Woburn Abbey, where he was 'of all their parties of pleasure!'; and the visit was repeated several times.[1] Such a continuing relationship is more significant of true society than a dozen marriages between noble blood and bourgeois gold *pour redorer le blason*.[2]

Below the level of the gentry, there was no barrier between land and trade—not even a permeable membrane. Given the rural character of most industry and the intermittent claims of agriculture, many cultivators were at the same time manufacturers or middlemen or both. This was true not only of textiles, but of branches like metallurgy where one might think the nature of the manufacturing process would have imposed a more rigorous division of labour: witness Isaac Wilkinson, Aaron Walker, Jedediah Strutt and others. Note that where similar conditions prevailed on the Continent, one found the same combination of activities: the land brought forth industrial enterprise and enterprisers. Yet again, what sets Britain apart is a question of degree. Nowhere else, as we have seen, was the countryside so infused with manufacture; nowhere else, the pressures and incentives to change greater, the force of tradition weaker. It was all of a piece: improving landlords, enclosures, commercial farming, village shops, putting-out, mines and forges, the active mortgage market—all combined to break the shackles of place and habit, assimilate country and city, and promote a far wider recruitment of talent than would have otherwise occurred. In a society of which four of five people lived on the land, this was a powerful stimulus to overall development.

By the same token, the flow of entrepreneurship within business was freer, the allocation of resources more responsive than in other economies. Where the traditional sacrosanctity of occupational exclusiveness continued to prevail across the Channel, enforced sometimes by law but in any case by habit and moral prohibitions, the British cobbler would not stick to his last nor the merchant to his trade. It was not merely a kind of negative phenomenon—that is, the absence of confining regulations or opprobrious strictures; rather it was a positive drive, an ambitious versatility that was always alive to the main chance. One

---

[1] Conrad Gill, *Merchants and Mariners of the Eighteenth Century* (London, 1961), p. 138.

[2] There was much of that too—on the Continent as well as Britain. But inter-class alliances are to be found in all but rigid caste societies. The real test is not the union; it is what follows: how many great families in such circumstances are willing to know their new relations after the wedding?

cannot but be impressed by a man like this Thomas Griggs, grocer and clothier of Essex in the mid-eighteenth century, who invested and speculated in real estate, fattened cattle for market, malted barley, lent money on pawn.[1] Or like Thomas Fox, Quaker clothier of Wellington, who was moved by hard times in the wool trade to look into the possibilities of lead, calamine, or copper mining—or all three.[2]

One could extend the list considerably, but one final example will have to suffice: Samuel Garbett of Birmingham, originally brassworker, then merchant and chemist, partner in spinning, chemical (Birmingham and Prestonpans, near Edinburgh), iron-smelting (Carron works, Scotland), and flour-milling (Albion Mills, London) enterprises, and shareholder in the Cornish Metal Co. (copper mines). To appreciate the force of this drive for wealth, one must remember that these men were risking their fortunes at each throw of the entrepreneurial dice. With rare exceptions, there was no haven of limited liability. Garbett went bankrupt in 1772 because of the failure of one of his partners.

Similarly, the structure of the firm was more open and rational in Britain than in the continental countries. Everywhere, the fundamental business unit was the individual proprietorship or the family partnership, but where, in a country like France, the family firm was almost always closed to outsiders, British entrepreneurs were far more willing to enter into association with friends or friends of friends. Indeed, this seems to have been the preferred way of raising capital to expand or of attracting and attaching special skills to the enterprise. In textiles, a capitalist like George Philips would seek out and take as partner an experienced manager like George Lee, late employee of Peter Drinkwater; or an already hardened flax spinner like John Marshall, faced with a crisis in the trade, could throw out his partners ('As they could neither of them be of any further use, I released them from the firm and took the whole upon myself'); and when, shortly after, though mortgaged to the hilt, he determined to expand, would bring in new ones for much larger amounts.[3] In brewing, where the need for capital was so great and urgent 'that it could not be produced fast enough from the profits of the firms', 'established concerns welcomed into their partnerships bankers and merchants, who of necessity brought in the social and political consequences of vast wealth made in other fields'.[4] In machine building, it was probably skill more than capital

[1] K. H. Burley, 'An Essex Clothier of the Eighteenth Century', *Econ. Hist. Rev.* 2nd ser. XI (1958), 289–301.

[2] Herbert Fox, *Quaker Homespun* (London, 1938), pp. 46 f.

[3] These were the Benyons, woollen merchants of Shrewsbury. W. Gordon Rimmer, *Marshall's of Leeds, Flax-Spinners 1788–1886* (Cambridge, 1960), pp. 40–4.

[4] Peter Mathias, 'The Entrepreneur in Brewing, 1700–1830', *Explorations*, X (1957), 73–6.

that was the scarce factor, though it took thousands of pounds to turn a repair shop into an engineering plant. Boulton and Watt are perhaps the best model of this alliance of money and talent, but one could cite many similar associations, with varying division of contributions and responsibilities.[1] The pattern was probably most widespread in metallurgy; there the requirements of both capital and talent were heavy, and the partnership was the normal business form.[2] Even where a firm was essentially a family affair—the Crawshay smelting mill at Cyfarthfa or ironmongery in London, for example—outsiders were brought in as needed; bought out later if advisable; and new partners found. Professor Ashton has pointed out the importance in this connection of interfamilial associations of Dissenters: the bonds of a common, persecuted religion proved almost as effective a business tie as blood itself.[3]

The cohesiveness and mutual support of the nonconformist business community was only one element in their commercial success. They suffered numerous disabilities because of their religion, and business was in many ways the most convenient outlet for their energy and ambition; and their faith itself, with its stress on diligence, thrift, and rationality as a way of life, was often a competitive advantage. They may also, as a result of child-rearing practices that gave early scope for initiative and freedom, have inculcated on their young a peculiarly intense need for achievement. This at least is the contention of David McClelland, who asserts that an independently established index of the need for achievement in England turns up sharply at the beginning of the eighteenth century, just in time for the Industrial Revolution.[4] In any event, it is surely no coincidence that Dissenters were most numerous in the North and Midlands, the centres of most rapid industrial development; or that a disproportionately large number of the leading entrepreneurs of the

---

[1] Thus Bateman and Sherratt of Salford: Fenton, Murray and Wood of Leeds; Hazeldine, Rastrick and Co. of Bridgnorth (Salop); and somewhat later, Maudslay, Son and Field of London; Nasmyth, Gaskell and Co. of Manchester; Sharp, Roberts and Co. of the same city; et al.

[2] To be sure, some of the facilities available in textiles were present in metallurgy as well. Thus landowners, desirous of increasing their incomes, were often ready to let mineral rights on favourable terms and otherwise promote enterprise on their estates; sometimes, as at Cyfarthfa and Dowlais, leases fixed at absurdly low rates ran for a century. Also, it was often possible to rent plants already built for a moderate sum. Nevertheless, it took a thousand pounds or more to launch even a modest furnace or forge; and a giant like Carron, capitalized at £12,000 at its founding in 1759–60, had fixed plant valued at £47,400 a decade later. R. H. Campbell, 'The Financing of Carron Company', Business History, I (1958), 21–34.

[3] Ashton, Iron and Steel in the Industrial Revolution (2nd ed.; Manchester, 1951), ch. IX: 'The Ironmasters'.

[4] David C. McClelland, The Achieving Society (Princeton, 1961). The argument

Industrial Revolution were from this group.[1] On the other hand, Britain was not alone in having Calvinists, who played the role of an entrepreneurial leaven throughout Europe. What distinguished Britain was the extent to which her religious nonconformists conformed to a wider social pattern; the entrepreneurial differences were differences of degree, and not of kind.

The same observations are relevant to the oft-cited thesis that price inflation brought bigger profits, and that bigger profits made possible industrial change.[2] Even if it could be shown that profits did increase over the century and that it was higher prices that were responsible—and the usual demonstration proves nothing of the sort—the fact remains that Britain was not the only nation to have price inflation in this period; that the best enterprises on the Continent made just as high rates of profit and relied more, if anything, on self-financing.[3] The point again is not so much the rate of return as the manner of its use: where British firms ploughed profits back into the business, their competitors abroad too often transferred them from trade to more honorific callings, or held them as a reserve in the form of land, mortgage loans, and similar non-industrial placements.

Finally, a word should be said about the role of banks and bank credit. In no country in Europe in the eighteenth century was the financial structure so advanced and the public so habituated to paper

has been subjected to careful scrutiny by M. W. Flinn, 'Social Theory and the Industrial Revolution', in Tom Burns and S. B. Saul, eds., *Social Theory and Social Change* (London, 1967), pp. 9–32. Flinn finds significant differences in the child-rearing practices of Dissenter sects: by McClelland's criteria, some were far less conducive to the inculcation of 'need-achievement' than others. Flinn gives low marks to the Methodists, whom McClelland makes much of; and gives the highest marks to the early Quakers and the Congregationalists. On balance, he is inclined to give some weight to McClelland's thesis.

[1] Cf. the survey of Everett Hagen, *On the Theory of Social Change* (Homewood, Ill., 1962), pp. 305–8, based on men mentioned in Ashton's little classic on the Industrial Revolution.

[2] The *locus classicus* is Earl J. Hamilton, 'Profit Inflation and the Industrial Revolution', *Quart. J. Econ.* LVI (1941–42), 257–70. See also his earlier article, 'American Treasure and the Rise of Capitalism, 1500–1700', *Economica*, IX (1929), 338–57, and his reply to the criticisms of John U. Nef, 'Prices and Progress', *J. Econ. Hist.* XII (1952), 325–49.

[3] See the excellent analysis of the problem in David Felix, 'Profit Inflation and Industrial Growth: the Historic Record and Contemporary Analogies', *Quart. J. Econ.* LXX (1956), 441–63. One should note that most of the price increase in the second half of the eighteenth century occurred in the 1790's. Felix argues that such expansion of profits as did take place was the result of greater productivity rather than a combination of price inflation and wage lag. This is clearly so: the very industries that were making the most rapid technological advances were the ones whose prices were falling and the nominal wages of whose workers (or real wages, for that matter)

instruments as in Britain.[1] Nominally, the credit offered by the growing multitude of private banks was for short periods—up to ninety days—to cover commercial transactions; in fact, much of it was in the form of revolving and open credits, or even of standing overdrafts, which served as quasi-capital.[2] What is more, the development of a national network of discount and payment enabled the capital-hungry industrial areas to draw for this purpose on the capital-rich agricultural districts. The system was just developing in the last quarter of the eighteenth century. By the 1820's and 1830's, however, when the problem of disposing of the products of British factories had become more difficult than that of financing technological change, bank credit was a pillar of the industrial edifice.

The role of bank credit was the more important because, in the early decades of the industrial revolution, working capital was still far more important than fixed capital. This was true even of enterprises in heavy industry—in mining, metallurgy, machine manufacture. Thus Sidney Pollard offers a sample of business accounts of firms in copper mining, copper refining, tinmaking, engineering, and light metals manufacture for dates ranging from 1782 to 1832: the lowest proportion of fixed capital to total inventory valuation of assets is 8·8 per cent; the highest, 33·2 per cent.[3] Other measures of this relationship—for example, comparisons of fixed capital with accounts receivable or payable—for other

were rising through most of this period (1760–1830). The mule spinners were a privileged group. What is more, there is considerable direct evidence that rates of profit in these industries were not increasing over the long run, but rather reached a peak with the introduction of the critical mechanical innovations (Schumpeter's entrepreneurial profits) and then declined as new firms were attracted into the field.

[1] Note, in this regard, the experience of Robert Owen, who found in 1797 that the toll collectors of the Glasgow–New Lanark turnpike preferred the notes of the local banks to gold coin. *The Life of Robert Owen by Himself*, ed. M. Beer (New York, 1920), p. 71.

[2] Not to speak of accommodation paper, which was a means of obtaining credit, if only for short periods, with or without the co-operation of the banks. With the connivance of banks or discount houses, accommodation paper could be the basis for generous medium- and long-term credit. On all this, see W. T. C. King, *History of the London Discount Market* (London, 1936); L. S. Pressnell, *Country Banking in the Industrial Revolution* (New York, 1956); D. S. Landes, *Bankers and Pashas: International Finance and Economic Imperialism in Egypt* (London, 1958).

[3] S. Pollard, 'Fixed Capital in the Industrial Revolution in Britain', *J. Econ. Hist.* XXIV (1964), 299–314. Actually Pollard's analysis requires one modification. The low ratio of fixed to circulating capital does not hold for the start of an enterprise when accounts receivable have not yet accumulated. See, for example, the year-by-year accounts of Oldknowe, Cowpe & Co., cotton manufacturers, whose proportion of fixed capital dropped from 90 per cent in the first year (1786), to 35 per cent a decade later. Chapman, *The Early Factory Masters*, p. 126. Thus initial fixed-capital requirements could be large and a bar to entry; and if the banks provided little long-term capital, it was not necessarily because little was demanded.

firms at other times show similar results. And Pollard argues that some of the largest, most heavily capitalized enterprises of the Industrial Revolution were actually in trouble because they found it hard to raise circulating capital commensurate with the size of their fixed plant. Paradoxically, they were too rich for their own good.

Although the development of an integrated national money market clearly promoted an easier, more abundant flow of resources from land to industry, the nature and direction of the balance of payments between these two sectors are less obvious. It is a commonplace of economic literature that one of the major aspects or criteria of development is the shift of resources from agriculture to manufacturing; and that a condition of rapid development is an increase of productivity in husbandry that will generate the savings to finance industrial expansion. The best example of such a sequence is Japan, where output per head in agriculture almost doubled in the space of a generation (1878/82–1903/7) at little expense of capital; and where, especially in the early years, the land tax drained a substantial fraction of farm income for investment in development.[1] The British case, however, differs sharply. For one thing, gains in farm productivity were assuredly far lower. The statistics available are in no way comparable to the Japanese but such as they are, they have led one authority to speculate that 'output per head in agriculture increased by about 25 per cent in the eighteenth century, and that the whole of this advance was achieved before 1750'.[2] The same source suggests that the real output of the farm sectors rose about 43 per cent in the course of the century, 24 per cent during the critical decades from 1760 to 1800;[3] by contrast, Japanese agricultural product about doubled from the late 1870's to the early 1900's.

Moreover, the increase in British farm output was due in large measure to enclosures and the improvements they made possible: concentration of holdings, elimination of fallow, more productive choice and rotation of crops, selective breeding of livestock, better drainage and fertilization, more intensive cultivation. It is still a matter of dispute how rapidly these new techniques spread or how quickly they followed on enclosure itself. What is clear is that both the division of the land and the subsequent improvements in its use cost money: for legal expenses, roads, ditches, and fences, to begin with; and eventually for buildings, equipment, drains, and materials. Unfortunately, we

[1] Kazushi Ohkawa and Henry Rosovsky, 'The Role of Agriculture in Modern Japanese Economic Development', *Econ. Devel. and Cult. Change*, IX, no. 1, part II (October 1960), 43–67; also G. Ranis, 'The Financing of Japanese Economic Development', *Econ. Hist. Rev.* 2nd ser. XI (1959), 440–54.

[2] Deane and Cole, *British Economic Growth*, p. 75.

[3] Deane and Cole, *op. cit.* p. 78.

have no figures of the area affected, but such partial statistics as are available—enclosure of commons and waste, for example, by parliamentary act—suggest that from 1760 to 1815 Britain enclosed millions of acres at an initial cost of redistribution of upwards of £1 per acre, and at an eventual cost of anywhere from £5 to £25 per acre, depending on the original condition of the soil and the nature of its use.[1] Such investments paid, as the higher yields and rents on consolidated land show. But it may well be that in the early decades of heavy enclosure, that is, the very years that also saw the birth of modern industry, British husbandry was taking as much capital as it was giving; while in the period from 1790 to 1814, when food prices rose to record levels, the net flow of resources was probably toward the land. The great contribution of agriculture to industrialization came after 1815, when both enclosure and the breaking of marginal soil slowed and proprietors and tenants reaped the fruits of earlier efforts. Yet even then, these returns depended on protection against foreign corn and were therefore not a net addition to the savings generated by the economy. Rather, they were bought at the price of a certain misallocation of resources, and abundant and responsive though they may have been, they were probably less than what the land would have provided under more competitive conditions. Still, it was thanks to enclosures and what is sometimes called the 'Agricultural Revolution' that Britain fended off as well as she did Ricardo's 'stationary state'—that end of growth and accumulation wherein the pressure of population on the supply of food has so raised the cost of subsistence and hence wages, that manufacturers can no longer make a profit and the wealth of the nation flows as rent to the owners of the land.

To sum up: it was in large measure the pressure of demand on the mode of production that called forth the new techniques in Britain, and the abundant, responsive supply of the factors that made possible their rapid exploitation and diffusion. The point will bear stressing, the more so as economists, particularly theorists, are inclined to concentrate almost exclusively on the supply side. The student of economic development, impressed on the one hand by the high cost of industrialization, on the other by the low level of savings in underdeveloped countries, has devoted most of his attention to the problem of capital formation: on ways to raise the rate of net investment from, say, 5 per cent to 12 or more; and on devices to prevent increased income from

---

[1] On the cost of enclosure, cf. Great Britain, Board of Agriculture, *General Report on Enclosures* (London, 1808), p. 97. On subsequent expenses of improvement, Albert Pell, 'The Making of the Land in England: A Retrospect', *Journal of the Royal Agricultural Society of England*, 2nd ser. XXIII (1887), 355–74.

dissipating itself on increased consumption.[1] His approach is essentially analogous to that of an economic historian like Hamilton, with his thesis of industrial revolution born of and fed by profit inflation. And indeed, many a planner has seriously contemplated the deliberate use of inflation, which tends to shift resources from consumers to savers, to promote industrialization.

Yet however justified this concern with saving and capital may be in this age of costly equipment and facilities and abysmally poor would-be industrial economies, it is less relevant to the British experience. To begin with, eighteenth-century Britain enjoyed, as we have seen, more wealth and income per head than the unindustrialized countries of today; she started, in other words, from a higher base. Furthermore, the capital requirements of these early innovations were small—usually within reach of a single person or family; and the successful enterprise could build the growth of each period on the profits of the one before.[2] Finally, these critical innovations were concentrated at first in a small sector of the economy, and their appetite for capital was correspondingly limited; while on the larger scale of the economy as a whole, just as within the smaller world of the enterprise, growth built on this narrow base by a process of derived demand that fed on earlier success.[3] It was the flow of capital, in other words, more than the stock, that counted in the last analysis. So much for the preoccupation with primitive accumulation.

Under the circumstances, it is not surprising to learn that the aggregate volume of investment was a relatively small proportion of national

[1] One could cite numerous examples. For some idea of the wide spectrum of thought along this one line, cf. W. A. Lewis, *The Theory of Economic Growth* (London, 1955), pp. 201 f.; W. W. Rostow, 'The Take-off into Self-Sustained Growth', *Econ. J.* LXVI (1956), 25–48; and a review by O. Ehrlich of Gerald M. Meier and Robert Baldwin, *Economic Development: Theory, History, Policy* (New York, 1957), in *J. Econ. Hist.* XVIII (1958), 74.

[2] On the ability of British enterprises to grow by reinvestment of profits, see the statistics assembled by François Crouzet, 'La formation du capital en Grande-Bretagne', *Deuxième Conférence Internationale d'Histoire Economique*, pp. 622–3. He offers a sample of fifteen firms from the textile manufacture, metallurgy, and brewing. In the first two branches, compound growth rates range from 3·5 to 29·8 per cent per year, and some of the companies show for several decades semi-logarithmic curves of growth that are almost straight lines. What is more, these figures give only an incomplete idea of the ability of these enterprises to generate profits. In the years 1794–1828 the capital of John Marshall & Co. (linen manufacture, Leeds) rose from £14,000 to £272,000; but in the years 1804–1815, that is, in about a third of the time, Marshall and his partners earned some £446,000. Admittedly these war years were especially favourable. *Ibid.*, p. 619, n. 3; Gordon Rimmer, *Marshalls of Leeds, Flax-Spinners 1788–1886* (Cambridge, 1960), pp. 69, 71 ff.

[3] So much for hypotheses of balanced growth; the historical experience, under conditions of relatively unplanned development, followed other lines. See below,

income in these early decades of the Industrial Revolution, and that it was only later, when a more elaborate technology required large outlays and Britain had increased her product per capita to the point where she could save more, that the proportion rose to the level that economists once looked upon as a characteristic of industrialization. Thus according to Phyllis Deane, the ratio of net capital formation to income did not go above 5 or 6 per cent through most of the eighteenth century, rising to perhaps 7 or 8 per cent only in the last decade, when the Industrial Revolution was in full swing. Not until the railway boom of the 1840's did the proportion rise to 10 per cent.[1]

The same pattern seems to hold for other industrializing countries, though it would be dangerous to make fine comparisons between the rough estimates of capital formation currently available. For France, we have the tentative findings of Jean Marczewski's research group at the Institut de Science Economique Appliquée which propose an implausibly low average net rate of 3 per cent of net domestic product for France until the railway years of the 1840's, when it rises to 8 per cent; not until the Second Empire, with even more railway construction and extensive urban improvement, does the proportion go up to 12·1 per cent.[2]

For Germany, unfortunately, we have no figures for the period before the 1850's. By that time mining, heavy industry, and the railway network were all expanding rapidly; even so, the rate of net capital formation for the two decades 1850–70 averaged less than 10 per cent.[3]

In general, there is good reason to believe that until very recently economists and economic historians were wont to exaggerate the significance of capital formation as a motor of economic growth.

pp. 314 ff., 321, 338. Also John Hughes, 'Foreign Trade and Balanced Growth: the Historical Framework', Amer. Econ. Rev. XLIX, no. 2 (May 1959), 330–37; and Goran Ohlin, 'Balanced Economic Growth in History', ibid. pp. 338–53.

[1] Deane, 'Capital Formation in Britain before the Railway Age', Econ. Development and Cultural Change, IX, no. 3 (April 1961), 352–68; Deane and Cole, British Economic Growth, ch. viii.

[2] Marczewski, 'The Take-Off Hypothesis and French Experience', in W. W. Rostow, ed., The Economics of Take-off into Sustained Growth (London, 1963), p. 121.

[3] Simon Kuznets, 'Quantitative Aspects of the Economic Growth of Nations, VI: Long-Term Trends in Capital Formation Proportions', Econ. Development and Cultural Change, IX, no. 4, part II (July 1961), 14. For Japan, Henry Rosovsky suggests rates averaging between 7 and 9 per cent for the decades from 1887 to 1917; rates of gross capital formation ran about 5 per cent higher. Much of this, moreover, was military expenditure, which contributed only in part to economic growth. If one excludes military outlays, one arrives at decennial average net rates between 4·5 and 6·8 per cent. Capital Formation in Japan, 1868–1914 (Glencoe, Ill., 1961), pp. 9, 15. On all the above, cf. Rondo Cameron, 'Some Lessons of History for Developing Nations', American Econ. Review, LVII, no. 2 (May 1967), 313–14.

Newer research has made clear that increase of capital will account for only a small fraction of gains in aggregate output; indeed that the combined inputs of the traditional factors of production—land, labour, and capital—play a minority role in the overall process.[1] Whence these gains, then? They seem to derive from the quality of the inputs—from the higher productivity of new technology and the superior skills and knowledge of both entrepreneurs and workers. And here again, as we have seen, the Britain of the Industrial Revolution was especially favoured.

Technological innovations are only part of the story. The question remains why they had the effect they did. An institutional order is a remarkably complex and elastic system; not everything can turn it upside down. Only changes of a certain quality and scope could have transformed the mode of production and initiated a self-sustaining process of economic development.

The manufacture of almost any textile may be analysed into four main steps: preparation, in which the raw material is sorted, cleaned, and combed out so that the fibres lie alongside one another; spinning, in which the loose fibres are drawn and twisted to form a yarn; weaving, in which some yarn is laid lengthwise (the warp) and other yarn (the weft) is run across over and under the longitudinal lines to form a fabric; finally, finishing, which varies considerably with the nature of the cloth, but may comprise fulling or sizing (to give the cloth body), cleaning, shearing, dyeing, printing, or bleaching.

At the beginning of the eighteenth century, only a handful of these processes had as yet been mechanized. In the wool manufacture, the fulling mill, its heavy hammers driven by water, was known on the Continent as early as the eleventh century and by the thirteenth had spread widely over the English countryside. The gig mill, which raised the nap on the cloth preparatory to shearing, dated from the sixteenth century; and though legal prohibition and the opposition of the shearmen delayed its diffusion, the repeated clamour against the device is the best evidence of its gains. There had also been two major improvements on the immemorial loom: the knitting frame, a complex, hand-run contrivance for weaving hosiery (invented by William Lee in 1598);

[1] On this whole question of the residual—that part of growth which cannot be explained by the conventional factor inputs—see S. Kuznets, *Modern Economic Growth: Rate, Structure, and Spread* (New Haven and London, 1966), pp. 79–85. Kuznets offers calculations of the value of the residual for the United States and Norway in the twentieth century, and for Soviet Russia. They seem to indicate a rise in the significance of quality as against quantity as industrialization proceeds. It may be, then, that comparable calculations for the Britain of the Industrial Revolution would show a much smaller residual than now.

and the Dutch or small-wares loom, invented at about the same time, and designed to weave as many as twenty-four narrow tapes or ribbons simultaneously.

Another precocious mechanical innovation was the silk-throwing machine, which twisted the filaments to form a thread. It was invented in the seventeenth century in Italy, where the secret was jealously guarded. But the plans were smuggled out by an Englishman named John Lombe in 1716–17, and within a few years John's brother Thomas built a huge throwing mill at Derby, a 500-foot power-driven factory of five or six stories and some 460 windows that was one of the wonders of the age. By the middle of the century, similar plants had been established in London and the provinces, some of them even larger than Lombe's monster.

In addition to these complex devices, which anticipate in their ingenuity and relative efficiency the better-known inventions of the mid-eighteenth century, a number of less spectacular advances had occurred, gradually and almost unnoticed. Over the centuries, the spinning wheel, large or small, had replaced the distaff, and the wheel itself had been altered to work faster and turn out a more even yarn. At the same time, those processes that required the use of fuel— dyeing, for example—had from the sixteenth century on learned to use coal instead of the more expensive wood. Finally, a variety of small improvements had been made in preparing the fibre for spinning, weaving the yarn in more complex patterns, and finishing it with the sheen and smoothness that betokened quality.

None of these advances, however, was sufficient in itself to trigger a process of cumulative, self-sustaining change. For it took a marriage to make the Industrial Revolution. On the one hand, it required machines which not only replaced hand labour but compelled the concentration of production in factories—in other words, machines whose appetite for energy was too large for domestic sources of power and whose mechanical superiority was sufficient to break down the resistance of the older forms of hand production. On the other hand, it required a big industry producing a commodity of wide and elastic demand, such that (1) the mechanization of any one of its processes of manufacture would create serious strains in the others, and (2) the impact of improvements in this industry would be felt throughout the economy.

Neither the knitting frame nor the Dutch loom nor the throwing mill could satisfy these conditions. The first two, hand driven, were quite suited to domestic manufacture; and all three were employed in the production of goods whose actual market was small and potential demand limited. It was not until the techniques of spinning and weaving cheap textiles were transformed that the threshold of revolution was crossed.

It was crossed first in the cotton manufacture. Why in cotton? One would have expected the passage to occur in wool, which was far and away the most important industry of the day, whether in terms of numbers employed, capital invested, or value of product. In England, imports of raw cotton (net of re-exports) in the first decade of the century averaged a little over a million pounds a year, worth perhaps £30,000 or £35,000; at that time, if we are to rely on available estimates, the woollen industry was consuming about 40 million pounds of material, valued at some £2 million. Even some decades later, in 1741, when both cotton consumption and prices were up and the price of wool had fallen, the disparity was still enormous: something over 1½ million pounds of raw cotton worth around £55,000, as against almost 60 million pounds of wool valued at perhaps £1,500,000.[1] In the other countries of Europe, the comparison was equally in favour of the older industry.

It has long been customary to explain this apparent paradox by denying it, that is, by asserting that it was just because the cotton industry was new, hence free of traditional restrictions on the scale and character of production, that it was able to adopt new techniques. The argument will not stand scrutiny. In England—which is the country that counts for our purposes—the extensive development of putting-out in the West Country and East Anglia and the rise of independent clothiers in Yorkshire had long freed the bulk of the wool manufacture from guild controls; indeed, in so far as legal restrictions entered into account, they favoured the older industry, on which the economic prosperity of the nation had been built.

On the other hand, the smallness of the cotton manufacture on the eve of the Industrial Revolution should not deceive us. For so young a creation, it was a spectacularly lusty child, and so rapid were its gains that almost from the beginning the older wool and linen trades were impelled to demand succour from the state. In England, a whole series of laws and decrees were passed from the late seventeenth century on to stimulate the consumption of domestic wool cloth: sumptuary laws like the Act requiring that all dead be buried in wool shrouds; prohibitions on the import of competitive fabrics; restrictions on the output of calicoes at home (1721). To no avail. The closing of England to East Indian cottons simply encouraged the domestic producers, whose fustians and linen-cottons (they were not yet able to turn out pure

[1] Cotton figures from Wadsworth and Mann, *Cotton Trade*, pp. 520–2; wool from P. Deane, 'The Output of the British Woollen Industry in the Eighteenth Century', *J. Econ. Hist.* XVII (1957), 220.

cottons) did not come under the interdiction. By the middle of the century, gains at home and abroad had made the cotton manufacturers a vested interest too powerful for even the still pre-eminent wool trade to overcome.

Still more important, cotton lent itself technologically to mechanization far more readily than wool. It is a plant fibre, tough and relatively homogeneous in its characteristics, where wool is organic, fickle, and subtly varied in its behaviour. In the early years of rudimentary machines, awkward and jerky in their movements, the resistance of cotton was a decisive advantage. Well into the nineteenth century, long after the techniques of mechanical engineering had much improved, there continued to be a substantial lag between the introduction of innovations into the cotton industry and their adaptation to wool. And even so, there has remained an element of art—of touch—in wool manufacture that the cleverest and most automatic contrivances have not been able to eliminate.

Once mechanization did come to cotton, of course, it was successful far beyond what it could have hoped to be in wool. On the one hand, the elasticity of supply of the raw material was substantially greater: one can increase acreage sown far more rapidly than the number of sheep. Thus cotton prices rose by about half in the 1770's and 1780's under the pressure of demand from the new spinning machines, while imports increased more than sixfold. Once the North American plantations entered the market, moreover, and the cotton gin made slave labour profitable, imports kept rising spectacularly while prices fell. In the peak year of 1860, Britain purchased over 1·4 milliard pounds of cotton at about the same 7½ pence it cost at the start of the eighteenth century.

On the other hand, the market for cotton goods was more elastic than for wool. Not only was the trend of taste in favour of the new fibre—for centuries, there had been an irregular but almost uninterrupted shift in the direction of lighter fabrics—but the availability of a cheap, washable textile gave rise to new patterns of dress of unforeseen potential. No longer was it the wealthy alone who could enjoy the comfort and hygiene of body *linen;* cotton made it possible for millions to wear drawers and chemises where before there had been nothing but the coarse, dirty outer-garments. A new kind of work-clothing was born—tough, yet comfortable to the skin and easy to clean and maintain. Even the rich, impressed with the colour and elegance of cotton prints, learned to distinguish more and more between the seasons and dress for the summer in muslins and calicoes.

At the same time, the bulk of the untapped markets in the pre-industrial areas of the world lay in the warmer climes or in temperate areas with hot summers. Already in the sixteenth and seventeenth centuries, a good part of Britain's gains as an exporter of wool cloth had been in the countries bordering the Mediterranean, the western plantations, and India; similarly, the spurt in re-exports of Indian calicoes that marked the late seventeenth century was due to the new demand of semi-tropical lands enriched by sugar, tobacco, and other 'colonial wares'. The story was no different in the eighteenth and nineteenth centuries: the commercial frontier of Britain lay overseas—in America, Africa, south and east Asia. The first was by far the most important: the West Indies and mainland colonies together bought 10 per cent of English domestic exports in 1700–1, 37 per cent in 1772–3, about 57 per cent in 1797–8.[1] Wool had played a big part in these gains: the sale of cloth in the new Atlantic market (America and Africa) grew sixfold from the beginning of the century to the eve of the American Revolution.[2] Now it was cotton's turn.

And so, although the first of the famous series of inventions that transformed the textile industry—both the fly-shuttle of Kay (1733) and the spinning frame of Wyatt and Paul (1738)—were designed for the manufacture of wool, the requirements of technology and the logic of the economic situation willed otherwise.

There is neither time nor space to review at this point the history of these inventions, which will be familiar to most readers. A number of summary observations, however, are indispensable.

(i) They came in a sequence of challenge and response, in which the speed-up of one stage of the manufacturing process placed a heavy strain on the factors of production of one or more other stages and called forth innovations to correct the imbalance. We have already noted the difficulty of supplying weavers with yarn. Kay's fly-shuttle, which did not really catch on until the 1750's and 1760's, only aggravated an already serious disequilibrium. The problem was solved by a family of spinning devices: carding machines by Paul and others (in use from the

---

[1] Deane and Cole, *British Economic Growth*, p. 34. These figures show a somewhat more rapid increase to the 1770's than those of Ralph Davis, 'English Foreign Trade, 1700–1774', *Econ. Hist. Rev.* 2nd ser. xv (1962), 292.

[2] *Ibid.* p. 291. The sale of 'other manufactures'—nails, tools, metal wares, leather goods, cordage, other textiles, and the like—grew even faster, to almost nine times its volume at the beginning of the period. As a consequence, the share of wool manufactures in total exports shrank from more than two-thirds to perhaps 27 per cent over the course of the century. Even at the end, however, they were still worth twice as much as cotton exports. Deane and Cole, *British Economic Growth*, pp. 30–1. Cottons followed a deviant geographical pattern: major expansion in overseas areas to about 1770, that is, the eve of technological revolution; then the most rapid gains, in Europe. Wadsworth and Mann, *Cotton Trade*, p. 146.

1750's); Hargreaves's jenny (c. 1765; patent 1770); Arkwright's water frame (1769); Crompton's mule (1779)—so called because it combined some of the features of the frame and the jenny.[1]

The mechanical advantage of even the earliest jennies and water frames over hand spinning was enormous: anywhere from six up to twenty-four to one for the jenny; several hundred to one for the frame. The spinning wheel, which had taken some centuries to displace the rock, became an antique in the space of a decade. Moreover, the victorious jenny scarcely outlived its victim; even the later models, with eighty and more spindles, could not compete in productivity—to say nothing of quality—with power-driven mules of two and three hundred. By the end of the century, the jenny was obsolete.

What is more, the quality of the machine-spun yarn was better than anything the distaff or wheel had been able to produce. A thread spun by hand is necessarily uneven in thickness and strength; and no two hanks are ever the same. One of the most difficult tasks of the manufacturer of the eighteenth century was to assemble suitable assortments of yarn. On occasion, he paid a premium for the work of an especially gifted spinster. The machine changed all this. Not only was its work more regular and stronger in proportion to weight, but the mule, which drew and twisted the roving simultaneously and continued to draw even after the twisting stopped, could spin higher counts than man had ever known: where the most skilful Indian spinner working with the wheel, or Swiss spinster using a distaff, could barely surpass

[1] Technically the family was composed of two branches. On one side were the throstles (beginning with the water frame and continuing through various avatars down to the cap and ring machines of the present day), which drew the roving out first and then imparted twist. On the other were the jenny and mule, which imitated the action of the human spinner by drawing and twisting simultaneously. Because the weakness of the untwisted thread limited the length of the draw, the throstle could not produce fine counts and was used primarily for the production of warps. In the early period, this was extremely important since the jenny—and later the mule—spun too loose a thread for this purpose. On the other hand, because the long draw gave more play to the twist, which concentrated in the thinner spots and built them up, the mule made a more regular thread than the frame; moreover, later improvements enabled the mule to produce a harder twist, and from 1800 the throstle tended to fade from use. There was a renewal of favour in the 1820's and 1830's, however, with the development of the ring principle and the growing use of power looms, which especially at first needed the strongest possible warps. Nevertheless, the British cotton industry, with its steady shift to finer yarn and cloth, has never made so much use of the throstle as the continental countries. Cf. Daniels, *The Early English Cotton Industry*, p. 164; also Julia de L. Mann, 'The Textile Industry: Machinery for Cotton, Flax, Wool, 1760–1850', in Ch. Singer *et al.*, *A History of Technology*, vol. IV: *The Industrial Revolution* (Oxford: Clarendon, 1958), pp. 283–91 and the sources cited there; and F. Nasmith, 'Fathers of the Machine Cotton Industry', *Trans. Newcomen Soc.* VI (1925–6), 167–8 (letter of E. J. Welffens).

150 hanks to the pound, the better mule operatives were able to approach 300 by the start of the nineteenth century.

The tremendous increase of the supply of yarn that resulted from these inventions—reflected in a more than twelve-fold increase in cotton consumption from 1770 to 1800[1]—made improvements in weaving imperative. This was the golden age of the hand-weaver, whose unprecedented prosperity was a shock to all, a scandal to some. The answer was the power loom, invented by Cartwright in 1787. It caught on with difficulty owing to mechanical shortcomings (the main problem was how to achieve speed without excessive breakage of the threads), and its diffusion can be linked directly to fluctuations in the demand for cloth and hence the cost of hand labour. Thus its adoption was slow during the first two decades of the century, when war and, later on, tariff barriers cut Britain off from important markets. In the meantime, performance was improved, and where, in the first decade of the century, the machine worked hardly faster than the traditional hand loom, the technical advantage had risen by the mid-1820's to as much as $7\frac{1}{2}$ to 1, and one boy on two looms could do up to fifteen times as much as the cottage artisan.[2] At that point, the aim seems to have been not so much to speed the machine as to simplify its operation so that one person could handle more units at the same time: in 1833, a young man with a twelve-year old assistant could run four looms and turn out as much as twenty times the output of a hand worker.[3]

Such figures are clearly impressionistic and unstandardized. Yet they convey a general picture of the growing gap between machine and man, a gap reflected in the statistics, themselves approximate, of power looms in operation in Great Britain: 2400 in 1813, 14,150 in 1820, 55,500 in 1829, 100,000 in 1833, 250,000 by mid-century.[4] By contrast, the number of hand-loom weavers declined, although at a rate that testified to the obstinacy and tenacity of men who were unwilling to trade their independence for the better-paid discipline of the sheds. In the teens, their number actually rose to about a quarter of a million, and hung steadily there for another decade, though wages had fallen

---

[1] Average net imports, 1768–72; 3,703,000 lb.; 1798–1802, 47,233,000 lb.

[2] Cf. Edward Baines, *A History of the Cotton Manufacture in Great Britain* (London, 1835), p. 240, citing R. Guest, *A Compendious History of the Cotton Manufacture* (Manchester, 1823).

[3] It is not clear how common this practice was. The impression one gets from comparisons between British and Continental practice is that the usual work load in a British cotton shed remained two looms until the 1870's, when conflicts arose over the effort to double the assignment.

[4] The figures up to 1833 are from Baines, *History of the Cotton Manufacture*, pp. 235–7. The 1850 number is from the factory reports, cited by T. Ellison, *The Cotton Trade of Great Britain* (London, 1886), pp. 76–7.

by over a half; by 1830 these reached an apparently irreducible minimum of about 6s. a week. The next two decades saw attrition shrink the weavers—in spite of recruitment of Irish immigrants whose subsistence level was even lower than that of the English artisans—to a remnant of 40,000. It is likely that many, if not most of these, were employed only part time—a reserve supply of labour in the event of unusual demand. A dozen more years, and there were perhaps 3000 left.

One point remains to be made about the pattern of challenge and response. The prominence of the inventions in spinning and weaving has tended to obscure the importance of this principle for all stages of textile manufacture. In particular, the mechanization of spinning would have been unthinkable without a corresponding speed-up of the preliminary processes of cleaning, carding, and preparation of the roving. The eighteenth century saw, therefore, the development of an entire complex of pre-spinning machines, linked in rationally calculated combinations to the frame and the mule; the early machine builders often sold their products in sets or 'assortments' covering the various stages of manufacture from raw fibre to yarn. Similarly, the finishing processes were transformed: it was no longer feasible to bleach cloth in open meadows when more of it was being turned out than there was ground available. The answer lay in the use of chemical agents: often sulphuric acid at first; from the 1790's on, chlorine. In the same way, cylinder printing was introduced in place of the block press in London in 1783; it had been known for some time before; but by then the need was ripe, and it spread quickly to the rest of the country.

(ii) The many small gains were just as important as the more spectacular initial advances. None of the inventions came to industry in full-blown perfection. Aside from the trial and error of creation, there were innumerable adjustments and improvements—in articulation of parts, transmission of power, and the materials employed—before these primitive contrivances would work commercially. The first decades of industrialization saw a ceaseless war against breakdowns. By the turn of the century, however, not only the heavy motionless frame of the machine could be built of iron, but also the moving parts; leather belts had replaced pulley-ropes of cotton-mill waste. In subsequent decades, improvements in the steam-engine produced a smoother stroke; gearing and shafting were rationalized; and increasing automaticity achieved its consummation in Roberts's self-acting mule (1825).

(iii) Nothing illustrates better the continued importance of purely technological considerations than the persistent lag of mechanization in the woollen industry. It was not until the 1780's that the jenny came into general use in the Leeds area, and the mule was not really a success until the 1830's. In worsted, where the combed fibres will take more strain, machines came in faster: in the 1780's and 1790's, Yorkshire mills and shops were using jennies, hand- or animal-powered mules, and modified water frames. The first use of the steam-engine dates from before the turn of the century, and by 1820 there were perhaps two dozen steam-powered factories in the West Riding. By then hand spinning was almost a curiosity.[1]

Even when mechanized, the wool industry was compelled to work more slowly than cotton. William Fairbairn, probably the greatest authority of the period on factory design, has the mules of his sample cotton plant running at 232 r.p.m., those of his hypothetical woollen mill at 152.[2] Limitations of speed were still more serious in weaving, where the power loom offered nothing like the gains in productivity characteristic of the new spinning equipment. Thus Fairbairn's cotton looms were working at from 140 to 160 picks per minute, while his woollen equipment was doing 46. To be sure, it was harder to weave woollen yarn than the tougher worsted, but even in worsted the power loom came in slowly. The transition in the West Riding came in the late 1830's and 1840's: 2768 power looms in 1836, 11,458 in 1841, 19,121 in 1845, 35,298 in 1856.[3] The woollen manufacture was about a decade behind (6275 power looms in Yorkshire in 1856, 5733 in Lancashire, 14,391 in the whole of Great Britain); and even after the hand loom had been driven from the sheds of larger enterprises, it survived in the Yorkshire countryside—*a fortiori* in the West Country, the home of the old-fashioned broadcloth trade.

Because of its subsequent importance, the iron industry has sometimes received more attention than it deserves in histories of the Industrial Revolution. Looking back from the vantage of one hundred years and more, living in a world in which heavy industry is the basis of the economy, writers have tended to overemphasize the immediate

---

[1] The best source is Eric Sigsworth, *Black Dyke Mills: A History* (Liverpool, 1958), chs. I–II; see also J. James, *A History of the Wool Manufacture in England from the Earliest Times* (London, 1857).

Another reason for the slower mechanization of the woollen, as against the worsted, manufacture was the relatively high cost of the raw material. Figures for 1772 show the raw wool accounting for one third of the value of the finished product in the cloth branch; for only one sixth, in the worsted branch. The share of labour was thus far greater in the latter, and the potential economy offered by the use of machinery was that much larger a proportion of total price. Cf. Deane, 'The Output of the British Woollen Industry', p. 215.

[2] *Treatise on Mills and Millwork* (2nd ed.; 2 vols.; London, 1864–5), II, 187, 195.

[3] H. Heaton, *The Yorkshire Woollen and Worsted Industries* (Oxford: Clarendon, 1920), p. 357; *Parl. Papers*, 1857 Sess. I, XIV, 180. The last is for the county of Yorkshire as a whole; the vast majority, however, were in the West Riding.

significance for the eighteenth century of the technological advances in smelting and refining. Not in number of men employed, nor capital invested, nor value of output, nor rate of growth could iron be compared with cotton in this period. If the unit of production, larger at the start than in other industries, grew under the stimulus of technical change, the social impact of this growth was nowise comparable to that of the transition from putting-out to factory in textiles. On the other hand, the growing supply of ever-cheaper metal did facilitate enormously the mechanization of other industries, the shift from water to steam power and, eventually, the transformation of the means of transportation. In the process, the units of manufacture in metallurgy grew until they overshadowed in their vastness and Vulcanian energy the largest cotton mills in the kingdom.

To understand the history of the iron and steel industry, a knowledge of the purely technological determinants is indispensable. In this regard, three points must be kept in mind:

(1) Metallurgy is a chemical process: the problem is to reduce the ore, which is iron in compound form, to a suitably pure metal. The reaction requires large quantities of carbon as well as heat, and the fuel, which serves a double purpose, is necessarily placed in direct contact with the ore. This in turn poses special difficulties. All fuel, whether vegetable or mineral, contains substances other than carbon—oils, as well as minerals like sulphur and phosphorus—that are harmful to the final product. Charring will get rid of the volatile impurities; already in ancient times, smelters and smiths were using charcoal rather than wood, and the introduction of coal as a fuel in the late Middle Ages was soon followed by the development of the analogous coked form. But charring or coking will not get rid of mineral impurities, which are far more serious in coal than in wood. So that although techniques were developed by the seventeenth century for using coke in glass-making, malting, dyeing, and other heavy energy-consuming industries where fuel and raw material can be kept separate, efforts to employ it in iron smelting failed.[1] Not until a semi-adventitious mix of fairly clean ore and coal was achieved by Darby at Coalbrookdale in 1709 did coke-blast iron become a commercial reality.[2] Even then, the process did not spread until half a century later, after decades of empiricism had achieved a knowledge of mix and finished product that made

---

[1] A simple point, but generally overlooked. Thus J. W. Nef, 'Coal Mining and Utilization', in C. Singer et al., A History of Technology, III, 79.

[2] There is some question about the exact date. See M. W. Flinn, 'Abraham Darby and the Coke-smelting Process', Economica, n.s. XXVI (1959), 54–9; and R. A. Mott, '"Coles": Weights and Measures, with Special Reference to Abraham Darby and the Coke-smelting Process', ibid. pp. 256–9.

it possible to make use of less favourable materials and improvements in the blast had yielded the higher temperatures required. Moreover, another generation had to pass before innovations in refining made it possible to convert coke-blast iron into competitive wrought iron, comparable in tenacity and malleability to metal made with charcoal.[1] Britain was only the first country to face the problem: the late adoption of coke smelting on the Continent was in large measure due to the same chemical difficulties. Similar considerations were to prove decisive in the second half of the nineteenth century in the application of new techniques for the mass production of steel.

(2) The charcoal or coke used in the blast furnace must be at once porous enough to provide as large a surface as possible to combustion and passage to heat and flames, yet at the same time strong and rigid enough to withstand the weight of the charge. This is one reason why there have always been limits—especially before the coming of the railway—to the transport of either fuel; once crumbled by jolting and handling, they are useless. This also explains why not all coal is suitable for metallurgical coke: if it is very oily, the end product of carbonization is too hollow, hence friable; and if it has little or no oil, like anthracite, the result is too solid for combustion. To be sure, there is a certain amount of leeway, and indeed modern metallurgy has made major advances in mixing otherwise unsuitable qualities of coal to produce a satisfactory coke. Nevertheless, differences in quality impose differences in costs, and in the nineteenth century especially, the distribution of coking coal—which was particularly favourable to Britain and western Germany—was a critical factor in the location and competitive position of metallurgical enterprise.

(3) Efficient combustion in the blast furnace requires a powerful, forced draught; the larger the furnace, the more powerful the draught. The substitution of coke for charcoal required and encouraged the use of ever bigger furnaces. Efforts to increase the blast of traditional water-powered leather bellows were on the whole unsatisfactory. Not until the cast-iron blowing cylinder (c. 1760 at Carron) was combined with the rotative steam-engine (1776 at John Wilkinson's furnace at Willey in Shropshire) was the problem solved.[2] Even then, furnace technique fell far short of the chemical possibilities of the combustion process. To exploit these, one had to alter the character of the blast itself. The first and most rewarding step on this path was to preheat the air (Neilson in

---

[1] In 1765 Jars wrote: 'the production of good wrought iron from pit-coal pig iron is considered impossible.' Gabriel Jars, *Voyages métallurgiques* (3 vols.; Lyons, 1774-81), I, 250.

[2] H. R. Schubert, *History of the British Iron and Steel Industry* (London, 1957), pp. 332-3; cf. Gabriel Jars, *Voyages*, I, 277.

1829; see below, p. 92). The next, not taken until after the Second World War, was to modify the wind by maintaining humidity constant and/or by enriching it with oxygen.

(4) The product of the blast furnace is pig iron, a hard metal too brittle to work. The only way to shape it is to cast it in moulds; even then, the resulting pieces will not stand up to pressure, strain, or blows. To change this form of iron into one that can be worked and will support stress (what is called wrought or malleable iron), one must refine it by removing most of the remaining carbon and such other chemical impurities as diminish its malleability, tensile strength, ductility, and other virtues. In the early eighteenth century, this was done by heating and reheating the metal in charcoal fires and pounding out the dross with hammers—a long, costly process that yielded a product of high, though uneven, quality and irregular shape.

From the 1730's on, British forgemasters devoted great effort and expense to finding a shorter, surer technique that would use mineral rather than vegetable fuel. The search took half a century. The first advance provided only a partial solution: by introducing a refinery hearth and sometimes also a reverberatory fire (one in which the flames did not play on the metal directly) between the furnace and the forge, it was possible to use coal or coke rather than charcoal for some and eventually all of the fining process. The operation was still slow and the resulting product was not so good as charcoal bar, but it was cheaper, and by 1788 according to one estimate, about half the wrought iron in the kingdom was being made with mineral fuel.[1] By this time, however, the definitive triumph of coal was assured by the invention of a quite different technique—Henry Cort's combination of puddling and rolling (patents of 1784 and 1783). The former process made use of a reverberatory furnace to decarburize the pig in one step, alternately heating and cooling the metal until the wrought iron could be separated out by reason of its higher melting-point. After some preliminary hammering, the rolling mill—long used for such light work as slitting rods—then squeezed rather than beat out the dross, shaping the iron the while. This application of the rotative principle (see below, p. 309, n. 1) offered two great advantages over the reciprocating action of the tilt-hammer: it worked perhaps fifteen times as fast; and by grooving or otherwise preforming the rolls, one could now turn out an almost unlimited range of those standardized crude shapes—beams, bars, rails and the like—that have come to constitute the framework of industry, construction, and transport.

The course of technological change in metallurgy suggests the following generalizations:

[1] Ashton, *Iron and Steel*, p. 88. No source given.

(1) There is in iron-making, as in textile manufacture, a see-saw of challenge and response. Thus the diffusion of coke-smelting put new pressure on refining, in spite of the ingenuity of ironmasters in developing new applications for cast iron. Cort's combination of puddling and rolling temporarily eased the difficulty, but the construction of new and larger furnaces gave rise in the course of the nineteenth century to a new imbalance. The fundamental difficulty was the physical hardship of puddling, which called for exceptional strength and endurance. There was simply a limit to what flesh could stand, and after a while the only way to increase output was to train more men and build more hearths. Much money and effort was expended on finding a way to mechanize the process. In vain: the imbalance was not corrected until Bessemer and his successors learned to make cheap steel.

(2) Again, in iron as in textiles, small anonymous gains were probably more important in the long run than the major inventions that have been remembered in the history books. And again, as in textiles, the reason is to be found in part in the empirical approximateness of these early advances. Patents were a beginning as well as an end, and ironmasters found that each combination of ore and fuel or metal and fuel required its own recipe. The word is used advisedly. Iron manufacture was essentially a kind of cookery—requiring a feel for the ingredients, an acute sense of proportion, an 'instinct' about the time the pot should be left on the stove. The ironmasters had no idea why some things worked and others did not; nor did they care. It was not until the middle of the nineteenth century that scientists learned enough about the process of converting ore to metal to provide a guide to rational technique and measures for testing performance. As late as 1860, Bessemer was baffled by the failure of his converter on phosphoric ores.

Aside from the adaptation of the processes of smelting and refining to ores and fuel of different characteristics, the lesser improvements in iron technology were concentrated for the most part in three areas:

(a) *Fuel economy*. The gains are hard to measure because of statistical incomparability. In South Wales, changes in the blast and in the shape and size of the furnace cut coal consumption (including engines and lime and ore kilns) per ton of pig from perhaps 8 tons in 1791 to 3½ in 1830. The most important single advance was Neilson's hot blast, introduced in Scotland in 1829: with some materials, it yielded a fuel saving of over a third if coke was employed, more than two-thirds if coal, the while increasing output per furnace markedly. The hot blast was the beginning of a surge of Scottish iron production: the make of pig rose from 29,000 tons in 1829 to 825,000 in 1855. Results were impressive but less spectacular south of the Tweed, and certain areas, like the Black Country and South Wales, were decades in switching to the new technique. In general, British interest in fuel economy was limited by the cheapness of coal; much of what improvement there was, was simply a by-product of growth—larger, more efficient furnaces tended to burn less coke per unit of output.

In refining, the traditional techniques had consumed 2½–3 tons of charcoal per ton of crude iron produced. The use of mixed fuel (part coke, part charcoal) reduced the ratio to about 2 to 1. Puddling then brought it down to 1½ to 1, and with further improvement, to about ¾ to 1 by the middle of the nineteenth century.[1] The gains were thus substantial, though less important than in smelting. One should keep in mind, however, that every technique that permitted the substitution of mineral for vegetable fuel added that much to man's energy resources.

(b) *Economy of metal.* The problem was especially serious in refining: in the early puddling furnaces, half the pig was drawn off in the slag. A series of changes, culminating in the late 1830's in Joseph Hall's furnace bed of roasted tap cinder (instead of iron-hungry sand), cut waste to 8 per cent while speeding the conversion process. Hall's innovation pushed iron economy almost to its limit; at the end of the nineteenth century, waste still amounted to about 5 per cent.[2]

(c) *Adaptation to growth.* The constant enlargement of the blast furnace was aimed, not so much at saving raw materials as at raising output and, if possible, the productivity of labour; it brought with it a great increase in the number of puddling furnaces. At the same time, greater familiarity with the uses of iron brought a demand for ever-larger pieces of metal. With this growth of both output and size of product came difficulties in moving the raw materials and in handling and shaping the work. These were solved by a variety of devices: elevated platforms for loading the blast furnace, rails for transportation within the plant and even within the forge sheds, overhead chain pulleys and cranes to lift the blooms and finished pieces. The steam hammer, conceived in 1839 by Nasmyth and first applied by Bourdon of Le Creusot (the debate over priority has assumed the character of a national quarrel), was in effect a way of placing in the hands of the forge worker unprecedented power and strength, subject to precise control; large boring machines were an analogous advance.

---

[1] Over the same period, the producers of charcoal-wrought iron fought hard to hold their market. Among other things, they succeeded in cutting their own fuel consumption to less than 1½ tons of charcoal per ton of crude bar. On this phenomenon of the technological stimulus of obsolescence, see below, p. 260.

[2] David Mushet, *Papers on Iron and Steel* (London, 1840), p. 32; W. K. V. Gale, 'A Technological History of the Black Country—Iron Trade' (typewritten MS.), p. 58. I am grateful to Mr Gale for allowing me to consult his extremely informative study.

The development of the British iron industry was directly linked to these technological considerations. Up to the middle of the eighteenth century, the pecuniary and material limitations on the transport of charcoal or wood restricted growth and often compelled the ironmaster to halt work for as much as several months while sufficient fuel was collected for another run; the effect was to raise overhead charges enormously. The irregularity of the supply of water for power, due to drought in the summer and, less often, frost in winter, imposed similar interruptions. Both difficulties combined on occasion to push the furnaces and forges into lonely rural areas, where abundance of fuel and water was largely offset by isolation from the market.

It has long been customary to argue that the excessive appetite of the British iron manufacture had by the eighteenth century so exhausted its supply of wood that numerous furnaces and forges were forced to shut down, that overall output fell or at least stood still from about 1660 to 1760, and that only the introduction of mineral fuel saved the industry from slow starvation. Recent studies, however, have modified the picture, noting that the wood employed by the furnacemaster was coppice rather than construction timber; that much of this was systematically cultivated for the iron industry, so that in some areas, at least, the supply increased; and that a substantial number of new furnaces and forges were fired after 1660, more than compensating for those that had to be abandoned.[1] The fact remains that charcoal was getting ever costlier in some of the traditional iron-making areas; far more of the new furnaces were founded before 1700 than after; much of the industry survived in the face of Swedish and Russian competition only thanks to customs duties; and production, though rising, was rising far more slowly than imports or the output of more prosperous industries. Mr Flinn has suggested an increase of 'upwards of 10,000 tons' from 1660 to 1760; this would imply at most a gain of 75 per cent. By comparison, purchases of iron from Sweden and Russia more than doubled from 1711–15 to 1751–5.[2]

As early as 1740, Great Britain was using perhaps 10 or 11 pounds of wrought iron per person a year. In the next fifty years, consumption about doubled. By comparison, the French were using around 5 pounds per head at the later date, and the average for the Continent as a whole

---

[1] See especially M. W. Flinn, 'The Growth of the English Iron Industry, 1660–1760', *Econ. Hist. Rev.* 2nd ser. XI (1958), 144–53; G. Hammersley, 'The Crown Woods and Their Exploitation in the Sixteenth and Seventeenth centuries', *Bull. of the Institute of Historical Research*, XXX (1957), 136–61.

[2] H. Scrivenor, *History of the Iron Trade* (London, 1854), p. 58; K. G. Hildebrand, 'Foreign Markets for Swedish Iron in the 18th Century', *Scandinavian Econ. Hist. Rev.* VI (1958), 4–15.

was far lower. These gross estimates are confirmed by the qualitative impressions of observers: thus Arthur Young, who notes with surprise that 'the wheels of these [French] waggons are all shod with wood instead of iron'.[1] Whatever the sources of this ferruginous temper—which Alfred Marshall attributed to 'that sturdy, resolute Norse character' of his ancestors[2]—it is the more impressive for having developed in the face of the growing scarcity of fuel; until well into the eighteenth century, Britain used iron because she wanted to, not because it was abundant or cheap. (To be sure, the most likely substitute, wood, was perhaps even dearer.) Even so, one can but wonder what would have happened, had she had to go on depending on costly and inelastic foreign sources for much, if not most, of the principal structural material of modern technology.[3]

In any event, the problem was solved by the substitution of coal for wood, which, thanks to Britain's exceptional resource endowment and favourable transport conditions, changed a high-cost industry into the most efficient in the world. The make of pig iron rose sharply (the 1780's seem to mark a definite break in the curve), and where, in 1750, Britain imported twice as much iron as she made, by 1814 her exports alone amounted to five times her purchases. Some of this rapid increase in output reflected the special needs of the war years. But the coming of peace simply brought other sources of demand to the fore: engineering; the construction of factory plant and equipment; the manufacture of agricultural implements, hardware, piping for water and gas, and, especially after 1830, rails. Most important, exports of iron rose almost twentyfold by the middle of the century (57,000 tons in 1814; 1,036,000 in 1852). In the 1780's Britain's output of iron was smaller than that of France; by 1848 she was smelting almost two million tons, more than the rest of the world put together.

The development of mechanized industry concentrated in large units of production would have been impossible without a source of power greater than what human and animal strength could provide and independent of the vagaries of nature. The answer was found in a new converter of energy—the steam-engine; and in the exploitation on a tremendous scale of an old fuel—coal.

Each of these called the other forth. The strongest source of demand

[1] Young, Travels, I, 46. [2] Industry and Trade (London, 1919), p. 60.
[3] On the rigidity of the Swedish supply after 1750, cf. Eli F. Heckscher, An Economic History of Sweden (Cambridge, Massachusetts: Harvard, 1954), p. 178. On Russia, cf. M. Goldman, 'The Relocation and Growth of the Pre-Revolutionary Russian Ferrous Metal Industry', Explorations in Entrepreneurial History, IX (1956-7), 20; R. Portal, L'Oural au XVIIIe siècle (Paris, 1950); R. Portal, 'Une route du fer au XVIIIe siècle', Revue historique, CCXI (1954), 19-29.

Table 1. *Pig-Iron Output of Great Britain (in long tons)*

1740	17,350	1830	678,417
1788	68,300	1835	940,000
1796	125,079	1839	1,248,781
1806	258,206	1848	1,998,568
1825	581,367	1852	2,701,000

SOURCES. For the years 1740–1830 and 1852, Scrivenor, *History of the Iron Trade*, pp. 136, 302; for 1835, M. Meisner, *Die Versorgung der Weltwirtschaft mit Bergwerks-erzeugnissen*, I, *1860–1926* [in *Weltmontanstatistik*, pub. by the Preussische Geologische Landesanstalt] (Stuttgart, 1929), p. 84; for 1839, Mushet, *Papers on Iron and Steel*, p. 421; for 1848, Ludwig Beck, *Geschichte des Eisens in technischer und kulturgeschicht-licher Beziehung* (5 vols.; Braunschweig, 1894–1903), IV, 665. Note that all of these are informed guesses. The first official returns of iron production do not come until 1854. Cf. R. Hunt, 'The Present State of the Mining Industries of the United Kingdom', *J. Royal Statistical Soc.* XIX (1856), 317; Howard G. Roepke, 'Movements of the British Iron and Steel Industry—1720 to 1951' [*Illinois Studies in the Social Sciences*, vol. XXXVI] (Urbana, 1956), p. 24.

for increased power was mining, especially coal mining. From the sixteenth century on, as we have noted, the need for new sources of thermal energy in a country almost denuded of its forests led Britons to substitute mineral for vegetable fuel in a wide variety of heat-absorbing industrial operations. At the same time, the consumption of coal for domestic purposes rose steadily: there was perhaps a time, in the six-teenth century, when the Englishman recoiled at the acrid, sulphurous fumes of burning coal; but by the modern period, such scruples were laid by familiarity and necessity.

The more coal man used, the deeper he dug; until, by the end of the seventeenth century, the pits in many areas had penetrated beneath the water table and flooding threatened to put an end to further extraction. (The same difficulties were beginning to afflict the tin, lead, and copper mines of Cornwall.) Ingenious systems were devised to lead off the water, when possible, or to pump or raise it out of the pits by animal power. But the task was fast getting out of hand: in one colliery in Warwickshire, five hundred horses were employed to hoist the water, bucket by bucket.

The use of five hundred horses is evidence of a simple but sometimes neglected fact: there is in principle no limit but numbers to the amount of work that can be accomplished or power that can be generated by human or animal labour. One thinks, for example, of the construc-tion of the pyramids or of such comparable tasks as the removal of a 327-ton obelisk in Rome in 1586 by the massed efforts of 800 men and

140 horses working forty capstans in the presence of the official executioner.[1]

Yet the use of gangs or of veritable herds of animals poses logistical difficulties that increase sharply with the number of labour units: there is the problem of co-ordination, first, and linked to it, the sheer limitations of space and the high cost of a complex system for the transmission of power. Moreover, man and beast are subject to fatigue; they must be relieved, and the more there are, the more difficult the passage from one team to the next. Mass labour of this kind is reasonably effective— if certain precautions are observed and discipline is maintained—in the performance of sporadic work demanding intense effort for short periods. It is ill suited to providing the steady, concentrated power required by industry.

Here lay the great advantage of the steam-engine. It was tireless, and one could direct its tens of horsepower far more effectively than one could combine the efforts of five hundred horses. Moreover—and in the long run, this was the key to the steam-engine's revolutionary effects on the pace of economic growth—it consumed mineral fuel and thereby made available to industry, for the provision of motive power as against pure heat, a new and apparently boundless source of energy. The early steam-engines were grossly inefficient, delivering less than 1 per cent of the work represented by their thermal inputs. This was a far cry from the performance of organic converters: both animals and man can deliver from 10 to 20 per cent of inputs, depending on conditions. But neither man nor beast can eat coal. And since the supply of organic nourishment was and is limited—as the Malthusian checks of famine and disease abundantly testify—it is this increment of fuel made available by the steam-engine, however wastefully used, that counted.

To make the point clear, compare man's consumption of coal with its hypothetical alimentary equivalent. By 1800 the United Kingdom was using perhaps 11 million tons of coal a year; by 1830, the amount had doubled; fifteen years later it had doubled again; and by 1870 it was crossing the 100-million-ton mark. This last was equivalent to 800 million million Calories of energy, enough to feed a population of 850 million adult males for a year (actual population was then about 31 million); or to supply one-fourth as many people with the complete energy requirements of a pre-industrial society.[2]

[1] See the contemporary pictorial representation of this operation in T. K. Derry and Trevor I. Williams, *A Short History of Technology from the Earliest Times to A.D. 1900* (Oxford, 1960), frontispiece; also pp. 180, 245.

[2] That is, the energy required for heat and manufacture, as well as for the internal nourishment of the biological organism. C. Cipolla, 'Sources d'énergie et histoire de l'humanité', *Annales: E.S.C.* XVI (1961), 528.

Or—to approach the subject from a different angle—in 1870 the capacity of Great Britain's steam-engines was about 4 million horse-power, equivalent to the power that could be generated by 6 million horses or 40 million men.[1] If we assume the same patterns of food consumption as prevailed in the eighteenth century, this many men would have eaten some 320 million bushels of wheat a year—more than three times the annual output of the entire United Kingdom in 1867–71. And this does not take into account the even larger number of workers required for activities other than furnishing power, or the young, old, and other unemployed members of our hypothetical coal-innocent society.

It would be easy, by selecting a later date and a higher consumption of energy, to conjure up more awful pictures. From 1870 to 1907, the capacity of prime movers in British industry alone more than doubled, and from 1907 to 1930, doubled again; to this would have to be added the even greater increase of engines in land transport and shipping. Or, to shift to a larger scene, world consumption of commercial sources of energy multiplied six times in the fifty years from 1860 to 1900 and more than tripled in the next half-century. One can imagine an in-dustrial world compelled to depend exclusively on animal engines for work, a world swarming with so many men and beasts that every inch of the earth's surface, including mountain, desert, and icy tundra, would not suffice to feed them. But one need not persist in these fantasies. The point is obvious: no such industrial world could come into being. It is precisely the availability of inanimate sources of power that has enabled man to transcend the limitations of biology and increase his productivity a hundred times over. It is no accident that the world's industry has tended to localize itself on and near the earth's coal measures; or that the growth of capital has been proportional to the con-sumption of mineral fuel. Coal, in short, has been the bread of industry.[2]

At this point, some words of caution are advisable. Like food, coal has been a necessary but not a sufficient cause of industrial performance.

[1] This is a conservative estimate, for the equivalency is between capacities over brief periods of time, a working day, for example. And while many of these steam-engines undoubtedly operated only part of the time and then often at less than full load, it seems reasonable to assume that animal generators would deliver an even smaller fraction of capacity. Thus men, and the beasts they use, rest most of each day and a substantial portion of the days in each year; whereas many steam-engines worked around the clock, day in and day out, year after year. On balance, double the number of men or animals would seem a more accurate equivalent.

[2] The above discussion owes much to conversations with Professor Carlo Cipolla. See his *Economic History of Population* (London, 1962), ch. II. Also Fred Cottrell, *Energy and Society* (New York, 1955); E. A. Wrigley, *Industrial Growth and Population Change* (Cambridge, 1961); and idem, 'The Supply of Raw Materials in the Industrial Revolution', *Econ. Hist. Rev.* 2nd ser. XV (1962), 1–16.

One cannot work without eating; yet the availability of food will not make one work. We shall have several occasions in the course of this survey to consider feats of industrial accomplishment by localities or countries poor in energy resources. Some of these have benefited from compensating advantages; others have transcended their handicaps by acts of creative entrepreneurship. Usually, however, these triumphs have occurred in light industry, where energy requirements are a relatively small portion of total cost. It is (or was) hard to make bricks without straw; or iron and heavy chemicals without cheap fuel.

It should be remembered, moreover, that the coal-steam combination was not the only source of inanimate power available to the European economies of the eighteenth century. The force of the wind had been harnessed for millennia, first by means of sail for navigation, then from the Middle Ages on, through mills for pumping and grinding. Even more important was water power. Already known in antiquity, the water mill first came into wide use in the Middle Ages, perhaps as an answer to the growing scarcity of slave labour. Its introduction into British wool manufacture to drive the fuller's hammers gave rise to that rapid expansion of rural production that Professor Carus-Wilson has described as 'an industrial revolution of the thirteenth century'. In the eighteenth century and the first decades of the nineteenth, the water wheel accounted for the greater, though a diminishing, share of the power used by British industry; and there is no doubt that, had Britain been better endowed by nature with hydraulic energy, or had she been poorer in coal, the dominance of the wheel would have continued much longer than it did. This was the case in the United States, where the great coal deposits lay in what were at first the relatively inaccessible lands west of the Appalachians and where the eastern slopes of the same range offered superb sites for the erection of water-driven mills. The same was true of comparable areas in Europe, the whole Alpine region, for example—Dauphiné, Switzerland, Baden, Bavaria, northern Italy.

Coal and steam, therefore, did not make the Industrial Revolution; but they permitted its extraordinary development and diffusion. Their use, as against that of substitutable power sources, was a consideration of costs and convenience. The advantage of wind and water power was that the energy employed was free; their great disadvantage was that it was often not abundant enough and in any event was subject to variations beyond human control. The wind might not blow; the stream might dry up or freeze. By contrast, the steam-engine could be relied on in all seasons; but the initial outlay was higher and it was costly to operate. As one writer of 1778 put it, 'the vast consumption of fuel in these engines is an immense drawback on the profit of our mines, for every fire-engine of magnitude consumes £3,000 worth of coals per annum. This heavy tax amounts almost to a prohibition.'[1] This was clearly an exaggeration, for the use of steam was growing. Still, it cost only £900 a year to feed those five hundred horses in Warwickshire. Small wonder that the early engines were generally employed only where coal was extremely cheap—as in collieries; or in mines too deep for other techniques, as in Cornwall; or in those occasional circumstances—the naval drydock at Saint Petersburg for example—where cost was no object.

As a consequence, the leitmotif of steam technology was the effort to increase efficiency, that is, the amount of work performed per input of energy. By comparison, the goal of greater power, that is, work performed per unit of time, took second place, although the two objectives were linked and what made for the one, permitted or yielded the other.

This pursuit of fuel economy and power, like other movements of technological advance, had its multitude of small and often anonymous gains: better materials, closer tolerances, the introduction of safety valves and gauges, the recognition and adoption of coal specially suited to the production of steam, the collection of accurate information on the performance of engines under different conditions. But it was also punctuated by some great leaps forward, each marked by a critical innovation that widened substantially the commercial applicability of steam.

The first practicable device for the conversion of thermal energy into work was Thomas Savery's 'fire-engine' of 1698. It was in effect steam-engine and pump combined. There was no piston, no transmission of power to other machinery. Steam was heated in a boiler, then passed into a 'receiver', where it was condensed to create a partial vacuum. This drew in water from below (more accurately, the water was driven up into it by air pressure), which was then expelled upwards by the next injection of steam, and the cycle began again. The waste of energy was enormous, not only because of the alternate heating and cooling of the receiver, but also because, in the absence of a piston, the steam came into direct contact with the cold water. The system had one other serious drawback: one could increase the power only by raising the pressure, and some of the Savery engines were worked at as much as three atmospheres. That was about the limit of safety. Given the quality of the materials employed and of the metal work of the day, anything higher was almost certain to result in an explosion, as a number of operatives learned too late. The only alternative, in deep mining, for example, was to use two or more engines in tandem, a costly procedure and one especially vulnerable to breakdowns.

[1] Price, in the Appendix to *Mineralogia Cornubiensis*, cited by Robert A. Thurston, *A History of the Growth of the Steam Engine* (Centennial edition; Ithaca, New York, 1939), p. 71.

What Thurston calls the first true engine, that is, a device for generating power and transmitting it to a machine performing the work desired, was the contribution of Thomas Newcomen, ironmonger and blacksmith of Dartmouth, England, in 1705. Here the pump was separate from the cylinder that received the steam. The vacuum produced by condensation was used, not to draw in water, but to work a piston connected to one end of a see-sawing cross-beam, the other end of which rose and fell and thereby operated the rod of the water pump. Note that the steam was not used to drive the piston, but only to create a vacuum; ordinary air pressure provided the force that pushed the piston downward against the weight of the pump at the other end of the beam. Hence the name, 'atmospheric engine'.

Newcomen's method offered two advantages over Savery's conception. First, it eliminated the loss of heat due to contact with the water being pumped. The saving was not large and was almost dissipated in the transmission of force from engine to pump. Years later, when construction of both types had much improved, tests of the two engines showed duties generally ranging between five and six million foot-pounds per bushel of coal, a yield of less than 1 per cent. Still, every bit helped.

Far more important, the use of a piston made it possible to obtain more force without increasing the steam pressure; all that was required was a larger surface on which the atmosphere could push, that is, a larger piston. As a result, the Newcomen engines were at once more powerful, safer, and more dependable. Indeed, some of them were to remain at work for five decades and more, well into the nineteenth century.

Not that the Savery steam pump disappeared. Builders like John Wrigley in Lancashire were manufacturing improved versions of it to the very end of the eighteenth century, and so enterprising a cotton spinner as John Kennedy used 'Savary's' machine to drive his improved mules in Manchester in 1793. One would like to know how many of these there were, where they were used, and for what purposes. Those we know of were small, generating a few horsepower, and were used to raise water to drive the wheels of light industrial plants.

By contrast, the Newcomen engine dominated the market for large prime movers. Thurston writes that within a few years of its invention, 'it had been introduced into nearly all large mines in Great Britain'; and that many new mines were dug that could not have been exploited before. The statement may be exaggerated; we do not have statistics on this point. But we do know that the engineer Smeaton found 57 of these machines, totalling 1200 horse-power, in the Newcastle basin alone in 1767, and 18 large engines in the Cornish mines in 1780. In the Midlands, the Coalbrookdale foundry, better known for its pioneering of coke smelting, was the major supplier of Newcomen engines to the collieries of the region; and even after the introduction of the Watt engine, the older type continued in demand, for coal at pithead was cheap or even a free good (many boilers burned unsaleable slack), and the lower initial cost of the Newcomen engine, its simplicity of maintenance, and its remarkable durability gave it the preference.[1]

Yet the persistence of the Newcomen engine should not lead us to underestimate the crucial significance of Watt's contribution. By building a separate condenser (patent of 1769; first commercial application, 1776), he saved the energy that had previously been dissipated in reheating the cylinder at each stroke. This was the decisive breakthrough to an 'age of steam', not only because of the immediate economy of fuel (consumption per output was about a fourth that of the Newcomen machine), but even more because this improvement opened the way to continuing advances in efficiency that eventually brought the steam-engine within reach of all branches of the economy and made of it a universal prime mover. Watt himself effected some of the most important of these further gains (patents of 1782 and 1784): the double-acting engine, with the steam working alternately on each side of the piston; the use of steam to drive the piston as well as to create a vacuum; the cut-off stroke, which took advantage of the expansive force of the steam to obtain a substantial saving of energy; above all, the sun-and-planet gear, which converted the reciprocating stroke of the piston into rotary motion and made it possible to drive the wheels of industry.

Watt believed firmly in the low-pressure engine; and, indeed, most of the power of his machine derived, not from the force of the steam, which rarely went above $1\frac{1}{2}$ atmospheres, but from the vacuum on the other side of the piston. Other men were less dogmatic. Around the turn of the century, William Bull, Richard Trevithick, the American Oliver Evans, and others evolved the high-pressure engine (two or more atmospheres), which eventually yielded fuel economies of $1:1\frac{1}{2}$ and better. In the beginning, however, its main advantage lay in its simplicity and its ability to deliver the same work with a smaller piston; it was thus lighter and cheaper than the low-pressure engine and used far less water. This saving of space and materials was of primary importance in the construction of movable engines. The locomotive and steamboat would have been sharply restricted commercially had only low pressure been available.

[1] On the continued use of the Savery and Newcomen engines, see A. E. Musson and E. Robinson, 'The Early Growth of Steam Power', *Econ. Hist. Rev.* 2nd ser. XI (1959), 418–39; Thurston, *History of the Growth*, pp. 68 ff.

Moreover it was high pressure that made possible the effective application of compounding, which made use of the energy that remained in the steam after it had driven the piston, by leading it into a second cylinder (eventually a third and even a fourth) of larger dimensions. The principle was the same as that which made possible the cut-off stroke: theoretically there is no difference between the expansion of the steam in one cylinder or more than one. Practically, there is a significant gain in efficiency: the sum of the forces exerted by more than one piston varies less throughout the action than that of a single piston; more important, the temperature of each cylinder varies less if the range of expansion of the steam is divided than if it is confined to one vessel. The result was a major saving of fuel: by the middle of the nineteenth century, an average compound engine used slightly over $2\frac{1}{2}$ pounds of coal per horsepower-hour; Watt's machine needed about $7\frac{1}{2}$, and the Newcomen engine of 1769 used 30.[1] Jonathan Hornblower built a two-cylinder engine on these lines as early as 1781, but he used steam of low pressure, and his machine was found to be no more efficient than that of Watt; moreover the latter sued him for infringement of patent, and when Hornblower was unable to pay royalties and fine, he was clapped into prison. It was Arthur Woolf who, in 1804, produced the first commercially successful compound engine. He used high pressure and a separate condenser—by this time Watt's patent had expired. In the long run, compounding found its widest application in shipping, where the saving on fuel was multiplied by the space released thereby for cargo and passengers.

Unlike the wooden machines for spinning and weaving cotton or wool, the steam-engine required from the start a corresponding revolution in the relevant fields of metallurgy and construction. Smeaton predicted that Watt would not be able to build his engine because it required more accuracy than the techniques of the day permitted; and indeed some seven years elapsed between the patent and the first commercial realization. The difficulty was solved in part through the ingenious efforts of John Wilkinson, who learned to bore cylinders with some precision; as Watt put it, he could 'promise upon a seventy-two inch cylinder being not farther distant from absolute truth than the thickness of a thin sixpence [say 0·05 in.] at the worst part'. Even this was hardly close enough for an effective vacuum, and Watt and engineers after him continued to use packed rope or hemp and tallow to plug the gaps between piston and cylinder. Not until well into the nineteenth century had materials and machine construction advanced

[1] For figures on coal consumption and a discussion of the statistical difficulties involved, see W. Stanley Jevons, *The Coal Question* (London, 1906), pp. 145–9; also Conrad Matschoss, *Die Entwicklung der Dampfmaschine* (2 vols.; Berlin, 1908), I, 506–7.

to the point where full advantage could be taken of the intelligence of Watt's conception.

This raises the related but larger issue of the connection between science and technology. It is often stated that the Newcomen machine and its forerunners would have been unthinkable without the theoretical ideas of Boyle, Torricelli, and others; and that Watt derived much of his technical competence and imagination from his work with scientists and scientific instruments at Glasgow. There is no doubt some truth in this, though how much is impossible to say. One thing is clear, however: once the principle of the separate condenser was established, subsequent advances owed little or nothing to theory. On the contrary, an entire branch of physics, thermodynamics, developed in part as a result of empirical observations of engineering methods and performance.[1] Nor is it an accident that this theoretical work was begun in France, where a school like the Polytechnique devoted its efforts explicitly to the reduction of technique to mathematical generalization. All of which did not prevent England from continuing to lead the world in engineering practice and invention.

Because of the steam-engine's early shortcomings, it was less suited than the gently turning water wheel for work requiring a certain smoothness and regularity of motion. This, together with purely economic considerations like relative size of firm, goes far to explain the slower adoption of steam in wool than in cotton. As late as 1850, more than a third of the power available to the wool manufacture of England and Wales came from water (12,600 h.p. steam; 6800 water); for the cotton industry of all of Great Britain, the corresponding figure was about one-eighth (71,000 steam; 11,000 water). The biggest users of steam power among the other industries were mining and metallurgy; unfortunately, overall figures are not available. We are thus reduced to crude estimates for the kingdom as a whole. Thus it has been suggested that there were no more than one thousand engines in use in 1800; guessing at an average size of 10 h.p. (it would not matter to the argument if one chose a multiplier twice as large), one arrives at an aggregate capacity of perhaps 10,000 h.p. Fifteen years later, according to the French observer Baron Dupin, this total had risen, for Great Britain alone, to 210,000 h.p.; and by the middle of the century it had further increased more than sixfold. For the United Kingdom in 1850, Mulhall estimates 500,000 h.p. of stationary engines, 790,000 h.p. of mobile engines, mostly in the form of railway locomotives. The latter had constituted an insignificant category a generation earlier.

[1] T. S. Kuhn, 'Energy Conservation as an Example of Simultaneous Discovery', in M. Clagett, ed., *Critical Problems in the History of Science* (Madison, Wisc., 1959).

One of the cherished myths of economic history is the image of a swift and drastic shift from rudimentary hand tools to machines. According to this, we begin with carpenters and millwrights with chisels and files, cutting and scraping by eye and feel; and then, within two generations, we have machinists and engineers operating precision power tools and working to specifications and blueprints. In fact, as is so often the case with revolutions, the old and new were not that far apart, and the change was slower than usually pictured.

The craftsman of the mid-eighteenth century, particularly in fields like clock-making, was familiar with an impressive variety of machines, including lathes, punches, drills, and screw- and wheel-cutting engines. These were slow and only moderately accurate; yet they were adequate to the industry of the day—both pre- and post-innovations—and indeed have survived in some out-of-the-way places to the present.[1] Of the great mechanical inventions of this period, only the Watt steam-engine required, as noted above, an immediate advance in metal-working technique.

In the long run, however, the diffusion of mechanized manufacture called forth major improvements in tool design. For one thing, the productivity of the new machines for making consumers' goods was directly related to speed of operation and efficient utilization of power; both of these in turn demanded precise, smoothly working parts. For another, the scarcity of skilled wood and metal workers created a need for the kind of equipment that would enable a mechanic to do more in less time and with as little training as possible. And both these considerations were reinforced by the growth of an autonomous, specialized machine-construction industry in which imaginative artisans had an opportunity to modify old tools and devise new ones; the same process of gradual, cumulative technological advance by anonymous increments that characterized the consumers'-goods industries was equally important in the manufacture of capital goods.

Because of the anonymity of many of these improvements and the great diversity of practice, it is impossible to convey more than an approximate notion of the overall pace of advance. In the cotton industry we can at least count spindles and categorize them under rubrics like 'mules' or 'water frames', which, though embracing equipment of different efficiencies, are homogeneous enough to be meaningful. In machine construction, we have no counts, and even

[1] On the technical competence of wood and metalworkers before the Industrial Revolution, see especially Musson and Robinson, 'The Origins of Engineering in Lancashire', *J. Econ. Hist.* xx (1960), 209–33. Also M. Daumas, 'Precision Mechanics', and K. R. Gilbert, 'Machine Tools', in C. Singer *et al.*, *A History of Technology*, iv: *The Industrial Revolution*, c. *1750*–c. *1850* (Oxford, 1958), 379–441.

if we had, the range of variation between tools of the same name is so great as to render classification illusory and even the timing of innovation uncertain. Two examples will suffice. We know that gauges were being employed by machine builders as early as the 1770's and 1780's; indeed, the use of the word to designate an instrument for measuring dimensions dates to the late seventeenth century. Yet it hardly seems likely that men were 'working to gauge' in this early period, that is, using these devices, not only to measure size or scribe lines, but to assure standardization. Where and when the latter technique was introduced, and how fast it spread, is impossible to say. Similarly, we know that the slide rest was in wide use in the eighteenth century. Yet the invention of this basic instrument of precision work, which took the cutting tool out of the fallible hands of the artisan and made possible control of the direction and depth of its action, was attributed by Nasmyth and others to Maudslay. A myth? Perhaps. More likely, however, contemporaries who credited him with it had in mind some change in its character or innovation in its use, perhaps simply insistence on its use where others were content to work by hand.

But if we cannot measure the state of technique at a given point in time we can speak of the trend. In the space of two generations, in large part owing to a handful of gifted figures who learned from each other and formed as it were a family of toolmakers, wood- and metal-working techniques were transformed, at least at the margin.[1] Tools became heavier and more rigid (Maudslay's all-metal lathe), more automatic and precise (Clement's self-regulating lathe and double-driving centre chuck, Nasmyth's self-acting nut-milling machine and shaper, a whole succession of improvements in planing), more versatile and easier to operate (the turret-lathe and milling machines). By the middle of the nineteenth century 'the majority of the machine tools now in use...had been brought into existence',[2] and men like Nasmyth were toolmakers to machine builders, stocking standard models and selling from catalogue descriptions.[3]

The means of performance came first; the standards of accuracy after. The invention of power tools did not change the personal

---

[1] For the family tree of innovations and innovators in machine-tool manufacture, see Joseph W. Roe, *English and American Tool Builders* (New Haven, 1916), p. 7; Gilbert, 'Machine Tools', p. 418. This pattern of direct employer–employee contact as a source of technical training and seed-bed for entrepreneurship characterized the continental industry as well. On Germany, see F. Redlich, 'The Leaders of the German Steam-engine Industry during the First Hundred Years', *J. Econ. Hist.* IV (1944), 146.

[2] Gilbert, 'Machine Tools', p. 441.

[3] See A. E. Musson, 'James Nasmyth and the Early Growth of Mechanical Engineering', *Econ. Hist. Rev.* 2nd ser. X (1957). Nasmyth expressed his intention of

character of the work. Each craftsman remained judge of his own performance, working to approximate specifications that were not always uniform even within the shop. The assembling of any piece of machinery required a costly and time-consuming adjustment of all the parts, which were individually filed down to fit the whole. Reproduction or replacement was similarly approximate. Every screw had its individual thread.

Maudslay and Clement made an effort to correct some of these shortcomings by insisting on the use of true plane surfaces and standardizing the screws produced in their shops. But the major work in this area was done by one of their pupils, Joseph Whitworth, who, building on the work of his masters, worked out standard threads for bolts and screws of all sizes and developed the gauges that bear his name. Diffusion of these principles and techniques was another matter. Whitworth's contributions go back to the 1830's and his methods were made public in 1840, yet in 1856 he was still pleading for accuracy.

Generally speaking, standardized precision work, which made possible interchangeable parts, preceded the adoption of common, industry-wide norms. Thus if working to gauge was still the exception before 1850, it was spreading rapidly, and a number of machine makers, like Roberts of the self-acting mule, had long made use of templets and jigs to facilitate the performance of repetitive operations. Uniformity of standards of screw and bolt manufacture, on the other hand, came only in the second half of the century (common within the enterprise by 1860) and for a long time stood alone; all the weaknesses of human vanity combined with habit and the cost of change to deter acceptance of general patterns by particular producers.

One field in which standardization of product was achieved early was stampings. The principle went back to antiquity, when dies were used to mint coins of uniform design. In the early modern period, the punch was introduced, and made possible regularity of shape and size. In industry proper, the technique was obviously appropriate to the manufacture of buttons, gewgaws, buckles, and similar small objects. Birmingham, if not the first to use it, was the city that made the most of it while limitations of power restricted its application to the light metal trades; in the nineteenth century, a number of minor industries—pen nib manufacture, for example—were revolutionized by adaptations of this process.

Such products are clearly not to be compared to interchangeable parts, which must be exact enough to fit and interact with others in a

operating on this principle as early as 1836 in letters to his future partner Gaskell. Cited in R. Dickinson, 'James Nasmyth and the Liverpool Iron Trade', *Trans. of the Historical Society of Lancashire and Cheshire*, CVIII (1956), 99.

larger mechanism. Nor are they—and the less so in this early period—
so strong as pieces wrought, forged, and milled in the traditional
sequence. (Even today a drop-forged blade commands a premium over
a stamped one.) Nevertheless, the principle was as promising as that of
precision machining, which would always be more expensive, and the
application was enormously broadened by the introduction of power
presses and similar big equipment. By the middle of the century, the
steam hammer was beginning to be used in the manufacture of railway
wheels. This was only a beginning, but it was the herald of a new kind
of machine construction that was eventually to make possible the
streamlined, inexpensive hard goods of the twentieth century—automobiles, refrigerators, bicycles, television sets.

Like the machine-building and engineering trades, the chemical
industry has tended to be neglected in textbook histories of the Industrial Revolution, in part for the same reasons: the complexity and many-
sidedness of its development, and the need for technical knowledge that
the historian rarely possesses. Probably even more important, however,
in promoting this oversight have been (1) the unrevolutionary character
of this development—the organization of labour remained essentially
unaltered while gains in productivity were usually smaller in chemicals
than in those areas where mechanization was feasible; and (2) the
secondary position of the industry in this early period—its growth was
largely a response to the needs of other branches of manufacture, in
particular, textiles, soap, and glass. We are accustomed today to look
on the chemical manufacture as a giant, partly because of its success in
creating wondrous new materials like nylon or plastics, partly because
of the 'miracle' drugs that pour out of its laboratories in an endless
stream; we are less aware of the enormous output of what is generally
known as the heavy chemical industry, which is concerned with those
inorganic agents, acid and alkali, used in the production of other
commodities.

Yet the derivative character of this growth in our period in no way
diminishes its importance. The transformation of the textile manufacture, whose requirements of detergents, bleaches, and mordants were
growing at the same pace as output, would have been impossible without a corresponding transformation of chemical technology. There was
not enough cheap meadowland or sour milk in all the British Isles to
whiten the cloth of Lancashire once the water frame and mule replaced
the spinning wheel; and it would have taken undreamed-of quantities
of human urine to cut the grease of the raw wool consumed by the mills
of the West Riding.

The solution was found in a simultaneous advance along several lines:

(1) by substituting where possible vegetable for animal sources of raw material; (2) by substituting inorganic for organic raw materials; (3) by making use of the by-products of each reaction to produce other reactions yielding useful compounds; and (4) by improving the tools and equipment of the industry—furnaces, vats, mixers, piping, and the like—so as to permit the more rapid processing of larger quantities with greater safety. The first two were analogous in significance to the substitution of coal for wood in metallurgy: they freed the industry from the bondage of inelastic supplies. The third is particularly characteristic of the chemical manufacture and largely accounts for the conditions of increasing return that prevailed in the heroic age of early innovation. The fourth yielded perhaps the smallest gains in our period, but was to grow increasingly important as innovations in the other areas were absorbed and the increasing scale of production shifted attention to the physical plant and the logistical problems of work flow.

The course and character of this advance are best conveyed by examining the changes in the production of those key compounds that are the basis of the heavy chemical manufacture and the industrial commodities derived from them. The most important of these, even then, was sulphuric acid, a substance of such versatility (oxidizing agent, dehydrating agent, acid, electrolyte) that its use has come to serve as a rough index of industrial development. In the first half of the eighteenth century, sulphuric acid was employed chiefly as a nostrum, occasionally as a bleach. The method of preparation was slow, constrained, inefficient; the price, 1s. 6d. to 2s. 6d. an *ounce*, prohibitive for most industrial use. Within the space of a few decades, however, the introduction from the Continent of the bell process (first successful application by Joshua Ward and John White at Twickenham in 1736) and then the substitution of large lead-lined vats for the much smaller glass 'bells' (John Roebuck and Samuel Garbett at Birmingham in 1746) increased the scale of operation a thousand-fold and pushed the cost down to $3\frac{1}{2}d$. a *pound*. By the end of the century Britain, which had once eked out the home supply with purchases from Holland, was exporting up to two thousand tons a year.[1]

In industrial chemistry, one compound leads to another. Sulphuric acid, in combination with salt, yielded as one product hydrochloric acid, from which chlorine could be freed for use as a bleaching agent. The method of accomplishing this was wasteful, and chlorine in its pure form was dangerous and so corrosive that it tended to rot the

[1] A. and N. Clow, *The Chemical Revolution: a Contribution to Social Technology* (London, 1952), pp. 132–9; Pub. Record Office, T. 64/241: 'An Account of the Exports of British Manufacturers from Scotland to Holland....' I am indebted to Dr T. C. Barker for this material.

fabric being treated. Yet it offered important advantages over such older bleaches as sunshine, buttermilk, and even dilute sulphuric acid, and the search began for chlorine compounds or mixtures that would handle more easily. The first of these were liquors, the most important of which, potassium hypochlorite or Javel water, was invented in France in 1796 and has remained a household cleaning agent ever since. For the textile manufacture, however, the major advance was Charles Tennant's invention of bleaching powder (patents of 1797 and 1799), made by absorbing chlorine in slaked lime. Tennant's output of the powder rose from 57 tons the first year, to 239 tons in 1810, 910 tons in 1825, 5719 tons in 1850; in 1852, production for Great Britain as a whole was 13,100 tons. In the meantime, the price fell to one-tenth its original level—from £140 to £14 per ton.[1]

Alkalis too were indispensable to the manufacture of textiles; and of a wide variety of other commodities as well. Two types were employed: potassium carbonate (commonly in the form of potash or the purer pearl ash) and sodium carbonate (generally called *soda*), along with compounds related to one or the other. Potassium alkalis were combined with tallow or other animal fat to make soft soap, used especially by the woollen industry for scouring and fulling; were mixed with sand to produce one of the silicates that we call glass; went into the manufacture of gunpowder and alum; and were employed in bleaching and cleaning cloth and in the softening of leather. For all their versatility, however, they had the disadvantage of deriving from raw materials in scarce and inelastic supply. Potassium carbonate was obtained from prepared wood ash in a ratio of perhaps 1 part of pure compound to 600 parts of wood, necessitating a rate of consumption that was out of the question in timber-starved Britain. Europe and America were combed for supplies, and from the middle to the end of the century imports grew from about 1500 to 9000 tons. Moreover England was not the only country in the market; as demand outstripped supply, the price went up substantially, doubling in the period from 1780 to 1815. Not until the 1860's, when the Germans began to exploit the rich deposits of mineral potash in the Stassfurt area, did this bottleneck ease. By that time, a revolution in the manufacture of sodium carbonate had altered drastically the relative importance of the two alkalis.

Sodium alkali is as versatile as the potassium variety; indeed, the two are substitutable for each other in many of their applications. The main difference industrially is that soda is used in the manufacture of hard soaps and curd soaps—hence, of a household staple as well as of a

[1] These and other details of this discussion are taken from L. F. Haber, *The Chemical Industry during the Nineteenth Century* (Oxford, 1958), ch. II.

production good. In the eighteenth century, sodium alkali also was obtained from the ashes of plants: the saltwort, which grew chiefly in Spain and the Canary Islands and yielded barilla, containing 20–35 per cent by weight of soda; and dried seaweed from western Scotland and Ireland, from which was derived kelp, with a soda content of from 5 to 10 per cent. The latter was able to compete because barilla, though richer, paid duty; moreover imports were just about cut off during the Napoleonic wars.

The supply of sodium alkali was more elastic than that of potash but could not possibly keep pace with increasing demand. Once again, the answer was found in the substitution of mineral for vegetable raw materials—in this instance, an especially abundant mineral, common salt. The actual technique was worked out in France in the 1780's by Nicolas Leblanc: conversion of salt to saltcake (sodium sulphate) by means of sulphuric acid (whose usefulness was multiplied thereby many times); and burning the saltcake in mixture with coal and calcium carbonate (usually in the form of limestone) to yield sodium carbonate and wastes.

British producers, who were certainly aware of the Leblanc process by the end of the eighteenth century, were slow to adopt it; large-scale manufacture began only in 1823. Scholars have usually attributed this delay to the effects of the tax on salt; more important, probably, was Britain's continued access to the traditional vegetable sources, combined with the conservatism of alkali users, who were reluctant to change over to the synthetic product even after James Muspratt made it available at a favourable price.[1] By contrast, France, which was cut off from Spanish barilla during the Napoleonic wars, had begun commercial manufacture in 1808 and within a decade was producing between ten and fifteen thousand tons of Leblanc soda a year.[2] Once the initial resistance was overcome, however, British output of synthetic alkali increased spectacularly, from the few hundred tons of 1820 to almost 140,000 tons in 1852. (French output at the latter date was perhaps 45,000 tons.) This rise was accompanied by a sharp fall in the price of soda; crystals, for example, went from a wartime peak of £59 a ton, to £36. 10s. on the eve of Leblanc, to £5. 10s. by mid-century.

Owing to the importance of bulky raw materials in chemical manufacture—it took ten to twelve tons of ingredients to make one ton of soda—the industry was sharply localized almost from the start. The

[1] Cf. T. C. Barker, R. Dickinson and D. W. F. Hardie, 'The Origins of the Synthetic Alkali Industry in Britain', *Economica*, n.s. XXIII (1956), 158–71.

[2] Based on J. A. Chaptal, *De l'industrie françoise* (2 vols.; Paris, 1819), II, 70, 173, which gives the price as 10 frs. per quintal and output as 2–3 million francs.

three main centres were the Glasgow area, Merseyside and Tyneside. The first was oriented originally to the local textile industry. Its resource position was not so strong as that of the other two, and its continued importance was a tribute to the technical creativeness and commercial energy of the Tennant firm. This enterprise built its fortune on bleaching powder and branched out from there into the manufacture of acids, alkalis, fertilizer and related commodities. Overall, it was the biggest chemical producer in the world in the thirties and forties, and its giant works at St Rollox, with its skyscraper chimney of $455\frac{1}{2}$ feet to dissipate the noxious fumes high above the countryside, was the world's largest chemical factory.

Merseyside was favoured by the availability of coal on one side and salt on the other, a network of excellent waterways, and proximity to the biggest textile market in the world. Its major product was soda ash, whose availability promoted the related soap manufacture: by 1835, the output of hard soap along the Mersey was 47,750,000 lb., as against 32,650,000 in London; output had tripled since 1820, as against a 75 per cent increase for the nation as a whole. Cheap soda and saltcake (sodium sulphate) were also factors in the rapid growth of glass-making in Lancashire—though less important than in soap; where in 1832 the factories in the Liverpool area paid less than an eighth of the excise on glass, by 1870, this region was probably making half the glass manufactured in England.[1]

The greatest centre of chemical manufacture was the Tyne basin, again an area with easy access to water transport and an abundant supply of cheap coal. Salt, on the other hand, had to come across the island from Cheshire; and the local market for chemical products was small, for there was no textile industry in the area and little manufacture of soap and glass. Yet the Tyneside firms found ample compensation in London and abroad, especially in northern Europe. From a late start— output of alkalis and acids was negligible in 1820—the north-east came by mid-century to account for half of the chemical plant, labour force and output of the entire kingdom.[2]

The encouragement given by the mass production of heavy chemicals to other branches of manufacture was only in part a function of the supply and price of the chemicals themselves. On the one hand, the availability of relatively pure compounds made possible the adoption of new raw materials that would otherwise not have been susceptible of treatment. Thus the development of purer soda ash made it feasible to

---

[1] T. C. Barker and J. R. Harriss, *A Merseyside Town in the Industrial Revolution, St Helens, 1750–1900* (Liverpool, 1954), pp. 202, 363. Unfortunately for our statistical evidence, the excise duty on glass was removed in 1845.

[2] For a partial census in 1852, see Haber, *The Chemical Industry*, p. 18.

use palm oil instead of animal fat in soap manufacture. The importance of this is apparent: the demand for fats was growing even faster than population and the traditional sources of supply were relatively inelastic; by mid-century, vegetable oils were being used in food, candles, and lubricants as well as soap.

On the other hand, the manufacture of synthetic compounds gave rise to enormous quantities of waste, which, by a kind of paradox not uncommon in technology, were a powerful stimulus to innovation. There was the positive lure of profit: waste turned to use had value; and the negative goad of expense: unexploited waste had to be disposed of. There were two tons of 'galligu' for every ton of soda made, and land for dumping cost a small fortune. Moreover, much of the waste was noxious and brought down on the chemical manufactures a hail of lawsuits, the attention of Parliament, and eventually official inspection and controls.

It would be impossible here to follow in detail the various solutions to this problem, or the interaction of these new techniques with one another and with outside processes to open new possibilities for growth. The story of chemicals in the first two-thirds of the nineteenth century is in large part this effort to use up all the materials, an effort which stemmed largely from soda manufacture but in specific instances originated elsewhere, in the production of chlorine for bleaching, for example. Every operation undertaken led to others, and the size of the productive unit grew with the proliferation of commodities. Yet this was not an industry that employed large numbers of men; as in metallurgy, plant and materials were the most important factors of production. In 1851 the industrial census gave 9172 adult workers in chemical manufacture, as against 292,340 in cotton, 152,205 in woollen and worsted, some 390,000 in the building trades.[1] The importance of chemicals, however, was clearly out of proportion to its numbers, or even its capital investment.

One aspect of the industry is worthy of special note. More than in any other, development derived from scientific research. This is not to say that the research itself was always conducted along correct theoretical lines—there was much empirical trial and error in the laboratories of this period—or that the industry made as much use of scientific knowledge or scientists as it might have. On the contrary, many of the advances were the work of self-taught 'chemists' and the more successful enterprises were characterized not so much by innovations in chemical process as by the effective organization of the factors of production within the prevailing scientific and technological framework.

[1] *Parliamentary Papers*, 1852–3, LXXXVIII, Part I, Table XXVIII, pp. ccxl–cclxii (males and females, twenty years of age and over).

The fact remains, however, that the laboratory was indispensable, at least to the invention of new procedures, whereas it was to all intents and purposes unknown in other fields. In this regard, the really important research in theoretical and applied chemistry was being done abroad, where the education of chemists was already more systematic and thorough than in Britain. For the moment, however, the abundance of cheap raw materials and economies of scale gave Britain a tremendous competitive advantage: soda exports, for example, went from 75,704 cwt. valued at £44,575 in 1840 to 2,049,582 cwt. worth nearly £1 million in 1860.[1] Not until the last quarter of the century did new techniques in both light and heavy chemicals threaten this hegemony.

Machines and new techniques alone are not the Industrial Revolution. They meant gains in productivity, a shift in the relative importance of the factors of production from labour to capital. But by revolution we mean a transformation of the organization as well as the means of production. In particular, we mean the assemblage of large bodies of workers in one place, there to accomplish their tasks under supervision and discipline; we mean, in short, what has come to be known as the factory system.

In this regard, two important questions call for consideration. The first is the relationship between the supply of labour and the extension of the new mode of production; the second, the place of the factory system in the overall pattern of economic change.

The first—the recruitment of a factory labour force—has been the subject of much debate. The facts are reasonably clear. By 1830 there were hundreds of thousands of men, women, and children employed in factory industry.[2] They had entered the mills in spite of a strong fear of the unknown, an aversion to supervision and discipline, and resentment of the unremitting demands of the machine. The rules of the early factories are our best indication of the importance of these issues: the heaviest fines were reserved for absence (the cardinal sin, often worth several days' pay), lateness, and distraction from the job.

The interpretation of these facts is something else again. For a long time, the most accepted view has been that propounded by Marx and repeated and embellished by generations of socialist and even non-

[1] *Hansard's Parliamentary Debates*, 3rd ser., vol. CLXVI, col. 1455.

[2] Even after passage of the Act of 1833 and the institution of regular inspection, we have no full count of the factory labour force at a given point of time. For one thing, the official definition of factory limited the term to power-driven textile mills; for another, employment varied constantly, and the different inspectors collected their statistics over a period of some months. See the data for 1835 in A. Ure, *Philosophy of Manufactures* (London, 1835), Appendix.

socialist historians. This position explains the accomplishment of so enormous a social change—the creation of an industrial proletariat in the face of tenacious resistance—by postulating an act of forcible expropriation: the enclosures uprooted the cottager and small peasant and drove them into the mills. Recent empirical research has invalidated this hypothesis; the data indicate that the agricultural revolution associated with the enclosures increased the demand for farm labour, that indeed those rural areas that saw the most enclosure saw the largest increase in resident population.[1] From 1750 to 1830, Britain's agricultural counties doubled their inhabitants. Whether objective evidence of this kind will suffice, however, to do away with what has become something of an article of faith is doubtful.

A more recent interpretation takes the opposite tack and argues that, since the factories were manned in the long run, there was never any problem of recruitment; that in the deceptive language of common sense, there was no labour shortage.

The proposition is non-refutable, hence meaningless. From the hindsight of any given level of resource utilization, the resource in question has proved adequate to that level. Besides, the economist knows no shortage; he knows only relative prices. The meaningful question is the influence of labour supply on the choice of techniques and rate of investment.[2]

Here, unfortunately, we are confronted by the apparent contradictoriness of the relationship. On the one hand, as we have seen, the high and rising cost of English labour was an encouragement to mechanization, hence growth, in the eighteenth century. Even after the initial period of industrialization, the rate of substitution of machines for men reflected fluctuations in wages or wage demands; thus the textile manufacturers introduced automatic spinning equipment and the power loom spasmodically, responding in large part to strikes, threats of strikes, and other threats to managerial authority. That famous apologist for the factory system, Andrew Ure, wrote a happy chapter on the

[1] See the important article of J. D. Chambers, 'Enclosure and the Labour Supply in the Industrial Revolution', *Econ. Hist. Rev.* 2nd ser. v (1953), 318–43.

[2] Cf. Morris Morris, 'Some Comments on the Supply of Labour to the Bombay Cotton Textile Industry, 1854–1951', *Indian Economic Journal*, I (1953), 138–52; and his 'Recruitment of an Industrial Labor Force in India, with British and American Comparisons', *Comparative Studies in Society and History*, II (1960), 305–28. This position derives in part from the experience of industrialization in India, where the pressure of an almost unlimited labour reserve and the development of a kind of symbiotic relationship between factory employment and village subsistence facilitated recruitment. Similar forces eased the transition in Japan as well. Characteristic of both economies has been the extreme paternalism of the industrial employer: 'A job with Tata's is like a piece of land.' It would be most dangerous, however, to infer from the Asian to the British experience.

capacity of the machine for taming labour.[1] In sum, high wages were a stimulus to innovation and technological advance.

On the other hand, one can have too much of a good thing. British industry could not have grown much if factory labour had been so much more costly than, say, agricultural labour, or so much more costly than labour in other countries that it no longer paid to invest in manufacturing. Something of the kind was happening in the late eighteenth century when, with the power loom not yet practicable and English weavers enjoying the unprecedented demand consequent on the introduction of machine spinning, it began to pay to ship British yarn to central Europe, there to be woven by peasants accustomed to a far lower standard of living than Englishmen.[2] The difficulty that certain isolated country mills found in obtaining workers at commercially feasible wages, to the point of being compelled on occasion to leave new equipment idle, is another example.[3]

Fortunately, the supply of labour increased substantially in Britain from the mid-eighteenth century on, almost as much, indeed, as the demand. In the first place, the rapid growth of population created a surplus of labour in the countryside, much of which found its way into the new urban centres of the North and Midlands. Secondly, while eighteenth-century England does not fit the economists' model of the pre-industrial society with unlimited supplies of labour,[4]—there were two societies nearby which do fit it and were in a position to send some of their surplus humanity to England—Scotland and, even more, Ireland. And finally, though least important, the same highly developed rural textile industry that had absorbed the free labour of the English countryside released an increasing number of workers as mechanization of weaving advanced and immigrant Irish labour began to compete for employment. The hand-loom weavers went into the mills reluctantly, but they went.

Even so, the task would have been immeasurably more difficult had the technological requirements of manufacture, especially in the early years of the jenny and water-frame, not allowed the employment of marginal elements—children, women, vagrants when necessary; and had social and political institutions not permitted a certain amount of explicit and concealed conscription, especially of parish apprentices.

[1] Ure, *The Philosophy of Manufactures*, pp. 364–70.

[2] It was this yarn trade that brought Nathan Rothschild to Manchester in 1797, to lay the foundations of the British dynasty. It was this also that inspired Wm. Radcliffe to write his *Origins of Power Loom Weaving* (London, 1828).

[3] Cf. A. Redford, *Labour Migration in England, 1800–1850* (Manchester, 1926), p. 88.

[4] The excellent analysis of W. Arthur Lewis, 'Economic Development with Unlimited Supplies of Labour', *The Manchester School*, xxi (1953), 139–91, is applicable to Britain only with major modifications.

With the coming of the power mule, however, grown men were required in increasing numbers and the employer was compelled to turn to the free labour market. This time it was the familial organization of factory labour that eased the change: the employer could hire parents and children together, which not only increased the financial incentive but also, by preserving the parents in their tutorial role, reconciled them the more easily to the undesirable features of factory work. By the time further technological advances—the introduction of long mules and the self-actor in the twenties and thirties—and limitations on child employment once again changed the composition of the labour force, a new generation had grown up, inured to the discipline and precision of the mill.[1]

How, now, does one reconcile the advantages of scarce labour and abundant labour in explaining Britain's economic development? It is not possible yet to give a definitive answer; we need to know a lot more of the facts before generalizing from them. At the moment, one can only advance the tentative hypothesis that the factor cost pattern required for a technological breakthrough is different from that needed for exploiting the possibilities of that breakthrough. Scarce labour seems to have encouraged a deepening of capital in eighteenth-century Britain; while a more abundant supply facilitated widening in the following decades.

Our second question is the place of the factory in the economy as a whole. There was a time when the coming of the factory system was pictured as a cataclysm, overwhelming the old order and transforming British industry within a generation. This was certainly the impression of contemporaries who, engaged in a fierce polemic over the social consequences of technological change, inevitably starkened the issues and saw everything in black and white. Some of the early economic historians accepted this view, though largely for different reasons. Among other things, the tendency to see the factory system as the last

---

[1] On the recruitment of the factory labour force in cotton, see, in addition to Redford's classic study of *Labour Migration*, George Unwin, *Samuel Oldknow and the Arkwrights* (Manchester, 1924); R. S. Fitton and A. P. Wadsworth, *The Strutts and the Arkwrights, 1758–1830* (Manchester, 1958); F. Collier, 'An Early Factory Community', *Econ. Hist.* II (1930), 117–24; Frances Collier, *The Family Economy of the Working Classes in the Cotton Industry, 1784–1833* (Manchester, 1964); Neil Smelser, *Social Change in the Industrial Revolution: An Application of Theory to the Lancashire Cotton Industry, 1770–1840* (London, 1959). For comparable problems in other industries, see D. C. Coleman, *The British Paper Industry 1495–1860: a Study in Industrial Growth* (Oxford, 1958), ch. XI; A. H. John, *The Industrial Development of South Wales, 1750–1850* (Cardiff, 1950), ch. III. Also D. F. Macdonald, *Scotland's Shifting Population, 1770–1850* (Glasgow, 1937), chs. III and IV; and J. E. Handley, *The Irish in Scotland, 1798–1854* (Cork, 1945), ch. IV.

of a sequence of ascending stages of industrial organization, beginning with the craft shop and passing through putting-out, implied the mutual exclusiveness of these forms and obscured those peculiar competitive advantages of each that have made possible their co-existence to the present day. Only in this century have scholars reversed the interpretation by stressing continuity rather than change. Clapham's classic *Economic History of Modern Britain* is a monument to this new point of view; it is, in Herbert Heaton's words, 'a study in slow motion'.[1]

The economic basis for the survival of the older modes of production is to be found partly within them, partly in the demands of the factory system and the general growth attending its development. Thus both craft shop and factory make possible the control of the work process from above (in the shop, the employer is usually worker as well); and while the factory is able to turn out more goods cheaper, the shop can work far more economically to special order. So that although factory production meant the end of many shops, it meant the beginning of many more. Machine building and maintenance, in particular, called forth a swarm of small artisanal enterprises; but large-scale industry in general found it desirable, for rational pecuniary reasons, to subcontract for much of its work.

The putting-out system is weak on both scores: the domestic artisan is rarely skilled enough to make individual finished products of the highest quality; nor can he compete with the factory in mass production of standardized items. Yet the weakness of putting-out is in many ways deceptive. For one thing, the capacity of dispersed manufacture for improvements in productivity should not be underestimated. Thus the division of labour made possible remarkable levels of output in certain trades—the metal-working ones in particular—well before the coming of machinery. Moreover, while the simplification of the work process implicit in such specialization is an invitation to mechanization, the devices that result often reinforce at first the position of the home worker; the early punching, cutting, and stamping machines were eminently suited to the cottage or the cellar. It is only when a higher stage of machine construction is reached, with the building of large, power-driven devices, that factory manufacture wins out.

Even where specialization and simplification cannot be pushed very far, in textiles for example, the home worker has one great advantage: he is cheap. He is usually able to draw some of his sustenance from the soil, if only from a garden plot; and his affection for the freedom of home work is such as to reconcile him to wages that a mill hand would not tolerate. For the manufacturer, moreover, he is dispensable; the immobilization of capital in plant and equipment is minimal, and in

[1] Heaton, 'Industrial Revolution', *Encyclopedia of the Social Sciences*, s.v.

time of difficulty work may be halted without fear of heavy, uncompensated fixed costs.[1]

For these reasons, the putting-out system proved hardier than might have been expected. It dragged on unconscionably in those trades where the technological advantage of power machinery was still small (as in weaving) or where the home artisan could build himself a rudimentary power device (as in nail-making and other light metalwork). And it often survived in symbiosis with the factory; many manufacturers found it profitable to install only so much machinery as would supply a conservatively estimated normal demand, relying on a reserve pool of dispersed labour for additional output in time of prosperity.

At the same time, much of the ground that the craft shop and putting-out lost in the newly mechanized industries was made up in other fields. On the one hand, the gains in productivity in certain stages of manufacture, with resultant reduction in price and rise in demand for the finished product, increased the labour requirements of the other, traditionally organized stages. Thus the clothing trades profited from the transformation of spinning and weaving, and lace-making and embroidery from the availability of cheap yarn. On the other hand, certain kinds of technological advance created craft and domestic industry where they had not existed before or extended them far beyond their traditional boundaries. The sewing-machine is an excellent example: it made ordinary women seamstresses and seamstresses tailors, and so doing hastened the transformation of what had once been the task of every woman into a professional activity.

In general, the whole tendency of industrialization and urbanization was to specialize labour ever farther and break down the versatility of the household. A whole range of occupations—baking, butchering, the manufacture of things as diverse as candles, soap, and polish—expanded or appeared in response. Along with this, the growth of population and *per capita* real income—as a result of productivity gains in agriculture as well as industry—augmented consumption and increased the portion devoted to manufactures and services, with consequent stimulation of the traditionally organized trades as well as the newly mechanized ones. Housing alone required an army of carpenters, masons, plumbers, plasterers, glaziers, tilers, and plain labourers.

All of this is clearly brought out by the occupational statistics. The British census of 1851—for all its inaccuracies—shows a country in which agriculture and domestic service were far and away the most

---

[1] For a theoretical analysis of some of the competitive advantages of putting-out, see A. Hirschman, 'Investment Policies in Underdeveloped Countries', *Amer. Econ. Rev.* XLVII (1957), 557–60.

important occupations; in which most of the labour force was engaged in industries of the old type: building trades, tailoring, shoemaking, unskilled work of all sorts. Even in the cotton manufacture, with over three-fifths of its working force of over half a million (of a total of almost sixteen millions) in mills,[1] almost two-thirds of the units making returns employed less than fifty men;[2] the average mill in England employed less than 200; and tens of thousands of hand looms were still at work in rural cottages.

Yet just as it would be wrong to picture the factory system as a tidal wave, so we would be deceiving ourselves to see it as a gentle erosion of the traditional order. For one thing, there was the trend: in the period from 1834, when the factory inspectors sent in their first returns, to mid-century, the number of cotton mill operatives in Britain increased from 220,825 to 330,924—and this in spite of substantial gains in productivity. In other industries—leather, paper, the metal trades—factory employment was growing even more rapidly; they were where cotton had been two generations earlier. Moreover the speed of the shift from old to new was increasing *pari passu* with the rate of technological change. In particular, the improvements in the technique of machine construction meant the rapid translation of concepts and devices developed in one industry to analogous operations in others; it is a short jump from cutting cloth to cutting leather or metal. They also meant larger and faster equipment that demanded power and was incompatible with domestic manufacture.

In a class by themselves, but following a similar path to factory organization, were those industries in which work had always been separated from the home and dispersion of labour was impossible. Iron, chemicals, machine work, shipbuilding all fall into this category. Long before the coming of the cotton mill, these branches of manufacture had been characterized by large units of production. A charcoal iron furnace of the early eighteenth century might employ eight or ten men, plus as many as a hundred digging ore, cutting and charking wood, transporting materials, and generally servicing the smelters. In the same period, the naval arsenal at Chatham employed upwards of a thousand men, all of them carefully assigned and supervised, so that 'tho' you see the whole Place as it were in the utmost Hurry, yet you see no Confusion, every Man knows his own Business...'.[3]

---

[1] The figures are of population and working force ten years of age and older.

[2] This is a guess based on the assumption that most of those employers who did not give the number of their men employed less than fifty. J. H. Clapham, *An Economic History of Modern Britain* (3 vols.; Cambridge, 1932–9), II, 35.

[3] Daniel Defoe, *Tour thro' the Whole Island of Great Britain*, ed. G. D. H. Cole; 2 vols. (London, 1927), p. 108.

Should such units be designated as factories? From the standpoint of the two critical criteria—concentration of production and maintenance of discipline—the term certainly fits. At the same time, they differed in one important regard from the textile mills that were in fact the prototype of the factory as we know it: however thoroughly the work in these forges and yards was supervised, the pace was set by men and not machines. It was spasmodic rather than regular. There were moments that required a burst of concentration and effort: when the furnace was tapped or the vat poured; the mast hoisted or keel launched; the hot blooms moved or turned. And there were quiet moments, while the mix boiled or the men waited for the next piece to be ready. At their loosest (disregarding the question of mobility), these production units were very much like the assemblage of craftsmen and assistants on a building job; or the construction gang on a canal or railway project.

Such enterprises multiplied and grew considerably in average size as a result of industrial expansion. In 1849 Dowlais, probably the largest iron plant in the kingdom, employed 7000 men to work its eighteen blast furnaces, its puddling ovens, rolling mills, mines, and the rest.[1] Yet the difference from the foundries and forges of the eighteenth century was more one of degree than of kind, and the social impact of this development was not so great as that of the rise of a disciplined proletariat in the textile mills.

On the other hand, the effect of improved technology was to push the man-paced industries toward the precision and regularity of spinning and weaving. In iron and steel, the rolling mill, steam hammer, and more effective handling equipment all led in this direction; and throughout the metal trades, the development of special-purpose machine tools and more precise parts was a portent of the assembly lines of the twentieth century.

Secondly, the contribution of factory industry to the economy was out of proportion to its share of total production. Thus the factory promoted a higher rate of investment, hence of growth, than other forms of manufacture. Partly this was simply a consequence of capital intensity: the man who lived by the machine was more likely to be interested in and save for mechanical improvements than the merchant who relied on cheap cottage labour.[2] Even more, it reflected the

[1] Beck, *Geschichte des Eisens*, IV, 663.

[2] Cf. A. O. Hirschman and G. Serkin, 'Investment Criteria and Capital Intensity Once Again', *Quarterly Journal of Economics*, LXXII (1958), 470, who cite the contrast in this regard between the owner of the land-intensive hacienda and the operator of the capital-intensive plantation. On this point, see also E. R. Wolf and S. W. Mintz, 'Haciendas and Plantations in Middle America and the Antilles', *Social and Economic Studies*, VI (1957), 380–412.

technological orientation implicit in concentrated production. In contrast to putting-out, where the entrepreneur was primarily a seller, a merchandiser of goods turned out by others by methods inattentive to market needs and opportunities, the factory placed the emphasis on making: the mill owner was first and foremost a production man, able within fairly wide limits to alter the techniques and conditions of work at will. As a result, technique was responsive to economic opportunity as never before. The pressures for change already inherent in the new technology—with its calculus of efficiency, its systematization of empirical investigation, its implicit and growing ties to a growing body of scientific theory—were thereby enormously reinforced. The factory was a new bridge between invention and innovation.

In sum, one must not mistake the appearance for the reality. The census returns and other numbers to be found between the covers of dusty parliamentary papers are the economic historian's butterfly under glass or frog in formaldehyde—without the virtue of wholeness to compensate for their lifelessness. As described by occupational data, the British economy of 1851 may not seem very different from that of 1800. But these numbers merely describe the surface of the society—and even then in terms that define away change by using categories of unchanging nomenclature. Beneath this surface, the vital organs were transformed; and though they weighed but a fraction of the total—whether measured by people or wealth—it was they that determined the metabolism of the entire system. We have seen that, in so far as small-scale enterprise continued to flourish, it did so largely because of demand derived from the growth of concentrated manufacture: the demand of the large producers themselves; of their employees; and of the urban agglomerations that grew up around them. But not only small industry was tied in this way to the modern sector. Agriculture, trade, banking—all came increasingly to depend on the needs, the products, the bills of exchange, the investments of Lancashire, the Midlands, and the other nodes of British factory industry. The people of the day were not deceived by the pristine air of much of Britain's landscape. They knew they had passed through a revolution.

It was, moreover, a revolution like nothing ever experienced. Previous transformations, political or economic, had always finished by stabilizing at a new position of equilibrium. This one was clearly continuing and bid fair to go on indefinitely. Many Britons would have stopped it in its course, or even turned it back. For good reasons or bad, they were distressed, inconvenienced, or outraged by its consequences. They mourned a merrie England that never was; deplored the soot and ugliness of the new factory towns; bemoaned the growing political power of crass *parvenus*; cried out against the precarious poverty of a rootless proletariat. This is not the place to assess these judgements, which have remained a matter of controversy to the present day. But it is worth noting that these pessimists, vociferous though they were, were a small minority of that part of British society that expressed an opinion on the subject. The middle and upper classes were convinced by the marvellous inventions of science and technology, the increasing mass and variety of material goods, the growing speed of movement and convenience of everyday activities, that they were living in the best of all possible worlds and what is more, a world getting better all the time. For these Britons, science was the new revelation; and the Industrial Revolution was the proof and justification of the religion of progress.

The 'labouring poor', especially those groups by-passed or squeezed by machine industry, said little but were undoubtedly of another mind.

CHAPTER 3

Continental Emulation

It is something of a commonplace that the Crystal Palace Exposition in 1851 marked the apogee of Britain's career as the 'workshop of the world'. True, the historian can detect premonitory indications of successful emulation by other nations, even evidence of foreign superiority in special areas of manufacture. But then, there is little the historian cannot detect if he sets his mind to it, and such harbingers of trouble hardly alter the general picture. This little island, with a population half that of France, was turning out about two-thirds of the world's coal, more than half of its iron and cotton cloth. (The figures are approximate, but they furnish orders of proportion.) Her income *per capita*, which cannot be compared precisely with that of the continental countries, all ingenious efforts to the contrary, was correspondingly higher than that of her neighbours.[1] Her merchandise dominated in all the markets of the world; her manufacturers feared no competition; she had even—in a move that marked a break with hundreds of years of economic nationalism—removed almost all the artificial protections of her industrialists, farmers, and shippers against foreign rivals. What other country could follow suit? She was, in short, the very model of industrial excellence and achievement—for some, a pace-setter to be copied and surpassed; for others, a superior economic power whose achievements rested on the special bounty of an uneven Providence, hence a rival to be envied and feared. But all watched and visited and tried to learn.

[1] An impressionistic estimate of 1832, by the Baron de Morogues, *De la misère des ouvriers et de la marche à suivre pour y remédier* (Paris, 1832), gave French *per capita* income as 198 fr. 30; English at 800 fr. Cited by E. Buret, *De la misère des classes laborieuses en Angleterre et en France* (2 vols.; Paris, 1840), I, 126. The gap would seem too large. More recent calculations, presumably more accurate (but *caveat lector!*), indicate that *per capita* income was about £32·6 for the United Kingdom in 1860, £21·1 for France (1859), and £13·3 for Germany (1860–9 average, 1913 area). Francs and marks have been converted to £s at 25·18 and 20·42 to 1, respectively. Sources: for the United Kingdom, Mulhall estimate, as given in P. Deane, 'Contemporary Estimates of National Income in the Second Half of the Nineteenth Century', *Econ. Hist. Rev.* 2nd ser. IX (1957), 459; for France, F. Perroux, 'Prise de vues sur la croissance de l'économie française, 1780–1950', in S. Kuznets, ed., *Income and Wealth*, Series V (London, 1955), p. 61; for Germany, P. Jostock, 'The Long-term Growth of National Income in Germany', *ibid.* p. 82.

Actually the learning process had started long before. By the middle of the eighteenth century, it was already obvious that British industrial technique had advanced significantly beyond that of the rest of the world. Government representatives and private businessmen came from the Continent on tours of inspection; their reports, often published, are among our best sources for the industrial history of the period. The heyday of these visits was roughly the third quarter of the century, before the British became aware of the competitive advantage afforded by their methods and began, in the best historical tradition, to erect barriers to their diffusion.

In this effort to study and emulate British techniques, the nations of western Europe were favoured by a number of advantages. To begin with, they had behind them an experience of organized and increasingly effective political behaviour. In one decisive respect, their 'age of troubles' was over: the issue of central *versus* fragmented authority had been largely settled in favour of the former, and the remnants of feudal jurisdiction and provincial autonomy were being steadily eroded by the limitless pretensions of the *Beamtenstaat*. Here, indeed, lay the basis and justification of monarchical supremacy: the creation of a standing bureaucracy administering a known corpus of law and separating the function and prerogative of office from personal interest. This it was that made possible the elaboration of coherent policy and the pursuit of continuing objectives; this, that insured the victory of the crown over insubordinate vassals who could fight better than they could govern. And if, in this struggle, the rising commercial and industrial interest generally found itself on the side of the king, it was in part because the bureaucratic state offered that definition and stability of the political environment that is propitious, if not indispensable, to business.

Similarly, their supply of capital and standard of living were substantially higher than in the 'backward' lands of today. And with this went a level of technical skill that, if not immediately adequate to the task of sustaining an industrial revolution, was right at the margin. Culturally, of course, the outlook was even brighter. The continental countries were part of the same larger civilization as Britain; and they were certainly her equals, in some respects her superiors, in science and education for the elite. In short, if they were in their day 'underdeveloped', the word must be understood quite differently from the way it is today.

Nevertheless, their Industrial Revolution was substantially slower than the British. Although they were able to study the new machines and engines almost from the start and indeed acquire them in spite of prohibitions on their export, they were generations in absorbing them and even longer in catching up to British practice.

Why the delay? Surely, the hardest task would seem to have been the original creative acts that produced coke smelting, the mule, and the steam-engine. In view of the enormous economic superiority of these innovations, one would expect the rest to have followed automatically. To understand why it did not—why even the quickest nations marked time until the third and fourth decades of the nineteenth century—is to understand not only a good part of the history of these countries but also something of the problem of economic development in general.

The industrialization of continental Europe may be broken down analytically into two aspects: (1) the response to endogenous pressures toward change, of the kind that precipitated an economic revolution in Britain; and (2) the reaction to the new methods developed across the Channel.

In order to clarify the first, one must examine briefly the character of continental industry in the pre-factory period. For one thing, nature had not been so kind to the lands across the Channel as to Britain. The key consideration was space: these countries were larger in proportion to population; and size, combined with difficulties of terrain, made for higher transport costs and fragmentation of markets. Roads were bad everywhere in the eighteenth century, but the British roads were possibly a little better and certainly shorter. And Britain had the sea. On the Continent, only Holland was so well served by water transport. The rivers of western Europe were used as much as possible for the movement of goods, but their usefulness was often vitiated by natural shortcomings—they were too shallow in the dry season, too rapid and treacherous at the full—and by poor communication between the different basins.

On the supply side, the contrast between Britain and the Continent was less sharp. Yet the resources of the mainland countries were in fact less favourable to industrial expansion than those of Britain even before the change in raw materials requirements consequent on the Industrial Revolution. The cloth industries of France, the Low Countries, and Germany, for example, had to import the bulk of their fine wool from abroad. And the lack of concentrated, easily accessible known deposits of coal led to a neglect of the possibilities of mineral fuel; here, indeed, even nature's bounty hurt, for the *relative* abundance of timber seems to have encouraged retention of the traditional technique.

Too often, moreover, man aggravated the handicaps that nature had set in his way. Thus the very best roads and waterways were dotted along their length by toll stations, whose exactions were so outrageous and formalities so tedious as to drive shippers miles out of their way and compel them on occasion to break and remake cargoes in an effort at evasion. Political boundaries were a further obstacle. Germany especially—and what are now Belgium and Italy somewhat less—was a patchwork of kingdoms, archduchies, duchies, bishoprics, principalities, free cities, and other forms of sovereignty, each with its own laws, courts, coinage and, above all, customs barriers. Even France, a unified polity by the end of the seventeenth century, continued to be divided economically into trade zones reflecting the gradual accretion that had built the nation-state. And these formal barriers were complicated by a network of informal boundaries defining markets and zones of supply for goods, like grain or wood or salt, that were vital to local survival. Finally, there were instances of the deliberate use of power to cripple trade. What is now Belgium was the worst victim: the natural access of the southern Low Countries to the sea via the Scheldt had been interrupted by the Dutch in the early seventeenth century and was to remain blocked until the annexation of the area by France during the revolutionary period. Efforts to make Ostend another Antwerp were only partly successful. The manufacturers of Wallonia, the industrial heart of the country, were compelled to turn to central Europe for markets.

These direct obstacles to the flow of goods were compounded by social and institutional limitations on demand. We have already had occasion to note that income and wealth were more unequally distributed on the Continent than in Britain, that indeed the societies of the mainland were cleft by deep horizontal fissures that discouraged emulative consumption of standardized products. The contemporary thesis linking luxury and prosperity—which Sombart picks up, with a wealth of illustrative detail, in his *Luxus und Kapitalismus*—makes some sense in this context. Some of the most important industrial enterprises were largely dependent on the orders of the wealthy few: the numerous courts, large and small, ranging from Versailles to the *Hof* of some German princeling; the Catholic Church; the socially aspiring *haute bourgeoisie*. By contrast, the great mass of near-subsistence consumers operated in an entirely different market. They could afford only the shoddiest articles, requiring a minimum of craft skill. What they could, they made at home; the poor of the eighteenth century entered the market as little as possible. Nor was what they bought standardized or mass-produced—in spite of its coarseness and simplicity. It was almost always the work of local artisans, turning out textiles and even tools in accordance with local tradition rather than some regional or national standard. Thus provincial patterns of dress lingered much longer on the Continent than in Britain, and longest in those semi-isolated rural areas where status and home were most firmly fixed.

Moreover, the poor of Europe were, as already noted, far worse off than those of Britain. The diaries of travellers offer abundant testimony to the contrast: one finds repeated references to bare feet, meatless tables, glassless windows, and the absence of iron where one would expect to find it—on the wheels of wagons, for example. Listen to Arthur Young's indignant reflections on the poverty of the Dordogne:[1]

> Pass Payrac, and meet many beggars, which we had not done before. All the country girls and women are without shoes or stockings; and the plough-men at their work have neither sabots nor feet to their stockings. This is a poverty, that strikes at the root of national prosperity; a large consumption among the poor being of more consequence than among the rich: the wealth of a nation lies in its circulation and consumption; and the case of poor people abstaining from the use of manufactures of leather and wool ought to be considered as an evil of the first magnitude.

Of the large number of similar comments, I shall confine myself to one, chosen to convey the progressive diminution in the demand for manufactures as one proceeds eastward. In 1835 a young German officer named Moltke travelled down the Danube on his way to an assignment in Turkey. Seeking means of land transport in Wallachia, he observed that the common vehicle of the country was 'like a child's wagon... so short and narrow that one man could hardly sit in it, if he brought along even so little baggage as we. On the whole waggon, there is not the smallest piece of iron: hub, axle, everything of wood. Nor is there any more point in looking for any kind of metal in the horse's harness'.[2] Nothing conveys better the circular link between poverty, the absence of industry, and a pattern of consumption that reconciles need with means and confines means to need.

Continental producers were similarly handicapped in foreign markets. Aside from higher costs due in large part to the material difficulties discussed above, they paid more for all the accessory commercial and financial services—insurance, bank credit, shipping. To be sure, the assistance of the most efficient middleman of the day, Holland, was available in principle to all. In fact, however, the nation that stood most to gain from this, France, systematically discouraged recourse to Dutch intermediaries in an effort to build up her own merchant marine—in spite of the cost and occasional impracticability of this challenge to the rules of comparative advantage.[3]

On the supply side, we have the same combination of political and

[1] *Travels* (2 vols.; Dublin, 1793), I, 38.
[2] Cited in Karl Braun-Wiesbaden, *Eine türkische Reise* (2 vols.; Stuttgart, 1876), I, 339.
[3] On this form of self-impoverishment, cf. Adam Smith, *Wealth of Nations*, Book IV, ch. ii. Navigation Acts were a far more serious handicap to the French than to

social considerations compounding natural handicaps. Thus, far more than in Britain, continental business enterprise was a class activity, recruiting practitioners from a group limited by custom and law. In France, commercial enterprise had traditionally entailed derogation from noble status; and although the monarchy made repeated efforts from Louis XIII on to make trade, especially international trade, and large-scale manufacture compatible with aristocracy, it found social values more powerful than decrees. In much of Germany, the cleavage was even wider, for there class prejudice was reinforced by law, and lines were carefully drawn between noble, burgher, and peasant enjoining each from trespassing on those areas reserved to the others. Indeed, the farther east one goes in Europe, the more the bourgeoisie takes on the appearance of a foreign excrescence on manorial society, a group apart scorned by the nobility and feared or hated by (or unknown to) a peasantry still personally bound to the local *seigneur*.[1]

This is not to say that European aristocrats did not engage in industrial activity, especially in those fields, like mining and metallurgy, that depend heavily on the ownership of land; or that they did not on occasion invest in manufacturing at the behest of a mercantilist sovereign intent on promoting economic development. Even there, however, their entrepreneurship was more often than not vicarious, and the few aristocratic industrialists who have caught the attention of scholars are not enough to alter significantly the picture of a class deriving its material strength at best from agriculture and estate management, at worst from rents, feudal dues, state offices, royal favours, and other perquisites of gentle birth. Here, as always, attitude is more decisive than law or fiat; and the attitude of most continental noblemen was summed up in the sententious quip of one Austrian magnate: 'Geschäfte macht kein Windischgrätz'.

The effect of this invidious social segregation of business enterprise was to discourage outside talent and capital from entering the field and to draw out the most successful of those already engaged. If the aristocrat was too high to stoop to trade, the ambitious, capable *novus homo* preferred to by-pass it and seek eminence via the professions and government service. Those who, for want of instruction, because of religious discrimination, through personal opportunity, or for other

the British, and Paris had to make numerous exceptions to insure the flow of goods to and from the colonies. E. Levasseur, *Histoire du commerce de la France* (2 vols.; Paris, 1911), I, 489–90.

[1] Foreign often in the literal sense: it is precisely in these traditionalistic agricultural societies, with their strong suspicion of trade and the trader, that commerce was left almost entirely to the metic, the stranger in the midst—Jew, Greek, or western European.

reason, sought their fortunes in manufacturing or commerce found financial assistance hard to obtain. Free capital flowed to the land, whose price was bid up to a point where a substantial and persistent gap developed between the rate of return in agriculture and industry. One does not find on the Continent the opportunities that offered themselves in Britain to the small man with more skill and ambition than money. The owners of non-business wealth, of land and buildings, were not awakened to the possibilities of gain that lay in converting such property and renting it for industrial use. Contrast, for example, the facilities offered in South Wales and the royalty policy of a firm like Boulton and Watt with the Draconian terms imposed on mining firms leasing Newcomen steam-engines in the Hainaut in the mid-eighteenth century: the machines had to be worked at minimum force (thereby multiplying fuel consumption per horsepower many times) for fear of straining them; and royalties ran as high as 10 per cent of gross output.[1] Mineral resources usually belonged to the state and were conceded on terms that made them inaccessible to thin purses. Loan funds, even at short term, were scarce and expensive; in those rural areas where industry would ordinarily be expected to locate, interest rates of 15 per cent and more were not uncommon. In effect, capital was limited to those who had received it from their ancestors or accumulated it by their own efforts.

At the same time, capital accumulated in business was continually draining off into more honorific channels: land, office, aristocratic status. So seriously were industry and trade weakened by this chase after prestige that the state intervened. In France, patents of nobility began to stipulate that the new rank was conditional on continuance of the family enterprise. On the whole such efforts to keep the bourgeois a bourgeois were no more successful than those to turn the gentleman into one. A majority of the descendants took their capital into the country to finance a life of gentility, while a handful carried on the business, at least for a while.

Turning from the supply of talent and capital to industry and trade to the actual conduct of business affairs, one is again struck by the contrast between continental confinement and inhibition and British freedom. The effect of mercantilist and guild controls on the scale and techniques of production is too well known perhaps to require discussion here. Suffice it to say, simply, that almost to the end of the eighteenth century the tendency of continental governments was to extend and reinforce these restrictions, partly from a conviction that this was the only way to maintain quality of production and hence

---

[1] A. Toilliez, 'Mémoire sur l'introduction et l'établissement des machines à vapeur dans le Hainaut', in Société des Sciences, des Arts, et des Lettres du Hainaut, *3e anniversaire de la fondation de la Société* (Mons, 1836), pp. 57–8.

sales (particularly sales abroad), partly because both the enforcement of regulation and derogations therefrom were excellent sources of revenue. A country like France actually reversed the decay of this medieval institution, bolstering the guilds where they were declining, establishing them where they never had been. Even when the state accorded rural craftsmen in 1762 the right to weave cloth for market, it did so not in belated recognition of a sphere of free enterprise, but in order to bring this growing volume of unregulated output under inspection and control.

Yet enterprise, like love, usually finds ways to laugh at locksmiths, and institutional restrictions will explain only a small part of the shortcomings of continental industry. More important, probably, were social and psychological attitudes unfavourable to effective entrepreneurship.

We have already had occasion to allude in passing to some of the differences between Britain and the Continent in this regard. To begin with, the business firm in France, the Low Countries, or Germany was far more likely to be exclusively familial, indeed to be so closely identified with the family as to be almost indistinguishable from it. The British entrepreneur had come a long way toward seeing a given industrial venture as a means to an end, as a device to be rationally utilized for making money. For his competitors across the Channel, however, the firm, *in conjunction with* the family whose reputation it contributed to and whose way of life it made possible, was an end in itself. This in turn had important consequences for the conduct of the enterprise. It made it difficult to view techniques and products impersonally, to sacrifice when necessary quality to quantity, to abandon traditional ways when more efficient and profitable tools and methods became available. It placed a premium on security and led to an overestimation of risk in investment decisions. It discouraged the use of outside capital, whether in the form of long-term loans or share investment, and, by throwing the firm on its own resources, drastically limited its opportunities for expansion while encouraging a policy of pricing that maximized unit rather than total profit.[1]

This pattern of behaviour was reinforced by the dominant values of the society as a whole. Thus the identification of the producer with his

---

[1] This reluctance of family firms to borrow, except *in extremis*, goes far to explain the paradox of the large and persistent gap between the interest paid by state funds and other 'safe' investments and that charged industrial enterprise. For an analysis of this entrepreneurial pattern and its implications for growth, see D. S. Landes, 'French Entrepreneurship and Industrial Growth in the Nineteenth Century', *J. Econ. Hist.* IX (1949), 45–61; and *idem*, 'French Business and the Businessman: a Social and Cultural Analysis', in E. M. Earle, ed., *Modern France: Problems of the Third and Fourth Republics* (Princeton, 1951), pp. 334–53. Also A. Gerschenkron, 'Social Attitudes,

tools and methods and his reluctance to scrap old ways for new was closely related to a worship of thrift that characterized the bourgeoisie as well as the peasantry to a degree unknown in Britain. I use the word 'degree' advisedly, for we are not dealing here with differences of kind. Yet it seems clear that along the wide spectrum of attitudes on this issue, ranging from the prodigality of an American family trained to look on a three-year-old automobile as unfashionable, even unpatriotic, to the parsimony of Maupassant's peasant bending to pick up a piece of string, the Englishman of the eighteenth century was substantially closer to a psychology of abundance than the Frenchman or the German. The reason lay partly in the fact of abundance: the English entrepreneur, as noted above, simply had more and cheaper resources at his disposal. But it also reflected greater security. The British farmer or burgher did not know war as did the Walloon or Bavarian; it was generations since his land had last been wasted by armies, his home pillaged; and no one in Europe could afford to be so confident of freedom from arbitrary exactions and confiscation. He had, in short, less fear of a 'rainy day'.

Similarly, the entrepreneur's preference for the greatest possible profit per unit of sale, as against higher total profit at some larger output, accorded with a general condemnation of competition, particularly price competition, as unfair and even socially subversive. The societies of the Continent and the local communities of which they were composed tended to see the total product of the group, as well as the aggregate demand for that product, as more or less fixed, growing only slowly over time with population. Under the circumstances, a man could become rich only at the expense of his neighbours, who, however inefficient they might be, had a right to sustenance appropriate to their station so long as they performed work of acceptable quality and satisfied thereby the needs of the community. The rich man who built his fortune on the ruins of less productive or talented competitors was not a model of achievement, a culture hero; he was a *mangeur d'hommes.*[1]

Entrepreneurship, and Economic Development', *Explorations in Entrepreneurial History*, vi (1953-4), 1-19; Landes, 'Social Attitudes, Entrepreneurship, and Economic Development: a Comment', *ibid.* vi (1953-4), 245-72; Gerschenkron, 'Some Further Notes...', *ibid.* vii (1954-5), 111-19; Landes, 'Further Comment', *ibid.* vii (1954-5), 119-20.

[1] This attitude, like the obsession with thrift, once again derives originally from the conditions of the rural community. Given a limited supply of land for cultivation, the peasant does in fact add to his holdings at the expense of his neighbour, who may well finish as his tenant or—in other times and societies—his debt bondsman. With the rise of towns and cities in the Middle Ages, this fear of the impoverishment and dependency consequent on inequality was transferred to the urban community, where

These generally accepted sanctions go far to explain why those continental enterprises that stood out above their fellows in size and efficiency did not take advantage of their superiority to wipe out smaller competitors and impose their technology on industry as a whole. For one thing, there were serious social penalties for inconsiderate behaviour, penalties that should not be underestimated in societies that place so much emphasis on 'connections'—in all matters, from profitable business transactions to honorific marriages. For another, social attitudes were translated into political institutions, and local authorities in countries like France and Prussia could on occasion interpose real obstacles to free-wheeling enterprise. Finally, there was a serious material deterrent: in a market dominated by a few large units amid a swarm of small, aggressive price competition by one giant is sure to invite painful reprisal from the others.

This is not to say that there was no competition or that there was no elimination of inefficient firms. The contrary is clearly true. The point is that these patterns of behaviour diminished the effectiveness of the price mechanism as a force for rationalization and slowed the diffusion of technological change. The effect varied from industry to industry. In one sense it was most significant—that is, it made the most difference— where it was *not* reinforced by and inextricably bound up with contributory factors—in textiles and other light manufactures, for example, where transport costs were not high enough to cut down competition regardless of entrepreneurial policy.

As a result of this combination of natural and human limitations on the demand for manufactured products and the supply of effective industrial enterprise, pre-industrial, pre-Revolutionary Europe was a conglomeration of small, semi-autarkic markets, each with its own fairly complete array of trades. The scale of operations of the individual enterprise was small enough to make locational resource and supply considerations almost irrelevant. Textiles were produced everywhere, most often with local flax or wool; small out-croppings of iron fed the local furnaces and forges, placed along streams in wooded areas to insure a provision of fuel. Only a few industries were compelled by special requirements to concentrate in suitable localities: porcelain manufacture, certain branches of the chemical industry, non-ferrous metallurgy.

To be sure, even in those industries that were most dispersed, there were centres of exceptional activity catering to more than local needs:

it inspired much of the guild regulation of production and competition. The guilds have long since disappeared, but in countries like France and Germany, the reprobation of judgment by the market place prevails to this day.

French Flanders, Verviers, Saxony, Normandy, Languedoc in woollen cloth; Switzerland, south Germany, Normandy in cottons and fustians; Wallonia, the Nivernais and upper Marne valley, the Siegerland, Silesia, and Styria in iron. Some of this localization reflected a specially favourable resource position: large flocks of sheep in Saxony; easy access to overseas cotton sources in Normandy; generous iron deposits in the Liégeois, Nivernais, or Siegerland; rapid streams in the Sauerland for the refining and working of the crude pig. Sometimes it rested on long tradition and a consequent inheritance of special skills: thus weaving in Flanders or the cutlery manufacture at Solingen and Thiers. Sometimes it was largely a product of entrepreneurial initiative, as in the textile centres created by Calvinist refugees at Krefeld, Elberfeld, and other points in the Rhine valley; and sometimes a *fabrique* was created by the state, as the fine-cloth manufacture at Sedan. Usually, as in the metal industries of Liège, it is a combination of two or more of these that accounts for growth. Finally, the localization of industry, particularly in textiles, was a function of the availability of cheap rural labour; spinning and weaving were most active in areas where the parsimony of the soil or the excessive fragmentation of the land compelled the peasant to eke out his living with the wages of industry. All the better if he was engaged in livestock raising or mixed husbandry rather than simple cultivation; his hands would be the smoother for handling yarn and fabric.

It is hardly surprising that the most successful of these centres—those growing most rapidly if not always the largest in absolute output—were almost invariably those unhampered by guild regulation. In France, where most industry was in principle subject to control, a city like Lille waged a long, vain struggle against the overgrown textile villages of the *plat pays*, which were stimulated by competition 'to by-pass the regulations, seek new processes, and vary their fabrics continually'.[1] In the Low Countries, the woollen trade of Liège declined steadily, while a few miles away, the free *fabrique* of Verviers throve; what is more, freedom raised a rival to Verviers itself, as from the middle of the eighteenth century the weavers of Dison pushed iconoclasm almost to the limit and built their prosperity on the use of waste yarn, the so-called *queues et pennes*.[2] In Aachen, the introduction of regulation merely served to drive the most enterprising producers to the suburb of Burtscheid.[3]

[1] A. de Saint-Léger, in a review of J. Crombé, *L'organisation du travail à Roubaix avant la Révolution* (Lille, 1905), in *Annales de l'Est et du Nord*, II (1906), 414.

[2] Pierre Lebrun, *L'industrie de la laine à Verviers pendant le XVIIIᵉ et le début du XIXᵉ siècle* (Liège, 1948), part III, section I, ch. iii.

[3] C. Bruckner, *Aachen und seine Tuchindustrie* (Horb am Neckar, 1949); cf. the failure

What *is* in some ways surprising is the superior performance of free industry to that of state-supported enterprise. The seventeenth and eighteenth centuries saw most of the governments of continental Europe—foremost among them France, Prussia, and the Austria of Maria Theresa—engage in extensive and costly programmes of industrial development. Their objectives were more or less the same: political aggrandizement through wealth and employment; but their methods, which were essentially empirical and dependent on uncertain resources, varied with place and time. In the beginning, the emphasis was usually on direct participation in economic life: almost every nation had its state enterprises producing the staples of royal consumption—armaments first, and then decorative furnishings like mirrors, tapestries, and porcelain. In Prussia the monarchy, with its large Silesian properties, was the largest producer of iron and coal in the kingdom.

Yet the economic ambitions of the state surpassed its resources in men and money, and compelled it from the start to rely heavily on private industry. Assistance sometimes took the form of direct investment, but more often of fiscal favours, assignment of labour, patents on techniques or exclusive sales privileges, guaranties of supplies, technological advice, loans at low interest or no interest, outright subsidies, or some combination thereof. From 1740 to 1789 the French monarchy lent without interest some 1·3 million *livres* and gave away 5 million more; to this, certain regional authorities like those of Brittany and Languedoc added their own subventions. All of these did not add up to much; but they were intended as 'seed money', planted in pilot enterprises in the hope that it would bring forth a crop of imitators. The state also designated numerous *manufactures royales* and *privilégiées*, and when necessary gilded the honour with monopoly rights as an inducement to the foundation of new industries or importation of new techniques. Finally, it sent observers abroad on technical missions; engaged inventors and manufacturers, for the most part Britons like Kay and Wilkinson, to teach their methods to French industry; and encouraged foreigners like Holker and Milne to settle in France and set up their own enterprises.

In Germany, Prussia was most active in this campaign of forced industrialization. Businessmen, even noblemen and local governments, were urged to set up 'factories' for the production of textiles, glass, chemicals, nonferrous and ferrous metals. This royal invitation was usually equivalent to a command, particularly to those Jewish merchants and court purveyors whose situation in a virulently anti-

of similar efforts to contain enterprise in the wire industry of western Germany. R. Sommer, 'Die Industrie im mittleren Lennetal', in *Spieker: Landeskundliche Beiträge und Berichte* (Münster), no. 7 (1956), p. 37.

Semitic country was utterly dependent on the pleasure of the ruler. Hundreds of enterprises were brought into existence in this manner, many in the newly conquered province of Silesia, which was an object of special solicitude.[1] The other governments of central Europe were less energetic only by comparison: witness Maria Theresa and her consort Francis, whom Frederick the Great called 'the greatest manufacturer of his time'; or the successive Kurfürsten of Saxony; or on a modest scale, the rulers of such lesser states as Württemberg, Hesse and Nassau-Saarbrücken.

In the long run, however, these efforts were only moderately successful. The state of the seventeenth and eighteenth centuries was incapable of planning development nationally or allocating resources efficiently. It lacked the conceptual tools, even the empirical statistical data, required; it had a strong affection for the wrong products, for labour-intensive luxuries like Gobelins tapestries and Dresden figurines; it promoted monopoly, when nothing could have been more harmful to long-run development; and it was not even sure of its own purposes in the face of resistance from conservative interests—corporate industry, landed proprietors, military leaders with their own ideas how to spend the nation's money.

In the particular, state assistance was more often than not an encouragement to laxity and a cover for incompetence. With some notable exceptions, privileged manufactories were sloppily managed and required repeated transfusions of royal capital. Often they turned out an inferior product that could be disposed of only to captive customers —army regiments or, in Germany and Austria, Jewish and foreign merchants. As the elder Trudaine put it, 'the money of the king brings bad luck to those who receive loans or advances'.[2] Many of these enterprises failed the moment a change in government personnel or an ideological shift toward *laissez-faire* cut them off from state largesse. Within his own lifetime, Frederick the Great saw dozens of his creations fold; most of the rest followed soon after his death.

This is not to say that this effort to promote industrial development from above was a complete waste of energy and money. It clearly was not. If it did nothing else, mercantilism did prepare many of the bearers of economic change. Thus these abortive manufactories and factories were often training grounds for the next generation; the fine-cloth 'factory' at Brno in Moravia was a stumbling undertaking that eventually collapsed, but its alumni helped to make the city the

[1] The standard work remains H. Fechner, *Wirtschaftsgeschichte der preussischen Provinz Schlesien in der Zeit ihrer provinziellen Selbstständigkeit, 1741–1806* (Breslau, 1907).

[2] Cited in Ch. Schmidt, 'Les débuts de l'industrie cotonnière en France, 1760–1806, II. De 1786 à 1806', *Revue d'histoire économique et sociale*, VII (1914), 30 n. 2.

centre of textile manufacture in what is now Czechoslovakia.[1] Similarly, there were few British technicians who emigrated to the Continent to set up shops and mills who did not teach, sometimes inadvertently, some of their eventual competitors. Finally, one must not underrate the long-run importance of the technological civil service—with men like Trudaine and Jars in France, Heinitz, Stein and Reden in Prussia—which continued to influence economic development on the Continent after the other aspects of mercantilistic policy had been discarded. The zeal of these officials was no substitute for a high general level of skill and empirical ingenuity; but they were a force for the rational study and promotion of change, and once the initial steps had been taken on the path of industrial revolution, once the process of cumulative advance had begun, they did channel innovation effectively.

In striking contrast, the industrial centres of west Germany—Krefeld, Monschau, the Wuppertal in textiles, Solingen and Remscheid in metalwork—grew rapidly without assistance and gave rise to large firms of international reputation. It was these and similar areas like Verviers-Hodimont that were the potential sources of technological revolution, for it is here that we find those bottlenecks in the supply of the factors which triggered change in Britain. The shortage of water power was already compelling a costly dispersion of iron-working in the Sauerland and Siegerland.[2] And the growing demand for labour led the merchant clothiers to seek spinners and even weavers, first in the nearby countryside, and then far afield in heavily populated agricultural areas like the Limburg, which lay at the centre of the triangle marked off by Verviers, Monschau and Aachen. Spinning was the worst bottleneck: sometimes the state intervened and prohibited the export of yarn in an effort to protect the supply of its own nationals. In the meantime, embezzlement seems to have increased, in spite of repressive measures comparable to those imposed in England.[3]

How heavy was this growing pressure on supply? Clearly much less than in Britain. Such evidence as we have indicates that up to the last decade of the century, the flow of cheap labour on the Continent continued to be abundant; the marginal cost of this factor was not

[1] See the unpublished dissertation of Herman Freudenberger, 'A Case Study of the Government's Role in Economic Development in the Eighteenth Century: The Brno Fine-Cloth Factory' (Columbia University, 1957).

[2] Max Barkhausen, 'Staatliche Wirtschaftslenkung und freies Unternehmertum im westdeutschen und in nord und südniederländischen Raum bei der Entstehung der neuzeitlichen Industrie im 18. Jahrhundert', *Vierteljahrschrift für Sozial- und Wirtschaftsgeschichte*, XLV (1958), 234, 239. An important article.

[3] Cf. C. Schmidt, 'Une enquête sur la draperie à Sedan en 1803', *Revue d'histoire des doctrines économiques et sociales*, V (1912), 100, 103; A. Crapet, 'L'industrie dans la Flandre wallonne à la fin de l'Ancien Régime', *Revue d'histoire moderne*, XII (1909), 28.

rising. On the contrary, the growth of population was outstripping that of industry and giving rise in some areas to the kind of pauperized rural proletariat that is a signpost of economic backwardness. Some of the strongest opponents of mechanization in the late eighteenth century were officials and peasants who feared that increased productivity would reduce thousands to unemployment and starvation. There was still room to expand industry in the burgeoning villages of Flanders, the Limburg, Saxony, and Bohemia-Moravia. In the last-named area, to take one example, the number of wool weavers rose from 12,700 to 24,800 between 1775 and 1788/9, while spinners more than doubled, increasing from 26,400 to 59,000; taken together, they represented 1 in every 90 persons at the earlier date, 1 in 50 at the later.[1] Similarly, the very slowness of certain technological changes is negative evidence of abundant labour: in France, the spinning wheel did not widely displace the distaff until the middle of the eighteenth century;[2] in Flanders, it was only in the early years of the nineteenth century that Liévin Bauwens introduced the fly-shuttle into the cotton industry of Ghent.

How long growth could have continued without necessitating a change in technique is another matter. Yet the issue is an idle one, for the continental countries did not have the opportunity to work out their own destinies. The changes across the Channel drastically changed their economic and political situation. For private enterprise, the immediate effects were frightening: traditional domestic industries, wherever they were unprotected, began to smother under the weight of cheap British goods. By the same token, exporters found their competitive position in international trade gravely undermined; and while most were reconciled by this time to seeing English manufactures win a privileged position in overseas markets, they were not prepared to

[1] H. Freudenberger, 'The Woollen-Goods Industry of the Habsburg Monarchy in the Eighteenth Century: a Case Study in Development', *J. Econ. Hist.* xx (1960). This increase gave rise, however, to institutional bottlenecks. In spite of the readiness of individual lords to allow manufacturers to hire serfs on their estates, the inability of the rural population to move toward work made impossible the swollen villages that had characterized East Anglia and Lancashire. Manufacturers began to compete for labour, wages went up, and the state attempted to ease the pressure by allotting regions to each establishment. So long as serfdom prevailed, however, concentrated factory production was unfeasible. In 1781 the state recognized the nature of the problem and declared that the abolition of serfdom would 'usefully influence the improvement of agriculture and industry'. A. Klima, 'Industrial Development in Bohemia, 1648–1781', *Past and Present*, no. 11 (1957), 96–7.

[2] Cf. P. Leuilliot, 'Commerce et industrie en Europe du XVIe au XVIIIe siècle; les industries textiles; problèmes généraux et orientation des recherches', in Comitato Internazionale di Scienze Storiche, X Congresso Internazionale di Scienze Storiche, *Relazioni*, vol. IV: *Storia Moderna* (Florence, n.d. [1955]), 287.

abandon the struggle entirely. Moreover change had its positive attractions; the British had opened a mine of profit for all the world to see.

For the state, British progress was a direct, unavoidable challenge. The governments of Europe had long come to look upon economic development as the key to a favourable balance of trade—hence wealth; to large tax revenues—hence power; and to stable employment—hence public order. They had traditionally encouraged enterprise as best they knew, cherishing especially those trades that furnish the means of war. Now they found the entire balance of economic forces upset. Industrialization was, from the start, a political imperative.

Admiration of British performance was one thing, however; emulation, another. The same objective obstacles to industrial expansion and technological change remained, aggravated in some respects by the nature of the innovations across the Channel. Thus Britain's advantage in industrial resources was greater than ever, now that cotton, a material of overseas origin, replaced wool as the chief textile fibre, and coal replaced wood as the main source of fuel. The continental countries not only had too little coal. What they had was widely dispersed, usually at a distance from associated raw materials like iron and, more often than not, of the wrong kind. France, for example, had little coking coal to begin with and has discovered little since. The rich deposits of the Ruhr were as yet unsuspected. Only in Belgium and Silesia were there known to be substantial, accessible coal measures, and in both places, particularly in Silesia, oil content was too high; the coke obtained was friable and not suited to furnaces above a certain size.

More than ever, therefore, the producers of the Continent found themselves confined by cost disadvantages to home consumers; and now the problem of scale was more acute as a result of the higher productive capacity of the new equipment. The old geographical and social limitations on demand were still there, and the same abundance of untapped rural labour that had made possible the expansion of the pre-factory period now acted as a deterrent to mechanization and concentration. Moreover, the lack of requisite technical skills posed an obstacle to innovation that only time could overcome.

Actually, time seemed to work at first against the continental economies. In France, a bare handful of cotton mills were built in the 1770's and 1780's, using jennies and water frames; one official estimated at 900 the total number of jennies in the entire country in 1790. Clearly mechanization was proceeding far more slowly than in Britain. The pace may have quickened, however, as a result of the Eden treaty of 1786, which opened the French market to British cottons and made modernization a matter of survival.

In metallurgy, the government promoted efforts to learn and apply the technique of coke smelting. William Wilkinson, ironmaster of Bersham, was brought over to act as technical adviser; it was he who suggested Le Creusot as a promising site, and it was there in 1785, in a furnace apparently built to his specifications, that Ignace de Wendel produced the first coke-blast iron on the Continent. For the moment, however, he had no imitators. Nor did anyone attempt to introduce Cort's puddling and rolling processes for another generation. French metallurgy was growing in scale but changing little in technique.

Le Creusot was also the first place in France to use the rotative steam-engine—one in 1784 to drive the hammers of the forge, in addition to four other Watt-type machines for pumping the mines and blowing the furnaces.[1] But in this too it was exceptional. Elsewhere the steam-engine, particularly the separate-condenser type, was a curiosity. On the other hand, it was in large measure a French-built curiosity (beginning in 1780–1, the brothers Perier were constructing *pompes à feu* at their works at Chaillot just outside of Paris), and this was in itself a major technological advance.

The other continental countries were even slower to change. The first German cotton-spinning mill, using Arkwright's water frame, was established in 1794 in a village appropriately named Kromford, east of Düsseldorf. In Saxony, the frame and mule came in just before the turn of the century; in the Low Countries (Verviers and Ghent) slightly later. In metallurgy, it was Silesia that took the lead, thanks to the pertinacity of Reden and the financial support of the Prussian government; the resemblance to the French experience is striking. The first coke-blast iron was tapped in 1791–2 from a charcoal furnace in the royal works at Malapane, and in 1794–6 a true coke-blast furnace was built at Gleiwitz by a Scots engineer named John Baildon (formerly employed at Carron) and two gifted German technicians, Bogatsch and Wedding. Similar attempts in western Germany, beginning in the 1760's in the Saar, were unsuccessful.[2] The Low Countries, by contrast, seem to have done little in this sphere before the 1820's.[3]

---

[1] The first atmospheric engine to be used in France had been installed at the Fresnes coal-mine near Condé (Nord) in 1732. The second came at Anzin in 1737; the third at Littry in Normandy in 1749. For purposes of comparison, around 1765 there were 127 atmospheric engines in the Newcastle district alone. Jean Chevalier, 'La mission de Gabriel Jars dans les mines et les usines britanniques en 1764', *Trans. Newcomen Soc.* XXVI (1947/8 and 1948/9), 59, 67.

[2] These were financed by Prince Wilhelm Heinrich of Nassau-Saarbrücken. The ore smelted well, but the iron produced was of poor quality, and the death of the Prince in 1768 put an end to the experiment. Beck, *Geschichte des Eisens*, III, 985–6.

[3] Pierre Lebrun, 'La rivoluzione industriale in Belgio: Strutturazione e destrutturazione delle economie regionali', *Studi storici*, II (1961) [special number: Studi sulla rivoluzione industriale], 610, mentions one brief attempt in the Liégeois.

In engineering the story was reversed: here the long experience of the Walloons in metal work enabled them to become machine builders to Europe. The first Newcomen engine on the Continent was erected in Liège in 1720-1, and by the middle of the century the ironworks of the vicinity were making copies for the Hainaut and other nearby mining districts. No area in Europe took so quickly to steam: in the period to 1790, thirty-nine atmospheric engines were installed in the Mons basin, and twenty of these were still operating at that date.[1] As these figures show, the adoption of steam power in the Low Countries was closely linked to the needs of mining. Thus the Liégeois, where the nature of the coal deposits permitted drainage by adit, exported its engines and made use of only a few in its own pits. As for other industries, neither the techniques employed nor the scale of manufacture called for more power than the water wheel could provide. Hence the slow adoption of the Watt engine: the first, a single-acting model, seems to have been introduced in the late 1780's, and the first rotative machine may well be the one imported by Bauwens around 1801 for his mule-spinning mill in Ghent.[2]

We know something of one of the peripatetic mechanics of Liège, Jean Wasseige, whose career in the 'Austrasian coal field' (that complex of deposits which extends from the Pas-de-Calais in northern France through Belgium to the Ruhr) covered almost the entire second half of the eighteenth century:[3] in 1751 he built what may well have been Germany's first steam-engine, for a lead mine near Düsseldorf; thirty-five years later, he is mentioned as installing a machine at Eschweiler (near Aachen).[4] He and others like him were carrying on the old

[1] Pierre Lebrun, ibid. pp. 625 f., 637.

[2] On a Watt machine installed in a mine at Produits 'fifty years ago', see N. Briavoinne, De l'industrie en Belgique (Brussels, 1839), p. 240. On the first rotative engine, Jan Dhondt, 'L'industrie cotonnière gantoise à l'époque française', Revue d'histoire moderne et contemporaine, II (1955), 241 and n. 2. This seems to correct Briavoinne, Sur les inventions et perfectionnemens dans l'industrie, depuis la fin du XVIIIe siècle jusqu'à nos jours [Mémoires couronnés par l'Académie Royale des Sciences et Belle-Lettres de Bruxelles, Série in-4°, vol. XIII] (Brussels, 1838), pp. 35–6. Toilliez, 'Mémoire' [see p. 359, n. 1, above], pp. 52 f., shows that for an area specializing in coal-mining like the Hainaut, the wasteful but simple Newcomen engine was preferred to the Watt machine well into the nineteenth century.

[3] For the definition and concept of the Austrasian field, see E. A. Wrigley, Industrial Growth and Population Change (Cambridge, 1961); also the older, but still valuable, book by Guy Greer, The Ruhr-Lorraine Industrial Problem (New York, 1925).

[4] Beck, Geschichte des Eisens, III, 984, is in error when he calls the steam-engine at Griesborn (1773) the first steam mine pump in what was later Germany. (Griesborn was then in Lorraine.) On the Düsseldorf engine, see Irmgard Lange-Kothe, 'Die Einführung der Dampfmaschine in die Eisenindustrie des rheinisch-westfälischen Industriegebietes', Stahl und Eisen, LXXXII (1962), 1669.

tradition of an international community of skilled craftsmen and technicians and anticipating the heavy contribution that Belgium was to make to the industrialization of Germany in the nineteenth century.

In spite of Belgian and British assistance, however, Germany made relatively little use of steam in this period. By the turn of the century, 'a few' Newcomen machines were operating and even fewer Watt engines. The first of these was erected by order of that extraordinary technocrat Reden, at Tarnowitz (Silesia) in 1788; and after an initial failure in 1785, a second was set to work near Mansfeld (Province of Saxony) in 1789.[1] Both used cylinders and other parts of English manufacture. Not until 1791 did German engineers succeed in building a machine in its entirety. It was a Newcomen engine, ordered in 1788 by the Freiherr von Stein from Silesia for use in the Ruhr and completed in 1791. By the time the parts made their way down the Oder, through the Baltic and North seas to Amsterdam, and up the Rhine to Ruhrort in 1792, the mine they were destined for no longer wanted them. They lay in storage eight years, until the Freiherr von Romberg decided to buy them and erect the engine at the Vollmond mine, near Bochum. This was the pre-Homeric age of industrial Germany, when steam-engines made odysseys and became subjects of fable to subsequent generations.[2]

At this point, the course of technological advance on the Continent encountered a political roadblock—the series of upheavals and wars that began with the French Revolution and ended with Waterloo. They brought with them capital destruction and losses of manpower; political instability and a widespread social anxiety; the decimation of the wealthier entrepreneurial groups;[3] all manner of interruptions to trade; violent inflations and alterations of currency. Above all, they cut

[1] On Reden, see W. O. Henderson, *The State and the Industrial Revolution in Prussia, 1740–1870* (Liverpool, 1958), ch. 1; on the Mansfeld engine, Lange-Kothe, 'Die Einführung', p. 1671.

[2] Lange-Kothe, 'Die Odyssee der ältesten Dampfmaschine des Ruhrgebietes', *Der Ausschnitt*, VII (1955), 24–6. The new and important researches of Miss Lange-Kothe have turned up a whole array of myths and misconceptions about the pre-history of German steam power. See her article on 'Johann Dinnendahl', *Tradition*, VII (1962), 32–46, 175–96.

[3] Pecuniarily, as a result of business fluctuations, interruptions of trade, and destruction of capital: and sometimes physically, for political reasons. Cf. P. Masson, ed., *Les Bouches-du-Rhône: encyclopédie départementale* (16 vols.; Marseilles, 1913–38), IX, 7–21, for the effects of the Terror in Marseilles; Schmidt, 'Une enquête sur la draperie à Sedan en 1803', *Revue d'histoire des doctrines économiques et sociales*, V (1913), 99, for the purge at Sedan. Or consider the disruptive effects of proscription and exile on such enterprises as the Wendel iron-works in Lorraine. Arch. Hayange, *passim.*

continental Europe off, sometimes by formal restrictions, from active intercourse with Britain and did more than anything else, certainly more than the British embargo on the emigration of artisans and export of machinery, to hinder the diffusion of the new techniques across the Channel.

Some areas were more seriously affected than others. In the beginning, it was France who suffered the most. Her economy, already weakened by the commercial treaty of 1786 with England and by the financial disorder of the monarchy, was racked between the requirements of a revolutionary government at war with enemies without and within and a general withdrawal of confidence by producers in all sectors. Internally, the demand for quality manufactures fell precipitately; abroad, she was deprived of almost all her foreign and colonial markets. In the decade following 1789, the output of some of her major textile centres fell by a half and more; only cotton seems to have held up, in part no doubt as an inferior good. Even metallurgy, which benefited from the increased demand for arms, seems to have declined: the make of pig iron was probably not much greater in 1815 than in 1789, in spite of a distinct rise during the Empire. Some parts of France, notably the west and south-west, underwent during these years what François Crouzet has called a process of pastoralization, from which they have never recovered.[1]

From the late 1790's on, the fortunes of politics changed. Now the states of northern Italy and central Europe bore the brunt of the fighting; they were the scene of combat, the source of much loot and continuing levies; the French discriminated against their economies in favour of the Empire; their governments were disrupted and too demoralized to continue their programmes of development. Yet even France, profiting from the spoils of war and the commercial advantages of 'imperial preference' and beneficiary of the most solicitous economic paternalism, lost ground in the long run. Commerce was naturally hardest hit: the Atlantic trade was never to be the same again. But industry also suffered: the cotton manufacture, which had expanded with spectacular rapidity, collapsed in the depression of 1810–12; wool advanced, but no more and probably less than it would have under conditions of peace; ironmaking grew in capacity but changed little in technique—there was no coke smelting or puddling, and only some isolated uses of rolling for the production of special shapes; the steam-engine was neglected.

With government assistance, a few industrial giants arose—Richard

[1] See his informative article, 'Les conséquences économiques de la Révolution: à propos d'un inédit de Sir Francis d'Ivernois', *Annales historiques de la Révolution française*, XXXIV (1962), 182–217.

Lenoir and Liévin Bauwens in cotton, Douglas in machine construction—but like the hothouse creations of the *ancien régime*, they shrivelled in the first winds of adversity. In general, the tendency to rely on state aid and protection, already excessive, was aggravated by this experience. The last five years of the Empire were years of spasmodic crisis that left the economy much enfeebled and momentarily helpless to meet the rush of cheap British products that came with peace.

To be sure, war and isolation had some favourable effects, at least prima facie. Technology, for example, was stimulated by the need to create substitutes for overseas imports; thus the invention of beet sugar and the spread of the Leblanc soda process. Similarly, the need and opportunity to increase rapidly the output of certain commodities encouraged mechanization, as in the woollen manufacture of Verviers and the cotton industry of Saxony. Here indeed were the greatest beneficiaries of the 'new order'—those small industrial states long locked in a tight tariff cage and now released into the huge spaces of Napoleon's Europe.

Yet it would be fallacious to assume that even these advances were a contribution to long-run development. They were the products of economic distortion, and if some, like the Leblanc technique, were fundamentally sound, others were unviable in normal circumstances. The trouble was that not all of these wartime anomalies were ready to disappear once peace returned. For every substitute that died quietly, like the woad of Languedoc, another remained as a vested interest and a burden on the consumer or taxpayer. Thus mechanized textile manufacture in central Europe, essentially a product of wartime shortages, made a strong effort to convert momentary advantage into permanent privilege, with some success; and one may reasonably attribute much of the persistent backwardness of the cotton industry in a region like Saxony to the legacy of small-scale primitive plant inherited from the period of the continental blockade.

More helpful in the long run were certain changes in the institutional climate of enterprise. In particular, traditional restraints on the mobility of capital and labour were removed or so undermined as to be incapable of blocking innovation further. Admittedly these restraints, as embodied in the corporate organization of production or, in central Europe, in the formal attribution to the various classes of society of functions and of legitimate objects of investment and expenditure, were already moribund before the Revolution. They were incompatible with the leading trends in economic life: the rise of a new industry like cotton, the spread of production into rural areas, the growing interest of the aristocracy in the possibilities of business investment, the shift toward freer enterprise and *laissez-faire*. The Revolution, however, hastened this movement, and in some areas consummated it. In France the Loi Le Chapelier of 1791 abolished the guilds, and the subsequent triumphs of the revolutionary and imperial armies brought these principles of free enterprise into the Low Countries, western Germany, and northern Italy. Where the French did not impose their institutions directly, the state was sometimes moved by French influence or success to take independent action: thus the reforms of Stein in Prussia, which were aimed not only at freeing the peasant from corporal and pecuniary servitudes (with obvious implications for the supply of industrial labour), but at opening the great mass of occupations to all comers and removing restraints on the movement of capital.

However introduced, freedom was contagious. In subsequent decades, all the lesser states of western and central Europe succeeded in eliminating this political expression of medieval economic and social values—despite tenacious opposition from craftsmen whose numbers and prosperity were often increasing as a result of overall economic growth.[1]

So much for the direct consequences of the Revolutionary upheaval. More important in the long run were the secondary effects of the delay. In particular, the gap between continental and British industrial equipment had increased, and while such a spread may mean in theory a greater incentive to modernization, it constituted in fact an obstacle.

Already under the Empire, best practice had long passed the stage of the jenny shop or garret factory. The few technicians, mostly British, who were capable of constructing textile machinery, were asking anywhere from 7500 to 12,000 francs for an 'assortment' of the equipment required for yarn manufacture, including four spinning devices (probably mules of 80 spindles each, operable by animal power, of the type used in Britain in the 1780's).[2] By the 1820's, however, the mule had become a long machine of up to a thousand spindles, workable only by steam or water power and costing more than a thousand pounds.

[1] For a general discussion of the consequences of the Revolutionary and Napoleonic wars for economic development in Western Europe, see F. Crouzet, 'Wars, Blockade, and Economic Change in Europe, 1792–1815', *J. Econ. Hist.* xxiv (1964), 567–88; also E. Labrousse, 'Eléments d'un bilan économique: la croissance dans la guerre', in Comité International des Sciences Historiques, Vienne, 29 août–5 septembre 1965, *Rapports*, I: *Grands thèmes* (Vienna, n.d.), 493–7.

[2] Of the three cotton mills founded in Ghent in 1805, one cost 80,000 fr. (about 550 spindles), another 90,000 fr. (about 600 spindles), and the third 400,000 fr. (about 2000 spindles). Dhondt, 'L'industrie cotonnière', *Revue d'histoire Moderne*, II (1955), 244–5. It is not clear that some of this did not in fact pay for post-spinning (weaving, finishing) equipment.

Blast furnace, puddling furnace, rolling mill, and coke oven had all grown in size; the story was the same in chemicals. Even where important capital-saving improvements had occurred—as in the case of the steam-engine, thanks to changes in design and the techniques of metal working—the increased scale of the other stages of the industrial process more than compensated by pushing up the size of the minimal effective unit. The early factory steam-engines were often of 6 and 8 h.p.; by the 1820's, machines of 50 h.p. and more were not uncommon.[1]

There are two points to note here. First, increased capacity meant that the latest equipment was sometimes less suitable to the post-Waterloo continental market than the rudimentary pre-Revolutionary machinery. After all, although legislation and decree had removed many of the man-made barriers to trade, central Europe still remained in 1815 a patchwork, and the fundamental topographical obstacles were yet to be overcome. Nor was the consumption pattern significantly different, though effective domestic demand was certainly larger.[2] As for outlets abroad, not only was the higher cost of materials on the Continent a continued bar to export, but Britain had made use of the war years, as noted above, to enter the preserves of her blockaded continental rivals (France and Holland, primarily), destroy their shipping, and ruin their merchants—all the while building up her own connections in South America, Africa, and the Orient. As a result, markets remained small. The potential yield of the most efficient production

[1] It seems likely that as a result of improvements in the techniques of machine-building and economies of scale in the engineering trades, the ratio of capital to real output in textile manufacture fell rapidly from the Napoleonic period to the 1830's and then tended to level off. Witnesses before the tariff inquiry of 1834 estimated the initial cost of spinning plant at 32 francs per spindle; in 1860, at from 40 to 55 francs. (Of course, output per spindle had increased in the meantime.) The English experience was probably similar. Mark Blaug, 'The Productivity of Capital in the Lancashire Cotton Industry during the Nineteenth Century', *Econ. Hist. Rev.* 2nd ser. XIII (1961), 359, has the ratio of total capital to net output rising from 2·0 in 1834 to 3·3 in 1860. The important point for us, however, is not so much the efficiency of capital as the minimal competitive investment required. And this depended, not only on the production function and relative factor costs, but also on the schedule of returns to scale and the size of competitive units of production—both machines and plant as a whole. From this point of view, best practice became far more costly as time passed.
[2] If only as a result of the increase in population, which grew in a country like France, in spite of the losses and dislocation of revolution and war, from about 26 to over 29 millions. For what they are worth, estimates of French national product indicate an even faster rate of growth, from 6,100,000,000 to 8,290,000,000 francs at current prices. Perroux, 'Prise de vues sur la croissance de l'économie française, 1780–1950', *Income and Wealth*, Series V, p. 61. The reader should treat such figures as gross indicators of direction.

methods was thus lower on the mainland, and the marginal gain over less capital-intensive techniques correspondingly smaller.[1]

Second—rate of return aside—the size of the initial lump of investment now required was itself an obstacle to change. Not only was it often beyond the reach of the small, prudent, self-financed family enterprise, but even those that could raise the money were reluctant to sink so much of their capital at one stroke. What we have here in effect is the well-known phenomenon of the differential evaluation of deprivation and incremental income: it was usually far more painful to contemplate the loss of a large fraction of the family's wealth than it was agreeable to envisage increasing the firm's income by some conjectural amount.

As a result, the mechanization of continental industry in the post-Napoleonic period did not follow the usual model that correlates newness and modernity. The bulk of the entrepreneurs of France, Belgium, and Germany did not take advantage of their opportunity to install the latest equipment and surpass the British in productivity. Rather they chose to invest in plants less efficient and *often less remunerative* than the best available. Many made do with used machines, and indeed there came to be a regular flow of used equipment from the richer, more advanced centres of manufacture to the more backward areas, with many pieces passing through several avatars on the way to the scrap heap. This voluntary obsolescence, in so far as it exceeded the dictates of the production functions and relative factor costs, helped maintain Britain's competitive advantage in third markets, confirmed many continental industrialists in their sense of inferiority, and reinforced the pressure for those artificial devices, such as prohibitive tariffs, which solved the immediate problem of economic survival at the expense of long-run growth.

On balance, then, emulation of Britain was probably harder after Waterloo than before. The gap in technique had widened, while most of the fundamental educational, economic, and social obstacles to imitation remained. The story of the generation after 1815 is in large measure the elimination or diminution of these, in part by state action, even more by private entrepreneurial effort.

The most immediate difficulty was technological ignorance: continental industry needed mechanics as much as machines. In the early years, while a native cadre of technicians was being formed and a

---

[1] The more so because the newer as well as the older models of industrial equipment were essentially labour-saving rather than capital-saving; the later steam-engines were a notable exception.

machine-construction industry developed, the continental countries imported skills and equipment from abroad, at first from Britain, with time, from secondary centres like Belgium and France as well. Indeed, the Industrial Revolution is an excellent case study—one of the best documented on record—of the larger phenomenon of cultural diffusion.

The transfer of techniques was not easy. Aside from the alleged shortcomings of the pupils (and the sources have an abundance of references to the awkwardness and incompetence of continental labour), the teachers were not always free to move or bring their paraphernalia with them. The emigration of British artisans was forbidden until 1825; the export of what appeared to be the most valuable types of machinery —in particular, the major textile inventions and parts and plans thereof —until 1842.[1] Yet there were so many loopholes and the ingenuity of smugglers and industrial spies was such, that these efforts were in the long run unavailing. By 1825 there must have been two thousand— and perhaps more—skilled British workers on the Continent. Similarly, while we will never know precisely how much machinery crossed the Channel illicitly, legitimate exports (by special licence of the Treasury) amounted to £600,000 (official value) in 1840 alone; the sources on the continental countries are full of evidence of the successful purchase and installation of British equipment.

The best of the British technicians to go abroad were usually entre-preneurs in their own right, or eventually became industrialists with the assistance of continental associates or government subventions. Many of them came to be leaders of their respective trades: one thinks of the Waddingtons (cotton), Job Dixon (machine-building), and James Jackson (steel) in France; James Cockerill (machine con-struction) and William Mulvany (mining) in Germany; Thomas Wilson (cotton) in Holland; Norman Douglas (cotton) and Edward Thomas (iron and engineering) in the Austrian empire; above all, John Cockerill in Belgium, an aggressive, shrewd businessman of supple ethical standards, who took all manufacturing as his province and with

[1] Paradoxically, steam-engines and machine tools were permitted to be exported by special licence—the former, because they were considered 'only a moving power', and not machines; the latter because it was felt to be impracticable to discriminate between tools used for the manufacture of machines and those used for other pur-poses. See the testimony of J. D. Hume in the 'First Report of the Select Committee ...Exportation of Machinery', *Parl. Papers*, 1841, VII, p. 5. Q. 17. The export of otherwise prohibited machinery by licence of the Board of Trade began some time before 1825—the parliamentary inquiry of that year could not ascertain the origin of the practice, its basis in law, or the extent to which it had been carried. *Ibid.* Second Report, p. iv.

the assistance of first the Dutch and then the Belgian governments made a career of exploiting the innovations of others.[1]

Some of these immigrants were early examples of what we today would call business executives, combining managerial and technical skills: thus John Maberley, who in 1838 became director of a joint-stock company to build flax-spinning machinery at Amiens; or in a later period, Charles Brown, who directed the machine shops of the Sulzer firm at Winterthur. Most, however, were simply foremen or skilled craftsmen. They were a costly investment, especially since many were not at all prepared to stay long enough for the employer to amortize the initial expense of bringing them over. In view of the size of this original outlay, manufacturers had a strong incentive to hire such workers away from competitors; the sources are full of complaints about such 'dishonest' practices. In this way, the high salaries originally promised were pushed higher, to the intense discomfort of employers, who not only found this a heavy levy on their purses but also learned that better pay often meant less rather than more work. Most of these technicians were used on jobs where they set their own pace; often they were paid by time rather than output; and many placed a high premium on leisure—the more so since they were generally homesick, unhappy, and prone to drown their sorrows in alcohol. They had a keen sense of their indispensability, and this combined with national pride to make them arrogant and fractious.

Thus in 1824 François de Wendel, ironmaster at Hayange and Moyeuvre in Lorraine, sent the chief of his English workmen back to Britain to bring back some technical information, two more of his countrymen, and the wives of those who were already employed. When his return was delayed, Wendel wrote him a letter, the rough copy of which has come down to us: 'I have received you letter from febr your absence me nuit beaucoup je paye your worckmans [?] and they do not worck the carpentar is an ivrogne, one can not employe him. I believe it is better for you to kom and to remaine her;...'[2] Small wonder that industrialists like Fritz Harkort, pioneer of the German engineering industry, could not wait for the day when German moulders were trained, 'so that the Englishmen could all be whipped out [herausgepeitscht]: we must even now tread softly with them, for

---

[1] The most convenient source is W. O. Henderson, *Britain and Industrial Europe*, 1750–1870 (Liverpool, 1954). Of the many specialized articles, see the interesting case study of Paul Leuilliot, 'Contribution à l'histoire de l'introduction du machinisme en France: la "Biographie industrielle" de F. C. L. Albert (1764–1831)', *Annales historiques de la Révolution française*, XXIX (1952), 3–22.

[2] Archives. Les Petits-Fils de François de Wendel et Cie, Hayange, Carton 856.

they're only too quick to speak of quitting if one does so little as not look at them in a friendly fashion'.[1]

The day came. Perhaps the greatest contribution of these immigrants was not what they did but what they taught. Employers or employees, they.trained a generation of skilled workers, many of whom became entrepreneurs in their own right. Thus the Cockerill firm sold its machines as far east as Poland, and every *assortiment* brought with it a mechanic, to install the equipment and live on the job while instructing the customer in its operation and maintenance. Needless to say, some of these never returned to the home office. As continental technology improved and the stirrings of industrial revolution moved eastward and southward, the countries on the western edge of the land mass— Belgium and France in particular—served increasingly as reservoirs of capital and skills. This secondary flow was especially important from the 1840's on, not so much in manufacturing industry, however, as in the construction of railways, roads, canals, and bridges.[2]

The growing technological independence of the Continent resulted largely from man-to-man transmission of skills on the job. Of less immediate importance, though of greater consequence in the long run, was the formal training of mechanics and engineers in technical schools. France and Germany in particular created a veritable hierarchy of such institutions: on the highest level, the *Ecole Polytechnique* (and its graduate affiliates of *Mines* and *Ponts-et-Chaussées*), the Berliner *Gewerbe-Institut*, the Prussian *Hauptbergwerks-Institut*; a middle range of mechanical training schools, the *écoles des arts et métiers* in France and provincial *Gewerbeschulen* in Prussia; and at the bottom a heterogeneous group of local courses, sometimes private, sometimes public, in manual arts, design, and the rudiments of calculation.

Here the state made the major contribution. Initial costs were too high and pecuniary rewards too distant for private enterprise to do more than offer its benediction and support to those lower-level schools whose short courses were aimed at training people to go directly into

---

[1] Cited in Franz Schnabel, *Deutsche Geschichte im neunzehnten Jahrhundert* (4 vols.; Freiburg, various editions and dates), II (2nd ed.; 1954), 287. In later years, Harkort used to say: 'I had at that time to cut several of my Englishmen down from the gallows, so to speak, if only in order to get some of them.' L. Berger, *Der alte Harkort* (Leipzig, 1890), p. 153.

[2] On the contribution of the Belgians and French to German industry, particularly in the Rhineland, see B. Kuske, in H. Aubin, Th. Frings, *et al.*, *Geschichte des Rheinlandes von der ältesten Zeit bis zur Gegenwart* (2 vols.; Essen: Baedeker, 1922), II, 198–9; Jean R. Maréchal, 'La contribution des Belges et des Français à l'essor de la grande industrie allemande', *Rev. universelle des mines*, 8e ser. XIII (1937), 517–31; Rondo Cameron, 'Some French Contributions to the Industrial Development of Germany, 1840–1870', *J. Econ. Hist.* XVI (1956), 281–321.

the mills. Only the government could afford to send officials on costly tours of inspection as far away as the United States; provide the necessary buildings and equipment; feed, clothe, house, and in some cases pay students for a period of years. Moreover, these pedagogical institutions were only part—though the most important part—of a larger educational system designed to introduce the new techniques and diffuse them through the economy; there were also non-teaching academies, museums, and, most important perhaps, expositions. The importance of the last is hard to realize in this age of world fairs for tourism and propaganda. There were no midways or aquacades in these early industrial competitions. All was business, and the medals awarded were a source of profit as well as pride to the victorious firms. They were, in a way, a kind of advertising before the age of the penny paper and mass publicity. As a result, the expositions did much to stimulate technological emulation and diffuse knowledge. In this, their influence ran counter to a deep-rooted tradition of secrecy, the stronger for the ineffectiveness of patent protection and the depth of technological ignorance. The rarer the skills, the greater their value. There were clashes on this score, but the juries made clear by their awards that they did not like secretive firms.

Finally, the government provided technical advice and assistance, awarded subventions to inventors and immigrant entrepreneurs, bestowed gifts of machinery, allowed rebates and exemptions of duties on imports of industrial equipment. Some of this was simply a continuation of the past—a heritage of the strong tradition of direct state interest in economic development. Much of it, in Germany particularly, was symptomatic of a passionate desire to organize and hasten the process of catching up.

In so far as this promotional effort stressed the establishment of rational standards of research and industrial performance, it was of the greatest significance for the future. At the middle of the century, technology was still essentially empirical and on-the-job training was in most cases the most effective method of communicating skills. But once science began to anticipate technique—and it was already doing so to some extent in the 1850's—formal education became a major industrial resource and the continental countries saw what had once been compensation for a handicap turned into a significant differential asset.[1]

---

[1] The cultivation of systematic instruction as a cure for technological backwardness fits well into Professor Gerschenkron's model, which postulates the establishment of private financial institutions or—under circumstances of severe retardation—the intervention of the state to mobilize capital for economic development. See his 'Economic Backwardness in Historical Perspective', in B. Hoselitz, ed., *The Progress of Underdeveloped Areas* (Chicago, 1951), recently reprinted in A. Gerschenkron,

It was not enough, of course, to bring techniques and technicians over from Britain; they would have remained curiosities had there not been a growing demand for them. Indeed this marked the main point of contrast between the eighteenth and nineteenth centuries: where before the government had been preaching in a kind of wilderness and had been obliged to take upon itself the task of implanting some of the new methods, it now faced a sympathetic business community moving ahead in its own right, to the point of anticipating the state and exploiting its resources.

In explaining this change, it is useful to distinguish between those factors that were essentially a continuation of eighteenth-century forces— though writ larger—and those that were new. Thus, as noted earlier, much of this heightened entrepreneurial interest in industrial development was part of a general process of growth: of accumulation of capital, of increasing demand, of the imbalances consequent on growth, of the contact with the British example. The rise in population was an important part of this story: it seems clear, in spite of the lack of census figures, that numbers were already mounting steadily in the eighteenth century; in the nineteenth they rose even more sharply—in France, from about 27·5 million in 1801 to 34 million in 1850; in Germany, from about 23·5 million in 1810 to 33·5 million in 1850; in Belgium from perhaps 3 million to 4·3 million in the same period.

On the other hand, changes in the economic and institutional environment after 1815 gave a strong push to this long-term rise in demand for manufactures and supply of the factors of production. On the demand side, the internal unification of national markets was substantially completed in western Europe by the formation of the German *Zollverein*: the long lines of wagons waiting through the cold night for the toll gates to open on the New Year of 1834 were eloquent testimony to the new opportunities that opened with them.[1] Analogous, and less important only by comparison, was the opening of the Rhine mouth to German shipping after centuries of mercantilistic restrictions. These changes probably more than compensated for such tariff increases as occurred in the areas affected.[2]

All of western Europe, moreover, profited by improvements in

Economic Backwardness in Historical Perspective (Cambridge, Mass., 1962), pp. 5–30. A school system is in this sense simply a device for mobilizing and developing productive skills and knowledge.

[1] For France and what was to become Belgium, the task had been achieved before 1815. Indeed, for both of these, the end of the Empire was a step backward, a return to a smaller sphere. This was far more serious for Belgium, which was cut off from the bulk of its potential market; the injury was aggravated by the secession from Holland in 1830.

[2] The trend was more complicated than might appear at first glance. On the one

transportation. These took the form, first, of better channels for move-ment—this was a period of active road building, river work, and a cer-tain amount of canal construction; and second, of faster, more capacious vehicles. To some extent, the two went hand in hand: it was impossible to shift from pack animals (the main method of transport in most areas of the Continent) to wagons until roads were better; and the use of steamboats and steam barges required waterways of greater depth and dependability.

The railroad was a special case. Except in Belgium, whose major lines were completed by mid-century, and to a much smaller degree, Germany, which built an important part of its network by that time, the railroad did not significantly affect the structure of the market in this period. The economic gains from a transport system increase in a kinked line, with steep jumps in results when certain junctions are made; the key connections for western Europe were not made until the 1850's and 1860's.

In other respects, however, the impact of the railway on industry is not to be underestimated. In the short run, it created an unprecedented demand for iron (as well as wood, glass, leather, stone, and other sub-stances used in the manufacture of cars and construction of fixed facilities); moreover, it wanted these materials in a wide variety of finished forms, ranging from relatively simple items like rails and wheels to complicated engines and machines, all of which gave a special push to the metalworking and engineering trades. If to this we add the general effect of this huge investment on the demand for consumers' goods, it seems fair to say that by the 1840's railroad construction was the most important single stimulus to industrial growth in western Europe.

It is doubtful, however, whether the influence of railway demand on technology was as consistently favourable as on output. In so far as the railroad required new products, it promoted innovation; witness the growing ability to mould and manipulate large masses of metal. On the other hand, the increase in demand for traditional products like pig iron in markets sheltered from outside competition was often an invitation to easy expansion along old lines. The 1840's saw in both France and Germany an increase in the output of charcoal pig iron and wrought iron.[1]

hand, Prussian tariff rates tended effectively to rise through most of this period; on the other hand, all states joining the *Zollverein* were compelled to accept the Prussian tariff, which was usually lower than their own.

[1] The increase was smaller in Germany, which imported large amounts of Belgian and British coke-blast pig. From 1837 to 1850 output of charcoal pig in Prussia went from 87,449 to 98,521 metric tons (up 12·66%); charcoal wrought iron went during the decade 1837–47 from 39,092 tons to 45,841 (up 17·26%). Beck, *Geschichte des Eisens*, IV, 714–16. In France, the make of charcoal pig went from 246,000 metric

One can hardly imagine a major technological or institutional change in the economic environment affecting demand and not supply. Thus cheaper, faster transport meant cheaper materials and more mobile labour, as well as wider markets. It also was the equivalent of a substantial increase in entrepreneurial capital: funds once sunk in stocks of raw cotton or buried for months in warehouses until bulky iron products could move on thawed or flowing streams were now freed for investment in plant and equipment.[1] By the same token, the growth of population yielded more abundant manpower as well as a larger outlet for manufactures.

On the other hand, more people needed more food, and this rising demand for nourishment might well have necessitated in the long run a diversion of productive factors to agriculture and higher costs for industry. Fortunately, on the Continent as in Britain, new methods of cultivation and a revolution in land tenure increased the surface cultivated, the yield per unit area, and the productivity of the agricultural worker.[2] As a result, it was possible to feed a growing industrial force at constant or diminishing prices while releasing the surplus farm population for industrial employment.[3]

Finally, the provision of capital for industrial ventures increased substantially in this period. Part of this was simply an aspect of the rise in overall income; part was the fruit of rapid accumulation in industry— as in Britain, the enterprises of these early years financed themselves as much as possible out of earnings.

Changes in the credit structure, however, by easing the flow of capital, accounted for much of the gain. To begin with, the countries of the Continent began in this period—long after Britain—to develop national

tons in 1835 to 339,000 in 1847 (up 37·8%). During the same period, however, output of charcoal wrought iron remained about the same. France, Min. des Travaux Publics, *Statistique de l'industrie minérale* (1893), pl. 10; idem, *Résumé des travaux statistiques de l'Administration des Mines en 1847*, p. 13.

[1] For a good case study of the effects of transport difficulties on capital requirements, see some of the material in G. Thuillier, 'Fourchambault et la sidérurgie nivernaise de 1789 à 1900' (thesis: Institut d'Etudes Politiques, Paris [Th 1081], n.d.).

[2] Thus for a country like France wheat crops averaged 51,719,000 hectoliters (10·78 per hectare) from 1815 to 1824; 79,590,000 (13·68 per hectare) from 1841 to 1850—a rise of over 50%. Average potato crops over the same period went from 28,755,000 hectoliters to 71,329,000, a rise of 150%. Population, by contrast, went from 29,380,000 in 1815 to 35,630,000 in 1850. *Annuaire statistique*, xxv (1905), Résumé rétrospectif, pp. 10*, 32*–33*.

[3] Here, too, as in the case of railway demand, the effects were clearly more favourable to output than to technological change as such. It is interesting to speculate on what a sustained demand for manpower in agriculture would have done to relative factor costs in industry and thus to the rate of substitution of capital for labour. Compare the American experience and the implications of the frontier.

capital markets, that is, markets that bound together the major business centres and the provinces and allowed funds to flow from local industry and even agriculture into other areas of activity. Clearly, little of this investment went into manufacturing proper; the favourite placement was government bonds. Yet had it not been for this new source of mobile capital, *rentes* would have siphoned off much of the liquid capital potentially available to industry and trade. This is what happened in Austria, where the incessant demands and disorderly finances of an impecunious government made loan contracting and speculation in the funds so profitable that the merchant bankers of Vienna had no eyes for anything else. It took the railway, with its large appetite for metal and fuel, to win their attention and some of their resources from imperial finance to industry.

All of this, as the reader will have already remarked, implies that the supply of capital was limited. For all the controversy that still attends this point, this was certainly the case in the aggregate, as the heavy demands of railroad building made clear.[1] In France, the boom of the forties immobilized enormous sums—spasmodically, as syndicates assembled hundreds of millions of francs to bid against one another for concessions, then released the greater part of these monies once the award was made; and progressively, through these ups and downs, as one company after another began work. Both the money and capital markets were squeezed dry, and the anticipatory scare of 1845 became the collapse of 1846–7. Many of France's most solid enterprises found themselves on the brink of disaster because of funds frozen in railway shares—not only coal and iron firms, which stood to win sales by promoting construction, but textile mills and merchant banks as well. Bertrand Gille has even speculated that the poor harvest of 1846 owed something to the diversion of disposable funds from agriculture to railways.[2]

The hypothesis is worth careful investigation; at least this is what seems to have happened in Germany. There, Prussia and other states had established Landschaften as far back as the 1760's, to finance agricultural development by issuing mortgage bonds to the general public and lending the proceeds to landowners at low rates of interest.[3] Over

[1] On Germany, see the important article by Knut Borchardt, 'Zur Frage des Kapitalmangels in der ersten Hälfte des 19. Jahrhunderts in Deutschland', *Jahrbücher für Nationalökonomie und Statistik*, CLXXIII (1961), 401–21, which argues, in large part from the low rate of interest on funds and best commercial paper, that capital was relatively abundant.

[2] See the analysis in his *La banque et le crédit en France de 1815 à 1848* [Mémoires et documents publiés par la Société de l'Ecole des Chartes, vol. XIV] (Paris, 1959), pp. 349 ff., especially p. 358.

[3] Note, however, that some of the funds lent by Landschaften went to manu-

the years, tens of millions of thalers had been drawn in this way from the savings of the industrial and commercial sectors. In 1835, however, the volume of Pfandbriefe in circulation, which had more than doubled since the beginning of the century, stopped growing and remained about the same for a decade.[1]

It is obvious that, despite increased mobility of capital, the continental countries had less to work with than Britain. On the other hand, their very weaknesses in this area led them to an innovation that was to give them eventually a real advantage over their precursor: the joint-stock investment bank. The effectiveness of this institution lay in its combination of capital resources, larger by far than those of merchant or private banks, and great freedom of action. The pioneer here was Belgium, with its Société Générale and Banque de Belgique, both investors on a large scale in mining and heavy industry. The precocious development of the Belgian coal industry—in the 1840's the biggest on the Continent—and the efficiency of its iron and machine industries—the only ones able to compete to some extent with the British—owed much to this injection of outside capital.[2]

France and Germany accomplished less in this area, the former largely because of official hostility, the latter partly for that reason, partly because the very shortage of capital that called for such institutions was still too serious to permit their establishment. The French brought forth a number of substitutes in the form of joint-stock partnerships (the so-called *caisses*). Visionaries and businessmen of both countries talked excitedly of the need for credit banks to finance industrial development: propagandists like the Saint-Simonians and bankers like Jacques Laffitte in France; Mevissen, Camphausen, Hansemann, and the rest of their Rhenish circle in Germany. By the 1840's, the stage was set in both places for a financial revolution; owing to depression and political upset, however, it was not to come until the following decade.[3]

facturing enterprises borrowing on their land; and that some were invested by landowners in industry. Cf. Bergenroth, 'Ueber deutsche Anstalten zur Förderung des Kredits', *Zeitschrift des Vereins für deutsche Statistik*, I (1847), 753–4.

[1] Value of Pfandbriefe of Prussian Landschaften in circulation:

1805	53,891,638 thaler	1835	100,915,598 thaler
1815	62,677,898 thaler	1845	103,339,223 thaler
1825	83,141,365 thaler	1855	118,353,373 thaler

C. F. W. Dieterici, *Handbuch der Statistik des preussischen Staats* (Berlin, 1861), pp. 574–5. I am indebted to Prof. Hans Rosenberg for this reference.

[2] P. Schöller, 'La transformation économique de la Belgique de 1832 à 1844', *Bull. de l'Institut de Recherches Economiques et Sociales* (Louvain), XIV (1958), 525–96.

[3] See D. Landes, 'Vieille banque et banque nouvelle: la révolution financière du dix-neuvième siècle', *Revue d'histoire moderne et contemporaine*, III (1956), 204–22.

In the meantime, the scarcity of capital in France and Germany was eased by flows from two sources. There was, to begin with, a certain amount of government investment and subvention of the traditional variety. This was much diminished, however, especially in France, where the budget-balancing governments of the Monarchie Censitaire concentrated almost all of their development expenditures on public works. In Germany, the state gave more generously to industry. The most active agency in this regard was the Prussian Seehandlung, which, under the direction of Christian von Rother, invested not only in the seaborne trade covered by its nomenclature, but also in roads, railways, and a variety of manufacturing enterprises. It was the Seehandlung, for example, that financed in 1842 Prussia's first mill to weave worsted by power, at Wüste Giersdorf. By the 1840's this policy of industrial promotion was under sharp attack, on the grounds that it was prejudicial to unsubsidized private enterprise and that it did not pay. The last reproach was true enough, although Rother argued that an official institute of this kind, whose primary aim was national development, should not be judged by ordinary criteria of profit and loss. Nevertheless, under pecuniary and political pressures, the See-handlung divested itself of almost all its industrial holdings by the mid-1850's.[1]

The Belgian pattern was closer to the German than to the French. In the Dutch period especially, the government gave generously to private industry, partly through a special Industrial Fund, partly through such corporate organisms as the Société Générale, already mentioned, and the Nederlandsche Handel Maatschappij. In the years from 1824 to 1830, the Fund lent 5,821,052 florins to shipbuilding. About four-fifths of the money went to the Belgian provinces.[2] This solicitude was moti-vated largely by political considerations: the government was anxious to placate the south, whose nationalistic resentment of Dutch rule was exacerbated by commercial policies more favourable to the trade of Holland than to the industry of Wallonia and Flanders.

After 1830 the flow of direct subsidies and investments continued, though less abundant than before. The new government made a special effort to assist the cotton and linen industries, both suffering from the competition of cheap British textiles. In general, however, the regime reacted sharply against the irregularities that had marked the manage-ment of the Industrial Fund and preferred to let private institutions like the Société Générale and the Banque de Belgique assume the burden of industrial finance.

[1] Henderson, *The State and the Industrial Revolution in Prussia*, ch. vii.
[2] R. Demoulin, *Guillaume I*ᵉʳ *et la transformation économique des provinces Belges, 1815–1830* (Liège and Paris, 1938), pp. 152 ff., 179.

It is always difficult to assess the contribution of such aids and sub-ventions. Where they furthered the growth of demonstrably successful enterprises—as with Cockerill in Belgium, Jackson in France, or the Egells machine shops in Berlin—they may well have hastened techno-logical change by freeing talented entrepreneurs from the limitations of impecuniosity. But too often, the state seems to have chosen the wrong enterprises or the wrong entrepreneurs and to have permitted by its assistance sloppy performance. And sometimes it was clearly on the side of reaction, as in Belgium, where hundreds of thousands of francs went to sustain an antiquated, unviable linen manufacture in the Flemish countryside.[1]

More useful, perhaps, in the long run, was the flow of funds from Britain to the Continent, which grew steadily as capital accumulated in the United Kingdom and reached a high point during the railway boom of the 1840's. Most of this went into government securities and public works, in France more than any other country. But substantial amounts went farther east, and these were augmented after a while by French and Belgian capital, attracted not only by higher returns but also by the abundant mineral resources of countries less experienced in the ways of industrial capitalism—witness the development of non-ferrous metal-lurgy in the Rhineland.

Unfortunately, we know relatively little as yet about these early capital movements. It seems clear, however, that they were more complex than one might think, and that there was a substantial amount of return investment from Germany and eastern Europe, particularly in the funds of western governments. Moreover, the criss-cross of flows, in so far as we can follow it, leaves the distinct impression that it was enterprise and opportunity that drew the capital rather than the reverse. Thus this same movement of German investment into British, French, and Belgian funds slowed down markedly once railway pro-motion and industrial development began competing for capital; whereas French investors and financiers—who early found it difficult to place their money in home enterprise owing to institutional and material limitations on growth and the repugnance of family entre-preneurs for outside assistance—were among the first and most active in financing the development of poorer nations to the east and south.

We may now turn to the technological evolution of the major industries on the Continent. Here, as before, we shall begin with the textile manufacture, although for reasons to be examined later, its

---

[1] Cf. G. Jacquemyns, *Histoire de la crise économique des Flandres, 1845–1850* (Brussels, 1929), pp. 173–93.

place in the overall transition to a factory system was less important on the mainland than in Britain.

Two preliminary remarks are in order. First, the sequence of technological change was different on the two sides of the Channel. Where in Britain the new machines spread in cotton far more rapidly than in wool, on the Continent the interruption of the supply of raw cotton during the Napoleonic period and the sharp increase in the military demand for woollen cloth temporarily reversed the order. It was two clothiers of Verviers who brought John Cockerill to the Low Countries to build spinning machinery; and it was the wool manufacturers of France, Spain, and the Germanies who bought the bulk of the equipment produced under the Empire by Cockerill and rivals like Douglas in Paris or Spineux in Liège. Within a decade after Waterloo, however, the return to peaceful trade relations and the natural susceptibility of the vegetable fibre to mechanical manipulation restored the cotton industry to its earlier technological pre-eminence. It was never to lose its lead again.

Second, there was nothing on the Continent comparable to the rapidity of British localization of manufacture in one, perhaps two, naturally advantaged centres: Lancashire and the Glasgow area in cotton; the West Riding of Yorkshire in woollen and worsted. In countries like France and Germany, the textile manufacture was highly dispersed to begin with. In the course of the nineteenth century, the transformation of technique and the triumph of factory manufacture were accompanied in each by a steady but slow localization of production in a handful of centres—not one, but three or four. The less efficient, smaller *fabriques*, moreover, proved surprisingly tenacious; it took a cotton famine, tariff changes, and the Great Depression of 1873–96 to kill even the weakest of them off. Finally, in so far as manufacture did thrive more in certain regions than in others, material advantages seem to have been a less important determinant of success than in Britain; human factors, especially entrepreneurship, played a decisive role.

In France the great bulk of the cotton industry lay north of the Loire. In 1815 there was still a major concentration of spindles and looms in Paris itself, but these firms faded quickly—the capital, with its high costs of land, labour, and raw materials, was no place for cotton mills.[1] By 1830 the map of the industry had taken on the appearance it was to keep for the rest of the century: heavy patches of enterprise in Normandy (centre Rouen), the North (Lille and Roubaix-Tourcoing), and

[1] See David Pinkey, 'Paris, capitale du coton sous le Premier Empire', *Annales: E.S.C.*, v (1950), 56–60.

the East (Alsace and the Vosges); and scattered dots throughout the rest of the country, with occasional clusters in places like Dauphiné or the Cholet area where cheap labour compensated somewhat for poor location and poor entrepreneurship.

Of the big three, the most progressive was Alsace, in particular the region around Mulhouse. There the industry grew out of cotton printing; the finished product was of high quality, competitive in foreign markets; the fortunes accumulated in this field, plus funds advanced by capitalists of Basel, enabled the entrepreneurs of the area to build large spinning and weaving mills almost from the start. More-over, the Mulhousian industrialist, usually a dedicated Calvinist of the Weberian type, early evinced considerable initiative in improving technique, especially the chemistry of dyes; this interest in rationalizing the finishing process carried over to the other stages of manufacture when the industry integrated backwards.

The Mulhousians began comparatively late—the first mill using mules and throstles was built apparently in 1802; the fly shuttle was unknown before 1805. Growth was rapid, however:

Table 2. *Cotton Manufacture: Department of the Haut-Rhin*

	Spindles	Hand looms	Power looms
1786	—	c. 1,900	—
1806	—	1,900	—
1809	24,000	—	—
1811	—	3,600	—
1812	48,000	—	—
1822	—	18–20,000	—
1826	—	30,000	—
1827	—	—	426
1828	466,000	—	—
1831	—	—	2,123
1834	—	31,000	3,090
1839	—	—	6,000
1844	—	19,000	12,000
1849	786,000	—	—
1856	—	8,657	18,139

SOURCES. Ch. Ballot, *L'introduction du machinisme dans l'industrie française* (Paris, 1923), pp. 150–2; A. Penot, 'Notes pour servir à l'histoire de l'industrie cotonnière dans le Haut-Rhin', *Bull. Soc. Indust. de Mulhouse*, XLIV (1874), 167–8.

As can be seen from the figures on hand and power looms, expansion and technological advance went hand in hand. In spinning the most rapid gains in productivity occurred between 1815 and 1830 (replace-ment of water frames and hand mules by power-driven mules), and from 1855 to 1870 (adoption of the self-actor); in weaving, it was the period in between that saw the decisive shift from hand looms to power. The timing reminds one of the alternating imbalance between spinning and weaving in the British cotton industry. The readiness of the Alsatian manufacturer to invest in up-to-date equipment owed much to the development of a creative local machine-construction industry. By the 1840's Mulhouse had become a centre of mechanical invention and was exporting mules and looms in competition with Britain throughout Europe.

In some ways, the pattern of development in the North was similar to that of Alsace: growth was impressively rapid; technology, well above average; entrepreneurship, dedicated and yet supple. Like his counterpart in the East, the northerner was a production man.

There were, however, important differences. The northerner was not so rich as the Alsatian: he had less wealth of his own, less access to the wealth of others, and was less willing to introduce foreign capital into the enterprise. The result was a smaller scale of production: where the average cotton mill in the Haut-Rhin counted 14,375 spindles in 1845, the figure for Lille in 1848 was 7,040; for Tourcoing in 1844, 4,000. Capacity for the department as a whole rose from about 112,000 spindles in 1818 to some 550,000 in 1849, of which 128,000 were in Roubaix and 60,000 in Tourcoing.

Technologically, the North was in some ways ahead of Alsace. Owing to the shortage of water, it was never able to use hydraulic power; there was hardly enough water even for the steam-engine, which did not come in until 1819. Nevertheless, there was clearly no alternative, and steam capacity rose faster than in the East. Similarly, the self-actor was introduced in Roubaix on a large scale in 1843—18,000 spindles in the plant of Motte-Bossut—and was starting to spread by mid-century. On the other hand, the weaving of cotton was somewhat neglected in the North, which exported most of its yarn to other parts of the country or twisted it into thread; as a result, the power loom was adopted quite late—there is evidence of a few around 1845, but they did not really come in until the mid-1850's.

The largest, yet most backward, of the major cotton centres was Normandy. It was the oldest and best located: convenient to the Paris market and overseas; rich in water power; close to the point of entry of the raw material. Rural labour was almost as cheap as in the North. As might be expected, however, these very advantages were a deterrent to technological change, the more so as they compensated, hence encouraged, a kind of inbred entrepreneurial conservatism. The *cotonniers* of the area were notorious for their penny-pinching and short-sighted avidity; the Alsatians looked down upon them as merchants and speculators rather than as industrialists. They were among the first groups to try the mule, yet were the slowest to improve their machines and replace them by later models. They were late in adopting steam power, primarily because water was so cheap, but also because steam-engines cost a lot of money and the Norman was reluctant to sink so much into his business. In 1847 there were still eighty-three mills in the area driven by hand or animal power; eighteen of these contained over ten thousand spindles each.[1] The use of such techniques had, so far as we know, disappeared in Alsace and the North. The availability of cheap water power was also a deterrent to innovation in other equipment; one of the reasons the self-actor was adopted so late—it was first coming in around 1860—was that it called for more power than water wheels could provide, and thus imposed a shift to steam.

In the meantime, cheap cotton and power helped the industry expand in these early decades before the self-actor. The last years of the Empire and the first of the Restoration were wretched: continental blockade, commercial crisis and, finally, the inundation of long-pent-up British cottons reduced the number of active spindles from a high of almost 400,000 in 1808 in the Seine-Inférieure to 98,000 in 1818. In the next decade and a half, however, years of prohibition of foreign yarn and cloth, the number decupled; in 1834 there were 960,000. And by 1847 there were 1,200,000, plus several hundred thousand in the Eure.

As fast as spinning capacity grew in this area, weaving outstripped it. Around 1860 tens of thousands of full-time rural workers (estimated at from 30,000 to 50,000) in Normandy itself, as well as an almost equal number of part-time weavers in Picardy and Artois, processed all the local yarn and more.[2] Wages were extremely low; workers were easily hired and fired with fluctuations in trade, and the availability of a reserve pool of labour in other regions was an enormous convenience to the manufacturer. Little wonder that the power loom did not make serious inroads until the 1850's and 1860's.[3]

There are a number of general points to be made about French cotton technology in this first half of the century. First, the range of efficiency from one region to another, or even within regions, was very wide; as backward as Normandy was, it was far ahead of the small centres of the West and South. There are instances of northern firms

[1] Claude Fohlen, *L'industrie textile au temps du Second Empire* (Paris, 1956), p. 193.

[2] A. Corneille, *La Seine-Inférieure commerciale et industrielle* (Rouen, 1873), pp. 185, 195 ff., gives 60,000 hand looms for this department alone in the late 1860's. Some of these, however, were used for linen manufacture.

[3] About ten thousand in 1859. Alphonse Cordier, *Exposé de la situation du coton et des produits chimiques dans la Seine-Inférieure et l'Eure, 1859–1869* (Rouen, 1869), pp. 116–23.

selling their discarded equipment to silk enterprises of Lyon, which, after getting all possible use out of them, sold them in turn to mills in places like Nîmes, where the cotton manufacture was a generation behind the times. 'Everyone remembers,' wrote Jules Simon, 'the obsolete mules of M. Jean Dolfus [Dollfus, one of the leading manufacturers of Mulhouse], which he wanted to sell as scrap and which, to his great astonishment, were bought as mules and functioned for a long time in the Vosges.'[1]

Second, this range of technique, which was explained above by divers market and entrepreneurial considerations, does not follow the usual pattern. One would expect those enterprises specializing in cheaper goods of standard quality to be the first to mechanize. Yet in France such firms were usually the most backward. It was Normandy that was known for coarse cottons, much of it used in the manufacture of working clothes; places like Flers and Laval turned out ticking; Cholet specialized in cotton handkerchiefs and fustians for domestic use.[2] By contrast, Alsace and the North not only turned out the finer fabrics, but early devoted much of their effort to what the French call *tissus de fantaisie*. In both regions, the enterprise aimed at diversification and flexibility rather than specialization; the result was short runs that helped raise unit costs substantially above those of comparable mills in Britain. This was especially true of the northern firms and no doubt explains in part their delay in adopting the power loom.

Why this inversion of the usual relationship between price of good and mechanization? The answer would seem to be partly historical, partly social. For one thing, under the conditions of hand manufacture—in the eighteenth century, for example—there was no doubt more profit in the manufacture of more costly products. Not only was the margin per unit greater, but only the fabric that was somewhat better than the home-made article could compete in more than a local market. It was the merchant-manufacturers of the better cloth who accumulated the wealth that built the mills of the industrial revolution. For another, and partly as a result of the first, there was traditionally much more prestige attached to the production of quality products—prestige reinforced by government policy from Colbert on. The exact importance of this consideration is hard to assess, but it was not negligible: we have instances of northern firms making their fortunes in cheap cloth and then abandoning it to turn to fashion fabrics. Finally, and paradoxically, technological considerations often made it

[1] J. Simon, *L'ouvrière* (4th ed., Paris, 1862), p. 101. Cf. Claude Fohlen, *Une affaire de famille au XIXe siècle: Méquillet-Noblot* (Paris, n.d. [1955]), pp. 30, 45–6.

[2] On the analogous pattern in Germany, F. O. Dilthey, *Die Geschichte der niederrheinischen Baumwollindustrie* (Jena, 1908), pp. 18–19.

inadvisable to mechanize the production of cheaper articles. One must distinguish here between coarseness and standardization; where the latter was always a spur to mechanization, the former sometimes had the opposite effect. Thus in the early days of power weaving, when machine looms were not much quicker than skilled craftsmen, it cost less to turn out a coarse fabric by hand: the thicker the yarn, the smaller the proportion of labour required for weaving proper, as against that employed in still unmechanized processes like dressing the warp.

In general, the French cotton industry continued to lag far behind that of Britain. Plants were smaller; machines were older, less efficient;[1] even allowing for differences in equipment, labour was less productive. It was a high-cost industry, unable except for certain enterprises in Mulhouse to compete outside the country. It profited in the first half of the century from growing wealth and population at home and the opening of overseas markets like Algeria. (See Table 3.) But its expansion, which rested on the exclusion of competition, was paid for in slower overall economic growth; and with few exceptions, enterprise was inordinately cautious, even sluggish.

Nevertheless, France was the most important manufacturer of cotton goods on the Continent. The Belgian industry, active early in Napoleon's reign, was hard hit by the continental blockade and the inrush of British goods at the end of the Empire, then suffered from low protection under Dutch rule. The producers complained bitterly, and indeed output fluctuated widely from boom to crisis and back again; thus the make of yarn in eastern Flanders, including the main centre of Ghent, went from 443 tons in 1806, to 693 in 1810, down to 374 in 1817, then up to 1720 in 1826. For all these uncertainties, capacity more than doubled—from 129,000 mule spindles in 1810 to 300,000 in 1829. Separation from Holland brought new difficulties: the colonial market, such as it was, disappeared, and home demand was cut almost in half. From 1829 to 1839, spindlage in the Ghent area actually dropped from 300,000 to 250,000. Yet this purge seems only to have strengthened the industry by eliminating the least efficient enterprises. During the same years, output of yarn in eastern Flanders rose to 4500 tons, and this trend continued into the forties. By 1846 there were perhaps 360,000 spindles in the kingdom, producing about 6500 tons of yarn, or 18 kg. per spindle. Compare this with the 5·4 kg. per spindle of 1810 and remember that owing to the increasing fineness of the product, the

---

[1] In 1848 the effort of the spinners of the North to introduce spinning machines of 480–600 spindles aroused sharp labour resistance. The British manufacturers had fought and won the battle to install the so-called long mules of 1000 spindles in the 1820's.

Table 3. *Consumption of Raw Cotton in Western Europe, 1815–1850*
(in metric tons)

	Great Britain	France	Belgium	Zollverein
1815	36,932	—	—	—
1816	40,245	—	1,349	—
1817	48,956	—	811	—
1818	49,864	—	1,788	—
1819	49,684	—	2,198	—
1820	54,582	—	1,100	—
1821	58,530	—	1,970	—
1822	66,011	—	2,245	—
1823	69,918	—	2,054	—
1824	74,955	—	1,175	—
1825	75,680	—	2,372	—
1826	68,149	—	3,213	—
1827	89,473	—	3,115	—
1828	98,866	—	2,311	—
1829	99,455	—	4,804	—
1830	112,341	—	3,016	—
1831	119,192	28,217	971	—
1832	125,634	33,623	2,435	2,422
1833	130,217	35,534	3,071	1,814
1834	137,657	36,881	2,032	7,536
1835	144,327	38,712	4,784	4,498
1836	157,620	44,294	6,673	7,618
1837	165,923	43,789	6,978	10,219
1838	189,062	51,173	6,853	8,996
1839	173,182	40,301	4,053	6,823
1840	208,208	52,812	9,049	12,835
1841	198,771	55,689	7,508	11,148
1842	197,410	57,141	6,107	12,145
1843	235,294	59,584	7,482	15,336
1844	247,181	58,506	6,680	13,310
1845	275,582	60,377	8,452	17,048
1846	279,076	63,952	4,823	16,008
1847	200,631	45,191	6,807	13,830
1848	262,153	44,760	6,924	15,427
1849	286,335	63,903	10,709	19,815
1850	222,046	59,273	7,222	17,117

SOURCES. United Kingdom: Ellison, *Cotton Trade*, table no. 1; France: *Annuaire statistique*, LVII (1946), résumé rétrospectif, p. 241*; Belgium: 1816–1830, from Robert Demoulin, *Guillaume Ier et la transformation économique des provinces belges*, p. 423 (I am indebted to Prof. L. Dupriez for calling my attention to this source); for the years after 1830, from Min. des Finances, *Tableau général du commerce de la Belgique avec les pays étrangers pendant les années 1831, 1832, 1833 et 1834*, and subsequent volumes (Brussels, 1835–); Zollverein: K. F. W. Dieterici, *Statistische Uebersicht der wichtigsten Gegenstände des Verkehrs und Verbrauchs im preussischen und im deutschen Zollverbande* [title varies] (6 vols.: Berlin, 1838–57), *passim*.

machines had to work that much faster to turn out a given weight of yarn.

The weaving sector seems to have done even better than spinning, largely because British yarn was available at low cost and the producers were ready to shift over to power. Machine looms, first adopted around 1825, numbered 700 in 1830, 2900 in 1839, 3500 in 1845–6. By that time hand weaving had disappeared entirely in Ghent, though it persisted in the countryside. In part the completeness of this transition was due to the usual difficulty of compelling performance by cottage workers; in part, interestingly enough, it was a reaction to the poor quality of hand work, itself no doubt a consequence of the frictions inherent in putting-out.

Weaving was only one of several areas in which the Belgian cotton manufacture was more modern than the French. North of the border, with coal cheap and water dear, the steam-engine rapidly displaced all other sources of power; by the mid-1840's the process was complete. The self-actor came in about the same time: in 1845–6, there were three mills (of fifty-three) in the Ghent area using the new machines, which cut labour requirements by a half or more, markedly diminished the physical demands on the spinners, and by eliminating the rapidly swinging hand cranks of the old mules, removed a prolific source of accidents.[1]

In many ways, the German industry was comparable to that of Belgium in this period. Tariff protection was relatively low, though higher on the coarser yarns and fabrics. As a result, there was a substantial import from Britain; indeed, large numbers of rural weavers, traditionally occupied with linen, shifted over to cotton manufacture and rested their survival on cheap yarn from abroad. Nevertheless, domestic spinning took hold, particularly after the establishment of the *Zollverein* in 1833: in 1844 there were 815,000 'factory' spindles; in 1849, some 900,000. Consumption of raw cotton increased eightfold from the early 1830's to the late 1840's. Even so, the German industry was no more than a third, perhaps only a quarter as large as the French at the end of our period.

Structurally and technologically, however, the German industry

---

[1] On the Belgian cotton industry, see particularly Belgium, Ministère de l'Intérieur, *Enquête sur la condition des classes ouvrières et sur le travail des enfants* (3 vols.; Brussels, 1846–8), vol. III: Société de Médicine de Gand, *Enquête sur le travail et la condition physique et morale des ouvriers employés dans les manufactures de coton à Gand*; also L. Varlez, *Les salaires dans l'industrie gantoise*, I. *L'industrie cotonnière* (Brussels, 1901). Figures on output of yarn are from Demoulin, *Guillaume Ier*, p. 329; and Belgium, Min. de l'Intérieur, *Exposé de la situation du Royaume...de 1851 à 1860*, vol. III (Brussels, 1865), p. 148. The great bulk of the Belgian factory cotton industry was concentrated at Ghent.

was close to the French. It was dispersed, with concentrations in the Rhine valley, Saxony (the most important in the period before 1850), Silesia, and Bavaria. The typical enterprise was small, family-run; in Prussia, for example, the average spindlage was 828 in 1837, 1126 in 1846; in Saxony it fell from 4300 in 1830 to 4100 in 1845. As contemporaries put it, 'when a peasant or a miller was feeling too good, he built a cotton mill'.[1] Finally, the older centres gave evidence in this period of an extreme conservatism; Saxony in particular, endowed like Normandy with cheap water power, lost ground as it clung to outdated equipment and methods. The manufacturers of the Gladbach-Rheydt area (Rhineland) did not build their first up-to-date spinning mills until the 1840's. Up to then, such mills as were founded operated on the so-called 'French' system, based on the British machinery of the 1780's as adapted and diffused on the Continent under the Empire. Only the preparatory cleaning and carding engines were power driven, sometimes by water, sometimes by animals; the final spinning was accomplished by hand mules. Some plants did no more than prepare the raw cotton for the traditional wheel; as late as 1858 there were still eight roving machines supplying cottage spinners.

In the 1840's a new generation of entrepreneurs founded joint-stock companies to build and operate large factories of the British type. These were not very successful; few survived the depression that marked the last part of the decade. For a while it seemed as though their unhappy example would serve to discourage others. In fact, however, they were accurate harbingers: the trend toward concentrated manufacture by corporate enterprise resumed in the 1850's, beginning in south-west Germany, where Swiss capital found a fertile soil. Thus in Baden, the average mill increased in size from 73 to 110 employees from 1849 to 1861. Where there were only two steam-engines (130 h.p.) in the cotton industry of the Grand Duchy in 1847, in 1861, the occasion of the first industrial census of the *Zollverein*, there were 46 (1160 h.p.). At the same time, spindlage doubled, from 155,000 to 296,000; power looms increased from 1960 to 5190 (22 per cent of the *Zollverein* total); while hand looms in mills fell off from 2535 to 391 (3 per cent of the *Zollverein*).[2]

It is instructive to contrast the Swiss and German cotton manufactures in this period. Until 1850 the Swiss had no tariff on foreign

[1] 'Wenn ein Bauer oder ein Müller sich zu wohl fühlte, baute er eine Spinnerei.' G. Schmoller, *Zur Geschichte der deutschen Kleingewerbe im 19. Jahrhundert* (Halle, 1870), p. 455. The spindlage figures are taken from the same work, p. 162. For the *Zollverein* as a whole, the average was 2740 spindles in 1844. Germany, *Amtlicher Bericht über die Industrie-Ausstellung aller Völker zu London im Jahre 1851*, II, 21.

[2] Franz Kistler, *Die wirtschaftlichen und sozialen Verhältnisse in Baden 1849–1870* (Freiburg i. Br., 1954), p. 92.

yarn or cloth, their only protection being the cost of transport from Lancashire or closer centres like Alsace. For British goods, this was already a substantial obstacle, though probably not so great as the combined barrier of freight charges and customs duties that shielded the German and Belgian manufacturers.

In spite—or more correctly, because—of this, the Swiss cotton industry thrived and stood at mid-century as one of the most modern on the Continent, comparable in equipment and method to those of Alsace and Belgium. Manufacturers were compelled to turn out a competitive product. Fortunately they had the means to do so. On the one hand, Switzerland was unusually well endowed for light industry. She possessed in her rapid streams a cheap source of power that enabled a small entrepreneur to undertake machine spinning with a minimum of capital. Most of her mills began, as in Britain, as small carding and mule shops, the work of putters-out or of weavers who had managed to set a small sum aside over years of hand labour. And as in Britain, those with larger ambitions or insufficient resources could get support from a prosperous, active merchant class—Switzerland had long been the middleman between central Europe and the Mediterranean.

Many of these merchants were Calvinists, of native origin or descendants of refugees from the wars and persecutions of the lands to the west. Their membership in a cohesive, yet dispersed 'in-group' was a major commercial advantage: the Swiss merchant-banker had access to a wide-flung network of trustworthy correspondents, commanded in other words rapid, accurate intelligence on business conditions and opportunities.[1] Capital was abundant, so much so that by the end of the eighteenth century the bankers of Basel were financing some of the Alsatian cotton printers. (Switzerland was probably the first country on the Continent to invest substantial sums directly in foreign industry.)

As a result, the tiny spinning mills spawned by the continental blockade, with their handful of hand-operated mule jennies and their two or three dozen employees, had just about disappeared by the late 1830's. They had been sustained for a while by their easy access to rural weavers, but this advantage faded quickly before the competition of large, semi-automatic mules. As the number of firms diminished, spindlage increased from around 400,000 in 1830 to about a million in 1851; from 1827 to 1842, the average per firm in the canton of Zurich went from about 1900 to 4800. At the same time, the spinners learned to turn out ever-finer counts: by the early 1840's, about a third of the output was no. 60 and higher. At that point, Swiss mills were supply-

---

[1] On the advantages and success of Calvinist merchant-bankers, see D. S. Landes, *Bankers and Pashas: International Finance and Economic Imperialism in Egypt* (London, 1958), pp. 20–4, and the references cited there.

ing all home requirements of coarse and medium yarn and beginning to look elsewhere for markets.

Mechanization was slower in weaving. Rural labour was cheap and it was hard to import good British equipment before 1842. As in Alsace, the weaving shed followed on the development of domestic machine manufacture. Thus, although the first power looms came in 1825 and the first weaving factory was established in 1830, the new technique did not catch on until the 1840's, when Caspar Honegger developed an improved loom and thereby founded an industry. At mid-century, there were an estimated three thousand power looms in operation.[1]

At the end of our period, therefore, the cotton manufacture on the Continent was still strongly characterized by the dispersion and provincialism of the beginning. There were great international and interregional differences in productivity and skill, but these had not yet compelled the kind of concentration and rationalization that they implied. Technology was a generation or more behind that of Britain. For the moment, natural and artificial barriers protected local markets, and the general growth of population and wealth left room for all.

The woollen manufacture was, of course, even slower to mechanize, and this in spite of its early start. Here too, we find a pattern of dispersion and provincialism, and here too, the growing gap between progressive and backward centres.

In France, the leading firms were to be found in Roubaix (an impressive entrepreneurial achievement that involved shifting from cotton to wool), Reims, and, to a much smaller degree, Saint-Quentin and Elbeuf. There were also a few plants in Alsace, as usual among the most modern in the country. At the other end of the scale were the small residual centres of the south—Lodève, Carcassonne, Castres—and the specialists in luxury cloth—Sedan, Louviers, Paris. In general, the industry suffered from all the obstacles to technological advance inherent in the fibre, heightened in this case by special circumstances: the uneven and inferior quality of the raw wool employed, and the effort to turn out a great variety of fabrics and stimulate rapid shifts in fashion. This effort was, it should be noted, successful, and the manufacturers of the finer, softer fabrics earned international reputations; the British tried vainly for decades to imitate the French merino worsteds.

Historically, the first process mechanized was the spinning of woollen yarn; by the early 1820's, only the more backward regions

[1] Oscar Haegi, *Die Entwicklung der zürcheroberländischen Baumwollindustrie* (Weinfelden, 1925), p. 57; A. Jenny-Trümpy, art. 'Textilindustrie: a, Baumwollindustrie', in *Handwörterbuch der schweizerischen Volkswirtschaft, Sozialpolitik und Verwaltung*, ed. N. Reichesberg, vol. 3, II (1) (Bern, 1911), p. 889.

spun carded wool on the wheel or jenny. Yet in the long run, the worsted spinners were to move far ahead, partly because of the greater resistance of combed wool to mechanical treatment, partly because the demand for the harder, lighter cloths was more elastic. There are isolated instances of machines in worsted spinning before 1820, but they did not really spread until the late 1820's and early 1830's; by the mid-1840's, over half a million spindles were in operation. As early as 1844, there were a few self-actors at Reims.

Weaving was another matter. The mechanical advantage of the power loom over the hand loom was even smaller than in cotton, and the variety of the finished product precluded long runs, increasing considerably labour cost per unit of output. Once again, it was Reims that seems to have introduced the new technique, in the 1840's; but power looms remained a rarity and their diffusion dates from the end of the next decade.

In what is now Belgium, wool manufacture was concentrated in and around Verviers, which we have already noted as a vigorous, forward-looking centre, well able to compete in distant markets and alert to changes in technique and fashion. Verviers had prospered enormously under Napoleon, thanks to the widening of the market and the heavy government demand for woollen cloth. The dissolution of the Empire, however, hurt all the more, and the injury was compounded, as it was for the cotton industry of Ghent, by the pro-commercial tariff policy of the Netherlands. Nevertheless, capacity and output rose, to the point where a number of firms over-extended themselves; the crisis of 1830 brought the greatest harvest of failures in history. In the mid-1830's, the expansion resumed, owing in large part to a shift from standard cloth [*drap*] to novelty stuffs and mixed fabrics; this was the path that Roubaix-Tourcoing, Reims, and the other French centres were taking. All in all, an impressive achievement; yet growth was not so rapid as in Roubaix or even Elbeuf: statistics indicate an increase from 35,000 to 64,000 pieces between 1809 and 1852. Woollen yarn output seems to have grown faster—from 11,300 to 25,000 kg. between 1842 and 1849 alone.[1]

Although Verviers was the first wool centre on the Continent to use machines, it did not maintain its technological advance. Not until 1818 was the mule introduced—hand-driven, wooden devices of 120–180 spindles each—and it was not until the 1860's that the self-actor came in; further, it would seem that the true throstle [*continu saxon*] was

---

[1] Apparently these figures refer to the city alone, and not the area. J. S. Renier, *Histoire de l'industrie drapière au pays de Liège et particulièrement dans l'arrondissement de Verviers* (Liège, 1881), p. 108; Lebrun, 'La rivoluzione industriale', *Studi storici*, II (1961), 606 n. 51.

not adopted until around 1840. Worsted spinning was even slower to develop, in part perhaps because there was no local market for the yarn. In
1822 Mme Biolley, one of those legendary woman entrepreneurs who
seem to be a by-product of the continental family firm, founded the
first mill for the working of combed wool. It was a commercial
success, but was slow to develop technically—the mules employed in
1840 had only 40 spindles each—and did not mark the beginning of a
trend. When, in 1870, Verviers began to weave worsteds, it was compelled at first to import the yarn from Roubaix. As in the cotton industry
of Ghent, the quickest gains came in the use of steam power; the river
Vesdre was already inadequate for the fulling mills of the area by the
late eighteenth century. The first engine was installed in 1816, and by
1845, of 214 in the province of Liège, 99 were used in the woollen
manufacture, and 68 of these were at Verviers.

The wool industry had never been strong in Germany. As in
Belgium, linen was the popular fabric: it was far cheaper than wool,
and flax was cultivated everywhere. The statistician Dieterici, who
estimated *per capita* consumption of wool around 1800 as half an ell a
year, wrote: 'It is notorious how poor in woollen clothing the rural
populace, in other words, the mass of the nation, were before 1806. The
woollen coat of the peasant had to hold out many years, and servants
and day labourers often appeared before the landlords and on court days
in the coldest winter in linen blouses.'[1]

In such a situation, the introduction of mechanical spinning and
weaving profited primarily the cotton industry, which—aside from its
technical affinity for machinery—produced the poor man's substitute
for linen cloth. Two of Germany's outstanding statisticians estimated
consumption per head of the three principal fabrics in 1849 as follows:
wool, 1 ell; linen, 5 ells; cotton, 16 ells.[2] With the supply of the raw
material inelastic and demand weak, the wool industry grew slowly,
clinging the while to antiquated techniques.

The jenny came in toward the beginning of the century and spread
easily among the more well-to-do drapers, who found this a fairly
cheap way to secure the bulk of their yarn requirements within the
shop. The usual enterprise could and did get along with only two or
three of these devices. Mechanization did not constitute therefore an
immediate threat to the hand spinners in rural areas; where the peasant
wove, he spun, and some of the knitting and hosiery yarn continued to
be made on the wheel right past the middle of the century.

There were, to be sure, a few centres of factory manufacture—
Aachen, Monschau, Reichenbach and other towns of the Saxon Vogt-

---

[1] Cited by Schmoller, *Deutschen Kleingewerbe*, p. 473.
[2] *Amtlicher Bericht* (cited above, p. 395, n. 2), II, 86–7.

land, Augsburg, Kottbus. But the word 'factory' is probably too grandiose. Most plants were no more than large shops attached to a putting-out weaving operation. The equipment comprised some preparatory machinery and a jenny or two; average spindlage in Prussia in 1837 was only 103. The largest firms were in the Aachen area (around 1000 spindles in 1843), Saxony (570 in 1837), and Silesia.

The major deterrents to the development of large-scale machine industry were the extraordinary cheapness of labour and the pressure of British competition. Most small firms rested their survival on the development of a speciality not produced abroad; the effect was to place a ceiling on demand and constrict the opportunities for growth. The official German commission at the Crystal Palace Exposition criticized their countrymen for their lack of imagination, their persistence in making a given style of cloth. And yet the 1840's had seen sundry new factories, large by German standards, very modest by British. Alongside these the small, shop-like mills found themselves in difficulty. Their rough product looked poor by comparison with the highly finished fabrics of the larger, more experienced centres, and with improvements in transport, the local market was no longer an isolated preserve. Confronted with falling sales, the small manufacturer tried the traditional remedy—adulteration. He cut prices, but gave thinner, poorly fulled and shorn cloth for the money—which only increased his difficulties. Long before the machine loom sealed his fate, he was on his way out, and with him his tiny spinning shop. Between 1837 and 1849 average spindlage in Prussia more than doubled, from 103 to 235; by 1861 it was up to 592. The largest mills were still in Silesia (average 784), the kingdom of Saxony (914), and the Rhineland (1246). For the *Zollverein* as a whole, with 1,117,870 spindles, the mean was 629, representing perhaps half-a-dozen machines; the average work force was 15—a far cry from the West Riding.

By contrast with the woollen manufacture, which drew on a supply of domestic wool more than sufficient to its needs, the German worsted industry suffered from a lack of long-fibre wool suitable for combing. Moreover the reverse of these circumstances, that is, the availability of home-grown long wool, made British yarn almost unbeatable and seriously discouraged German ambitions of competition. In 1840 there were 56,258 worsted spindles in Prussia, as against 380,839 woollen. By 1846 the number had actually shrunk to 32,470, distributed among 253 enterprises; the average of 128 per firm was equal to the capacity of three jennies or a pair of small hand mules. Saxony did better: she had 14 mills in 1836-7, averaging 1400 spindles; a quarter-century later, there were 39 and the mean size had almost doubled, to 2680. For Germany as a whole, Viebahn estimates worsted spindlage in 1845 at about 300,000. This presumably includes cottage wheels and jennies; otherwise one is confronted with a serious overall decline to the 252,000 factory spindles of 1861.[1] Yet such a contraction is not inconceivable. Increasingly in these years, the German wool manufacture relied on foreign yarn, imports of which rose from an insignificant amount in 1836, to 53,000 cwt. in 1850, and 213,000 cwt. in 1864. Most of this was English combed yarn; and if we generously estimate the consumption of worsted yarn at one-half that of woollen yarn, these imports already accounted for about a quarter of the supply of the weavers of worsted and mixed cloths by the middle of the century. By the early 1860's, when the domestic output of worsted yarn ran about 110,000 cwt. a year, imports probably supplied over half the requirements of the industry.

The stagnation or decay of much of the German worsted yarn manufacture and the small scale of production betray the technological backwardness of the industry. Which was cause and which effect, would be hard to say. Probably the influences worked both ways. In any event, hand spinning, which seemed on its way out in the thirties, got a new lease on life when English yarn prices rose in the forties, and survived in the countryside past the middle of the century on the cheap labour of old men, women and children. Weaving, as might be expected, was even slower to change. The power loom, which came in woollens in the early 1830's, in worsted at Wüste Giersdorf (Silesia) under semi-official auspices in 1843, remained a rarity until the 1850's. Prussia had some 1200 of them in woollen and worsted in 1849, as against 26,700 hand looms.[2] For a long time they offered little pecuniary advantage, though they did weave a tighter, more regular cloth and found use in the manufacture of simple, solid fabrics.

Because of this relatively small margin between new and old techniques, the penalties of obsolescence were far lighter in weaving than spinning. More important than equipment were the style and finish of the fabric, and these depended on the skills and taste of labour and management. Whereas the Germans imported an increasing share of their yarn from abroad, their exports of cloth throve: that of woollens

[1] [G. W. von Viebahn], *Amtlicher Bericht über die allgemeine deutsche Gewerbe-Ausstellung zu Berlin im Jahre 1844* (3 vols.; Berlin, 1845), I, 174–93, especially p. 185; Idem, *Statistik des zollvereinten und nördlichen Deutschlands* (3 vols.; pagin. cont.; Berlin, 1858–68), pp. 885–8.

[2] A. Wache, *Die volkswirtschaftliche Bedeutung der technischen Entwicklung der deutschen Wollindustrie* (Leipzig, 1909), p. 81; Schmoller, *Deutschen Kleingewerbe*, p. 523. For the *Zollverein* as a whole, there were 2592 power looms in woollen mills in 1861, as against 11,818 hand looms; 3655 power looms in worsted mills, as against 9068; plus 67,343 hand looms in cottages and shops. O. Schwarz, 'Die Betriebsformen der modernen Grossindustrie', *Zeitschrift für die gesamte Staatswissenschaft*, xxv (1869), 580.

tripled from 1836 to 1864, when it represented perhaps two-thirds of total output; in an even shorter period, from 1843 to 1864, that of worsteds rocketed from 313 to 108,082 cwt. Viebahn was anxious for the spinning branch, which clearly was one of the weak points of German industry. But he could be well pleased with the cloth manufacture: 'Even if the English still have an advantage in many strong and solid articles, or the French in a few very fine and patterned fabrics, the German wool industry still stands in its specialities at the head of this branch of civilization.'[1]

As in textiles, so in heavy industry the first half of the century saw, not a transformation of techniques as in Britain, but a slow, spasmodic diffusion of new methods alongside the old. There were, however, major differences. In metallurgy as against light manufactures, material factors—availability and quality of resources, costs of transportation—were of critical importance. Good entrepreneurship often seems to have been a decisive advantage in textiles: how else explain the success of such centres as Mulhouse, the Roubaix-Tourcoing area, or Krefeld—or, for that matter, Brno or Lodz—which were not significantly favoured by nature or were even worse situated than less prosperous competitors? In iron-making, however, cheap ore and coal could cover a multitude of sins, and all the ingenuity in the world could not compensate for their absence.

Furthermore, the shift in the continental iron industry from old to new techniques took place under special external stimulation. Thus the improvement of transportation did much more to promote industries producing commodities of great weight and volume in proportion to value than light manufactures. At the same time, demand grew more rapidly (that is, the demand curve shifted farther to the right) for industries whose market grew not only with the increase in population and wealth but also with the general change in technology: the substitution of mineral for plant fuel, of metal for wooden machinery; the use of iron pipe for gas, water, and sewage; the diffusion of the steam-engine; the coming of the railroad. In Britain, the Industrial Revolution had been built on the cotton manufacture, which grew more rapidly than other branches of industry before 1800 and drew them with it. On the Continent, it was heavy industry—coal and iron —that was the leading sector. This reversal, it should be emphasized, was essentially the consequence of the timing of growth—not of some structural law of economic development. The clustering and interaction of technological changes made this an age of metal, and even in Britain, where the cotton trade sold most of its goods abroad and con-

[1] Viebahn, *Statistik*, pp. 917–18, 921, 923.

tinued to enjoy a highly elastic demand curve, the make of iron grew faster in these years than that of yarn or cloth.

The effect of this strong and growing demand for metallurgical products on technique was something else again. On the one hand, by pressing on the capacities of the old plant and promising substantial rewards to innovation, demand encouraged change. On the other, the very security of outlets permitted many an ironmaster to sit back and rake in substantial profits with obsolete equipment, especially where—as was often the case—his market was naturally or artificially protected from outside competition. To be fair, his location did not always permit him to convert to mineral fuel; and even where there was coal, conversion was expensive; modernization required a larger initial outlay than in the textile manufacture.

As a result, the development of the continental iron industry in this period, unlike that in Britain, was two-pronged. On the one side, there was the introduction and considerable diffusion of the new mineral-using techniques; on the other, there was an expansion of old-type plant, improved to some degree, but obsolescent.

The process varied, of course, from one country to another. In France, iron-making, like textile manufacture, was hard hit by the flood of British imports before and after Waterloo. At that point, the only plant to make coke-blast iron was Le Creusot, and Le Creusot made it poorly; the firm failed in 1818. Around the turn of the decade, however, a number of ironmasters succeeded in overcoming the technical difficulties (the biggest of which was the unsuitability of the coal, the ore, or both to the coke-smelting process) and established the new method on a firm basis: Gallois at Terrenoire, Dufaud at Fourchambault, Wendel at Hayange in particular. In the mid-1820's, the national output of coke-blast pig was perhaps four or five thousand tons; within a decade it had increased eightfold, and by 1846 amounted to 187,411 tons. During this interval, however, the number of charcoal blast furnaces increased by about two-thirds—there were some 375 in 1825 and 623 in 1846—and output rose slightly faster, from 194,000 to 335,000 tons.[1] Indeed, not only did the old smelting technique thrive, but even the so-called Catalan forge, a descendant of the antique oven that antedated the blast furnace, dragged out a stubborn existence on the slopes of the Pyrenees and in the Massif Central.

In contrast to Britain, where puddling came more than half a century after coke smelting, the continental countries learned to refine with coal first. This is the normal sequence technologically: the fuel and ore

[1] The second figure includes production by a mixture of wood and coal. Within this mixed category, more than two tons of wood or charcoal were used for every ton of coal or coke. *Résumé des travaux statistiques de l'Administration des Mines en 1847*, p. 11.

economies are greater in refining; the absence of direct contact between fuel and metal excludes some of the most serious difficulties associated with the chemical composition of the materials employed; and the initial cost of the shift to coal in refining is much less than in smelting.

In France, the period of innovation was the later 'teens and early 1820's; the innovators, again men like Wendel, Dufaud, Gallois, and somewhat later, Frèrejean at Vienne and Manby and Wilson at Charenton and Le Creusot. This is just what one would expect: the greatest economy lay in combining coke smelting with puddling and rolling, and the pioneers in one area were bound to be pioneers in the other. Within a few years, the new technique had spread throughout the country: at the beginning of 1826 there were probably well over 150 puddling furnaces in activity (only about a third of which were operated in conjunction with rolling mills), and some 40 per cent of the total output of malleable iron was being made with coal. Two decades later, in 1845, there were some 437 puddling furnaces (of which 382 employed according to the *méthode anglaise*, that is, in combination with rolling mills) turning out 226,788 tons of wrought iron and rails, or two-thirds of a total make of 335,267 tons.

Along with the shift from vegetable to mineral fuel went various improvements in the construction and operation of plant and equipment. As in Britain, the blast furnace grew. In 1825 a 15-metre furnace at Le Creusot was exceptional; the average French unit turned out some 1325 metric tons of pig a year. In 1846 this was a characteristic height for coke-blast furnaces, and output averaged 3400 tons. Similarly, the make of wrought iron per puddling furnace doubled, going from 300 tons at most, to almost 600 in the same period.

The Belgian iron industry changed over to mineral fuel faster than the French, for a number of reasons: the relative abundance of coal and its proximity to the ore—in the 1830's and 1840's, Belgium was the largest coal producer on the Continent; the lower tariff barrier and consequent pressure of British competition; the unity of the national market and resulting inter-regional competition; and the availability of substantial venture capital from such institutions as the Société Générale.

The first blast furnace to use coke was that of Haudires, near Couillet —a small affair originally intended to burn charcoal. The first built for coke was that of Cockerill at Seraing in 1823. The years thereafter were, as in France, a period of trial and error; most of the early coke furnaces—there were ten in 1830—were small and uneconomical. Then came an alternation of boom and stagnation. The early 1830's saw a rapid advance (there were twenty-three coke furnaces in 1836), which was followed by a severe setback in 1837–9. Cockerill was forced to liquidate and was reorganized as a corporation; the Banque de Belgique temporarily suspended payment; numerous iron firms failed; the number of active coke-blast furnaces fell to seventeen. Expansion resumed in the 1840's, however, and by 1847, forty-six coke furnaces were in operation. During the same period, from 1830 to 1847, the number of active charcoal units fell from ninety-one to twenty-five.[1]

This expansion and rationalization reflected in part the opening of the German market to Belgian iron. As in textiles, the main difficulty of the Belgian ironmasters was the inadequacy of local demand and the consequent inability to achieve the economies of scale implicit in the new techniques. In the 1830's, the Belgian government tried to solve the problem by forming a customs union with France, but the opposition of French manufacturers, for obvious reasons, and of the British government for reasons of state, killed the project. A similar effort to join the *Zollverein* in the 1840's (as did Luxembourg in 1842) failed because of French political opposition, but the Belgian government did succeed in obtaining a 50 per cent reduction in the German duty on iron. At a time when German consumption of iron was breaking records owing to the railway boom, this advantage gave the Belgian industry a tremendous push: where Belgium had accounted for a sixth of German iron imports in 1842-3, it provided over two-thirds in 1850; shipments of pig to the *Zollverein* jumped from 9500 to 76,000 tons.

In Germany, by contrast, these were decades of extremely slow progress. The greatest advances came in the manufacture of those finished goods—steel and steel objects, for example—that demanded special skills and high inputs of labour, as against the initial, mass-production processes. This preference reflected in part the craft traditions of the people and relative factor costs; but it was also the result of a tariff policy that treated pig and even wrought iron as a raw material and exposed the antiquated German furnaces and forges to the competition of Belgium and Britain.

The bulk of the German iron manufacture, like that of France, was

---

[1] These figures are from Beck, *Geschichte des Eisens*, IV, 688. They do not accord with the figures cited on p. 687, and the inconsistencies probably reflect the diversity of sources. The official *Exposé de la situation du Royaume, 1840–1850*, part IV, p. 118, gives the following statistics:

Blast Furnaces in Belgium

	Active		Idle	
	Coke	Charcoal	Coke	Charcoal
1845	33	23	19	52
1846	44	33	13	37
1847	50	35	12	34

based throughout this period on ore, wood, and water. The largest centre was in the Rhineland: in the hills around Siegen, where high-quality iron was easily accessible in small, dispersed outcroppings; and on the Sauerland plateau to the North-West, heavily forested and cut deeply by numerous rivers driving dozens of forge and mill wheels. The Siegerland concentrated on smelting; the Sauerland, on refining and finishing. Here lay the internationally known centres of Solingen, its coat of arms flaunting an anchor on crossed swords; Remscheid, with its sickle under a lion rampant; Iserlohn, home of a pin and needle industry whose division of labour recalls the famous chapter of Adam Smith.

The effect of growing demand on these districts was essentially to intensify output along traditional lines; more mines, more water wheels, more forges. Coal came in slowly, and then in those works that lay close to the Rhine and could import it by water from the Ruhr. It was used at first in refining only; indeed, the Sauerland developed a flourishing forge and shaping industry to process Belgian and British pig, or convert *Spiegeleisen* from the Siegerland into steel. Not until the 1840's was coke-blast pig manufactured in the Rhineland.

By comparison, the Ruhr was insignificant. No one realized as yet the extent and quality of the coal that lay beneath its still-green fields. As late as 1852 the official German commissioners to the Crystal Palace Exposition were able to write: 'It is clearly not to be expected that Germany will ever be able to reach the level of production of coal and iron currently attained in England. This is implicit in our far more limited resource endowment.'[1] Besides, in the 1830's and 1840's, Belgian and British pig iron was, or at least seemed, too cheap to compete with. Almost all of such pig as the Ruhr did turn out went into castings, and the first coke-blast furnace in the area was not blown in until 1851.[2] Here, too, puddling and finishing developed on the basis of imported iron and local fuel: in 1844, of some 35,000 tons converted into various forms of merchant iron, tinplate, and steel, less than 5 per cent came from Westphalian furnaces.

Several of the newer forges of the Ruhr and Sauerland were among the most modern on the Continent. And in one field, steel, Germany was in the van of technical progress. In 1849 Lohage and Bremme founded a company to exploit their process for producing steel by

[1] *Amtlicher Bericht* (cited above, p. 167 n. 1), I, 238.
[2] According to Dr Irmgard Lange-Kothe, the Friedrich-Wilhelms-Hütte in Mülheim, which is usually credited with having blown in the first coke-blast furnace in the Ruhr (1849), ran in fact into technical difficulties and had to extinguish the fires shortly thereafter; not until 1853 did the furnace work successfully. In the meantime, coke smelting had been introduced by the Eintrachthütte at Hochdahl (near Düsseldorf) in 1851 and by Detillieux at Bergeborbeck (near Essen) in 1852.

puddling, the first major advance on the road to cheap steel since the invention of the crucible process in the eighteenth century. Two years later Krupp startled the Crystal Palace Exposition by exhibiting a huge two-ton block of cast steel, the result of a marvellous co-ordination of labour and supervision in the pouring of dozens of crucibles simultaneously.

Silesia was the only area whose output in this period was comparable to that of the Rhineland. It would be difficult, however, to find two districts so different in vocation and in the character of their development. Where the one was thickly settled, western in social structure and political tradition, located near the heart of what for centuries had been one of the main thoroughfares of European civilization and commerce, the other was heavily forested, thinly populated, parcelled into large estates of privileged aristocratic landowners, a frontier march won in war and therefore closely administered by the Prussian government.

Silesia did not compare with the Rhineland in markets, capital, or enterprise; but she had minerals, including valuable deposits of non-ferrous metals and apparently inexhaustible coal measures; she also had the solicitous patronage of the state. The earliest of the great Silesian iron-works and coal-mines were royal establishments; the names often announced the fact: Königshütte, Königshuld, Königsgrube. As noted earlier, these state enterprises were among the first in continental Europe to smelt with coke successfully, thanks to the assistance of British technicians and the work of civil servants like Reden.

By contrast, the private sector remained backward. Most of the mineral and forest wealth was held by noblemen whose entrepreneurial ambitions were limited to a diffuse appetite for gain and whose horizon was restricted to the traditional agrarian vocation of the domain. For most of them, coal and iron were a kind of treasure trove, an unexpected addition to wealth yielded by cultivation and husbandry; it took decades before a few pioneers realized that there was more to iron-making than the small forge or smithy that serviced the estate and that industry was a greater potential source of income than agriculture. Their fellows were slow to follow suit, partly no doubt because of inertia, partly because wood was so cheap that, given the differences in quality, charcoal blast iron could compete with the coke-smelted pig; for many, indeed, wood seems to have been almost a free good (save for cost of labour)—if it was not used in the furnaces, it simply went to waste. As a result, the share of coke-blast pig in the total output of Upper Silesia rose from 28 per cent in 1838 (9108 out of 32,426 tons by eleven out of eighty furnaces) to only 35 per cent in 1847 (13,050 out of 37,550 tons, by eighteen out of sixty-three furnaces.)

Germany was thus the slowest of the west European countries to develop a modern iron industry, in spite of the early start in Silesia; and Belgium the fastest. In all, however, the scale of enterprise was smaller than in Britain. No company on the Continent was capable of turning out 80,000 tons of pig a year, as the fifteen furnaces of Dowlais did in 1845. The Wendel firm of Lorraine, probably the largest in France, produced 22,000 tons in 1850; the Forges de Decazeville, some 16,000 tons at the height of the boom of the 1840's. As late as the end of the 1850's, the six furnaces of the S. A. John Cockerill were producing 11,000–12,000 tons. The German enterprises were on average even smaller; the Laurahütte, newly created in 1838 and a giant of the Silesian industry, had four blast furnaces and a capacity of about 16,000 tons.

Similarly, British equipment was larger. The biggest Welsh furnaces were smelting 120 tons a week in the late 1840's; the average was 90; for Britain as a whole, the mean was 89. On the Continent, only Belgium was comparable, with a general average of 60 tons. By contrast, the make of French coke-blast furnaces in 1846 was 66 tons a week; of all furnaces, less than 18. And in Germany, where the coke-blast furnaces of Silesia were restricted in size by the friability of the fuel, even these averaged only 14 tons a week in 1847.[1]

The same differences in scale of output and size of equipment characterized the refining processes. Only in certain special cases—Seraing's rail-rolling mills or Krupp's steel-pouring shed—were continental plants comparable to those of the United Kingdom. Nor was it coincidence that both of these installations were developed to supply the state. Private demand seemed too limited and fickle to justify investment on the British scale.

In one respect, however, the best practice on the Continent was moving ahead of that of Britain. The higher cost of fuel, otherwise a serious disadvantage, was an incentive to technological innovation. Where British ironmasters continued to allow the flames and gases of their furnaces to illuminate the night, the best continental producers took steps to use this once waste energy for refining the pig, heating the blast, or driving the steam-engines. Similarly, Neilson's hot blast spread fairly rapidly among French manufacturers of coke-blast pig: in 1846 some forty-three out of fifty-five active furnaces were so equipped. Belgium was slower in this regard, perhaps because cost conditions were closer to those of Britain; but Belgium was the leader in putting to use the waste gases of carbonization.

[1] Beck, *Geschichte des Eisens*, IV, 700. This figure does not accord with statistics for the same year cited on p. 699, which indicate an average of 21 tons a week.

To be sure, these savings were not large enough to offset the British cost advantage; until the systematic exploitation of Lorraine ore and Ruhr coal in the second half of the century or, indeed, the application of the Thomas process in the 1880's and 1890's, no iron was cheaper than British iron. The fact remains, however, that continental iron-masters were making more of their resources than their competitors across the Channel; and since fuel economy was the key to efficiency in almost every stage of manufacture, these tentative advances of the 1830's and 1840's were the starting-point of a scientific metallurgy that was to pay off in major improvements a generation later. For the moment, however, nothing could compare with the wealth of British resources or the ingenuity of such inventors as Neilson, Mushet, and Hall.

On the Continent, even more than in the United Kingdom, the steam-engine was linked to mining and metallurgy. For where it was still possible in the second third of the century to use water to drive the smaller, obsolescent types of textile machinery (which, as we have noted, were competitive under continental conditions), the coke-blast furnace and rolling mill usually required far more power than the water wheels could provide and were less compatible than the equipment of other industries with a fluctuating supply of energy. Once again, we do not have adequate statistical evidence for the United Kingdom, but the data, such as they are, give the impression of a relatively high concentration of steam power in the cotton industry. France seems to have occupied an intermediate position, with 42·2 per cent of her rated steam horsepower in mining and metallurgy (including engineering) and 29·5 per cent in textiles. Belgium was at the other extreme: in 1851 over 55 per cent of her steam power stationary engines were in coal-mining, another 15 per cent in iron-making, only 11 per cent in textiles. Here, as in heavy metallurgy, the Belgian achievement was by far the most impressive of the period. In 1846 she had some 38,000 h.p. for 4,337,000 people (8·76 per thousand), as compared with 50,000 h.p. for France (1·5 per thousand).[1] Germany was slow by comparison: 26,400 h.p. in 1846 (approximately 0·76 per thousand).

Technologically, steam power on the Continent followed the same path as metallurgy; that is, far more emphasis was placed on fuel economy than in Britain. From the very start, the Woolf compound engine (patents of 1803 and 1804; commercial realization *c.* 1812), which made use of high pressure to operate two cylinders alternately

---

[1] These are stationary engines only. Briavoinne, *Sur les inventions*, p. 38, remarks wryly: 'If it is correct to say with M. Chaptal that the extent of the industry of a country is measured today less by its population than by the machines it possesses, the disproportion between France and Belgium would not seem to be very great.'

and offered a fuel economy over the Watt machine of about 50 per cent, found its greatest market in France. Unfortunately the compound engine was costly to build and difficult to maintain, handicaps particularly serious in capital- and skill-poor countries, and for some time it was confined primarily to marine and river shipping. Instead, the continental industrialists preferred simple engines working at medium or high pressure; as pointed out earlier, these were cheaper to build as well as more economical of fuel than the Watt-type machine.[1] They were also more dangerous, however, and it was some years before metal-workers learned to build reliable boilers and even more years before the public would put any faith in them. Acceptance did not come until the 1830's, in large part as a result of improvements in marine engines and the development of the steam locomotive.

Whenever possible, the continental manufacturer used water power. In the textile districts of Normandy, steam was used only as a *pis aller*: where the streams were so crowded there was no room for another wheel; or where energy was required over and beyond what water already furnished. Even in heavy industry, water continued to play a far greater role than is usually thought: as late as 1844, the French iron manufacture was using hydraulic engines of 21,710 h.p., as against steam-engines of only 5982 h.p. (3213 fuelled by coal, 2769 by gas from the furnaces).[2] In general, it was the coal-short French who were most active in developing the technology of water power. The key figures are J. V. Poncelet, whose undershot wheel with curved vanes achieved efficiencies about three times as great as the ordinary wheel; and Fourneyron, whose turbine (1827) holds a place in hydraulics comparable to that of Watt's engine in the field of steam power.

In the eighteenth century, almost all of the continental steam-engines came from England: if it was hard for British metal-workers to achieve the precision required, it was almost impossible for French or German craftsmen. Not only did they lack the manipulative skills, but their materials were inadequate to the task—too soft or brittle and uneven in quality.

---

[1] As of the end of 1836, of a total steam-engine capacity of 38,173 h.p. in France, 35,440 was so-called 'high-pressure' (that is, high and medium), and 2733 low. The corresponding figures for 1846 were 103,739 and 5196. France, Ministère des Travaux Publics, *Compte rendu des travaux des ingénieurs des mines, pendant l'année 1847* (Paris, 1848), p. 88. The figures are necessarily approximate, since they rest in large part on declarations made for the purpose of securing authorization for the machines in question. Also, they probably include machines authorized but not installed as yet; this is no doubt compensated, however, by machines installed in anticipation of authorization.

[2] *Ibid.* 1845, pp. 26–43.

By the 1820's, however, the combination of imported British labour, continental determination, and, in some countries, high tariff barriers and similar constraints on foreign competition led to the development of a home machine industry. At first, the mainland producers were essentially copyists, reproducing British models with negligible alteration—and then largely in the direction of economy of material, even at the expense of solidity. The French and Belgians were the first to break away and conceive their own machines, increasingly on the basis of theoretical speculation; observers contrasted them with the practical British in this regard. At mid-century, Germany was just beginning to enter this 'independent' stage. Some of her engineers still had difficulty in obtaining proper materials locally, and many firms continued to import accessory machine tools from abroad.

Few continental machine construction firms worked for export, and the industry as a whole was much smaller than the British. The division of labour within the trade reflected these limitations of scale. Thus while the industry tended, as in Britain, to split into light and heavy sectors, there were not on the Continent such pure machine-tool firms as Maudslays and Nasmyths.[1] Instead, most of the engineering houses —Schneider, Gouin, or Calla in France; Cockerill in Belgium; Harkort, Borsig, Egells in Germany—were ready to undertake anything ordered, from locomotives and marine engines to distilling apparatus and lathes. Some even tried their hand at textile equipment, although it was soon recognized that this was the kind of product best left to specialists.[2]

In these circumstances, the industry made little attempt at standardization, except in the manufacture of spinning machinery and similar apparatus, where the volume of demand permitted and encouraged the appearance of types and models. Even here, however, the manufacturer made everything to order, and every order was in some way different from the one before. There was no production on speculation

---

[1] The witnesses before the Select Committee on Machinery of 1841 asserted that while continental machine shops were able to make special-purpose machine tools for themselves, they did not ordinarily manufacture them for sale, that industrialists needing tools imported them from Britain. According to one machine maker, William Jenkinson of Manchester, three-fourths, if not four-fifths of the machine tools made in England were intended for export. The figure seems very high. *Parliamentary Papers*, 1841, VII, QQ. 1312–29, esp. 1326, 3182, 4459–62.

[2] Even in Britain, however, most machine shops in the 1840's and 1850's were general shops. The producers of textile equipment were the major exception. A more advanced division of labour did not come until the 1870's, and it was another decade or two before specialization became the mark of the modern efficient enterprise. J. B. Jefferys, *The Story of the Engineers 1800–1945* (n.p., n.d.), p. 53.

of the kind that Nasmyth attempted.[1] Interchangeable parts were unknown; there was little or no working to gauges; and the file was still the machinist's most important tool.

There was far more improvisation than in Britain. Engineering shops made their own equipment, and the larger manufacturing firms—in textiles, for example—often maintained machine departments large enough to stand on their own. Some of these did in time split off and become independent enterprises. Smaller factories depended on local mechanics and repair men, ready to put their hands to anything. This was an expensive way of doing things: 'home-made' machines cost a lot more than the products of the large national firms. But local production meant immediate attention and easier maintenance, and most manufacturers were agreed that these versatile, on-the-spot artisans were indispensable. Besides, repair shops were factories in embryo, and many a small mechanic became an industrialist by ploughing back profits and borrowing from sympathetic and dependent manufacturers. In few trades was entrepreneurial advancement so rapid.[2]

Much more than in Britain, machine-building on the Continent grew with heavy industry. Not only was textile manufacture relatively less important but, as noted above, much light manufacturing continued to rely on water power. It was mining and metallurgy at first, the railroad later, that provided the major market for engines and complex metal shapes. Railway construction was particularly important. It called forth a large number of machine shops, encouraged as in Britain the diffusion of major innovations in the working and handling of heavy forms—among them the steam hammer and overhead cranes—and provided for the first time so large a demand for machine tools that specialization in their manufacture became feasible. But this was not to come until after mid-century.[3]

---

[1] See above, p. 106 and note 3. To be sure, Nasmyth was an exception even in England. The German commissioners at the Exposition of 1851 noted that many British firms did not have price lists, preferring, 'in view of the great diversity of requirement', to quote on order. *Amtlicher Bericht* (cited above, p. 167, n. 1), I, 589.

[2] To choose but two areas where this kind of promotion from shop to factory took place on a large scale: on St-Etienne, cf. L. J. Gras, *Histoire de la métallurgie dans la Loire* (St Etienne, 1908), pp. 223f., 267–9, 220, 265f., 393f.; L. Thiollier, *Notices industrielles* (St Etienne, 1894), pp. 41–50; on central Germany, G. Aubin, *Die wirtschaftliche Einheit Mitteldeutschlands* (Merseburg, 1927), pp. 17–19.

[3] Switzerland was an exception. There, lack of coal and iron and an abundance of cheap water power made metallurgy and engineering relatively less important. As a result, machine building grew, not so much out of the independent metal trades, as out of the young factory textile industry. Cf. Bruno Lincke, *Die schweizerische Maschinenindustrie und ihre Entwicklung* (Frauenfeld, 1910), pp. 9–12; Walter Bodmer,

The chemical industry encountered the same problem in more serious form; the effects of weak demand were aggravated by the dispersion of the critical raw materials. The market was limited to begin with: the textile industry was, as we have seen, nowise comparable to that across the Channel, and this was the most important single customer for chemical products. Moreover the market was cut up: chemicals were cheap in proportion to volume, sometimes hard to handle, and liable to spoilage and breakage of containers; no industry suffered so much from the high cost of transport. Finally, these geographical handicaps hurt on the supply side as well: there was nothing like the Merseyside concentration of coal and salt in combination with water carriage. All of which limited the scale of operations, raised costs above the British level, and led producers to stress versatility rather than volume. Most chemical manufacturers were kitchen cooks on a large scale.

Their equipment and techniques were consonant with this kind of industrial cuisine. On the one hand, the thriftiness of the small producer and official regulations on the capture and disposal of noxious wastes encouraged rationalization, which meant in effect the recuperation and exploitation of by-products. On the other hand, proper recuperation cost money and sometimes made other processes more difficult; thus the apparatus for the recovery of hydrochloric acid in the manufacture of sodium sulphate (Glauber's salt) cut down on furnace draught and made it that much harder to effect the initial reaction. The result was often a compromise between rationality and compliance on the one hand, and penny-pinching shortcuts on the other. In Belgium, where the chemical industry was comparatively well endowed by nature, government inspectors noted in 1854 the poor condition of the equipment, the sloppiness of the work: the glass bells for hydrochloric acid installed outdoors, where changes in temperature cracked them; the dosage of materials, approximate and variable; little effort made to maintain the purity of the reagents. Most of the firms producing sulphuric acid counted themselves fortunate to obtain 75 per cent of the theoretical yield.

Rationality of techniques would seem to have advanced further in France. At least this is the impression one gets from the report of a Belgian inspector, J. S. Stas, who visited the Kuhlmann plant at Lille in the same year: 'I had a great deal of trouble convincing myself that I was dealing with furnaces for the manufacture of sodium sulphate.' In Belgium, he notes, such furnaces 'sweat hydrochloric acid and remind one constantly, by their state of disrepair, more of ruins that are painful to look at, than of active equipment belonging for the most part to wealthy industrialists'.[1]

Yet one must not confuse Kuhlmann with the run of French firms. As in Belgium, the large, rationalizing establishment was the exception; the small pot boiler, the rule. At mid-century Kuhlmann's Madeleine plant was recovering 158 kg. of hydrochloric acid per 100 kg. of salt, a loss of perhaps 2 per cent in view of the impurity of the salt; at Aniche (Nord) results of up to 183/100 had been achieved under better conditions. Yet a decade later, the plants in southern France were still losing two-thirds of their by-product acid, and even in Britain there were losses of as much as a half.

The main difficulty was lack of apparent financial incentive. As one Belgian manufacturer, whose recovery ratio of hydrochloric acid was 70/100, put it, there was no profit in doing any better. Yet the argument should not be taken at face value. For one thing, there were a number of producers in both countries who did better and sold their acid at a profit. For another, few if any of the manufacturers of the period could really say in a precise way what paid and what did not. Scientific standards of performance were still confined to laboratories, and there was as yet no clear-cut choice of technique that imposed itself on the investing entrepreneur. As a result, each firm had its own procedures or combinations thereof.

In Germany the chemical industry of this early period gave little hint of the great things to come. The textile manufacture was far weaker than that of France; the standard of living, lower; and soap and glass consumption, that much smaller. On the supply side, as we have noted, the mineral wealth of Westphalia was as yet unsuspected. Not until 1840 was soda produced by the Leblanc method, and as late as the 1870's, when the Solvay process was beginning to transform the industry, German output was less than that of France a generation earlier.[2] Indeed, demand far outstripped supply, and soda imports rose in a decade (1836–45) from 634 to 6913 metric tons, almost all of this from Britain;[3] not until the 1880's did Germany become a net exporter of soda. Similarly, the make of sulphuric acid long remained

[1] Belgium, Chambre des Représentants, 1854, *Fabriques de produits chimiques*, Annexes, p. iv.

[2] Output did not pass the 40,000 metric ton mark until 1872. The plants in the Marseilles area alone were turning out this amount by the 1840's. L. F. Haber, *The Chemical Industry in the Nineteenth Century* (London, 1958), pp. 47, 41. According to R. Hasenclever, 'Über die deutsche Soda-Fabrikation', *Chemische Industrie*, VII (1884), 280 ff., soda output was 58,000 tons in 1872, shrinking to 42,000 by 1878 under the pressure of British competition. The higher figure, however, does not alter the significance of the comparison.

[3] Gustav Miller, *Die chemische Industrie in der deutschen Zoll- und Handelsgesetzge-*

low, amounting in 1878 to about half of that of France.[1] Here, however, supply early passed demand and by the mid-1840's Germany was selling more acid abroad than she imported.

Yet if the German chemical industry was productively weak at mid-century, it had important technological assets. It was more scientific than that of other nations, to the point of what might appear superficially as economic inefficiency. The typical German firm outdid those of the other continental countries in diversity of output; the largest producers of sulphuric acid and soda also turned out the rarest pharmaceuticals, alkaloids, and organic acids. The experts attributed this versatility to the skill and training of the young technicians—not the *savants*, but the production men:

...most of our chemical manufacturers are in a position, because of a much stronger scientific education, and because of the ease with which they [can draw], partly on our array of pharmacists, whose scientific knowledge goes so far beyond that of the apothecaries of other countries, partly on the large number of other young chemists, to obtain at any time the kind of help that is only rarely to be had elsewhere and then only with great expenditure. These circumstances enable them to compose, alongside the most extensively active products of the trade, a great many preparations that can be entrusted only to educated and experienced men.[2]

Wissenschaftliche Bildung was to pay handsomely in the second half of the century.

At mid-century, then, continental Europe was still about a generation behind Britain in industrial development. The relative disparity showed clearly in the population figures. Where in 1851 about half of the people of England and Wales lived in towns, in France and Germany the proportion was about a quarter; not until the last years of the century did urban population pass rural in Germany, and in France the even point did not come until after the First World War. The occupational distribution tells a similar story. At mid-century, only a quarter of the British male working force (twenty years and older) was engaged in agriculture. For Belgium, the most industrialized nation on the Continent, the figure was about 50 per cent.[3] Germany took another twenty-five years to reach this point; indeed, as late as 1895,

---

bung (1902), cited in H. Schultze, *Die Entwicklung der chemischen Industrie in Deutschland seit dem Jahre 1875* (Halle, 1908), p. 7.

[1] An estimated 112,000 against 200,000 tons. *Ibid.* p. 71.

[2] *Amtlicher Bericht* (above, p. 167, n. 1), I, 262. The original is grammatically incomplete.

[3] According to the Belgian census of 1846, 1,075,000 were engaged in agriculture,

there were more people engaged in agriculture than in industry.[1] And in France industry was outnumbered until the Second World War and the economic recovery that followed.

By the same token, the continental proletariat was very different from the British. The concentration of large numbers of workers in huge factories was only just beginning, and then more in heavy industry than in textiles. There was nothing yet like the new slums of Manchester and Leeds, filled with pallid mill hands crowding into a smokestack jungle. Continental slums were different. They were usually the run-down older quarters, comparable to the wynds of Edinburgh, and were inhabited primarily by artisans and domestic workers—handloom weavers in the damp cellars of Lille or the tenements of Liège; woodworkers in the Faubourg Saint-Antoine. Here and there were new mill towns on the British pattern; but Roubaix, Mulhouse, and the cities of the Wuppertal were so much smaller than their counterparts in Lancashire and the West Riding that they were really a different species.

Much more than in Britain, industry was dispersed through the countryside. The continued reliance on water power was one factor; the greater place of metallurgy and mining, which were bound to locate at the sources of raw materials, was another. As late as 1858, 19 of 49 spinning mills, 49 of 57 blast furnaces, 75 of 152 wire mills, 158 of 167 steel plants, and 15 of 28 machine factories in Westphalia were *auf dem platten Lande*.[2] To be sure, this was a legalistic definition, and many of these plants were in fact situated in communities that deserved to be called urban. Many, however, were located in what were in effect swollen villages, essentially rural in character. There was, as in Lancashire in the eighteenth century, a thickening of the countryside; it had not yet thickened enough, however, to form a continuous industrial conurbation.

There was, moreover, a great expansion of rural putting-out, a continuation of the trend of the eighteenth century, paradoxically accelerated by the mechanization of some—but not all—of the stages of manufacture. Thus the availability of cheaper semi-processed materials—yarn, rough metal shapes, tanned leather—increased the demand for the corresponding finished goods and stimulated the trades that

660,000 in industry. Counting dependants, agriculture supported 2,220,000, industry 1,400,000, and commerce 290,000 of a population of 4,340,000. B. S. Chlepner, *Cent ans d'histoire sociale en Belgique* (Brussels, 1956), p. 13.

[1] Of a working force (including unemployed) of 22,913,683, 8,292,692 were engaged in agriculture, forestry, and fishing, as against 8,281,220 in mining and industry. *Statistisches Jahrbuch für das deutsche Reich*, XIX (1898), 7 (Table I, 9).

[2] Peter Quante, *Die Flucht aus der Landwirtschaft* (Berlin-Grünewald, 1933), p. 5.

made them. Here differentiation of product was often pushed to the extreme, and the importance of skill or painstaking labour gave the shop and cottage an advantage over the factory. Even the march of the machine did not always favour power-driven, concentrated manufacture. When the embroidery loom was finally improved in Switzerland to the point of commercial effectiveness in the 1850's, it was installed at first in large weaving sheds; a device of this complexity was beyond the means of most home workers. But before long the manufacturers found that it paid to place these machines in cottages, as the stockingers of Nottingham had done with their frames two hundred years before; and in subsequent decades the loom found its way into the most isolated villages of the Voralberg.[1]

The extension of putting-out on the Continent owed much to the pattern of land tenure. In Britain, the enclosures had promoted the absorption of small holdings into large, commercial exploitations. In east-Elbian Europe, the emancipation of the serfs had similar consequences: the debts imposed on the peasants as the price of their freedom and property so burdened them that many had no choice but to sell their land and either hire out as labourers or leave. Much of western Europe north of the Alps and Pyrenees, however, lay in the hands of independent proprietors; moreover, the prevalence of partible inheritance (written into the Code Civil in France) led to a progressive fragmentation of their already small holdings. The system held an ever larger population on the land, for the children of each generation tended to stay on to work their shares of a diminishing patrimony. On the other hand, even with improved techniques, these small plots were less and less adequate to nourish their occupants. Increasingly, the peasant had to eke out his income with earnings as a farm labourer or cottage worker. Poor soil and division of holdings were the parents of rural industry.

This persistence of the old social framework was a source of great satisfaction to many continental statesmen and writers. In France particularly, where the traditional structure was most tenacious and British industrial success least palatable, society was wont to congratulate itself on being spared the penalties of unbalanced and immoderate growth: the white slavery of the factories; the filth and misery of the cities; the godlessness and radicalism of a rootless proletariat.

In fact, the Continent had its poverty, as conscientious observers were quick to perceive, but much of it was dispersed and, as one investigator put it, latent.[2] In societies where population was increasing

---

[1] Lincke, *Die schweizerische Maschinenindustrie*, pp. 46–7.
[2] Buret, *De la misère des classes laborieuses*, I, 209, 249.

more rapidly than the demand for factory labour, there was a heavy flow into cottage industry, depressing wages in the short run and creating in the long run huge pools of depressed humanity, barely subsisting until the day when even the wages of hunger would not be low enough. The same thing happened in Britain, but to a much smaller degree. For one thing, there was more alternative opportunity: industry drew people; people did not press into industry. The Irish hand-loom weaver was an exception, but, little as he earned, he was probably better off in Lancashire than in Mayo. At least he survived. For another, as we have already noted, it was the Continent that supplied much of the hand labour required to process the semi-finished manufactures of Britain. The weavers of Silesia, Saxony, and central France (the tulle trade of Tarare) were in one sense beneficiaries of British industrial progress; they were also its victims. In effect, they were taking part of the burden of adjustment to the new economic order from Britain's shoulders. The reckoning came in the 1840's, both for those processing British exports and those—in linen, for example—working up home materials. Technological advance, trade depression, and famine combined to produce misery and death on a scale that Britain never knew. Only in Ireland was there anything comparable to the tragedy of the Silesian woollen weavers or the flax spinners of Flanders.[1]

The principal reason for the long survival of putting-out on the Continent was undoubtedly the low cost of rural labour. Linked to this, however, was the docility that normally accompanied dispersion: the entrepreneur found the cottage worker easier to deal with. Again and again, businessmen and officials note the dissipation and indiscipline of the urban proletariat, whether employed in mills or at home. The British hardly discuss the issue—and this in spite of the greater militancy and effectiveness of their labour movement.

The contrast is significant. It reflects, first of all, the difference in entrepreneurial response to factor costs. For the British employer, the best remedy for insubordination was technological unemployment. It hardly occurred to him to allow social considerations to modify the rational organization of his enterprise. Secondly, it reveals the insecurity of the continental bourgeoisie, the deep-rooted fear of another political and social upheaval like 1789. To be sure, England could have and did have her scares: witness Peterloo, or the emergency constabulary of 1848. But these passed, cured by good sense, humour, or both.

[1] On Silesia, see, in addition to Hauptmann's classic, *The Weavers*, the study by S. B. Kan, *Dva vosstaniia silezskikh Tkachei (1793–1844)* [Two uprisings of Silesian weavers] (Moscow, 1948). On Flanders, the standard work is the above-cited (p. 158, n. 1) Jacquemyns, *Histoire de la crise économique des Flandres (1845–1850)*.

Generally speaking, Britain took social order for granted. The industrialist had no illusions about the hostility of the working class or the possibility of violence; but he never doubted that the law would prevail. His French counterpart—and to a lesser extent, the German or Belgian manufacturer—was never sure when labour unrest or unemployment would turn into political revolution. Hence his readiness to equate working-class poverty and criminality—*les classes laborieuses* and *les classes dangereuses*.

Finally, the continental entrepreneur had a different conception of his role from the British. In societies with a strong feudal and manorial tradition, the successful factory owner tended to see himself as master as well as employer, with the duties as well as the privileges that such a position entails. He placed himself *in loco parentis*, treated his workers as minors in need of a firm tutorial hand, and felt a certain responsibility for their job security and welfare—always, of course, at the very modest level suitable to their station. This paternalistic sentiment varied considerably from person to person and place to place; just as Britain had her benevolent manufacturers, especially among the owners of the country mills, so the Continent had its 'exploiters'.[1] On the whole, however, the continental industrialist never achieved that freedom of manœuvre and conscience that comes from looking on labour as just another factor of production, to be hired and fired as needed.

To be sure, even his paternalism was not entirely idealistic. Some of it was a response to the danger and inconvenience of losing a working force collected with difficulty and only too easily dispersed. This was one reason why, in contrast to what Marxist doctrine might lead us to expect, he often encouraged and assisted his men to become proprietors; or why he kept his working force on part time in moments of crisis, even at some sacrifice.[2] Moreover, there was the pressure of public and official opinion. In these early decades of industrialization,

---

[1] Michelet's generalization, impressionistic as it was, probably sums up the situation as well as anything short of a detailed empirical study. The paternalistic employers, he argued (*Le peuple*, ed. L. Refort (Paris, 1946), p. 87), were the very large factory owners and the very small; those in between were hungry, hard, indifferent to everything but their own material interests. Even if they began with some feeling for their men, he noted, they lost it on the battlefield of trade. He might also have noted the opposite phenomenon—the assumption, with prosperity, of the 'enlightened' role expected of the responsible employer. For an analogous phenomenon of assimilation to responsibility with success, this time in banking, cf. Landes, *Bankers and Pashas*, p. 40 and n. 3.

[2] For an analysis of paternalism as a means of training and fixing the industrial labour force, cf. Carl Jantke, *Der Vierte Stand: die gestaltenden Kräfte der deutschen Arbeiterbewegung im XIX. Jahrhundert* (Freiburg, 1955), pp. 175–8.

both the traditional elites and the governments they dominated had serious qualms about the implications of a concentrated proletariat. There were many who felt that economic strength was not worth the price of social subversion. If many of these doubtful elements were won over in the long run to industrial capitalism, it was partly because they accepted the image of the paternalistic entrepreneur and saw in the maintenance of traditional personal bonds between employer and employed a powerful instrument of social control. And when the employer forgot his obligations, the state was prepared to remind him of them. In France, the government was sensitive to factory unemployment as to nothing else, keeping close watch on hiring and firing and utilizing political pressure when necessary to limit the number of jobless, even in—or rather, especially in—severe crises.

What we have, in short, is the usual phenomenon of legitimation by means of assumption of a role acceptable to the society as a whole. In the process, these attitudes, whatever their original motivation, tended to become an integral part of the entrepreneurial personality. The paternalistic manufacturer of the Continent believed that he was father to his men. And it was the very sincerity of this belief that often made him inflexible in his dealings with organized labour. For the British employer, a union may have been an adversary, a strike vexing and costly, the effort of labour to raise wages chimerical. He did not like these things, but he was prepared to face up to them. For the continental employer, however, a union was a conspiracy against public order and morals; a strike, an act of ingratitude; the effort of labour to raise wages, the indiscipline of an impatient son. All of this was evil. And there is no negotiating with evil.[1]

Similarly with the efforts of the state to dictate hours or conditions of work: any such move was an intolerable intrusion that could only undermine the authority of the master. To the requirements of the factory act of 1841, the family enterprises of France, of northern France especially, opposed a deep, indignant immobility that discouraged examination and disarmed enforcement. The law called for voluntary inspectors from among the manufacturers themselves, active and retired. It was a fiasco: few volunteered and many of these soon resigned in despair or under pressure of friends and colleagues. There is no collaborating with evil.

[1] This paternalism will seem to some incompatible with that deep-rooted fear of the people discussed above. On the contrary: the paternalistic businessman rarely feared his own men; presumably he knew them and they trusted him. But they were children, even savage children, and could be led astray. See the reaction of Gaston Motte to a strike in his great-grandfather's plant in 1847: it was probably the work of outside agitators, as was not infrequently the case. L. Machu, 'La crise de l'industrie textile à Roubaix au milieu du XIXe siècle', Revue du Nord, XXXVIII (1956), 72, n. 1.

CHAPTER 4

Closing the Gap

The period from 1850 to 1873 was Continental industry's coming-of-age. It was a period of unprecedentedly rapid growth, which may be best conveyed—in the absence of year-by-year calculations of national income or product—by certain critical time series:[1] railroad mileage, coal consumption or output, steam-power capacity, make of pig iron, consumption of raw cotton. In all these areas (with the exception of cotton, whose manufacture suffered a grievous setback in the 1860's), whether for France, Belgium, or Germany, the *compound* rate of increase runs between 5 and 10 per cent a year (see Table 4).

These were also years of technological maturation. They were marked in essence by the working-out on the Continent of those innovations that constitute the heart of the Industrial Revolution and had been developed and diffused in Britain a generation or more earlier. In textiles the self-actor and power loom replaced the mule and hand

[1] We have annual estimates of the national income of Great Britain from 1870 on. There are several series at the historian's disposal; they differ in detail, but are essentially congruent. See the brief discussion and the literature cited in William Ashworth, *An Economic History of England 1870–1939* (London and New York, 1960), pp. 186–9. For the earlier period, we have occasional contemporary estimates, critically analysed by Phyllis Deane (see above, p. 47, n. 1), and the decennial figures (1801 on) calculated by Deane and Cole, *British Economic Growth* (1962), pp. 166–7. The nearest thing we possess to an *annual* estimate of national product is Walter Hoffman's series of industrial output. See his *British Industry 1700–1950* (Liverpool, 1955).
We now have decennial averages of French national product (goods, not services) going back to the late eighteenth century. These have been calculated at the Institut de Science Economique Appliquée by a group headed by Jean Marczewski. He offers a preliminary statement of the results, which represent the first step in a long-range programme to develop an annual series, in 'Some Aspects of the Economic Growth of France, 1660–1958', *Economic Development and Cultural Change*, IX (1961), 369–86; see also W.W. Rostow (ed.), *The Economics of Take-off into Sustained Growth* [papers of a Conference of the International Economic Association at Konstanz, 2–11 September 1960] (London, 1963).
German figures of national income, in the form of decennial averages, have been worked out by W. G. Hoffmann, J. H. Müller, F. Knoll and associates back to 1850. It is hoped to develop an annual series and to push the data farther back in time. Cf. the chapter by Hoffman, *ibid.*, pp. 95–118. See also Hoffmann and Müller, *Das deutsche Volkseinkommen 1851–1957* (Tübingen, 1959); and Wagenführ's estimates of industrial output cited below, p. 329, n. 1.

Table 4. *Economic Development in the Third Quarter of the Nineteenth Century*

	Railroad mileage (statute miles)	Coal production or consumption (1000 metric tons)[b]	Steam-power capacity[e] (1000 h.p.)	Pig iron output (1000 metric tons)	Raw cotton consumption (1000 metric tons)
Germany					
1850	3,639	5,100[c]	260	212	17·1
1869	10,834	26,774	2,480	1,413	64·1
1873[a]	14,842	36,392	—	2,241	117·8
France					
1850	1,869	7,225	370	406	59·3
1869	10,518	21,432	1,850	1,381	93·7
1873[a]	11,500	24,702	—	1,382	55·4[g]
United Kingdom					
1850	6,621	37,500[d]	1,290[f]	2,249	266·8[f]
1869	15,145	97,066	4,040[f]	5,446	425·8[f]
1873	16,082	112,604	—	6,566	565·1[f]
Belgium					
1850	531	3,481	70	145	10·0
1869	1,800	7,822	350	535	16·3
1873	2,335	10,219	—	607	18·0

SOURCES AND NOTES

Railroad mileage. G. Stürmer, *Geschichte der Eisenbahnen* (Bromberg, 1872), pp. 90–1, 54–61, 137, 149, 154–8; William Page, *Commerce and Industry* (2 vols.; London, 1919), II, 170–1; *Statistisches Jahrbuch für das deutsche Reich*, XII (1891), 90; *Annu. statistique de la France*, VII (1884), 456; *Annu. statistique de la Belgique*, XXI (1890), 326, 328.

Coal. We have no official estimates for Britain before 1854. The unofficial guesses before that date all proved to be serious underestimates when complete returns came in. For this early period, see the 'Report of the Commissioners Appointed to Inquire into

[a] All German figures for 1873 are swollen by the annexation of Alsace-Lorraine; conversely the French achievements are diminished.

[b] For Germany, production; for the U.K., France, and Belgium, consumption. (The one country for which consumption figures are indispensable is France, which was importing almost 40 per cent of its coal requirements in 1850, almost 30 per cent in 1869.) For Germany, production of ordinary coal only; to this would have to be added lignite (7,569,000 tons in 1869, 9,752,900 tons in 1873), with a calorific content roughly equal to two-ninths that of regular coal.

[c] An estimate based on extrapolation of a ratio of Prussian to German output of 82 to 100 (the ratio of 1860). Prussian coal output in 1850 is given as 4,153,000 tons.

[d] By extrapolation from post-1854 figures.

[e] Estimates for 1850 and 1870 (on 1869 lines) only.

[f] Great Britain, rather than United Kingdom.

[g] A bad year; consumption in 1872 was 80,257 tons.

the Several Matters Relating to Coal in the United Kingdom, Report of Committee E', in *Parliamentary Papers*, 1871, XVIII (C. 435–II). These have been reprinted in such other sources as J. R. McCulloch's *Commercial Dictionary*, and A. J. Mundella, 'What Are the Conditions on Which the Commercial and Manufacturing Supremacy of Great Britain Depend, and Is There Any Reason to Think They May Have Been or May Be Endangered?' *J. Roy. Statistical Soc.* XLI (1878), 109. For the period after 1854, there are the annual volumes of Robert Hunt's *Mineral Statistics*: or the 'Final Report of the Royal Commission...Coal Resources' (Cd. 2363), in *Parliamentary Papers*, 1905, XVI, 24–5. For Germany, official figures for the entire *Zollverein* go back to 1860; cf. the *Statistisches Jahrbuch*, I (1880), 30; XIV (1893), 128. For earlier years, we have figures of output in Prussia in A. Bienengräber, *Statistik des Verkehrs und Verbrauchs im Zollverein* (Berlin, 1868), p. 260; and K. F. Dieterici, *Statistische Uebersicht der wichtigsten Gegenstände des Verkehrs und Verbrauchs im preussischen Staate und im deutschen Zollverbande* (6 vols.; Berlin, 1838–1857), passim. For France, *Annu. statistique*, rés. rétro. LVII (1946), 230*–1*. For Belgium, Amé Wibail, 'L'évolution économique de l'industrie charbonnière belge depuis 1831', *Bull. de l'Inst. des Sciences Economiques* (Louvain), VI, no. 1 (1934), 21–2.

Steam power. From Mulhall, *Dictionary of Statistics* (4th ed.; London, 1899), p. 545.

Pig iron. As with coal, official British iron statistics begin in 1854; the subsequent returns are given in Hunt, *Mineral Statistics*. See also the *Iron and Coal Trades Review*, Diamond Jubilee Number (December 1927), p. 133. For the years before 1854, see British Iron and Steel Federation, *Statistics of the Iron and Steel Industries* (London, 1934), p. 4; H. Scrivenor, *History of the Iron Trade* (London, 1854); and W. Oechelhäuser, *Vergleichende Statistik der Eisen-Industrie aller Länder* (Berlin, 1852), p. 144. For Germany, see Beck, *Geschichte des Eisens*, IV, 731–2, 982; *Statistisches Jahrbuch*, III (1883), 34. For France, *Annu. statistique*, rés. rétro. LVIII (1951), 134–5. For Belgium, A. Wibail, 'L'évolution économique de la sidérurgie belge de 1830 à 1913', *Bull. de l'Inst. des Sciences Economiques*, V, no. 1 (1933), 50–1, 60.

Raw Cotton. For Britain, T. Ellison, *The Cotton Trade of Great Britain* (London, 1886), appendix, table 1. For Germany, Bienengräber, *Statistik*, pp. 202–3; *Statistisches Jahrbuch*, III (1882), 134. For France, *Annu. statistique*, LVII (1946), 241*–2*. For Belgium, *Annu. statistique de la Belgique*, II (1871), 226–7; VI (1875), 236–7.

loom. The iron industry consummated the shift from vegetable to mineral fuel. The steam-engine sealed its triumph over the water wheel. The heavy chemical industry was firmly established and the technical possibilities of the salt-soda-acid complex exploited along the lines implicit in the Leblanc process. Finally, the machine spread ever more widely—into nail-making and the cutlery trade, the stamping of heavy metal forms, tailoring, the manufacture of paper, and other fields too numerous to list.

This description of the middle decades of the century as a period of technical maturation, of the working-out and diffusion of earlier developments, is not meant to imply that invention had ceased and that the gains of productivity were all made behind a stable technological frontier. On the contrary, these were years of sustained creativity which saw some of the most important innovations of the century.

But these innovations were either complementary to the original bundle of changes that constituted, as we noted, the heart of the Industrial Revolution; or they anticipated the future and did not come to fruition until the last third of the century. The machine comber, steam hammer, and the compound steam-engine—all of them actually introduced in the 1840's—fall in the former category. The Bessemer converter and Siemens-Martin hearth, the industrial use of electricity, the gas motor, artificial coal tar dyes, and the Solvay ammonia process belong in the latter; with their ramification and elaboration in later decades, they laid the basis for a new long wave of expansion that some writers have come to call the Second Industrial Revolution.

The quickening of the pace of development in the 1850's can be understood only in terms of a remarkable conjuncture of endogenous and exogenous stimuli to growth. Negative, first: the nations of western and central Europe had lifted the mortgage of pre-capitalist institutions, broken the strongest of the bonds of tradition, and, thanks to the railroad, were well on the way to eliminating those natural obstacles to the movement of the factors of production and to the exchange of goods that had fragmented and straitened economic activity since time past memory. We noted above that the productivity of a transportation facility is discontinuous, jumping sharply with each of the connections that turn isolated lines into a coherent network. Belgium had her north–south, east–west cross by 1844. For Germany, the critical gains came in the late 1840's: by 1850 goods and passengers could move by rail—with numerous changes, to be sure—from Aachen to Breslau and from Kiel to Munich. France was the slowest of the three: as of the middle of the century, she still had only the beginnings of a radial network out of Paris, plus some scattered pieces in the provinces. But the early 1850's were years of rapid construction, and by the end of 1854 lines were open from Lille to Bordeaux and Marseilles and from Le Havre to Strasbourg.

The economic implications of cheaper transport have already been discussed; the effect on the market and competition, however, deserves to be stressed again. Rapid growth and technological advance do not necessarily go hand in hand. On the contrary, an increase in demand may so raise prices as to make obsolescent methods profitable and encourage producers to retain, or return to using equipment that would otherwise be abandoned. If the decades of the 1850's and 1860's were characterized by both major gains in output and a drastic purge of industrial enterprise, it was in large measure because certain of the changes in the technological and commercial climate were at once excitant and cathartic. The railroad was basic here: it provided the means by which competitive pressures could be applied and marginally inefficient units, once protected by distance and topography, squeezed out.

On the other hand, rail transport by itself was simply a means. In societies like those of the Continent, where human values, habit, and law joined to deprecate and diminish price competition, an incentive or compulsion to struggle was needed if the market mechanism was to be effective in diffusing technological change. Periodic crises, with their abrupt contractions of credit and deflation of demand and prices, served in their times as 'moments of truth'; that of 1857 was especially purgative. At the same time, however, a conjuncture of institutional changes exercised over these decades a persistent pressure toward rationalization—(1) within the individual national economies, by facilitating the entry of new firms and the expansion of the more efficient and ambitious; and (2) between economies, by opening them to foreign enterprise and manufactures.

Thus, already before 1850, the limitations on *Gewerbefreiheit* that persisted in some parts of central Europe were essentially confined to the traditional handicrafts and had little effect on the development of a factory labour force. But in the early 1860's even these vestiges of control disappeared in all but a few areas, and freedom of enterprise was incorporated in the *Gewerbeordnung für den Norddeutscher Bund* adopted by the North German Confederation in 1869 and introduced into the southern states from 1870 to 1872.[1] Similarly, restrictions on the establishment of joint-stock corporations—a form of enterprise indispensable in economies poor in capital and yet compelled to create much of their industry *de novo*—were mitigated by increasing complaisance of the state or evaded by recourse to substitute forms not requiring official authorization, in particular, the *société en commandite par actions* (*Kommanditgesellschaft auf Aktien*). In Germany, moreover, the very multiplicity of jurisdictions proved an advantage. In fields like banking and insurance, where location was not rigidly dictated by material considerations, it was often possible to obtain from the smaller states the authorization refused by Prussia or Frankfurt.

In the meantime, the growing demand by projectors, industrialists, and investors for easier conditions of company formation overcame the suspicions and hostility of the governing bureaucracy and the general

---

[1] The most convenient introduction to the history of *Gewerbefreiheit* is the articles on 'Handwerk' and 'Zunftwesen' by Wilhelm Stieda in the *Handwörterbuch der Staatswissenschaften* (3rd ed., Jena 1911). The classic study of the subject is Kurt von Rohrscheidt, *Vom Zunftzwang zur Gewerbefreiheit* (Berlin, 1898). See also T. Hamerow, *Restoration and Reaction* (Princeton, 1958), ch. II and bibliographical notes, pp. 295–6, and Wolfram Fischer, *Handwerksrecht und Handwerkswirtschaft um 1800* (Berlin, 1955), ch. III, which in spite of the title deals with later developments.

resentment and fear of free speculation and secured the right to limited liability by simple registration. The first country to take this step was Britain, in 1856 (generalized by Act of 1862). In 1863 France created the *société à responsabilité limité*, a true limited-liability corporation, but restricted in size; the complete abolition of controls did not come until 1867. Germany was somewhat slower. A number of jurisdictions, Hamburg and Lübeck for example, had always permitted free incorporation. The vast majority, however, including Prussia, required authorization, and while the state proved tolerant in certain areas—insurance, transportation, public utilities—it tended to be difficult about manufacturing ventures and intolerant of banking projects. Nothing illustrates more clearly the dampening effect of these controls than the increase in company formation in Prussia after the establishment of automatic registration in June 1870: 123 firms capitalized at 225 million taler in all the years before 1850; 295 firms capitalized at 802 million taler from 1851 to 1870; 833 firms at 843 million taler from 1870 to 1874.[1] Even allowing for the stimulating boom conditions of the last years, the power of this release from constraint is impressive. A similar explosion took place in Britain in the early 1860's and another, though much weaker, in France after 1867.[2]

There were other legal changes in the direction of freer, easier enterprise. The prohibition of usury was dropped in Britain (1854), Holland (1857), Belgium (1865), Prussia and the North German Confederation (1867).[3] Increasingly, foreign corporations were permitted to cross boundary lines and operate on a basis of equality with home firms without special authorization (thus agreements by France and Belgium, 1857, and France and Britain, 1862). New commercial instruments like the cheque were legalized and domesticated; the penalties for debt and bankruptcy were eased; patent law was amended to include trademarks and other intangible forms of business property; and commercial relations in general were simplified by the codification of the

---

[1] *Jahrbuch für die amtliche Statistik des Preussischen Staates*, IV, 1 (1876), 134. See also Ernst Engel, *Die erwerbsthätigen juristischen Personen, insbesondere die Actiengesellschaften, im preussischen Staate* (Berlin, 1876). On the general question of legal structure, company formation, and economic development, see D. S. Landes, 'The Structure of Enterprise in the Nineteenth Century: the Cases of Britain and Germany', in Comité International des Sciences Historiques, XIe Congrès International des Sciences Historiques, Stockholm, 21–28 août 1960, *Rapports*, vol. v: *Histoire contemporaine* (Uppsala, 1960), pp. 107–28, and the sources cited there.

[2] On the British boom of the 1860's, see Landes, *Bankers and Pashas*, ch. II.

[3] By law of 9 June 1857, the Bank of France was permitted to set its rate of discount at more than 6 per cent; this privilege was extended by judicial interpretation to all banking houses.

congeries of statutes and decrees accumulated over the years (French law of 13 June 1866; *Allgemeines Deutsche Handelsgesetzbuch*, 1861 [Prussia] *et seq.*).

In all these and other areas, the gains of the middle decades were simply a continuation of trends that went back to the eighteenth century and beyond. The history of commercial and civil law in the West is in large measure the story of the progressive adaptation of the usages of an agrarian, community-centred, tradition-bound society to the requirements of an industrial, individualistic, and rational—hence mobile—capitalism. The full story remains to be told; unfortunately, this is an area that economic historians have tended to ignore or leave to legists.[1] Yet one should not confuse indifference or dismissal with a considered judgment, and it would be a mistake to construe the paucity of material as evidence of the triviality of the subject.

On the other hand, lack of data and analysis does make it difficult to integrate legal considerations into the complex of factors shaping economic growth. Clearly, many of these changes are simply surface manifestations of a deeper transformation; the law is the reflection—frequently a belated reflection—of man's values and material needs. But the fact that it is often belated is evidence that it is not simply a dependent variable in the service of economic development. Not only do economic interests conflict and pull both legislation and administration in different directions; non-economic considerations have their say, and questions of morality and social prejudices intervene. Finally the law has a rationale of its own—a conservatism built on precedent and the niggling complexity of institutionalized justice.

As a result, the timing of changes in legal institutions can and does materially affect the pace and character of economic development. The impact on short-run growth—on the rhythm and amplitude of the cycle, for example—is most obvious. The long-run effect is less easily discernible, and indeed the nature of the relationship between short and long run is still a subject of debate among economic theorists and historians. Suffice it to note here that this reciprocal adjustment of law and industrial capitalism did take place over a period of more than a century; that one of the periods of most rapid change in both areas was the middle decades of the last century; and that the legal changes of that period, especially those establishing the charter of modern corporate enterprise, contributed substantially to continental Europe's new-found ability to compete with Britain.

One modification of the politico-legal climate of enterprise deserves special mention: the general lowering of barriers to international trade.

[1] One of the few books that have attempted to deal with the problem is Georges Ripert, *Aspects juridiques du capitalisme moderne* (2nd ed.; Paris, 1951).

This took three forms: (1) the elimination or reduction of restrictions and levies on the traffic of such international waterways as the Danube (1857), the Rhine (1861), the Scheldt (1863), the lower Elbe (1861), upper Elbe (1863 and 1870), the Danish Sound and the channels between the Baltic and North Seas (1857); (2) the simplification of the confusion of currencies that was the monetary counterpart of Europe's political fragmentation (German union thaler of 1857; uniform Austrian florin, 1858; Latin monetary agreement among France, Belgium, Switzerland, and Italy, 1865); and most important (3) a series of commercial treaties providing for a substantial diminution of tariff rates between the leading industrial nations of Europe (Britain–France, 1860; France–Belgium, 1861; France–Prussia, 1862; by extension, France–*Zollverein*, 1866; Prussia-Belgium, 1863 and 1865; Prussia–Britain, 1865; Prussia-Italy, 1865; and numerous others).

This cluster of trade agreements is unique in economic history. It would be impossible here to examine in detail the particular reasons why each of the signatories decided to sacrifice traditional protections of home industry and trade for the benefits of increased exchange and the risks of competition. We may note in passing, however, that aside from the usual pressure of selected business groups for lower tariffs and the special political considerations that motivated, first, Napoleon III and then the government of Prussia to seek freer trade by treaty, these accords reflected a general mood of optimism and of doctrinal acceptance, in political and intellectual if not in business circles, of the pacific as well as economic virtues of international exchange. *Aperire terram gentibus* was the slogan of the day. Here we rejoin in effect the legal liberalization discussed above. It was as though the very expansiveness of the economy, the general euphoria of growth and prosperity, had persuaded nations and people to let their guard down, to trade control for freedom, parochialism for universalism, tradition for change, the safety of exclusiveness for the danger yet potential profit of the open world.

Freedom was, as we shall see, a fleeting mood, an aberration. The period from the late 1870's on was one of steady closure and constriction, reversed—and then for how long?—only after the Second World War. While the mood lasted, however, it gave a powerful impetus to specialization along lines of comparative advantage, with concomitant economies of scale and increases in return. To the surprise of adamant protectionists—if not to their discomfiture—all nations saw their volume of exports grow. Home industries did not collapse before British competition, but rather changed and grew stronger in the process. Marginally inefficient firms, vegetating in the shelter of protective duties, were compelled to re-tool or close. In France especially, where the high tariff had long been a fetish, the effect of the commercial treaties, coming as they did on the heels of a severe commercial crisis (1857-9), was to purge manufacturing enterprise and hasten its relocation along rational lines.[1] In Germany and Belgium, where customs rates had been lower, the impact was necessarily weaker.

Even more important than these negative stimuli in shaping the conjuncture of the 1850's and 1860's were the positive forces for expansion: (1) improvements in transport, (2) new sources of energy and raw materials, (3) a sharp increase in the supply of money, and above all (4) a creative entrepreneurial response to this combination of long-run opportunity and short-run facility.

1. Transportation first: the most important advance was the continued ramification of the railroad system.[2] Fifty thousand miles of new line were laid in Europe between 1850 and 1870, as against 15,000 in all the years before, at a cost of 30 milliard francs. Of these, the French built 9300, at an outlay of over 7 milliard francs, while the Germans, profiting from lower land costs and economizing on the roadbed, built 7500 miles for about 4 milliards. Even so, almost three quarters of the share capital invested in Prussian joint-stock companies from 1850 to 1870 went to railway firms. And these expenditures do not take into account investment in and production of rails and rolling stock for lines in other countries. Already in the 1840's, Britain had played an important role in the construction of the early continental railways, exporting labour and skills as well as capital and material. In the 1850's Britain turned her attention increasingly to areas outside of Europe—Egypt, India, North America—while France became the most active promoter and builder of European roads—in Spain, Switzerland, Italy, the Danube valley, and Russia. Exact figures are not available, but it would seem that France was placing more than half as much money in foreign railways in this period as she put into her own.[3]

---

[1] Cf. A. L. Dunham, *The Anglo-French Treaty of Commerce of 1860 and the Progress of the Industrial Revolution in France* (Ann Arbor, 1930); and C. Fohlen, *L'industrie textile au temps du Second Empire* (Paris, 1956). The archives of individual firms—for example, De Wendel and Le Creusot in iron and steel manufacture—offer eloquent evidence of the retooling undertaken in response to the new conditions of international competition.

[2] On the contribution of the railway to economic growth, see above, p. 153.

[3] On Britain, the best treatment remains Leland Jenks's classic *Migration of British Capital to 1875* (New York, 1927). On France, see Rondo Cameron, *France and the Economic Development of Europe, 1800–1914: Conquests of Peace and Seeds of War* (Princeton, 1961), who estimates French investment in foreign transport at 5250 million francs from 1852 to 1881 (see table 3, p. 88). A team at the Centre de Recherches sur l'Histoire des Entreprises (which is in turn part of the Centre de Recherches Historiques) in Paris is currently preparing, under the direction of Bertrand Gille, a series of studies

From mid-century on, the railroad, by its demand for capital goods
and labour and the cumulative effect of these expenditures as they
worked and reworked their way through the economy, had displaced
textiles as the drummer of industrial activity, setting the beat for short
cycles and long trends alike.

2. Manufacturing industry is from one point of view the use of
energy to transform raw materials into finished products. With the
growth of industry, the appetite of European economies for both these
ingredients grew enormously; one can follow the hunt for new
sources of supply from the Middle Ages on. And clearly, if this search
had not been successful or if substitutes for commodities in short supply
had not been found, the Industrial Revolution as we have known it
would have been impossible. The reader will recall in this connection
the importance of coke smelting to the British iron manufacture, of
the replacement of vegetable by mineral sources of alkali to the
chemical industry, of Eli Whitney's gin and American cultivation to
the cotton trade.

The discovery or creation of new sources of energy and raw materials
is in part responsive to need, in part fortuitous. Both factors give rise
to irregularity in the growth of the stock of resources at the disposal of
the economy: there are fat periods and lean. The middle decades of the
nineteenth century were bonanza years in both respects. Bird droppings
(guano) were collected from islands in the Pacific and brought as
fertilizer to the fields of Europe. Wool and hides from Australia, South
Africa, and South America began to pour into the European market
and submerge domestic sources of supply; the wool was the more welcome for the cotton famine of the 1860's, which cut severely into the
output of cotton cloth and clothing.[1] Vegetable oils, mainly from Africa,
became increasingly important as a substitute for traditional animal

---

on the export of French capital. A number of preliminary articles on the subject have
already appeared in the *Bulletin* of the Centre. Germany, poorer to begin with and
investing more heavily in home industry, was slow to join the competition for concessions and contracts; even then, her role was never comparable to that of Britain or
France.

[1] Imports of raw wool into the United Kingdom by source (annual averages in
millions of pounds weight):

	South Africa	Australia and New Zealand	South America
1840–4	1·4	14·0	5·0
1850–4	6·7	43·7	6·5
1860–4	18·9	75·0	14·3
1870–4	37·1	188·6	18·2

SOURCE. *Statistical Abstract for the United Kingdom.*

fats in the production of soap and candles.[1] The effort of a French syndicate of the 1830's to exploit a monopoly of Sicilian sulphur and squeeze the European chemical trade led to the perfecting of processes using sulphides as the raw material for the manufacture of sulphuric acid and to the discovery of new deposits of pyrites in the United Kingdom, Norway and, above all, Spain. By the 1870's, well over 90 per cent of Britain's acid was prepared in this manner.[2] The world was indeed opening up.

More important, however, and second only to the railroad as a focus of investment and stimulus to entrepreneurial activity, was the availability of newly found or exploited energy resources, above all, coal. The existence of deeper beds beneath the marl of Westphalia was known as early as the 1830's, but the first efforts at extraction were handicapped by lack of capital, and a precise apprehension of the nature of the deposits took decades. The discovery and prospection of the Pas-de-Calais extension of the Northern field in France came later, in 1845–7. In both cases the real harvest came in the 1850's. Coal output in the Ruhr went from 1,640,000 tons in 1850 to 11,812,500 in 1869; the gains in the Pas-de-Calais were equally spectacular: 4672 tons in 1851 to 2,188,247 in 1871. At the same time, as noted earlier, overall extraction rose substantially in both countries—in Germany, from 4,192,000 to 23,761,000 tons; in France, from 4,434,000 to 13,330,000.[3]

The Germans were doubly favoured in their exploitation of the deeper Ruhr beds. Not only did the coal extracted provide energy; it produced a coke ideally suited to the blast furnace; and iron ore was found interspersed with some of the measures, yielding a *Kohleneisenstein* comparable to the blackband that had made possible the great expansion of Scottish metallurgy in the 1830's. From 1852 to 1860 ore extraction in the Ruhr jumped from 5000 to 227,000 tons. Once the Westphalian industrialists realized the potentiality of this providential

[1] Annual averages of imports of vegetable oils into the United Kingdom:

	Palm oil (thousand cwt.)	Coconut oil (thousand cwt.)	Olive oil (thousand tuns)
1840–4	395·0	57·2	10·9
1850–4	593·9	125·8	12·8
1860–4	773·4	267·0	19·1
1870–4	1001·7	244·8	28·7

SOURCE. *Statistical Abstract for the United Kingdom.*

[2] In the period from 1840 to, say, 1880, Britain's annual consumption of pyrites increased from a negligible amount to perhaps 700,000 or 800,000 tons. Cf. Haber *Chemical Industry*, p. 103.

[3] For statistics of the output of coal in the Ruhr, see Prussia, Königliches Statistisches Bureau, *Jahrbuch für die amtliche Statistik des Preussischen Staates*, IV, 1 (1876), 235.

combination, they went over to coke-blast iron with a vigour that not only redeemed the technological retardation of the first half of the century but has tended to obscure the very memory of this earlier lag.

3. The contribution of new gold to European industrial development in the 1850's is only partially measurable in terms of the direct increase in the supply of money. This was impressive enough: even allowing for a responsively swelling export of silver to the East, the net gain was a substantial fraction of the pre-existing metallic circulation, especially important in countries like France and Germany where popular mistrust and the conservatism of financial and official circles inhibited the use of paper money. At the same time, issue of paper money increased on the strength of the growing stock of bullion: note circulation of the Bank of France more than tripled, rising from 450 million francs in 1850 to 1550 million in 1870;[1] while that of the Preussische Bank, desirous of replacing with its own paper the notes of other German institutions, shot upward at a dizzy pace—from 18,370 million taler in 1850 to 163,260 millions in 1870.[2]

More significant, however, were the indirect consequences of easy money. The rate of interest fell, momentarily to as little as 2 per cent on short-term paper in Britain, 3 per cent in France, slightly higher in Germany (always hungrier for capital). Concomitantly, the volume of credit expanded. This was the critical consideration, for—as mentioned earlier—it is not so much the price of capital that counts as its availability. Supply and demand curves may be smooth and continuous in theory; they may even be so in practice for certain commodities in certain markets at certain times. But the short-run supply curve of bank credit—as against that of all credit, usurious and otherwise—is truncated by the banker's values, by his sanctification of prudence, security, liquidity. Up to a point, the institutional lender tries to ration funds by price; beyond that point, he fixes quotas, or simply waits for the outlook to improve. And while there are other lenders, these are often limited in resources or set conditions so onerous as to make borrowing irrational—without choking it off, however: desperation is notoriously deaf to reason.

Moreover, this increase in the volume of credit was far out of pro-

---

[1] *Annuaire statistique*, LVII (1946), rés. rétro. pp. 140*–1*.

[2] H. von Poschinger, *Bankwesen und Bankpolitik in Preussen* (3 vols.; Berlin, 1879), II, 373. Some of this increase is explained by laws of 1855 and 1857 that forbade the circulation of banknotes of other German States within the Prussian monarchy. But Poschinger seems to have underestimated the increase. According to the *Jahrbuch für die amtliche Statistik des Preussischen Staats*, IV, 1 (1876), 469, the note circulation of the Preussische Bank in 1870 was 586,437,000 marks (equal to 195,479,000 taler).

portion to that of the money supply. The critical consideration was the rediscount policy of the central banks, and this was essentially a function of bullion reserves. These jumped for the Bank of England from £8·3 millions in October 1847, to an average of £21·8 million in the third quarter of 1852; for the Bank of France, from one of 122·6 million francs in 1847 to 584·8 million in 1852.[1] And when the central banks were ready to take paper, everybody was ready to take paper. The great pyramid of debt could be built higher, fostering speculation in commodities and securities, facilitating the formation of new companies and the operation of old. Like the merchants of the Medina del Campo and the Antwerp *bourse* in the sixteenth century, the traders and bankers of nineteenth-century London and Paris waited eagerly for the first word of sails off Land's End or l'Ouessant bringing golden cargoes from the Pacific. The amounts involved were a tiny fraction of debts outstanding in the money and securities markets; but they made all the difference between easy and hard liquidation at month's end.

To be sure, the stimulus afforded by such an injection of money weakened rapidly as inflation vitiated the incremental advantages of investment and the exponential demand for credit pushed the rate of interest upward. Nevertheless, one must not underestimate the long-run significance of such periodic excitants. For one thing, they can change the pattern and significance of the business cycle, making upswings more buoyant and downturns milder, with obviously favourable consequences for the rate of growth.[2] Thus the industrial as well as commercial development of this period is in large measure the story of three great credit booms: 1852–7 (Britain, Germany, France); 1861–6 (more Britain than Germany or France); and 1869–73 (primarily Germany). The last, like the others, was built on easy money, derived, however, not from an influx of gold, but from a transfusion of five milliard francs—Bismarck's unprecedented war indemnity after the triumph of 1870. For another, they facilitate the accomplishment of technological and institutional changes of continuing importance.

4. These bring us to what may be called the 'financial revolution' of the nineteenth century. This was closely associated with the credit inflation of these years, both as cause and effect, and was the counterpart and companion piece in the banking sphere to the technological transformation of industry.

[1] For the Bank of England, T. Tooke and Newmarch, *A History of Prices and of the State of the Circulation from 1792 to 1856* (5 vols.; New York [reprinted], n.d.), p. 566; see also J. R. T. Hughes, *Fluctuations in Trade, Industry and Finance: A Study of British Economic Development 1850–1860* (Oxford, 1960), p. 290. For the Bank of France, *Ann. statistique*, LCII (1946), rés. rétro. p. 140*.

[2] Cf. the analysis of I. Svennilson, *Growth and Stagnation in the European Economy* (Geneva: United Nations Economic Commission for Europe, 1954), pp. 12–13.

The revolution had two aspects. One was a drastic widening of the clientele for banking services and credit. Here, as in industrial mass production, Britain pioneered. Her early 'vulgarization' of the money market was, as we have seen, a source of great economic strength, and the rise of the great discount houses and the joint-stock commercial banks (London and Westminster Bank, 1834) continued the process.[1] If one sets aside certain early efforts, generally abortive, the diffusion of these principles to the Continent dates from the 1850's. There were, first, the joint-stock discount banks established to ease commercial credit during and after the crisis of 1848: the French and Belgian comptoirs d'escompte; the Union du Crédit in Brussels (1848); the Schaff-hausen'sche Bankverein in Cologne (1848); the Discontogesellschaft in Berlin (1851); the Frankfurter Bank (1853). These were followed by such institutions as the Crédit Industriel et Commercial in Paris (1859), explicitly intended to introduce English commercial banking practice to France and a pioneer on the Continent in the use of the cheque as an instrument of payment. Finally, the great branch banks rounded out the system, some resulting from the proliferation of the institutions in the great financial centres (including central banks like the Banque de France), others developing out of local enterprises like the Crédit Lyonnais (1863). The result was a vastly more efficient sweep of financial resources: the new banking networks were able to draw in the rapidly growing savings and working capital of myriads of small and middling tradesmen and producers; for the first time, they brought country as well as city into the money market. Thus the Continent began to approach that mobility of capital that Britain had achieved half a century before.[2]

More important, however, for industrial development was the second half of this revolution: the rise of the joint-stock investment bank. This was a continental innovation and went back at least as far as

[1] The best source is W. T. C. King, History of the London Discount Market (London, 1936); see also S. Evelyn Thomas, The Rise and Growth of Joint-Stock Banking, vol. 1: (Britain to 1860) (London, 1934).

[2] The literature on the banking history of this period is fairly abundant. Among the more useful secondary sources are, for France: R. Bigo, Les banques françaises au cours du XIXe siècle (Paris, 1947); A. Courtois fils, Histoire des banques en France (2nd ed.; Paris, 1881); P. Dupont-Ferrier, Le marché financier de Paris sous le Second Empire (Paris, 1925); E. Kaufmann, La banque en France (trans. A. S. Sacker; Paris, 1914); Jean Bouvier, Le Crédit Lyonnais de 1863 à 1882 (2 vols.; Paris, 1961); and G. Ramon, Histoire de la Banque de France (Paris, 1929).

For Germany, see Poschinger, Bankwesen und Bankpolitik; A. Krueger, Das Kölner Bankiergewerbe vom Ende des 18. Jahrhunderts bis 1875 (Essen, 1925); F. Hecht, Bank-wesen und Bankpolitik in den süddeutschen Staaten 1819–1875 (Jena, 1880); K. Jackel, Gründung und Entwicklung der Frankfurter Bank, 1854–1900 (Leipzig, 1915).

For Belgium, see B. S. Chlepner, Le marché financier belge depuis cent ans (Brussels,

those years after the Congress of Vienna when Europe set out once again on the path to a modern economy. As early as 1819 a plan for a Bavarian National Bank included a provision for mortgage loans to industrial enterprise; the Estates tabled the proposal.[1] A more specific project by a group of French bankers and manufacturers to found a *Société Commanditaire de l'Industrie* failed in 1825 owing to opposition from the defenders of the power of landed wealth. It was in Belgium that the institution got its start. There the *Société Générale* (founded 1822; began with mortgage loans to industrial enterprise in the 1820's; turned to intensive investment banking in 1835) and the *Banque de Belgique* (1835) promoted a company boom in mining and metallurgy in the years 1835–8 that accounts for the precocity of Belgian industrialization.[2] In the 1840's the French returned to the charge and established what were in effect investment banks (*caisses*), which took the form of limited share partnerships for want of official approval for regular *sociétés anonymes*. But it was only in the 1850's that the corporate finance company took hold—first in France, where the brothers Pereire founded the *Crédit Mobilier* (1852) that gave the institution one of its generic names, then in Germany, Austria, Spain, Italy, and Holland, and finally, from the 1860's on, throughout the business world. For only then were the political and economic conditions for easy company formation and flotation satisfied: in France, a new regime anxious to build a counterpoise to older financial interests; in Germany and elsewhere, impecunious governments hungry for outside capital and amenable to pecuniary persuasion; and an easy, indeed, exalted, capital market.[3]

It would be impossible to do justice in a few paragraphs to the contribution of the investment bank to the economic development of these decades. We will have to confine ourselves to a few general points:

(1) The principal virtue of the investment banks lay in their ability to channel wealth into industry. Bigger and richer than the traditional

1930); A. van Schoubroeck, *L'évolution des banques belges en fonction de la conjoncture de 1850 à 1872* (Gembloux, 1951).

For Holland, H. M. Hirschfeld, *Het Ontstaan van het moderne Bankwezen in Nederland* (Rotterdam, 1922).

[1] W. Zorn, *Handels- und Industriegeschichte Bayerisch-Schwabens 1648–1870* (Augsburg, 1961), p. 129.

[2] Cf. P. Schöller, 'La transformation économique de la Belgique de 1832 à 1844', *Bull. l'Institut de Recherches Economiques et Sociales* (Louvain), XIV (1948).

[3] D. S. Landes, 'Vieille banque et banque nouvelle: la révolution financière du dix-neuvième siècle', *Revue d'histoire moderne et contemporaine*, III (1956), 204–22; R. Cameron, 'The Crédit Mobilier and the Economic Development of Europe', *J. Political Economy*, LXI (1953), 461–88; R. Cameron, 'Founding the Bank of Darm-

private houses, they were, like the joint-stock commercial banks, an active force for widening and deepening the capital market. They sought out the largest possible clientele for their promotions, which they advertised as one would a patent medicine. And whereas the old private merchant banks viewed industrial credit as a hazardous operation incompatible with the character of their resources, and even the more versatile joint-stock commercial banks looked upon it as an accessory activity at best, the finance companies made it their *raison d'être*.

(2) The contribution of the *crédit mobilier* was manifestly most important where the opportunities for industrial investment were abundant and the supply of capital limited or hard to mobilize. Thus it came late to Britain (1860's) and then did comparatively little for the improvement or expansion of the transport network and manufacturing plant. Rather, it concentrated its activities in the lucrative but risky areas of commodity speculation, secondary short-term financing, overseas trade and investment.

By contrast, Germany is the best illustration of the generous yield of systematic investment in a backward economy of high potential.[1] Already in the 1840's, the more far-sighted missionaries of national development were calling for banks to promote industry and transport as well as to perform the traditional functions of commercial credit and exchange. Several of these projects were well advanced when stifled by the economic and political crisis of 1846–8. In the 1850's, however, hard on the heels of the *Crédit Mobilier* and with its assistance, Mevissen founded his *Darmstädter Bank* (1853); Hansemann reorganized the *Discontogesellschaft* (1856); a syndicate of leading Berlin merchant bankers formed the *Handelsgesellschaft* (1856); and so on to the capital sum of over 200 million taler (equal approximately to 740 million francs) in new banks by 1857.[2]

Not all of these were explicitly *crédits mobiliers*. But even those that

---

stadt', *Explorations in Entrepreneurial History*, VIII (1955–6), 113–30. A translation of the last, with supporting documents, appeared in *Tradition*, II (1957), 104–31.

[1] Cf. A. Gerschenkron, 'Economic Backwardness in Historical Perspective', in B. Hoselitz, ed., *The Progress of Underdeveloped Areas* (Chicago, 1952), pp. 3–29, which develops a theme that goes back through Schumpeter and a number of German students of banking history to such contemporary promoters and observers as Mevissen and Horn.

[2] According to Max Wirth, *Geschichte der Handelskrisen* (4th ed., Frankfurt-am-Main, 1890), p. 310. This sum comprises all banks, including the purely commercial institutions. But it is difficult to assemble figures on investment banks specifically because so many firms refused in practice to confine themselves to the activities provided for in their statutes. For purposes of comparison, new railroad shares in this period totalled 140 million taler, plus a substantial sum in bond issues.

were nominally commercial banks found it hard to resist the opportunities of industrial finance. Moreover, the investment banks were generally mixed in function, that is, they received deposits and performed the traditional commercial services at the same time as they promoted companies, floated securities, and lent at long term. This was the most revolutionary feature of the new institution. By all that was sacred in good banking practice, sight and demand claims were incompatible with the immobilization of assets in speculative ventures. The mixed bank was in principle an unviable monster; many did in fact collapse when crisis followed boom. But the great majority throve, in large measure because this combination of deposit and investment functions could also be a source of tremendous strength. For it multiplied many times the ability of these institutions to accumulate resources, and this in turn meant greater support for the banks' industrial and commercial protégés, enabling them to expand easily in prosperity and sustaining them in adversity.

The result was a circle of mutual assistance and reinforcement. Under unfavourable circumstances, this interdependence could bring all down together, and many a Cassandra predicted the direst of consequences for all concerned. In an economy growing so rapidly as the German, however, the effect was one of general stimulation. During the decades preceding the First World War, the system seemed to march from success to success, the so-called *Grossbanken* fattening on their triumphs, absorbing competitors, sowing the land with branches and subsidiaries.[1] It is no coincidence that German economists were the first to develop the conception of a new stage of economic organization —finance capitalism.

The French case was strikingly different. They were, after the Belgians, the first to develop joint-stock investment banking; and after the debacle of 1848, nowhere did the new financial era begin with so much *éclat*. Yet the long-run impact of the innovation was small, not so much for lack of means, that is, capital, as of opportunities to use it. Two factors were determining here. First, the French investor—in particular the *rentier* from outside the industrial sector—preferred fixed-interest securities, especially bonds issued or guaranteed by governments, to more speculative industrial shares. Promotional possibilities were biased accordingly. Second and more important, French business

---

[1] They also drew capital from outside Germany, particularly from France, in the form of short-term advances on their commercial paper. In effect, the same French deposit banks that were reluctant to provide capital for French industry were furnishing it to German producers: not directly—this would have violated good practice; but indirectly, by 'proper' loans to financial intermediaries more enterprising than themselves.

firms—the family partnership particularly, but joint-stock companies as well[1]—preferred to finance expansion out of profits, to build on the past rather than anticipate the future, and were willing to have recourse to long-term bank credit only *in extremis*. Hence high-quality borrowers were scarce. The *Crédit Mobilier* of the Pereires found it necessary from the start to look abroad for employment of much of its resources. And this was a development bank. The great commercial and deposit banks—the *Crédit Lyonnais, Société Générale* (1864), and others—made some tentative gestures in the direction of industrial investment in their early years but were rapidly disenchanted. As time passed, their coffers swelled with savings swept in by a growing net of branch banks, savings that might have provided a substantial addition to the capital of French industry; instead they went in large part into the funds of other lands. In the first decade of this century, when French banking was under attack for failing to develop home industry—the comparison was explicitly with Germany—Henri Germain of the *Crédit Lyonnais* put the lender's viewpoint brutally: there were, he said, no industrialists in France worthy of support. There were, of course, but they were not interested in borrowing.

So much for the long run, which resembles somewhat the British experience. For the period that immediately concerns us, that is, the middle decades of the century, the mobilization of savings initiated by the *Crédit Mobilier* and effected by a variety of Parisian and local *sociétés de crédit* was a significant stimulus to growth. Money that would have been hoarded was put into circulation; and even capital that went abroad often returned in the form of contracts for French enterprises and orders for French manufactures. The push was not so direct or strong as in Germany or in the Belgium of the 1830's and 1840's. In part it was merely psychological, a heightening of euphoria. But it was a major element in the expansive conjuncture of these years.

We are now ready to consider the implications of this conjuncture for technological change and economic development. To save time and space, we shall focus the discussion on three points already adumbrated:

(1) the realization of the economic possibilities of the core innovations of the Industrial Revolution; specifically, the triumph in the more advanced European nations, of mechanization in textile manufacture, of the use of coal in iron-making, and of steam power;

(2) the concentration of production in ever-larger units; and

(3) the rationalization and relocation of industry along new regional lines.

[1] On the entrepreneurial behaviour of the French family firm and its implications

TECHNOLOGICAL ADVANCE

Textiles

By the middle of the century, Britain had more or less completed the transformation of her major textile industries. This was especially true of cotton, where the self-actor had gained its most obvious victories, the hand-loom weavers had consummated their agony, and those pioneers of the Industrial Revolution, the country water mills, had abandoned the struggle with the chimneyed factories of Lancashire. To be sure, there were survivals: the mule still accounted in 1850 for half the spindles in the industry; one spoke of 'a few thousand' draw looms in 1856; and here and there the big, cool wheels turned as before. But against these holdouts, the new techniques continued their remorseless advance: the self-actor won ground in the face of a steady shift to fine yarn that favoured the mule; the last hand looms vanished in the 1860's and 1870's, no longer because remuneration was inadequate but because there were no young people to carry on a dying trade; spindles and looms worked ever faster and better. Thus the giant steps were past. It was now a question of marginal gains in productivity, of filling in corners, of waiting for mechanical improvements to increase slightly the economic advantage of the new equipment, or for a contraction, cyclical or adventitious—as in the cotton famine of the 1860's—to squeeze out the inefficient producers.[1]

Change continued more important in wool, as might be expected of an industry that, for all its age, was technologically younger than cotton. In the woollen manufacture, the condenser filled in the otherwise complete sequence of mechanized operations: it replaced the hand piecers in taking off the loose strips of wool from the carder, and the old 'slubbing billy' in preparing the roving for the mule. The condenser was invented and perfected in New England around 1830 and was commonplace there by 1850. In Britain, Edward Baines was still speaking of it in 1858 as a 'new machine', but within another decade it was widespread in Yorkshire. Elsewhere it was still almost unknown.

for growth, see the sources on p. 131, n. 1, above. On the investment policy of joint-stock companies and its similarity to that of the family firm, see Bouvier, Le Crédit Lyonnais, pp. 390–7.

[1] We need a history of the British cotton industry in the period after 1780, to link up with G. W. Daniels, The Early English Cotton Industry, and A. P. Wadsworth and Julia de L. Mann, The Cotton Trade and Industrial Lancashire. The best work is still T. Ellison, The Cotton Trade of Great Britain (London, 1886); see also S. J. Chapman, The Lancashire Cotton Industry: a Study in Economic Development [a term used half a century too soon] (Manchester, 1904).

Worsted was, as usual, more enterprising than its sister branch. In spinning, the cap frame began to replace the throstle in the 1840's; this and accessory improvements—more precise machine construction, increased power, better lubrication, more efficient transmission—made it possible to double or more in the 1850's the equipment tended by each worker. In weaving, power achieved from 1840 on the success it had won in cotton from the 1820's; by 1867, there were some 71,500 machine looms and the contest was over. But the biggest gain was in the preparation of the yarn: the machine comber, like the condenser, eliminated the one remaining gap in the sequence of mechanization and was, in its effects on productivity and employment, the last of the great textile inventions. Within a decade of its adoption around the middle of the century, it killed off a large and once-flourishing handicraft that, like the hand weaving of a generation before, had already begun to feel the pressure of the first, rudimentary combers and was shrivelling in anticipation of death. The perfected machines of the 1850's left no room for competition: one of them could turn out over 20,000 kilograms of combed wool a year, as against perhaps 350 kilograms for the best hand worker, with his pots to heat his combs, his oils to minimize breakage of the fibres, and his wife and children to bite out the knots that formed in the skeins of wool. The great beneficiary of the new machine was Britain, and specifically Bradford, the world's greatest centre of worsted manufacture: spindlage for England and Wales as a whole (85 per cent or more of it in Yorkshire) went from 864,750 in 1850 to 2,087,000 in 1867.[1] The price of the gain was the displacement of some 21,900 hand combers in the Bradford district alone, less than half of whom found employment in the machine industry.[2]

The continental textile industries had much further to go at mid-century. For them, the innovations discussed above were accessory to more fundamental advances: the diffusion of the self-actor in cotton manufacture; and the substitution of the power loom for the draw loom in cotton and wool. In both areas progress was slow. Both of these innovations were essentially labour-saving and fuel-consuming, hence less remunerative on the Continent; and the self-actor in particular required more force than the ordinary water wheel could provide. Most serious, however, were the human resistances: the determined

---

[1] Since localization is generally promoted by mechanization, which enhances the importance of fuel costs and external economies, it is significant that, at the turn of the century, the West Riding still accounted for only a half of the woollen spindles of the kingdom. Clapham, *The Woollen and Worsted Industries* (London, 1907), p. 20. Compare the 85 % or more of worsted spindlage in this area.

[2] The best source on worsted technology is Sigsworth, *Black Dyke Mills*, pp. 30–4 88–92.

opposition of factory weavers to increase of the work load, which diminished proportionately the economic advantage of power equipment; and the slow response of conservative enterprises, most of them family-owned and run, to technological opportunity.

As before, it was the centres producing the better—though not the very best—fabrics that were most advanced in method and equipment. In France, Alsace, with its fine prints, and the relatively young industry of the Vosges led the way in cottons: from 10 per cent in 1856, the portion of their spindles that were self-acting rose to 73 per cent in 1868; and by 1870 over 90 per cent of Alsatian looms were powered. The North and Normandy followed suit—the former bravely, the latter painfully. The late 1850's and 1860's were a misery: contraction, lower tariff protection, cotton famine, and then another contraction followed one another in unremitting succession. The small *cotonnier* cried out his anguish to Paris; he had to wait for the Third Republic to obtain satisfaction.[1]

The worsted centres of Roubaix and Fourmies, in the Nord, and Reims, in Champagne, were the pace-setters of the French wool industry. Modernization was especially rapid in the 1860's, when the American Civil War pushed the price of cotton fabrics up and stimulated enormously the demand for the lighter textile substitutes. Of 450,000 worsted spindles added to national plants from 1862 to 1867, most of them self-acting, some three quarters were installed in the department of the Nord; in roughly the same years, Roubaix and Reims tripled their power looms, which numbered respectively 12,000 in 1869 and 7000 in 1866. By contrast, a top woollen *fabrique* like Elbeuf had only 370 such looms in 1870; many of the others had none.

In Germany it was the southern centres—Bavaria, Württemberg, and Baden—with their new joint-stock companies and, interestingly enough, their persistent use of water power in conjunction with steam, that took the lead in cotton (72 per cent self-actors in 1867); the Gladbach area (Rhineland) was not far behind. Even so, the spinning mills were unable to satisfy the demand of the weaving section of the industry, favoured as always by the low cost of rural labour. Imports of yarn actually increased. But their share of total consumption fell rapidly and almost uninterruptedly—from 70·6 per cent in 1836–40, to 52·6 per cent in 1851–5, to 22 per cent in 1867–9. This progressive emancipation is the measure of the development in Germany of a modern, all-factory industry.

By comparison with cotton, or even with the French wool industry,

[1] The best source is C. Fohlen, *L'industrie textile au temps de Second Empire* (Paris, 1956).

the German wool manufacture was poor in resources and hesitant in performance. Production of worsted yarn was little developed: not until the 1870's and 1880's did Germany begin to free herself from dependence on British imports. And woollen spinning, as everywhere, was a stronghold of conservatism. Yet the important branch was weaving, and here, in both worsteds and woollens, the use of power increased sharply, while draw looms began for the first time to decline absolutely as well as relatively, from 74,000 in 1861 to 47,000 in 1875.[1] The figures measure an important industrial advance; but who will translate them into a measure of the puzzlement, pain, and dull resentment of those ground by the wheels of an impersonal progress?

The picture obtained of the continental textile technology in these middle decades is thus far less serene than that of its British counterpart. There are brilliant highlights that recall, in smaller degree, the great strides of Lancashire and Yorkshire; but these are flecked with grey and black, and whole sections of the canvas are dull and even sombre. By comparison with the more homogeneous techniques and advanced localization of the British industries, all is still confusion.

One passes also from a large to a small canvas. Continental progress notwithstanding, Britain's textile manufacture remained far ahead of competitors. Its dominance was most striking in cotton, where it had three-fifths of the spindles in the world at the end of our period, more than half of those in Europe as late as 1913 (see Table 5). Britain's equipment was the latest available; her factories the largest; her labour force the most efficient. Comparisons with the best French and German practice toward the end of the century show Oldham mills using less than half, sometimes less than one-third as many workers per thousand spindles. The margin was presumably even greater around 1870. It is not easy to make the same comparison in weaving because of differences in the final products. Yet where the hand loom had all but disappeared in Britain, France still counted 200,000 of them in 1866, as against 80,000 power looms;[2] while for the Germany of 1875 (not including Alsace) the numbers were 125,000 of the old type and 57,000 of the

[1] The most convenient assemblage of statistical material on the development of the German cotton and wool industries in the nineteenth century is to be found in G. Jacobs, *Die deutschen Textilzölle im 19. Jahrhundert* (Braunschweig, 1907).

[2] G. Roy, 'Industrie cotonnière—tissage', in M. Chevalier, ed., *Exposition universelle de 1867 à Paris: Rapports du Jury international* (13 vols., Paris, 1868), IV, 39. This volume contains useful data on the other textile industries. It should be remembered that the rate of output of a machine loom was substantially greater than that of a draw loom. Fohlen, *L'industrie textile*, p. 456, gives a ratio of six to one. G. von Viebahn, *Statistik des zollvereinten und nördlichen Deutschland*, p. 926, gives one of slightly over three to one. Much would depend on the kind of looms used, the skill of the workmen, and the type of fabric woven.

new. Other things equal, moreover, it would appear that English power looms ran faster and wasted less; while the English weaver minded more machines—generally twice as many as his French or German counterpart.

Table 5. *Cotton Spindlage in Major Countries (in thousands)*

	1834	1852	1861	1867	1913
Great Britain	10,000	18,000	31,000	34,000	55,576
U.S.A.	1,400	5,500	11,500	8,000	30,579
France	2,500	4,500	5,500	6,800	7,400
Germany	626[a]	900	2,235	2,000	10,920
Switzerland	580	900	1,350	1,000	1,389
Belgium	200	400	612	625	1,469
Austria-Hungary	800	1,400	1,800	1,500	4,864[b]

[a] 1836.
[b] Areas of post-war Austria and Czechoslovakia only.
SOURCES. For 1834 and 1861, G. Jacobs, *Die deutschen Textilzölle im 19. Jahrhundert* (Braunschweig, 1907), p. 26, n. 1; P. Benaerts, *Les origines de la grande industrie allemande* (Paris, n.d.), p. 487; Viebahn, *Statistik*, p. 877.
For 1852 and 1867, Mimerel Fils, 'Filature du coton', in M. Chevalier, ed., *Exposition universelle de 1867 à Paris*, IV, 20.
For 1913, Comm. on Industry and Trade, *Survey of Textile Industries: Cotton, Wool, Artificial Silk [Being Part III of a Survey of Industries]* (London, 1928), p. 151.

Britain's lead in wool was smaller but still substantial: 2,087,000 worsted spindles in 1867, against perhaps 1,750,000 for France; 71,500 worsted power looms against perhaps 20–25,000. Germany, with her 320,000 spindles and perhaps 10,000 looms was a poor third. We do not have comparable figures for woollens, but here it would appear that Germany rather than France held second place.

All in all, it was an impressive hegemony. To be sure, Britain's margin diminished with time—as the return of protection closed valuable markets, as the younger textile industries of the Continent grew into a manhood nourished by rising standards of living, as newcomers in distant lands entered the competition. Even so, no other established British industry, perhaps, showed so much vitality and adaptability in the difficult years from 1870 to 1914. But that is another story.

Iron and steel

It is something of a relief to move on from textiles—heterogeneous and subtle—to metallurgy. The history of iron and steel is simple by comparison with that of woven fabrics: far less diversity of raw material or final product; technological changes uncomplicated by competition between modes of production; an overwhelming primacy of resources in determining location and competitive ability, which contrasts sharply with the subtle interplay of human and material considerations in the lighter industry.

In the middle decades of the nineteenth century the major development in continental metallurgy was the definitive triumph of mineral fuel. Coal had long come to dominate the refining process, and the traditional 'Walloon' or 'Champagne' techniques had given way in most places to the puddling furnace and rolling mill. But smelting remained a stumbling block owing to the direct contact between ore and fuel in the blast furnace, and right past the middle of the century charcoal-blast iron continued to command a premium for quality. For uses demanding special tenacity—axles, for example—it was almost obligatory.

In the long run, however, the inelasticity of the supply of wood and the forced dispersion and limited capacity of wood-burning furnaces made charcoal smelting uneconomic. The Belgians, with their abundant coal deposits and long mining experience, were, as we have seen (above, p. 176), the first on the Continent to make the shift to mineral fuel: by 1845, 90 per cent of their pig iron output, 121,000 out of 134,500 tons, was being made in coke-blast furnaces. (The reader should remember that almost the entire British make was produced with coke by 1800.) By contrast the French, who started on this path even earlier (Le Creusot in the 1780's) and possessed at least as much technical competence in this domain, were slow to accomplish the transition. For one thing, they were perennially short of coal, especially the kind that makes good metallurgical coke; only too often, moreover, the coal was located far from the ore, and costs of transport in the pre-railway age were discouragingly high. For another, much of their iron industry was in the hands of small, technically ignorant furnacemasters, bound by resources and habit to poor locations and protected from the incursions of more efficient producers by prohibitive tariffs, costly transport, and a tacit avoidance of price competition.

In the early 1850's France's industrial expansion gave the traditional technique a new lease on life; the make of charcoal pig actually rose, though nowhere near so fast as that of coke-blast iron. But then the crisis of 1857 brought a sharp contraction in demand, and the old-fashioned furnaces were the first to suffer. They settled at a new, lower level from 1858 to 1860, whereupon the new competition of the low-tariff 1860's, facilitated by cheap transportation, all but killed them off. The nature and timing of the shift is apparent from Table 6.

Germany was the last of the three to develop a large coke-blast smelting industry. As late as 1840 the only furnaces to use mineral fuel were in Silesia, and even there the great majority burned charcoal. It was around that time that the coke technique was successfully intro-

Table 6. *Substitution of Mineral for Vegetable Fuel in Smelting Iron*
(*Production in thousands of metric tons*)

	France		Prussia		Belgium	
	Coke or mixed	Charcoal	Coke or mixed	Charcoal	Coke	Charcoal
1825	5	194	—	—	—	—
1830	31	194	—	—	—	—
1835	49	246	—	—	—	—
1837	—	—	9	87	—	—
1840	82	321	—	—	—	—
1842	—	—	18	80	—	—
1845	193	305	—	—	121	13·5
1850	176	230	33	99	131	13·3
1855	488	361	158	123	280	14·1
1856	548	375	225	120	306	15·9
1857	619	373	270	110	288	14·5
1858	546	326	295	110	313	11·5
1859	531	333	281	110	309	9·6
1860	582	316	299	96	315	5·3
1861	691	276	377	73	306	5·9
1862	817	274	461	65	353	3·6
1863	901	256	568	70	386	6·1
1864	989	224	631	75	444	5·5
1865	1010	194	712	60	466	4·6
1866	1076	184	750	54	482	0·6
1867	1074	155	838	78	422	1·4
1868	1104	131	973	80	435	0·9
1869	1262	119	1104	77	532	2·2
1870	1088	90	1086	69	563	1·8
1875	1332	116	1341	57	540	1·3
1880	1670	55	2021	32	—	—
1885	1602	29	2634	31	—	—
1890	1950	12	3269	20	—	—

SOURCES. For France, Jean-Paul Courthéoux, 'Délais d'innovation, états des coûts, évolution des prix dans l'industrie sidérurgique', in Jean Fourastié, ed., *Prix de vente et prix de revient: recherches sur l'évolution des prix en periode de progrés technique* (8e série) (Paris, n.d.), table I.

For Prussia, Beck, *Geschichte des Eisens*, IV, 714; V, 1069; *Zeitschrift für das Berg-, Hütten-, und Salinenwesen* (1856–71).

For Belgium, I have not been able to obtain figures of actual output of charcoal- and coke-blast furnaces before 1845. There are, however, data on the number of such furnaces which would seem to indicate that output of coke-blast iron passed that of charcoal blast some time around 1833–5 (assuming a ratio of I to 4 for the average annual outputs of the two types of furnace: cf. E. Flachat, A. Barrault, and J. Petiet, *Traité de la fabrication du fer et de la fonte* (Paris, 1842), p. 1287). *Exposé de la situation du Royaume, 1840–1850*, part IV, p. 118; *ibid. 1850–1860*, III, 114; *1861–1875*, II, 726.

duced into the Saar basin; five or six years later it was the turn of the Rhineland; not until 1849 was the first coke-blast pig poured in the Ruhr. At that date, barely one-tenth of the make of iron in the *Zollverein* was smelted in this manner.

Once the decisive step was taken, however, the new technique took hold rapidly and drove out the old in a matter of years. For Prussia as a whole, representing about 90 per cent of the iron output of the *Zollverein*, the proportion of charcoal-blast iron fell from 82 per cent in 1842, to 60 per cent in 1852, to 12·3 per cent in 1862. In a new smelting industry like that of the Ruhr, the demise of vegetable fuel was even more rapid; it accounted for 100 per cent of iron output in 1848, 63 per cent in 1850, 4·2 per cent in 1856, 1·3 per cent in 1863.[1]

Along with this went a continued increase in size of equipment and plant, which was made possible by and stimulated in return the kind of technological improvements that are not spectacular or revolutionary in themselves but constitute severally a major transformation. The blast became more powerful and hotter; cooling, more efficient (the more heat generated, the more acute the problem of dissipating it), and smelting runs consequently longer; loading, easier. Other things equal, the latest-model furnace doubled in height and more than doubled in capacity from 1850 to 1870; while the shift from charcoal to coke brought with it an even greater increase in the size of the average furnace. In France the make per coke-blast furnace rose from 2450 tons in 1846 to 5800 in 1870; for all furnaces, from 1250 to 4400 tons over the same period. Prussia began with smaller, less efficient equipment: in 1850 the average furnace produced 720 tons. By 1871, however, the figure was over 5000 for Germany as a whole and slightly higher for Prussia.

The gains in refining were by contrast small. The puddling furnace remained the bottleneck of the industry. Only men of remarkable strength and endurance could stand up to the heat for hours, turn and stir the thick porridge of liquescent metal, and draw off the blobs of pasty wrought iron. The puddlers were the aristocracy of the proletariat, proud, clannish, set apart by sweat and blood. Few of them lived past forty.[2] Numerous efforts were made to mechanize the puddling furnace—in vain. Machines could be made to stir the bath, but only the human eye and touch could separate out the solidifying decarburized metal. The size of the furnace and productivity gains were limited accordingly.

[1] Benaerts, *Les origines de la grande industrie allemande*, p. 457; Beck, *Geschichte des Eisens*, IV, 990.

[2] See the fascinating article by J. P. Courthéoux, 'Privilèges et misères d'un métier sidérurgique au XIXe siècle: le puddleur', *Révue d'histoire économique et sociale*, XXXVII (1959), 161–84.

The answer was eventually found in an entirely different direction—in the manufacture of cheap steel and its substitution for wrought iron in all but a handful of uses. The Bessemer process dates from 1856; the Siemens–Martin open-hearth technique from 1864. Yet each, as we shall see, did not make real headway until almost a decade after its introduction. Steel still accounted for less than 15 per cent of the finished iron (cast or refined) produced in Germany around 1870, less than 10 per cent of that made in Great Britain. Its commercial triumph and the revolutionary impact of this triumph on industrial technique belong to the next period of economic development, and we shall accordingly postpone our discussion of these innovations so as not to separate them from their effects.

One final point to place matters in their proper perspective: the spectacular expansion of the continental iron industry in these decades should not blind the reader to the continued progress and dominance of the British manufacture. Her rate of growth (5·2 per cent per year, 1848–70) was not so rapid as that of Germany (10·2 per cent, 1850–69) or even that of France (6·7 per cent, 1850–69), but for an old industrial power it was eminently respectable. Her equipment was bigger than that of her major competitors; her enterprises were larger and stronger. The *most powerful* furnaces in the Ruhr yielded around 250 tons of pig a week in 1870;[1] the *average* British unit did almost as much (183 tons), and the new eighty-foot 'monsters' (the expression is Clapham's) of the Cleveland district, with gas recovery and superheated blast, were turning out 450–550 tons a week in 1865.[2] Nor were there any firms on the Continent like Dowlais and Gartsherrie, with eighteen and sixteen blast furnaces respectively in the 1850's. By way of comparison the largest German firm, the Hörder Verein, had six furnaces in 1870, averaging 180 tons a week.[3] When all is said and done, the United Kingdom was still manufacturing half the world's pig iron in 1870, three-and-one-half times as much as the United States, more than four times as much as Germany, more than five times as much as France.

---

[1] Z. f. das Berg-, Hütten-, und Salinenwesen, XIX (1871), Statistischer Theil, 169, 171.

[2] Beck, Geschichte des Eisens, v, 964; I. L. Bell, Principles of the Manufacture of Iron and Steel (London, 1884), p. 24. Clapham, Economic History, II, 50, incorrectly gives this as output per day. Interestingly, the world leader in this regard was Belgium, whose blast furnaces averaged over 230 tons a week. See C. Reuss, É. Koutny and L. Tychon, Le progrès économique en sidérurgie: Belgique, Luxembourg, Pays-Bas 1830–1955 (Louvain and Paris, 1960), p. 58 (Table 11). Aggregate Belgian output of pig iron, however, was less than one-tenth of the British make.

[3] Z. f. das Berg-, Hütten-, und Salinenwesen, XIX (1871), 168. These were built in 1853 and 1854, and were slightly under 50 feet in height (48 Prussian feet).

Power

With the diffusion of those new techniques on the Continent went larger power requirements and an increased reliance on the steam-engine as prime mover. It appeared in areas and trades where it had never been used before; it was adopted by firms desirous of supplementing their supply of water power or of replacing their hydraulic installations by something more dependable; and its use spread within enterprises already familiar with it. A large iron or engineering works might employ a dozen or more engines of varying capacity—to drive the blast, turn the rolls, work the hammers, power a diversity of machine tools, and operate lifts, cranes, and other manipulatory devices.

Our figures of steam power in this period are seriously defective: for most countries, including Britain, we have only more or less informed private estimates; and differences in methods of calculating capacity (a difficulty that persists into the twentieth century) make international comparisons especially hazardous.

Such as they are, however (see Tables 7 and 8), the statistics make clear the importance of these years for the adoption of the steam-engine in the continental countries. All the more advanced were by 1840 on the steep middle slope of the 'S-curve' of increasing capacity, which doubled or more every decade until the 1870's. At mid-century, France led by a wide margin in number of fixed engines—more than the rest of continental Europe combined—and clearly no economy had gone so far in adapting steam to a wide variety of uses. But her power units were small compared to those of Belgium and Prussia, with their heavy stress on mining and metallurgy, and the aggregate capacity of the Belgian plant, totalling perhaps 25 per cent less than that of France, continued to justify Briavoinne's invidious comparison of the 1830's (see above, p. 181, n. 1).

In the years after 1850 Belgium maintained her rate of advance; French capacity grew faster than before; while Prussia leaped forward at a rate (quintupling from 1849 to 1861, then increasing almost seven times from 1861 to 1878) that took her past Belgium in the mid-1850's and a few years later left France far behind. Together with the spectacular rise in her output of iron and coal, this leap heralded the appearance of a new industrial giant. We have no comparable figures, unfortunately, for Britain, where the *laissez-faire* of the executive power in the nineteenth century has cost the economic historian dear—though he has been more than compensated by the curiosity of Parliament; but if total steam power is a valid indication, the increase of British fixed engine capacity was already beginning to slow in the 1860's.

Table 7. *Capacity of All Steam-engines (in thousands of horse-power)*

	1840	1850	1860	1870	1880	1888	1896
Great Britain	620	1,290	2,450	4,040	7,600	9,200	13,700
Germany	40	260	850	2,480	5,120	6,200	8,080
France	90	370	1,120	1,850	3,070	4,520	5,920
Austria	20	100	330	800	1,560	2,150	2,520
Belgium	40	70	160	350	610	810	1,180
Russia	20	70	200	920	1,740	2,240	3,100
Italy	10	40	50	330	500	830	1,520
Spain	10	20	100	210	470	740	1,180
Sweden	—	—	20	100	220	300	510
Netherlands	—	10	30	130	250	340	600
Europe	860	2,240	5,540	11,570	22,000	28,630	40,300
U.S.A.	760	1,680	3,470	5,590	9,110	14,400	18,060
World	1,650	3,990	9,380	18,460	34,150	50,150	66,100

SOURCE. Mulhall, *Dictionary of Statistics*, p. 545; Wl. Woytinsky, *Die Welt in Zahlen* (7 vols.; Berlin, 1926), IV, 59. Woytinsky correctly stresses the approximate character of these estimates.

Table 8. *Fixed Steam-engines and Capacity by Country
(Capacity in thousands of horse-power)*

	Prussia		France		Belgium	
	Number	Capacity	Number	Capacity	Number	Capacity
1837	419	7	—	—	—	—
1838	—	—	—	—	1,044	25
1839	—	—	2,450	33	—	—
1843	462	16	3,369	43	—	—
1844	—	—	3,645	46	1,448	37
1849	1,445	29	9,949	62	—	—
1850	—	—	5,322	67	2,040	51
1855	3,049	62	8,879	112	—	—
1860	—	—	14,513	178	4,346	99
1861	7,000	143	15,805	191	—	—
1869	—	—	26,221	320	—	—
1870	—	—	27,088	336	8,138	176
1878	34,431	958	37,589	484	—	—
1880	—	—	41,772	544	11,752	273

SOURCES. For Prussia, Engel, 'Das Zeitalter des Dampfes', in *Z. Königlichen Statis-tischen Landesamtes* (1880), p. 122; also available in Woytinsky, *Die Welt in Zahlen*, IV, 63; for France, *Annu. statistique*, LVII (1946), *rés. rétro.* p. 116*; for Belgium, *Exposé de la situation du Royaume, 1840–1850*, part IV, p. 113, and Woytinsky, *Die Welt in Zahlen*, IV, 70.

INCREASING SCALE AND CONCENTRATION

The ever-greater size and cost of industrial equipment and the new competitive pressures produced by cheaper transport and freer trade gave a strong stimulus to two trends already under way—increasing scale and, to a lesser degree, concentration.

The enterprise was growing steadily larger. Some of this was a statistical illusion, for the elimination of marginally inefficient units tended to move the statistical average up. But much of it was real growth, as successful firms expanded and new ones were established on a scale never dreamed of. It is here that the joint-stock company made its greatest contribution. Almost all the new iron-works and coal-mines in Prussia were founded as corporations, as they had long been in Belgium. The same was true in French heavy industry, though often the *commandite par actions* was employed in order to reconcile personal direction and responsibility with widespread ownership. Yet this compromise in itself, which had been resorted to from the 1830's on in an effort to by-pass the government's suspicion of and hostility to the corporation as a business form, was eloquent testimony to the exigencies of increasing scale. Even in Britain, where the accumulation of capital within the enterprise and the efficiency of the money market made recourse to the investment public unnecessary, the trend to joint-stock was strong and growing stronger. From the 1850's on, the larger new firms were established as companies, like the railroads before them, and from the 1860's on, numerous private ventures, especially in capital-intensive industries like metallurgy, converted to the corporate form: thus John Brown in Sheffield, Ebbw Vale in Wales, Bolckow-Vaughan at Middlesbrough. Some of these reorganizations reflected the biological problems inherent in individual proprietorship and partnership—death, illness, unwillingness of heirs to carry on the business; some of them were inspired by a desire, occasionally only too well justified, for the shelter of limited liability; but many were a response to the increased capital requirements of production.[1]

The most rapid increase in scale came, as would be expected, in heavy industry. In 1853 the largest smelting firm in the Ruhr, the Borbecker Hütte at Essen, with its three blast furnaces and steam-engines totalling 252 h.p., employed 450 men to make 19,500 tons of

---

[1] The best discussion is in J. B. Jefferys, 'Trends in Business Organization in Great Britain since 1856' (unpublished Ph.D. thesis, University of London, 1938). See also the above-cited (p. 198, n. 1) essay by D. S. Landes, 'The Structure of Enterprise in the Nineteenth Century: the Cases of Britain and Germany', and references given there.

pig iron. By 1870 a dozen enterprises surpassed this output, and the leader, the Hörder Verein, produced three times as much. (Thanks to increased productivity, however, growth as measured by number of employees was slow; the more efficient enterprises of 1870 were getting as much as 100 tons per man per year or more, as against the 43 of the Borbecker Hütte.)[1] And one could show similar developments in France, where a firm like Wendel saw its output of pig iron rise from 22,370 tons in 1850 to 134,470 in 1870; or in Britain, where Schneider, Hannay and Co. (later merged in the Barrow Haematite Steel Co.) began in Barrow in 1859 with two furnaces and added to its plant at intervals until by 1871 it had twelve in operation, all in a row like the pretty maids of the nursery rhyme.[2] The reader may perhaps object that I have chosen these examples to make my point; as indeed I have. And he may adduce numerous instances of ventures that did not grow so quickly, or even failed. Yet the firms mentioned were not alone; one could cite enterprises like Cockerill in Belgium, Krupp in Prussia, Schneider in France, John Brown in England, which expanded if anything faster. And the figures of increasing employment per firm in a period of rising productivity and capital intensity make the general tendency manifest.

The trend was not so strong in a light industry like textiles, for several reasons: technological change had slowed and with it the increase in optimum size of plant; it is probable that economies of scale were smaller; because non-material and entrepreneurial factors were of more weight than in heavy industry, a small but imaginative firm was better able to compete; and finally, since initial capital requirements were lower, there was less pressure toward the formation of joint-stock enterprises with their built-in penchant for bigness.[3] Generally speaking, the less advanced the industry, the more rapid the growth of scale; or more accurately, average size increases most rapidly in the period of transition from the dispersed shops and tiny man- or animal-powered mills of early mechanization to the steam- or water-driven factory. Thus spindlage per mill in the cotton industry of Great Britain rose by about half from 1850 to 1878; that of firms in northern France about doubled from 1850 to 1870; while in Prussia it

[1] *Z. f. das Berg-, Hütten-, und Salinenwesen,* II (1854), A. 286; XIX (187), B. 168–9.
[2] See the illustration in Beck, *Geschichte des Eisens,* V, 236. The layout was unquestionably unusual in its simplicity. See also J. D. Marshall, *Furness and the Industrial Revolution* (Barrow-in-Furness, 1958), pp. 220–2, 249–54, 342, who gives the figure of sixteen furnaces, against Beck's twelve.
[3] Jefferys, 'Trends in Business Organization', p. 92 n., gives a figure of £250,000 for an up-to-date iron-and-steel works in the 1870's and 1880's, £75–100,000 for 'the most expensive' new cotton mill.

increased seven times (828 to 5738) from 1837 to 1861.[1] The same phenomenon may account for the somewhat faster trend to bigness in the British woollen industry, by comparison with cotton, in spite of smaller economies of scale: in the years 1850–75, spindles per mill almost doubled in woollens and increased by 158 per cent in worsteds.[2] On the other hand, the Prussian experience was the reverse—a sixfold increase in wool from 1837 to 1861 (from an average of 103 to one of 587 spindles), as against the sevenfold gain in cotton mentioned above.

Increasing scale is usually accompanied by the concentration of an ever-greater share of the assets or output of industry in the hands of the largest firms. Yet the available statistics, which are discouragingly sparse, do not permit a categorical affirmation on this point. We do not, for example, have data on size or production of individual firms in the textile industry, and even in metallurgy, where the surveillance by government bureaus of equipment and practice at the level of the plant has left the historian a heritage of invaluable information, our coverage is incomplete and not always homogeneous. Still certain inferences seem justified. In the textile manufactures of the Continent, the purge of marginal enterprises in the 1850's and 1860's by easier transport, lower tariffs, and—in cotton—by the interruption of American supplies and a concomitant sharp rise in the requirements of working capital, almost surely promoted a higher degree of concentration: the rich got richer, and the poor went under. Britain had nothing like this, save for the travail of the cotton famine; her day of reckoning came after 1873, when the prolonged depression of prices and trade, combined with the loss of some of her finest markets to resurgent protectionism and the energy of younger competitors, effected a comparable catharsis. In the meantime, however, the new ease of company formation and the accumulation of capital in Lancashire favoured the creation of cotton enterprises of an unprecedented size as early as 1860. These were the so-called 'Oldham limiteds'—huge, standardized joint-stock spinning mills established in and around Oldham, outside Manchester, beginning in 1858 and continuing *crescendo* to a spate in the mid-1870's. They were built in large measure with the savings of local shopkeepers, professional men, even workers, who bought shares in denominations

---

[1] Ellison, *Cotton Trade*, p. 72; Fohlen, *L'industrie textile*, pp. 228–9, 450–1; *Amtlicher Bericht über die allgemeine Gewerbe-Ausstellung zu Berlin im Jahre 1844*, I, 238; Viebahn, *Statistik*, p. 877. The figures for France are not complete enough to permit more than an informed guess about the rate of increase. It was apparently faster in Roubaix-Tourcoing than at Lille.

[2] *Parl. Papers*, 1850, XLII, 458–60, 467–8; 1875, LXXI, 68, 74. See also F. J. Glover, 'The Rise of the Heavy Woollen Trade of the West Riding of Yorkshire in the Nineteenth Century', *Business History*, IV (1961), 1–21.

as small as one pound. The largest ran well over 100,000 spindles; the average to between 60,000 and 70,000. In the two peak years of 1874–5, about three million spindles were floated in Oldham alone, as much, roughly, as there were in all of France or Germany. The propagation of these giants almost surely meant an increase in concentration. Yet when all is said and done, the textile industry is not one that lends itself to monopolistic tendencies: entry is too easy as we have seen; the economies of scale are not great enough. In 1885 the ten largest public companies in Oldham accounted for only 22 per cent of the assets or spindlage of such joint-stock enterprises in that locality alone; their share of the national totals was far smaller.[1]

One would expect, and one finds, a higher degree of concentration in metallurgy; though the trend is by no means powerful or unambiguous. In France, the ten largest firms produced 14 per cent of the total make of wrought iron and steel in 1840–5; in 1869, one company alone, De Wendel, made over 11 per cent, and the top ten together were up to 54 per cent.[2] In Germany, however, these same years saw little movement in this direction. The top ten smelting enterprises made 32·6 per cent of the pig iron in 1852, 35·9 per cent in 1871.[3] And while we do not have the data that would permit a similar analysis of the British iron manufacture, the subsequent pattern would seem to indicate that both assets and output were more evenly shared than in France and possibly even Germany. As late as 1927, the twelve largest concerns made only 47 per cent of the country's pig iron and 60 per cent of its steel.[4] This lack of concentration was apparently linked to the geographical dispersion of the industry.

In general, the historical experience of concentration is almost *terra incognita*. The fairly abundant literature on the structure of industry in the nineteenth century has concerned itself almost exclusively with such questions as scale, integration (were spinning mills and weaving sheds combined? smelting and refining?), and localization; and even those studies that purport to deal with concentration generally treat rather of these other issues.

---

[1] Based on Roland Smith, 'An Oldham Limited Liability Company 1875–1896', *ibid.* pp. 52–3.

[2] On France, see Bertrand Gille, 'Analyse de l'industrie sidérurgique française à la veille de 1830', *Rev. d'hist. de la sidérurgie*, III (1962), 83–111; 'Les plus grandes sociétés métallurgiques françaises en 1845', *ibid.* II (1961), 207–19; J. B. Silly, 'La concentration dans l'industrie sidérurgique en France sous le Second Empire', *ibid.* III (1962), 19–48.

[3] *Z. f. das Berg-, Hütten- und Salinenwesen*, I (1853), A. 157–65; XX (1872), Statistischer Theil, 153–64.

[4] T. H. Burnham and G. O. Hoskins, *Iron and Steel in Britain, 1870–1930* (London, 1943), p. 210.

15

NEW REGIONAL PATTERNS

Increasing scale and the forces that brought it about combined to recast the economic map of Europe. The process took two forms: localization, the spatial concentration of industrial activity; and relocation, the rise of new centres of production.

In regard to the first, one can distinguish positive and negative stimulants. On the one hand, bigness gave added weight to the advantages of rational location; the larger the appetite for raw materials, the more important it was to be placed near convenient sources of supply. Moreover, the advance of technology gave rise to new external economies in those branches characterized by a complex interweaving of mutually supporting activities. In short, the rich got richer. On the other hand, we have already noted the dissolving effect of cheaper, easier transport—especially when reinforced by lower barriers to foreign competition—on the mosaic of local autarkies. The poor got poorer, and many were simply snuffed out. The net result was a coalescence of manufacturing activity at a few favoured points and a de-industrialization of the countryside that gave new impetus to the age-old pumping of rural population by urban centres.[1]

Relocation was closely related to the new resource base of heavy industry consequent on the substitution of mineral for vegetable fuel and the invention of new steelmaking techniques (more of these later). Each country had its areas of opportunity. In France, it was the north-east corner (the departments of the Meurthe and the Moselle) and the northern apex (the Nord and the Pas-de-Calais). The former had the largest, most easily exploited beds of iron ore in Europe—the relatively poor (iron content about 30–33 per cent), once despised *minette*—in reasonable proximity to the coal of the Saar. With the construction of the eastern railway in the late 1840's, new smelting installations were built, and the area swiftly rose from one of the lesser ironmaking districts to the most important in France. Its greatest gains came after 1856, when first the commercial crisis, then low tariffs and cheaper transport put heavy pressure on the antiquated forest furnaces of Champagne, the Franche-Comté, the Nivernais, and Dauphiné. In an economy in which competition was damped by entrepreneurial forbearance and formal *ententes*, no purge was so effective as a forced purge. Output in Lorraine quadrupled (109,000 tons in 1857 to 420,000 in 1869), and where in 1847 the two departments accounted for 10·6 per

[1] See the detailed local study of Ph. Pinchemel, *Structures sociales et dépopulation rurale dans les campagnes picardes de 1836 à 1936* (Paris, 1957). It was not the purely agricultural areas of Picardy that lost by emigration in the mid-nineteenth century, but the regions of declining domestic industry.

cent of the nation's make of iron and in 1857 for 11 per cent, the proportion had risen by 1869 to 30·5 per cent.[1] By comparison, the
growth of smelting in the Nord and the Pas-de-Calais was far slower,
but there the availability of relatively cheap fuel furnished a stronger
base for refining, finishing, and that multitudinous family of energy-
consuming industries called by the generic name of metalworking. In
addition, the area possessed long-established textile trades—heavy
consumers of machines, engines, and other metal products—a powerful
chemical manufacture, and a prosperous industrial agriculture centring
on the sugar beet. The result was a far more diversified economy than
in the north-east.

This pattern of balanced growth also characterized the Ruhr, though
on a far larger scale; indeed in one sense, the big story of these years is
the emergence of Westphalia as the greatest centre of industrial
activity in western Europe. The bases of this development were coal
and iron: once the extent of local mineral resources became apparent,
German bankers and investors, often seconded or anticipated by French
and Belgian capital, hastened to create a rash of joint-stock mining and
metallurgical corporations. Twenty-seven coke-blast furnaces were
built from 1851 to 1857, more than had existed in the entire *Zollverein*
at the earlier date; after a short pause during the crisis of 1857–9, the
boom resumed and continued until the prolonged depression of the
1870's. From 1851 to 1871 output of pig iron in the Dortmund district increased *over 35 times*, to 421,000 tons, almost twice as much as in
all of Germany at mid-century. By that time, the Dortmund and Bonn
districts combined (the latter included enterprises situated in southern
Westphalia) turned out over two thirds of Prussian output and five
eighths of that of the entire Empire.[2]

Nevertheless, the spectacular rise of a smelting industry in the Ruhr
should not obscure the growth of other forms of manufacture. Here
too, cheap coal encouraged all the metalworking and engineering
trades, including the long-established manufacture of small hardware—
screws, nuts, knives, locks, and the like—whose demand for semi-
finished iron and steel further stimulated the furnace and heavy forge
sectors. The most striking thing about Westphalia to this day is not so
much the thick stacks of the *Hochöfen* or the hoists above the coal pits,

[1] France, Ministère des Travaux Publics, Direction des Routes, de la Navigation
et des Mines, *Statistique de l'industrie minérale*, 1893, p. 10. Twenty years later, in 1888, in
spite of the loss of much of this area to Germany, the mills of Lorraine produced 54 %
of the country's pig iron.

[2] Excluding the newly acquired territory of Lorraine, the figures for 1870 were:
799,000 tons in the Bonn and Dortmund districts, 1,156,000 tons in Prussia, 1,391,000
tons in the *Zollverein*. Beck, *Geschichte des Eisens*, v, 254–60.

as the slender chimneys everywhere. In this regard it resembles, though on a larger scale, the well-named 'Black Country' around Birmingham. Moreover, as in northern France, though again on a larger scale, metallurgy was tied into a broad regional complex that included the textile manufactures of Gladbach-Rheydt and Elberfeld-Barmen and the lusty infant chemical trades of the Frankfort and Cologne areas.

Britain too saw a relocation of her industry, though less drastic in its impact. Staffordshire (with Birmingham and the Black Country) and Wales were merely marking time. Scotland, which had risen in two decades to second place among British iron-producing districts on the strength of blackband and the hot blast, continued to gain slightly and held the first position for a while in the late 1850's and 1860's. But by the end of our period output had levelled off and it was only a matter of time before the rising cost of the blackband ores brought about contraction. Two-thirds of the entire increase of the national make of pig iron (from 2,700,000 tons in 1852 to 5,963,500 in 1869) took place in two new areas: in the north-east (centre Cleveland), which went from about 145,000 tons in 1852 to something over 1,600,000 in 1869; and north-west (Cumberland and north Lancashire), with 16,570 tons in 1855, 169,200 tons in 1860, 678,000 in 1869, 1,045,000 in 1875. (Here was growth even more rapid than that of the Ruhr: an increase of 63 times in twenty years!) The first built its prosperity on the proximity of ore and coal in the valley of the Tees; its social expression was the grimy boom town of Middlesbrough. The second was really a creature of the 1860's, when its deposits of haematite iron proved to be the only major source of ore suitable to the acid Bessemer process in the British Isles; it too had its frontier mill town—Barrow-in-Furness.

By 1870 the industrial map of Europe was substantially what it is today. The only major deposits of minerals to enter the pool of resources since then are the northern Swedish ores (opened up by railway transport in the late 1880's), the Briey extension of the Lorraine beds (late 1890's and 1900's), the Lincolnshire ores in England (developed after the First World War), and the Lorraine extension of the Saar coal field (developed on an important scale only since the Second World War). All of these have been essentially ancillary and none has had an impact on location comparable to that of the new fields of the middle decades of the nineteenth century. It is no coincidence that the discovery and exploitation of these in different countries fell so close in time. Prospecting was a reflection of economic pressures and opportunities. The results constituted as much a consummation as a commencement. Individually, each of the new fields marked a new area of growth; together they represented the effective completion of the material base of the Industrial Revolution.

The 1850's and 1860's then were the years when western Europe caught up with Britain. Not in a quantitative sense; that was to come later, and then only in certain areas. Nor even qualitatively, whether in scale and efficiency of production of given industries, or in degree of industrialization of the economy as a whole. Britain, as we have seen, was not standing still. If one envisages development as a sequence of stages—traditional (or pre-industrial) economy, industrial revolution, and maturity—the nations of western Europe were still in the second stage during these decades, that is, they had broken through the 'crust of custom', had cleared away institutional obstacles to growth, and were engaged in transforming the technology of their basic industries; while Britain, which had accomplished this transition around the turn of the century in metallurgy, by the end of the 1830's in cotton, had spent the decades since diffusing the core innovations and their derivatives throughout the economy. Britain achieved maturity by the middle of the century; Germany, not until the 1890's, and even then not to the same degree.

Yet such comparisons are misleading. Stage systems, which go back in economic history to the German historical school (List, Roscher, Bücher and, off to the side, Marx), have their virtues.[1] They clarify and synthesize the inconsiderate confusion of reality. But they also have their weaknesses, the most serious of which is their inability to encompass historical time. The Industrial Revolution in France or Germany was very different from what it was in Britain—and this, not only because of the peculiar circumstances and endowments of each of these countries, but also because they made their moves later and indeed skipped certain moves altogether. So that while taxonomically Britain

[1] One of the latest is that of W. W. Rostow, which refines the traditional tripartite schema into a five-part taxonomy. The pre-industrial stage is divided into traditional and preparatory ('transitional') phases; and the maturity stage, into maturity proper and the affluent age of surplus output (which may be devoted to high mass consumption, armament, or such other goals as the society may choose). Much of Rostow's system consists in calling old flowers by new names. The Industrial Revolution, which he has vividly labelled 'take-off', remains the heart of the process. His 'leading sectors' are Schumpeter's areas of entrepreneurial innovation. The 'backward' and 'lateral' linkages are the derived demand of neoclassical economics; the 'forward linkages' are a combination of the traditional notions of response to bottlenecks and of external economies. Aside from such nomenclatorial merits as the system may possess (in my opinion, questionable), it has the virtue of reaffirming the distinctive historical importance of the industrial revolution in the history of any economy. It also has the fault, however, almost inescapable in stage analysis, of oversimplifying and overgeneralizing to the point of discomfort. On all this see Rostow, 'The Take-Off into Self-Sustained Growth', *Econ. J.* LXVI (1956), 25–48; Rostow, *The Stages of Economic Growth* (Cambridge, 1960); above all, Rostow (ed.), *The Economics of Take-off* (cited above, p. 193, note).

was still far more advanced than her continental emulators around 1870, was 'mature' where they were 'immature', in terms of capacity to grow her lead had disappeared. As a result of a generation of drastic institutional changes and selective investment, the nations of western Europe now had the knowledge and means to compete with Britain *in certain areas* on an even plane. (The analogy to the rivalry between the Soviet Union and the United States will not fail to strike the reader.) Face to face with opportunities for growth and development, they were as free—perhaps freer—to pick their methods and opportunities. Their very lateness now turned to their advantage. In the jargon of sports, it was a new race.

CHAPTER 5

Short Breath and Second Wind

The years from 1873 to 1896 seemed to many contemporaries a startling departure from historical experience. Prices fell unevenly, sporadically, but inexorably through crisis and boom—an average of about one-third on all commodities. It was the most drastic deflation in the memory of man. The rate of interest fell too, to the point where economic theorists began to conjure with the possibility of capital so abundant as to be a free good. And profits shrank, while what were now recognized as periodic depressions seemed to drag on interminably. The economic system appeared to be running down.

Then the wheel turned. In the last years of the century, prices began to rise and profits with them. As business improved, confidence returned—not the spotty, evanescent confidence of the brief booms that had punctuated the gloom of the preceding decades, but a general euphoria such as had not prevailed since the *Gründerjahre* of the early 1870's. Everything seemed right again—in spite of rattlings of arms and monitory Marxist references to the 'last stage' of capitalism. In all of western Europe, these years live on in memory as the good old days—the Edwardian era, *la belle époque*.

Their memory is brightened by the contrast with the years of death and disenchantment that followed. In every field, the war seems to be the great divide: between optimism and pessimism, parliamentary democracy and fascism, progress and decline. The massive mobilization of people and resources for conflict and their destruction in conflict seemed to throw everything out of kilter, never to be set right again. In economic life, the war saw the introduction of 'temporary' controls and restrictions—of trade, prices, investments, movements of funds and persons—that have persisted in one or another form ever since. The quietly self-adjusting international economy gave way to a sputtering, inefficient mechanism, kept operating only by repeated adjustments and repairs.

Yet a closer examination makes clear that the war was only a catalyst, a precipitant of changes already under way. The signs of a turning from optimism and freedom are apparent well before 1900, in literature and philosophy as well as in politics and economics. This is not to deny the enormous impact of the war, but simply to place it in its context. The system was already undergoing a painful transformation, which was itself more source than consequence of international rivalry and conflict. Here, however, we touch on a subject both complicated and polemical, and we had best put off discussing it for the moment.

Superficially, the intercyclical trends of the European economy in this period have appeared to most analysts to be a repetition of earlier alternations of long-term contraction and expansion. Monetary theorists have pointed to a diminution in the supply of money relative to demand from 1873 to 1896, followed by a sharp increase in the stock of bullion consequent on gold strikes in South Africa and the Klondike. This argument received its fullest analytical development, perhaps, in the work of Simiand, who generalized the nineteenth-century experience and constructed a model of alternating inflationary and deflationary long trends, the former characterized by rapid quantitative growth on a relatively stable technological basis (analogous to what we now call widening of capital), the latter by qualitative improvement (deepening of capital) and the forced elimination of inefficient enterprises.[1]

Generally opposed to this interpretation are those economists and historians who see investment as the primary determinant and prices as a symptom. Schumpeter is perhaps the best known of this group, with his model of an economic machine powered by bursts of innovation. Also in this camp is Rostow, with a more nuanced analysis based on shifts of investment among uses with different rates of gestation: the longer the lag between outlay and return (infinite in the case of expenditure on armaments), the greater the immediate inflationary effect.

Between these two positions falls a man like Kondratiev, who argues that the upswing of the long cycle *is associated with* increases in both investment (due to new inventions, resources, and markets) and money supply. Kondratiev does not look upon these concomitants of fluctuation as causes, but rather as products of the conjuncture, and speaks cryptically of 'causes which are inherent in the essence of the capitalistic economy'. It is nevertheless clear—questions of ideology aside—that they hold the same explanatory place in his schema as they do, *mutatis mutandis*, in those of the other writers on the subject.[2]

---

[1] F. Simiand, *Le salaire, l'évolution sociale et la monnaie* (3 vols., Paris, 1932).

[2] His classic article, 'Die langen Wellen der Konjunktur', appeared in the *Archiv für Sozialwissenschaft und Sozialpolitik*, LVI (1926), 573–609. This has been translated in short form as 'The Long Waves in Economic Life', *Rev. Economics and Statistics*, XVII (1935), 105–15; the English version has been reprinted in *Readings in Business Cycle Theory* (Philadelphia, 1944), 20–42.

On one point, however—the periodization of the long trends—all agree. Beginning with the late eighteenth century, they would punctuate the economic history of the industrial era roughly as follows: 1790–1817, inflation; 1817–50, deflation; 1850–73, inflation; 1873–96, deflation; 1896–1914, inflation. (The exact dates will vary from one analysis to another, but the schema and the approximate points of demarcation remain the same.) Moreover, most would agree on the cyclical character of these fluctuations. To be sure, a Marxist like Kondratiev would presumably qualify this (though he does not do so explicitly) by confining the pattern to capitalist economies and subjecting its repetitiveness to the influence of underlying, even longer-range changes in the total system. Similarly, the recent work of Rostow on stages of industrialization would seem to imply the possibility that the rhythm and character of these waves alter with maturation of the economy. Yet these reservations would not affect the accepted periodicity of the nineteenth century.

This picture seems to me inaccurate and leads in my opinion to a misunderstanding of the relationship between the underlying process of industrialization and the other aspects of economic change. The main source of difficulty is the optical illusion produced by the contrast between the boom of the 1850's and the depression of the 1870's: each stands out and seems to usher in a new era, marking off a period of inflationary upswing from 1850 to 1873. In fact, the price series show no such long trend. The long deflation that begins after the Napoleonic wars is momentarily reversed by the influx of bullion and the credit boom of the 1850's. But the inflation lasts no longer than the upturn of the short cycle. Prices break in 1857, and while they have their ups and downs over the next decade and a half, the trend is slightly falling (at most, level in some cases), with a sharp decline setting in from 1873.[1]

In sum, the nineteenth century was marked by a protracted and sharp deflation, stretching from 1817 to 1896 with only one short interruption of some six or seven years. In the long history of money and prices from the Middle Ages to the present, there is nothing like it—with the possible exception of milder declines in the decades following the Black Death and in the seventeenth century. Moreover, unlike these earlier periods, when falling prices were linked to catas-

---

[1] The path of prices varied somewhat from one country to another, for each felt the impact of boom and bust differently according to political as well as economic circumstances. For all the major economies of western Europe, however—Great Britain, Germany, France, Belgium—the trough of 1873–96 is an extension of the path traced in 1820–50. See Graph no. 1 in Gaston Imbert, *Des mouvements de longue durée Kondratieff* (Aix-en-Provence, 1959), pocket.

trophe, depopulation, and widespread depression, the nineteenth century was a period of peace, of unprecedented increase in numbers and rapid economic expansion. Otherwise, with or without the connivance of kings and governments, the long run is all debasement and inflation.

The explanation for the aberration of the nineteenth century seems to lie precisely in the productivity gains that stimulated and made possible this economic growth. Over the century, real costs dropped steadily, at first mainly in manufacturing, and then—after a revolution in transport that opened vast new lands to commercial cultivation—in food production as well. (It is the harvest of advances in both sectors that accounts for the particularly sharp drop of the years 1873–96.) To be sure, technological improvements and cost economies had occurred before. Why, then, this uniquely persistent deflation? The answer lies of course in the uniqueness of the innovations that constituted the Industrial Revolution; never before had there been a cluster of novelties so general in their application and so radical in their implications.

The price decline of the nineteenth century, then, is the consequence and barometer of European industrialization. Needless to say, this does not imply that, because the course of price changes was more or less the same for all the countries of Europe, the course of industrialization was also the same. Given the commercial and monetary communication that prevailed, a synchronization of price trends was inevitable. This is in the nature of a market. But patterns and rates of growth are another matter. Although the same international communication that gave rise to general deflation was also conducive to sympathetic movements of technology, here differences in material resources and institutions and lags in the timing of development were determining. The result was substantial variation from one country to another.

The economy whose career the course of prices fits best is that of Britain. This is hardly surprising. The first nation to industrialize, she remained, into the twentieth century, the bellwether of the international market. Even after she lost her supremacy in critical branches like iron and coal to the United States and Germany in the 1890's, her position as mediator of world trade and finance sustained her predominant influence on commodity prices.

It is not my intention to undertake at this point a detailed examination of the British experience. We may note simply that such calculations as we have of her rates of industrial growth and increase in productivity—and they are confirmed by the major industrial time series—show a distinct falling-off after the mid-century decades of high prosperity. They do not turn up again until after 1900. From 1870 on, with the exception of a branch like steel, which was transformed by a series of fundamental advances in technique, British industry had exhausted the gains implicit in the original cluster of innovations that had constituted the Industrial Revolution. More precisely, it had exhausted the big gains. The established industries did not stand still. Change was built into the system, and innovation was if anything more frequent than ever. But the marginal product of improvements diminished as the cost of equipment went up and the physical advantage over existing techniques fell.

Not until a series of major advances opened new areas of investment around the turn of the century was this deceleration reversed. These years saw the lusty childhood, if not the birth, of electrical power and motors; organic chemistry and synthetics; the internal-combustion engine and automotive devices; precision manufacture and assembly-line production—a cluster of innovations that have earned the name of the Second Industrial Revolution. Conceivably the energetic exploitation of the cost-saving possibilities of these innovations might have yielded a further decline in prices—though, given the state of technology, their relative impact was bound to be smaller than that of the path-breaking advances of the eighteenth century. In the event, however, Britain did not take full advantage of the opportunities offered, and the initial boost to prices imparted by bullion inflows from South Africa (Witwatersrand, 1887), West Australia (1887), and the Klondike (1896) was relayed and reinforced by a pattern of investment that yielded slow returns in consumable goods and services. And then, of course, came the First World War, bringing with it pressures toward inflation that render comparison with the earlier period impossible.

Even so, this cluster of innovations marked the start of a new upswing, a second cycle of industrial growth which is still in course and whose technological possibilities are still far from exhausted. It is in this context that one may understand the debate about the timing of Britain's 'climacteric'. Change of life there was; the question is, did it take place in the 1870's or 1890's?[1] The answer clearly depends on the point of view. The end of high prosperity after 1873 and the persistent malaise of the following decades signal in effect the evening of the Industrial Revolution; whereas the hinge of the 1890's marks the beginning of a new career.

Germany offers a striking contrast. Hers was an economy that, for

---

[1] Cf. the debate between E. H. Phelps-Brown and S. J. Handfield-Jones, 'The Climacteric of the 1890's: a Study in the Expanding Economy', *Oxford Econ. Papers*, IV (1952), 266–307; and D. J. Coppock, 'The Climacteric of the 1890's: a Critical Note', *The Manchester School*, XXIV (1956), 1–31.

On the general problem of the so-called Great Depression, see the valuable article of A. E. Musson, 'The Great Depression in Britain, 1873–1896: a Reappraisal', *J. Econ. Hist.* XIX (1959), 199–228. Also Coppock, 'The Causes of the Great Depression, 1873–

all its capabilities, was well behind Britain in 1870 in assimilating and diffusing the technology of the Industrial Revolution. Large sectors of industry remained to be mechanized; domestic manufacture continued to predominate in many branches; the rail network was far from complete; the scale of production, generally small. So that once the setback of the mid-1870's was behind her, Germany resumed her high rate of growth. And she had not yet exhausted this momentum when the new opportunities at the end of the century gave her economy another push. As a result, one has the impression of an uninterrupted rise. For Germany too, however, the 1890's were a watershed.

France presents still another pattern. With Belgium, she had been the first on the Continent to follow the British example. But her overall rate of industrial growth had been the slower for her tentative decades of preparation and experiment, and for the development within her body social of psychological and institutional antibodies to the virus of modernization. 'France', wrote Clapham, 'never went though an industrial revolution.' She did, but it was muffled. The contours of the spurt that accompanied the shift to mechanization, steam power, the factory system, and rail transport are rounded both before and after. After the relatively rapid expansion of the Second Empire, the Third Republic was a period of measured autumnal advance, accelerated finally by the upturn of 1900-13, which was based partly on the new technology, partly on the opening of valuable iron ore deposits in Lorraine. Previous to this revival—and even after, for opinion always lags in these matters—the somnolence of the French economy called forth repeated warnings from Cassandras aghast at the increasing gap between the French and German economies. 'Growthmanship' is by no means an invention of contemporary American political debate.

Alongside the advanced economies, a number of what we would call today 'underdeveloped' nations embarked during these years of technological transition upon their own industrial revolutions. Some among them, like Sweden and Denmark, effected the change smoothly and achieved rapid gains in productivity and real income per head. Others, like Italy, Hungary, and Russia, assimilated only pieces of modern technology, and these advances, achieved at discrete points of the economy, were slow to break down the tenacious backwardness of most branches of economic activity. In these countries, moreover, industry accounted for so small a fraction of national wealth and income, that even rapid gains in this sector did relatively little at first for total output or the standard of living. Nevertheless, their industrial

96', The Manchester School, XXIX (1961), with critique by J. Saville and reply, ibid., XXXI (1963); and H. Rosenberg, 'Political and Social Consequences of the Depression of 1873-1896 in Central Europe', Econ. Hist. Rev. XIII (1943), 58-73.

growth was generally more rapid in this period than that of the more advanced countries, even Germany. Partly this reflects a statistical fallacy: their product was so small in these early stages that even modest increments appear proportionately large. But even more it reflects the poverty of their technological base and the enriched content of their industrial revolutions: the gap between what they had and what they might do was that much greater than it had been for the early industrializers.[1]

The exhaustion of the technological possibilities of the Industrial Revolution coincided with changes in the structure and size of the market that aggravated the dampening effect of diminishing autonomous investment. These changes did not all work in the same direction; but they added up on balance to a failure of demand to keep up with the increasing capacity of industry. There were customers for those who knew how to find and win them; but one had to look for them in new places and woo them in new ways. And the task was not so easy as it had been for the pioneer industrialists of the first half of the century.

The historical relationship of demand to supply over the course of the nineteenth century is not a simple one. We have noted the pressure of rapidly increasing domestic and foreign demand on the industrial system of Britain in the eighteenth century; it was this pressure that gave rise to bottlenecks and tensions resolved finally by a transformation of the means and mode of production. This Industrial Revolution in turn radically altered the terms of the problem. On the one hand, it shifted the emphasis from consumption to investment: capital was needed to build industrial plant and realize the potentialities of the new techniques. On the other, it made foreign outlets that much more important, for even a domestic market whose purchasing power was in no way constrained by a higher rate of saving would have been unable to keep up with the rapid increase in the output of manufactured goods.

In fact aggregate domestic demand did rise substantially in all the industrializing countries, even during the period of most rapid capital formation. How much it increased, however, is hard to say. Here we run into the question of the alleged 'immiseration' of the working

---

[1] This statement begs certain questions about the advantages and disadvantages of an early start that are best left in abeyance at the moment. For statistics of industrial growth, see S. J. Patel, 'Rates of Industrial Growth in the Last Century, 1860–1958', *Economic Development and Cultural Change*, IX (1961), 316–30; R. W. Goldsmith, 'The Economic Growth of Tsarist Russia, 1860–1913', *ibid.* 441–75.

classes, which has aroused an extraordinary amount of discussion, particularly with regard to the British experience.[1]

Did the standard of living of the poorer classes fall as a result of the Industrial Revolution during the years, say, from 1780 to 1850? It would be presumptuous to attempt to settle so complicated and emotional an issue in a few lines. The arguments commonly advanced are concerned with the consumption not only of manufactures, but of all goods and services, and rest as much or more on theoretical deductions, political dogma, and sympathy as on empirical data—for what they may be worth. Much of this lies outside our range of interest. What does concern us is first, that average as well as total home demand for *manufactures* rose. Consumption of cotton goods, for example, increased from some 35,600,000 lb. per year in 1819–21 to 149,600,000 in 1844–6 (the Hungry Forties!), a fourfold leap at a time when population rose by somewhat less than a third.[2] And if comparable statistics on other commodities were available, on iron in the form of consumers' goods, for instance, they would no doubt tell the same story.

Even so, home demand could not keep up with supply. From the start, Britain had to rely heavily on overseas outlets, and the interruptions of normal trade relations by war and blockade before 1815 and protectionist tariffs after only stirred her to search for new markets in distant corners of the globe. The picaresque expedition of Popham to Buenos Aires in 1806 is dramatic evidence of both commercial anxieties and dynamic response: here was a naval commander who took it upon himself to sail his squadron across the Atlantic in time of war to pluck a piece of the Spanish empire for British trade. And when His Majesty's Navy took umbrage and instituted court martial proceedings, Popham saved himself by rallying the British mercantile community to his defence.[3]

As early as the period 1819–21, two-thirds of the cotton yarn produced in Britain were sold abroad either directly or in the form of

[1] An extensive bibliography would take too much space. The interested reader may consult R. M. Hartwell, 'Interpretations of the Industrial Revolution in England: a Methodological Inquiry', *J. Econ. Hist.* XIX (1959), 229–49.

[2] Ellison, *Cotton Trade*, p. 59. How much of this rise in demand was due to the substitution effect (that is, to the purchase of cotton in preference to other goods because of its relatively greater fall in price) and how much to increased real income consequent on this fall in price is another question, one directly related to the controversy over the standard of living in these years. But it is not immediately relevant to our concern with the evolution of the market for manufactures, except in so far as the rise in consumption of cotton was compensated by a fall in that of other textiles. This does not seem to have happened in Britain, even in the case of linen, which was cotton's most direct competitor. Cf. Deane and Cole, *British Economic Growth*, p. 204.

[3] H. S. Ferns, *Britain and Argentina in the Nineteenth Century* (Oxford, 1960), ch. 1.

cloth; almost three-fifths of the yard goods manufactured were similarly disposed of. Sixty years later, in 1880–2, the respective proportions
were 84·9 and 81·6 per cent. The biggest gains were in the Orient: in
1814 less than a million yards of cloth were shipped to ports east of Suez;
by 1830 the figure had risen to 57 million yards; by 1850, 415 million;
and by 1870, 1402 million, or some 43 per cent of total exports.[1]

To be sure, no other major commodity depended so heavily as
cotton on foreign markets. But almost all manufactures showed the
same trends: a substantial increase in both absolute volume sold abroad
and the proportion of such sales to total output. We do not have
direct estimates of the overall export proportion over time; but
Schlote has calculated a ratio of the *index* of exports of finished goods
to an *index* of industrial production (in both cases, 1913 = 100) that
shows a rise from about 45 per cent in the 1820's to almost 90 per cent
by the early 70's.[2]

This steady extraversion of the economy was the principal motor of
the persistent, if spasmodic expansion of British imperialism throughout the century. Until recent years, scholars were inclined to underestimate the scope of this expansion. They allowed themselves to mistake the principles and even the policy embodied in the slogan 'Little
England' for performance; and more serious, they neglected what,
from an economic point of view, is the most important and lucrative
variety of imperial dominion—informal control.[3] The fact was that
not only did Britain annex during these years large areas in India,
Oceania, and South Africa, but her sphere of commercial influence
broadened enormously to embrace most of Latin America, coastal
Africa, and south and east Asia.

By the last third of the century, however, the conditions of commercial expansion had altered drastically. Monopoly had given way to
competition; Britain no longer stood alone as the workshop of the
world. This had always been true of certain articles: the fine cottons of
Alsace and Switzerland had held their own with those of Lancashire

[1] Ellison, *Cotton Trade*, pp. 59, 63; S. B. Saul, *Studies in British Overseas Trade,
1870–1914* (Liverpool, 1960), p. 14.

[2] W. Schlote, *British Overseas Trade from 1700 to the 1930's* (Oxford: Blackwell,
1952), pp. 75–7, 154–5. The export index includes finished goods, metals, coal, and
processed foodstuffs. The source of the index of production is not given, but Schlote
apparently used the index later published by W. Hoffmann in his *Wachstum und Wachs-
tumsformen der englischen Industriewirtschaft von 1700 bis zur Gegenwart* [Kiel, Institut
für Weltwirtschaft, 'Probleme der Weltwirtschaft', Vol. 63] (Kiel, 1939)—see
Schlote's reference, p. 50. Schlote's ratios are useful only as indicators of trend.

[3] See J. Gallagher and R. Robinson, 'The Imperialism of Free Trade', *Econ. Hist.
Rev.* 2nd ser. VI (1953), 1–15; John S. Galbraith, 'Myths of the "Little England"
Era', *Amer. Hist. Rev.* LXVII (1961), 34–48.

from the early nineteenth century, while French 'merinos' proved an admittedly inimitable rival of Yorkshire worsteds. But from 1870 on, there was a sharp increase in such competitive exports, particularly from the younger industrial nations—Germany, the United States, even India and Japan.

British commercial observers of the nineteenth century were wont to indulge in a little game, which we may call 'Count the customers', by analogy with chicken counting and similar pastimes. They would estimate the number of people in a given area, note their consumption of British products by comparison with more established markets, and then calculate the gain that would result if sales could be increased to this hypothetical standard. China was a favourite subject for such suppositions. A population of well over 300 millions! If her consumption *per capita* of British cotton could be raised to the Indian level, Ellison reckoned, sales would total £25 million per annum instead of the £5 million of 1883. Nothing illustrates the commercial implications of the industrial surge of newcomers like India and Japan better than what happened to these daydreams. From 1885 to 1913 British sales of yarn in China fell from 20 million to 2 million pounds. In 1905 India alone sold 200 million pounds there.[1] And in 1913 the Japanese figure was 156 millions, and her total export of yarn and thread was worth well over twice as much as that of Germany and about 40 per cent of that of the United Kingdom.[2]

This shift from monopoly to competition was probably the most important single factor in setting the mood for European industrial and commercial enterprise. Economic growth was now also economic struggle—struggle that served to separate the strong from the weak, to discourage some and toughen others, to favour the new, hungry nations at the expense of the old. Optimism about a future of indefinite progress gave way to uncertainty and a sense of agony, in the classical

[1] From the late 1880's, British exports of cotton cloth to India levelled off, while sales of yarn fell. In the meantime, the proportion of Indian yarn output exported rose from 15 per cent in the 1870's to over 75 per cent by 1913. Saul, *Studies in British Overseas Trade*, p. 189. India's first mechanized cotton mill was founded in the Bombay area in 1851. A decade later she had 338,000 spindles, which became almost 5 million by the turn of the century; by 1913 the number had grown to 6,917,000. In that year, her consumption of 2,177,000 running bales of raw cotton placed her fourth in the world, after the United Kingdom, the United States, and Russia. A. Rai, *Die indische Baumwoll-Industrie* (Delhi, n.d.), pp. 46–7; Committee on Industry and Trade, *Survey of Textile Industries*, p. 154. (G. E. Hubbard, *Eastern Industrialization and Its Effect on the West* [Oxford, 1938], p. 256, gives spindles working in 1913–14 as 5,848,000.)

[2] Committee on Industry and Trade, *Survey of Textile Industries*, p. 156; J. E. Orchard, *Japan's Economic Position* (New York, 1930), pp. 93–4. The growth of the

meaning of the word. All of which strengthened and was in turn strengthened by sharpening political rivalries, the two forms of competition merging in that final surge of land hunger and that chase for 'spheres of influence' that have been called the New Imperialism.

From 1876 to 1914, the colonial powers of the world annexed over 11 million square miles of territory. This was the high-water mark of that expansion of Europe that began in the eleventh century on the East Elbian plains, the plateau of Castille, and the waters of the Mediterranean. Politically the gain was a source of gratification to many: the sun never set on the British flag. Economically the results were distinctly less impressive. Already by 1870, little but the chaff remained: the best markets had already been formally annexed or informally integrated into Europe's expanding economy. There were still gains to be made in Africa and especially Asia, and indeed, the share of exports that went to these areas increased in subsequent decades. But given the poverty of these countries and their low rates of growth, their demand for manufactures was limited: on the eve of the First World War, the industrial powers of the world were still *each other's* best customers.

Even more, they were *their own* best customers: as the potentialities of overseas outlets diminished, the domestic market acquired increasing importance. And rightly so. Here were the richest consumers in the world; and both their numbers and wealth were increasing faster than those of the more backward areas. From 1870 to 1910 the population of Europe rose from 290 to 435 millions and that of the leading industrial nations (the United Kingdom and Germany) from 72 to 110 millions, while national incomes doubled or tripled. (France, of course, was an exception: her population was just about standing still.) If the days of easy commercial expansion were over and the time had

Japanese cotton industry may be gauged from the following data:

	Number of spindles (thousands)	Output of yarn (million pounds)	Export of yarn (million pounds)	Export of cloth (thousand sq.yd.)
1880	13	—	—	—
1890	358	42	—	—
1900	1361	268	83	572
1913	2287	672	187	4302

SOURCES. Spindles from Manji Iijima, *Nihon bōsekishi* [A history of the Japanese spinning industry] (Tokyo, 1949), pp. 489–91; yarn output from Japan, Naikaku Tōkeikyoku [Cabinet Bureau of Statistics], *Nihon Teikoku tōkei nenkan* [Japanese Imperial Statistical Yearbook], vols. XII, XXIV–XXV, XL; exports of yarn and cloth from Nihon sen'i Kyōgikai [Council of the textile industry of Japan], *Nihon sen'i sangyōshi* [A history of the Japanese textile industry] (2 vols., Tokyo, 1958), pp. 944–5.

come to cultivate demand in depth, there was no better place to work than at home.

More important than the growth in aggregate purchasing power was the change in the pattern of consumption. The steady rise in income *per capita*, which reached down into the lowest strata of the population, released increasing amounts for the purchase of manufactures as against food, of conveniences as against necessities.[1]

A number of factors reinforced this process. First of all, food prices dropped relatively to others after 1875 as a result of massive flows of grain from the great plains and steppes of North America and South Russia and ever larger imports of meat from Argentina and of oils and fruit from tropical and semi-tropical areas. It took a combination of technological improvements to make this radical increase and diversification of Europe's food supply possible: the railroad, which linked interior agricultural regions to the sea; more efficient marine transport, which led to a sharp rise in capacity and a corresponding fall in freight rates; new techniques of cultivation, especially dry farming of open plains; new methods of food conservation, among them canning and refrigeration.

This competition from outside producers called forth in turn a vigorous technological response from certain sectors of European agriculture. Some countries or regions turned to specialization, choosing those products where nature and skill combined to yield differentiated quality that defied competition. Denmark is the best example, with her pork and dairy products (the cream-separator was the vital innovation here). But Switzerland and France had their cheeses

---

[1] Real wages rose substantially, even allowing for cyclical unemployment. Thus so anticapitalist an author as J. Kuczynski shows gains of the order of two-thirds in Britain from 1850 to 1900; of one-third in Germany from 1870 to 1900. *Die Geschichte der Lage der Arbeiter in England von 1640 bis in die Gegenwart*, Bd. IV, 3. Teil: *Seit 1832* (Berlin, 1955), pp. 132–3; *Die Geschichte der Lage der Arbeiter in Deutschland*, Bd. I, 2. Teil: *1871 bis 1932* (Berlin, 1954), pp. 96–7.

Whether labour's share in national income rose, is another question. Such statistics as we have point to a significant increase in the share of income going to salaried employees and wage-earners combined in France and Germany; in Britain in our period the change is negligible. But there is no way of separating out the higher-salaried brackets from the lower. See S. Kuznets, 'Quantitative Aspects of the Economic Growth of Nations, IV. Distribution of National Income by Factor Shares', *Economic Development and Cultural Change*, VII, no. 3, part II (April 1959), and the sources cited there.

As for equality of distribution of income, our data are incomplete, grossly approximate, and scarcely comparable; the picture is consequently obscure. Cf. Colin Clark, *The Conditions of Economic Progress* (2nd ed., London, 1951), pp. 530–41; also the discussion in Wm. Ashworth, *An Economic History of England, 1870–1939* (London, 1960), pp. 247f.

and every large city had its ring of market gardens. At the same time cultivators obtained much higher yields per acre for all crops by extensive use of fertilizer, especially the new mineral and artificial varieties and rich organic imports like Peruvian guano (another dividend of the revolution in transportation.) The result was the highest standard of eating that the world had known. For the first time, man could afford to feed his own staff of life, grain, to animals to fatten them for his table.

Secondly, the same improvements in transportation that did so much to diminish the cost of food also worked to reduce the price of manufactures. Not only was shipment less expensive, but the creation of truly national markets conduced to the elimination of local peculiarities of taste and hence to the economies of mass production.

Thirdly, consumer wants increased significantly. There was, to begin with, the steady process of urbanization, which introduced millions of rustics to a more expansive way of life. Nor was this appetite for creature comforts confined solely to those who settled in the cities. It slowly but inexorably seduced the countryside, traditionally self-denying to the point of avarice. Some, who visited the city, largely thanks to the railroad, were never more the same; and some felt the need to emulate city cousins, whether for the sake of self-esteem or to meet the competition of a more comfortable, varied existence for the loyalty of children, girl-friends, and wives. Seen in the large, the process was painfully slow and uneven; the material backwardness of most rural homesteads is a problem even today. And it was inevitably erratic: the same peasant who sold his cheese and ate curd, who raised bees to avoid buying sugar and made a Sunday suit last a lifetime, might buy himself a watch, give a gold bauble to his daughter, let his son visit a vacation resort, or allow his wife to decorate the house.[1] (In all this, the increased influence of women and children on consumption, a tendency that has continued to the present, is obvious.) In the long run, however, this internal 'demonstration effect' has been probably the most important factor—more important than the increase in income—in developing a market of high consumption (to adapt W. W. Rostow's term), that is, a body of consumers able and willing to buy above the line of necessity.

Once again, larger economic and social processes owed much to technological innovation, in this case to the introduction of new methods of retail distribution. It is these decades that saw the spectacular development of the department store and the chain store (multiple

---

[1] Cf. A. G. Manry, 'En Limagne, entre 1865 et 1905', *Annales: Economies, Sociétés, Civilisations*, v (1950), 114–19.

shop), with all their associated devices for the temptation of the consumer: fixed prices, right to return purchases without charge, standard packaging, catalogue orders, effective display, periodic sales, advertising.[1] And to these should be added the efforts of merchants and manufacturers to increase their market by cultivating fashion changes and establishing the reputation of trademarks and brand names.

All of this was the more important because of the relationship of the new industrial technology to the character of consumption. As we shall see, the great advances of these decades—cheap steel, precision manufacture, electric power—made possible a whole new range of consumers' goods, what we now call consumers' durables: the sewing machine, cheap clocks, the bicycle, electric lighting and eventually electrical appliances. The consequent expansion of production, after the earlier surge based primarily on capital goods and the complex of demands associated with the railway, was possible only in this new kind of supraminimal market.

The severity of competition for foreign outlets and concomitantly increasing importance of domestic demand led to a sharp reaction against the economic freedom, hence insecurity, of the mid-century. The liberalization of commerce was barely achieved when the tide changed. In France, agitation against the new policy of low protection never ceased; from the start, the representatives of the manufacturing interest put protocol aside and denounced the agreement with England as an abusive, even fraudulent, act of fiat. (In a sense, the Empire began to die in January 1860.) Every ill of French industry was imputed to 'the Treaty'; every success was achieved in spite of it. The campaign for a return to protection grew stronger with the crisis of 1867, achieved some minor successes in the early years of the Third Republic, and finally attained its goal with the passage of the Méline tariff in 1892. In Germany, the depression of the 1870's and Bismarck's desire for the support of the new alliance of industrialists and Junkers led to a rejection in 1879 of the traditional policy of low duties, which had reached its extreme with the free admission of pig iron in 1873. Italy adopted

---

[1] One of the best indirect indicators of this commercial transformation is the spectacular rise in production of plate glass, used extensively for store windows and mirrors. From 1870 to 1901, British imports of plate jumped from some 36,000 to 464,000 cwt., while the output of Britain's largest producer, who entered the field in 1876, rose from 1,078,000 sq. ft. in 1877 to over 5 million in 1903–4, to over 14 million in 1912–13. Barker, *Pilkington Brothers*, pp. 161, 189. The Pilkington figures are for the Cowley Hill works only.

On the significance of the new techniques of retail selling, see J. B. Jefferys, *Retail Trading in Britain, 1850–1950* (Cambridge, 1954); P. Bonnet, *La commercialisation de la vie française du Premier Empire à nos jours* (Paris, 1929); G. d'Avenel, *Le mécanisme de la vie moderne*, 1re série (7th ed.; Paris, 1922), pp. 1–79.

high protection in 1887; Austria and Russia returned to it in 1874/5 and 1877 respectively; Spain established new rates in 1877 and 1891; and so on throughout Europe. Overseas, American import duties tended to rise with each new tariff law from the Civil War onward. Even Britain, the home of classical economics, saw its faith in free trade shaken. The commercial interdependence of these increasingly specialized economies multiplied the impact of these increases; each action brought its reactions, until tariff rates were established as much for bargaining as for protection. The spiral continued upward with few pauses or reversals until the constraints of war made these earlier restrictions look like freedom.

Along with this encapsulation of national markets went efforts to minimize intranational competition. Cartels for the control of prices and output—an institution that went back to the seventeenth century and beyond (cf. the Newcastle Vend)—began to multiply, especially after periods of prolonged or severe depression. Characteristically they were found in industries like coal, iron, or chemicals, where homogeneity of product facilitated the specification of quotas and prices, and where lumpy capital requirements yielded important economies of scale, the number of competing units was consequently small, and entry was difficult. They were most numerous and effective in Germany, where entrepreneurial psychology, the structure of industry, legal institutions (cartels could enforce their contracts in the courts), and tariff protection against interlopers all combined to promote agreements in restraint of trade.

Cartels were less important in France, for reasons that may be deduced from the analysis of their success in Germany. For one thing, light industry was far more important than heavy, and the family firm, with its attachment to entrepreneurial independence, held a large place, even in capital-intensive branches of manufacture. Secondly, the emphasis on diversity and differentiation of product made group control difficult. Finally and most important, French industry had long maintained tacit limits on competition that were about as effective as formal contracts. Not only the entrepreneur, but labour and indeed society in general looked upon price warfare as essentially unfair (déloyale) and subversive. And given the modified oligopoly characteristic of many industries—a few big, efficient enterprises amid a swarm of small, backward ones—these moral sentiments were reinforced by counsels of prudence; vigorous competition could only invite reprisal from rivals just as big and capable as oneself. In short, France did not need cartels. She did develop a few, in iron and steel manufacture particularly. But their role was more one of convenience than influence.

British industry found itself in a mixed position in matters of com-

bination. In the first place, conspiracies in restraint of trade were forbidden by common law; yet cartels went back centuries in Britain, and
it was Adam Smith who wrote: 'People of the same trade seldom meet
together, even for merriment and diversion, but the conversation ends
in a conspiracy against the public, or in some contrivance to raise
prices.'[1] Secondly, the absence of a tariff barrier was a serious obstacle
to collusive fixing of prices or output; yet costs of transportation or
local productive advantages served to protect certain trades, regionally
or nationally, and make combination profitable. Finally the structure
of the enterprise, unlike that in Germany, was ill-suited to formal
co-operation: most firms, even nominally public companies, were
private in character and independent in behaviour; moreover there was
little vertical integration or bank control. Yet as in France, there was
also a strong tendency to the kind of gentleman's agreement that makes
cartels unnecessary.

With these contradictory forces in play, Britain developed a mild
trend toward mild combination. Cartels appeared in metallurgy,
milling, chemicals, glass-making, but they were less rigid than their
German analogues, less compulsory in character, less effective in times
of contraction, less enduring. The foreign interloper was always a problem. Thus the highly effective British Glass Manufacturers' Association
found its efforts to maintain prices at home continually thwarted by
Belgian competition. Offers to establish an international agreement were
disregarded for decades, until labour troubles in the early 1900's convinced the Belgian producers that the security of union more than
compensated for the constraints. As finally established, the Plate Glass
Convention of 1904, the most successful of the international glass
cartels, included not only the United Kingdom and Belgium, but
Germany, France, Italy, Austria-Hungary, and the Netherlands.
Similar accords were negotiated in fields like rail-making and tobacco,
where, because the bulk of demand lay overseas or because value in
proportion to weight was so high that transport costs offered no protection, national agreements were ineffective. Such international cartels
worked well on the whole so long as there was agreement but showed
little resistance to dissension and rupture; their histories have an
on-again-off-again beat.[2]

Aside from cartels, that is, associations of independent enterprises,
there were also a number of 'combines', monopolistic or would-be
monopolistic concerns that grouped a sizable fraction of the productive
units in a given trade in various degrees of amalgamation. In some
cases, these coalitions were simply what the Germans call an *Interes-*

[1] On the glass cartels, see Barker, *Pilkington Brothers*, chs. VIII, IX, and XIII.
[2] *Wealth of Nations*, Book I, ch. X.

sengemeinschaft; each participant retained his autonomy, and centralized direction was provided by a sometimes unwieldy body whose influence depended on the good will of the member firms. The original English Sewing-Cotton Company (1897) and the Calico Printers Association (1899) were of this type. Others were true mergers, like the Salt Union of 1888, which claimed to control 91 per cent of the salt output of the United Kingdom; or the United Alkali Company, formed in 1891 in a last-ditch effort of Leblanc producers to hold their own against the competition of the Solvay process.

The combines were Britain's answer to the integration and concentration of German industry. On the whole, they were a poor answer: they appeared in the wrong industries, or if in the right ones, for the wrong reasons; they were often founded by promoters rather than producers, and the initial over-evaluation of capital burdened subsequent performance; the very multiplicity of their adherents complicated their task; and here too the absence of tariff protection exposed the prosperous ones to the incursions of interlopers—success was almost as dangerous as failure.

The consequences of this new, commercial version of the enclosure movement are not easy to disengage from the multitude of other factors that determined the character and volume of world trade; nor do they lend themselves to easy generalization. The return to protection discouraged some forms of international exchange, but served to stimulate rivalry in open markets. Similarly, cartels worked to restrain competition and stabilize prices and output up to a point; but their very success nourished ambitions that led to eventual rupture and wider fluctuations than before. And even when accord was maintained, the effort of the individual members to secure larger quotas often stimulated a development of capacity more rapid than free competition would have produced or a rational investment policy based on anticipated return warranted. In the last analysis, however, these new institutional arrangements are of interest to us as efforts to cure, hence as indicia of, an internal malaise. That they did not always accomplish their purpose should not surprise.

What, then, is the larger significance of this welter of developments, sometimes mutually reinforcing, sometimes contradictory? The answer would seem to lie in that vivid word of Phelps-Brown, 'climacteric'— applied not to Britain alone, however, but to the world economy as a whole, and conceived primarily in terms of the relations of the component national economies to one another. What we have, in short, is a shift from monarchy to oligarchy, from a one-nation to a multi-nation industrial system; if we want to retain the biological metaphor, from a one-celled to a many-celled organism. That this change of life coincided

with an equally fundamental technological transformation only complicated what was intrinsically a difficult adjustment—so difficult, indeed,
that the most determined efforts of the wisest men did not avail to
appease the resentments and enmities that grew out of the consequen-
tially altered balance of political power. Marxist students of history
have been wont to see the international rivalries that preceded the
First World War as the thrashing of a system in process of decline and
dissolution. *The fact is that these were the growing pains of a system in
process of germination.*

It was not the first time that the world economy, as an interacting
system, had passed through such a climacteric. A comparable crisis had
attended Britain's breakthrough to a modern industrial order. There too,
as we have seen, the balance of both economic and political force
shifted drastically, posing a severe challenge to all nations pretending
to membership in the concert of first-class powers. That the international
consequences were not so unhappy as they were to be during the next
climacteric reflects *in part* market considerations: on the one hand, the
availability in the earlier period of a still untapped, highly elastic world
demand for manufactures; on the other, the opportunities for fruitful
interaction between the one major centre of production and its still
pupillary emulators.

If the climacteric of the late nineteenth century was not the first of
this international system, neither has it been the last. In so far as the
historian can understand his own age, it would seem that we are now
going through still another change of life, once again brought about by
the entry into the lists of a new group of industrial and industrializing
nations, the most important of which is Soviet Russia. This time,
however, the problem of adjustment is complicated by fundamental
differences of social structure and organization between old and new.
In effect, the newcomers are competing with the older industrial powers
not so much economically as politically, and economic efforts are
directed not to the pursuit of wealth, with such unfortunate political
consequences as that may or may not entail, but to the pursuit of power,
with more probably disastrous results. Here a certain wistful and wish-
ful reserve, as well as the historian's customary prudence, counsels
against any attempt at prediction.

With that brief allusion to the unhappy present, inserted only to
complete the logic of this analysis, we may turn with relief to the
anodyne details of the history of technology.

By the last decades of the nineteenth century, technological advance
was proceeding within the older industries on so broad a front that the
task of the historian is enormously complicated. And this in turn goes

far to explain why the subject has been neglected.[1] Broad advance, as Rostow notes, is the hallmark of maturity: the basic innovations spread from the small group of industries that are at the heart of the revolution to the rest of the productive sector. Under the circumstances, we shall have to abandon our concentration on a few selected foci of change. Instead, we shall attempt to organize the data of technological progress along analytical lines, grouping them according to principle rather than area of application: I. New materials and new ways of preparing old materials. II. New sources of energy and power. III. Mechanization and division of labour.

The order chosen is not intended to imply relative importance, since there is no way of assessing the impact of each of these on general productivity. Rather, my intention is to reconcile as much as possible the analytical schema, which is in a sense timeless, with the chronological sequence of technological change, so that the reader will not lose track of economic history *qua* history. For this reason, the bulk of the space will be allotted to topics I and II, for they lend themselves best to description as process, as development through time. More than the others, also, they permit the historian to introduce those general issues of comparative economic growth that are the *leitmotif* of the chapter.

NEW MATERIALS

The subject of new materials and new ways of making old materials is multifarious and would, were we to pursue it to its limit, take us into every branch of industry. For the sake of economy, however, we shall concentrate on two themes: the invention and diffusion of cheap steel and the transformation of the chemical industry.

The age of steel

Man is a naming animal. He loves to pin labels on things. And no one is more prolific of nomenclature than the historian, who cannot resist the opportunity to designate each chronological section of his subject by some pithy title—the Age of the Enlightenment, the Era of Good Feeling, the Age of Reform—partly for pedagogic or heuristic convenience, partly for proclamatory effect, partly as a surrogate for understanding.

So we have the Age of Steel. It is one of the better of these slogan-titles. If one were to seek out the primary feature of the technology of

[1] Cf. R. J. Forbes, 'The History of Science and Technology', in XIe Congrès International des Sciences Historiques, *Rapports*, I, 72.

the last third of the nineteenth century, it would be the substitution of steel for iron and the concomitant increase in the consumption of metal per head.

It is a commonplace to note that modern industry was built (and indeed continues to be built, even after the development of plastics and concrete) on a framework of metal, particularly ferrous metal. It is worth pausing, however, to consider why this was and is so. The answer lies not so much in the separate characteristics of metal, some of which are duplicated by other materials, but in their combination, which is unique and thus far unapproached by any other product of man's ingenuity.

The salient advantages are three: great strength in proportion to weight and volume; plasticity; and hardness. The first is implicit in the elasticity of metal, that is, its resistance to the various forms of stress-compression (including the variety known as percussion), pull, and bending or torsion. Even so remarkable a material as reinforced or pre-stressed concrete, light in proportion to volume and capable of sur-prising performances as an enclosing or supporting member of standing structures, cannot compete with metal where economy of space and movement are important considerations. In the earliest days of the Industrial Revolution, when metalworking techniques were rudi-mentary and craftsmen voluntarily employed whatever substitute materials offered themselves—wood, particularly, but also leather and rope, depending on the use—the most important pieces of the machines, the spindles for example, were already made of iron. And it was not long before everything, including the frame, was so made. No better material for articulated parts has been discovered since.

The superiority of iron in such uses derives from its exceptional strength—greater than that of other metals—and from its plasticity and hardness. It can be shaped without significant loss of elasticity—hammered (malleability); drawn (ductility); cut, stamped, and drilled; filed and ground; melted and cast. And it can be worked with precision: one can make a clean cut in it, a smooth hole, a sharp impression. Finally, it holds its shape well under abrasion and heat: the edge re-mains straight and, when necessary, keen; the holes remain smooth; the impression stays sharp.

As a result of this intimate connection between ferrous metals and machines, the consumption of iron *per capita* has always been one of the most accurate measures of industrialization. We have already had occasion to note the precociously 'ferruginous temper' of the English in the eighteenth century. The introduction of puddling and rolling accentuated this tendency, which was ever a source of astonishment to visitors from poorer lands. Thus the French ironmaster, Achille Dufaud of Fourchambault, in 1823: 'Internal consumption is said to be 110,000 tons; a frightening quantity, but when one has gone through England, it does not seem incredible.'[1] Only a generation later, in 1849, she was consuming perhaps fifteen times as much.

Steel is a superior variety of iron. It possesses all the advantages attributed above to metal and especially ferrous metal, in higher degree. Chemically, the two are distinguished by carbon content: pig iron, 2·5–4 per cent; steel, 0·1 per cent to about 2 per cent; wrought iron, less than 0·1 per cent. The higher the carbon content, the harder the metal; the less carbon, the softer, more malleable, and more ductile. Tenacity reaches a peak at about 1·2 per cent carbon, in the steel zone, then tapers off rapidly to 3 per cent, where the drop slows. As a result, pig iron is hard, but it is also brittle. It cannot be worked without breaking; to be used at all it must be cast. And it cannot withstand stress; hence it is suited only for the manufacture of such things as pots and pans, radiators, or engine blocks, where compression and torsion are negligible. Wrought iron, on the other hand, can be made so soft it can be worked by hand. In India the farrier tests his nails by bending them on his forehead. By the same token, however, wrought iron is extremely susceptible to wear and tear, is easily altered by shock, and offers low resistance to pull or bending. Where pig iron will crack or snap, wrought iron will yield.

Steel combines the advantages of both. It is hard, elastic, and plastic. It can be ground to a sharp edge and then hold it; nothing else is so well suited to cutting and shaping other metals. Its resistance to percussion and abrasion makes it ideal for hammers, anvils, nails, rails and other objects subject to pounding or wear and tear. Its strength in proportion to weight and volume makes possible lighter, smaller, and yet more precise and rigid—hence faster—machines and engines. And the same combination of compactness and strength makes steel an excellent construction material, especially in shipbuilding, where the weight of the vessel and space left for cargo are of primary importance.[2]

Metalworkers were aware of the peculiarities of steel in ancient times. The old bloomery furnace, which made malleable iron directly from the ore, produced a mass of heterogeneous metal whose degree of

[1] Guy Thuillier, *Georges Dufaud et les débuts du grand capitalisme dans la métallurgie, en Nivernais, au XIXe siècle* (Paris, 1959), p. 230.

[2] Within the category of steel, there are mild and hard steels, again distinguished by carbon content. The former (less than 0·25% carbon) are much like wrought iron: they will not take a temper, but are very tough and ductile, and are especially suited to structural uses, rails, and such forge work as riveting. The latter are the high-carbon steels, used for edged and other tools, the moving parts of machines, and structural pieces of unusual strength.

decarburization varied with the effectiveness of oxidization and contact with the fuel. Most of the bloom was wrought iron (*fer doux*), but some, especially the matter on or near the surface (the *fer fort*), had the quality of steel or even pig iron.

The reaction of the earliest smiths was to reject this recalcitrant material as unworkable. With time, however, the virtues of steel were recognized, especially for the production of edged tools and weapons. Somewhere, sometime in the ancient world, smiths learned to make steel deliberately, rather than accept what the accident of the bloomery yielded. The principal technique employed was carburization of wrought iron by cementation, that is by soaking it at a high temperature in a solid bath of carboniferous matter; the result was what came to be known as blister steel, so called because of the characteristic blistering of the surface when carburization was completed. An alternative method, though less satisfactory, was the direct one of interrupting the refining process before the carbon had burned completely away.

Because of the nature of the cementation process, in which the hot but solid metal absorbed its carbon from outside, blister steel was uneven in quality, ranging from soft steel at the core to iron at the surface. Greater homogeneity could be achieved by breaking the blister steel into small pieces, packing them in a sheath, and pounding them together at welding heat, thereby distributing the carbon more evenly through the mass and yielding what became known as shear steel. The resultant bars could then be bent double and the process of hammering repeated as often as necessary to obtain the quality desired. In Britain, one pounding was deemed sufficient for most purposes, and twice-hammered shear steel was considered the best made. In Germany craftsmanship was pushed further, and the so-called *viermal raffinierter Stahl* consisted of tough, nervy bars that consolidated in their 30–centimetre cross-section some 320 separate layers of charcoal steel.

This kind of work took time: one to two weeks to complete cementation and several days of forge work afterward. Moreover, the alternate heating and hammering called for a prodigal expenditure of fuel. Small wonder that first-quality steel was a costly commodity worth up to several hundred pounds sterling a ton. In effect, this was a metal sold and used by the pound for small objects of high value in proportion to weight: in particular, razors, surgical tools, blades, shears, files and rasps. Even ordinary blister steel was too costly to use in quantity: the blade of the peasant's scythe—when he could afford a scythe—usually consisted of a steel surface welded on to the iron core. The one area in which there was little or no stinting was the manufacture of arms: man has rarely quibbled about the cost of instruments of death.

This was the status of steel technology on the eve of the Industrial

Revolution. The first major innovation in this area since the anonymous, dateless invention of cementation was Huntsman's crucible technique (1740-2), which yielded decisive gains in the quality of the product. Huntsman took blister steel, achieved a high enough temperature to melt it in small vessels along with a flux of carbon and other metals, skimmed off the slag and poured. The result was (1) a purer steel, for the natural separation of foreign matter from the molten iron was far more effective than the pounding or squeezing out of drossy juices ever could be; and (2) a more homogeneous steel than could possibly be achieved by hammering solid metal on the anvil (compare the difference between stirring batter and kneading dough).

Crucible steel was harder and tougher than even the best shear steel; its one weakness was that it could not be treated at more than red heat, hence was hard to work, especially with the tools of the eighteenth century. (It could, of course, be cast.) Moreover, in the early days of Huntsman's monopoly or near-monopoly, its price was higher than that of shear steel in spite of the labour economies consequent on the elimination of repetitive forge work. As a result, smiths were hostile, and the use of the new metal was limited to those objects where the price of material was a negligible fraction of total cost—watch and clock parts, for example, and the finest edged tools. It did not really take hold until after 1770.

With time, however, the entry of competitors brought the price down. The effect of monopoly may be judged in part from the French experience: in 1815 cast steel had to be imported from Britain at £700 or £800 per ton; in 1819, after plants had been established at Badevel (Doubs) by Japy and near Saint-Etienne by James Jackson (English, as the name indicates), the price was £140.[1] Improvements in technique conduced to the same result. Producers learned to work with cheaper ingredients, to start with wrought iron, for example, and build up to steel by addition of powdered carbon. By the middle of the nineteenth century, Swedish steelmakers were mixing pig iron and iron ore with charcoal and selling the product at £50-£60 per ton.

The crucible technique had one further advantage, which opened the door to modern steel technology: it made possible—implicitly at first, effectively by the mid-nineteenth century—the manufacture of large pieces. Not that the individual crucibles could be made very big: they were perhaps 9-11 inches tall at first—the size of a vase—and more than a century later (1860) were still only about 16 inches in height; they held perhaps 45 to 60 pounds, though larger sizes were occasionally used. But they could be heated and poured *en masse*, or rather

[1] [W. F. Jackson], *James Jackson et ses fils* (Paris: privately printed, 1893), p. 17, gives a lower figure—£120 per ton in 1818.

in close succession; and with time manufacturers learned to co-ordinate the labour of a small army of men, teeming hundreds of crucibles, to produce ingots weighing many tons. Krupp was the pioneer here, and his 2¼-ton cylinder was the sensation of the Crystal Palace Exposition; scarcely a generation later, in 1869, Vickers was using 672 crucibles at a time to make pieces ten times as heavy.[1]

The products of these *tours de force* were intended for boring as cannon; at £100 or more a ton, large ingots of crucible steel were far too expensive for ordinary industrial purposes. Yet the advantages of steel over wrought iron were manifest, and considerable money and effort was devoted to discovering a method to produce cheap steel in bulk.

The first step was the development of puddled steel; the major contribution was made in the early 1840's by two German technicians, Lohage and Bremme. The principle was simple: if the puddling process could refine pig iron into carbon-free wrought iron, why not stop it before completion, while there was still enough carbon in the metal to make steel? Execution was another matter. It was particularly difficult to know when the steel was ready and yet not too cooked; and the temperature had to be kept high enough to melt the pig iron, while low enough to let the steel separate out as a pasty mass because of its higher melting point. As a result, puddled steel was rarely as homogeneous and hard as crucible steel, or as tough as shear steel. Often it was simply substituted for blister steel or iron in the crucible process. On the other hand, it was cheap—by the 1850's it was selling in Germany for about £22 a ton—and could be produced in large masses for such peaceful uses as tyres, wheels, gears, and drive shafts. The process was adopted more rapidly on the Continent than in Britain, where the ore apparently yielded pig iron too impure to serve as a base for acieration by puddling.[2] In France the new metal passed all other forms of steel in importance in 1857; the German figures do not permit a similar comparison (puddled and blister steel are combined), but the scissor year probably came at least as early.[3]

For lack of better, puddled steel would have been the nearest approach to mass-production steel—costs were eventually squeezed to around £10 per ton—had it not been for the invention of the Bessemer and Siemens–Martin processes, in their acid and basic variants.

---

[1] Sidney Pollard, *History of Labour in Sheffield*, p. 160.

[2] See the report of M. Goldenberg in Michel Chevalier, ed., *Exposition Universelle de 1867 à Paris, Rapports du jury international* (14 vols., Paris, 1868), v, 393f.

[3] France, Min. de l'Agric., du Comm., et des Trav. Publics, Direction des Mines, *Statistique de l'industrie minérale; Résumé des travaux statistiques de l'Administration des Mines en 1853, 1854, 1855, 1856, 1857, 1858 et 1859* (Paris, 1861), pp. 484–99; G. Viebahn, *Statistik des zollvereinten Deutschlands*, pp. 439ff.

(1) *Bessemer.* Again the inspiration came from armament. Henry Bessemer (1813–98), who was not a metallurgist but rather a kind of high-class tinkerer already wealthy by his ingenuity and versatility, devised in the early 1850's an artillery shell that required an exceptionally long and strong gun. The problem was to make steel cheap enough to render the mass production of such large pieces budgetarily feasible. (Even the military gagged at the cost under existing techniques of acieration.)

Bessemer found one of those solutions that amaze by their simplicity —once they are discovered. Instead of refining the pig iron by the traditional application of heat to its periphery, he blew air into and through the molten metal, using the heat thrown off by the oxidization itself to keep the iron liquid.[1] As a result, decarburization was extremely rapid: three to five tons in the early days in ten or twenty minutes, as against perhaps 24 hours for the equivalent amount of puddled steel.[2] A Bessemer converter in blast fairly erupts with the sudden release of energy. It is a little hell. With its flames and its shooting sparks of changing hue, it is also one of the most exciting sights that industry has to offer.

The consequent saving in labour and materials (Bessemer entitled the paper in which he announced his discovery in 1856, 'The Manufacture of Iron without Fuel') made possible the first steel that could compete in price with wrought iron—£7 (including royalty of about £1) per ton as against about £4 per ton. Yet adoption was slow. For one thing, iron-makers and users were reluctant to admit that the greater strength and durability of steel more than made up for the remaining difference in price; indeed, the very advent of cheap steel was enough to put producers of wrought iron on their mettle and

---

[1] Due credit should be given to the earlier invention (*c.* 1851) of this technique (with minor differences) by William Kelly in the United States. Kelly kept his operations secret until 1856, when his application for a patent ran up against a previous grant to Bessemer. He finally succeeded in getting his priority recognized in 1857—too late, however, to save himself from bankruptcy. It is doubtful, in any event, whether his process was suitable to mass production. See W. Paul Strassmann, *Risk and Technological Innovation: American Manufacturing Methods during the Nineteenth Century* (Ithaca, N.Y., 1959), p. 30. Nor should one overlook the vital contribution of Robert F. Mushet, who corrected the tendency of the converter to produce a 'burned-out' (over-oxidized) iron, by adding *Spiegeleisen*, that is, an iron containing manganese, to the molten metal. This process proved especially valuable in refining British pig iron. Owing to an unfortunate combination of circumstances, Mushet's patent was allowed to lapse before he could reap the fruits of his inventiveness. Cf. R. F. Mushet, *The Bessemer-Mushet Process, or Manufacture of Cheap Steel* (Cheltenham, 1883).

[2] Moreover, there was no intrinsic limit to the size of the converter. In puddling, the capacity of the furnace could not exceed the amount of molten iron a strong workman could stir by hand. The usual charge was about 200 kg. In the Bessemer process,

stimulate them to more strenuous efforts. For another, the Bessemer process was attended by technical difficulties, some the inevitable concomitants of breaking-in, others inherent in the process itself.

The most serious of these was the inability of the converter to burn off the phosphorus along with other impurities in the pig iron; anything more than a minute proportion of this element made the steel unworkable. It was mere chance that Bessemer was using the right kind of pure pig iron when he invented his technique. (Compare the good fortune of Darby, one hundred and fifty years earlier.) His licensees were less lucky: hardly had they gone into production when they had to stop. The contretemps came, in Bessemer's words, 'as a bolt from the blue'.

A new start was made with haematite ores, which are non-phosphoric. The difficulty was that these were rarer and costlier than ordinary ironstone. In the entire industrial world, only the United States had an adequate supply: about half the Lake Superior basin was non-phosphoric. Britain had a major deposit of haematite in the Cumberland–Furness area, which boomed as a consequence, but almost from the start had to import additional supplies from Spain; the beds of non-phosphoric ironstone in the Bilbao area were probably the richest in Europe. Germany had small amounts in the Siegerland, but had to provide the great bulk of her needs from Spain and Austrian Galicia. France had only scattered outcroppings of haematite in the Centre and had to bring in ore from Elba and Algeria to supplement imports from Spain. Belgium had nothing. Small wonder that the use of the Bessemer technique developed slowly on the Continent, and that for almost a decade after its invention puddled steel continued to predominate.

(2) *Siemens–Martin.* The second major advance in steelmaking simply re-emphasized the ore problem: the Siemens-Martin process also required non-phosphoric iron. As the name implies, the innovation was twofold. The furnace itself was the work of Frederick and William Siemens, brothers and members of a German family that will go down as the most inventive in history. (The main branch of the family were, as we shall see, pioneers in electrical communication and engineering.) The originality of the furnace lay in its utilization of the regenerative principle, by which the waste gases of oxidization were used to heat a honeycomb of bricks that in turn superheated the air and gaseous fuel in combustion; at the same time, the generation in a separate unit of the gas required made possible the employment of low-grade coal. The result was the achievement of far higher tempera-

by contrast, the only limit was the ability of machines to tilt the container and pour its contents. The early converters ran from 2 to 5 tons; by the end of the century, 20- and 25-ton vessels were common.

tures—the only immediate limit was the resistance of the furnace itself—at a substantial saving of fuel.

The potential contribution of the regenerative principle was not confined to metallurgy; it was an efficient method of heat production applicable to any energy-consuming industrial process. Its first appearance in iron manufacture was in the hot-blast stove of E. A. Cowper, an associate of Siemens, in 1857; from the start it yielded a blast of 620° C. and thereby increased the output of pig by 20 per cent.[1] The open-hearth version developed by Charles William Siemens found its first employment in 1861 in a flint-glass works in Birmingham. Early efforts to use it in steelmaking, where along with the Bessemer converter it had the advantage of being able to melt the pig completely (the puddling furnace produced at best a viscous mass), were failures. Commercial success was not achieved until 1864, when Pierre Martin introduced scrap iron into the bath to facilitate the process of decarburization. Even then, diffusion had to wait until the different centres of steel manufacture, each using its own qualities of ore, iron, and coal, learned by trial and error the proper combination of ingredients. Some used a mix that was more than half scrap; others added no more than a seasoning of iron chips; some used old steel as well as, or instead of, iron; Siemens himself used iron ore. The effective use of the open-hearth technique really dates from the 1870's.

Table 9. *Production of Bessemer and Siemens–Martin Steel (Flusseisen)*
(in thousand tons)

	1865	1869	1873	1879
Great Britain	225	275	588	1030
Germany[a]	99·5	161	310	478
France	40·6	110	151	333
Belgium	0·65	2·9	22	111

[a] Includes Luxembourg. New boundaries from 1873.

SOURCE. Beck, *Geschichte des Eisens*, v, 233, 308.

(3) *Basic steel.* As a result of her favourable resource position, Britain dominated the early age of steel—in spite of the fact that no country had a greater stake in the old way of doing things. To the end of the 1870's she accounted for more than half of the Bessemer and Siemens–Martin production of the four major industrial countries of western Europe. This weakness of the continental countries in a new technological situation was potentially of critical importance both economically and politically. For Germany in particular, the great

[1] H. R. Schubert, 'The Steel Industry', in Singer *et al.*, ed., *History of Technology*, v, 58.

advances of the 1850's and 1860's were substantially offset and the new balance of power called into question. It is obviously hard to say what would have happened if the ore problem had not been solved (compare the fuel issue in eighteenth-century England). The conjuncture gives no clue. One is tempted to ascribe the severity of the depression of the German iron industry in the 1870's—five years of red ink and a 19 per cent drop in output from peak to trough—to structural reasons: approaching inanition for want of nourishment. Admittedly the decline was shared, though in lesser degree, by Britain, and by France and Belgium as well. Still, it seems most unlikely that the spectacular rise of the Reich to a position of economic pre-eminence in Europe by the end of the century would have been possible without a strong steel industry, and one may doubt whether the steelmakers of the Ruhr could have thrived as they did had they been forced to seek their raw material in the Mediterranean area and northern Spain in competition with British producers, already advantaged by haematite deposits at home.[1] Lorraine, of course, far from good coking coal and dependent on cheap but high-phosphoric *minette*, would have gone out of competition with wrought iron and the puddling furnace.

The answer was found in 1878–9 by two Englishmen: Sidney Gilchrist Thomas, by occupation a clerk in a police court; and his cousin Sidney Gilchrist, chemist in a Welsh iron-works. They put basic limestone in the molten iron to combine with the acid phosphorus in a slag that could then be drawn off; and they lined the converter with basic matter in place of the usual acid siliceous bricks in order to prevent this basic slag from eating away the walls and releasing phosphorus back into the metal. The solution was a simple one, founded on a widely known principle. Success lay in the ingenuity of the practical arrangements—the combination of basic flux and lining—and it is probably no coincidence that the idea came to an amateur who approached the problem with an open mind.[2] Thomas is comparable in this regard to Bessemer, who for all his experience as a professional inventor was not a steel man. But whereas Bessemer had done his work a generation earlier when metallurgical chemistry was still in its infancy, Thomas solved a problem that had engaged the attention of some of Europe's most highly trained engineers for years. He was

[1] Beginning in the 1890's, the Ruhr came to rely increasingly on Swedish ores, which averaged about 60% iron content. They were too phosphoric, however, for acid steel, and would have played a far smaller role had technology remained the same as in the 1870's.

[2] This twofold character of the innovation is often overlooked. See the discussion in Schubert, 'The Steel Industry', p. 60; similarly, J. Jewkes, D. Sawers and R. Sillerman, *The Sources of Invention* (London, 1960), p. 51.

one of the last and perhaps the most important of the line of tinkerers that had made the Industrial Revolution. After him, the professionals just about had the field to themselves.

The invention of basic steel was an event of world import. Thomas was besieged by offers; the petitioners would not even let him eat his breakfast in peace. The story is told that two of the leading German iron firms sent representatives on a Phineas Fogg-like race to Middlesbrough; the one who did not stop for sleep won. The tale may be apocryphal, but it conveys something of the excitement of the occasion. In the end, a handful of industrial giants on the Continent (Schneider in France; Wendel in German Lorraine; the Hörder-Verein and Rheinische Stahlwerke in Germany) leased the patent rights for sums that, though not so inconsequential as tradition would have it, were a wonderful bargain; most of them sublet them in turn to other producers. The commercial manufacture of Thomas steel began in late 1879; within four years there were eighty-four basic converters in operation in western and central Europe (including Austria-Hungary), with a capacity of 755 tons. Output in 1883 totalled over 600,000 tons; compare acid Bessemer output, which took well over a decade to reach that level.[1] The adaptation of the process to the open hearth was almost as rapid.

(4) *Steel* v. *wrought iron.* Together, the Bessemer, Siemens–Martin, and basic processes drove the real cost of crude steel down some 80 or 90 per cent between the early 1860's and mid-1890's and opened the iron ore deposits of the earth to fruitful exploitation. The consequences may be followed in the curve of output, which behaves in its steep upward trend like that of a new substance confronted by an extremely elastic demand. The combined production of Britain, France, Germany, and Belgium in 1861—before the Bessemer process had taken hold—was approximately 125,000 tons; in 1870 the total was perhaps 385,000 tons; in 1913 it amounted to 32,020,000 tons, a gain of 83 times (10·8 per cent per year) over the forty-three-year period.

Against this must be set the decline of wrought iron, long the frame of the industrial structure. At first, the older malleable form resisted: it was cheaper, and in countries like Britain there was a fortune invested in puddling plant. Moreover, the homogeneity of early Bessemer steel left something to be desired, and even the open-hearth variety, costlier to begin with, was not good enough for more exacting uses—large rolled plates, for example. Nor should one underestimate the strength

---

[1] In the absence of statistics separating converter from open-hearth production for France, 1872 would seem to have been the year when Bessemer output in western and central Europe passed the 600,000-ton mark. Cf. Beck, *Geschichte des Eisens*, v, 967, 1057, 1110, 1134, 1177.

of inertia and conservatism in these matters—the scepticism of the British Admiralty, the reluctance of French railway men to admit that steel rails could outlast iron by a factor of six to one. Before long, however, steelmakers learned to correct the flaws in their product; and improvements in efficiency wiped out enough of the price difference to make competition in most uses impossible. The railways were the first major consumer (after the military, of course) to adopt the new metal. The changeover was substantially accomplished in the 1870's; it was stimulated by the diminishing ratio of steel and iron rail prices—2·65 to 1 in 1867, 1·50 in 1871, 1·16 in 1875.[1] Shipbuilding, by contrast, which set higher standards under the watchful eyes of insurers like Lloyd's, began to accept steel in place of iron only in the late 1870's. In 1880 38,000 tons of steel shipping were added to the register of the United Kingdom, against 487,000 of iron. Five years later iron still predominated—308,500 to 185,000 tons—especially in the building of sailing vessels, where initial cost was a decisive consideration. Another five years of savings in the manufacture of open-hearth plates, however, and the tables had turned: 913,000 tons of steel to 46,000 of iron in 1890.[2]

Actually, the high point of wrought-iron manufacture was not reached in Britain and France until 1882 (2,841,000 and 1,073,000 tons respectively) and in Germany until 1889 (1,650,000 tons). As late as 1885 Britain was turning out more puddled iron than steel; in Germany the curves of output do not cross until 1887; and in France, not until 1894.

This Indian summer of growth and achievement in obsolescence is a common economic phenomenon: witness the golden age of coaching after the coming of the railway; or the development of the clipper and the large intercontinental schooners after the introduction of the steamship. It derives from one or more of several factors: (1) a creative technological response to the challenge of the new competitor; (2) a compression of cost and elimination of waste in the struggle for survival; (3) opportunities derived from the demand created by the more efficient technique (cf. the role of coaches as feeders to railway trunk lines in the 1830's and 1840's).

Wrought iron attempted the first without success (above, p. 218). The goal proved a will-o'-the-wisp. Given the qualitative advantages of

[1] This is the French ratio, but the trend was substantially parallel in the other producing countries. Jean Fourastié, ed., *Documents pour l'histoire et la théorie des prix* [Centre d'Etudes Economiques, 'Etudes et Mémoires: Recherches sur l'évolution des prix en période de progrès technique'] (Paris, n.d. [1959]), pp. 122–3.

[2] *Encyclopaedia Britannica*, 11th edition, 'Ship'. These figures differ somewhat from those of the British Iron Trade Association. See W. A. Sinclair, 'The Growth of the British Steel Industry in the Late Nineteenth Century', *Scottish J. Political Economy*, VI (1959), 35, 41 f.

Table 10. *The Manufacture of Cheap Steel in the Nineteenth Century*

	Acid	Technology and economic consequences	Basic	Technology and economic consequences
Bessemer		Half-hour or less for carbonization; rapidity of output compels extensive mechanization; consequently important economies of scale		Long reputed the poorest of cheap steels. Yet produces metal of high ductility and excellent welding quality—especially good for tubes and wire
Siemens–Martin	Uses relatively scarce non-phosphoric ores. Long reputed to produce a tougher steel than the basic process	Six to eighteen hours for decarbonization; closer quality control; smaller scale of production. Higher cost; but differences mitigated by feasibility of using scrap	Uses cheaper ore; costs less. Produces by-product phosphates that make excellent fertilizer. High proportion of slag leads by way of compensation to larger scale of production	Especially abundant supply of scrap iron since most wrought iron was phosphoric

steel, it is most unlikely that mechanization could have done more than delay the inevitable. More effective was a general rationalization of methods and reduction of wages (compare the compression of wages of hand-loom weavers in earlier decades) that made it possible to cut prices by about half from the early 1870's to mid-1880's.

As for the third, wrought iron and steel were essentially substitutes rather than complementary, especially after the invention of basic steel. To be sure, the general demand for metal—all metals—was increasing, and the income effect of cheap steel may have redounded somewhat to the benefit of the older substance. In the end, however, iron came to be confined to uses where softness was not a handicap and resistance to corrosion was especially desirable: anchors and anchor chains, ornamental grill-work and gates, garden furniture and the like.

(5) *International division of labour and competition.* It would take too long to discuss in detail the different technical characteristics of Bessemer and Siemens–Martin steel, acid and basic, and analyse their implications for industrial development. They are summarized in the accompanying table. Very briefly, Bessemer was cheaper, more approximate in quality, and was produced in larger, more capital-intensive plants; Siemens–Martin steel was more homogeneous, closer to specification, and better suited to custom work. The one found its most important early use in rails; the other in plates. As production standards rose and railway construction slowed, the long-run trend was toward Siemens–Martin; but it was much more rapid in Britain, the world's greatest builder of ships, than in continental Europe (Table 11).

Table 11. *Percentage of Steel Produced by Siemens–Martin*

	1890	1913	1930
Great Britain	43·6	79·2	94·3
Germany	17·4	40·2	52·3[a]
France	36·8	33·8	27·5
Belgium	Negligible	Negligible	Negligible

[a] Had been as high as 60·6 per cent in 1920.

SOURCE. T. H. Burnham and G. O. Hoskins, *Iron and Steel in Britain 1870–1930* (London, 1943), p. 183.

Some of this diversity was due to differences in resources. Britain, with her haematite ores, long remained faithful to the acid process. The continental countries, on the other hand, compelled by the absence of haematite ironstone and encouraged by the abundance of phosphorus-rich ore in Lorraine and Sweden to concentrate on the basic technique, found Thomas steel (that is, basic Bessemer) especially remunerative.

Yet one should not underestimate the human factor. Stimulated by necessity, the continental steelmasters worked at the basic process with a scientific will: they achieved and maintained a proper mix and produced a metal of good, uniform quality. The British tinkered and improvised, and the irregularity of their product merely confirmed the doubts of consumers, which in turn discouraged experiment and investment. The whole situation was self-reinforcing. By about 1890, the continental countries were turning out more basic than acid steel; whereas the latter accounted for 92 per cent of Britain's open-hearth make and 73 per cent of her converter output as late as 1897.[1] The respective proportions were 63 and 65 per cent in 1913, and it took the First World War to wean Britain from her allegiance to the older, more costly process.[2]

This specialization by type of process both shaped and was shaped by the growth patterns of the respective national steel industries. Britain had relatively small plants; Germany large. Around the turn of the century, the *biggest* British mills were turning out only as much as the *average* Westphalian works. (Contrast the situation a generation earlier; see above, p. 219.) Nor was this simply a matter of delayed response to opportunity: *new* British plants in the 1890's were a quarter to a third of the size of their German competitors.

The disparity extended backward to the smelting stage: the median member of the German steel cartel (1903) was four times as big as its British analogue (1900), more than twice as big as the median iron firm in the Cleveland area. And the disadvantage to Britain was cumulative, for Germany put big and big together and Britain left small and small apart. In 1902 only twenty-one open-hearth firms of seventy-two in Britain, with one quarter of the make, had adjacent blast furnaces; whereas integration with smelting was almost universal in the Reich. The same was true of ties to later stages of manufacture: where the tendency of Westphalia was to build rolling mills on to steel works, British rerollers were relying increasingly on outside sources for their crude metal.

Size of plant and integration, moreover, were closely related to technique and productivity. German equipment, originally smaller and less efficient than the British, grew rapidly in size and performance until, by the turn of the century, it outstripped that of her precursor by a wide margin.[3] In 1870 the average British blast furnace made 74 per

[1] See the discussion *ibid.*; also I. F. Gibson, 'The Establishment of the Scottish Steel Industry', *Scottish J. Political Economy*, v (1958), 22–39.
[2] *Iron and Coal Trades Rev.* Diamond Jubilee Issue, 1867–1927 (1927), 134; Burnham and Hoskins, *Iron and Steel in Britain*, pp. 179–80.
[3] The above is based primarily on the discussion in Burn, *Economic History*, ch. x. The recent article of Sinclair argues that Burn neglected the open-hearth sector, with

cent more pig iron than its German counterpart—8700 against 5000 tons. By 1910 the positions were reversed: Germany, 49,000 tons; Britain, 30,000. Similarly in steel: by 1890 the average German open hearth was half again as large as the British—15 against 10 tons—and output was correspondingly higher; and German converters poured out an average of 34,000 tons in 1901, where British equipment produced 21,750.[1]

What is more, the very size of German equipment imposed extensive mechanization. A furnace turning out 3000 tons of pig iron a week consumed 6000–9000 tons of ore, perhaps 1000 tons of limestone, some 4000 tons of coke. It took some six hundred freight trucks, averaging 20 tons capacity, just to bring materials to the mill.[2] (It would have taken twelve hundred or more of the smaller British trucks.) And once there, these materials had to be fed somehow to the flames. The traditional winch and counterweight systems for hauling small tilt wagons to the lip of the furnace—supplemented on occasion by human brawn and hand shovels—were hopelessly inadequate. In their place appeared continuous conveyors, travelling cranes, and suspended railways powered by electricity.

And then there were the 3000 tons of iron to be tapped, poured into moulds, lifted, and broken for remelting; or better yet, delivered directly to the refinery for conversion into wrought iron or steel. As noted earlier, the rapid Bessemer process required mechanization from the start. By comparison, the lengthier period required for decarburization by Siemens–Martin encouraged a certain tolerance of interruptions for transport and manipulation: with proper facilities it took

consequent depreciation of the achievements of British metallurgy by comparison with the German. The reproach, it seems to me, is exaggerated. For one thing, Burn makes a number of salient points about the weaknesses of open-hearth steel though he tends to pass over the strengths. For another, and more important, the comparison is not so much between sectors of the British steel industry, as between British and foreign manufacture. It would be equally unreasonable to measure the growth of German steel by the Thomas sector alone.

What is more, Sinclair carries his story only into the 1890's; yet the discrepancy between German and British rates of growth is even more striking after that date than before. Even if we measure British open-hearth against German total steel output, we find, taking 1890 as 100, an increase by 1913 to 387 for the former, to 825 for the latter. Taking total output for both countries, the respective indexes are 214 and 825. *Iron and Coal Trades Rev.* Diamond Jubilee Issue, 1867–1927 (1927), 130, 134.

[1] Burnham and Hoskins, *Iron and Steel*, pp. 145, 181; S. J. Chapman, *Work and Wages*, part 1: *Foreign Competition* (London, 1904), p. 89.

[2] British trucks were much smaller, and coal wagons were typically of 10-ton capacity. Cf. K. G. Fenelon, *Railway Economics* (London, 1932), pp. 168–73; S. E. Parkhouse, 'Railway Freight Rolling Stock', *J. Institute of Transport*, XXIV (1951), 213–15.

some $3\frac{1}{2}$ hours to fill a 40-ton hearth by hand.[1] But here too the trend toward mechanization was inexorable. By the end of the century, German steelmakers especially were imitating the best American practice and building tiltable furnaces of 100–300 tons capacity, equipped with hydraulically or electrically powered charging apparatus. The effect of mechanical loading alone was to reduce a work force of 46 skilled and unskilled labourers per hearth to 16 and cut labour costs (allowing for the amortization of the additional capital) by 58 per cent.[2]

Finally, and perhaps more important, there was a strong tendency toward increased automaticity of the forge. The development was along two lines. One, resuming the advance implicit in Cort's combination of puddling and rolling, was to eliminate as much as possible the hammer and have all the work of squeezing and shaping done by the mill. Powerful and fast as the steam hammer was, it was of its nature intermittent in operation and gave rise to a costly and difficult problem in manual manipulation. One has only to look at any of the hundreds of sketches of mid-nineteenth-century forges that have come down to us to appreciate the disadvantages of the old technique: the shop is generally a vaulted cavern, illuminated by the glow of the furnaces and the hot ingots and blooms; the floor is a Vulcanian jungle of puffing steam-driven machines, heaps of incinerating iron, tools momentarily discarded, the suspended vines of the overhead cranes; and in the middle, hanging dumb but deadly in its chain sling is the large cylinder or block of white-hot metal, teased and nudged on to the anvil, then twisted and released into a new position, and then another, by the pincers and rods of as many as dozens of black and sweating pygmies. To which one must add what the sketches cannot convey: the clash and clangour, the enervating heat, the burning, dust-filled air that killed.[3]

Around 1870, direct rolling of big masses was confined essentially to rails; otherwise it was thought necessary to 'consolidate the structure' of the ingot by pounding before squeezing. Some of the British began to get away from this intermediary step in the 1860's, and the contraction of the 1870's helped spread the practice by sharpening

[1] 'On Charging Open-hearth Furnaces by Machinery', *J. Iron and Steel Institute*, LI (1897), 90–1. Actually 48 tons of materials were charged per heat in a hearth of this size, 'and that in the face of a furnace radiating a considerable amount of heat'. Four men were used, each charging about 3·4 tons per hour. The 'great physical and constitutional strength' required can easily be imagined.

[2] Von Kammerer, 'Entwicklungslinien der Technik', *Technik und Wirtschaft*, III (1910), 16.

[3] See Pollard, *A History of Labour in Sheffield*, pp. 168–9. The average age at death of rollers and forgers in Sheffield who died in the period 1864–71 (85 cases) was 37 years; the only group that was consumed more rapidly was the puddlers, who averaged a brief 31 years.

competition. At John Brown's in Sheffield, one mill and eighteen men did the work of three hammers and fifty-four men.[1]

Note, however, the factor of three: even with the mill it took eighteen men to send the metal on its way, then receive it as it completed its run and send it back for another pass. The task was just as difficult as that of guiding ingots under the hammer; if there was less need for strength and precision, more agility was required to handle the billet or sheet as it spewed from between the rolls. Fatigue could be fatal, and indeed most of the accidents occurred in the early morning hours.[2]

The answer—and this is the second of the two lines of development referred to above—lay in minimizing handling by automating the mill. One improvement, which was first introduced in Britain in 1866, was to apply a reversing engine to the rolls, so that the metal could be run back and forth without leaving the machine. The saving in labour and time was such that capacity was more than doubled; but the strain on the engine, which every few seconds had to fight its momentum and that of the rolls to start back the other way, was tremendous. The American solution, extensively adopted in Germany, was the three-high mill, where a third roll placed above the usual two made it possible to pass the metal back on an 'upper level', shaping it the while.

Faster work called for improvements in feeding techniques, for the task of catching the metal on a three-high mill and lifting or lowering it to send it back on the other track was if anything more arduous and dangerous than on two-high mills. By the turn of the century, best practice was moving the metal on roller tables, turning it by automatic tumbling bars, raising and lowering it by lifts, putting it into and removing it from the reheating furnaces by hydraulic (later, electric) cranes fitted with giant pincers. Reheating itself was progressively eliminated as the rapidity of the shaping process increased. There were even continuous mills for narrow shapes, with ten or more sets of rolls that stretched and shaped the billet in a single pass. It required great precision to effect such a result: at one end the much reduced, almost finished metal came rushing through the final rolls at forty to sixty miles an hour; while at the other end the same piece of metal, thick and unshapen, was still feeding slowly into the roughing rolls. It also required ingenuity and heavy capital outlays to process the final product: 'flying shears' for cutting, facilities for cooling, stacking, and

[1] Burns, *Economic History*, p. 56, citing *Iron and Coal Trades Review* (1874), 760.
[2] See the analysis of a realistic painting of the forge at Königshütte (Silesia) in the 1870's: K. Kaiser, *Adolph Menzels Eisenwalzwerk* (Berlin: Heuschelverlag, 1953). Compare the jacket illustration of Pollard's *Labour in Sheffield*, which shows sheet rolling at the Atlas Steel Works in 1861.

moving. These were the ancestors of the modern wide strip mill. The continuous system was first invented in Britain, where one or two examples were built in the 1860's to make rods and rails. But it did not find general acceptance, and it was not until the 1890's that the idea was picked up again in the United States and spread thence to Europe. On the whole, the continental engineers, especially the Germans, were quickest to adopt it.[1]

Efficiency promotes efficiency: indeed, it makes it necessary. Just as size and integration facilitated in Germany greater intensity of capital, so capital intensity encouraged a more rational organization of work and a simplification of the product mix. The reader will recall that one of the most serious obstacles to the diffusion of the power loom was the high cost of immobilizing valuable machinery to change patterns; by the same token, the need to change rolls was an impediment to the adoption of longer and faster mills. In order to make the most of their equipment, the Germans were compelled to standardize and in that way stretch their production runs. As early as 1883 the United Societies of German Architects and Engineers drew up a complete set of standard sections for rolled iron in shipbuilding, engineering, and construction.[2] And where in 1900 British steelmakers were turning out 122 channel and angle sections as a matter of course, the Germans made 34.

Finally, there was the question of waste. In the eighteenth and early nineteenth centuries, the best British enterprises were internationally renowned for their neatness, their attention to detail, their meticulous inventory controls. Wedgwood was uncompromising on this point; continental visitors to Crawshay's iron mill in Wales, coming as they did from poorer lands, found this one of the most impressive and congenial features of his production organization. By the end of the century, however, the tables had turned. British visitors to German steel plants marvelled at bins to catch oil dripping from the lubrication boxes and steam captured, condensed, and re-used.[3] Above all, they

[1] On German 'arrangements for relieving labour of its more exhausting characteristics', see British Iron Trade Association, *The Iron and Steel Industries of Belgium and Germany* (London, 1896), p. 13 and *passim*.

[2] Burn, *Economic History*, p. 199. It is impossible to say what was the effect of such a list on industrial practice. But the very fact of its preparation is significant (Burn notes the preoccupation of German engineers with the advantages of different sections in the 1870's), and the characteristics of the cost curves, to say nothing of the ideological commitment to rationality (see below, pp. 352–4) undoubtedly influenced the German enterprise in this direction. Cf. W. H. Henman, in discussion of W. H. A. Robertson, 'Notes on the Mechanical Design of Rolling Mills', *J. Birmingham Metallurgical Soc.* VII (1919), 40.

[3] See British Iron Trade Assn., *The Iron and Steel Industries of Belgium and Germany*, pp. 36, 42, 45, 47. German superiority in this field continued right through to the war and after. Cf. Robertson, 'Notes'.

admired the Germans' efficient use of fuel, so often the best criterion of metallurgical performance. The discrepancy here was apparent at every stage—from coking, where continental ovens supplied energy for steam-engines and produced by-product tar and ammonia for the chemical manufacture;[1] to smelting, where the German *mise au mille* was 15–25 per cent lower than good British practice and the hot gases of their blast furnaces drove internal-combustion engines whose output transcended the requirements of the enterprise and furnished electric power to outside consumers; to steelmaking, where German vertical integration made it possible to work their metal hot from start to finish, while the British, whose high pig–scrap ratio made such methods even more profitable, had to move and reheat pigs and blooms at several stages. The statistics on fuel consumption in post-smelting processes are eloquent: 22·5 cwt. per ton of output in Britain in 1929 (31 cwt. in 1920), 4·9 in the average Belgian plant, 3·2 in an integrated Belgian plant, even less in Germany.[2]

The effects of greater capital intensity and more rational organization were apparent in productivity, where output per man-year (a necessarily gross approximation of real productivity) in steel melting and rolling ran to 77 tons in Germany in 1913, against 48 tons in Britain in 1920, when productivity was presumably higher than before the war.[3] It also showed in prices. British rails and plates, originally the cheapest in the world, became dearer than comparable German products around the turn of the century, both on the respective home markets and for export. On the eve of the war, the difference in quotations on plate at Essen and on the Clyde was 20–25 per cent.

As a result, superior technology went hand in hand (I use the expression advisedly because there was clearly a reciprocal relationship) with industrial expansion. A semi-log graph of iron and steel output

---

[1] The best history of coke technology is F. M. Ress, *Geschichte der Kokereitechnik* (Essen, 1957).   [2] Burn, *Economic History*, p. 439 and n. 4.

[3] *Ibid.* p. 417. The figures are ambiguous and comparison is correspondingly hazardous. Thus we have such statistical anomalies as an output per man-year in Germany in 1913 of 345 tons in steel melting, 104 tons in rolling, but only 77 in melting and rolling combined.

Smelting productivity gives rise to even more serious problems. Chapman, *Work and Wages*, p. 76, simply asserts that 'no trustworthy figures are obtainable'. The statistics given by Burnham and Hoskins, *Iron and Steel*, pp. 315–17, and Burn, *Economic History*, p. 417, show some brutal variations in productivity from year to year but concur in showing Britain ahead—as much as 40% ahead—before the war. Everything we know about comparative size, capacity, and mechanization of blast furnaces, however, and the relationship of these to productivity throws doubt on these data. The trouble would seem to lie in the count of workers assigned to smelting. (There is also the question of actual hours worked, but this is probably much less important as a source of bias.)

offers the most vivid illustration possible of the course of international economic rivalry in the period 1870–1914: the British lines bend over like wilting flowers, while the German continue their steep ascent to the very eve of the conflict. In the early 1870's, Britain was making four times as much iron and twice as much steel as the *Zollverein*. In the quinquennium 1910–14, by contrast, Germany averaged almost twice as much iron, more than twice as much steel. The point of passing was 1893 for steel, 1903 for pig iron.

One more point is worth making about Britain's loss of metallurgical hegemony, which actually dated from 1890, when the United States permanently took over first place in both iron and steel output. For a long time, the painful effects of expansion abroad were somewhat mitigated by the absorption of the great bulk of the incremental make by the markets of the producing countries; both the United States and Germany needed vast quantities of steel for their own economies. By 1910, however, Germany was exporting more iron and steel than Britain, which had been the leading supplier to the world for over a century; worse yet, the steelmasters of the Ruhr were selling some of their production in the United Kingdom itself. The royal crown was slipping, and the doctrines of economic theorists on comparative advantage and international division of labour were cold comfort.

A new chemical industry

Chemical manufacture, which by definition is the transformation of matter for productive use, is the most miscellaneous of industries. Thus metallurgy is technically a branch of applied chemistry, and among our new materials of the turn of the century (see p. 249 above) would have to be alloy steels and non-ferrous metals like aluminium. Similarly, glass-making and paper-making are branches of the chemical trade, and so are cement and rubber manufacture and ceramics.

In all of these areas, the late nineteenth century saw important technological innovations. Of chemical improvements proper, we may note the invention and perfection of wood-pulp paper from about 1855 onward (there are bibliophiles and scholars who would not accept this as an advance); the Hall-Héroult electrolytic process for deriving aluminium from bauxite (1886), which changed a precious metal used for spoons at the table of Napoleon III to a light, non-corrosive industrial substitute for iron and steel in some of their applications; and the development of more refractory materials in the manufacture of furnace brick (magnesite and dolomite, 1860 on), indispensable for the higher temperatures become customary in heat-consuming processes. At least as important, probably, in raising productivity in the chemical trades were mechanical and instrumental innovations: the introduction of the regenerative furnace (late 1850's) and the semi-automatic bottle machine (1859 on) in glass-making; the use of automatic presses, extrusion and hose-making machines in rubber; of the continuous long-chamber kiln, special presses, and extrusion machines in brick-making and ceramics; of the shaft kiln (developed in the 1870's; intro-duced to Britain from Germany in the 1880's) and rotary kiln (perfected early 1890's) in cement manufacture.

Yet all of these improvements took place in what were still minor areas of industrial activity—the great days of rubber and cement, for example, still lay in the future; or, occurring as they did in the manu-facture of final products, their impact on the economy as a whole through indirect savings and derived demand was limited. The great advances in chemical manufacture in our period had these qualities of immediate scope and ramifying consequences. The two most impor-tant were the Solvay method of alkali manufacture and the synthesis of organic compounds.

1. L. F. Haber has called the period from 1860 to 1880 'the golden age of the Leblanc soda industry'. The demand for alkalis increased with that for textiles and soap, consumption of which rose with income, improved sanitation, and higher standards of living; and the introduction of esparto grass into paper manufacture, to supplement the manifestly inadequate supply of rags, called for large quantities of bleaching powder. In the generation from 1852 to 1878, British production of soda ash tripled, from 72,000 to 208,000 tons; the make of soda crystals rose almost as fast, from 61,000 to 171,000 tons; and output of bleaching powder increased almost eight times, from 13,000 to 100,000 tons. Most of these alkalis were consumed at home, but a significant and growing proportion went abroad, first to the United States, and then to France after the commercial treaty of 1860 and to the *Zollverein*. Exports went from 16,500 tons in 1847 to 273,000 in 1876, a leap of over 1500 per cent. The production of the continental countries, though growing, was a small fraction of the British.[1]

This growth evoked several improvements in technique, mostly of an instrumental character and more labour- than material-saving: larger decomposing pans; mechanical roasters; the revolving furnace (late 1860's); and the Shanks vat (1861), which made it possible to extract the black ash by means of hydrostatic pressure rather than by laborious shovelling from tank to tank.[2] Yet when all is said and done, the industry had never used much labour, and the impact of such innovations was

---

[1] Haber, *Chemical Industry*, pp. 59, 55.

[2] See T. I. Williams, 'Heavy Chemicals', in Singer *et al.*, eds., *A History of Techno-logy*, v, 235–56.

correspondingly limited. In 1862, around 10,000 men were employed in the Leblanc manufacture of England and Wales, as against 400,000 in textiles. Of these, a fraction (less than a fifth probably) were needed to perform the chemical process proper; the rest were engaged in packaging, handling, and maintenance.[1]

Even so the supply barely kept ahead of demand. The long-term level of alkali prices during these years was unchanged; bleaching materials alone showed a significant decline, and then only after the crisis of 1873, when general deflation had set in. It was at this point that ammonia soda entered the picture.

The Leblanc technique was an offence to chemist and manufacturer alike. Even after Gossage had developed in 1836 his towers for the condensation of by-product hydrochloric acid, whose fumes were poisoning the countryside in the neighbourhood of every alkali plant, the chlorine therein was lost to industry. Moreover, the process continued to waste valuable sulphur, to say nothing of calcium and large amounts of unchanged coal, in the form of a noisome mud that the inhabitants of Lancashire expressively baptized 'galligu', which added to the injury of loss the insult of costly disposal.

By comparison the ammonia-soda technique was more elegant (in the mathematical sense of neatness and simplicity), and gave every promise of being more profitable. The chemical reaction was discovered by Fresnel as early as 1811: one could obtain sodium bicarbonate and ammonium chloride from concentrated solutions of salt (sodium chloride) and ammonia (NH_3) by treating with carbonic acid (H_2CO_3). The sodium bicarbonate, on heating, yielded the sodium carbonate (soda) desired, plus water and carbon dioxide. The one practical difficulty—and it proved serious—was the inability to recover the ammonia, a costly compound in those days, from the by-product ammonium chloride.

The problem was essentially one of plant—to build equipment to do what everyone knew should and could be done. Dozens of scientists and empiricists spent tens of thousands of pounds to find a solution. 'Never before was the industrial realisation of any process attempted so frequently and for such a long period of time....'

Ernest Solvay (1838–1922), born in the small Belgian village of Rebecq, inherited his interest in chemical manufacture. His father was a salt refiner, among other things; his uncle, the director of a gas works, the one place where ammonia was almost a free good. It was in his uncle's factory that he first observed its wastage in coal distillation; and it was there he conducted his first experiments in soda manufacture,

[1] Cf. D. W. F. Hardie, *A History of the Chemical Industry in Widnes* (n.p., Imp. Chemical Industries, 1950), pp. 118–19.

devised his tower to mix carbon dioxide with ammoniacal brine, built his still to recover the ammonia. In December 1863—he was only 25 years old—Solvay founded with outside assistance the firm that bears his name and remains to this day one of the giants of the world chemical industry.

The years immediately following saw numerous disappointments, continued experiments. It took another decade to perfect the process; but by the mid-1870's, Solvay alkalis, even with the burden of royalty payments, could undersell Leblanc products as then produced by about 20 per cent. The greatest saving was in materials.

There then ensued a struggle that is technologically analogous to that between cheap steel and wrought iron and economically analogous to the competition between the British and German steel industries. The new technique spread rapidly on the Continent, predominantly in the Solvay version but to a small extent in variant forms. In France, less than a quarter of the alkali produced in 1874 was made by the ammonia process; a generation later, in 1905, the figure was 99·65 per cent. Germany was slower at first; of the comparatively small quantity of soda produced in 1878, some 42,500 tons, only 19 per cent was of the ammonia variety. By 1887, however, the proportion was 75 per cent; by 1900, it was over 90 per cent of some 300,000 tons.[1]

Only Britain lagged. She had a large investment in Leblanc plant, which entrepreneurs were unwilling to abandon. And these hard-pressed producers squeezed new economies and additional income out of their Leblanc works by closer attention to costs, the introduction of more efficient equipment, and recovery of chlorine from the by-product hydrochloric acid (Weldon's process, 1869–70). Prices of Leblanc alkalis fell by 1890 to about a third of their peak on the eve of Solvay (1872–3).

At these levels, British alkalis were competitive, and the firmness of the price of by-product bleaching powder was an unexpected dividend. British exports more than doubled in tonnage from 1870 to 1883 and remained at almost that high level until 1895. Then the agony began. It was partly technical in origin. The introduction of electrolytic methods of preparing chlorine and caustics in the 1890's hit directly at the Leblanc industry's most profitable operation. Once again, Britain watched other countries take the lead: by 1904 all the American and 65

---

[1] On the competition between the two processes, see, in addition to Haber, G. Lunge, *The Manufacture of Sulphuric Acid and Alkali* (3rd ed.; 4 vols.; London, 1911), III, 737–44; R. Hasenclever, 'Ueber die gegenwärtige Lage der Leblanc'schen Soda-fabriken in Concurrenzkampf mit der Ammoniak-Soda', *Die Chemische Industrie*, X (1887), 290–1; *idem*, 'Die Lage der deutschen Sodafabrikation im Jahre 1901', *ibid.* XXV (1902), 73–5.

per cent of the German output of chlorine was electrolytic; the corresponding figures for France and the United Kingdom were 19 and 18 per cent.[1] And it was partly the result of protectionism abroad; the United States Dingley tariff of 1897 was particularly harmful. Total exports fell from 312,400 to 188,500 tons; output decreased by much less, about 10 per cent, but the point is that it decreased—for the first time since the beginning of the Industrial Revolution. German output rose the while and was beginning to compete even in those tropical areas that had always been a British preserve.

Thus disappeared the last resource of the Leblanc manufacture (the gains afforded by the Chance-Claus sulphur recovery process—at last a way to save the sulphur!—were not enough to compensate). The formation in 1890 of the United Alkali Co. Ltd., uniting in one large trust the bulk of the country's Leblanc capacity, and the subsequent negotiation of price and commodity agreements with the major producer of ammonia soda, Brunner, Mond and Co., served only to delay the demise. In spite of all the determination and ingenuity the company could muster, disappointment followed disappointment, dividends stopped, the equity shrank to a fraction of its original value, to the point where there was not enough capital to scrap the old and build anew. In 1920, not quite a century after its introduction, Britain's once great Leblanc industry shut down.

As in steel, differences in technique were reflected in rates of growth. We do not have British figures on alkali manufacture for the years immediately preceding the First World War; and such German statistics as we possess are not comparable because the products are measured at different degrees of purity. But we do have estimates of the respective outputs of sulphuric acid, 'the most important inorganic chemical for technical purposes'. It is used for the production of such other inorganic compounds as sodium sulphate; in the manufacture of fertilizer, particularly the superphosphates; in petroleum refining, iron and steel, and textiles; in the production of explosives; and in dyemaking and other branches of organic chemistry. As a result, its consumption is a rough yardstick of general industrial development. As late as 1900, British output of sulphuric acid was almost twice the German: about 1 million as against 550,000 tons. Only thirteen years later the positions were almost reversed: Germany, 1,700,000 tons; Britain, 1,100,000.[2]

[1] Clapham, *Economic History*, III, 173.

[2] These figures are derived from W. Woytinsky, *Die Welt in Zahlen*, IV, 316; the *Statistisches Jahrbuch des deutschen Reichs*; Haber, *Chemical Industry*, pp. 104, 122; and League of Nations, Economic and Financial Section, International Economic Conference, Geneva, May 1927, Documentation: *The Chemical Industry* (Geneva, 1927), pp. 23, 127. An effort has been made to convert all figures to acid of 100 % concentra-

2. The theoretical and experimental work that lay at the basis of the organic chemical industry was largely German and British. Some of the landmarks are Faraday's isolation of benzene in 1825, Wöhler's discovery of the isomerism of organic compounds (1828), the analysis and fractionation by Hofmann and his pupils of coal tar (Mansfield's historic paper, 'Researches on Coal Tar, Part I', was published in 1849), and Kekulé's theoretical reconstruction of the benzene molecule (1865). The practical discoveries that were the substance of the new industry were the work of Britons, Germans working in Britain, and Frenchmen. In 1856 Perkin fortuitously synthesized the first aniline dye, a purple that took the French name *mauve*; Natanson and Verguin in France perfected aniline red, or magenta, in 1859; in 1863 Martius, building on the researches of Griess, made the first commercially successful azo dye, Bismarck brown;[1] finally, in 1869 Perkin in England and Graebe and Liebermann in Germany produced alizarin, the first artificial dye to replace a natural colourant, in this case madder. This was the last of the great British developments and the first of a long series of major discoveries by German laboratories; it marked a shift in the locus of innovation. It also symbolized the arrival of an era of purposive research: Perkin came upon mauve by accident, but he sought and found alizarin, while Graebe undertook his research on direct orders from his master Baeyer. The two turning-points—in location and character of research—were interrelated.

One final remark about the scientific background: as in other examples of industrial innovation, so in organic chemicals it is tempting to recall the famous achievements and take the rest for granted. The fact was that experimental syntheses were a far cry from commercial processes. The transfer of these reactions from laboratory to factory called for the development of new sources and patterns of supply, accessory techniques for the inexpensive manufacture of scarce test-tube materials, and the invention of reliable equipment for effecting what could be dangerous reactions. In one early British works, the nitration shed was known as 'the shooting gallery'. At the same time, the utilization of these dyes in textile manufacture called for further innovations: mordants for recalcitrant fabrics; and patterns that would take advantage of the opportunities presented by these new and fast colours. Here the French contribution was decisive.

tion (monohydrate); the indifference of even the most expert writers to this elementary detail does not make the task easy.

[1] Azo dyes are so called because of the presence of nitrogen (French *azote*) in the molecule. Haber notes that they were the first to be produced directly on cloth and became the most fruitful source of artificial colourants—385 out of 681 commercial dyes in 1902, 461 of 1001 in 1922. *Chemical Industry*, p. 83.

As this account implies, the first years of the new branch of chemical manufacture belonged to Britain, with France in second place. Not only was the bulk of the early research conducted in English laboratories, but in no other country had the distillation of coal tar for commercial purposes advanced so far. The same enterprises that produced heavy oils for wood preservatives (Bethell patent of 1838) and 'naphtha' for use in the manufacture of rubber and varnish could easily turn out 'light oils' as well. Conditions of supply were therefore especially favourable, and indeed several of the pioneers of the British organic industry went from coal tar to dye-stuffs.

In France, the emphasis on highly coloured, imaginatively designed fabrics provided a ready-made market for the new dyes. Lyons, the home of the silk manufacture (silk took aniline dyes better than other fibres), was one centre. Alsace, with its high-fashion cotton-print industry, an old pioneer in textile chemistry, was another. The Paris area was a third. In 1864 one of the strongest producers joined with the young Crédit Lyonnais to found what was probably the largest dye firm in the world, La Fuchsine, capital 4 million francs.

In both countries, however, this early development was soon blighted. In Britain, the coal-tar amateurs were out of their depth, and the specialists lost their best German scientists to the enterprises of their native country. All but a few firms stagnated or failed. They found themselves undersold at every turn by foreign competitors and in so far as they prospered, they did so on sufferance, by means of price or market agreements. Venture capital was frightened off, accentuating the spiral of decline. In France, many of the producers ruined each other by a costly patent war in the 1860's. La Fuchsine went bankrupt in 1868, doing more than anything else to convince Henri Germain, the crusty director of the Crédit Lyonnais, that there was no industrialist in France worthy of his support.[1]

German output of dyestuffs soared. In the late 1860's, the industry was still small, dispersed, and essentially imitative. Scarcely a decade later, Badische Anilin, Höchst, AGFA, and the others held about half of the world market; by the turn of the century, their share was around 90 per cent. Moreover, this does not take into account the output of subsidiaries and affiliates in other countries. Thus in France, only one of the major dyestuff plants on the eve of the First World War was French-owned and managed; six were German, two Swiss; and the four or five small native firms were dependent on foreign, principally German, firms for intermediate products.

[1] See the account in Bouvier, *Le Crédit Lyonnais*, pp. 374–81, and the sources cited there.

In technical virtuosity and aggressive enterprise, this leap to hege-mony, almost to monopoly, has no parallel. It was Imperial Germany's greatest industrial achievement. Of the other nations of the world, only Switzerland succeeded in developing a vigorous dyestuffs manufacture in the face of this competition. By importing raw chemicals and inter-mediates from north of the border, concentrating on special tints requiring the highest production skills, and offering their customers the latest technical advice, CIBA, Geigy, and the other Basle manu-facturers won and held an important share of the international market. Swiss output in 1895 was almost a fifth as large (by value) as the Ger-man and just about as big as that of all other countries combined.

In Germany, the organic sector accounted for well over half of the work force and capital investment of the chemical industry by the First World War; other countries, though far slower, were following the same path. For dyes were only one corner of a new world: the scientific principles that lay behind artificial colourants were capable of the widest application. There was the whole range of products derived from cellulose, that remarkable family of carbohydrates that constitutes the chief solid element of plants. Nitrocellulose explosives (Schönbein's gun-cotton, 1846) came first, followed by lacquers, photographic plates and film, celluloid (the first modern plastic, by Hyatt in 1868, and for all its flammability still useful, for the manu-facture of table-tennis balls among other things), and artificial fibres (Chardonnet's *soie artificielle*, 1889; C. F. Cross's viscose in 1892). Viscose in turn gave birth to a family of its own, including cellophane (Brandenberger in 1912), sizing compounds, sausage casings, and sundry other items of greater or lesser usefulness. And in 1909 Baeke-land patented the first of the synthetic resins, the so-called 'plastic of a thousand uses', bakelite. The point to be noted is the almost incredible ingenuity of these techniques, their ceaseless ramification in new direc-tions and products. As the title of one history of a chemical firm put it, *One Thing Leads to Another*. Here in unexpected form was a surrogate for the long-sought secret of transmuting and creating matter.

NEW SOURCES OF ENERGY AND POWER

The subject divides itself logically into three parts:

(1) The sources of energy proper: falling water; burning carbon (in the form of coal, wood, gas, oil, or the like); the sun; chemical sub-stances that liberate heat or electrical current in reaction.

(2) Motors and the conversion of energy into movement.

(3) The distribution of energy. It is under this last rubric that the economic historian will most conveniently place electricity as a techno-

logical innovation. Electricity is not a source but a form of energy. Electrical dynamos and similar generators are essentially converters, turning water, steam, or other primary power into current, which can then be stored in batteries, used directly for illumination, heat, or communication, or transformed into motion by means of motors.

Because of the inextricable relationship of these three elements, however, it is not convenient to dissect the historical development along these lines. Instead, we shall build the story around those areas of innovation that had the widest economic significance, keeping the above schema in mind as a guide to the technological rationale.

Steam and steam-engines

The closing decades of the nineteenth century saw the gradual exhaustion of the technological possibilities of the reciprocating steam-engine. Earlier advances had shown the way to greater power and efficiency—first higher pressures, and then compound expansion—and by the end of our period, the forty-pound pressures of the 1850's had increased four- and five-fold, while triple- and quadruple-expansion engines had been developed to channel these concentrations of energy.

Compounding, known for decades (see above, pp. 181 f.) but neglected, came into its own at mid-century. It was adopted most rapidly for ships, where power plant tended to be larger than on land and fuel economy was of crucial importance—every foot taken for coal was lost to cargo. A kind of improvised compound engine was achieved by M'Naught in 1845 when he joined a high-pressure cylinder to the old low-pressure one and used both to drive the beam. This was a relatively inexpensive solution to the problem of inadequate power and dozens of engines were 'M'Naughted' in subsequent years. It was not until 1854, however, that the first compound engine built as such was installed on a vessel; within the decade they were the rule on large ocean steamers. The triple-expansion variety was introduced in 1874, but did not spread until the 1880's; it was standard for big plant, both on land and at sea, by the end of the century.[1]

The main contribution of these technical improvements was power: compare, for example, the first steamer of the Peninsular and Oriental, launched in 1829 with paddle wheels and a 60 h.p., low-pressure machine, with the *Campania* or *Lucania* of 1893, each equipped with twin screws and triple-expansion engines totalling 30,000 h.p.; or the 10

---

[1] As is so often the case with mechanical improvements, this success owed much to the employment of superior materials—in this instance, high-quality open-hearth steel plate that could withstand greater boiler pressures.

and 20 h.p. industrial engines of the opening decades of the century with the 3000 h.p. superheated giants of the close. By contrast, the gains in fuel economy were less impressive. Even if one discounts the extraordinary reported performances of the Cornish beam engines in the 1830's and 1840's, it is clear that the great reduction in energy consumption per unit of output had already occurred by the 1850's, when well-run machines were using less than 4 pounds of coal per horsepower-hour. At the end of the century, best performance was down to around 1½ and the curve was running along the asymptote.

Yet still the demand for power grew, especially for high power in proportion to space. The way to get more power was to increase the running speed of the engine, but here the need to convert reciprocating to rotary motion posed a serious difficulty. The assembly of the piston, piston rod, cross-head, and connecting rod had to be started and stopped with each half-turn of the crank; and the force required to reverse this momentum rose with the speed of the stroke. Eventually the stresses were such that the engine broke down. So that although piston velocities had been pushed as high as 1000 feet a minute by the turn of the century, they were beginning to rub against a ceiling of commercial feasibility: one could build bigger and stronger engines, but at disproportionately higher costs for both materials and space.

At this point the steam turbine made possible a new technological breakthrough, both in power and economy. The principle was simple: instead of turning force into reciprocating motion and converting that into rotary, one went directly into rotary by driving against appropriately shaped vanes or buckets branching off a turning axis. Every child who has ever played with a pinwheel is familiar with the technique.

As noted earlier, the water-driven turbine went back as far as 1827 and had been much improved in subsequent decades, particularly in connection with the utilization of high-fall power. A practical steam turbine, however, in spite of experiments going back to the eighteenth century, was not achieved until 1884, when Charles H. Parsons learned to tame the kinetic energy of the steam jet by joining a series of turbines together and letting the pressure drop off by stages. Here again was the principle of the compound engine, in an idealized form: one put almost all the useful heat to work by letting the steam cool by expansion only, driving as it went. Used in tandem in this way, each wheel had an efficiency of between 70 and 80 per cent, as high as that of water turbines and far higher than that of even the best reciprocating steam-engines.

The Parsons machine was more powerful than any motor built up to that time. It had been devised to run electric generators, but no generator could handle it—the maximum speed of existing dynamos was 1200 r.p.m. Parsons therefore developed his own generator, running at 18,000 r.p.m., and patented it at the same time as the turbine. The two together represent the greatest innovation in the use of steam power since Watt's construction of an engine to produce rotary motion; they also made possible an efficient, large-scale electrical power industry.

In subsequent years, a number of variant types of turbine appeared, of which pure impulse machines like those of C. G. Curtis in the United States and of C. G. P. de Laval of Sweden, proved most useful. The latter, a one-stage affair, proved particularly effective for low- and medium-horsepower installations. The Parsons, however, dominated the high-power field. On the eve of the First World War, a few tandem turbo-alternators were generating over 10,000 kW. (13,400 h.p.), and ships like the *Lusitania* and *Mauretania* (1907) were equipped with twin turbine sets totalling 68,000 h.p. each.[1]

Internal combustion and new fuels

The principle of an internal combustion motor is that of a channelled explosion: the rapid expansion of gases in a confined space, a cylinder for example, drives an object, generally a piston, in the direction desired. The earliest and most elementary form of internal-combustion engine is a gun. This remark may seem facetious to some, or at best a *curiosum*, and indeed single-stroke mechanisms of this type have up to now been of little or no productive use. In recent years, however, it has proved feasible to shape by explosion pieces of metal too large for presses, thereby eliminating the need for costly and intrinsically unreliable welds, and if technological change follows its usual pattern, the principle will find an increasing variety of applications in years to come.

The most important use of the internal-combustion engine, of course, has been in motors. The possibility of such a device, driven by regularly repeated explosions, was conceived as far back as the seventeenth century, when the Abbé Hautefeuille proposed (1678) and Huygens actually constructed an experimental machine powered by gunpowder. Not until 1859, however, when Etienne Lenoir brought forth a motor fired by a mixture of gas and air, was a potentially practical version achieved.

Lenoir's prototype consumed too much gas to be commercially competitive. But it furnished the pattern, and from then on a large number of engineers and tinkerers devoted themselves to the problem.

[1] See, among others, R. H. Parsons, *The Development of the Parsons Steam Turbine* (London, 1936), and J. W. French, *Modern Power Generators* (London, 1908).

The crucial conceptual contribution was made in 1862 by Beau de Rochas, whose four-stroke cycle has since become standard. But no one put this principle to effective use until N. A. Otto combined it in 1876 with precompression of the charge to produce the first practical gas engine. The Otto 'silent' engine, as it was called, swept the market: within a few years, more than 35,000 of them were at work all over the world.[1]

This form of internal combustion offered the industrialist important advantages over steam. It was more efficient, especially when working intermittently or at less than full load,[2] conditions frequently found in small industry. It was cleaner, and the nature of the fuel was such that it was easy to automate the feed; the saving on labour costs was often substantial. Finally, gas was often obtainable as a by-product of other industrial operations—coking and smelting for example—and, so obtained, was far cheaper than when deliberately distilled from coal, or than coal itself.[3]

The major weakness of the gas engine was its immobility. It was tied to its source of supply, whether feeder line or furnace. This was not a serious handicap for most industrial purposes, but it did make gas less suitable as a source of power in transportation.[4] The answer was found in liquid fuels—primarily petroleum and its distilled derivatives. These burned about as efficiently as gas and produced about twice as much work per weight as coal, while taking half as much space;[5] like gas, moreover, they could be fed cleanly and mechanically, with automatic controls. All of this was especially important at sea, for there economy counted double and everything saved on fuel or crew meant that much more income from cargo and passengers. Not least important was the elimination of the stokers, who generally accounted for more than half the crew. It was getting increasingly hard to find men for this

[1] D. C. Field, 'Internal Combustion Engines', in Singer et al., A History of Technology, v, 159.

[2] See the figures in William Robinson, Gas and Petroleum Engines (2nd ed.; 2 vols.; New York, 1902), I, 4, 136, 198, and passim.

[3] Around 1900, a blast furnace would give off 158,000 cubic feet of gas per ton of iron smelted. It was a dirty gas, which often had to be cleaned for further use, and a poor one, yielding from 70 to 120 B.Th.U. per cubic foot (as against perhaps 480 B.Th.U. for illuminating gas).

[4] Although man's ingenuity has surmounted this difficulty in times of crisis, when no other fuel has been available. Frenchmen of the immediate post-war years will not forget the automobiles circulating with tanks of gas on their roofs. But it should be noted that even then, such vehicles were most common in the south, near the centre of natural gas production in the Toulouse area, and disappeared rapidly as petrol once again came on the market. I am told that the English resorted to the same expedient.

[5] In most cases, it was possible to free the space given over to coal bunkers entirely and store the oil in the double-bottom spaces once used only for water ballast.

back-breaking work, and those hired were not surprisingly notorious for their intractability and their appetites.

The principal objection to oil was its cost—anywhere from four to twelve times that of coal in Britain around 1900. Yet the price of petroleum products fell rapidly as new sources of supply were opened up and the industry perfected its methods of refining and techniques of distribution. The earliest commercially practical oil engines were probably those used in Russia from the 1870's to burn *ostatki* waste from distillation of Baku crude in the manufacture of kerosene and lamp oil. According to Lunge, 'practically all the steam power in South Russia, both for factories and navigation of the inland seas and rivers', was being raised *c.* 1910 from *ostatki* fuel.[1] In the West, however, in spite of widespread and successful experimentation with oil engines, petroleum did not really catch on until the opening of the Borneo (1898) and Texas fields (Spindletop Well, 1901) made available an oil especially suited by chemical composition to serve as fuel. Shortly thereafter (1902) the Hamburg-Amerika Line adopted petroleum in place of coal on its new liners and was followed by one after another of the great steamship companies. At the same time, the navies of the great European powers began the process of conversion: Italy installed an oil burner as early as 1890; Britain began in 1903 with vessels operating in waters near sources of petroleum—the Far East particularly—but within a decade built a world-wide storage network that permitted the use of liquid fuel throughout the fleet.

Acceptance for land use was slower, although some British railways and a few industrial firms on the Thames tried petroleum and abandoned it only when rising prices made it too expensive relative to coal. The one application in which it gained ground steadily was in the form of what contemporaries called petroleum spirit, our present-day petrol or gasoline. Nevertheless, the automobile was still a luxury in pre-World War I Europe, roads were atrocious, breakdowns frequent, and no one could possibly anticipate the enormous expansion in the demand for liquid fuel for road vehicles that has taken place since. The oil companies themselves moved their products by horse and wagon.

Electricity

From the standpoint of the economic historian, the significance of electricity lay in its unique combination of two characteristics: transmissibility and flexibility. By the first we mean its ability to move

[1] J. Fortescue-Flannery, in article, 'Fuel', *Encyclopaedia Britannica*, 11th ed. A masterly survey.

energy through space without serious loss. And by the second we mean its easy and efficient conversion into other forms of energy—heat, light, or motion. An electric current can be used to produce any or all of these, separately or together, and the user can switch from one to the other at will. He can also draw precisely the amount of power needed, large or small, and can change it when necessary without time-consuming adjustments or sacrifice of efficiency. And he pays for what he uses.

From these characteristics two major consequences emerge. On the one hand, electricity freed the machine and the tool from the bondage of place; on the other, it made power ubiquitous and placed it within reach of everyone. Both of these—and they are inextricably linked together—merit detailed consideration.

Up to the latter half of the nineteenth century, the machine had always been closely bound to its prime mover. It could not be placed too far off because of the inefficiency of belts and shafting as a method of distributing energy: each gear, joint, or wheel was a source of power loss, and the torsion on long shafts was such that rigidity and smooth rotation could be maintained only by the use of disproportionately heavy materials. Similarly, the machine was rooted to its emplacement or restricted to positions along the path of the shafts, for only there could it draw on the source of energy.

These were not serious disadvantages in such industries as the textile manufacture, where neatly aligned banks of equipment worked side by side at the same pace, although even there shafting longer than 200 feet posed costly problems.[1] But they gave rise to all manner of difficulties in trades like iron or engineering, where the work was dispersed, the pace uneven, and much of the equipment was always being moved about. The answer in such cases was a multiplicity of steam-engines, large and small. It was an expensive solution, not only in capital outlays but in operating costs. As we have already seen, these smaller engines, often working at less than full load, were extremely inefficient; by the same token, they had a voracious appetite for labour. Not least important, they were a nuisance, with their piles of coal scattered about, their noise and dirt, their exhaust gases, their need for separate maintenance.

Energy can be transmitted economically over longer distances than a few hundred feet only by fluids or gases, which can be delivered under pressure in rigid pipe or flexible hose, or by electric current. Each technique has its own merits and area of application; all are highly

---

[1] Yet in Coventry, entrepreneurs erected in the 1850's a number of so-called 'cottage-factories', rows or enclosures of weavers' houses, which drew power from a central engine over a distance of several hundred feet. John Prest, *The Industrial Revolution in Coventry* (Oxford, 1960), ch. VI.

efficient. In the last half of the nineteenth century, all three of these methods began to be used, in the order given.

Fluid systems generally use water—there is no liquid cheaper—or oil, which lubricates as it works; gas systems almost always use air. They are especially suitable to short and medium-range transmission, at distances up to a few miles between prime mover and machine. Their forte is work where incompressibility is an advantage and the mechanical action is direct—in lifts, pumps, presses, punches, and brakes. Their effect in these operations has a certain inexorable quality, and their work is characterized more by force than by motion—as anyone who has ridden in a hydraulic lift will testify.

In principle, water and air pressure may also be used with turbines to produce rotary motion (cf. the windmill). Here, however, they are not so flexible as electricity nor so suitable to heavy work. But compressed air, especially, is excellent with light motors—it has found a new application today in dentistry, where it has proved the most convenient drive for high-speed drills—and is almost indispensable in fields like mining where the presence of inflammable dusts precludes the use of sparking motors.

Historically, pneumatic pressure systems have almost always been the work of the individual enterprise, whereas hydraulic pressure has usually been distributed from central power stations. The development of these installations dates from the invention in 1850 of the accumulator, which made it possible to store pressure and to economize on peak capacity. At first water was obtained simply by tapping public mains. But by the last two decades of the century, the technique had reached the point where private capital was ready to invest in independent pumping works and distribution systems. British enterprise was particularly active in this regard, and as late as the middle 1890's, there were engineers who were convinced that hydraulic pressure was superior to any other means of power transmission. In 1894 Antwerp actually tried to use it to distribute energy to electrical power stations scattered through the city, rather than send current directly from the central power plant. The operation was not profitable.

The fact was that hydraulic and pneumatic power owed much of their success to their priority. They came along first. But once electricity came on the scene, they were bound to lose ground. They were strongest where one or both of two conditions prevailed:

(a) Where the primary power source had been constructed for other purposes and existed independently, as in the case of public water works or of air pumps used in underwater excavation. In such circumstances, the water or air used for motor purposes is a by-product whose marginal cost is very low. The municipal hydraulic systems of Geneva and

Lyons, both cities abundantly endowed with flowing water, fall in this category.

(b) Where the industrial operations of the area lent themselves to these techniques—in ports, for example, like Liverpool and London, where there is a great deal of lifting work to be done; or in a cotton town like Manchester, with its hundreds of packing presses.

Otherwise—beginning in the very last years of the nineteenth century—electricity had the field of power transmission to itself. The history of this development is worth following—as an example of scientific and technical co-operation, of multiple invention, of progress by an infinitude of small improvements, of creative entrepreneurship, of derived demand and unanticipated consequences. The symbiotic growth of electric power and electric motors is like that of textile machines and the steam-engine in the eighteenth century: a new technique and system of production were now available, with boundless possibilities. This was once again Genesis.

At the start of the nineteenth century, electricity was a scientific curiosity, a plaything of the laboratory. As the result of widespread investigation and experiment, however, it became a commercially useful form of energy, first in communication,[1] shortly thereafter in light-chemical and metallurgical processes,[2] and finally in illumination. Of these, the last had the greatest economic impact because of its implications for power technology in general.

The invention of the incandescent filament lamp, especially Edison's high-resistance variety, was crucial here. For the first time electricity offered something useful not only in industry, or in commerce, or on the theatre stage, but in every home. None of the earlier applications had been particularly voracious of energy; and each enterprise, given the scale of its requirements, could profitably generate its own. Now, however, a demand existed—incalculably large *in toto* yet atomized into a multitude of individual needs—that could be satisfied only by a

[1] A brief list of the key inventions and landmarks will be helpful: Electromagnetic telegraph, in Britain, by Cooke and Wheatstone, c. 1837; in the United States, by Morse and Vail, c. 1838; undersea cable, across the Channel, 1851; across the Atlantic, by C. W. Field, 1866. Telephone, by A. G. Bell, 1876. Wireless, by Marconi, 1895.

[2] Light industrial electrochemistry went back to the 1830's. It found its principal applications in galvanoplasty, that is, the manufacture of exact moulds of sculptures, engravings, and the like for purposes of reproduction (invention in 1838 by Spencer in England and Jacobi in Russia), and electroplating (John Wright of Birmingham, in 1840, followed by a host of others). These processes, originally effected with batteries, were greatly stimulated by the availability of cheap, abundant current from central stations. A new range of industrial applications opened up, especially in plating with baser metals (galvanized iron).

centralized system of power generation and distribution. This too was Edison's conception, and it made all the difference between electric lighting for a wealthy few and for everyone.

The development of central power was the work of the last two decades of the nineteenth century. It was a tremendous technological achievement, made possible only by almost a century of large and small theoretical advances and practical innovations. The landmarks stand out: Volta's chemical battery in 1800; Oersted's discovery of electromagnetism in 1820; the statement of the law of the electric circuit by Ohm in 1827; the experiments of Arago, Faraday, and others, climaxed by Faraday's discovery of electromagnetic induction in 1831; the invention of the self-excited electromagnetic generator (Wilde, Varley, E. W. von Siemens, Wheatstone, et al.) in 1866–7; Z. T. Gramme's ring dynamo, the first commercially practical generator of direct current, in 1870; the development of alternators and transformers for the production and conversion of high-voltage alternating current in the 1880's. Less well known but equally vital, however, were advances in the manufacture of cable and insulation, in the details of generator construction, in the operation of prime movers, in the linkage of the component units of the system, in the choice of current characteristics, in the registration of flow and consumption.[1]

The first public power station in Europe was established at Godalming in England by Siemens Brothers in 1881.[2] Within the next decade and a half others sprang up throughout western Europe, a patchwork multitude of market-situated local units, each with its own equipment and method of transmission. In Britain, particularly, where the Electric Lighting Act rested on the proposition that each parish should have its own power station, the resultant multiplicity of techniques was to be a costly legacy.

Very early, however, entrepreneurs realized that important savings might be achieved if the generating plant were located at or close to the source of energy and the current were sent out from there. To be sure, the longer the lines the greater the loss of power, but this could be minimized by the use of high-voltage alternating current.[3] The first

---

[1] The above is based largely on C. M. Jarvis, 'The Generation of Electricity' and 'The Distribution and Utilization of Electricity', in Singer et al., eds., History of Technology, v, 177–234. Other treatments sometimes give other dates and even other names. The history of technology has yet to be endowed with a commonly accepted chronology.

[2] G. F. Westcott and H. P. Spratt, Synopsis of Historical Events: Mechanical and Electrical Engineering (London: H.M.S.O., 1960), p. 18, give 1882 as the date of the first central station in England (Holborn) and note that it was designed by Edison.

[3] Both alternating and direct current have their advantages. The latter is cheaper to generate, among other things, because it is possible to store the surplus current of

large station of this kind was that which Ferranti built in 1887–9 at Deptford on the Thames to supply London at 10,000 volts. In the meantime, experiments on the Continent, where there was a great incentive to use hydro-electric power, were demonstrating the possibility of transmitting energy over even longer distances. In 1885 power was sent from a 150 kW. generator in Creil to Paris, a distance of 56 km., on an experimental basis; and in 1891 the decisive breakthrough came when Oscar Müller and the Swiss firm of Brown, Boveri and Co. delivered 225 kW. over 179 km. at 30,000 volts, from Lauffen on the upper Neckar to Frankfurt-am-Main.[1] Twenty years later current was being transmitted over lines operating at as high as 100,000 volts, and the principle of regional distribution grids was established. It was now possible to develop large, integrated power districts in which agricultural and industrial enterprises of all kinds, to say nothing of homes and shops, could draw on an efficient energy source in common. To the substantial economies of scale in the generation of power were thus added the advantages of diversification: the more heterogeneous the demand, the more favourable the load and capacity factors.

The Germans took the lead here. The most rapid development occurred in Westphalia, where the waste heat of the blast furnaces and the gases of the coking ovens constituted an exceptionally cheap source of energy; even so, demand outstripped supply, and huge coal-fired steam generating plants were built to meet the needs of industrial and domestic consumers. The largest producer of current was the Rheinisch-Westfälische Elektrizitäts-A.-G., founded in 1900, whose network of lines ran the length and breadth of the Rhine valley, from Koblenz to the Dutch border; from 2·7 million kWh. in 1900/1, its output leaped to 121·7 million in 1910/11 and 388 million in 1915/16. Other companies were smaller only by comparison; and to these should be added the several coal and iron firms that doubled as independent suppliers of

periods of low demand in batteries and release it as needed; one thus obtains more favourable load and capacity factors. On the other hand, alternating current is easier to transmit over long distances. The reason is that such transmission calls for high voltages and low amperage (energy losses increase proportionally with amperage), and alternating current lends itself far more readily than direct to substitutions of voltage for amperage and vice-versa, which it effects by means of transformers. The two systems competed fiercely in Britain for many years. In the long run, however, victory lay with centralized generators and long-distance transmission.

[1] G. Olphe-Galliard, *La force motrice au point de vue économique et sociale* (Paris, 1915), p. 104; A. Menge, 'Distribution of Electrical Energy in Germany', in *Trans. First World Power Conference, London 1924* (London, n.d.), III, 528. Menge gives the figure of 135 kW.

power.[1] In the rest of Europe, however, the realization of these possibilities did not come until a decade or more later.

Yet electrical current was more than a convenient means of distributing established fuels. Thanks to long-distance transmission, falling water once again came into its own as a source of energy, which could now be delivered to the factory as coal to the steam-engine. The addition to the world's resources was enormous: in 1913 world output of water power, most of it used to generate electricity, was 510 million kWh., the equivalent of 800,000 long tons of coal (at a consumption of 3·5 lb. of coal per kWh.); sixteen years later, in spite of a world war, hydro-electric output was over 120 billion kWh., equivalent to slightly over 100 million tons of coal (at a more efficient rate of 1·0 lb. per kWh.) and representing 40 per cent of the total world production of electricity.[2] By that time electric generating plants were taking up about two-thirds of the prime mover capacity of the principal industrial countries.

While the precipitating cause of large-scale generation of power was electrical illumination, this was soon surpassed as a demand factor by other and heavier applications of the new form of energy. The first of these was traction. It was in 1879, at about the same time as the incandescent filament lamp came on the market, that Siemens demonstrated the first electric railway at the Berlin Industrial Exposition. Within the next generation electrical drive had become standard in tramways and subways and had been successfully introduced into full-gauge rail systems. The second was heavy electro-chemistry: both the Hall–Héroult method of aluminium manufacture (1886) and Castner's sodium, sodium cyanide, and caustic soda processes (1886 and 1894) required enormous quantities of energy.[3] The third was electrometallurgy: the key innovation was Sir William Siemens's electric furnace (1878). This technique, whose great virtues are its cleanness and high temperatures, received considerable impetus from the development of special alloy steels around the turn of the century.

The fourth and most important application was fixed motor power. Ironically enough, producers and engineers were long in appreciating its potential. As late as 1894, some six years after Tesla's invention of the a.c. induction motor and polyphase a.c. systems had 'made alternat-

---

[1] Hans Spethmann, *Die Grosswirtschaft an der Ruhr* (Breslau, 1925), pp. 86–91.

[2] G. Olphe-Galliard, *La force motrice au point de vue économique et sociale* (Paris, 1915), p. 104; A. Menge, 'Distribution of Electrical Energy in Germany', in *Trans. First World Power Conference, London 1924* (London, n.d.), III, 528. Menge gives the figure of 135 kW.

[3] Around 1910 the consumption was 9 kWh. per pound of metal produced.

ing current as suitable for power purposes as it had been for lighting',[1] the President of the British Institute of Mechanical Engineers was saying that the chief purpose of public generating plants 'was, and probably always would be, to supply energy for lighting purposes'.[2]

He could not have been more mistaken. By its flexibility and convenience, electricity transformed the factory. Now the motor could be fitted to the tool and the tool moved to the job—an especial advantage in engineering and other industries engaged in the manufacture of heavy objects. And now one could clear away the jungle of shafts and belts that had been the most prominent feature of machine rooms since the water mills of the 1770's—a threat to safety, an interference to movement, a source of breakdowns, and a devourer of energy.

But electricity did more than change the techniques and decor of the factory: by making cheap power available outside as well as inside the plant, it reversed the historical forces of a century, gave new life and scope to dispersed home and shop industry, and modified the mode of production. In particular, it made possible a new division of labour between large and small units. Where before the two had almost inevitably been opposed within a given industry—the one using new techniques and thriving, the other clinging to old ways and declining—now a complementarity was possible. Both types could use modern equipment, with the factory concentrating on larger objects or standardized items that lent themselves to capital-intensive techniques, while the shop specialized in labour-intensive processes using light power tools. And often the complementarity became symbiosis: the modern structure of sub-contracting in the manufacture of consumers' durables rests on the technological effectiveness of the small machine shop.

New uses and cheaper power promoted capital formation. The increased efficiency of prime movers was more than compensated by the larger demand for energy and the multiplication of motors and machines, not only in industry but in agriculture and eventually the household. To be sure, the great expansion promised by electrification of the home still lay far ahead: in Europe, the refrigerator, electric heater, washing machine, and similar big power users (by contrast with electric lighting, the radio, and the gramophone, which consume little current) do not come in on a large scale until after the Second World War. As late as the 1950's the overwhelming majority of houses and flats made do with entry circuits of ten amperes or less; the

---

[1] C. H. Merz, 'The Transmission and Distribution of Electrical Energy', in *Trans. First World Power Conference*, III, 809.

[2] Clapham, *Economic History of Modern Britain*, III, 193, citing A. W. Kennedy, *Trans. Institute of Mechanical Engineers* (1894), 181.

hungriest piece of equipment was the electric iron. Yet this secular proliferation and diffusion of electrical equipment, which is far from exhausted, goes back to these decades before the First World War. There was now no activity that could not be mechanized and powered. This was the consummation of the Industrial Revolution.

Some of this investment represented simply a shift from working to fixed capital, as resources once set aside for fuel supplies and furnace labour were freed for other uses. But by far the greater part of it was new capital, created in response to the opportunities offered by new production functions. In this respect, one should not forget the electrical industry itself—tens of thousands of enterprises generating and distributing current and building and servicing electrical equipment.

Here, as in chemicals, the most striking achievements occurred in Germany. The parallels are numerous: the belated start, the rapid rise based on technological excellence and rational organization, the concentration of production, the strong position on the world market. Up to the very eve of the First World War, Britain was possibly still ahead in consumption of electrical power, though the statistics of the two countries were established on so different a basis that comparison is hazardous.[1] Within less than a decade, however, Germany had overtaken her rival and left her far behind—in spite of heavy losses of territory due to the war. Thus by 1925, regular output of German prime movers totalled 21,186,825 h.p., as against 16,808,700 in Britain in 1924; the corresponding figures for electric generators were

[1] The only overall figures we have are those collected by each country in the industrial censuses of 1907. The British returns give capacity of engines and motors; the German, the power produced in regular operation (the instruction explicitly states that this does not mean capacity [*Höchstleistungsfähigkeit*]). The British statistics show total prime mover capacity (including engines producing energy for electric generators) as 10,749,000 h.p., generator capacity as 2,341,900 h.p. German figures of power production are respectively 8,008,405 and 1,830,000 h.p. These last do not include industrial enterprises in the public sector, far more important in Germany than in Britain; the power output here was 733,520 h.p. overall, 151,800 h.p. by electric generators.

On Britain, *Parl. Papers*, 1912–13, cix (Cd. 6230): Final Report, First Census of Production; on Germany, *Statistik des deutschen Reichs*, N.F. vol. ccxiv, tables 8, 11, 15.

Furthermore, we have reason to believe that the difference in the basis of inquiry biased the results in favour of British power production even more than appears at first examination. We do not have the relevant figures for 1907, but post-war data (1929 for Germany, 1928 for Britain) show that German electrical generator plant had a capacity factor 67% higher than the British, that is, each unit of German generator capacity produced two-thirds more current in the course of the year. Wilhem Leisse, 'Die Energiewirtschaft der Welt in Zahlen', in *Vierteljahrshefte zur Konjunkturforschung*, Sonderheft 19 (Berlin, 1930), p. 34. This is the kind of ratio that reflects the pattern of power distribution and the structure of the electrical industry and presumably did not change much in the course of these two decades.

13,288,800 and 8,510,000 h.p. respectively. What is more, as the higher German capacity factor implies, her stations and distribution nets were on the average larger: her current characteristics more uniform; and her performance more efficient.

Even more impressive was the progress of the German electrical manufacturing industry. It was the largest in Europe—more than twice as big as that of Britain—and second only by a small margin to that of the United States.[1] The firms, as in the chemical industry, were large, well-financed enterprises, strongly supported by the capital market and the great investment banks. The largest, Emil Rathenau's Allgemeine Electricitäts-Gesellschaft (or AEG) and the Siemens-Schuckert combine, were holding companies of extraordinary versatility and complexity. Their products were ingenious, solidly made, competitively priced; financial support made possible generous credit to customers. As a result, German exports on the eve of the war were the largest in the world, more than two-and-one-half times the United Kingdom total, almost three times the American.[2]

Yet one should not overemphasize the importance of capital. As in the chemical manufacture, scientific knowledge, technical skill, and high standards of performance weighed more heavily in the market place than price. Here too a small country like Switzerland was extraordinarily successful, and names like Brown-Boveri, Oerlikon, Eggi-Wyss, and C.I.E.M. (Cie de l'Industrie Electrique et Mécanique) acquired international renown. And for the same reasons, even an agrarian economy like that of Hungary could produce an enterprise like Ganz of Budapest.

Some general considerations

There are two points that deserve emphasis: the underlying stability of the resource base of industrial power; and the continued growth of power consumption. The spectacular contribution of new methods of power production and distribution tends to obscure the continuities of this aspect of industrial history. This is an optical illusion: the eye is always caught by movement. For all the development of new sources

[1] According to the estimates of the British Electrical and Allied Manufacturers' Association, German output of electrical products and equipment in 1913 was worth about £65 million, that of Britain £30 million, that of France £7,700,000. The United States Census of Manufactures gave American output in 1914 as $359 million. Great Britain, Comm. on Industry and Trade, *Survey of Metal Industries...Being Part IV of a Survey of Industries* (London, 1928), pp. 282, 331. Note that British industry had made substantial gains in the decade before the war: the Census of Production of 1907 returned only £14·4 million for electrical manufactures.

[2] *Ibid.* pp. 338–9. Because there are statistical difficulties in making this comparison, approximate ratios are preferable to meretricious precision.

of energy—hydro-electricity, oil, gasoline, gas—coal retained its commanding position. It lost ground, to be sure: in 1913 it accounted for about 88½ per cent of the world's energy output; in 1925 75½ per cent; in 1931 only 66½. Yet these figures tend to exaggerate the decline, for a high proportion of the power derived from other sources has always gone to transportation and domestic consumption; by contrast coal holds a much stronger place in industry, either directly by means of steam engines or indirectly through the intermediary of the electric generator.

Table 12. *Proportion of Primary Power Derived from Steam-engines*

	1911 (%)	1925 (%)
Great Britain	92	90
Germany	82	82
France	73	71
Italy	29	22
Switzerland	20	6

SOURCE. G. F. Hiltpold, *Erzeugung und Verwendung motorischer Kraft* (Zürich, 1934), p. 12.

The proportion of energy derived from coal varied in each country with resources. Mineral-rich Britain and Germany relied heavily on the steam-engine as prime mover; Belgium, a flat land with no high-fall streams, even more so. By comparison, France, with a perennial coal deficit but abundant hydro-electric endowment (Alps, Pyrenees, Vosges, Massif Central), made less use of heat engines, while Italy and Switzerland, with almost no coal but lots of mountains, came to depend almost entirely on water power.

To this day coal remains the primary source of industrial energy and thus the basic resource of an industrial economy. How long this will continue is impossible to predict, given the rapidity of technological change, the progressive exhaustion of the more accessible deposits, the competition of cheap petroleum, and the potential competition of nuclear power.[1] Even in ferrous metallurgy, where coal would seem most firmly ensconced because of its role as both source of energy and reducing agent, recent innovations in smelting practice have made it possible to work with natural gas, and it would be rash to predict the course of technique. Even so, coal has the advantage of cheapness and elasticity of supply, for important deposits are yet to be exploited and the ratio of output to reserves remains comparatively low. Coal—one

[1] Cf. A. P. Usher, 'The Resource Requirements of an Industrial Economy', *J. Econ. Hist.* VII, supplement (1947), 40, 46.

is tempted to say King Coal—is not likely to be dethroned in our lifetime.

Whatever the source, however, the use of power in and out of industry grew rapidly. Even allowing for the egregious shortcomings of our statistical data, particularly resistant to international comparisons, the trend over time is too strong to be missed. World production of commercial sources of energy is estimated to have increased from the equivalent of 1674 million megawatt hours in 1870 to 10,840 million in 1913.[1] As for national developments, we are best informed about the continental countries:

Table 13. *Steam Power in Industry (capacity in thousand horse-power)*

	Germany	France	Belgium
c. 1860[a]	100	169	102
1875	949	401	212
1895	3357	1163	—
1907[b]	6500[c]	2474[d]	1038

[a] 1861 for the *Zollverein*; 1859 for France; 1861 for Belgium.
[b] 1909 for Belgium.
[c] 8,008,000 h.p. from all energy sources.
[d] 3,191,500 h.p. from all energy sources.

SOURCES. Germany: G. Viebahn, *Statistik des zollvereinten und nördlichen Deutschlands*, pp. 1036–7 (his figure does not seem to accord with that of Engel, 'Das Zeitalter des Dampfes', *Z. Königlichen Preussischen Statistischen Landesamtes*, xx [1880], 122, who shows 142,658 h.p. for *Prussian* agriculture and industry in 1861); F. Zweig, *Economics and Technology* (London, 1936), pp. 119–20; G. F. Hiltpold, *Erzeugung und Verwendung*, p. 68.

France. *Annu. statistique*, LVII (1956), *rés. rétro.* pp. 116*–117*.

Belgium: *Exposé de la situation du royaume, 1861–1875*, II, 834–5; *Annu. statistique* (1911–12), p. 349.

We cannot offer comparable statistics for Britain, but the figures on coal consumption tell the story (Table 14).

It should be noted, moreover, that these figures on coal underestimate if anything the rapidity of the German industrial advance. In Britain, transportation, in particular shipping, accounted for a large and growing share of energy consumption in the last decades of the nineteenth century. Estimates by Mulhall give power of fixed engines as 20 per cent or less of total steam capacity; other guesses range as high as 33 per cent, but this is still a small fraction.[2] In Prussia, by contrast, shipping engines could provide less than a tenth of total steam power, while fixed plant accounted for about 85 per cent.

[1] United Nations, Dept. of Economic and Social Affairs, *Acts of the International Conference on the Utilization of Atomic Energy for Peaceful Ends*, vol. I, table xxiii B, p. 28.
[2] Woytinsky, *Welt in Zahlen*, IV, 66–7.

Table 14. *Coal Consumption in Selected Countries (in thousands of tons)*[a]

	United Kingdom		Germany		France		Belgium	
	Amount	Index	Amount	Index	Amount	Index	Amount	Index
1861	77,657	100	13,957[b]	100	15,403	100	6,140	100
1913	189,074	244	187,000[c]	1340	64,834[d]	421	26,032	424

[a] Long tons for the U.K.; metric tons for the rest.
[b] Includes 4522 tons of lignite, deflated at a 9:2 ratio.
[c] Includes 94,160 tons of lignite, deflated at a 9:2 ratio.
[d] To which one might add approximately 10,000 tons consumed in Alsace-Lorraine.

SOURCES. United Kingdom: Finlay A. Gibson, *The Coal Mining Industry of the United Kingdom* (Cardiff, 1922), p. 77, and William Page, *Commerce and Industry* (London, 1919), II, 154, 180.

France: *Annu. statistique* LVII (1946), 230*–31*.

Germany: Bienengräber, *Statistik des Verkehrs und Verbrauchs im Zollverein*, pp. 259, 263, for the year 1861; *Statistisches Jahrbuch für das Deutsche Reich*, XLI (1920), 149, for the year 1913.

We may conclude this discussion with a few thoughts on the wider significance of these somewhat tedious statistics of power production and fuel consumption. They are of interest for their own sake, but even more as indicators of industrial growth and capital formation. The coefficient of correlation between energy consumption and such cal-culations as have been made of industrial capital stock is astonishingly high—for the United States from 1880 to 1948, 0·9995; for the United Kingdom from 1865 to 1914, 0·96 or 0·99, depending on the series employed.[1] Indeed, one is almost tempted to ask whether direct, com-posite measurement of capital formation is worth the effort.

At first thought, this parallelism may be surprising: technological improvements have tended to increase the ratio of energy output to input and therefore to diminish capital requirements at a given level of power consumption. But this has been counteracted, as we have seen in the discussion of electricity, by the spread of motors and machinery into activities previously left to hand or animal labour; in effect, every improvement in the efficiency of the production or utilization of energy has encouraged the substitution of fixed for working capital. In a sense, the story of power is the story of industrialization.

MECHANIZATION AND DIVISION OF LABOUR

Any effort to follow the diffusion of mechanization in all its ramifica-tions is bound to welter in a confusion of details. The basic principles, however, established by 1850, were few. As noted above, the machine

[1] A. G. Frank, 'Industrial Capital Stocks and Energy Consumption', *Econ. J.* LXIX (1959), 170–4.

that will punch metal can be made to punch leather; the die press that will stamp coins can be made to shape pipe or stamp out body parts for automobiles; the knife that will cut cloth can be made to slice metal. The period from 1850 on was rich in new adaptations of this type. One example, chosen for its social as well as its economic significance, will suffice: the sewing machine.

Credit for invention of the sewing machine is not easy to assign: as is frequently the case, there is the distinction to be made between nominal and effective discovery and between inventor and innovator; and in this instance matters are complicated by parallel and not-so-parallel invention. The earliest workable machine was that of Barthélemy Thimonnier of St Etienne, patented in 1830. It was made of wood, was slow and clumsy, but it did take hold in the manufacture of army uniforms, where quality was a secondary consideration and standardization was feasible. In 1841 there were perhaps eighty-one of the machines in operation in a large shop in Paris; they were wrecked by a mob in an almost forgotten outbreak of Luddism. Thimonnier improved his model in subsequent years, but the disturbances arising from the revolution of 1848 and the development of superior techniques by others disappointed his efforts. He died poor and unknown in 1857.

The main line of sewing-machine development runs through Elias Howe (the eye-pointed needle, underthread shuttle, and characteristic lock-stitch in 1846), Isaac Singer (the treadle and the straight needle, in 1851 and later years), and Allen B. Wilson (rotary hook and bobbin, making possible continuous rather than reciprocating motion, and four-motion feed, in 1850 and 1854). Singer was the Arkwright of the industry. He had a vision of the role the new device could have, not only in industry but in the home; it was the first domestic appliance. He advertised it widely, provided courses in its use, made it available on the instalment plan, pioneered the sale-and-service contract. In the face of fierce opposition from tailors and professional seamstresses, the machine caught on rapidly. It was bound to—not only because industry found it so economical but because women found in it liberation from an old bondage. The sewing machine did not mark the end of exploitation and sweating in the clothing manufacture; on the contrary. But it did make needle and thread obsolete and so doing put an end to the 'weary hand' and 'stitch-stitch-stitch' of the dolorous 'song of the shirt'.

The sewing machine gave birth to a family of related devices: machines for band stitching, button-holing, blind-stitching, embroidery, lace-making. Even more important were its applications in other industries: in glove-making, harness work and saddlery, book-binding, above all, in boot- and shoe-making (Blake-McKay machine for sewing uppers to soles, 1860; Goodyear welt machine, 1871 and 1875).

Its versatility made it the most radical innovation in the production of consumers' goods since the power loom.

The result was a further extension of the factory system and a substitution of the large shop (often sweatshop) or putting-out arrangements for the seamstress's table and artisan's bench. Machine clothing manufacture, especially, required relatively little initial capital (a new sewing machine in 1870 cost from £4. 10s. to perhaps £14);[1] the supply of labour, nourished by immigration from central and eastern Europe, was abundant; and production could be dispersed, subcontracted, or given out to home workers. As a result entry was easy; but so was exit.

In the long run demand was elastic and steadily increasing. The early producers of ready-made clothing had confined themselves to sailors' uniforms, army orders, and the plantation market overseas. People of means had their clothes made to taste; the poor made their own. By the end of the century, however, the acceptance of store clothing was widespread, beginning with those articles—coats, shirts, undergarments—where fit was a less important consideration. The 'Sunday suit' was a major factor in this change of attitude: the workman who had been content to spend his life in corduroy or denim trousers and cotton or knitted pullover now had some dress clothes. And for the more fastidious clientele, there was the special order department, turning out factory garments to personal measure. Unfortunately, we do not have statistics on the output of the clothing industry over time; but such partial and qualitative evidence as we do have testifies to the rapidity of its expansion and to the importance of this new class of commodities for the field of retail trade.

Shoe manufacture was another story: the equipment was too expensive and bulky for home use and was ill-suited by its functional specialization to dispersed production. Indeed, all the efforts of the industry were directed toward fragmenting the work into steps simple enough to be carried out by single-purpose machines. In 1858 it took one cobbler 1025 hours to produce 100 pairs of women's shoes, at a labour cost of $256.33; in 1895 it took 85 men 80 man-hours to accomplish the same work, at a total labour cost of $18.59.[2]

This was in the United States, where the price of labour was relatively high and consumers were more favourable to mass-produced, standardized clothing. In Europe the advance of the machine shoe industry

[1] Joan Thomas, *A History of the Leeds Clothing Industry* [Yorkshire Bulletin of Economic and Social Research, Occasional Paper no. 1] (Leeds, 1955), p. 37.

[2] U.S. Bureau of Labor, *Thirteenth Annual Report of the Commissioner of Labor, 1898: Hand and Machine Labor* [55th Congress, 3rd Session, House Doc. 301] (2 vols.; Washington, D.C.: G.P.O., 1899), I, 28–9.

was slower, that of factory manufacture slower yet. Nevertheless, the example of American development and, in Britain, the pressure of cheap imports from across the Atlantic encouraged the adoption of the new techniques. Between 1890 and 1903 the value of imports of leather footware into the United Kingdom rose by £607,000, while exports fell by £53,000. Even so hard-shelled an opponent of mechanization and a defender of the pristine virtues of the craftsman as the Union of Boot and Shoe Operatives was shaken, and reluctantly reconciled itself to the necessity for change.[1]

The entrepreneurial reaction was appropriately vigorous: 'There can be no doubt that the boot and shoe industry is now in process of a more sudden and complete revolution from a hand to a machine industry than any other great English industry', noted an observer in 1904.[2] The statement was true only of the larger plants, which made up *most* of the technical lag by about 1907. The industrial census of that year showed 75 per cent of the workers in the British shoe trade (105,200 out of 140,500) in 'factories' using some amount of power; the rest were outworkers (13,700) or handicraftsmen in shops (21,600). These factories were for the most part small enterprises using light equipment; total power capacity was only 20,171 h.p., or about $\frac{1}{5}$ h.p. per man.[3] They accounted, however, for 88 per cent of the industry's output.

German figures are not strictly comparable. But allowing for differences in classification, they show an industry somewhat smaller than the British and probably more mechanized. One thing is clear: the German shoe manufacture relied far more on electrical power.

For all the sewing machine's impressive proliferation in variant forms, its technological significance resides perhaps even more in the conditions of its own production. The introduction of such a complex device into the home offered a great opportunity to manufacturers of machinery, but posed new problems of technique. For one thing, the machine had to work smoothly and quietly: no housewife was going to take the din of the factory into her bedroom or sitting-room if she could help it. For another, repairs had to be simple and cheap: a mill could afford to have a maintenance staff on hand at all times; the

---

[1] See the discussion in Alan Fox, *A History of the National Union of Boot and Shoe Operatives 1874–1957* (Oxford, 1958), ch. xxiv.

[2] U.S. Dept. of Labor, *Eleventh Special Report of the Commissioner of Labor: Regulation and Restriction of Output* (Washington, D.C., 1904), p. 841, cited by S. B. Saul, 'The American Impact on British Industry, 1895–1914', *Business History*, iii (1960), 20. An important article.

[3] *Parliamentary Papers*, 1912–13, cix, 420–1 (Final Report, First Census of Production).

individual home, or even small shop, could not. Both these conditions called for precision manufacture with interchangeable parts—a subject we shall come to in a moment.

With mechanization went the pursuit of speed, both in the literal sense of faster movement of machines and in the related sense of greater output per unit of time.

No field saw greater gains in this respect than metalworking and engineering. Not only were machine tools more powerful and convenient, but the development of hard steel alloys put in the hands of the workman cutting edges worthy of the mechanical force at his disposal. The earliest of these special materials was simple high-carbon steel; it could work economically at cutting speeds of about 40 feet a minute. In the 1850's and 1860's, Köller in Austria and Mushet in England developed tungsten, vanadium, and manganese alloys that were self-cooling, outlasted regular tool steel five or six times, and could cut 60 feet a minute. This, moreover, was under unfavourable circumstances: machines of the day were not strong enough to support the speed that the steel made possible. The discrepancy was quickly corrected, however, and by the 1890's tools had been developed that could cut 150 feet of mild steel a minute without lubricants. Finally, in 1900 F. W. Taylor and Maunsel White demonstrated their high-speed chromium-tungsten steel at the Paris Exposition. The metal ran red-hot, yet did not soften or dull. Again it was the machine that lagged, and heavier models had to be built, four to six times as powerful as those using carbon steel, before the possibilities of the new metal could be exploited. By the First World War, speeds of 300 and 400 feet per minute had been achieved on light cuts, and it was common for a single tool to remove twenty pounds of waste a minute. Little remembered now, this innovation was one of the wonders of its day. One senses, reading contemporary accounts, the near incredulity of observers at seeing steel pierced and cut like butter.

Yet metalwork offers but one example, admittedly impressive and important, of a general phenomenon. The improvement of textile machinery in this period consisted primarily in more revolutions or picks per minute. Thus from the 1830's to the 1890's, the time needed for the mule carriage to run out and back was cut by one- to two-thirds, depending on the fineness of the yarn; the speed of spindle rotation more than doubled from the throstle to the ring frame; similarly, the pace of the simple power loom. In heavy industry, the invention of the steam hammer meant more rapid as well as heavier blows; the progressive substitution of rolling for hammering speeded the output of wrought iron and steel considerably; and increased automaticity of the rolling equipment led, as we have seen, to continuous mills that moved the hot metal along at the speed of a railway train.

And so on. It would take too long to review these numerous and varied gains in detail; what is important is to consider those underlying improvements that made faster driving practicable. Three changes were crucial.

The first was improved lubrication. This is a subject that has been much neglected by observers and students of technology and its history. The great international expositions of the nineteenth century collected and displayed industrial activities and products of man with a comprehensiveness and taxonomic enthusiasm that never fails to astonish. They assembled all manner of tools and machines, the raw materials they worked, the finished articles they made. They did not neglect the products of the soil or the sea, even the take of the hunt. But they took grease for granted.

And yet from the very start of the Industrial Revolution, lubrication was a matter of critical importance. In 1823 the young French iron-master Achille Dufaud wrote home to Fourchambault that Cyfarthfa was using only first-quality Russian fat as grease. The cost was high—6d. a pound—but in the summer, when the water was low, the use of this fat had gained ten revolutions per minute for the mill wheel; the total annual saving was £3000.[1] And a generation later Fairbairn wrote in his classic *Treatise on Mills and Millwork*: 'In large cotton mills I have known as much as ten to fifteen horses' power absorbed by a change in the quality of oil used for lubrication; and in cold weather, or when the temperature of the mill is much reduced (as is generally the case when standing over Sunday), the power required on a Monday morning is invariably greater than at any other time during the week'.[2]

Few manufacturers gave lubrication the attention it deserved— small wonder the historian has ignored it. Fairbairn again notes that in most plants the task of oiling the shafts was given to the sloppiest worker in the enterprise: 'the result is, that every opening for the oil to get to the bearings is plugged up, the brass steps are cut by abrasion, and the necks or journals of the shafts destroyed'. With time, however, the construction of heavier, faster equipment made it impossible to be indifferent to the cost of lost motion and wear and tear. Experience gave rise to an awareness of the numerous facets of what had seemed at first a simple problem. Industrialists and engineers learned to differentiate solid, semi-solid, and liquid lubricants; and to distinguish them by viscosity, oiliness, freezing and melting points, flammability, tendency to gum or thicken, to stain fabrics, or to decompose and deposit acid or

[1] Thuillier, *Georges Dufaud et les débuts du grand capitalisme dans la métallurgie*, pp. 227, 230.   [2] Second edition; 2 vols.; London 1865, II, 77.

carbon. They learned to suit the material to the use, often by mixing two or more types of lubricant to secure the advantages of each; the introduction of mineral oils and greases from the 1850's on opened a whole range of new possibilities. They also invented ingenious ways to maintain the lubrication of rapidly moving parts without interrupting motion: placing the rubbing surfaces in a standing bath; saturating a pad against which parts moved: cutting grooves down which the oil could run by gravity or be siphoned; and installing automatic pumps or spray guns. A major advance was the use from 1890, first in steam-engines and then in other machines, of forced lubrication, which made possible quiet running at high speeds with little wear and without risk of seizing.[1]

The second of our underlying advances was the substitution of steel for wrought iron in the construction of machinery—of a hard, smooth material, resistant to wear, for a comparatively soft metal, nervy in structure and irregular in abrasion. The result was less friction. And the third was greater precision in the manufacture of moving parts (of which more later), with similar gains.

These last two together made possible a major innovation designed to dispense with or diminish the need for lubrication. The principle of the spherical bearing is well known and as old as history; it is the same as that underlying the use of the wheel instead of the sledge in surface transport—the replacement of sliding friction by rolling contact. Benvenuto Cellini set 'four little globes of wood' to this purpose in the base of a statue as far back as the sixteenth century, and he was almost surely not the first to do so. Yet it was not until around 1880 that precision machinery and the development of hard steels made the spherical bearing a practical industrial instrument by making possible even distribution of the load and reducing the distortion produced by wear to tolerable proportions. The decisive patent was taken out in 1877 by William Bown of Birmingham, a manufacturer of sewing machine parts and roller skates. The first important application, how-ever, was in the form of ball bearings in the bicycle manufacture—Rudge was advertising their advantages in 1886—and for a time the technique seemed suitable only to light loads. The development of the roller bearing, however, by distributing the pressure over lines rather than points of contact, corrected this shortcoming and made possible savings of as much as 90 per cent of power losses in shaft transmission.[2]

[1] The inventor was A. C. Pain, a designer on the staff of Belliss and Morcom, Birmingham, who pioneered the innovation. A. Stowers, 'The Stationary Steam-engine, 1830–1900', in C. Singer et al., eds., A History of Technology, v, 136.

[2] For information on the introduction of ball bearings into modern manufacture, I am indebted to Mrs Smith of the University of Birmingham. From the evidence

Machines were not only faster; they were also bigger, as was the whole range of manufacturing plant. There is no need to labour the point. We have already observed the trend in the iron and steel industry and in the construction of prime movers. At the same time, and in large measure owing to this growth of the equipment unit, the scale of efficient working increased. The trend to size, already marked in the period from 1850 to 1873, continued.

It was most rapid in Germany, where industry was younger, growth more rapid, and the close ties between manufacturing and finance facilitated company formation, expansion, and mergers. In addition, the very prevalence of cartel arrangements in many fields made it often imperative to integrate vertically, in order to free oneself from the exactions of collusive suppliers or customers; and integration opened the way to new economies of scale. Over the period from 1882 to 1907 the proportion of workers in enterprises employing over fifty persons increased from 26·3 to 45·5 per cent; the number of people in works of over one thousand employees more than quadrupled, from 205,000 to 879,000.

As might be expected, the stronghold of big business was heavy, capital-intensive industry: iron and steel, where almost three-quarters of the men in 1907 worked in enterprises of over a thousand employees; machine construction and engineering, where 84 per cent were employed in what was designated as *Grossbetriebe* (51 or more employees); the manufacture of heavy electrical equipment (dynamos, generators, motors, transformers), with 96·4 per cent in the 51-plus category; and chemicals, where the alkali, explosives, and organic-dye trades showed proportions ranging from 82·6 to 98·2 per cent in this class. Yet the trend was clearly general, and even an industry like textile manufacture saw the share of the work force in *Grossbetriebe* increase in spinning from 71·1 per cent in 1882 to 89 per cent in 1907; in weaving from 34·3 per cent to 73·5 per cent.[1]

This increase in personnel, moreover, was accompanied by an even greater one in physical output per unit, for productivity was rising. We cannot always measure this growth directly because of variation in product over time, but where we are dealing with a homogeneous commodity, the evidence is clear. Thus in iron and steel, the average

she has collected, it is clear that the discussions in extant published sources are both incomplete and inaccurate. Even so, the reader may consult with profit Hugh P. and Margaret Vowles, *The Quest for Power from Prehistoric Times to the Present Day* (London, 1931), pp. 206–10; J. G. Crowther, *Discoveries and Inventions of the 20th Century* (4th ed., New York, 1955), pp. 118–19; C. F. Caunter, *The History and Development of Cycles*, part 1: *Historical Survey* (London: H.M.S.O., for the Science Museum, 1955), p. 15.

[1] *Statistik des deutschen Reichs*, N.F. CCXIV, table 11.

annual make of smelting plants increased seven-and-one-half-fold from 1880 to 1910—19,500 to 149,000 tons[1]—while that of Bessemer mills went from 109,000 tons in 1890 to 205,000 in 1905.[2]

What was happening in Germany was also happening in Britain, France, Belgium, and the other countries of Europe—though in lesser degree.[3] Some of this increase in scale is accounted for by new plants, risen full-blown from the soil as Venus from the foam. But much of it, and especially the giantism, consisted in the growth of established enterprises, some young, some old, adding machines, shops, entire buildings and works to their existing plant. Look at the maps that often adorn the proud anniversary histories of business firms—showing them either 'before and after', or distinguishing by colours and dates the stages of their growth.[4] Except for their linearity, they resemble nothing so much as historical maps of the expansion and consolidation of kingdoms and empires—here a frontier straightened out, there a salient established, there an enclave absorbed.

This accretionary character of industrial growth had important technological consequences. There was a certain rationality underlying it all, but opportunism and improvisation were of necessity equally determining. As a result, the matrix of past arrangements became ever more confining, and at each change of equipment or addition to plant, the gap between 'best possible' and 'best practicable' grew. Nowhere was this legacy a more serious handicap than in the organization of the flow of work—what we may call the logistics of production.

Increased intensity of capital and scale of production made the old demon of logistical strangulation more redoubtable than ever. This was inevitable—implicit in the general discrepancy between anticipation and event. The city is built to handle the population and traffic of today or at best a decade from today; with time the streets are too narrow, the courts inaccessible, the buildings cramped and inconvenient. By the same token, even the well-planned factory begins its obsolescence from the moment its doors open. Changes in technique alter to its disadvant-

[1] Sombart, Der moderne Kapitalismus, III[2], 889.

[2] Burn, Economic History, p. 220.

[3] We cannot follow the process so well in Britain, for lack of censuses comparable to those in Germany in 1861, 1875, 1882, 1895 and 1907. The trend is obvious, however (cf. inter alia Pollard, History of Labour, pp. 159–63, 224–6), though one must distinguish for our purposes true growth from consolidation. On the comparison of scale of enterprise between France and Germany, see D. S. Landes, 'Social Attitudes, Entrepreneurship, and Economic Development: A Comment', Explorations in Entrepreneurial History, VI (1954), 245–72.

[4] Thus the historical map of the Siemens plant at Woolwich in J. D. Scott, Siemens Brothers 1858–1958: an Essay in the History of Industry (London, 1958), opp. p. 268.

age the relationship between work and environment; increased speed and volume of work press against the confinement of fixed walls and equipment like the agitated molecules of a heated gas in a rigid container. To be sure, ingenuity and powerful handling and moving devices can ease the difficulty—as we shall see. But even these have their limits, and logistical problems of this kind—with the related costs they attach to any given innovation—have been perhaps the greatest single material obstacle to technical change in mature economies. Consider the comment in 1960 of an American steelman confronted with a new process that allegedly more than doubles the output of an open hearth: 'We can do the same thing on any one open hearth on any one day that we want to put on a demonstration. But I'd like to see them do it day in, day out, with all the furnaces in an open-hearth shop. That creates a tremendous congestion and enormous problems of heating the furnaces and keeping them properly heated, getting the metal away, and getting enough charging buggies.'[1]

By the same token, bigness increased the leverage of logistic operations and of workers' performance in general on the pecuniary results of the enterprise. We are often so impressed by the increase in productivity that results from labour-saving innovations, that we forget the other side of the coin—the multiplier effect on the costs of inefficiency. The greater the outlay on plant and equipment, the less one can afford bottlenecks, sloppiness, or slack; worse yet, inefficiency is infectious and tends to contaminate everything around.

The entrepreneurs of the late nineteenth century were thus goaded by necessity and spurred by the prospect of higher returns to find ways, first, to ease the movement of work through the plant, and second, to draw more output from each man with a given body of equipment. The two were interrelated, not only because a smooth flow of work led to higher productivity, but because a change in the organization and character of labour was, in fact, prerequisite to a revision of the traffic pattern within the plant.

Moreover, this drive to efficiency was reinforced by the underlying commercial and technological trends of the period after 1870. As we have seen, competition was growing keener both in national and international markets as capacity began to outstrip demand, and the pressure for economy grew with it. Yet at the same time, innovation in the older industries was slowing down; new equipment cost more and yielded less. So that the one area that offered large opportunities to cut costs was that of organization and administration; the one factor that was compressible was labour.

The actual progress of these efforts to rationalize production and

[1] *Wall Street Journal*, Pacific Coast edition, 20 May 1960, p. 22.

increase efficiency is hard to follow. Other aspects of technological change and industrial development lend themselves to quantification, and we have a rich statistical heritage to work with. But changes in plant layout and organization are not easily measured, and even where this is possible in individual cases, the variation in approach makes standardization and comparison difficult if not impossible. Perhaps for these reasons, these are subjects that have been relatively neglected by scholars. There are no general histories, and most contemporary accounts are concerned with ideal arrangements rather than actual practice. Our knowledge of the latter must be constructed from occasional case studies, passing references, and informed inferences. Most of the research remains to be done.

To clarify the issue, it is useful to divide industries into two classes, those that transform and those that assemble. The former would include most of the textile and chemical manufactures, metallurgy, glass-making, petroleum refining, food processing, and those other trades whose primary purpose is the conversion of a given body of raw material into some other form. The latter comprises fields like machine-building and engineering, clothing and shoe manufacture, and construction industries, all of which may undertake some transformation but whose salient characteristic is that they put their work together.

The distinction has direct implications for technique. The basic principle of industrial organization is smooth and direct work flow from start to finish of the manufacturing process; detours, returns, and halts are to be avoided as much as possible. For transforming industries, the conceptual problem is simple: there is one stream of activity and a sequential spatial arrangement of operations is all that is required. By contrast, the actual movement of the material may give rise to serious difficulties. It may be too hot to handle, as in metallurgy or certain chemical processes; it may be corrosive or noxious, as in the manufacture of acids and alkalis; it may be bulky or heavy. These problems stimulated a wide variety of ingenious arrangements for moving solid, liquid, and gaseous matter at all temperatures: conveyors and belts, elevators and hoists, pipe and valve systems, pumps, storage bins and tanks, meters, calibrators, gauges, and controls.

Solids gave the most trouble. To be sure, man is capable of astonishing feats of strength and adroitness: there are porcelain factories in Limoges today where porters carry almost one hundred expensive plates at a time, along corridors, around corners, through doorways and down steps—two-thirds of their precious burden in their hands, the rest heaped high on their heads! Moreover, the mechanics of manipulation have long been familiar; the basic devices—screw, pulley, lever, crank, and inclined plane—go back to antiquity. Yet the transmission of power to such machines was beset with difficulties. Moving equipment, by its very nature, could be tied to shaft-and-belt systems only within narrowly circumscribed limits. To some extent human strength was sufficient, if labour was cheap. Matschoss remarks that as late as the 1870's, hand-driven travelling cranes were still the rule in German industry;[1] and among the new installations in a modernizing French machine-construction plant in the 1920's were 'four small 2-ton travelling cranes worked by hand'.[2]

Yet the limitations of human power are obvious: it took four workers 50 minutes to raise five tons four metres by means of winches; two workers, $12\frac{1}{2}$ minutes using pulleys. An effort was made to use small, special-purpose steam-engines; probably the most frequent application of the locomobile—aside from its employment in agriculture— was in lifting and handling. But this was a wasteful and troublesome technique: the engines were generally worked well below capacity and then only intermittently; and the task of keeping the machine fueled was complicated by its movement. Steam was at its best where bulk was not a handicap and speed of action not particularly important—in surface excavation for example—or where weight was a positive advantage, as in the rolling of asphalt pavement.

The eventual solution was, as we have seen, threefold:

(1) Water or air pressure where the working radius of the machine was relatively limited and its action direct and simple. These came in on a large scale in the 1860's and dominated the scene until about 1900.

(2) Electricity where the radius was limited but freedom, rapidity, and versatility of action desirable. It was introduced in the 1890's in the United States, a decade later in Europe.

(3) Petroleum or gasoline where the range of action was very large, in dispersed construction projects for example.

Of these, electricity was the most important. Its most useful area of application was in the driving of 'travellers', where its quickness and responsiveness to control yielded productivity gains of the order of several hundred per cent. The electric crane revolutionized dock work and such industries as metallurgy, where it was often used in conjunction with giant magnets in the lifting of iron and steel objects. The latter technique was particularly effective in handling such things as scrap, the pieces of which were too large for shovels to handle and too irregular and small for claws. Here too, as everywhere, the trend was

[1] Matschoss, *Ein Jahrhundert deutscher Maschinenbau*, p. 137.
[2] This was the Soc. Anon. de Constructions Métalliques de Baccarat. International Labour Office, *The Social Aspects of Rationalisation* [Studies and Reports, Series B (Economic Conditions), no. 18] (Geneva, 1931), p. 114, citing a report published in the *Bulletin du Ministère du Travail* from 1924 to 1927.

to size, with machines of 100-ton capacity and more in common use in shipyards and of up to 75 or 100 tons in heavy engineering on the eve of the First World War.

How important was this mechanization of transport and manipulation within the plant? The answer would vary with the nature of the enterprise; in some processes, handling represents more than 85 per cent of the cost of the finished product; in light industries like textiles, very little. Moreover, big gantry cranes or mobile lifts are not in themselves an assurance of economy. Often enterprises were outfitted with equipment too big or elaborate for the work required. And sometimes labour was so cheap that machines were a luxury. It is only too easy to mistake the paraphernalia of modernity for efficiency.

Nevertheless, one may fairly say that handling was a focus of rapid advance in productivity—not so much because of the spectacular realizations in heavy industries like metallurgy, but because of the uncounted small improvements in every branch of manufacture. The backwardness of some enterprises in this period is astonishing: one reads of dozens of men carrying tons of earth or coal on their backs; of chains of workers standing on a ladder passing material from hand to hand. Often a simple hoist, a few small carriages, or the installation of lifting tables or a conveyor system made all the difference. In an age of ever costlier equipment and diminishing returns, this was the one area that repeatedly saw investments pay for themselves in months and even weeks.

Many of these advances were also important in assembling industries, as several of the examples show. Here the nature of the work had given rise to a complex and wasteful pattern of operations. First—and this was really determining—the assembly process was in most trades imprecise, a matter of repeated trial and error and adjustment; this character of the work is still reflected in our vocabularies, in English words like *fitter* and *steam-fitter* or the French term *ajusteur*. Secondly, few of these industries benefited from the long production runs of homogeneous products that characterized metallurgy and the chemical manufacture. Engineering and machine-building in particular did much of their work to order, and even basic components varied with the job. As a result, there was a great deal of repetitious movement of the wrong kind, with a given object going back and forth several times over the same path until it was satisfactory; and little repetitive movement of the right kind, in which object after object follows the same path, undergoes the same processes, and emerges from the production line with the expedition that comes from practice and mechanization.

In such industries two kinds of work arrangements were commonly employed:

(1) Machines were grouped by type—drills, planes, lathes, and so on in engineering and machine construction, for example—and the pieces were moved from one post to another until they were finally brought together for fitting in the assembly shop. This is the German *Platzarbeit*.

(2) If the work was extremely bulky, as in shipbuilding, construction, or heavy engineering, the men and tools would be brought to it, and components would either be prepared on the spot or wrought elsewhere, usually on the first system, and brought over as well.

Thus instead of the linear flow of the transforming industries, a nodal traffic arrangement prevailed, with material zigzagging back and forth between these work posts, different pieces following different paths. The one pattern may be compared to the smooth stream of vehicles on a through highway; the other to the spasmodic, irregular movement of city streets.[1] One may carry the analogy further. Just as an addition to a throughway increases travel time only in proportion, whereas the expansion of an urban complex increases it at a geometric or even exponential rate, so in *Platzarbeit*, the growth of the plant means greater distances between the posts and multiplies the time lost in the repetitive movement of material. The more successful enterprises gave entire floors, or even separate shops, to a single type of tool. Logistic difficulties thus set a low upper limit to economies of scale.

Finally, the same technological problems that gave rise to the nodal pattern—imprecision and variation on the one hand, custom work on the other—called forth and sustained social institutions that were a source of further inefficiencies. The assembling industries were the stronghold of skilled craftsmen, for in the period before gauges and automatic machine tools, only a deft hand could make components that were reasonably accurate or fit them together. These men were the aristocracy of the labour force. Masters of their techniques, able to maintain their tools as well as use them, they looked upon their equipment as their own even when it belonged to the firm. On the job they were effectively autonomous. Most of them paid their own assistants, and many played the role of subcontractors within the plant, negotiating the price of each job with management, engaging the men required, and organizing the work to their own taste and convenience. The best of them 'made' the firms they worked for.

Yet their independence was costly. Measured by modern time-and-motion methods, skilled labour tends to be less efficient than directly supervised semi-skilled or unskilled labour; and this is only to be

[1] For illustrations of plant and equipment layouts characteristic of the two systems, see Vienna, Kammer für Arbeiten und Angestellte in Wien, *Rationalisierung, Arbeitswissenschaft und Arbeiterschutz* (2nd ed., Vienna, 1928), pp. 189–95.

expected, for the skilled worker sets his own pace instead of accom-
modating to that of the machine. Furthermore, these master craftsmen
were proud, umbrageous, and usually well organized. Their vested
interest in the *status quo* was an obstacle to innovation, the more so
because their skill and virtuosity were incompatible with the fundamental principle of industrial technology—the substitution of inanimate
accuracy and tirelessness for human touch and effort.

The drives to mechanization and increased scale, on the one hand, and
toward a more rational organization of production, on the other, con-
verged at this point. In order to eliminate skill and push back the
logistic barrier, two steps were required: (1) the fragmentation of the
job into simple operations susceptible of being performed by single-
purpose machines run by unskilled or semi-skilled hands; and (2) the
development of methods of manufacture so precise that assembly
became routine, in other words, the production of interchangeable
parts. Only in this way could one change from a nodal to a linear flow;
only in this way could one move the work to the workers at a pre-
determined pace, to be processed and put together by a series of simple,
repetitive acts. The assembly line was thus far more than just a new
technique, a means of obtaining greater output at less cost. In those
branches where it took hold, it marked the passage from shop, however
big and heavily equipped, to factory.

Coherent sequences of machines and interchangeable parts are easier
to establish in some industries than others. The determining consideration is the degree of precision required, which varies not only with the
purpose of the product (compare a chronometer, a rifle, a pair of
pliers, and the frame of a house), but with the material employed
(compare textile fabrics or leather, which give, with metals, which
do not). It is largely because of its comfortable tolerances that shoe
manufacture was among the earliest assembling industries to develop
progressive machining, as it is sometimes called.

Metal devices—the kind that had to be wrought piece by piece and
assembled, as opposed to simple objects that could be stamped or
pressed out—were another matter. Here margins were often very fine,
measured in the hundredths and thousandths of an inch. As a result,
interchangeability was costly, and only the achievement of volume
manufacture made the effort worth while. (Eventually entrepreneurs
learned that the converse was also true: the effort, if successful, made for
low prices and a mass market.) It is no coincidence that the first
important applications of the principles of interchangeable parts and
line assembly were in the manufacture of small arms, which were
needed in quantity for military use.

History has traditionally assigned this critical innovation to Eli

Whitney, of cotton-gin fame, but his claim will not stand up under scrutiny. Robert S. Woodbury has noted that a Swedish mechanic, Christopher Polhem, was making uniform clock gears as early as the 1720's, and that a Frenchman named Blanc was turning out rifles in the government arsenals on an interchangeable basis before the Revolution. Neither of these early achievements took root, however, and it was not until a number of American gunmakers—among them, Whitney, though he was by no means the first—worked out the principles and developed the requisite tools in the first two decades of the nineteenth century that we have an unbroken record of diffusion.[1] In the beginning the technique found its widest application in the northeastern United States, in the manufacture not only of small arms, but also of locks, clocks, and agricultural machinery.[2] Not until the 1850's was it introduced into Britain, in the government arms factory at Enfield following a visit of inspection across the Atlantic. From there the techniques spread to two of the leading private firms, the London Small Arms Company and the Birmingham Small Arms Company (founded 1861). Even so, the size of the market was by no means so conducive to interchangeable manufacture as in the United States: Britain did not have a turbulent frontier. Nor was official policy helpful: the government rationed declining orders for small arms to three or four companies in set proportions, in effect vitiating competitive incentives to technological improvement.[3]

Yet the rifle and pistol are, so far as articulation is concerned, crude mechanisms. The contribution of the last half of the nineteenth century lay, first, in the invention of a number of non-military devices—the sewing machine, then the typewriter, bicycle, and finally the automobile —that required a much higher degree of precision and at the same time enjoyed the kind of demand that made the achievement of interchangeability worth while, if not indispensable; and second, in the development of the equipment and techniques required. Three areas of innovation were crucial: machine tools, grinding, and measurement.

We have already had occasion to discuss the early improvements in machines to make machines. By the middle of the nineteenth century,

[1] R. S. Woodbury, 'The Legend of Eli Whitney and Interchangeable Parts', *Technology and Culture*, I (1960), 235–53. John E. Sawyer, President of Williams College, is currently preparing a study of the 'American system of manufacturing' and its French antecedents.

[2] J. E. Sawyer, 'The Social Basis of the American System of Manufacturing', *J. Econ. Hist.* XIV (1954), 361–79; D. L. Burn, 'The Genesis of American Engineering Competition', *Econ. Hist.* [supplement of the *Econ. J.*], II (1931), 292–311; Merle Curti, 'America at the World Fairs, 1851–1893', *Amer. Hist. Rev.* LV (1950), 833–56.

[3] S. B. Saul, 'The Market and the Development of the Mechanical Engineering Industries in Britain, 1860–1914', *Econ. Hist. Rev.*, 2nd Series, XX (1967), 123.

the essential requirements were all present: the true plane, which supplied the uniform standard of reference; the slide rest, which took the cutting tool from the fallible hands of the artisan; and screw-threaded adjustments, which made possible fine work. What the next two generations did was essentially to adapt and elaborate on these techniques in developing more efficient forms of the basic tools: drills, lathes, planers, and the rest. There were, however, two major novelties, both connected to the growing demand for what are now consumers' durables:

(1) The turret (eventually automatic) lathe. The machine was equipped with a rotating turret that carried as many as eight cutting tools, each of which could be brought to bear on the work in turn. The next step was automatic rotation, achieved in 1861 if not earlier, and the concurrent invention of a device for gripping and feeding the work reduced the role of the worker to insertion, supervision, and removal. Though the idea came perhaps from Britain, the first extensive use of these machines was in the United States in the 1840's; the Civil War, with its demand for mass-produced metal wares, encouraged their diffusion. By the 1870's they were widely used in Europe.

Toward the end of the century the productivity of these machines was increased four or five times by the use of multiple spindles, which made it possible to work on several pieces simultaneously. Eventually, banks of these machines were set up, using cross-slides as well as turrets, to work away side by side like the array of spindles on a mule. The only labour required was for occasional tool setting and replenishing the supply of raw material.

(2) The milling machine. Its distinguishing characteristic is the use of a revolving multiple cutter, which resembles a small cylinder or truncated cone with saw-toothed sides. It offered several major advantages over the usual single-point tools, with their intermittent reciprocating actions:[1] relatively wide cutting edges; continuous motion; and the possibility of profiling the teeth to permit the production of any

---

[1] This was one example of a general principle that has found numerous applications in the history of technology. Some of these are already familiar: the substitution of the rolling mill for the hammer in forge work; of continuous rolling for reversing rolls in the mill; the replacement of the reciprocating steam-engine by the turbine. Other uses will also come to mind: the circular saw, rotary printing press, cylinder printing of textiles. In machine manufacture itself, we may note the increasing use in the late nineteenth century of high-speed drills, using bits with spiral cutting edges instead of the traditional smooth sides, in place of such tools as the slotting machine. Cf. the discussion of this 'Rotationsprinzip' in Sombart, Der moderne Kapitalismus, III[1], 109–10. On the innovation of the twist drill, see G. A. Fairfield, 'Report on Sewing Machines', in R. H. Thurston, ed., Reports of the Commissioners of the United States to the International Exhibition held at Vienna, 1873, vol. III: Engineering (Washington, D.C., 1876), p. 30.

geometrical shape desired. When the cutter, moreover, was combined with an adjustable swivel headstock to permit attacking the work from all angles or from changing angles, to cut spirals for example, the result was the so-called universal miller (1861), a marvel of versatility. Eventually this was further improved by a kind of compounding process comparable to that which had produced the multi-spindle lathe.[1]

The first milling cutter is said to go back to Vaucanson in the eighteenth century; the first milling machine was built by Eli Whitney in 1818. Again, however, it was the demand arising out of the Civil War that established the device in the United States; by the early 1870's it was standard in the manufacture of sewing machines. In Britain also, the sewing machine seems to have been a decisive factor in the adoption of the new technique. The largest factory in the world for the production of this combination capital good-consumers' durable was the Singer plant at Clydebank, Scotland, which began operations in 1870 and was turning out 8,000 machines a week by 1885. The Singer works installed some 216 milling machines in the decade of the 1870's and a total of 2,233 during the period 1870–1914. The vast majority of these, unfortunately, were built either at Clydebank or by the home company in the United States, so that there was little propagation of the new technology to independent British machine tool makers. To be sure, milling was taking hold in other branches of manufacture; thus some of the locomotive works were doing it to good effect in heavy machining in the late seventies and early eighties; but the real diffusion of milling waited until the bicycle boom of the 1890's opened a new field of application.[2]

Part of the difficulty was technical: for a long time, machine design and materials were not up to the conception. The wide cutting edges of the miller, more than one of which may be in contact with the work at once, subject the spindle and arbor to extreme stress, and only the stiffest construction will prevent the tool from vibrating and chattering; even then, the reciprocating planer and shaper will do more accurate work, especially on wide surfaces. Furthermore, the continuity and rapidity of milling call for tough metal, the more so because the uneven wear of any of the cutting edges necessitates the regrinding of all; as we have seen, the special tool steels required were invented only at the turn of the century.[3]

[1] The best source is R. S. Woodbury, *History of the Milling Machine* [Technology Monographs, Historical Series, no. 3] (Cambridge, Mass., 1960). It offers a brief but useful bibliography.

[2] Saul, 'The Market and the Development of the Mechanical Engineering Industries', pp. 124–5.

[3] The extent of the wear on the cutting tool, even with high-speed steels, was often such as to compel machine makers to sacrifice speed of operation to speed and ease of

The introduction of new and harder alloy steels, not only for tools but for machine parts, intensified the challenge already posed by the drive for speed and precision. Rapid, accurate work called for sharp cutting edges and nice finishing; both of these could be achieved only by grinding.

It is important to distinguish between these two basic functions of grinding—tool maintenance and shaping. Until the turn of the century, the first was by far the more important: grinding was generally confined to the irregular and unsystematic sharpening of tools by the individual workman. Gradually, however, abrasives came to be used as tools themselves. As in most other areas of metal working, the United States led the way: as early as the 1870's, one observer was able to write that 'the grandeur [Grossartigkeit] of the grindstone industry in America astonishes every foreigner'. In these early years, however, the technique was confined to fine finishing. It took a series of related advances in the preparation and manipulation of abrasives plus a creative reinterpretation of the nature and the possibilities of the technique to make possible what has since come to be known as production grinding.[1]

The major material problem was the achievement of a true, efficient abrasive surface of known and uniform characteristics. Up to the end of the nineteenth century, all industrial grinding was done with such natural abrasives as sandstone, emery (an impure aluminium oxide), or, beginning in the 1820's, corundum (almost pure aluminium oxide). The last of these was the hardest, but it was also the most costly, for until the 1870's it had to be imported from lands around the Indian Ocean. At that point, the discovery of large deposits in North America brought the price down, and in the next two decades, corundum largely displaced emery in shaping and finishing. At the same time, the desirability of a true and lasting abrasive surface led to the development of solid grinding wheels, in which the cutting grains were mixed with such bonds as glue, vulcanized rubber, clay, or silicates. The first of these date back at least to 1837 in England, 1843 in France, 1850 in Germany. Along with them went ingenious devices for dressing, that is, renewing the edge of the wheel (1860's on) and truing its shape (roughly the same period).

At the same time, machine builders were putting these wheels into

maintenance and to use milling heads with one tooth. This was a twentieth-century development. Cf. *Ludwig Loewe und Co., Actiengesellschaft Berlin, 1869–1929* (Berlin, 1930), pp. 87–8.

[1] Again the best source is R. S. Woodbury, *History of the Grinding Machine: A Historical Study in Tools and Precision Production* (Cambridge, Mass., 1959). See also Mildred M. Tymeson, *The Norton Story* (Worcester, Mass., 1953).

power devices that could operate them as a drill its bit or a miller its cutting head. The earliest of these grinders go back to the Renaissance, if not beyond, and they found considerable use in optical work, watch-making, and similar light trades in the following centuries; but their improvement and specialization for large-scale manufacturing was the work of the Industrial Revolution. British (Whitelaw, Bodmer, Nasmyth, Barker and Holt), German (Krupp), and above all American (David Wilkinson, Bridges, Wheaton, Darling, Poole) mechanics were engaged in this development, which reached its culmination in the work of Joseph Brown of Brown and Sharpe, the conceiver if not designer of the universal grinding machine (1875).

It is no coincidence that these concomitant improvements in abrasive surface and working mechanism quickened toward the end of the century and came to inspire a radically new concept of grinding technique. Once again the revolution in this domain was intimately connected with the growing demand for complex machines smooth and sturdy enough in operation to withstand the abuse of the mechani-cally incompetent household consumer. The sewing machine gave a foretaste of these derived technological consequences, as did the bicycle with its ball bearings; but neither had anything like the impact of the automobile. It is hard to overestimate this impact, which is comparable to that of the steam-engine in the eighteenth century. The automobile was not the first object of manufacture to call for complicated or delicate or precise work. But nothing before had ever demanded all of these, often in materials too hard to be shaped by traditional means, and in such quantity as to strain the supply of skilled labour. From the start, the automobile industry paid top wages for its craftsmen: it needed to and could afford to. And from the start it was compelled to do new things and find new ways to do old. Moreover, there was the economic carrot as well as the technological stick: the elasticity of demand for private transportation provided an enormous incentive for cost-saving improvements, which, given the nature of the work, almost invariably consisted in the substitution of capital for labour.

The answer to many of the new industry's production problems lay in replacing cutting and scraping by grinding. Not only did the new technique assure the greater precision required by interchangeable parts working at high speeds and temperatures, but it proved invaluable in rough work—in removing stock from crankshafts and camshafts, for example. And it permitted the use of light, hard alloys like vanadium steel, without which an economical automobile for general use would not have been feasible.[1]

---

[1] Cf. P. W. Kingsford, 'The Lanchester Engine Company Ltd., 1899-1904',

The advances that made this kind of production grinding possible were threefold: first, the invention of artificial abrasives, particularly carborundum (first commercial use, 1896), which was harder than the traditional natural materials (always excepting the diamond) and could be prepared in varying grits to suit the requirements of the work; second, the development of precision grinding machinery, of heavy, powerful construction, using larger and wider wheels; and finally, the introduction of plunge grinding, in which the wheel was given the shape of the part desired and fed into the work rather than run across it.

Production grinding affords an excellent example of the contribution of the engineer as innovator-entrepreneur. The pioneer here was Charles H. Norton, a giant in the tradition of Maudslay, Nasmyth, and Whitworth. Norton conceived the new technique, called attention to its larger economic implications, designed numerous machines to effect it, and worked out the principles of optimum operation, notably the choice of abrasive and grinding speed to fit the job. But his success and that of the other American pioneers in this area owed much to the entrepreneurial and technological orientation of the American automobile industry—the precocious emphasis on quantity, lightness, and low cost.

European practice was not far behind the American. To be sure, the extensive adoption of production grinding in the manufacture of automotive vehicles did not come in Britain and Germany until during the War or after. On the other hand, both countries anticipated the United States in the application of grinding to the construction and maintenance of locomotives. And in other industries, Europeans were quick to buy American equipment or manufacture machines after American patents; beginning in 1904, for example, Ludwig Loewe and Co. were turning out Norton-type grinders in Berlin. It was not long, moreover, before they and others were designing their own models to suit their own conceptions and the requirements of European manufacture.

In the meantime, the new standards of manufacture called forth a revolution in the other domain of grinding, that of the maintenance of cutting tools. Here the key gains were once again the introduction of improved abrasives and the development of precise, special-purpose machines. The effective utilization of this equipment, however, entailed a reorganization of the shop that often aroused sharp opposition from the highly skilled and correspondingly umbrageous metal workers. In particular, it was now necessary to appoint specialist grinders and create a separate tool room to stock work pieces and keep them in proper condition. This meant the abdication by the worker of control over his tools; it also deprived him of the pleasant relaxation of the grindstone queue—the nineteenth-century equivalent of the coffee break.[1]

Along with improved tools went standardized controls—not by means of measuring devices like the rule and calipers, but by instruments independent of the vagaries of the human eye, stable in their accuracy, and calling for little or no skill. Whitworth's plug and ring gauges were the prototypes of a whole family of contrivances—limit (go and no-go) gauges, difference gauges, adjustable gauges, reference disks, end measuring blocks—whose tolerance was sometimes as small as one fifty-thousandth of an inch and whose operation was almost foolproof. Even so, the gain was not in the quality of the final product, but in its cost. The nature of the change is well described by H. F. Donaldson, machine manufacturer from Woolwich and member of the Council of the Institution of Mechanical Engineers, in a lecture of 1909:

When I began to serve my time in the shops, I remember that 'a fine 1/64 of an inch' was about the closest measurement to which any workman, or for the matter of that, his superiors, referred to, but none the less, even with such a coarse nominal dimension, and the use of a pair of ordinary callipers, magnificent work was produced owing to the skill of the individual workmen and the precision of their sense of touch. Neither the workman, nor in many cases his superiors, had any real knowledge of the degree of accuracy to which the work was being done, but the fact remains that work of the highest quality was made and fitted together, having fits at least as close as those secured today by more systematic, and, as we believe, improved and certainly cheaper methods. The great difference which existed between then and now, is that though the work then was of the highest quality as regards each machine put together, the degree of accuracy ruling in each part was quite unknown, and the parts of one such machine were not interchangeable, or capable of mutual substitution in another machine, which was nominally of the same dimensions in all particulars. In other words, the machines were made and 'fitted' then with great care and with a large amount of expensive hand-work, where today, at least in the more progressive shops, machines are 'assembled' from parts made to a known degree of accuracy, and with a minimum of expensive hand-fitting, and with the added advantage that the parts of machines so made are interchangeable one with another if the work is done on a proper system of limits or limit-gauges.[2]

The quotation is as interesting for what it implies as for what it

[1] See the delightful photograph of such a queue in O. M. Becker, *High-speed Steel* (New York and London, 1910), p. 153.

[2] *Proc. Inst. Mech. Engineers* (1909), pp. 254–5.

says. Before the First World War, outside those few industries manufacturing mass-market items like the sewing machine, only the more
progressive enterprises in Britain worked with interchangeable parts.
A team of American automobile mechanics, sent by Cadillac to England
in 1906, caused a sensation when they set out the jumbled components
of three cars on the floor of a shed at the Brooklands track and assembled
the vehicles with wrench, screw-driver, hammer, and pliers.[1] Most
British firms of this period were caught in a vicious circle: output was
not big or uniform enough to warrant heavy outlays for specialized
precision equipment and a reorganization of plant layout; yet this was
the only way to achieve the lower costs and prices that would yield
increased demand and justify longer production runs. Many manufacturers would have plausibly argued that any effort to fix the form
and structure of their products would rob them of that flexibility that is
the strongest arm of the small or medium enterprise. It took initiative to
break this conservative chain of logic, and it was rarely forthcoming.
In most cases it took outside pressure, like the increasing inroads of
Henry Ford on the British market, or extraordinarily favourable
incentives, like the huge government orders of wartime, to induce a
change.[2]

If standardization within the firm was difficult, how much harder
was it to persuade manufacturers throughout an industry to accept a
national norm? The problem was complicated by the peculiarly
British institution of the consulting engineer, who tended to design
every project as though the manufacturer were a custom tailor working
in metal. Here too, however, outside competition made itself felt. The
Americans had been the first to adopt uniform shapes and sizes,
imposing them by fiat on manufacturing clients and consumers from
the eighties on.[3] The Germans had followed suit, in large part for
reasons of principle—simplification was rational; moreover, industrial
organization facilitated the introduction and enforcement of inter-firm
standards. Lagging British sales, both in these countries and in other
markets, and the increased concern of technicians finally led in 1901 to
the creation in Britain of an Engineering Standards Committee under
the auspices of the leading national engineering associations.

[1] Arthur Pound, *The Turning Wheel: the Story of General Motors through Twenty-
five Years* (Garden City, N.Y., 1934), p. 107.

[2] Cf. P. W. S. Andrews and E. Brunner, *The Life of Lord Nuffield: a Study in
Enterprise and Benevolence* (Oxford, 1955), pp. 59–71, 87–94.

[3] On the importance of entrepreneurial attitudes—the refusal of producers to
supply their clients with special shapes except on payment of a punitively high price—
see J. Stephen Jeans, ed., *American Industrial Conditions and Competition: Reports of the
Commissioners Appointed by the British Iron Trade Association to Enquire into the Iron,
Steel, and Allied Industries of the United States* (London, 1902), p. 256.

The first efforts of the committee were in the field of iron and steel manufacture, where British makers produced 122 angle and channel sections against 33 for the United States, 34 for Germany.[1] Here they achieved considerable success, for the manufacturers wanted to eliminate the waste of diversification and the very existence of standards gave them a ready-made reply to the idiosyncratic preferences of the client.[2] By 1914, 95 per cent of the output of five of the largest rolling mills in the United Kingdom was standardized.[3] Similarly, standardization made good progress in a new industry like electrical manufacturing, run by scientifically trained technicians and relatively forward-looking managers, though diversity of current supply complicated matters considerably.

By contrast, the older assembling industries like engineering were slow to change. Each firm took a proprietary pride in its own work, to the point where many were simply not interested in norms and the production techniques that went with them.[4] Moreover, labour in the engineering trades, strongly organized, craft-oriented, and fearful of technological unemployment, fought all changes in conditions of work.[5] Again it was the First World War with its great demand for machines of all kinds and short supply of skilled hands that gave impetus to the struggle against idiosyncrasy; indeed, the descriptions of the gains made after 1914 are our best source—implicit but valid—for the inefficiencies that prevailed before.[6] Even so, progress was slow in many branches, which were described in 1927 as 'still bound by

---

[1] Burn, *Economic History*, p. 199. See above p. 267.

[2] Cf. *Report of the Tariff Commission* [a private body], vol. 1: *The Iron and Steel Trades* (London, 1904), no. 631.

[3] Commission on Industry and Trade, *Factors in Industrial and Commercial Efficiency* [*Being Part I of a Survey of Industries*] (London, 1927), p. 294.

[4] Donaldson, 'Interchangeability', *Proc. Inst. Mech. Engineers* (1909), pp. 255f.

[5] The issue was at the heart of dozens of major and minor strikes in the industry from 1897–8 on. Cf. A. Shadwell, *The Engineering Industry and the Crisis of 1922* (London, 1922); Pollard, *History of Labour in Sheffield*, pp. 235 ff.; J. B. Jefferys, *The Story of the Engineers*, part III. The very existence of this conflict, of course, is evidence that a certain amount of rationalization was taking place.

[6] Cf. the Report of the Board of Trade Engineering Trades Committee of 1916–17: 'Old works have been added to, fresh machinery has been introduced from time to time to balance up old machinery. There has been generally an absence of totally new works with an economic lay-out. Whilst the country can point to many works of the highest class, with the most modern equipment worked at the highest efficiency, there can be no doubt that many of our older works are manufacturing at costs which could be greatly reduced if their works as a whole were on a larger scale, well-planned and equipped with plant, and, therefore, capable of being worked in the most efficient and economical manner.' Commission on Industry and Trade, *Survey of Metal Industries* [*Being Part IV of a Survey of Industries*] (London, 1928), p. 149.

tradition and drift[ing] along with an enormous number of spare parts, making no attempt to simplify'.[1]

By comparison with Britain, then, Germany was distinctly more advanced, though there is a tendency to concentrate on the most striking examples of German achievement in this domain, thereby exaggerating the discrepancy. Even so modern a plant as the Loewe machine-tool works in Berlin, built anew in 1898–99 according to the best American practice, did not set up 'Arbeitskreise', that is, switch over from a nodal to a linear-flow pattern, until 1926.[2] Similarly, the Wolf machine works in Magdeburg was turning out interchangeable parts with special-purpose equipment before the war, but these components were then used to mount rows of fixed machines in the assembly hall.[3] For both countries, the new system of mass production was essentially the work of the famous 'rationalization' of the 1920's.

As already implied, reorganization of work entailed reorganization of labour: the relationships of the men to one another and to their employers were implicit in the mode of production; technology and social pattern reinforced each other.

But labour is not a factor like other factors. It is active where equipment and materials are passive. It has a mind of its own; it resists as well as responds. Its performance independent of other considerations —what we may call its efficiency as opposed to its productivity—is not easily calculated except by modern systems of cost accounting, and the historical data are correspondingly impressionistic and sparse. It is especially difficult to separate pure effort, diligence, and skill from organization and supervision, which obviously make a difference. Fortunately, such fine discrimination is not necessary to our analysis, and we may lump these elements together without undue sacrifice of precision.

Our ignorance of the variations of labour efficiency over space and time is the more unfortunate because we have every reason to believe that it was an important determinant of the rate and character of economic development in any given country and as between countries; moreover, that its significance in this regard grew in the course of the Industrial Revolution until, by the turn of the century, this was one of the areas of greatest slack and, by the same token, of greatest potential gain in productivity.

In the days before power machinery, skill and rapidity were decisive

---

[1] Commission on Industry and Trade, *Factors in Industrial and Commercial Efficiency*, p. 295. [2] *Ludwig Loewe and Co.*, pp. 94–9.

[3] C. Matschoss, *Die Maschinenfabrik R. Wolf, Magdeburg-Buckau, 1862–1912* (Magdeburg, n.d.), pp. 103 f.

differentials. Defoe was well aware of this; comparing wages and work in England and France, he wrote:

I might examine this Article of Wages, and carry it thro' almost every Branch of Business in *England*; and it would appear, that the *English* Poor earn more Money than the same Class of Men or Women can do at the same kind of Work, in any other Nation.

Nor will it be deny'd, but that they do more Work also: So then, if they do more Work, and have better Wages too, they must needs live better, and fare better; and it is true also, that they cannot support their Labour without it.

And here I may grant, that a *French* Man shall do more Work than an *English* Man, if they shall be oblig'd to live on the same Diet; that is to say, the Foreigner shall starve with the *English* Man for a Wager, and will be sure to win: He will live and work, when the *English* Man shall sink and dye; but let them live both the same Way, the *English* Man shall beggar the *French* Man, for tho' the *French* Man were to spend all his Wages, the *English* Man will outwork him.

It is true again, the *French* Man's Diligence is the greatest, he shall work more hours than the *English* Man; but the *English* Man shall do as much Business in the fewer Hours, as the Foreigner who sits longer at it.[1]

In the early decades of the Industrial Revolution, however, when rapidly changing techniques offered large returns and mechanization in particular yielded spectacular gains in productivity over hand work, labour efficiency lost in relative importance and—wisely or not—was neglected. Eric Hobsbawm, in an important article on 'Customs, Wages, and Work-load in Nineteenth-Century Industry',[2] cites the *Carding and Spinning Master's Assistant* of 1832, which warned against rearranging machine installations, even if inefficient, on the grounds that the cost would probably exceed the savings.

Most entrepreneurs and managers in this period preferred fixed wages and relied on 'hard driving' by foremen and master workmen to get them value for their money in the short run, on the quiet effect of technological change to cut labour costs in the long. When the measurement of output was possible, piece wages were sometimes used as an incentive to diligence; but a number of considerations combined to nullify their stimulatory effect. Thus rates were usually calculated on the basis of customary norms and adjusted with changes in technique so as to reserve to capital the greater part of any gains in productivity. Such a division of the incremental product may or may not have been fair, but the effect on the worker was to convince him of the uselessness of assiduity. Moreover, labour, even in the factory, often had the kind

[1] [Defoe], *A Plan of the English Commerce* (Oxford, 1928), p. 28.
[2] In Asa Briggs and John Saville, eds., *Essays in Labour History* (London, 1960), pp. 113–39. This is a path-breaking effort to synthesize some of this material historically.

of backward-bending supply curve that had always characterized domestic work.[1] Just as wages tended to be customary, so the level of performance was fixed by tradition and income expectations—compare the still persistent ideal of 'a fair day's work for a fair day's pay'—and was enforced against the temptations of ambition by the strongest group pressure. It is the slack implied by this rationing of effort that goes far to account for the ability of labour to maintain output in the short run whenever hours were cut, as they were repeatedly in the course of the century; and conversely, for the almost universal failure of technological innovations to yield the productivity gains they theoretically made possible.[2]

The tendency of management to let custom set the level of work performance was shaken by adversity. The contractions of the late 1860's (in textiles especially) and mid-1870's (industry-wide), when wages held up better than profits, were crucial in this regard. Employers attempted to cut labour costs by increasing performance, and the question of the nature and size of the work load supplanted wages as the major issue in labour disputes. In textiles the *casus belli* was the attempt of management to increase the number of power looms per weaver; the struggle was particularly bitter on the Continent. In machine construction and engineering a serious bone of contention was the right of management to shift men about as needed, that is, to treat the worker as an interchangeable part of the production process. In all industries, there was general discontent at the replacement of skilled by unskilled and semi-skilled hands, easier to manage and more amenable to pace set from above.

The wage structure reflected the new policy. As the diversified work of the artisan, unmeasurable in homogeneous units of output, gave way to the routine operation of special-purpose machines, time wages gave way to piece wages. The change was felt most keenly in the engineering trades, where time rates had always been the rule. There were numerous protests. That there should have been any was testimony

---

[1] Cf. Pollard, *History of Labour in Sheffield*, p. 130, for this phenomenon in the light metal trades toward the end of the nineteenth century.

[2] A direct historical measurement of the cost of labour inefficiency and bad organization is impossible, but it does not seem far-fetched to draw, as Hobsbawm does, on the analogy of the cotton textile industry of Latin America in the mid-twentieth century. This was studied in detail in a pioneering attempt to measure the relative importance of determinants of productivity for an entire industry. The conclusion was, contrary to expectations, that the greater part of the excess of labour employed was due to administrative and organizational rather than technological deficiencies—and this in an industry where, far more than most, machines set the pace for labour, rather than vice-versa. United Nations, *Labour Productivity of the Cotton Textile Industry in Five Latin-American Countries* (New York: U.N. Dept. of Econ. Affairs, 1951), p. 10.

to the tensions and resentments produced by these changes in technique and organization. For labour, and particularly organized labour, ordinarily preferred piece wages. Admittedly, they led some men to overtask themselves (although collective restraints usually prevented this), encouraged hasty, even sloppy work (though it was not difficult to watch against this), and caused some to adopt the rush-slack rhythm that we know to have characterized the putting-out manufacture of the eighteenth century. Yet more important than all of these drawbacks was the conviction of most men that piece wages gave them their only assurance of a share of increased output consequent on advances in technique. Even where the employer tried to adjust the rates downwards, there was at least something to negotiate. With time wages, by contrast, the work could and did increase imperceptibly as productivity rose; and even when the process was manifest, the system of remuneration afforded little opportunity for redress.

To the English worker of the late nineteenth century, however, the piece wage seemed an instrument of exploitation rather than a defence. To be sure, it held out the promise of higher pay. But the workers alleged that the rates were set to the performance of the most rapid men; the slow ones followed suit or 'went to the wall'.[1] The higher pay, they felt, was nothing but sweetening to get them to swallow higher work norms; and in fact, the new rates were rarely maintained beyond what was felt to be a reasonable increase—a third or perhaps a half—over customary wages.

Here, as much as in the employer's appetite for gain, lay the heart of the difficulty. The employer, like most Englishmen of the 'propertied classes', took it for granted that his men and their children were destined to remain workers; and 'that the whole social, political, and industrial fabric would fall into a heap' if labourers suddenly became rich, discontented with their lot, and ambitious for higher status.[2] Now there may have been a time, as some assert, when the worker, or at least many a worker, did not believe this, when he honestly thought he could rise and was susceptible to appeals to diligence and 'self-help'. By the last decades of the century, however, disenchantment had clearly set in, partly owing to longer experience with the difficulties of advancement, partly to the heightened class consciousness of an organized labour movement ideologically fortified by militant doctrine. By this time the worker was prepared to see any initiative of the

[1] Comments of W. G. Bunn at the Industrial Remuneration Conference of 1885. See Industrial Remuneration Conference, *The Report of the Proceedings and Papers* (London, 1885), p. 169. There is a great deal of scattered information on this trend.
[2] U.S. Bureau of Labor, *Twelfth Special Report of the Commissioner of Labor: Regulation and Restriction of Output* (Washington, D.C., 1904), pp. 752-7.

employer as a trap. And to this should be added his fear of technological unemployment. Political economy notwithstanding, he
instinctively held to the 'lump-of-labour' doctrine: there was just so
much work to go around and what one man gained by faster work took
bread out of the mouth of his fellow. As a result, the worker tended to
resist, as a member of a group, even those innovations that were to his
advantage as an individual; and whereas, in the early nineteenth
century, the effort of labour to wrest improvements from the employer
was a stimulus to innovation, by the end of our period, the same effort
—more effective, but aimed more at conditions of work than at wages
—may well have been on balance a deterrent to technological change.
Certainly this was often true in the short run; and in history if not in
theory, the long run is often the short run enshrined as practice, tradition, or vested interest.

In the meantime, the effort to maximize the product of labour led to
a careful study of the worker as an animate machine, through the eyes
of a new kind of engineer. The initiative came from the United States,
as always preoccupied with this issue. It was in the Midvale Steel
Works in Pennsylvania in the early 1880's that Frederick W. Taylor
(1865–1915) met and learned, as worker and foreman in the machine
shop, the practice and tricks of ca' canny and developed the system that
came to be known as scientific management or Taylorism. As eventually
elaborated, his method comprised, first, careful observation, analysis,
and timing of workers' movements; second, precise measurement of
the labour cost of each operation; and third, the establishment of norms
based on these calculations. The introduction of these new standards,
almost invariably higher than those customary in the trade, was to be
sweetened by favourable piece rates, premium payments, or other
incentives.

Here the circle came full turn: the effort to improve the worker's
efficiency, an effort which grew out of the increased efficiency of
capital, opened the way to advances in the use of equipment. Scientific
management was logically linked both as cause and effect to the innovations in machine-tool operation, handling of materials, division of
labour in the shop, and organization of work flows discussed above,
for the establishment of norms rested on an analysis of the production
process and inevitably turned up both weaknesses and possibilities of
improvement. What Taylor preached was a substitution of reason for
habit, a new way of looking at familiar things. It is no coincidence that
he discovered high-speed steel; or that he worked out correct tensions
and speeds for power belting and an efficient procedure for the
maintenance of what had always been the responsibility of no one in
particular (like oiling or grinding). The point is that his search for an

optimum pace of work led him to study and set standards of efficiency for every aspect of production.[1]

Almost as early, however, Europeans were doing their own thinking and writing on plant management, and parallel ideas were finding occasional and discrete application. In 1896 J. Slater Lewis, head of the electrical engineering department of a Manchester steel works, published 'what is apparently the first modern book on factory organization'.[2] By the turn of the century, the leading engineering journals in England and Germany, as well as the United States, were full of the new gospel and supporting their preachments with examples of successful innovation. It is no coincidence, however, that the area of most rapid advance was accounting: it was easier to improve the flow and quality of intelligence than to act upon it. Nevertheless, closer cost controls made possible a more centralized administration of production; it is this, for example, that explains in large part the decline of the so-called 'butty system', in which management subcontracted jobs to master workmen who hired their own assistants on a time basis. The system was generally expensive, but its most serious disadvantages were its nasty implications for discipline and morale: the interposition of an entrepreneur between employer and worker made effective command difficult; and the competition for these contracts gave rise to the kind of wage squeeze that often accompanied the putting-out system. For all this, the butty system was almost indispensable in industries like shipbuilding, where it enabled management to calculate the costs of complicated jobs in advance. Without prediction, there could be no competitive bidding. From the 1890's on, cost accounting was the answer. The office was beginning, but only beginning, to dominate the shop.

Seen from the hindsight of the mid-twentieth century, scientific management was the natural sequel to the process of mechanization that constituted the heart of the Industrial Revolution: first the sub-

---

[1] See Hugh G. J. Aitken, *Taylorism at Watertown Arsenal: Scientific Management in Action, 1908–1915* (Cambridge, Mass., 1960), ch. 1; also M. J. Nadworny, *Scientific Management and the Unions, 1900–1932: a Historical Analysis* (Cambridge, Mass., 1955); Frank B. Copley, *Frederick W. Taylor, Father of Scientific Management* (2 vols.; New York, 1923).

[2] L. H. Jenks, 'Early Phases of the Management Movement', *Administrative Science Quart.* v (1960), 428. This is the best brief survey of the subject and offers an extremely useful bibliography on developments in the United States and Britain. On the latter, see also L. Urwick and E. F. L. Brech, *The Making of Scientific Management* (3 vols.; London, 1949), vols. I and II. There is some historical material on the movement in France in G. Bricard, *L'organisation scientifique du travail* (Paris, 1927). Yet these are poor substitutes for a scholarly study, and the best source remains the contemporary engineering periodicals.

stitution of machines and inanimate power for human skills and strength; then the conversion of the operative into an automaton to match and keep pace with his equipment. The third stage is now upon us: automation—the replacement of man by machines that think as well as do. How far and fast the new technique will go; whether, in combination with atomic power, it will mean a second (or third) Industrial Revolution, it is still too early to say. But it is some consolation to think that it is apparently easier to make machines like man than to turn man into a machine.

Behind this kaleidoscope of change—sometimes marked by brilliant bursts, sometimes tedious in its complex fragmentation, always bewildering in its variety—one general trend is manifest: the ever-closer marriage of science and technology. We have already had occasion to observe the essential independence of these two activities during the Industrial Revolution; and to note that such stimulus and inspiration as did cross the gap went from technology toward science rather than the other way. Beginning in the middle of the nineteenth century, however, a close alliance develops; and if technology continued to pose fruitful problems for scientific research, the autonomous flow of scientific discovery fed a widening stream of new techniques.

How did this marriage come about? The usual answer is that it was the inevitable consequence of increasing knowledge: as the cognitive content and range of both activities grew, they were bound to touch and join forces in certain areas of common concern. Yet in fact, they do not touch, and this is one marriage that requires permanent mediation to work; the gap between science and technology is far too wide for direct communication. The link is provided by two intermediaries: applied science, which has as its aim control rather than knowledge and converts the discoveries of pure science into a form suitable for practical use; and engineering, which takes the generalities of applied science, along with a host of other considerations, economic, legal, and social, and extracts those elements needed to solve a particular technical problem—whether it be building a bridge, designing a plant, or rating a machine.

When one speaks, therefore, of the marriage of science and technology, one really refers to a complex liaison, which was not consecrated at a moment in time but developed slowly and unevenly, and varies to this day from country to country and industry to industry. There are still areas of production that must rely heavily on inspired empiricism. Nevertheless, it was the second half of the nineteenth century that first saw close systematic ties between the two in important branches of industrial activity; and it was success in these areas that set the pattern and provided the incentive for further collaboration.[1]

The reasons for this development may be sought in both the supply of and demand for knowledge. On the side of supply, the establishment as early as the 1790's of institutions of engineering instruction, staffed in part by men of theoretical preparation and bent, made it possible not only to transmit to the students certain elements of contemporary science (which were sometimes erroneous) but more important, to equip them with the tools of analysis and attitudes of mind that make it possible to pass from the abstract to the concrete, the general to the specific. On the side of demand, the nature of the newer fields of industrial activity—organic chemistry and electrical engineering in particular—tended to diminish reliance on the traditional combination of empiricism and common sense and impose a more scientific approach. For these older methods are capable of handling well only what is susceptible to ordinary sensory perception and formulatable in terms of the familiar: one can see a lever lift a weight and deduce from that an accurate principle of mechanical advantage; it is another matter to infer the nature and possibilities of an electric current from observation of its effects. Admittedly the ingenuity of man as tinkerer and doer almost surpasses belief: note the lead of steam engineering over the theory of thermodynamics.[2] The fact remains that the task of invention was getting steadily more complex, the matter of invention more recondite. As a result, applied science was a more efficient key to the unknown, hence more prolific of innovations.

Nor were these accomplishments limited to the newer branches of industry. Everywhere, the growth of scale turned what once had been negligible elements of cost into potentially serious sources of loss: the smallest economy in a steam plant that consumes a ton of coal a minute can save thousands of pounds a year. The result was steady pressure

[1] The precise dating of this progressive marriage of science and technology is a matter of some dispute among students of the subject. There are those who would confine it to the twentieth century, even to the last generation, others who push it back to the nineteenth and in some areas farther. To an outside observer, it would seem that much of the disagreement inheres in the vagueness of the generalizations commonly offered. If a chronology must be attempted, it is clear that the evidences of collaboration from before the mid-nineteenth century are exceptional and often adventitious—essentially prodromes. See the discussion in John Jewkes et al., The Sources of Invention (London, 1960), chs. II and III.

[2] Conversely, there is often an enormous lag between applied science and engineering on the one hand and practice on the other. Thomas Savery's steam-engine of 1698 was a perfectly workable concept; but the metalworkers of the day were simply incapable of building it. R. Jenkins, 'Savery, Newcomen, and the Early History of the Steam Engine', Trans. Newcomen Soc. III (1922-3), 96-118; IV (1923-4), 113-30. We have already noted Watt's difficulties in this regard.

toward more exact and rational design, a trend reinforced by the greater complexity and precision of manufacturing equipment and the closer control of quality in a period of increasing competition. More than ever, the emphasis was on measurement, and the measuring instruments themselves were among the most ingenious applications of pure scientific principles to industrial needs: thus the modern refractometer-goniometer, used in chemical manufacture, and the pyrometer, used in all manner of high-temperature work. Other products of this collaboration between theory and practice were Parsons's steam-turbine, which required a combination of 'all the available resources of mathematics, science, and machine design', and such major innovations in non-ferrous metallurgy as the Hall–Héroult aluminium and Mond nickel processes. Even in iron manufacture, where empiricism and serendipity continued to play a fruitful role into the twentieth century, the need for new materials (as against traditional problems of smelting and refining) made recourse to precise measurement, chemical analysis, and microscopic metallography indispensable.[1] To be sure, these were often simply sharper tools in the service of empiricism. But the emphasis on accurate examination and systematic experiment opened the door to scientific principles, for the man trained to perform the one could often apply the other. And while he could get along without them—and usually did—he could do a lot more with them. Competition took care of the rest.

In general, there was a gradual institutionalization of technological advance. The more progressive industrial enterprises were no longer content to accept innovations and exploit them, but sought them by deliberate, planned experiment. To take just one example: until this century engineers were content to utilize in their work such materials as were readily available from metals producers; but beginning with a branch like the electrical industry, which introduced a whole range of new requirements, the demand for special alloys increased to the point where users were not ready to wait on the pleasure and imagination of suppliers. Laboratory techniques and equipment steadily improved; and increasing amounts were allocated to research. For those who were unable or unwilling to sink capital in permanent plant and staff, scientific and technical consultants were becoming available— division of labour that was evidence in itself of the growth of the market for knowledge. Eventually success nurtured in industry a veritable

[1] Cf. J. K. Finch, 'Engineering and Science: a Historical Review and Appraisal', *Technology and Culture*, II (1961), 329–30; J. K. Feibleman, 'Pure Science, Applied Science, Technology, Engineering: an Attempt at Definitions', *ibid.* pp. 313 f.; M. Kerker, 'Science and the Steam Engine', *ibid.* p. 388; Cyril S. Smith, 'The Interaction of Science and Practice in the History of Metallurgy', *ibid.* pp. 363–4.

mystique of the profitability of science—to the point where enterprise began to finance fundamental as well as practical research.

This cognitive tie between science and practice accelerated enormously the pace of invention. Not only did the autonomous expansion of the frontiers of knowledge yield all manner of unanticipated practical fruits, but industry could now order desiderata from the laboratory as a client a shipment from the mill. In a strange way, the importance of technology as a factor in economic change was thus both heightened and diminished. On the one hand, it became more than ever the key to competitive success and growth. The faster the rate of change, the more important to be able to keep up with the pacemakers. On the other, technology was no longer a relatively autonomous determinant. Instead, it had become just another input, with a relatively elastic supply curve at that.

SOME REASONS WHY

It is now time to pull the threads of our story together and ask our-selves why the different nations of western Europe grew and changed as they did. In particular—for lack of space compels us to select our problems—why did industrial leadership pass in the closing decades of the nineteenth century from Britain to Germany?

The larger interest of this question will not escape the reader. It is of concern not only to the student of economic growth but to the general historian who seeks to understand the course of world politics since 1870. The rapid industrial expansion of a unified Germany was the most important development of the half-century that preceded the First World War—more important even than the comparable growth of the United States, simply because Germany was enmeshed in the European network of power and in this period the fate of the world was in Europe's hands.

In 1788 a perceptive French demographer named Messance wrote: 'The people that last will be able to keep its forges going will perforce be the master; for it alone will have arms.'[1] He was somewhat in advance of his times. In subsequent years the Revolutionary armies and then Napoleon were to show what well-directed manpower—a nation in arms—using traditional weapons, could do to traditional armies. By the 1860's, however, Messance's analysis was borne out, first by the American Civil War, and then by the Franco-Prussian War. It was now *Blut und Eisen* that counted, and all the blood in the world could not compensate for timely, well-directed firepower.

It took a long time for people to adjust to this new basis of power.

[1] M. Messance, *Nouvelles recherches sur la population de la France* (Lyons, 1788), p. 128.

When the Prussian coalition defeated France in 1870, numerous Britons, including the Queen, rejoiced to see the traditional Gallic enemy and disturber of the peace humbled by the honest, sober Teuton. Within fifteen years, however, the British awoke to the fact that the Industrial Revolution and different rates of population growth had raised Germany to Continental hegemony and left France far behind. This was one of the longest 'double-takes' in history: the British had been fighting the Corsican ogre, dead fifty years and more, while Bismarck went his way.

In subsequent decades, this shift in the balance of power was the dominant influence in European international relations. It underlay the gradual re-forming of forces that culminated in the Triple Entente and Triple Alliance; it nourished the Anglo-German political and naval rivalry, as well as French fears of their enemy east of the Rhine; it made war probable and did much to dictate the membership of the opposing camps. It has, I know, been fashionable for more than a generation to deny this interpretation. In the reaction against Marxist slogans of 'imperialist war' and 'the last stage of capitalism', scholars have leaned over backwards to expunge the slightest taint of economic determinism from their lucubrations. Yet doctrine was never a valid guide to knowledge, at either end of the ideological spectrum, and this effort to rule out material considerations as causes of the World War betrays naïveté, or ignorance about the nature of power and the significance of power relations for the definition of national interests.

These political concerns go far to explain Britain's agitated response to German economic expansion. Germany was not, after all, the only country to compete with Britain in the home and foreign markets. American manufactures, particularly machine tools and other devices that placed a premium on ingenuity, invaded the United Kingdom as early as the middle of the century and continued to trouble British producers to the end of our period. And we have already noted the success of Indian and Japanese cottons in the competition for the potentially bottomless Eastern market.

Yet it was Germany that stuck in John Bull's craw. In the decades preceding 1870, she had gradually turned from one of the best markets for British manufactures to a self-sufficient industrial country; one can follow the process in her diminishing dependence on imports of such tell-tale products as cotton yarn (see above, p. 213) and pig iron ($57\frac{1}{2}$ per cent of consumption in 1843 at the height of the railway boom, 34 per cent in 1857, 11 per cent a decade later).[1] After 1870, with the home market won, German industry began to make an important place for itself abroad. Actually, the process had begun before, but it is

[1] Beck, *Geschichte des Eisens*, IV, 696; Benaerts, *Origines*, pp. 460–1.

from this point roughly that the increase in the volume of manufactured exports picked up and the British began to awaken to their new rival. From 1875 to 1895, while the value of British exports stood still, though volume rose by some 63 per cent, the value of German exports rose 30 per cent and volume correspondingly more. At the same time, where only 44 per cent of German exports were finished products in 1872, 62 per cent fell into this category in 1900 (as against 75 per cent for the United Kingdom).[1]

Moreover, the particulars of the trend were more disturbing than the general tide. There was, for example, the export of German iron and steel to areas that Britain had come to look on as a private preserve—Australia, South America, China, Britain herself. There was the marked superiority of Germany in the newer branches of manufacture: organic chemicals from the 1880's, electrical equipment from the 1890's. Above all, there were the 'unfair' methods allegedly employed by the Teuton: he sold meretricious, shoddy merchandise, often under the guise of British articles; he accepted training engagements with British houses in order to spy out a trade; he pandered to the tastes of the natives and seduced them by concessions to their ignorance—to the point of translating sales catalogues into their language. Complaints reached a peak during what Ross Hoffman called the 'midsummer madness of 1896'.[2] Parliamentary orators exercised their eloquence on government purchases of Bavarian pencils, or the importation of brushes made by German convict labour; newspapers denounced the purchase of cheap German garments, many of them produced from reclaimed British woollens. No item was too small to heap on the flames of indignation: playing-cards, musical instruments, buggy whips.[3]

To be sure, it is easy to demonstrate the exaggeration of these alarms. Germany's gains still left her far behind Britain as a commercial power: the volume of her trade in 1895 was perhaps three-fifths as great; the tonnage of her merchant marine only a sixth as large. British commerce was still growing, losses in one market were generally compensated by gains in another, her industry had not forgotten how to meet compe-

[1] Germany, *Statistisches Jahrbuch* (1908), p. 125; Schlote, *British Overseas Trade*, p. 125. The 1872 figure is from France, *Annu. statistique*, XLVIII (1932), *rés. rétro.* p. 408, which gives the 1900 German percentage as 65.

[2] *Great Britain and the German Trade Rivalry, 1875–1914* (Philadelphia, 1933).

[3] On all this, see D. S. Landes, 'Entrepreneurship in Advanced Industrial Countries: the Anglo-German Rivalry', in *Entrepreneurship and Economic Growth* (Papers presented at a Conference sponsored jointly by the Committee on Economic Growth of the Social Science Research Council and the Harvard University Research Center in Entrepreneurial History, Cambridge, Mass., 12 and 13 November 1954).

tition. Moreover, the difference in overall rates of growth between the two countries was considerably smaller than the discrepancy in rates of industrial growth would lead one to expect. Where British output of manufactured commodities (including minerals and processed food) slightly more than doubled from 1870 to 1913, against a German increase of almost sixfold, the ratio between the rising incomes of the two countries, whether calculated in aggregate or *per capita*, was of the order of 0·7 or 0·8 to 1.[1]

In part this paradox simply reflected a shift in resources. More mature than Germany, Britain was beginning to develop her service sector (distribution, transport, banking and insurance) at the expense of

Table 15. *Capital Formation as Share of National Product*
(in percentages)

		United Kingdom				Germany[a]		
		NDCF/NDP		NNCF/NNP		NDCF/NNP	NNCF/NNP	
U.K.	Germany	Cur-rent prices	Con-stant prices	Cur-rent prices	Con-stant prices	Cur-rent prices	Cur-rent prices	Con-stant prices
	1851–60					8·4	8·6	7·9
1860–9		7·2	8·6	10·0	11·5			
	1861–70					8·5	9·7	10·6
1870–9		8·2	7·3	11·8	10·9			
	1871–80					11·6	13·5	13·0
1880–9		6·4	3·4	10·9	8·1			
	1881–90					11·2	14·0	14·5
1890–9		7·3	3·0	10·1	6·0			
	1891–1900					13·9	15·4	15·9
1895–1904		8·8	4·8	10·5	6·7			
1900–9		8·2	4·1	11·7	7·8			
	1901–13					15·6	16·5	15·9
1905–14		6·7	1·2	13·0	8·0			

[a] 1913 boundaries.

ABBREVIATIONS
  NDCF Net Domestic Capital Formation.
  NDP   Net Domestic Product.
  NNCF Net National Capital Formation.
  NNP   Net National Product.

SOURCE. S. Kuznets, 'Quantitative Aspects of the Economic Growth of Nations: VI. Long-Term Trends in Capital Formation Proportions', *Economic Development and Cultural Change*, IX, 4, part II (July 1961), 58, 59, 64.

[1] On production of *Sachgüter*, see R. Wagenführ, 'Die Industriewirtschaft: Entwicklungstendenzen der deutschen und internationalen Industrieproduktion 1860 bis 1932', *Vierteljahrshefte zur Konjunkturforschung* (ed. Institut für Konjunkturforschung), Sonderheft 31 (Berlin, 1933), pp. 58, 69.

manufacturing industry; so that the share of the latter in national product diminished steadily. The increase in foreign holdings had similar statistical consequences.[1] In part, however, Britain's relatively good overall performance was the result of a more efficient allocation of resources. The rapidity of German industrial expansion had left important sectors of the economy behind, protected from the shock of obsolescence and the logic of marginal rationality by human foibles and such institutional devices as protective tariffs. A surprisingly large area of manufacturing, for example, clung tenaciously to hand processes and domestic production;[2] and where Britain had liquidated the less remunerative aspects of her agriculture, a sizable fraction of the German population continued to live on the soil.[3] The German economy, in

[1] On the eve of the First World War, Britain earned almost £200 million a year by business services to the rest of the world—just about as much as she derived from her enormous foreign investments. The two together represented more than a sixth of national income. A. H. Imlah, *Economic Elements in the Pax Britannica: Studies in British Foreign Trade in the Nineteenth Century* (Cambridge, Mass., 1958), table 4, pp. 70–5.

[2] Of 10,873,701 people engaged in mining and manufacture in 1907, almost 30 % (3,166,734) were self-employed or worked in enterprises of five persons or less. Dispersed home production was common in clothing and textiles, leather and woodwork, toy manufacture, food processing and a host of minor metal trades. In these areas Wilhelmian Germany was just beginning to go through the process of modernization that Britain had largely traversed by 1870, as the spate of contemporary studies on the problem of the *Hausarbeiter* testifies.
The best brief introduction to the subject is W. Sombart, 'Verlagssystem (Hausindustrie)', in J. Conrad *et al.*, eds., *Handwörterbuch der Staatswissenschaften* (3rd ed., Jena, 1911), vol. VIII. There is a convenient guide to the literature in Belgium, Ministère du Travail, *Bibliographie générale des industries à domicile* [Supplément à la publication: *Les industries à domicile en Belgique*] (Brussels, 1908). Sombart offers a list of materials published in the years immediately following.

[3] How large the discrepancy was between input and output in agriculture, not only in Germany, but throughout Europe, may be inferred from the following table:

Place of Agriculture in Selected Economies, c. 1891–96 (in percentages)

	Share of population dependent thereon	Share of national wealth	Share of national income
Russia	70	43	32
Austria	62	39	27
Italy	52	45	28
France	42	32	21
Germany	39	31	20
United States	35	25	16
Belgium	25	36	14
Holland	22	33	18
Great Britain	10	15	8

other words, presented some of those contrasts between advanced and backward sectors that we have come to call dualism and to associate with rapid, unbalanced growth.[1]

Even so, compound interest is a remorseless arbiter. The difference in the rates of growth cannot be blinked: any projection of the trends constitutes a judgment unfavourable to Britain. And this is the more true in that the discrepancy between the two countries applied not only to national income, that is, the yield of today, but also to capital formation, that is, the yield of tomorrow. Here the contrast was particularly striking: as Britain slowed down, Germany speeded up (see Table 15).

Table 16. *Germany and United Kingdom: Foreign Investment as Percentage of Total Net Capital Formation (at current prices)*

Germany		United Kingdom	
1851/5–1861/5	2·2	1855–64	29·1
1861/5–1871/5	12·9	1865–74	40·1
1871/5–1881/5	14·1	1875–84	28·9
1881/5–1891/5	19·9	1885–94	51·2
1891/5–1901/5	9·7	1895–1904	20·7
1901/5–1911/13	5·7	1905–14	52·9

SOURCES. The German series is from a manuscript kindly furnished by Professor Simon Kuznets and based on information from Professor Walter Hoffman. The series for the United Kingdom is based on Imlah's calculation of foreign balance on current account, *Economic Elements in the Pax Britannica*, pp. 70–5, and on estimates of net domestic capital formation kindly communicated by Miss Phyllis Deane.

At this point, moreover, our aggregate statistics join our qualitative and micro-quantitative data. All the evidence agrees on the technological backwardness of much of British manufacturing industry—on

SOURCE. M. G. Mulhall, *Dictionary of Statistics* (4th ed., London, 1909), p. 615.

On the winnowing of British agriculture, see T. W. Fletcher, 'The Great Depression of English Agriculture, 1873–1896', *Econ. Hist. Rev.* XIII (1961), 417–32.

[1] In this sense, the pre-First World War German economy was comparable to the Japanese. See Henry Rosovsky, *Capital Formation in Japan, 1868–1940* (Glencoe, Ill., 1960), ch. IV, who argues, however, that the persistence of a labour-intensive traditional sector released resources for the costly installations of the modern sector and thereby promoted Japanese growth. The thesis is a provocative one. It does not seem applicable to the German case.

One should carefully distinguish, incidentally, between this dualism of growth, inherent in the inevitable unevenness of development, and the dualism of the colonial economy, in which the modern installations of foreign administration and enterprise contrast sharply with the primitiveness of indigenous life; or the dualism of a semi-stagnant economy like that of Spain or southern Italy (at least until very recently), in which a few gleaming cities, or merely city districts, and other isolated expressions of modern technology are scattered over a countryside little different from what it was two millennia ago.

leads lost, opportunities missed, markets relinquished that need not have been. These are themes that have recurred in every official inquiry, every report of a travelling delegation, for the last two generations. And the very spurts that certain branches have made from time to time are evidence of an effort to catch up and of previously unexploited potential. There is no doubt, in short, that British industry was not so vigorous and adaptable from the 1870's on as it could have been. Why?

Before attempting to answer this question, it may be useful to clear the ground by ruling out the usual congenial explanations. Thus Britain's industrial resources were as good as those of any other European country in the late nineteenth century. In the whole world, only the United States surpassed her in coal output; and no country possessed better coal for power, metallurgy, or chemical manufacture. One of the ironies of economic history is that Germany, which almost monopolized the production of coal-tar derivatives, drew much of her tar from the United Kingdom.[1] Much has been made of the great Lorraine iron deposits and their suitability for the production of Thomas steel; but England had her own large deposits of phosphoric ores in the East Midlands, far closer to good coking coal than the Lorraine beds and just as easily mined. As for those industrial materials which had to come from the outside—cotton, for example, and almost all wool—England was better situated than her European competitors. No nation had so wide a commercial network at its command, and it was no accident that almost all the major primary commodities had their central markets in Liverpool and London. To be sure, England's relative importance as a re-exporter of the world's merchandise declined somewhat as countries like Germany, France and the United States learned to buy directly from producing areas; but they—and other countries still less—never learned to by-pass the British entrepôt entirely, and the absolute value of this re-export trade continued to rise right up to the war. Actually, commodities like cotton and wool tended to be a few pennies cheaper in Liverpool and other British ports than in Le Havre and Hamburg; and though the difference was not great, foreign industrialists thought it great enough to buy there.

Nor was the smaller size or slightly slower rate of increase of the British population a disadvantage. From the standpoint of labour

[1] Marshall, *Industry and Trade*, p. 195. On the advantageous resource position of the British chemical industry, both for organic and inorganic processes, and Germany's dependence on imports for a significant fraction of her consumption of things like pitch, tar, and anthracene, cf. *Parliamentary Papers*, 1901, LXXX, no. 2, 'Report on Chemical Instruction in Germany and the Growth and Present Condition of the German Chemical Industries', pp. 42, 68.

supply, it was Germany rather than Britain who found it difficult to meet the needs of growing industries toward the end of the century; among other things, she had to move tens of thousands of people from the villages of Pomerania and East Prussia clear across the country to the mills of Westphalia and the Rhineland. As for demand, although the German home market was no doubt growing faster and was potentially greater, British manufacturers actually had most of the known world for an outlet. Here again, their wide-flung, experienced commercial relations gave them an important initial advantage over potential competitors. Even in certain German colonies, British traders and planters long held a pre-eminent position because of their earlier establishment in these areas, their familiarity with the problems and possibilities of backward regions, and the greater willingness of the British investor to put his money into distant ventures.[1]

Finally, Britain had more capital to work with than Germany. Her role as precursor of industrialization had made possible an unprecedented accumulation of wealth, which spilled over her boundaries in increasing abundance from the late eighteenth century on. The first of a series of booms in foreign funds occurred in the 1820's, and by the middle of the century the London Exchange had taken on that cosmopolitan colour that distinguished it from all others. It was and remained, in spite of the rivalry of the Paris Bourse toward the end of the century, the world's most important international securities market, whether for funds, rails, mining shares, or industrial and agricultural ventures.[2]

Germany, by contrast, was a net importer of capital throughout the first two-thirds of the nineteenth century. And even after, the appetite of her burgeoning industry was such that foreign placements never took more than a small fraction of savings available for investment. For a long time indeed, the government discouraged the export of capital on the explicit ground that domestic needs were urgent and should receive priority. This attitude later yielded to other considerations—the desire to develop an empire and to extend German political influence abroad.[3] Even so, and in spite of the rapid ramification of German bank interests throughout the world, the outflow of funds was sporadic

[1] Cf. W. O. Henderson, 'British Economic Activity in the German Colonies, 1884-1914', Econ. Hist. Rev. xv (1945), 55-66.

[2] The best source remains L. H. Jenks, The Migration of British Capital to 1875 (New York, 1928). See also Landes, Bankers and Pashas, chs. I and II; A. K. Cairncross, Home and Foreign Investment 1870-1913 (Cambridge, 1953); and Imlah, Economic Elements in the Pax Britannica.

[3] The traditional hostility to foreign lending remained strong notwithstanding, and the ministries of Finance and Foreign Affairs were often divided on the issue. See Herbert Feis, Europe the World's Banker, 1870-1914 (New Haven, 1930), ch. VI.

and from the 1890's on represented a diminishing portion of net capital formation (Table 16).

This hunger for money was reflected in a continued gap of one to two points between the rate of interest in Berlin and those rates prevailing in the other markets of western Europe. Short-term funds moved back and forth with the business cycle, but the net balance favoured Germany, even *vis-à-vis* a country like France which discouraged lending to a former enemy. French banks may have been reluctant to entrust their funds to domestic industry, as undeserving of confidence; but they thought German banks a good risk, and these passed the money on to their own entrepreneurs. Financially this procedure was unexceptionable; politically it had the makings of a scandal.

No, the reasons for German success in the competition with Britain were not material but rather social and institutional, implicit once again in what has been called the economics of backwardness.

There were, first, certain disadvantages inherent in chronological priority: not so much, however, the oft-cited costs of breaking the path as the so-called 'related costs' of adjustment to subsequent change. The former have been much overemphasized. Admittedly a pioneer in any field incurs additional expense owing to ignorance and inexperience; and in theory those who follow may profit by his mistakes. Yet this assumes on the part of the imitators a wisdom that historical experience belies. If the pioneer often sins on the side of excessive modesty, the follower often suffers from excessive ambition; if the one does not quite know where he is going, the other knows too well and undoes himself by his eagerness. There is such a thing, as technicians of the late nineteenth century were careful to point out, as machines that are too big, engines too powerful, plants that are too capital-intensive.

Far more serious are the burdens imposed by interrelatedness, that is, the technical linkage between the component parts of the industrial plant of an enterprise or economy. In principle, the entrepreneur is free to choose at any time the most remunerative technique available. In fact, his calculus is complicated by his inability to confine it to the technique under consideration. For one thing—and here we shall stress the point of view of the enterprise—no piece of equipment works in a void: the engine, the machine it drives, and the means by which it transmits its power are all built to fit; similarly the number and kinds of machines employed, as well as the capacity and type of channels for supply, transfer, and removal of raw and finished material are rationally calculated in relation to one another. As a result, the replacement of one unit of equipment by another, or the introduction of a new device, can rarely if ever be considered in isolation. What is more, the decision on a given change does not always lie entirely within the enterprise but will depend rather, in greater or lesser degree, on the co-operation of out-side units. New assembly techniques, for example, may require new standards of accuracy, hence new equipment, in the plants of sub-contractors; more rapid loading facilities may yield far less than their possibilities if carriers do not adjust their methods to the new tempo. In such cases, the allocation of cost and risk poses a serious obstacle, not only because calculation is objectively difficult but even more because human beings are typically suspicious and stubborn in this kind of bargaining situation.[1]

On the other hand—and here we are considering the problem from the standpoint of the economy—large-scale, mechanized manufacture requires not only machines and buildings, but a heavy investment in what has been called social capital: in particular, roads, bridges, ports, and transportation systems; and schools for general and technical education. Because these are costly, because the investment required is lumpy and far exceeds the means of the individual enterprise, and because, finally, the return on such outlays is often long deferred, they constitute a heavy burden for any pre-industrial economy condemned by its technological backwardness to low productivity. Moreover, the burden has tended to grow with the increasing size of industrial plant, so that today many of the so-called underdeveloped countries are trapped in a vicious circle of poverty and incapacity. The much-vaunted freedom of the latecomer to choose the latest and best equip-ment on the basis of the most advanced techniques has become a myth.

There are thus two kinds of related costs: the one, micro-economic, falls most heavily on the early industrializer; the other, essentially macro-economic, falls most heavily on the follower country. The relative weights of the two have never been measured historically, nor is it likely that the information at our command will ever permit such a calculation. It would seem, however, that the ratio has varied over time. If the balance today favours the advanced countries, whose lead in output and in standard of living continues to grow, the advantage lay the other way in the middle and late nineteenth century. By that time Germany 1 ad built up a more productive stock of social capital than Britain (she was never so far behind as the 'backward' countries of

---

[1] On the comparative advantages and disadvantages of priority, see F. R. J. Jervis, 'The Handicap of Britain's Early Start', *The Manchester School*, XVI (1947); M. Frankel, 'Obsolescence and Technological Change', *Amer. Econ. Rev.* XLV (1955), 296–319; and an exchange between D. F. Gordon and Marvin Frankel on the same subject, *ibid.* XLVI (1956), 646–56. Also W. E. G. Salter, *Productivity and Technical Change* (Cambridge, 1960); and C. P. Kindelberger, 'Obsolescence and Technical Change', *Bull. Oxford University Institute of Statistics*, XXIII (1961), 281–97.

today), while the related costs of growth fell to the enterprises of the unhappy pioneer. All of British industry suffered from the legacy of precocious urbanization; the cities of the early nineteenth century were not built to accommodate the factories of the twentieth (logistics again!). Steel plants, especially, with cramped, ill-shaped sites, found it difficult to integrate backward to smelting or forward to finishing; and lack of integration in turn inhibited adoption of a number of important innovations, among them by-product coking. Similarly, railways and colliery owners were long unable to agree on the adoption of larger freight trucks; and the electrical industry was crippled for decades by the initial diversity of methods of supply. The very sight of the spacious arrangements of the Homestead plant in the United States made Windsor Richards wish he 'could pull down the whole works at Bolckow's and start afresh'.[1] If wishes were horses, beggars would ride.

Where, then, the gap between leader and follower is not too large to begin with, that is, where it does not give rise to self-reinforcing poverty, the advantage lies with the latecomer. And this is the more so because the effort of catching up calls forth entrepreneurial and institutional responses that, once established, constitute powerful stimuli to continued growth.

The French, among others, have a saying: 'It is easier to become rich than to stay rich' (compare the related apothegm, 'shirtsleeves to shirtsleeves in three generations'). However sceptical those of us who have not had the opportunity to test this aphorism may be of its general validity, it clearly rests on empirical observation of the rise and fall of fortunes. On the one hand, prosperity and success are their own worst enemies; on the other, there is no spur like envy.

Thus the Britain of the late nineteenth century basked complacently in the sunset of economic hegemony. In many firms, the grandfather who started the business and built it by unremitting application and by thrift bordering on miserliness had long died; the father who took over a solid enterprise and, starting with larger ambitions, raised it to undreamed-of heights, had passed on the reins; now it was the turn of the third generation, the children of affluence, tired of the tedium of trade and flushed with the bucolic aspirations of the country gentleman. (One might more accurately speak of 'shirtsleeves to hunting jacket—or dress coat, or ermine robes—in three generations'.) Many of them retired and forced the conversion of their firms into joint-stock companies. Others stayed on and went through the motions of entrepreneurship between the long weekends; they worked at play and played at work. Some of them were wise enough to leave the management of their enterprises to professionals, comparable in privilege and

[1] In the *J. Iron and Steel Institute*, LI (1897), 106.

function to the steward of the medieval domain. Yet such an arrangement is at best a poor substitute for interested ownership; at its worst, it
is an invitation to conflict of interests and misfeasance. The annals of
history are full of enriched and ennobled stewards, bailiffs, *Meier*, valets,
and the like.

Nor were corporate enterprises significantly better. For one thing,
family considerations often determined their selection of managing
personnel. For another, such scanty and impressionistic evidence as we
have indicates that private and public companies alike recruited too
many of their executives from the counting room rather than from the
shop.[1] And such production men as were elevated to high responsibility were more likely than not to be 'practical' people who had
learned on the job and had a vested interest in the established way of
doing things.

The weaknesses of British enterprise reflected this combination of
amateurism and complacency. Her merchants, who had once seized
the markets of the world, took them for granted; the consular reports
are full of the incompetence of British exporters, their refusal to suit their
goods to the taste and pockets of the client, their unwillingness to try
new products in new areas, their insistence that everyone in the world
ought to read English and count in pounds, shillings, and pence.
Similarly, the British manufacturer was notorious for his indifference
to style, his conservatism in the face of new techniques, his reluctance
to abandon the individuality of tradition for the conformity implicit in
mass production.

By contrast, the German entrepreneur of the late nineteenth century
was generally a *novus homo*; he was almost bound to be, given the
lateness and rapidity of the country's industrialization. Often he was a
technician, formally trained for his work; trained or not trained,
however, he was utterly serious. He worked long hours and expected
his subordinates to do likewise; he watched every *pfennig*, knew every
detail of his firm's operations. The observers of the day join in picturing
him as supple, ingenious, aggressive to the point of pushingness, and
occasionally unscrupulous. He had no antiquated veneration of quality
for its own sake, was skilled in meretricious presentation, accommodat-
ing on terms of sale, energetic in prospecting for new customers and
tenacious in serving them.

Yet these unflattering comparisons, which ring true and conform to
the historical experience of similar rivalries (compare the inflexibility
of the declining Italian cloth industry of the seventeenth and eighteenth

---

[1] Cf. Charlotte Erickson, *British Industrialists: Steel and Hosiery, 1850–1950* (Cambridge, 1959), ch. VIII, esp. p. 194.

centuries),[1] also contain a great deal of caricature. For one thing, a certain amount of exaggeration is built into any contrast of this kind. For another, the evidence is biased, to a degree that is hard to assess. Contemporary observers emphasized the failures of British entrepreneurship and the imminent dangers of German competition much as a newspaper cries up the morbid aspects of the news. That was the way one sold articles or attracted the notice of officials in London. Besides, there is such a thing as fashion in opinions, and this was clearly one of the popular dirges of the day.

The question is a complicated one. Berrick Saul has shown that a number of British enterprises in fields like engineering reacted vigorously and imaginatively to foreign competition in the years before the First World War. He cites an American consular report of 1906: 'No one who has not lived in England during the last seven or eight years can realize how great has been the awakening here nor how changed the British mental attitude is regarding new ways of doing things. There has been much wise and clever adaptation to British cheaper labor of American machinery ideas.'[2]

In certain fields, then, the lag was probably diminishing. Yet there was still a great deal to be accomplished, as the wartime inquiries into these same industries were to show. Moreover, this very irregularity of pace and this uneven distribution of technological advance pose important questions for the economic historian. If many older enterprises were complacent, why did younger units not take advantage of the opportunity to push them aside? In other words, why did not change diffuse more rapidly? And what of new industries like electrical engineering and organic chemicals, where hardening of the arteries had not set in?

A number of considerations suggest themselves. There were the usual market frictions. Macro-economic change is rarely abrupt, simply because the system works imperfectly. The nature of the competitive imperfections of the British economy before 1914 is a subject well worth investigating. This was in principle the freest market in the world—no barrier to outside products and, as we have seen, a limited movement toward formal cartelization. Yet only a close study of actual buying and selling practices will show the extent to which habit, personal ties, and sheer inertia distorted the play of competition.

A second support of conservatism was increasing difficulty of entry.

---

[1] See the interesting article by Carlo Cipolla, 'The Decline of the Italian Cloth Manufacture: the Case of a Fully Matured Economy', *Econ. Hist. Rev.* 2nd ser. v (1952), 178–87.

[2] S. B. Saul, 'The American Impact on British Industry 1895–1914', *Business History*, III (1960), 28.

This was most severe in heavy industry, especially in branches like metallurgy, where site and ready access to scarce mineral resources were critically important; but the increase in the scale of enterprise and consequently in initial capital requirements was general, and it was no longer an easy matter for an individual or even a group of partners to undertake the manufacture of a mass-market commodity.

There were exceptions. Trades like clothing, where taste played a role, the vagaries of fashion limited standardization, and equipment was inexpensive and shop production feasible, continued to beckon to newcomers. And there was a steady proliferation of small repair and maintenance units, not only in the older machine trades, but in new fields like bicycle and electrical repair. A few of these firms became giants—one has only to think of the beginnings of the British or, for that matter, any motor car industry. The bulk, however, performed modestly; economies of scale were limited, and with them the scope for entrepreneurial ability; and while the rate of entry was high, so was the death rate.

All of this was connected with a general turning away of talent from the older branches of manufacture, whose inadequacy of reward at once justified and was aggravated by this abandonment. The area of greatest opportunity for new men lay in catering to the needs of a long-enriched business class freed of the habit and necessity of abstinence, of a labour force enjoying for the first time an income above the minimum of decency, of a growing rentier class reposing on the returns from home and overseas investments. Mass leisure had become a powerful market force, for the first time in European history, and the service sector grew apace—not only banking, insurance and the professions, but the whole range of activities that provide for recreation and travel. It began to look as though Britons would soon be living by transferring back and forth the income received from the work of others. The image was caricature, but it testified to the direction of economic change. The situation offers some interesting analogies to that of eighteenth-century Holland.[1]

Finally, there were two difficulties that afflicted the entire industrial sector, but above all its newest branches: scarcity of skills and scarcity of venture capital.

Skills are learned. And the supply of skills to industry is essentially dependent on education. To observe this, however, is merely to state a truism. To do more, one must begin by breaking down this omnibus

[1] Cf. the studies of Charles Wilson: 'The Economic Decline of the Netherlands', *Econ. Hist. Rev.* IX (1939), 111–27; and *Anglo-Dutch Commerce and Finance in the Eighteenth Century* (Cambridge, 1941).

word 'education' and relating its content to the requirements of production.

By education we really mean the imparting of four kinds of knowledge, each with its own contribution to make to economic performance: (1) the ability to read, write, and calculate; (2) the working skills of the craftsman and mechanic; (3) the engineer's combination of scientific principle and applied training; and (4) high-level scientific knowledge, theoretical and applied. In all four areas, Germany represented the best that Europe had to offer; in all four, with the possible exception of the second, Britain fell far behind.

The first raises special problems of evaluation. It is not easy to define and assess the relationship of primary education to industrial efficiency. The more obvious connections are probably the least important. Thus, although certain workers—supervisory and office personnel in particular—must be able to read and do the elementary arithmetical operations in order to perform their duties, a large share of the work of industry can be performed by illiterates; as indeed it was, especially in the early days of the Industrial Revolution. Probably the main economic advantages of an extensive, well-run system of compulsory elementary education, therefore, are first, the foundation it provides for more advanced work, and second, its tendency to facilitate and stimulate mobility and to promote thereby a selection of talent to fit the needs of the society. It helps optimize, in short, the allocation of human resources.

Yet it is one thing to point out the significance of this mechanism and another to measure its effectiveness. No empirical studies of the relationships between education and selection on the one hand, between selection and industrial performance on the other, exist for our period. All we have is qualitative observations, plus data on length and generality of schooling and on some of the more elementary cognitive consequences of instruction—notably percentages of literacy. The rest we are obliged to infer.

For what these data are worth—and they are subject to serious caution when used for international comparisons—they show an enormous gap between British and German achievements in this area. On the one hand, we have a nation that until the closing decades of the century preferred to leave schooling to the zeal, indifference, or exploitation of private enterprise. It was not only a question of laissez-faire. For every idealist or visionary who saw in education the path of an enlightened citizenry, there were several 'practical' men who felt that instruction was a superfluous baggage for farm labourers and industrial workers. These people, after all, had been ploughing fields or weaving cloth since time beyond recall without knowing how to read or write; not only was there no reason to change now, but in the last analysis, all they would learn in school was discontent. As a result of this indifference and resistance, it was not until 1870 that local boards were empowered to draft by-laws of compulsory attendance; and not until 1880 was primary instruction made obligatory throughout the kingdom.

Under the circumstances, Britain did well to have roughly half of her school-age children receiving some kind of elementary instruction around 1860. At least this was the finding of the Newcastle Commission, which was exceptionally tolerant of hearsay evidence and tended to view the situation with invincible optimism.[1] There was good reason to believe that many if not most of these students honoured their classrooms by their absence more than their presence; and that in some of the large industrial centres, attendance was lower in the 1860's than it had been a generation before.[2] Even granting the accuracy of the Newcastle estimates, one notes that only two-fifths of these children went to schools inspected by the state; and only one quarter of these remained long enough to enter the upper classes, the only ones that were 'reasonably efficient'.

The situation improved considerably in later years. At least attendance increased sharply from 1870 on and the content of elementary education was enriched by the simple act of assimilating the instruction of the generality of schools to the modest standards of the inspected institutions. Even so, the system remained sterilized by invidious prejudice and the constraints of pathological social conditions. Thus it was widely assumed that aptitude for instruction—or more subtly, ability to use instruction—was a function of class, and that the content and level of training should be suited to the student's station in life. 'The Education Act of 1870,' wrote H. G. Wells, 'was not an Act for common universal education, it was an Act to educate the lower classes for employment on lower class lines, and with specially trained, inferior teachers who had no university quality.'[3] In short, it was not intended to find and advance talent. But one could go further: whatever the ostensible aims of compulsory elementary education, its essential function (what Robert Merton might call its latent function) was not even to instruct. Rather it was to discipline a growing mass of disaffected proletarians and integrate them into British society. Its object

[1] See *Parliamentary Papers*, 1861, xxi (Cd. 2794).
[2] Frank Smith, *A History of English Elementary Education, 1760–1902* (London, 1931), pp. 280–1.
[3] In his *Experiment in Autobiography*, cited by G. A. N. Lowndes, *The Silent Social Revolution: an Account of the Expansion of Public Education in England and Wales, 1895–1935* (London, 1937), p. 5.

was to civilize the barbarians; as Her Majesty's Inspector for London
put it, 'if it were not for her five hundred elementary schools London
would be overrun by a horde of young savages'.[1]

Compulsory elementary education goes back in parts of Germany to
the sixteenth century; in Prussia, Frederick the Great issued his *General
Landschulreglement* in 1763. The quality of the instruction was often
poor—teaching posts were long looked upon as excellent places for old
soldiers—but improved with time. By the early nineteenth century,
the school systems of Germany were famed throughout Europe, and
travellers like Madame de Staël and observers like Victor Cousin made
it a point to visit and examine this greatest achievement of a knowledge-
hungry people.

The obligation of children to attend primary school was enforced—
as laws usually are in Germany: in Prussia in the 1860's, the proportion
of children of school age attending class was about 97½ per cent;[2] in
Saxony, it was actually over 100 per cent.[3] More important than
quantitative results, however, were the character and content of the
system. To begin with, it was the expression of a deep-rooted conviction that schooling was a cornerstone of the social edifice; that the
state not only had an obligation to instruct its citizenry, but found its
advantage therein, since an educated people is a moral and strong
people. Secondly, the very antiquity of the system obviated the
emphasis on debarbarization that marked the first generation of compulsory education in Britain. Observers from abroad were impressed
by the neatness and decorum of German schoolchildren, from whatever class; the schools were consequently free to concentrate their
efforts on instruction. Thirdly, schooling tended to last longer than in
Britain, and the elementary classes were linked to so-called 'middle'
and secondary grades in such a way that some selection of talent
occurred. The process was only moderately effective; in large areas,
particularly rural districts, it was inoperative. Yet even in the middle
decades of the nineteenth century, visitors were impressed by the
catholicity of recruitment of the continuation (as well as the elementary) schools: 'They are generally very well attended by the children
of small shopkeepers,' wrote Joseph Kay in 1850, 'and contain also
many children from the poorest ranks of society.'[4]

---

[1] *Ibid.* p. 19.

[2] It had been 43% in 1816, 68% in 1846. Prussia, *Mittheilungen des Statistischen
Bureaus in Berlin* (ed. Dieterici), 1847, p. 47.

[3] The excess is to be accounted for by children under six or over fourteen years of
age, and by a number of foreign students. France, Min. de l'Agriculture, du Commerce et des Travaux Publics, *Enquête sur l'enseignement professionnel* (2 vols.; Paris,
1865), II, 7f.

[4] J. Kay, *The Social Condition and Education of the People in England and Europe*

It hardly needs saying that the above discussion does some violence to the complexity of the contrast between the two countries. One can find some striking bright spots in the British achievement—certain elementary and grammar schools, for example, which provided excellent instruction to poor scholars and children of well-to-do parents alike; just as one can find among the Junkers of East Elbia instances of a benighted hostility to education to match anything in Britain.[1] Similarly, one could discuss endlessly the merits of the educational philosophies of the two countries, not only because the subject is intrinsically open to contention, but because it is almost impossible to reconcile the contradictory mass of impressionistic evidence. Was one system of elementary instruction more given to 'cramming' than another? one more practical, the other more liberal? one more devoted to facts, the other to ability to think? No categorical answer is possible.

The link between formal vocational, technical, and scientific education on the one hand and industrial progress on the other is more direct and evident. Moreover, it became closer in the course of the nineteenth century, for reasons that can be deduced from our earlier discussion of technology. To begin with, the greater complexity and precision of manufacturing equipment and the closer control of quality, in conjunction with the growing cost of inefficiency and pressure of competition, conduced to higher standards of technical knowledge and proficiency, especially on the upper levels of the productive hierarchy and among the designers of industrial plant. Secondly, the high cost of equipment made on-the-job training increasingly expensive and helped break down an apprenticeship system that had long been moribund. And finally, the changed scientific content of technology

(2 vols.; London, 1850), II, 227. Kay returns to this theme repeatedly: '...I *constantly* found the children of the highest and of the lowest ranks sitting at the same desk....' *Ibid.* p. 209; also pp. 74–5, 80.

Compare the introduction of universal education in Japan in the 1870's, which was hastened and facilitated by similarly deep-rooted social values. According to Ronald Dore, the acceptance of the Confucian principle that virtue consists in knowledge of one's station and respect for one's superiors, implied the necessity of education for all, but especially for the lower classes, who had that much more virtue to acquire. (See his *Education in Tokugawa Japan* (Berkeley and Los Angeles, 1965), ch. x: 'The Legacy'.) The system ostensibly aimed, then, at least before the Meiji period, at reducing ambition and mobility. Yet latent functions are often more important than manifest ones, and history is full of unanticipated consequences.

[1] Cf. R. H. Samuel and R. H. Thomas, *Education and Society in Modern Germany* (London, 1949), pp. 6–7.

compelled supervisory employees and even workers to familiarize themselves with new concepts, and enhanced enormously the value of personnel trained to keep abreast of scientific novelty, appreciate its economic significance, and adapt it to the requirements of production.

It would serve no useful purpose to paint in detail the familiar chiaroscuro of the late and stunted growth of technical and scientific education in Britain as against the vigorous, precociously developed German system. Briefly, where Britain left technical training, like primary education, to private enterprise, which led in the event to a most uneven and inadequate provision of facilities, the German states generously financed a whole gamut of institutions, erecting buildings, installing laboratories, and above all maintaining competent and, at the highest level, distinguished faculties. Until the middle of the century, Britain had nothing but the young University of London, the good, bad, and indifferent mechanics' institutes, occasional evening lectures or classes, and courses in the rudiments of science in a few enlightened secondary and grammar schools. After that, improvement came slowly, though the pace picked up measurably after about 1880. The first gains came around the middle of the century in scientific education (Royal College of Chemistry in 1845; Government School of Mines, 1851; Owen's College, Manchester, 1851; university degrees in science, 1850's); they came at the highest level and for many years were partially vitiated by the above-mentioned failure of the primary and secondary schools to find and prepare recruits. Technical and vocational training had to wait another generation and suffered right through the inter-war period from the same handicap. On the eve of the First World War, the British system still had a long way to go to catch up with the German—at least from the standpoint of economic productivity. (There were social and psychological aspects of the Teutonic system that gave outsiders pause.) The long chorus of anguish from otherwise sober savants, writing in the press, addressing the public, or testifying before a remarkable series of parliamentary commissions from 1867 on bears witness to the high cost of this educational backwardness.

More important than the lag itself are the reasons. Essentially they boil down to demand, for a free society generally gets the educational system it wants, and demand was once again a function in part of British industrial priority and German emulation.

As we have seen, even elementary education encountered suspicion and resistance in England; a fortiori, technical instruction. There were those industrialists who feared it would lead to the disclosure of or diminish the value of trade secrets. Many felt that 'book learning' was not only misleading but had the disadvantage of instilling in its beneficiaries or victims—depending on the point of view—an exaggerated sense of their own merit and intelligence. Here management was joined by foremen and master craftsmen who, products of on-the-job apprenticeship, despised or feared—in any case, resented—the skills and knowledge of the school-trained technician. Still other employers could not see spending money on anything that did not yield an immediate return, the more so as the notions imparted by these classes and institutes almost invariably called for new outlays of capital.

A few were afraid of raising up competition.[1] But most would have snorted at the very idea: they were convinced the whole thing was a fraud, that effective technical education was impossible, scientific instruction unnecessary. Their own careers were the best proof of that: most manufacturers had either begun with a minimum of formal education and come up through the ranks or had followed the traditional liberal curriculum in secondary and sometimes higher schools. Moreover, this lesson of personal experience was confirmed by the history of British industry. Here was a nation that had built its economic strength on practical tinkerers—on a barber like Arkwright, a clergyman like Cartwright, an instrument-maker like Watt, a professional 'amateur inventor' like Bessemer, and thousands of nameless mechanics who suggested and effected the kind of small improvements to machines and furnaces and tools that add up eventually to an industrial revolution. She was proud of these men—listen to Lowthian Bell citing in reply to criticism of British technical shortcomings the names of Darby and Cort.[2]

In many trades there developed a mystique of practical experience. Consider the implications of the following question at the Parliamentary Inquiry of 1885:

You know perfectly well that in every mill there is one man who can spin very much better than anyone else, and if you wanted a finer number, that was the man that was put on. Without a technical school you have always some man of that kind; do you think any technical school would turn out any number of those men in a mill?[3]

And one manufacturer in the tinplate trade, denying the importance of trained engineers, remarked that what was needed was 'practical men who were in sympathy with their rolls and everything else. They

[1] In 1884 Huxley stigmatized this 'miserable sort of jealous feeling about the elevation of their workmen'. Cited in S. F. Cotgrove, *Technical Education and Social Change* (London, 1958), p. 24.

[2] *J. Iron and Steel Institute*, 1878, p. 315.

[3] *Parliamentary Papers*, 1886, xxi: 'Commission...on Depression of Trade and Industry', Q. 5173.

could do a lot with their machinery if they were in sympathy with it.'[1]

Moreover, even when employers did come to recognize the need for trained technical personnel, they yielded grudgingly. The underpaid 'scientists' were put in sheds, reclaimed workrooms, and other improvised quarters that hardly permitted controlled conditions and accurate tests. Their work was one cut above the rule-of-thumb techniques of the skilled workman; it was far below that of the German laboratory researcher.[2]

In sum, job and promotion opportunities for graduates in science and technology were few and unattractive. The most remunerative field, in spite of what has been said, was chemistry, and even there the best positions were often reserved for men trained abroad; undoubtedly the mediocre quality of many British graduates served to reinforce the scepticism of management. There was just about nothing for physicists until the last decade of the nineteenth century. The worst situation was in the lower ranks, on the level of vocational training, where students occasionally suffered for their ambition: a witness before the Committee on Scientific Education of 1868 testified that only one in four of those who attended vocational classes of the Science and Art Department in the 1850's got back into his trade.[3] In 1884 the Royal Commission on Technical Instruction reported:[4] 'We believe that many workmen are disposed to attach too little value to the importance of acquiring knowledge of the principles of science, because they do not see their application.' No wonder. No wonder also that the most gifted of those few young men who had the means to pursue their education beyond the intermediate level followed the traditional liberal curriculum to careers in the civil service, to pursuit of the genteel county life, or to the kind of post in industry or trade—and there were many—that called for a gentleman and not a technician.

The contrast with German attitudes is hard to exaggerate. For an ambitious nation, impatient to raise its economy to the level of the British, vexed if not humiliated by its dependence on foreign experts, an effective system of scientific and technical training was the foundation and promise of wealth and aggrandizement. A veritable cult of

[1] W. E. Minchinton, 'The Tinplate Maker and Technical Change', *Explorations in Entrepreneurial History*, VII (1954–5), 7.

[2] Cf. J. E. Stead, *J. Iron and Steel Institute*, XLIX (1896), 119; Burn, *Economic History*, p. 178; *Final Report of the Committee on Industry and Trade* (Cd. 3282; London: H.M.S.O., 1929), pp. 214f.

[3] *Parliamentary Papers*, 1867–8, Comm. on Scientific Instruction, pars. 301–28, cited by Cotgrove, *Technical Education*, p. 51, n. 1.

[4] *Parliamentary Papers*, 1884, XXIX: Royal Commission on Technical Instruction, Second Report, I, 523; cited *ibid.* p. 40.

Wissenschaft and *Technik* developed. The kings and princes of central Europe vied with one another in founding schools and research institutes and collected savants (even humanistic scholars like historians!) as their predecessors of the eighteenth century had collected musicians and composers; or as the courts of the Italy of the *cinquecento*, artists and sculptors. The people came to gape at the *Hochschulen* and universities with the awe usually reserved for historical monuments. Most important, entrepreneurs prized the graduates of these institutions and often offered them respected and often powerful positions—not only the corporate giants with their laboratory staffs of up to a hundred and more, but the small firms also, who saw in the special skills of the trained technician the best defence against the competition of large-scale production.

There is keen irony in all this. We have noted how a British observer of the mid-nineteenth century was impressed by the 'social democracy' of the German classroom; yet this is precisely what had struck continental travellers of the eighteenth century as one of the peculiar virtues of the British society of that period. To be sure, higher schooling in those days was confined to a very small fraction of the population; even the children of wealthy families often received little formal instruction; so that such equality as prevailed was as much or more one of ignorance than of knowledge. But that is the point: it did not make that much difference in the eighteenth century how much instruction a man had received. The recruitment of talent was on other grounds; wide avenues of mobility were open to the unschooled as well as the schooled; and many a man taught himself or learned by experience the knowledge and skills he required for his work.

With industrialization and the proliferation of bureaucracy in business as well as government, however, formal education took on steadily increasing importance as the key to occupational, hence social, preferment. This is not to say that the system or content of instruction was well suited to the requirements of the economy and polity; merely that schooling came more and more to govern recruitment of talent.

This is a task that a school system is in theory ideally equipped to perform. It is of its essence objective, grading and advancing students on the basis of ability and work—except where competition has been deliberately excluded from the classroom. Yet in fact, the selective efficiency of the system depends directly on its own circumstances and principles of recruitment, and these reflect in turn the values and attitudes of its creators and clientele.

Once again, timing and intent are crucially important. In Britain, where technological change came early, a new industrial society had already taken shape by the time the schools were built; so that these embodied not only the prejudices and cleavages of the established order, but the material inequalities. For members of the poorer classes, it was not only presumptuous to covet a more than minimal education; it was pecuniarily impossible—not so much because of the direct outlays required (though these were often a serious deterrent) as because of the earnings that would have to be foregone. It was the opportunity cost of instruction that made it the almost exclusive prerogative of the well-to-do. The school system, in other words, which might have been the great force for social mobility and advancement by talent, became a powerful crystallizer, defending the positions of a newly entrenched Establishment by giving it a quasi-monopoly of such knowledge and manners (including speech pattern) as the society valued.

Some of this was also true of German education, but to a much smaller degree—and differences in history are almost always a question of degree. The Germans developed their schools in advance of and in preparation for industrialization. The system was meant to strengthen the polity and economy not only by instruction, but also by finding and training talent, and while it necessarily fell short of its objectives, the elements of intent and direction were critically important. Hence one of the strangest paradoxes in modern history: that on the one hand, a liberal society standing out from all others in the eighteenth century for equality and mobility of status, should have lost something of these during the very period of its progressive political democratization; while on the other, a far more authoritarian society, characterized in its pre-industrial period by a clearly defined, fairly rigid hierarchy of rank, should have developed a more open structure, without corresponding political change.[1]

Needless to say, this contrast between two forms of social organization is not meant to imply an invidious moral judgement. Education and mobility are not virtuous ends in themselves, but means to ends, and their consequences, intended or not, may as easily be evil as good. One could easily argue that the *élite* produced by the British system—obnoxiously sure at times of its place and prerogatives but endowed with a keen sense of traditional morality and *noblesse oblige*—was in every way to be preferred to the hard, opportunistic, end-justifies-means specimens promoted by the German *cursus honorum*. But such a comparison would take us well beyond the limits of our subject.

Britain's relative lack of skills and knowledge (who could have imagined this eventuality in the first half of the nineteenth century?) was accompanied by, and contributed to, an equally astonishing inadequacy of venture capital. This statement may well strike the

[1] Cf. Kay, *Social Condition*, II, 74–5; also G. M. Trevelyan, *British History in the Nineteenth Century* (1st ed., London, 1922), p. 353.

reader as inconsistent with our earlier discussion of Britain's plethora of wealth. But savings are not necessarily investment, and there are all kinds of investment—foreign and domestic, speculative and safe, rational and irrational. The British had the capital. But those who channelled and dispensed it were not alert to the opportunities offered by modern technology; and those who might have used it did not want or know enough to seek it out.

The supply side first: the British banking system had grown more or less like industry—step by step, from the ground up, along with its clientele. Its greatest virtue was its remarkable ability to transfer resources from suppliers to demanders of capital through such traditional instruments as the bill of exchange, the open credit, the overdraft. Its greatest weakness, which became apparent only after the middle of the nineteenth century, was its inability to initiate or encourage the kind of industrial enterprise that would call for large amounts of outside capital. It was passive rather than active, responsive rather than creative.

Moreover, in so far as the capital market did direct the flow of funds, habit and predilection combined to give the preference to overseas governments and to public utilities, foreign and domestic. These were London's stock in trade, and London controlled the bulk of the country's liquid capital.[1] Industry was left to local markets: Manchester had its cotton enterprises; Birmingham, arms and hardware; Newcastle, coal and metallurgy. In such fields London itself was no more than a regional centre, trading the shares of shipyards on the Thames, a machine construction firm at Ipswich, local breweries, and the great department stores and hotels of the capital. As a result, the British corporation was often simply a partnership writ large—parochial in resources, direction, control, and scope. It was bigger than its predecessors of the first half of the century; but it was no match for the *Konzerne* and *Interessengemeinschaften* that were mushrooming across the North Sea.[2]

The sharply contrasting structure of German credit and finance is once again understandable only in terms of the economics of priority and backwardness. We have already observed that whereas British industry could build its resources from the ground up, the Germans found it necessary from the start to create institutions to mobilize scarce capital and channel it to a productive system taking its departure on an advanced level of technique and organization. These were the

[1] Cf. John Saville, 'A Comment on Professor Rostow's British Economy of the 19th Century', *Past and Present*, no. 6 (November 1954), pp. 77–8.

[2] Cf. C. W. von Wieser, *Der finanzielle Aufbau der englischen Industrie* (Jena, 1919), pp. 134–5; Lord Aberconway, *The Basic Industries of Great Britain* (London, 1927), p. 346.

joint-stock investment banks, and their increasingly intimate collaboration with manufacturing enterprise was to have major consequences for the rate and character of German development.

For one thing, it meant planned promotion and development of the individual firm. The banks had to learn to evaluate the possibilities for profit in a given business situation before undertaking to issue securities. To this end they not only consulted outside technicians, but developed their own specialists to examine and advise on industrial matters. There were some banks, to be sure, which were less careful than others, or less scrupulous. Germany had her *Gründerzeit*, and there were always financiers who felt that the only significant question in any promotion was its speculative potentialities. Yet most banks did not float and unload; they stayed with their creations, held on to some of their stock, kept an eye on their performance, and encouraged their growth as lucrative clients.

For another, bank financing implied continuing expansion of the industrial sector as a whole. If the profitability of *any given* promotional transaction depended on careful appreciation of the elements involved and on influence over later developments, the *total return* of this very important branch of the bank's operations depended on finding or inventing promotions. Thus the specialists in industrial finance were as concerned with discovering possibilities for growth or reorganization as with helping them come about. This was especially true from 1880 on, after the decline in railway construction and nationalization had deprived the market of its most popular staple. In the following years, the banks played an important role in stimulating as well as in supporting the growth of German heavy industry and its integration along vertical and horizontal lines. Throughout, their influence was on the side of a more thorough utilization of resources and a more effective combination of the factors of production.[1]

Yet it is easy to exaggerate the importance of these differences in the structure and behaviour of the capital markets of the two countries. Students of British economic history in particular have offered on occasion a simpler answer: they have assumed a straightforward inverse relationship between domestic and overseas investment; when the one waxed, the other waned.[2] More careful examination of the data has forced the abandonment of this simple model for a more complex,

[1] One of the best studies of this relationship is O. Jeidels, *Das Verhältnis der deutschen Grossbanken zur Industrie* (Leipzig, 1905).

[2] This point of view is implicit in W. W. Rostow's *British Economy of the Nineteenth Century* (Oxford, 1948), though nowhere does he state it so plainly as A. K. Cairncross, who affirms 'that in the *long* run foreign investment was largely at the expense of home investment or vice versa'. *Home and Foreign Investment* (Cambridge, 1953), p. 187.

more accurate, but less comfortable analysis.[1] Even so, many scholars have continued to take for granted that, *grosso modo*, the scale of British foreign investment was such as to deprive domestic industry of nourishment.

I am not persuaded by this thesis. It rests, first, on a misapprehension. Without going so far as Professor Rostow, who saw the period 1873–98 as one of a general shift from foreign placements toward 'intensive investment at home', one may note that there were times during these years when Britain sank large sums into domestic industry. In 1885 Goschen waxed fairly rapturous on the subject:

Never before has there been so keen a desire on the part of the whole community to invest every reserve shilling they may have in some remunerative manner. There is a competition between men who have a few tens of pounds and a few hundreds of pounds to put them into business, and into business they are put. Joint-stock enterprise has swept up all these available resources. Like a gigantic system of irrigation it first collects and then pours them through innumerable conduit pipes right over the face of the country, making capital accessible in every form at every point.[2]

Yet from the macro-economic standpoint, the results were a disappointment. Clearly, it is not money that counts, but what one does with it.[3]

Secondly, there is good reason to believe that capital flows to opportunity, that if there are borrowers who know what to do with it and seek it, there will be lenders to meet their needs. Admittedly such a generalization does violence to the facts of many individual cases and even perhaps to the experience of certain nations. And it slights the contribution that an imaginative, active banking system can make to industrial development—as we have seen. Yet it seems valid on balance for the major sectors, *qua* sectors, of the advanced industrial economies.[4]

This consideration, moreover, is reinforced here by the fact that, barring non-economic deterrents—lack of security, confiscatory exchange controls, and the like—home enterprise has first claim on the resources of an economy. It has all the advantage of the familiar,

[1] Cf. S. B. Saul, *Studies in British Overseas Trade*, pp. 90f.

[2] *Addresses on Economic Questions* (London, 1905), quoted in Rostow, *British Economy*, p. 70.

[3] In this connection, it is interesting to note that a recent comparison of production functions in different countries shows differences in the efficiency of capital as well as in the better known efficiency of labour. Indeed the two seem to be related.

[4] Cf. Alec K. Cairncross, 'The Place of Capital in Economic Progress', in Leon H. Dupriez, ed., *Economic Progress* (Louvain, 1955), pp. 235–48.

whereas foreign ventures are difficult to appreciate, relatively immune from verification and control, and intrinsically more speculative. Indeed the differences between the two are sufficient to give rise to a substantial gap in the expectations of return required to attract investment to each of the two sectors—a gap analogous to the cost of moving labour from one job to another. In sum, if Britain sent so much money abroad, it was partly for lack of initiative on the part of lenders, but even more because borrowers at home did not want it.

This brings us to the demand side of the equation, which, given the rough equality of the two economies in material resources, was essentially a function of entrepreneurship, that is, of those human elements— imagination, energy, aspiration—that shaped investment decisions in the two systems. Here again, the contrast is sharp enough to transcend the intrinsic limitations of qualitative evidence. The British manufacturer, strong in his admiration for experience and his preference for empiricist tinkering as against bookish experiment, was inclined to be suspicious of novelty. Riley, describing his finally successful efforts to introduce the use of hot pig in Scottish open-hearth mills to the Iron and Steel Institute in 1900, declared that 'the want of confidence in success and the passive resistance often met with in such cases was perhaps more discouraging than any possible difficulties which might arise in actual working, or in working out practical methods'. The conservatism of the tinplate trade was notorious: 'Generally speaking,' said one manufacturer in the years before the war, 'when anything new is introduced into any work, if it is not right away a success out it goes'. The response to something new was to ask 'if any other fool had tried it yet'.[1] One could cite similar examples from other branches of industry.

In the meantime the German system had institutionalized innovation: change was built in. There was no assurance of major discoveries— it is worth noting, for example, that the great advances in metallurgy in the second half of the century were English (Bessemer, Siemens, Thomas–Gilchrist), French (Martin, Carvès), or Belgian (Coppée). But there was some assurance that inventions of whatever origin would be tested and exploited; and there was within industry itself a steady flow of small improvements which cumulatively constituted a technological revolution.[2] The six largest German firms for coal-tar products took out 948 patents between 1886 and 1900, as compared with 86 by

[1] Minchinton, 'The Tinplate Maker', *Explorations*, VII (1954–5), 6.
[2] Cf. the discussion of W. N. Parker, 'Entrepreneurial Opportunities and Response in the German Economy', *Explorations*, VII (1954–5), 27: 'Economic opportunity in Germany has been an opportunity for the technologist of ingenious and limited range, and for the production engineer. It has not been aimed at devising striking new

the corresponding English firms.[1] And as Schumpeter put it in his description of the German electrical industry, the variety and frequency of innovation under the impulse of the technical departments of the big concerns gave rise to a race which 'though never displaying the formal properties of perfect competition, yet produces all the results usually attributed to perfect competition'.[2]

Furthermore—and again we come up against the complexity and inextricability of multiple factors in historical explanation—these contrasts in receptivity to innovation were strengthened by differences in entrepreneurial rationality. The British manufacturer remained faithful to the classical calculus: he attempted to maximize return by making those investments which, given anticipated costs, risks, and sales, yielded the greatest margin over what existing equipment could provide. He was handicapped, as we have seen, by the burden of related costs, which often made otherwise interesting outlays unprofitable. He often made the mistake of tying investment to current operations and returns rather than to expectations of what the future might reasonably bring. Either his tacit assumption was that tomorrow would be the same as today or, as Kindleberger suggests,[3] he was unconsciously trying to minimize the need to make decisions—as always, the most demanding and disagreeable duty of the entrepreneur. Finally, he was sometimes unreasonable enough to neglect one of the cardinal precepts of economics, that sunk costs are sunk, and cling to antiquated equipment because it worked. The theorist is reluctant to admit that people often behave this way, because irrationality does not lend itself to logical analysis; but they do. The weight of earlier advance and growth lay heavy on many a British producer. As Lowthian Bell put it in a comparison of British and American practice: 'The English ironmaster stood in a somewhat different position, inasmuch as if he spent £25,000 to effect [a] saving, he would have to sacrifice the £25,000 he had already laid out.'[4] And another remarked: 'One wants to be thoroughly convinced of the superiority of a new method before condemning as useless a large plant that has hitherto done good service.'[5] The latter

---

types of machinery....' On p. 29 he speaks of 'German possibilities and their introduction in small and incessant doses into existing technology...'.

[1] Cotgrove, *Technical Education*, pp. 20f.

[2] J. A. Schumpeter, *Business Cycles: a Theoretical, Historical and Statistical Analysis of the Capitalist Process* (2 vols.; New York, 1939), I, 440.

[3] Kindleberger, 'Obsolescence and Technical Change', *Bull. Oxford Univ. Inst. of Statistics*, XXIII (1961), 296, 298.

[4] *J. Iron and Steel Institute*, LIX (1901), no. I, p. 123.

[5] Alfred Baldwin, in his Presidential Address to the British Iron Trade Association, as reported in *Engineering*, 6 May 1898, p. 569; cited in Burn, *Economic History*, p. 186. Cf. Kindleberger, 'Obsolescence', p. 295.

statement, of course, may have been nothing more than an affirmation of the need for accuracy in comparing the profitability of old and new equipment—though one is troubled by the reference to past rather than future returns. Even when the British entrepreneur was rational, however, his calculations were distorted by the shortness of his time horizon, and his estimates were on the conservative side.

The significance of this pecuniary approach is best appreciated when it is contrasted with the technological rationality of the Germans. This was a different kind of arithmetic, which maximized, not returns, but technical efficiency. For the German engineer, and the manufacturer and banker who stood behind him, the new was desirable, not so much because it paid, but because it worked better. There were right and wrong ways of doing things, and the right was the scientific, mechanized, capital-intensive way. The means had become end. The economist, to be sure, considering the situation *ex post*, will simply distinguish between two pecuniary calculations: the German entrepreneur simply had a longer time-horizon and included in his estimates exogenous variables of technological change that his British competitor held constant. But this would miss the crucial difference in *ex ante* motivation that made the German behave as he did.

Given this non-rational motivation, there was of course no *a priori* reason why the German pattern should have paid better. It is clear that there can be such a thing as overmodernization—an excessive substitution of capital for labour—just as there can be overemphasis on one or two branches of economic activity at the expense of the rest. Here, however, Germany was fortunate, in that the long wave of technological change favoured science- and capital-intensive methods and industries, while the nature of her own human and material resources were such as to enable her to take advantage of the opportunities offered. In short, she took the right path, though in part for the wrong, or more exactly, irrelevant reasons.

Here some words of caution are in order. I have rested much of this discussion of Anglo-German economic competition on what sociologists call the analysis of ideal types, in this case, two contrasting types of entrepreneurs. This is inevitably a dangerous technique of historical comparison, because it rests on the averaging of the unmeasurable, hence unaverageable, and does violence to the complexity and variety of human behaviour. The economist would be the first to point out that it does not matter in the long run how backward the techniques or how inefficient the performance of the great majority of entrepreneurs, so long as a few are energetic enough to introduce change and force the rest to follow suit. And this is true enough—of the long run. The observation of Lord Keynes has been so often repeated that it has lost much of its pungency; but its correctness remains: In the long run, we are all dead. In the long run, under the pressure of American and German competition, British industry did change many of its ways. But in the meantime it lost ground; one war and then another intervened; new economic rivals appeared; and much talent and capital flowed in other channels. The world does not stand still for anyone, and the short-run weakness contributes, in ways that we are as yet unable to define and measure, to the long-run lag.

One final point. Even if one grants the importance of this human factor—the success of entrepreneurial and technological creativity on one side, the failure on the other—perhaps it was itself nothing more than a reflection of economic determinants. There is, for example, what we may call the 'feedback approach', which sees the growth of an economy or even an industry in any period as a function of its growth in the preceding period: the rate of expansion itself elicits the material and human responses required to sustain it. A succinct statement of this position is to be found in Svennilson:[1]

It may be assumed that the new capacity added in an expanding industry will be built in accordance with the latest technical knowledge, while the rest of the industry, representing the earlier capacity, will lag behind in modernization. The proportion of modern equipment in an industry will thus increase in proportion to the rapidity of the industry's growth. This leads to the conclusion that, *ceteris paribus*, the efficiency of an industry increases according to the rapidity of its expansion.

This line of explanation has been applied to the Anglo-German rivalry by Professor Habakkuk in his study of *American and British Technology*.[2] To begin with, he is inclined to depreciate the gap between British and German performance: he lays stress, for example, on the British bright spots of open-hearth steel and shipbuilding, the one related to the other. And while he concedes the backwardness of other branches, old and new, he lays great stress on related costs of change, on the burden of established plant and vested interest (for example, the obstacle posed by a widespread gas network to electrification), and above all, on the slow rate of expansion. This last, he feels, explains not only the lack of opportunity to build up-to-date plant, but also such entrepreneurial short-comings as may in fact have existed (here too,

[1] Svennilson, *Growth and Stagnation*, p. 10.
[2] H. J. Habakkuk, *American and British Technology in the Nineteenth Century: The Search for Labour-saving Inventions* (Cambridge, 1962).

Habakkuk feels that the usual indictment is exaggerated): 'Great generals are not made in time of peace; great entrepreneurs are not made in non-expanding industries.' Even the weakness of British scientific training and technical performance (once again, Habakkuk contends that it has been overdrawn) can be largely accounted for in analogous terms: 'the English industry failed to attract or retain the available scientific ability, and lacked the desire to train its own scientists, because its prospects deteriorated for reasons independent of the supply of scientific skills'. In sum, 'such lags as there were in the adoption of new methods in British industry can be adequately explained by economic circumstances, by the complexity of her industrial structure and the slow growth of her output, and ultimately by her early and long-sustained start as an industrial power'.[1]

I disagree. Not that the argument is wrong; it is simply incomplete and does justice to the behaviour of neither adversary.[2] In regard to Britain, there is the evidence that even the new investment of older industries was characterized by excessive caution and short horizons; and it is also necessary to account for the generally weak performance of the new science-based branches of manufacture. Moreover, it would be wrong to dismiss as incorrect or irrelevant a great mass of contemporary evidence not only testifying to entrepreneurial and technological shortcomings but attributing them to social values and forces independent of the economic system.

The explanation is equally incomplete for the German side of the rivalry. Here too, the analysis has much truth in it: the economic achievements of the *Zollverein* and then the Reich, in conjunction with the military triumphs of Prussia, promoted an atmosphere of euphoric confidence and thereby reinforced the material stimuli to investment and growth. But this is not all one has to explain. There is the question in particular, why the pattern of German investment deviates from what relative factor costs would lead one to expect. Until the last quarter of the nineteenth century, this was not the case: new German plant was less capital-intensive than British plant; equipment was smaller, often less advanced—and this in spite of a far higher rate of growth than in Britain, from 1850 certainly and perhaps from 1834. There is also the objective evidence of technological fecundity deriving from good and widespread scientific training; nowhere is this more

[1] The quotations are to be found *ibid.* pp. 212, 216, 220.
[2] Our concern here is specifically with the feedback part of the analysis, that is, the contention that Britain's slower rate of growth 'adequately' (perhaps 'substantially' would be more accurate) accounts for those aspects of her economic performance not explained by such direct limitations on entrepreneurial decisions as related costs. On these, already discussed above (see p. 334), one would find general agreement.

obvious than in organic chemicals, where the opportunities for research are in large measure independent of the character or volume of current production. Finally, there is again an abundance of concurrent contemporary testimony about the influence of entrepreneurial attitudes and technical standards on business performance that one would be ill-advised to dismiss except on the strongest grounds.

In other words, the feedback approach offers an explanation for one side of economic behaviour, that of the stimulus to economic activity which comes from the side of demand. But it slights the supply side and thereby truncates historical reality. Nothing succeeds like success ...but why do some succeed and others fail? Why do some front runners fade and laggards pick up?

Such questions take us into the most difficult problem of economic history, that of explaining why—not simply how or what—change occurs. This is not the place to undertake a discussion of the causation of development and growth, a subject that has already provoked a library of debate, much of it concerned explicitly with the issue posed by the Anglo-German rivalry, that is, the relative importance of human and non-human determinants. But one brief *wissenschaftsozio-logische* observation is worth making: when all is said and done, neither empirical evidence nor theoretical reasoning is likely to settle the dispute. Sharp differences of opinion will always remain. For one thing, so complex is the matter of history and so unamenable to the replicated analysis of the laboratory, that the precise imputation of weights to each of the many determinants of economic development—even in a limited situation, *a fortiori* in general—is impossible and likely to remain so. For another, this very complexity and imprecision precludes demonstration that any given explanation of events, however plausible, is the only possible explanation. And since scholars are human, with many, if not all, of the predilections and biases of other humans, they tend to choose and will no doubt go on choosing those interpretations that they find not only plausible but congenial.

This element of congeniality must not be underestimated. Economic development is a great drama. It is the puberty of nations, the passage that separates the men from the boys. It therefore carries with it, in a world that admires power and covets material prosperity, connotations of success and virility. Now some societies have effected this passage earlier than others and have consequently achieved greater wealth; some, though later starters, have been growing faster than some of their predecessors and promise (or threaten, depending on the point of view) to pass them; others have not yet been able to enter on the path of development at all. Because of the profound implications of this drama for the status of the participants, the explanations offered for success or failure are themselves crucial to the self-esteem of these societies and their members. Under the circumstances, the identification of the scholar with the problem he studies has often been as important a determinant of his approach as the objective data.

CHAPTER 6

The Interwar Years

THE ECONOMIC CONSEQUENCES OF THE PHONEY PEACE

It is not easy to write the economic history of the twentieth century. For one thing, it is too close to us; for another, it is messy by comparison with the halcyon nineteenth. For a hundred years Europe had not known a major war, and her economies had been free to develop with little distraction from political and military quarters. To be sure, all of them in some degree had started with the handicap of a pre-industrial social and legal structure, some of it not only not favourable to capitalism but developed in antagonism to it. But the history of economic policy in the nineteenth century is largely one of liberation from this legacy, and to the degree that this liberation was effective and the natural and human resources for growth were available, the economies of Europe transformed themselves and waxed mighty. The story of each, *mutatis mutandis*, fits closely to a kind of ideal model of modernization; the leitmotif is the process of industrial revolution.

The twentieth century by contrast is a confusion of emergencies, disasters, improvisations, and artificial expedients. One passes in a few weeks of 1914 from a quiet stream, as it were, to white water.

Yet economic history, more even than other branches of history, abhors chronological boundaries. As we have already had occasion to notice (see above, p. 231 f.), many of the economic aspects of the postwar period are manifest before 1914: the closure of markets against outside competition, the trend toward combinations in restraint of trade, the intervention of the state in matters once reserved to private enterprise or left to the free play of the market—all of these developments were well under way by the turn of the century. Their timing varied from country to country, depending on political and ideological as well as economic circumstances; thus prewar Britain withstood strong pressures to abandon free trade, in the face of a rising tide of neomercantilism elsewhere. Yet these developments constituted, as we have seen, a response to a climacteric of the industrial system, common to all advanced nations, and all found it necessary sooner or later to take the new path.

The war made it sooner—because it hastened the dissolution of the old international economy; because it gave rise to temporary expedients that, in so far as they conformed to the longer trend, tended to become permanent; and because it prepared people psychologically for changes that they might otherwise have been unwilling to accept. When Britain instituted in 1915 the so-called McKenna import duties with a view to saving shipping space, she was without realizing it demolishing a fundamental tenet of the national faith. The duties were retained after the war; from 1919 the countries within the Empire received a preference; and the Safeguarding of Industries Act of 1921 imposed duties of $33\frac{1}{3}\%$ *ad valorem* on the products of industries alleged to be vital to national defence. All that remained was to generalize the protection and drop the sham of emergency legislation, and this last step was accomplished with the Import Duties Act of 1932.

Britain's return to protection deprived the world of the largest free port it had ever known. At the same time, the economies of central and eastern Europe were fragmented by the dissolution of the multinational empires: Austria–Hungary in particular, but also Russia, which lost Finland, Poland, and the Baltic states, while she herself more or less withdrew from the international market. To be sure, some of these successor states moved with independence from higher tariff cover to lower. Yet this did not compensate for their separation from economically complementary regions that had once supplied them with raw materials and labour or taken their products. The separation was aggravated, especially in the beginning, by virulent animosities: for a time, none of the Austrian successor states was ready to allow its railway rolling stock to cross its borders for fear of seizure, and goods had to be unloaded and reloaded at every frontier station. Such absurdities were eventually eliminated; yet these small, scarcely viable economies persisted in their efforts at autarky, at high cost to themselves and others.

This accelerated tendency to closure was powerfully encouraged by the collapse of the prewar monetary order—here the War clearly effected a revolutionary change. The nineteenth century stands out in European history as a unique period of monetary stability. The buying power of money fluctuated, to be sure, though as we have seen, the long-term trend was deflationary, and this in itself was an almost unparalleled experience. But the paper currencies of Europe, with few exceptions, retained their relative values and remained throughout convertible into precious metal; so that the freedom of national and international money markets could be taken for granted. Very rarely was it necessary to impose explicit restrictions on the movement of funds, for in all but the most severe crises, the market took care of itself. An excess of demand for any currency was absorbed by a fractional shift in the rate of exchange. If the rates shifted enough, of course, it became cheaper to ship gold than to buy the currency concerned. But since this was an expensive way to make payment and an outflow of gold brought with it monetary stringency and credit restrictions, the system discouraged excessive spending and encouraged nations to measure their outgo to their income.

This was exchange under the gold standard, which even today some bankers and economists look back to nostalgically as the international policeman of responsible monetary behaviour. This opinion, unfortunately, rests on an erroneous reification. The gold standard had no autonomous existence. It was the product of a particular economic conjuncture—a multilateral balance of international accounts that permitted settlement within a very narrow range of exchange fluctuations. Moneys could float free because they did not float far.

The War changed all that. On the one hand, it sharply diminished the real value, that is, the buying power of all European currencies; on the other, it diminished them unequally and, so doing, altered their respective exchange values.

All wars are inflationary, if only because so much is spent for unproductive or, worse yet, destructive goods and services. But the First World War far surpassed in this regard any previous conflict; so that in spite of the most strenuous controls and ingenious fiscal expedients, prices rose considerably in all belligerent countries. This wartime rise, however, was only the wispy warning of a smouldering volcano; for a massive inflation lay beneath the surface, pent up by emergency ceilings, market quotas, rationing and the rest of the apparatus of economic compression. Once the war was over and these restrictions were removed, the lid was off and prices shot up.

The pattern of this explosion varied widely with military and political as well as economic circumstances. In a country like Britain, victorious, suffering little damage, the return to a kind of normalcy was relatively easy. Prices reached their peak in 1920—about three times prewar—and then subsided to about one-and-a-half to two times that level. In France, the war had destroyed a large part of her industrial plant, and peace was the signal for an already exhausted country to undertake a massive programme of reconstruction. To some extent, the cost of this investment was paid by Germany, but to a far lesser extent than required and expected. Prices rose as in Britain in the years immediately following the war, from an index of 356 in 1919 (1913 = 100) to 509 in 1920, and then subsided to 327 in 1922. But then, unlike in Britain, they climbed again, topping the 700 mark in 1926 and levelling off only with the Poincaré stabilization of 1926-7.

The most extreme cases of inflation, however, were found in central and eastern Europe, in countries wracked by defeat and civil strife: in Austria, where prices rose to 14,000 times the prewar level; in Hungary, where the multiple was 23,000; in Poland, 2,500,000; in Russia, 4,000 million. The limit was reached in Germany, where the burdens of reconstruction were aggravated by those of reparation for the war damage and costs incurred by the victorious Allies. The amounts called for were enormous—though they by no means exceeded what Germany would have exacted had she won. The fact remains that they were more than Germany could pay, and a desperate government had increasing recourse to the printing press to meet obligations. By 1923 banknotes were being issued in astronomical denominations; even so, Germans were using baby carriages to wheel sheaves of paper to the shops and spend them before they became worthless. At the end of the inflation in November of that year, the mark was worth one trillionth of its prewar value.[1]

The German experience is illustrative of the extent to which an adverse balance of payments, due partly in this case to reparations, can exacerbate an inflationary process. But the victorious Entente powers had their own difficulties on this score. Before the War, the industrial nations of Europe, Britain and France in particular, had accumulated enormous holdings abroad, the income of which not only sufficed to cover deficits on commodity account but was large enough to finance further capital formation. A part of these holdings was liquidated to pay for food and military supplies, mostly in the United States: Britain sold perhaps £207 million out of £800–900 million in dollar investments, plus another £54 million of sterling; while France sold 3·5 billion (milliards) out of 45. On the other hand, France lost over half of her holdings abroad (23 of 45 billion) because her debtors were wiped out—12 billion in Russia alone. And much of what was left stopped paying interest or dividends; annual income from holdings abroad fell

---

[1] It was worth even less in the occupied Rhineland, where the circulation of so-called emergency money (*Notgeld*) had attained incalculably large proportions. This *Notgeld* consisted of paper notes issued by provincial and local authorities, and even by private enterprises, to meet a demand for money that the printing presses of the Reichsbank were unable to satisfy. In principle, these issues required the preliminary consent of the Finance Minister and the deposit of cover in the Reichsbank in the form of cash or treasury notes. In 1923, however, the confusion and opportunity of hyperinflation and the difficulties of supplying the occupied areas with Reichsmarks led to an uncontrolled issue of this private paper, which the Reichsbank continued to accept at its counters until 17 November. Rolf E. Lüke, *Von der Stabilisierung zur Krise* (Zurich, 1958), p. 24. There is a large literature on the German inflation, which has served as a kind of monetary bugbear ever since. See, however, the recent study of Karsten Laursen and Jørgen Pedersen, *The German Inflation 1918–1923* (Amsterdam, 1964), which prefers inflation to growth-inhibiting deflation and attributes the collapse of 1923 to the lack of a correct monetary policy.

from 8,040 million francs in 1910–13 to 2,800 millions in 1920.[1] (This was one instance, however, where investors should have known what they were getting into: every Russian bond issue since the 1890's had encountered a storm of denunciation from émigré radicals, who circulated flysheets warning investors that the revolutionary regime—when it came—would not honour the obligations of the Tsar.)

Over and above this liquidation and these losses, the European belligerents all found it necessary to borrow to finance their military effort and that of their allies. The British, who lent some £1,741 million to their comrades in arms, including some £568 million to Russia, covered most of this by borrowing £1,365 million, of which £1,027 million from the United States. The French covered their foreign exchange deficit partly by public loans (more than 4·5 billion gold francs), but far more by direct borrowing from their Allies (more than 30 billions, mostly from the United States).[2]

As a result, the end of the War found all the European belligerents considerably impoverished. Nor did peace bring a respite from these extraordinary outlays: the costs of reconstruction were enormous. To be sure, these were supposed to be covered by German reparations. The slogan was: Germany will pay. Yet Germany could or would pay only a part of what she owed, and much of that was financed by borrowing from the United States, that is, her creditors' creditor. At a distance of almost half a century, the situation seems absurd enough to be almost funny. It was not amusing, however, to contemporaries, who found in it abundant food for mutual recrimination.

In the meantime, the inescapable fact was that Europe, shorn of much of her savings, was compelled to live beyond her means. The imbalance was eased considerably by postponement (eventually repudiation) of war debts to the United States and by a marked shift in the terms of trade in favour of manufactures. (This affluence at the expense of what we would call today the underdeveloped parts of the world was eventually to come home to roost when the economy of the industrial nations collapsed in 1930.) Even so, the net flow of capital continued to be from west to east across the Atlantic, reversing a pattern that went back more than a century. Much of it, unfortunately, was short-term funds, easily withdrawn in the event of stringency in the United States; and this precarious dependency was to prove disastrous in 1930–1.

[1] Charles Rist and Gaëtan Pirou, eds., *De la France d'avant guerre à la France d'aujourd'hui* (Paris, 1939), p. 534.

[2] Statistics of British war finance are taken from Sidney Pollard, *The Development of the British Economy 1914–1950* (London, 1962), pp. 74–5. French figures are from Rist and Pirou, eds., *De la France d'avant guerre*, pp. 531–3.

European statesmen and technicians expended considerable ingenuity and money in the 1920's in effort to restore monetary normalcy. The British succeeded in returning to the gold standard in 1925, with the pound at prewar parity with the dollar; but this *tour de force* was achieved only by systematic deflation, which cost the economy dearly in output and industrial peace. The result, moreover, was not a true equilibrium rate. The pound was slightly overvalued, and this was a continuing handicap to industries already on the defensive in foreign markets. France never managed to return to the *franc de germinal.* At the low point in 1926, it took 50 francs to buy a dollar, as against 5 before the War. Six months later, thanks to energetic intervention in the money market, Poincaré succeeded in pegging the franc at five cents. This rate held for a decade, but in the thirties the slide resumed, and on the eve of the Second World War, the franc was down to about two cents again. Needless to say, Germany simply wrote off the old currency and started anew.

In such conditions of monetary instability and imbalance of payments, the gold standard as a kind of fundamental law of international monetary relations was obsolete. No nation was ready to abandon its sovereign right to protect its currency as it saw fit; and few nations could afford to accept the constraints implicit in convertibility. The European states yearned after the orderliness of yore; the central bankers continued to cling to financial orthodoxy; and their efforts along these lines did effect short quasi-restorations in a number of countries. But the old order was dead, and these policies, instead of promoting stability, injected elements of rigidity and unevenness into the international monetary system. When the depression struck in the thirties, those few countries that had succeeded in returning to the gold standard were forced to abandon it; in most instances, they did so much too late.

It is impossible to assess with precision the consequences of monetary difficulties for the economic history of Europe in the interwar period. It was, after all, only one aspect of a general imbalance between means and ends and cannot be pulled out of that context without suffering distortion. But one can list some of the ways in which it exercised a harmful influence: (1) it made the conduct of business more difficult and costly, for traders now had to take into account not only market fluctuations in rates of exchange but a bureaucratic mess of regulations and restrictions designed to protect currencies against the penalties of deficit financing and unfavourable balances of payments; (2) it distracted funds from productive activities to speculation in exchange, whether in the form of actual trade in futures, or of hoarding, or of the export, licit and illicit, of capital to safer markets, or of investment in inventory as a hedge against depreciation; and most important (3) it reinforced the protectionist mechanisms of high tariffs, quotas, and similar obstacles to international trade.

This raises the subject of one of the most important but difficult aspects of post-World War I economic development. One of the marked characteristics of the period was the failure of trade to grow as fast as before (see Table 17, p. 366) or as fast as output. Not until 1924 did the volume of trade return to the 1913 level; it then picked up smartly for four years, growing at almost 5 per cent per annum, as against about 4 per cent in the period 1896–1913; and then collapsed in the thirties. Similarly, if one takes 1913 as 100, world output of manufactures (at constant prices) stood at 149 in 1928–9, and the volume of trade in manufactures at only 112; a decade later (1936–8) the two index numbers were 188 and 92 respectively.[1]

Some of this disparity was in a sense unavoidable: it reflected the increasing share in world production of the United States, a nation whose economy was largely self-sufficient; and of Soviet Russia, a nation excised from the world market by revolution and ideology. For the most part, however, the gap was the result of choice: the growing recourse to protection against foreign competition.

Yet even for western Europe protectionism is not the whole story. It can explain the slowing of trade in manufactures: the average European duty on finished goods rose by about 50 per cent from 1913 to 1927. But there was no such increase in rates on primary products. Here the analysis of W. A. Lewis is pertinent: trade slowed down because population growth had slowed down. The major factor was the war: Europe had some 22 million fewer people in 1920 than it should have had; if one adds Russia, the deficit was 48 million. By comparison, the decline in the birthrate was much less serious, though it picked up speed and became more important in the thirties.[2]

Fewer heads, the argument runs, meant less mouths to feed; Euro-

[1] Ingvar Svennilson, *Growth and Stagnation in the European Economy* (Geneva: United Nations Economic Commission for Europe, 1954), p. 218. Svennilson offers figures for the three major industrial nations of western Europe:

Volume of Output, Exports, and Imports of Manufactures, 1913–38 (1913 = 100)

	U.K.[a]			Germany[b]			France[b]		
	Output	Exports	Imports	Output	Exports	Imports	Output	Exports	Imports
1913	100	100	100	100	100	100	100	100	100
1928–9	106	81	139	107	90	113	(153)[c]	169	124
1936–8	137	82	137	124	65	40	(130)	86	93

[a] Excluding Ireland.   [b] Boundaries as of date.   [c] Including the Saar.

[2] W. Arthur Lewis, *Economic Survey, 1919–1939* (London, 1949), pp. 151–2.

Table 17. *Growth of World Trade*

A. 18th century to 1880–9, Mulhall data

	Volume of trade 1865–85 prices (millions of £)	Rate of growth per decade, successive periods (%)	Europe's share of total[b] (%)
1720, 1750, 1780[a]	153	—	72·6
1820, 1830	315	10·1	73·5
1830, 1840	410	30·2	72·6
1840, 1850	662	61·5	70·2
1850, 1860	1,058	59·8	69·0
1860, 1870	1,616	52·7	70·3
1870, 1880	2,483	53·7	71·0
1880, 1889	3,497	43·4	69·4

B. 1881–1913, League of Nations (Hilgerdt) data

	Volume of trade 1913 prices (billions of $)	Rate of growth per decade, decade periods (%)	Europe's share of total[b,c] (%)
1881–1885	15·69	—	65·4
1886–1890	18·13	42·0	65·7
1891–1895	19·97	27·3	64·6
1896–1900	22·54	24·2	65·3
1901–1905	27·52	37·8	62·8
1906–1910	32·88	45·9	58·5
1911–1913	39·07	47·6	60·0
1913	40·50	—	60·1

C. 1913–60, United Nations and Dewhurst data

	Index of volume of world exports (1913 = 100)	Rate of growth per decade, successive periods (%)	Western Europe's share of total (%)[b]
1913	100	—	51·8
1928	113	8·5	45·7
1937	114	1·0	43·9
1950	131	11·3	—
1960	244	86·0	39·1[d]

[a] Average of individual years indicated.

[b] Share of total in current prices.

[c] Includes the following countries: United Kingdom, France, Germany, Holland, Belgium, Switzerland, Scandinavia, Italy, Austria–Hungary, Spain, and Russia.

[d] 1958.

SOURCE: Kuznets, *Modern Economic Growth*, pp. 306–9.

pean agricultural output, moreover, had risen substantially during the war, and this new capacity pressed heavily on the market in the postwar decade. As a result, the prices of primary products lagged well behind those of manufacturers, and Europe's suppliers, many of whom had little to sell but food and raw materials, found it harder and harder to be Europe's customers. For Lewis, this was the heart of the problem: '*The decline of trade in manufactures was due neither to tariffs nor to the industrialisation of new countries.* The trade in manufactures was low only because the industrial countries were buying too little of primary products and paying so low a price for what they bought' (p. 155).

Lewis exaggerates; the word 'only' is much too strong. But even if one substitutes some such expression as 'in part', the statement still poses some difficulties. One would expect, for example, that if the demand for primary products were the source of the trouble, Europe's trade with overseas countries would suffer more than trade within Europe. It does; but not by very much. Thus imports from European sources accounted for 49·4 per cent of the total in 1913, 53·6 per cent in 1928; while exports to the same customers rose from 59·6 to 63·0 per cent. At the same time, if the slowing of population growth were having the effect postulated by Lewis, one would presumably see evidence of this in the trade in a commodity like wheat; yet wheat exports from the major producing countries rise sharply in the postwar decade: from 2·4 to 5·3 million metric tons from 1909–13 to 1928 for Argentina; 1·1 to 1·6 million for Australia; 2·0 to 9·9 million for Canada; 1·4 to to 2·1 million for the United States.[1]

Yet there was serious trouble brewing in the international market for agricultural products. Towards the end of the twenties, the prices of certain key commodities were softening. Cotton peaked in 1923, and by 1929 was down by a third. The fall of rubber began two years later but was far more precipitous, plunging from slightly over 70 cents a pound in 1925 to barely 20 cents by 1929—this in spite of almost a doubling of inventory. And wheat, which topped $2·10 a bushel in the winter of 1924–5, fell to about $1·15 a bushel in the spring of 1929. In the meantime, only the accumulation of large stocks kept the prices of tropical staples like sugar and coffee from collapsing—and even so, only until about 1927–8. In that year, for example, the stock of coffee in the state of Saõ Paulo leaped from 3·3 million to 11·7 million bags, and with the best of will, the Brazilian government could not keep up with the supply. The next year, in spite of a drop of one fifth in the world crop and of one third in the Brazilian crop, the price plunged from 180 to 98 gold francs a quintal.[2]

[1] League of Nations, *The Course and Phases of the World Economic Depression* (Geneva, 1931), p. 43. [2] *Ibid.*, pp. 58, 56, 46, 53.

In short, Lewis's model, while not a sufficient explanation of the lag in trade, does point to one of the weakest spots in the international economy.

In spite of the above-mentioned difficulties, the economies of Europe grew in the twenties, as Table 18 indicates:

Table 18. *Relative Changes in Real National Income and Manufacturing Output, 1920 to 1930*

	Income		Output	
	Number of years above 1913 level[a]	1928–9 as percentage of 1913	Number of years above 1913 level[a]	1928–9 as percentage of 1913
United Kingdom	8 (4)	113	4 (1)	106
Germany	4 (4)	109	4 (1)	118
France	7 (7)	124	7 (7)	139
Belgium				
Sweden	11 (10)	139	7 (7)	143
United States	11 (11)	166	10 (10)	172

[a] The figures in parentheses are the number of years income surpassed the 1913 level by more than 5 per cent.

SOURCE: Ingvar Svennilson, *Growth and Stagnation in the European Economy*, p. 28.

On closer scrutiny, however, this growth is less impressive than it seems. In the first place, it was extremely uneven. A country like Britain was not only gaining ground slowly and spasmodically but never succeeded in achieving full employment.[1] Indeed, from 1921 on, unemployment was never less than 9 per cent of the work force; there

[1] By using other indices, one obtains a somewhat better picture of Britain's economic growth in this period. Thus gross domestic product, which does not include earnings from abroad (these fell sharply as a result of the War), rose by 27·6 per cent from 1913 to 1928–9, or 1·45 per cer cent per year. Similarly the K. S. Lomax index of industrial production (excluding building) shows a gain of 20 per cent from 1913 to 1928–9 (22 per cent from 1913 to 1929). On the other hand, the OEEC index of manufacturing output shows no gain whatever for the period 1913–29. The Feinstein-Prest estimates of net national income (1900 prices, which tend to bias the gain upward) show an increase of 14·7 per cent from 1913 to 1929 (0·9 per cent per year). Angus Maddison, *Economic Growth in the West: Comparative Experience in Europe and North America* (New York, 1964), pp. 201–2 (gross domestic product); Mitchell and Deane, *Abstract of British Historical Statistics*, pp. 272 (Lomax), 367–8 (Feinstein-Prest); OEEC, *Statistiques de base de la production industrielle 1913–52* (Paris, n.d.), Table 1. For a revisionist view of British economic performance in the interwar years, see D. H. Aldcroft, 'Economic Progress in Britain in the 1920s', *Scottish Journal of Political Economy*, XIII (1966), 297–316, and 'Economic Growth in the Inter-War Years: A Reassessment', *Econ. Hist. Rev.*, 2nd ser., XX (1967), 311–26.

seemed to be a hard core of one million jobless, good times or bad. Germany, though growing faster in the twenties (she started after the war from a much lower base), faced the same problem.[1] Trade union returns (which are biased downward, especially from 1928 on) show that from 1923, the proportion of unemployed fell below 7 per cent in only one year, 1925. It was up to 18 per cent in 1926, and after a considerable decline in late 1926 and 1927, started up again in the following year; so that in 1929, with the economy still booming, at least in appearance, one in eight workers—some two million persons—was without a job.[2] The Scandinavian countries were, if anything, in worse shape. In Sweden, where one in four was jobless in 1921, the percentage of unemployed was reduced to 10·1 by 1924; but it was never to fall so low again in that decade; and at the height of prosperity, in 1928–9, the rate stood at 10·6 per cent. Denmark and Norway were in still deeper trouble; unemployment averaged 18·4 and 19·5 per cent respectively for the period 1925–9. Estimates for Europe as a whole show the number of jobless rising from between 3½ and 4 millions in the period 1921–5 to between 4½ and 5½ in the boom years 1926–9. And these figures clearly understate the real facts, for they are essentially confined to wholly unemployed male workers in urban industrial occupations.[3]

This persistent unemployment reflects the serious weakness of certain branches and sectors, aggravated by institutional and psychological impediments to the movement of labour between economic activities; while in a country like Britain, the difficulty was further exasperated by deflationary policies in defence of the pound. Almost everywhere the old consumers' goods industries—textiles, leather, pottery manufacture, woodworking—were in difficulty, as were coal mining, iron and steel, and shipbuilding.[4] And in those countries, Germany in particular, where the heavy industries were expanding in the middle and late twenties, this growth was accompanied by vigorous programmes of rationaliza-

[1] The OEEC index shows a rise in German manufacturing output of 22 per cent from 1913 to 1927 (the cyclical peak) and 18 per cent from 1913 to 1929. This corresponds closely to the Hoffmann index of production by sectors, which shows a rise of 19·5 per cent from 1913 to 1929 for industry, mining, and handicrafts combined. On the other hand, Hoffmann does not show a peak in 1927. Output goes up steadily in the period 1925–9 (with the exception of a slight dip in 1926), and the gain of 18 per cent registered in those years accounts for almost the whole of the improvement since 1913. Walther G. Hoffmann, *Das Wachstum der deutschen Wirtschaft seit der Mitte des 19. Jahrhunderts* (Berlin, 1965), p. 455.

[2] Svennilson, *Growth and Stagnation*, p. 31; cf. Carl T. Schmidt, *German Business Cycles 1924–1933* (New York, 1934), pp. 69, 106–7.

[3] Svennilson, *Growth and Stagnation*, pp. 30–1.

[4] For the distribution of unemployment by industry in the U.K., see Mitchell and Deane, *Abstract of British National Statistics*, p. 67.

tion and concentration that made it possible to close down the least efficient enterprises and eliminate 'redundant' labour. Meanwhile agriculture languished, and although unemployment and underemployment on the land do not show in the official statistics (except in so far as men left the country to seek jobs in the city and ended up on the dole), they were there—a burden on the economy and a threat to social and political stability.

The growth of the 1920's was uneven in another sense. The early years of the decade were a time of difficult political and economic adjustment, characterized by monetary instability and wide fluctuations in prices and punctuated by bitter labour disputes. It was only in the second half of the period that the resolution of these problems laid the foundation of a firm upswing, and then production responded vigorously enough to make some think that man had found the secret of eternal prosperity. (These naive optimists, it must be said, were usually persons who were dazzled by stock market prices, to the exclusion of other economic indicators.) In a country like Germany, for example, national income rose in 1925-9 from 60 to 76 billion RM., a rate of 6 per cent a year.[1] France was growing just about as fast, and even Britain only slightly slower.·

But this spurt, however impressive, rested on a peculiarly improvisational, hence precarious, foundation. The improvisation consisted in the *ad hoc* measures devised to overcome the imbalance of international monetary arrangements; and the precariousness, in the tentative, discretionary character of these measures.[2]

The fundamental difficulty, as we saw, was the disparity between means and ends. Europe had been forced to liquidate a substantial fraction of its assets abroad to pay for the war, while much of its real capital had gone up in fragments or smoke; and with these sharply reduced resources, it had to rebuild and grow again. In the last analysis, the difficulty—in every way analogous to the dollar shortage of the forties—was met by a flow of money and capital from the United States. The stimulus provided by this injection of funds was particularly important in the late twenties; indeed, given the strains in the system—the weak demand for consumers' goods, the depression in agriculture—the economy of those years is comparable to an overworked engine, vigorously stoked but near to cracking from the strain. Germany offers

---

[1] G. W. Guillebaud, *The Economic Recovery of Germany 1933-1938* (London, 1939) p. 14. This is in current prices. If income is deflated by the change in the price level, the rate of growth is slightly higher.

[2] Perhaps the best study of the meretricious prosperity of the late twenties, particularly in its monetary aspects, is Rolf E. Lüke's monograph on the German experience: *Von der Stabilisierung zur Krise.*

the extreme example, with capital imports totalling 17·5 billion RM. from 1924 to 1929, of which 3·9 billion in 1927 and 4·3 in 1928.[1] Even so, German economic expansion was slowing down well before the break of late 1929; investment in new plant, for example, peaked in 1928, and while the stock market collapse of that autumn can account for some of the drop in that year (see Table 19), it will not explain all of it. Entrepreneurial anticipations were clearly turning down, and this is reflected in the price of industrial shares, which levelled off as early as the winter of 1926–7 and had already fallen some 25 per cent by the summer of 1929.

Table 19. *Germany: Industrial Investments of Large Corporate Enterprise 1924–31[a] (in millions of Reichsmarks)*

	New plant	Replacement	Total
1924	193	513	706
1925	574	574	1,148
1926	301	647	948
1927	535	721	1,256
1928	711	789	1,500
1929	327	841	1,168
1930	116	791	907
1931	21	501	522

[a] All corporations with share capital of over one million RM, plus smaller firms whose shares were traded on a stock exchange. These represented at the end of 1931 roughly 90 per cent of the total share capital of all German corporations.

SOURCE: *Wirtschaft und Statistik*, 1 October 1933, as given in Germany, Untersuchungsausschuss für das Bankwesen 1933, *Untersuchung des Bankwesens 1933* (3 vols.; Berlin, 1933), I. Teil, vol. 1, p. 571.

In the earlier years, much of this flow took the form of capital movement, that is, the purchase of European securities by American investors. But by the late twenties, this source of supply thinned out, as rapidly appreciating American common stocks proved more attractive; and the transfer of funds took the far more dangerous form of short-term or call loans, placed in Europe by bankers who were attracted by higher interest rates. Once again Germany was the extreme case: fully one half of the money that came in from abroad from 1918 to 1931 (10·3 out of 20·6 billion RM.) took the form of short-term credits.[2] These served for a while to sustain the expansion, but then speculation on the American exchanges grew so frenetic that the price of short loans

[1] Lionel Robbins, *The Great Depression* (New York, 1934), p. 227. Over the same period, reparations deliveries amounted to 8·6 billions.
[2] Gustav Stolper, Karl Häuser, and Knut Borchardt, *The German Economy 1870 to the Present* (N.Y., 1967), p. 113.

to cover securities transactions on the United States rose well above the European level. By late 1928 and early 1929 American banks began calling their European loans, so that net exports of capital from the United States, which had risen from less than $200 million in 1926 to over a billion dollars in 1928, plunged to $200 million again in 1929.[1]

This withdrawal of support put tremendous pressure on the European banking system, particularly on the great German banks, which had always followed the policy of borrowing short and lending long. The result was a brutal contraction of credit, which made itself felt in every corner of the economy. The shock was the greater because it was reinforced by the rapid fall in the price of industrial shares (see Table 20). Meanwhile commodity prices tumbled, squeezing thousands of businessmen who had used inflated values as a basis for borrowing or had diverted liquid assets into what had seemed a short cut to riches. In a highly integrated economy, this kind of collapse builds up in mass and momentum like an avalanche or a sandslide. Each man calls upon his debtors for help in meeting the claims of his creditors, so that even the healthiest enterprises are hard pressed to meet the demands that crowd in upon them. So it was in the United States; so it was in Europe. The weaker firms, the swollen industrial empires with watered stock and large debts went first; but they dragged some of the strongest companies down with them.

Table 20. *Percentage Fall in Prices of Industrial Shares, 1927–31*

Germany	April	1927 to June 1931	−61·7
Netherlands	March	1929 to June 1931	−60·0
U.S.A.	September 1929 to June 1931		−59·7
France	February	1929 to June 1931	−55·7
United Kingdom	January	1929 to June 1931	−45·0
Sweden	July	1929 to June 1931	−30·6
Switzerland	September 1928 to June 1931		−29·3

SOURCE: League of Nations, *The Course and Phases of the World Economic Depression*, p. 175.

It is hard to give an analytical account of the crisis that does justice to the rush of disasters, tumbling one upon the other; or to give a narrative account that illuminates the confusion of events. Every branch of the economy was in trouble—trouble real enough in an objective sense but magnified out of proportion by panic. Manufacturing enterprises cut their output sharply and dismissed a large fraction of their work force. Unemployment in Britain more than doubled from 1929 to 1931, jumping from 1,249,000 to 2,698,000. In Germany the contraction was

[1] League of Nations, *Course and Phases of the World Economic Depression*, p. 98.

far more rapid, and from 1929 to the end of 1930 the official number of jobless had risen from slightly under 2 million to almost 4·5 million; two years later, the figure stood at almost 6 million, and this was certainly an understatement of the true facts. At the seasonal peak at the end of 1932, unemployment in Europe as a whole reached an all-time high of about 15 million persons.[1] At the same time, those business firms in difficulty hastened to realize every liquid asset, selling off stocks of materials and goods at a fraction of their cost and previous value.

Table 21. *Index of Bankruptcies* (*1928 = 100*)

	France[a]	Germany[b]	Italy[a]	United States[c]
1929	106	123	104	99
1930	111	142	117	119

[a] All traders.

[b] Firms inscribed on the official trade registers.

[c] Individuals, firms, or corporations engaged in ordinary commercial operations, including banks. Failure of stockholders, real-estate brokers, and similar traders not included.

SOURCE: League of Nations, *The Course and Phases of the World Economic Depression*, p. 186.

The others, reluctant to sell at a loss, held inventory but cut back production accordingly. Neither policy was conducive to prosperity, and the number of bankruptcies rose sharply everywhere. As Table 21 shows, Germany was the hardest hit: in 1931, the *annus terribilis* of mass unemployment, bitter political conflict and racist violence, and international enmity, some seventeen thousand enterprises closed down.

Among the branches that suffered most in this debacle was banking, especially in central Europe. Actual failures at the time of the stock market collapse were rare, as the different financial institutions tried to cover one another against the consequences of the contraction. But these ingenious stop-gap measures depended on the tacit good will of all concerned, and the extent and duration of the crisis tended to undermine this altruistic disposition; moreover, however sensible the bankers of any given country were prepared to be, the stability of the system depended on international co-operation. Germany in particular needed the help and forbearance of other countries, and by the end of 1930 she could no longer count on substantial assistance. Part of the difficulty was that her potential creditors were in trouble themselves; part was a reflection of justifiably diminishing confidence in German political stability; and part was a consequence of France's refusal to join with the

[1] Pollard, *The Development of the British Economy*, p. 225; Guillebaud, *The Economic Recovery of Germany*, pp. 14–31; Svennilson, *Growth and Stagnation*, p. 30.

United States and Britain in sustaining the German finances and economy.

It is interesting, in the light of France's recent diplomatic and economic policy (1965–7), to scrutinize her behaviour in 1930–1. Then as later, she had large gold reserves and appeared to the rest of Europe as a bloated moneybags hoarding her wealth while others starved. Then as later, she assumed a unilateral stance of nonco-operation with her former allies, conditioning her economic good will on the political complaisance of those who sought her help. At the same time, she was even less tender with her former enemies, combating in particular Germany's efforts to improve her commercial situation by trade agreements with the countries of eastern Europe—agreements that threatened to affect French economic and political interests adversely.

In defence of French policy, it should be noted that Germany gave her good cause to worry. It was hard, for example, for the French to accept German pleas of poverty when they knew full well that the Weimar regime was engaged, overtly and covertly, in a costly campaign to rearm—a campaign waged partly to steal the thunder of chauvinist elements on the extreme Right, partly with a view to general revision of the Versailles treaty. Similarly the proposal of a customs union between Germany and Austria was more than it appeared to be. Superficially the union was to be a purely economic arrangement, perfectly compatible in principle with the peace treaty. In fact, it was intended as the prelude to a closer political connection, even a merger, and Dr Luther of the Reichsbank was so indiscreet as to speak of going over, in foreign affairs, to 'a war of movement'. In any event, it is now clear that for all France's opposition to the *Zollunion*, she did not, as has long been believed, put pressure on Germany and Austria to drop the project by a massive withdrawal of short-term credits. What she did do, however, was close her capital and money markets to new German and Austrian borrowing. Once the bank crisis broke in May of 1931, this was enough to give the French strong leverage, and in August Germany and Austria promised to drop the plan for good.[1]

From the French point of view, then, financial strong-arm tactics were politically justified. Indeed the tragedy of the interwar years was that usually everyone was right politically, and there was simply no solution that would do justice to all. What was needed was a higher

[1] The best source for the effect of political considerations on Franco-German relations is Edward W. Bennett, *Germany and the Diplomacy of the Financial Crisis, 1931* (Cambridge, Mass., 1962). On the question of the withdrawal of short-term credits, see Karl Erich Born, *Die deutsche Bankenkrise 1931: Finanzen und Politik* (Munich, 1967), pp. 54–6, 64–5. Even so reliable a source as Lüke, *Von der Stabilisierung zur Krise*, pp. 268–9, repeats the conventional wisdom on this matter.

altruism that would have paved the way for compromises that, though diminishing the advantage of each, would have enhanced the general welfare.

The same contradiction of short and long run, of special interest and general, was to be found in the economic sphere. France's policy of financial coercion was not immediately expensive, except in so far as French capitalists were obliged to forgo opportunities for profitable investment—more profitable, that is, than alternative opportunities. The loss was surely small. Over time, however, egoism was a two-edged sword. The markets of Europe were too closely linked for any country to benefit from the business collapse of another. Germany and Austria went over the brink in the summer of 1931. For several years thereafter France, among others, was to feel the economic repercussions; and if one takes into account the more distant political consequences of the depression, it is clear that the world, including France, was still paying the bill for the 'victories' of 1931 a generation later.

The central European banking crisis began in May, when Austria's most important bank, the Credit-Anstalt, collapsed. The Credit-Anstalt was no ordinary big bank: it controlled two thirds of Austrian industry, either directly or indirectly; was the joint-stock arm of the Vienna Rothschilds; was the embodiment of enterprise *cum* solidity. When the Credit-Anstalt announced on 11 May that it had suffered losses almost equal to its capital, it brought on a run that cost it one quarter of its foreign funds (equivalent to over three times its capital) by the end of the month; while the gold and exchange cover of the National Bank of Austria fell in one week (by 15 May) from 83·5 per cent to 67·5 per cent of note issue.[1]

The Austrian debacle undermined the credit of all central European enterprise. Germany, already in deep economic trouble, was caught up in a whirlwind of calls and liquidations, as creditors and investors hastened to protect themselves. In the space of five or six weeks the Reichsbank lost almost 2 billion RM. in gold and foreign exchange. Private institutions lost heavily as well, especially the leading Berlin *Grossbanken*, which accounted for well over half the nation's foreign banking debits. Nor were foreign creditors alone in their haste to place their funds under shelter; German depositors rushed to withdraw their money, and once again it was the *Grossbanken* of Berlin that were hardest hit—some 2 billion RM. reimbursed in the months of June and July.[2]

[1] Born, *Deutsche Bankenkrise*, p. 65. Capital of the Credit-Anstalt was 145 million shillings. Foreign claims and holdings at the beginning of May totalled 1,800 million, including 700 million at short term.

[2] Guillebaud, *The Economic Recovery of Germany*, p. 20; A. Dauphin-Meunier, *La banque 1919–1935: Allemagne–Angleterre–France* (Paris, 1936), pp. 216–18.

The German governments, the Reichsbank, and the directors of the private banks spent the spring of 1931 scrambling to stop the leaks. On June 6 Chancellor Brüning declared that Germany was no longer in a position to meet her reparations payments, already much reduced as a result of the Young Plan. This repudiation was then sanctioned by the so-called Hoover moratorium of 20 June, which made a virtue of necessity and offered to suspend all intergovernmental debts for a period of one year. There were those who pressed for a delay of two years, but in a debate that seems otherworldly in the light of subsequent events, it was decided not to put off longer than necessary the return to normal business relationships.

Given the rate at which the German capital and money markets were haemorrhaging, the effectiveness of this first aid depended on speed of application. But here the old nemesis of international mistrust and self-interest intervened. The French were outraged by this further, indeed final, erasure of German reparations; and their outrage was exacerbated by the American authorship of the proposal. One French historian has described the event in a paragraph that sums up all the resentment of these interwar years:

The United States, after having played a preponderant role in fashioning the Treaty of Versailles, did not ratify it; they did not join the League of Nations; they refused to recognize any legal bond between their claims against their former allies and the claims of these allies against Germany. There they are now, intervening publicly, but for what purpose? to extend a protective hand to their old enemy! The contradiction may seem strange. It is explainable in terms of the blow that a complete failure of Germany would inflict on her American lenders. Hoover is the creature of the banks, and in his eyes their interests come before any considerations of public morality.[1]

As a result, the French delayed their acceptance of the moratorium until 6 July, and this reluctance not only deprived the measure of its shock effect but called attention to the rapid deterioration of Germany's financial position. Although the Reichsbank and the Golddiskontbank succeeded in obtaining abroad emergency credits totalling some 630 million RM, these could not compensate the outflow, and the reserves of the central bank dwindled rapidly. In desperation, it followed the orthodox banking technique of tightening credit, which just aggravated the distress. Any velleities, moreover, that the Reichsbank may have entertained of easing restrictions were swiftly stifled by those foreign banks whose assistance was desperately needed. As the President of the Reichsbank, Hans Luther, put it: '...it was impossible to give up the

---

[1] Jacques Chastenet, *Histoire de la Troisième République: Déclin de la Troisième 1931–1938* (Paris, 1962), p. 21.

restrictions, for any discussion of a moratorium with the principal foreign banks of issue presupposed that the Reichsbank would defend first of all its own position in a perfectly obvious way.'[1]

The events of these critical days of early July 1931 may have seemed to the tormented participants to pass in an agony of slow motion; to the historical observer, they have the whirlwind jerkiness of an early motion picture chase. On 8 July the president of the Reich announced a decree authorizing the government to establish a syndicate composed of all German business enterprises with a capital of more than 5 million RM, to guarantee, proportionately to size of firm, credits from the Deutsche Golddiskontbank of up to 500 million RM to those enterprises in need of help. Why the Golddiskontbank and not the Reichsbank? Because the central bank, like all banks of issue, could lend only on the security of good commercial paper, and Germany's banks, and behind them, Germany's industrial enterprises, had no good paper to speak of.

The plan, which recalls Schacht's scheme of 1923 to offer a mortgage on all the land in Germany as a guarantee for the notes of the Renten-bank, was never put into execution; the monetary situation was de-teriorating too fast as a result of the collapse on 7 July of one of Ger-many's most important textile combines, the Norddeutsche Wollkäm-merei und Kammgarnspinnerei (Nordwolle),[2] behind which stood the Danat bank (a merger of the Darmstädter Bank and the Nationalbank für Deutschland).

Now began another round of mendicant visits. This time Hans Luther, the President of the Reichsbank, went himself and by aero-plane, a still unfamiliar means of locomotion that only underlined the urgency of the crisis. The morning of 9 July he was in London talking to Montagu Norman, head of the Bank of England; that afternoon he entrained for Paris, where he spoke the next day to Moret of the Bank of France. But Moret told him that the size of the credit required was too large for the Bank of France and that it was now a matter for the government to decide—another way of saying that France would help only on condition that Germany provided the desired political guaran-tees. So Luther saw Pierre Flandin, the French Minister of Finance,

---

[1] Report to the General Assembly of the Reichsbank, 16 March 1932, cited in Dauphin-Meunier, *La banque*, p. 219.

[2] Rumours of the predicament of Nordwolle had been circulating for some time, fanned by the National Socialists, who saw here an excellent opportunity for anti-Semitic propaganda. Needless to say, these rumours did not help matters. On 10 June Nordwolle published a balance sheet announcing important losses, and when, less than a month later (7 July), it was revealed that liabilities amounted to about 200 million RM, the Stock Exchange suspended trading in Nordwolle shares. Cf. Léon Proskourovsky, *La crise des banques de crédit en Allemagne depuis 1931* (Paris, 1935), pp. 19, 26.

who demanded among other things a reversal of Germany's armament policy and further assurances of adherence to the Versailles treaty. Luther was then supposed to proceed from Paris to Basel, to attend a meeting of the Bank for International Settlements. Instead, he flew back to Berlin on the 11th, empty-handed.

Something had to give. On Monday, 13 July, the Danat Bank closed its doors. An emergency meeting of the leading Berlin bankers called that same day broke up in an exchange of insults and accusations. The Danat would not merge with the Dresdner; the Dresdner would not merge with the Deutsche Bank. At this point the German business community and public were seized with panic, rushed the counters, and in forty-eight hours brought about the closing of all banks and credit institutions—what the contemporaries called euphemistically a bank holiday. In the German case the holiday lasted three weeks, until 5 August, when the banks were permitted to resume normal operations subject to a Reichsbank discount rate of 15 per cent and a rate on collateral loans of 20 per cent.

Interest rates of 15 and 20 per cent were designed to be a deterrent to borrowing; but credit was desperately needed to prevent a complete collapse of German business life. To this end, the state created in July 1931 a Guaranty and Acceptance Bank (Garantie und Akzeptbank), with a capital of 200 million RM, of which 80 million subscribed by the national government, 12 million by the Prussian state, the rest by the major banking institutions. The new establishment acted as an intermediary between ordinary banks and the Reichsbank: for a small commission it endorsed bankers' bills and thereby made them eligible for rediscount. By the end of the year it had accepted in this way paper totalling some 1·6 billion RM. One quarter of this went to shore up the Dresdner Bank, to no avail.

This was only one of several areas in which the state moved to reconstitute the banking system and money market. It proceeded to guarantee deposits in shaky banks and to make good the losses of depositors in those institutions that had been forced to liquidate. Total outlays on this account eventually came to almost one billion marks. At the same time, it acted to meet a problem that, if not peculiarly German, was more acute there than elsewhere: the immobilization of bank assets in long-term, hence illiquid, loans to and investments in business enterprise. The device employed was the exchange of discountable state paper for the securities representing these loans and investments, and the system was regularized by the creation in December of 1932 of the Deutsche Finanzierungs-Institut (Definag). Finally, the state moved to refloat or merge a number of sinking financial institutions on a new, healthier base. Invariably, these reorganizations entailed drastic write-offs of capital and reserves, with the state obtaining a substantial share of what remained. Among the banks reconstituted in this way were the Dresdner (which absorbed the Danat), the Barmer Bankverein, the Commerz- und Privatbank, the Allgemeine Credit-Anstalt, the Sächsische Stadtbank, and the J. F. Schroeder Bank (Bremen). Only the Deutsche Bank of those houses in trouble was able to reorganize itself, and even there the government indirectly bought shares to the amount of 50 million RM. By the end of 1932, of 442 million RM of capital of the five remaining Berlin *Grossbanken* (Berliner Handels-gesellschaft, Deutsche Bank, Dresdner Bank, Commerz- und Privat-bank, and the Reichskreditgesellschaft), 282 million were held by the state, either directly or through the intermediary of the Golddiskont-bank.[1] The one bank to come through without government assistance was the Berliner Handelsgesellschaft.

At the same time, the state took measures to stop the outflow of foreign exchange, and these necessarily took the form of severe con-trols over commercial transactions. By decree of 18 July, all Germans liable to property tax were required to declare their holdings of foreign money or claims, either at home or abroad; and the Reichsbank was authorized to purchase such assets for marks, except where needed for legitimate business purposes. (Not coincidentally, a decree of the same day established rigid control of the press in an effort to halt a campaign of rumour and invective that was seriously undermining public confi-dence in the banking system and the government.)[2] Ten days later, another decree provided for registration of all debts to foreign creditors in excess of £25,000. And on 1 August, still more stringent require-ments were instituted: whereas before it had only been forbidden to sell German money for foreign currency, now even the right to dispose of foreign exchange or assets required the permission of the authorities. The enforcement of these controls was facilitated by a 'standstill agreement' of 1 September 1931 between Germany and her foreign creditors that provided for a moratorium on short-term indebtedness. This was subsequently renewed at intervals and prevented the loss of another 10 billion RM in foreign exchange. It gave rise, however, to a new species of blocked marks, the first of a large family of special currencies that proliferated later under the Nazi regime.

Finally, the state instituted controls over the banks themselves. An ordinance of 19 September 1931 established a commission of surveil-lance (Kuratorium für das Bankgewerbe), composed of three state officials and two representatives of the Reichsbank, whose mission was 'to remain informed of the situation of German banking and credit,

---

[1] Dauphin-Meunier, *La banque*, p. 258, n. 2.
[2] *The Economist*, 25 July 1931, p. 160.

especially in their relations abroad, and to influence general banking policy from the standpoint of the overall Germany economy'. These aims were as vague as they were broad; and the significance of the Kuratorium depended in the last analysis on the use it made of its powers. Here the historian runs up against the muteness of the sources: the Kuratorium almost never intervened publicly in the policy or conduct of banking enterprises. This may mean that it did not in fact intervene; or that it was able to achieve its ends by more discreet pressures. One is inclined to argue *ex silentio* that once the crisis of 1931 was past, the need for government supervision and control disappeared; and that the Kuratorium was important, not so much for what it did as for what it could do. In this regard it was, together with its executive organ, the Reichskommissar für das Bankgewerbe, the model for the analogous control bodies of the Nazi regime: the Aufsichtsamt and the Reichskommissar für das Kreditwesen.

Germany and Austria were the countries hardest hit by the financial crisis of 1929–31; but no advanced banking system emerged unscathed. Britain faced essentially the same problems as Germany, though in less acute form. At the end of March 1931 she owed some £400 million abroad at short-term, which were only partially offset by £150 million in short-term credits. These, moreover, were largely in the form of commercial acceptances, secured in principle by the commodities in transaction. But the value of these commodities had shrunk below the point of cover, and the paper was in effect unrealizable, the more so as some 40 per cent of these claims—£60 million, of which £45 million in trade acceptances—were against German debtors.

As a result, when Germany's banking system collapsed, Britain's was badly shaken. Foreign creditors began to withdraw funds from London. They were encouraged to make haste by the Macmillan Report of 14 July 1931, which called attention to Britain's dangerous deficit on short-term account; and by the May Committee report of 31 July, which offered a gloomy appraisal of Britain's budgetary position and hinted that so long as the Labour government pursued a policy of generous expenditures for unemployment insurance and social welfare, financial equilibrium was impossible.

The conventional defence against this kind of run would have been a sharp increase in the interest rate. But this would only have aggravated the hardships of the business community and with them the unemployment that weighed so heavily on the state's finances. Moreover, it was not at all clear that the kind of 'hot money' that was at the root of the instability of the international money market would respond to a higher rate of return. By the middle of 1931, capitalists and speculators were more concerned with security than with percentage points.

So the British, like the Germans, went shopping for loans, and like the Germans, found they had to pay a political as well as monetary price for help. In late July of 1931 the Bank of England borrowed £50 million from the Federal Reserve Bank of New York and the Bank of France, but when, in August, it tried to raise another £80 million, it was told that the money would be more easily forthcoming if the British government pledged itself to an economy budget and, in particular, to reduce the dole. Or perhaps it was the British banking community itself which put these demands in the mouths of the American and French lenders in order to give more weight to their own demands for economy. Or perhaps it was Ramsay MacDonald, Prime Minister of the Labour government, who cultivated this version of events as an excuse for his own surrender to City pressure. In any event, the cabinet split; the more welfare-minded members refused to support a 10 per cent cut in unemployment payments. This was Sunday, 23 August. The next day MacDonald met his colleagues again and informed them that they were out, but he was in. He was named that evening as Prime Minister of a National government, comprising four Conservatives, two Liberals, and three Labourites.

A coalition government had two virtues: it made it possible to shift to Labour the onus of reduced unemployment payments, which the Conservatives preferred to avoid; and it was a gage of stability and conservatism to the foreign bankers. These did indeed come through on 28 August with the keenly sought and dearly bought credit of £80 million, but Britain's financial troubles were far from over. The haemorrhage of funds continued, partly because the financial crisis was spreading from Germany to the Netherlands, partly because British depositors were becoming uneasy. Then the news broke that the Royal Navy had mutinied. The report was much exaggerated; there had been passive resistance (a refusal to muster or work) at the naval base at Invergordon (Scotland) in protest against pay cuts that hit hardest at the ordinary seaman. But the rumour sufficed to convince many that Crown, Empire, and the white cliffs of Dover were on the point of collapse. On Wednesday, the 16th of September, the Bank of England lost £5 millions in gold; the next day, £10 millions; the next, £18 millions. The credit of £80 million was almost gone; the Bank's gold reserves were down to £130 million; and the weekend promised no more respite than the minute of rest before the knock-out round of a fight.

Weekends are made for serious financial decisions, as anyone who has followed the history of monetary devaluations knows. On Saturday the 19th, the Bank of England advised the government to go off the gold standard, which it did on Monday, 21 September. At the same time, the Bank raised the discount rate from 4·5 to 6 per cent.

In contrast to the German debacle, the British banks stood up well to adversity. No house of any importance had to close its doors, even temporarily. This strength reflected in part a more cautious lending policy, in part the extent and diversity of the clientele of the great joint-stock banks. And then, there was the temperamental inertia of the British depositor—what a French historian has called his slow-wittedness [*lenteur d'esprit*]. Even so, almost everyone was bled white, and the smaller merchant banks, discount houses, and bill brokers were years in recovering.

It was the end of an epoch. Within a few months, the Commonwealth countries, Scandinavia, and Japan followed Britain off gold. Less than two years later, it was the turn of the United States. In the face of this abandonment of what for many was the sacred law of monetary morality, France, Switzerland, Holland, Belgium, Italy, and Poland formed a gold bloc: they would settle balances among them in gold, but would not export gold outside the bloc. It was a gallant gesture. but it had two serious disadvantages. First and less important, the chief gold market remained in London, so that the value of the currencies of the gold-bloc countries fluctuated with the price of gold outside the system. This dependence made little if any economic difference, but politically it was an irritant. Secondly, the trading position of the gold-bloc countries deteriorated by comparison with that of the deserters. The latter saw the exchange value of their currencies fall; the pound, for example, was down to $3·40 (from $4·86) by the end of 1931. This made imports more expensive, but it gave a strong boost to exports—a boost that was badly needed in a country like Britain, which had struggled for half a decade under the burden of an overvalued currency. At the same time, home prices remained steady, so that confidence in sterling returned and with it, foreign capital. By April 1932 the financial crisis was over.[1] By June the discount rate was down to 2 per cent, the sign of a safe, quiet, but also somnolent, money market. Business activity was almost at its low. Six months later, all the indicators had turned upward, and Britain was out of the woods.

In terms of liquid assets, France was the richest country in Europe, the one least vulnerable to panicky movements of hot money. The reserves of the Bank of France, in gold and foreign exchange (*devises*), had risen from some 20 billion (milliard) francs at the end of 1925 to 67·5 billion at the end of 1929. Two years later, at a time when Britain and Germany had trouble maintaining even the shadow of a reserve and then only by means of emergency transfusions, the Bank of France had increased its holdings to 88·5 billions. The cartoonists of the day

[1] Pollard, *The Development of the British Economy*, p. 229.

pictured Marianne as a bloated plutocrat, throning high on her money-bags while the other nations of Europe came begging for alms.

Yet France had her own financial and banking problems. Business activity levelled off in 1930, and a number of local banks found themselves in difficulty. The most important of these was the Banque Adam, a family enterprise of Boulogne (Pas-de-Calais) that had gone public and ramified as far afield as Guiana. The Banque Adam was caught up in the stock market speculations and manipulations of its principal shareholder, Oustric; when it was forced to suspend payments in November 1930, the rest of the banking community was shocked but attributed the disaster to the incompetence and malfeasance of the Adam management. Unfortunately, this kind of complacency is not easily communicated to the ordinary man. The failure of the Banque Adam triggered a run that brought down a whole series of local banks. The big branch banks then moved in to salvage the wrecks and absorb them. The Crédit Industriel et Commercial, for example, took over the Banque de la Vallée du Rhône, the Comptoir d'Escompte de la Sarthe, the Banque Privée Lyon-Marseille, and the best part of the Banque d'Alsace-Lorraine.

Even more serious in its consequences was the collapse of the Banque Nationale de Crédit, which had placed large sums in speculative industrial enterprises and in risky commercial paper, in particular in the drafts of traders in diamonds and precious stones. Looking back from the vantage of several decades, it is hard to believe that one of the major banks in Paris would rediscount the most blatant accommodation paper: often one and the same stone served as security for a whole array of bills; and sometimes there was no stone at all. But the B.N.C. was relying on that third signature of the smaller banks that dealt directly with the diamond merchants; and when these were caught up in the retreat of jewelry prices, the B.N.C. went with them.

This time panic threatened the major Parisian houses; and to avoid a moratorium, the government moved in, guaranteed deposits, and arranged to reorganize the B.N.C. as the Banque Nationale pour le Commerce et l'Industrie. Even so, a number of middle-sized houses, some of them a century old, succumbed in the ensuing run and liquidation: the Banque Syndicale de Paris, Banque Commerciale Africaine, Banque Courvoisier, and others in Paris; the Comptoir d'Escompte de Reims; Veuve Guérin et Fils at Lyons; Ramel, Tardif et Cie at Saint-Etienne; the Banque Charpenay in Grenoble. Other houses survived, but only at the price of drastic write-offs of debt and capital. Thus the Banque de l'Union Parisienne, which held large blocks of foreign and colonial securities in portfolio, was forced to reimburse some 600 million francs in two weeks; and having withstood this trial, to merge with the rival Crédit Mobilier Français, reduce its capital from 300 to 100 million francs, and then raise 100 millions in fresh capital.

All in all, some 670 banks failed from October 1929 to September 1937. Most of these, to be sure, were small exchange shops that hardly deserved the appellation of bank; but 276 were joint-stock corporations with an aggregate capital of 1,900 million francs; and given the tendency of nominal capitalization to lag behind the depreciation of money, their gross worth was far greater. A number of these were among the most important banking houses in France: five were capitalized at over 50 million francs; and nine, between 25 and 50 millions. What the overall loss was, it is impossible to say; but Henry Laufenburger made a partial calculation of the losses suffered by stockholders and depositors of some 91 major banks, 48 in Paris, 43 in the provinces. Not all of these had actually failed; some had simply been forced to write off bad assets by reducing their capital. The total loss came to five billion francs.[1]

These losses would no doubt have been far greater if the French government had not intervened directly by guaranteeing deposits and thereby reassured a public that was on the edge of panic. Nor did the state confine its support to banking. It moved to shore up other shaky branches of the economy and eventually spent some three billion francs in these rescue operations. This policy of 'socialization of losses' came in for considerable criticism, the more so as many of the beneficiaries would not have returned the favour, had the state needed their support; some indeed were among the political enemies of the Republic. But this would seem to be an unavoidable concomitant of this kind of policy: to save the 'innocent', one must help the 'guilty'. The trouble is that some of the 'guilty', at least, do much better than anyone else. In the meantime, contemporary critics did make the point that the privately owned Bank of France, whose coffers were bulging with bullion, could have done a lot more to support her sister banks. The one instance where she did lend a hand was in the reorganization of the Banque de l'Union Parisienne. But then this was the preferred corporate instrument of the *haute banque protestante*, that select group of old Calvinist houses which constituted the cream of French merchant banking; and the *haute banque protestante* was well represented on the Board of Regents of the Bank of France.

In the meantime, both the French government and the Bank of France had to face up to the international monetary crisis. We have noted their toughness and obduracy toward Germany—not entirely unjustified—in July of 1931. They were similarly unyielding in their

[1] The above data are taken from Marcelle Pommera et al., *Grandeur et déclin de la France à l'époque contemporaine* (Paris, n.d.), pp. 286-7.

response to Britain's abandonment of the gold standard two months later; and once again the decision was as much political as economic. To understand it, one must go back to the twenties and the years when France was struggling to stabilize the franc. By a law of 7 August 1926, the Bank of France was empowered to purchase foreign exchange and gold at market prices and use these as cover for note issue beyond the legal maximum. In effect, France went on to a gold exchange standard rather than on the gold standard, and in the following two years she acquired some 26 billion francs in exchange (*devises*), as against about 10 billion in gold. But the French were never happy with this arrangement, which they looked upon as a *pis aller* that left the franc at the mercy of the monetary policies of Great Britain and the United States.[1] Such dependency 'was understandable in the relations between a satellite state and suzerain state, but it did not accord with the independence of France or with the place she occupied at the time on the international chessboard.'[2] Indeed, the gold exchange standard seemed to some Frenchmen an Anglo–American plot to use money as an instrument of economic domination. Thus Edmond Lebée: 'This dogma, which like many others is of Anglo–Saxon origin, reconciles, in a singular fashion for the Latins, an ardent monetary mystique and the harsh defence of material interests.' The idea, he wrote, was to concentrate 'the world's stock of gold in a few well chosen places, in a few financial centres under [British] control. The gold exchange standard thus appears as that form of controlled money which the future controllers prescribe ...for the others'.[3]

So that when, in June of 1928, the franc was officially stabilized, the legislature forbade the Bank of France to buy foreign exchange and required it to take only gold in settlement of France's claims abroad.

[1] At least this is what the officers of the Bank of France asserted in later years. But it should be noted that the Bank earned large sums in interest on this foreign exchange, whereas gold would have lain sterile in its vaults. Indeed, in 1929 receipts from foreign assets accounted for 65 per cent of the Bank's gross profits. League of Nations, Economic, Financial and Transit Department, *International Currency Experience: Lessons of the Inter-War Period* (Princeton, 1944), p. 43. The vehemence of these denunciations of the gold exchange standard in the early 1930s was not unconnected to the Bank's loss on these holdings when Britain abandoned gold. In its successful effort to get the state to bear this loss, the Bank presented itself as the victim of a vicious system; and it justified its long retention of these assets, not on pecuniary grounds, but on altruistic considerations: it did not want to increase the pressure on the pound sterling. As is so often the case, the officers of the Bank were no doubt moved by both kinds of concerns, that is, they were happy to be paid for their abnegation.

[2] Pommera *et al.*, *Grandeur et déclin*, p. 309.

[3] E. Lebée, *Les doctrines monétaires à l'épreuve des faits*, cited in Pommera *et al.*, *Grandeur et déclin*, p. 309. This is probably an article: I have not been able to find a book of this name.

These were substantial in the late twenties, partly because Frenchmen were repatriating capital that had previously fled in search of more stable currencies, partly because the franc was now undervalued and France enjoyed a substantial surplus on current account. The result was an abrupt rise in the bullion reserves of the Bank of France, as may be seen in the following table:

Table 22. *Bank of France: Holdings of Precious Metal and Foreign Exchange (millions of francs)*

		Foreign Exchange		
End of	Gold reserve	Sight deposits	Bills	League of Nations figures (million dollars)
1925	18,142	316	— [a]	13
1926	18,146	418	—	116[b]
1927	18,126	252	—	850[b]
1928	31,977	13,510	19,215	1,287
1929	41,668	7,249	18,693	1,021
1930	53,578	6,792	19,387	1,027
1931	68,863	12,354	8,757	842
1932	83,017	2,938	1,545	176
1933	77,098	16	1,143	—

[a] The absence of a figure is not to be interpreted as meaning no holdings of bills of exchange. These were not distinguished, however, in the accounts of the Bank, being grouped with other holdings under such rubrics as 'Sundry Assets'. Hence the League of Nations estimates for 1926 and 1927.

[b] Estimated.

SOURCES: Holdings in francs are taken from Paul Einzig, *France's Crisis* (London, 1934), p. 130. The figures on the gold reserve correspond closely to the year-round averages in the *Annuaire statistique*, LVII (1946), Résumé rétrospectif, p. 142. These latter, however, offer the inconvenience of valuing holdings previous to stabilization in 1928 at the prewar parity, that is, in terms of the *franc de germinal*, and thereby exaggerate the increase of that year. League of Nations estimates of foreign exchange are from *International Currency Experience: Lessons of the Inter-War Period*, p. 234.

In contrast, holdings in foreign exchange remained fairly steady from 1928 through the first part of 1931, for the Bank was well aware that further gold purchases would seriously aggravate 'the monetary difficulties of other countries'.[1] But such abstinence was not enough; and when, in the summer of 1931, French capitalists and banks became anxious about their sterling assets and presented them for liquidation, the Bank had no choice but to turn them into gold, and the pressure on London became unbearable.

[1] League of Nations, *International Currency Experience*, p. 39.

Britain's abandonment of the gold standard cost the Bank of France the sizable sum of 2·3 billion francs—the loss on £62 million still in portfolio. By law of 23 December 1931 the French government was kind enough to take over this loss; but the narrow escape only confirmed the officers of the Bank of France in their conviction that Britain had committed an immoral act. Looking back at the monetary experience of the previous years, the Governor of the Bank saw the gold exchange standard as an open door to speculation and unsound enterprise. Convertibility, he proclaimed, was not 'a superannuated habit', but 'a necessary discipline'. He returned to the subject in his report on the year 1933:[1]

The experience of the year 1933 can only reinforce in our eyes the value of the doctrines to which we have always been and remain firmly attached. We remain more than ever convinced that the convertibility of money into gold is the indispensable condition of a healthy economic and social discipline. However tempting may be the artificial procedures that, as history shows, nations always have a tendency to resort to in time of crisis, they provide in reality only illusory and precarious advantages, soon followed by disappointments. The international exchanges that, in the modern world, insure in so large part the wealth of all countries, will not be able to resume their rise so long as the value of the major currencies is not definitely fixed. Monetary stability is thus the most effective means of preparing the return to a lasting prosperity. But it has in our eyes an even higher significance. It alone seems to us capable of guaranteeing, in order and justice, the progressive development of the societies of mankind. France will remain faithful to it. Our country instinctively rejects facile and adventurous solutions, which it senses are contrary to its profound interests and its genius.

France tended, therefore, to make the gold standard a question of national honour: 'we shall cling to it,' said Flandin, 'as we did to Verdun'. But this was poor consolation to those branches of the economy that felt the repercussions of this deflationist policy. France became an expensive country in a cheap world. Her capital charges were higher than those of her neighbours; her money, overvalued—as the price indices show (see Table 23).

Even Germany, which nominally stayed on gold, knew better than to imprison itself in a doctrinal cage. Instead it developed a variety of special arrangements that made it possible to sell cheaply abroad while not suffering the disadvantages of inflation at home. To be sure, the labyrinth of German currency manipulations and controls was no panacea; and it is no accident that German foreign trade came to depend increasingly on special bilateral agreements and barter. The fact remains that Germany, as well as the other nations that had devalued, did far

---

[1] Cited in Pommera *et al.*, *Grandeur et déclin*, pp. 313–14.

Table 23. *Index of Wholesale Prices, 1933–6 (1929 = 100)*

	1933	1934	1935	1936[a]
France, home market	63·6	60·0	54·0	59·0
France, export prices	58·0	50·0	42·0	40·1
Great Britain[b, c]	51·1	47·6	46·6	48·4
United States[b]	55·9	46·5	49·8	49·3
Japan[b]	33·0	28·8	28·8	31·0
Germany, export prices[d]	50·0	39·0	37·0	39·6

[a] First four months.
[b] Gold prices.
[c] Board of Trade figures.
[d] Average price per commodity ton exported.

SOURCE: Pommera *et al.*, *Grandeur et déclin de la France*, p. 325.

Table 24. *Change in the Volume of Production, Exports,*
and Imports of Manufactures, 1928–9 to 1936–8 (1928–9 = 100)

	Production	Exports	Imports
United Kingdom	129	101	99
Germany	116	72	35
France	85	51	75
World	126	82	82

SOURCE: Adapted from Svennilson, *Growth and Stagnation*, p. 219.

better than France and the other gold-bloc countries in the competition for trade.

This loss of ground in foreign markets, bad as it was, would have been far worse had French manufacturers not made a desperate effort to retain their customers by dumping—as the growing gap between export and home prices makes clear (Table 23, above). But these same high prices that made.dumping necessary (and possible) exposed the French producer to the competition of foreign goods in his own market. As a result, it was necessary to raise and re-raise customs barriers, thereby increasing costs to industries already suffering from excessive costs. Thus in 1929 customs receipts had accounted for 7·6 per cent of the value of imports; by 1935, the proportion was 29·4 per cent.[1] All of this made export that much more difficult, dumping that much more expensive.

Deflation may thus have been a triumph of ideology and virtue; but it was an economic failure. It was a severe impediment to business revival, to the point where France, alone of the major European industrial nations, saw her national product and industrial output decline from

[1] Pommera *et al.*, *Grandeur et déclin*, p. 327.

1933 to 1935. And because of this, it was a monetary failure. For this was the point that the worshippers of the golden calf forgot: that the value of money is based, not on gold in vaults, but on the goods it will buy. And French money bought less in these years than the money of other countries. It even bought less money. Ordinarily, deflation and the security of the gold standard should have kept the rate of interest low; whereas inflation and a floating currency tend to promote higher rates. Yet the bank rate in Britain stayed at a steady 2 per cent in these years, in spite of substantial growth and rising demand for capital; while the discount rate of the Bank of France rose from 2·5 per cent in 1933 to 4·17 per cent in 1936, and the open market rate more than doubled in the same period. But then, this is just what one might expect in an economy where business failures were increasing and the general economic malaise was radicalizing political opinion and fomenting public disorder.

What is more, the unfavourable balance of payments on commodity account produced by this overvaluation inexorably impaired the liquidity on which France's rugged individualism rested. In spite of high duties and absolute quotas, France bought more every month than she sold; and this drain was aggravated by a renewed flight of capital that recalled the outflow of the 1920's. Capitalists and speculators were less impressed by the form than by the substance, and the example of Britain was there to remind them that devaluation was never more than a weekend away. In the meantime, the state, always short of funds, continued to spend beyond its means: after four exceptional years of surplus from 1926 through 1929, the perennial deficits resumed and doubled from an average of 5 billion francs in 1930–2 to 10 billion in 1933–5.

As is usually the case, the pot came to a boil when political anxieties added fuel to the flames. The signal for panic was the alliance between Radical–Socialists, Socialists, and Communists and the victory of the Popular Front in the elections of May 1936. In the first nine months of that year the Bank of France lost some 16 billion francs' worth of gold, as against 3·5 billion in 1935. Prices rose sharply, partly owing to the cost of social legislation, partly as an almost reflex response of French merchants to uncertainty. The Popular Front government, which had made a point of reassuring France's timid *rentiers* that it would not sacrifice their income to socialism, was compelled in the end to devalue. On 1 October 1936 the government suspended convertibility and permitted the franc to float between a maximum of 74·8 per cent and a minimum of 65·5 per cent of its previous gold value (between 43 and 49 milligrams, as against 65·5 milligrams). Unfortunately, the remedy was too little, come too late. The flight of capital continued, and the new value of the franc was maintained only by heavy purchases in the open market by the Fonds d'Egalisation; so that in November 1938, another devaluation was necessary, reducing the franc to the equivalent of 8·5 centimes, less than one tenth of the prewar gold franc (27·5 as against 322·6 milligrams). Where before 1936, 75 francs equalled £1, now it took 170 francs to make one pound sterling. At this point, capital began to return. But then the war came and set the franc once again on the inflationary course begun in 1914.

Of all the European nations, France was the hardest hit by the Great Depression. Her difficulties began later than her neighbours': in 1930, when the other European economies were already in deep trouble, French output was 99·1 per cent of the 1929 figure. Even when business slowed markedly in the following years, it did not contract as much as in Germany, Austria, or for that matter, the United States. Then, for reasons already mentioned, partly economic, partly political, France sank deep into a morass that even the armament programme of the late thirties could scarcely pull her out of. Industrial output fell slowly but steadily, reaching a low in 1935 of 72 per cent of the level of 1929. Then it vacillated, rising to 82 in 1937, but falling back to 76 in 1938. The gravity and persistence of this depression is best brought out by the comparison with other countries.

But as Table 25 makes clear, most of Europe, and indeed the world as a whole, suffered grievously in these years. The best showing, by Greece, Finland, and Sweden, entailed a compound growth rate of slightly over 5 per cent per annum from 1929 to 1937. Britain's 24 per cent gain represented about 2·7 per cent a year; Germany's 16 per cent, about 1·9 per cent.[1] For the world as a whole, excluding the U.S.S.R., industrial output was up only 3 per cent over this period—roughly 0·4 per cent per year.

Why? Why the severity, the generality of this setback?

These questions gave rise, almost from the start, to keen debate. Contemporary opinion tended to divide into two camps: one, largely Marxist, saw the crisis as unique, a paroxysm of the collapsing capitalist system; the other, composed of a wide range of economic opinions, saw this as just another depression, although more than usually severe. In support of their interpretation, the Marxists pointed precisely to those aspects of the European economy that distinguished postwar from prewar: the failure of trade to grow as fast as before; the weakness of

---

[1] These rates are slightly lower than those implied by the statistics of manufacturing output assembled by the OEEC (see above, p. 368, n. 1): for the U.K., a gain of 27 per cent from 1929 to 1937, or 3 per cent a year; for Germany, 17·5 and 2 per cent respectively.

Table 25. *Effects of the Great Depression: Movement of Industrial Output in the 1930s (in percentages)*

	1932, as against 1929	1937, as against 1932	1937, as against 1929
Group I			
Japan	− 2	74·4	71
Greece	1	49·5	51
Finland	−17	79·5	49
Sweden	−11	67·4	49
Hungary	−23	77·9	37
Denmark	− 9	47·2	34
Rumania	−11	48·3	32
Norway	− 7	37·6	28
United Kingdom	−17	49·3	24
Group II			
Germany	−42	100·0	16
Austria	−39	73·7	6
Group III			
Canada[a]	−42	72·4	00
Italy	−33	49·2	—
Czechoslovakia	−36	50·0	−4
Belgium	−31	36·2	−6
United States	−46	70·3	−8
Netherlands	−38	46·7	−9
Group IV			
Poland	−46	57·4	−15
France	−31	4·3	−28

[a] Including construction and electric power.

SOURCE: League of Nations, *La production mondiale et les prix* (1937–8), cited in Pommera *et al.*, *Grandeur et déclin*, pp. 321 f.

the agricultural sector; the persistent unemployment, even during the boom of the twenties; and the unprecedented degree of contraction. As for such recovery as did take place in the middle and late thirties, Marxists argued this was an artificial by-product of heavy investment in armaments. Could the capitalist economies of Europe have recovered without this 'unnatural' stimulus—a kind of anti-investment in the means of destruction? Marxists thought not.

Non-Marxists rejoined that a difference in degree is not necessarily a difference in kind; and that the obvious maladjustments of the postwar years, the result largely of adventitious political circumstances, should not be mistaken for an incurable malady. True, recovery was painfully slow; and some countries, including the world's greatest industrial power, had yet to return to the 1928–9 peak a decade later. But this protracted convalescence was the result of poor diagnosis and in-appropriate treatment.

What would have helped? The remedy proposed varied—and con-tinues to vary—with the economic philosophy of the doctor. In the light of what we have learned since, however, two lines of treatment would seem to have been indicated. One was to increase demand for manufactures from the outside, by promoting trade; the other was what we would call today a Keynesian approach—to stimulate demand with-in the economy by promoting investment, whether indirectly by government expenditure, or directly, by easier credit.

The first of these—the promotion of trade—was never a serious possibility. On the contrary, the depression reinforced the impedi-ments to exchange that had originated in or been strengthened by the War. What was left of free convertibility vanished in the wave of de-valuations of the early thirties, to be replaced by an ever-changing array of defensive currency and exchange regulations. For the first time in perhaps centuries, barter transactions became a significant aspect of international trade. At the same time, each nation put up barriers to competitive imports in an effort to soften the impact of diminished home demand; the most spectacular development here was Britain's definitive abandonment of free trade, but this was only one piece of a much larger movement, which took the form not only of higher cus-toms duties but, harder to by-pass, of restrictive quotas on designated commodities.

These restrictions on imports were applied to agricultural as well as industrial products; and indeed, one of the features of economic policy in the thirties was the effort to shelter the individual economy from out-side disturbance by fostering a better balance between the various branches of economic activity. The effect of this autarkic tendency, however, was to diminish the demand for primary products in inter-national trade and to drive down their prices farther than those of manufactures (see Table 26). There was, from the European standpoint, a marked improvement in the terms of trade, which incidentally eased somewhat the impact of depression and unemployment on the Euro-pean standard of living. But from the standpoint of the primary-producing nations, and in particular of the unindustrialized parts of the world—Africa, South America, much of Asia—Europe's gain was an unmitigated disaster. Their balance of payments, at best deficient, worsened considerably, the more so as European creditors realized out-standing claims and reduced new investment to a trickle. Inevitably, the primary producers reduced their imports of European products. And so the initial disturbance was propagated by echo—each restriction inviting or compelling retaliatory restrictions.

Table 26. *Index of the Value per Unit of European Imports,*
by Area of Origin, 1928–38 (1928 = 100)

Industrial Europe[a]	95	Areas of recent settlement	68
Other Europe	84	All other	64
Total Europe	90	World	73
United States	73	World, less industrial Europe	69

[a] U.K., Germany, France, Italy, Netherlands, Belgium, Sweden, and Switzerland.

SOURCE: Charles P. Kindleberger, *The Terms of Trade: A European Case Study* (Cambridge, Mass., and New York, 1956), p. 195.

The consequences are apparent in the aggregate statistics. In 1928 the total value of Europe's trade was approximately $58 billion (see Table 27); by 1935 it had fallen to less than half that, $20·8 billion; and although it picked up in the next few years, to $24·1 billion in 1938, it was still at only 41·5 per cent of the peak level. If one deflates for population growth, moreover, the contraction is even more severe, from $157 per head in 1928 to $61 a decade later.

Table 27. *Value of Trade for Europe and the Rest of the World,*
1925–38[a] (in billions of 1934 gold dollars)

	1925	1928	1932	1935	1938
Imports					
Europe, less U.S.S.R.	30·90	32·38	13·78	11·67	13·63
U.S.S.R.	0·72	0·83	0·61	0·21	0·27
Rest of World	24·51	25·62	9·26	8·85	10·30
Total	56·13	58·83	23·65	20·73	24·20
Exports					
Europe, less U.S.S.R.	23·96	25·70	10·65	9·09	10·44
U.S.S.R.	0·55	0·71	0·50	0·32	0·25
Rest of World	28·91	29·19	10·67	10·16	11·97
Total	53·42	55·60	21·82	19·57	22·66

[a] Special trade only; that is, re-exports are excluded.

SOURCE: League of Nations, Economic Intelligence Service, *Europe's Trade* (Geneva, 1941), p. 10.

Trade, therefore, offered no exit to the sick and sulking economies of western Europe. The alternative was an increase in home investment— whether endogenous, that is, growing out of the natural performance of the economic system; or exogenous, in the sense of being promoted by the state or other 'outside' agency; or both.

Here the British experience is very much to the point. Great Britain, as we have seen, was less hard hit in 1929–33 than any other country in western Europe, with the exception of Scandinavia. To be sure, the dip experienced by the British economy, as contrasted with the plunge else-where, reflected in part the previous decade of persistent unemploy-ment and quasi-depression; that is, Britain did not sink so far because she was already half submerged. The fact remains that the British economy did stand up better to the crisis; that it began to recover earlier than those of the other western European countries; and that its upswing was both longer and stronger—again, with the exception of the Scandinavian economies (see Table 25).[1]

Various explanations have been offered for this recovery, only too often by monists who seek to advance their own hypothesis while excluding others. One school of opinion has laid great weight on the beneficent effects of government policy, in particular, the devaluation of the pound and the provision of cheap money. The former, as we have seen, made life a good deal easier for those export industries that had languished in the twenties under systematic deflation; but given the shift in the terms of trade and the sharp fall in the purchasing power of Britain's traditional customers, devaluation was at best a palliative. It helped Britain do better than France, for example; but by itself it can account for only a small part of the economic gains after 1932.

Table 28. *Recovery from the Great Depression*

	Real national income 1937–8 as % of:		Real income per head 1937–8 as % of:		Manufacturing output 1937–8 as % of:	
	1928–9	1913	1928–9	1913	1928–9	1913
United Kingdom	119	135	114	120	131	139
Germany	119	129	113	114	122	144
France	88	110	88	110	86	119
Sweden	135	188	131	169	161	231
United States	98	163[a]	92	123[a]	96	164[a]

[a] The denominator is 1909–18, rather than 1913.

SOURCE: Svennilson, *Growth and Stagnation*, p. 28.

Cheap money poses a more difficult problem of analysis. The discount rate of the Bank of England stayed at 2 per cent from 1932 to 1939, as compared with 5 per cent in the late twenties. In principle, this should have facilitated investment; and industrial issues did in fact increase from £70·9 million in 1931–2 to £244·1 million in 1935–6. But this coincidence is not in itself evidence of cause and effect; and one may well argue that entrepreneurs are concerned less about a few points of

[1] Sweden clearly did better than Britain in both decline and recovery. Denmark and Norway did better on the downswing, but some time series (e.g. OEEC manufacturing output) show them following her in recovery.

interest than about the prospect of good returns on their investment.[1]
On the other hand, entrepreneurs are concerned about the availability of
credit, and cheap money usually entails a more hospitable reception to
demands for loans.

Even so, easy money by itself is not enough—witness the low rates
that prevail in periods of prolonged stagnation. There must be a demand for venture capital, and such a demand rests on·business expectations. Here two forces made an important contribution to Britain's
economic recovery: housing and the new industries.

The housing boom of the 1930's, which saw the construction of
almost three million dwelling units—twice as many as in the 1920's—
was admittedly due in part to cheap financing.[2] The interest rate on
mortages fell from 6 per cent in 1931 to $4\frac{1}{2}$ per cent in 1935, which
meant a significant reduction in the size of weekly repayments. In
addition, lenders were willing to take longer mortgages, and to take
them from workers and others of low income whom they had formerly
looked upon as credit risks. Yet more important in the last analysis were
the autonomous sources of demand: the relocation of population from
the depressed industrial areas of the North to the more active centres in
the Midlands, South, and Metropolitan area; the return of emigrants
from colonial areas; the long-standing housing shortage, which had
built up to about one million units by the end of the twenties; the shift
of the work force into white-collar occupations, where standards and
expectations of housing were higher than in manual employment.[3]

A house, of course, is not a mere shell. It calls for electrical and
plumbing fixtures, domestic appliances, furnishings. The housing
boom, therefore, provided by derived demand a substantial stimulus to
a whole array of industries, some of them, like electrical power and
engineering, among the most dynamic and technologically progressive
in the economy. Moreover, in so far as the new housing was located in

[1] Cf. H. W. Richardson, 'The Basis of Economic Recovery in the Nineteen-
Thirties: A Review and a New Interpretation', Econ. Hist. Rev. 2nd ser., xv (1962),
346: 'it is probable that a rise in the marginal efficiency of capital was a stronger
influence.'

[2] H. W. Richardson, Economic Recovery in Britain, 1932–9 (London, 1967), pp. 159–
63.

[3] In his article of 1962 (pp. 349 f.), Richardson places particular emphasis on 'the fact
of rising real income for those in work'. Given the high level of unemployment, in
the early thirties, however, this was probably not enough to overcome the effects of
the fall in aggregate disposable income, especially in the depressed areas. What it did
do, presumably, was make it easier to sell and rent housing in the centres of new,
expanding industry.
In his recent book, Richardson returns to this theme (pp. 164–5)—this time, however, with reservations. The spatial and chronological congruency of income changes
and housing construction leaves something to be desired.

suburban neighbourhoods, at some distance from the residents' places of employment and poorly served by established means of public transportation, it encouraged the purchase of motor cars, with further derived-demand effects at one remove. On the other hand, these newer industries that profited indirectly from the housing boom themselves contributed to it. New electrical appliances and plumbing facilities made old housing obsolete and new housing desirable; just as the motor car made it possible for builders to build on tracts of cheaper land and for buyers to move to distant neighbourhoods that they would otherwise not have considered.

At the same time, these newer industries had a life of their own, based partly on a general rise in consumer expectations, partly on the ability of a rapidly advancing technology to whet these expectations. As a result, where the volume of all industrial output rose only 19 per cent from 1930 to 1935, that of electrical engineering increased by 133 per cent; motors and cycles, by 56 per cent; rayon, by 172 per cent; electrical power, by 73 per cent; chemicals, by 31 per cent; and so on. (We shall return to this story in greater detail below.) Because these industries also showed the greatest gains in productivity, employment did not rise proportionately; but by 1935 their work force numbered some 1,100,000, half again as many as in the building trades.[1]

This expansion rested on and called for heavy investment in new plant and equipment. In the late 1920's gross fixed capital formation in the United Kingdom (and Germany) was running about 500 million dollars a year. At the trough, this had shrunk only to 410 millions (as against 110 millions in Germany), and by 1937 investment had rebounded to 950 millions (750 millions in Germany). How much of this was accounted for by the new industries? Precise figures are unavailable, although, as Richardson argues, one may presume that their share was out of proportion to their output; electrical power alone absorbed some £272 million between 1930 and 1937—equal to about 5 per cent of total national investment.[2]

Although one can demonstrate by figures such as these the leverage exerted by the new industries in Britain's recovery, it is not clear why they should have more effect there than in other western European countries. The new technology, after all, was common property; and if it played the autonomous, primary role attributed to it, why was there not in the thirties the kind of generalized boom that was to mark the

---

[1] Richardson, 'Economic Recovery', p. 355. Richardson uses the classification of new and old trades employed by A. E. Kahn, *Great Britain in the World Economy* (1946).

[2] Richardson, 'Economic Recovery', pp. 359 f., citing the *Midland Bank Review*, May–June 1938.

fifties? The answer may lie in part in Britain's peculiarly poor performance in the 1920's.[1] This is not to say that there is, or has to be, some kind of compensatory mechanism that rewards in one time period those economies that went unrewarded or poorly rewarded in the previous period; though there probably is some such mechanism at work as a result of accumulated needs, the demonstration effect and technological imitation. But one might argue, as Richardson does, that the slow advance of the British economy was the result of 'inter-industry structural deficiencies'; that is, that the economy did not shift resources away from the older, declining branches fast enough; and that the depression was a moment of truth that imposed a more realistic assessment of investment opportunities and a more rational allocation of resources. Or one might take the other tack and argue that one consequence of Britain's economic difficulties of the twenties was an early start on the liquidation of obsolescent enterprise; and that it was precisely because branches like cotton had begun contracting then that the impact of the later crisis was not so severe as elsewhere. Britain, in other words, had partially discounted her depression by experiencing some of it ahead of time and, so doing, had laid the ground for the subsequent upswing.

The difficulty with this compensation model is that it is *ad hoc* and is applicable only with difficulty to the experience of other countries. If one argues that new industries boomed in Britain in the thirties because investment was freed from the habit and restraints of the twenties, one might expect the reverse to hold, that is, that an upsurge in the twenties would be followed by a loss of momentum in the thirties. The United States and France would seem to be good cases in point. But what does one do with Sweden, which grew faster than France (*a fortiori*, than Britain) in the twenties, and then after a brief setback in the early thirties, resumed her earlier rate of growth?

The trouble here, as in so many other cases of historical analysis, is that the search for a single pre-eminent cause inevitably truncates the reality. A major development of this kind, involving an entire economy, invariably depends on a conjuncture of circumstances. Britain's new industries thrived because of autonomous technological stimuli, which encountered a rising demand in the context of a more intelligent monetary and credit policy than had prevailed in the twenties.

The Great Depression was both mid-point and divide of the interwar generation. It was trauma following close on the trauma of World

[1] I say this in spite of the recent articles by Mr Aldcroft (see p. 368, n. 1). His reasoning is ingenious; but his statistics pose problems, and the argument does not persuade me.

War I; and it made the further trauma of World War II almost inevitable. Everywhere there was the unforgettable pain of these years of privation and humiliation—at all levels of society, but concentrated as usual in the 'lower orders'. The children of later, more affluent decades will never quite understand the shock of this experience; but the sociologists of political behaviour tell us that nothing—not religion, nor race, nor economic interests—has shaped the subsequent allegiances of the depression generation so indelibly as the calvary of unemployment and the dole. The numerical data cannot possibly convey the poignancy of the suffering; they are like Plato's shadows on the walls of the cave: a distorted image of reality. One has to go to the eye-witness descriptions, to the qualitative testimony, to get even a hint of what was going on; and even then, only a few pens, like that of George Orwell in *The Road to Wigan Pier*, are adequate to the task.

Even if one could recount the story of these years of travail in all its fullness, it would lie outside the scope of this essay on the determinants, course, and economic consequences of technological change. But the politico-economic responses to the crisis (one cannot separate the political and the economic) are another matter. As the British and French experiences show, these determined the institutional context of industrial activity in the 1930's and indirectly, therefore, the pace and character of technological development. These responses (remedies?), moreover, by their extremeness and violence in certain instances, give some measure of the gravity of the wound.

Of all responses, the most radical was the German. This was due in part to the extremity of Germany's predicament: we have seen that the drop in output was sharper, unemployment greater than in the other countries of western and central Europe, with the possible exception of Austria. But the depression was only the last ingredient in a complicated witches' brew that included a long, sick legacy of racist ideology, an even older tradition of national aggrandizement by force, the embitterment of defeat in the Great War, the resentment of a Carthaginian peace whose severity was surpassed only by that which the Germans would have imposed had they won, the political conflicts of a regime unacceptable to a large fraction of the population, and the social consequences of the fulminating inflation of 1923. And students of German history continue to devote a large share (some would say, an inordinate share) of their efforts to the allocation of responsibility for the disaster that was Hitler: to what extent was the Third Reich written in the errors and aberrations of Germany's more distant past? and to what extent was it a response to the misfortunes and mistakes of the postwar decade?

Again this is an issue that lies outside the scope of the present essay. But the economic aspects of the German experience of the thirties are of interest to us—for the light they shed on an important and increasingly popular response to economic problems, that of state intervention and control; and for the lessons they afford, or have been alleged to afford, on the character and destiny of the capitalist system.

In evaluating German econòmic policy of the 1930's, it is important to keep in mind that state intervention in times of economic crisis has an uninterrupted history that goes back as far as the written record. Crises have always entailed unrest, and no government can afford to stand idly by and allow the hardships of its subjects or citizens to provoke them to insurrection; besides, depressions are also costly to those well-to-do citizens whose taxes are the main support of the state and whose interests are thus an object of particular solicitude. So that even those regimes most reluctant in principle to interfere with workings of the economy—the July Monarchy of Louis-Philippe or the Republican administration of Herbert Hoover—have found it possible to sacrifice doctrine to expediency in this matter.

What was different about German economic policy of the thirties, and that of other European countries to a lesser degree, was that it constituted a partial abandonment of the notion that such intervention consisted essentially of temporary responses to an emergency, regrettable intrusions into what should be, and ordinarily is, a self-governing mechanism. It rested instead on the assumption that the hand of the state is indispensable in good times as well as bad; that indeed, only the state can assure continued economic growth in an atmosphere of social harmony; further, that the economy, like any other aspect of national life, should serve the state, rather than the reverse. (In this respect, the economic policies of the thirties must be distinguished from the conventional forms of government intervention in the commercial and monetary spheres, which were thought of, not as instances of economic direction, but as part of a larger process of definition of the rules and context of economic activity.)

Economic engineering, like emergency economic therapy, has a long history. The measures of the 1930's harked back in spirit to the mercantilism and cameralism of the Old Regime; and although the British example of *laissez-faire* and the autonomous technological stimulus afforded by the Industrial Revolution had led even the most convinced mercantilist states in the course of the nineteenth century to loosen their grip on their respective economies, some measure of economic engineering had persisted everywhere. The legacy was strongest in railway construction and operation, not only because this was a task that in most countries was beyond the resources of private enterprise, but also because no branch of the economy was so clearly linked to the effective exercise of political authority and military power.

The recourse to economic engineering in the interwar period was a function in part of national tradition and style. The British, who, it will be recalled, were the only ones in Europe to build their railroads without state aid, moved toward intervention reluctantly, for the conventional economic wisdom counselled against interference with the natural workings of the market. In the twenties the government stepped in where it had to, particularly in coal and cotton, but it viewed its efforts apologetically, as *ad hoc* improvizations. From late 1929, however, with unemployment fast increasing and business confidence shattered, the authorities were compelled to widen their scope of action. Even so, the British characteristically preferred to work indirectly, through the intermediary of the Bank of England and of private corporations established with government support for the purpose of promoting industrial rationalization, concentration, and growth. The state, in short, preferred to help business help itself.

The French were less uncomfortable in this sphere. They had a long mercantilist tradition behind them; and neither French society as a whole nor the French business community had ever taken the doctrines of *laissez-faire* as divine gospel. On the contrary, the French entrepreneur had long been accustomed to tariff protection, subsidies, and preferential tax treatment for selected branches of activity. The French state, moreover, had always been more highly centralized, organized, and active than the British. So that the shift to increased government participation in the economy, the proliferation after the war of state or mixed enterprises in banking, transport, electricity, and manufacturing, seemed a perfectly natural response to new economic circumstances. This tendency was accelerated in the thirties by political considerations: the Left was far stronger in France than in Britain, and the failure of the Centre parties to find adequate remedies to economic depression gave the Popular Front coalition an opportunity to introduce a new wave of controls and nationalizations. This in turn provoked an extremely hostile reaction from the business community, which was prepared to accept friendly government intervention, but viewed the developments of 1936–7 as the prelude to socialism. On the eve of the war, then, the economic role of the state was the most divisive of issues. The turn of the apolitical technocrats, who saw their task as the promotion of economic development rather than social justice, was not to come until the establishment of the Vichy regime, or even until the return of peace.

What the British undertook gingerly and with considerable reservation, what the French came to welcome or fear as the prodrome of political radicalization, the Germans took to without any difficulty. The reason was simple: business enterprise was already highly organized by private associations. Even before the War, cartel agreements had been enforceable at law, and the state had shown itself ready to impose price and output controls on those trades it had an interest in. Then during the War the government had found it necessary to impose all manner of restraints on production and distribution—though always with due and tender concern for the interests of business enterprise.[1]

With the return of peace came a yearning for normalcy, which in Germany meant a reversion to economic organization by cartels, syndicates, and employers' associations—a system described by various writers as *Verbandswirtschaft*, *Verbundene Wirtschaft*, or *Korporative Wirtschaft*. In key industries in which the state itself was a major producer—coal, lignite, potash—it established compulsory cartels (*Zwangskartelle*) to enforce a profitable stability. At the same time, wide powers to rationalize and plan economic activity were granted a variety of government agencies, in particular, the ministries of Trade, Labour, Food and Agriculture, and Economics.

Through most of the twenties, these powers remained dormant, except in so far as the state was itself a producer and participant in the economy; and this abstinence was the more surprising because the Weimar Constitution and Republic were strongly tinged with socialist convictions and aspirations. Yet the split between Socialists and Communists left labour and the radical movement divided; while the return of prosperity eased the pressure for government intervention on behalf of the workers.

Then came the depression, and as everywhere it compelled the state to take on the role of economic medicine man; but in Germany more than elsewhere, for social tensions were running high, political sentiment was increasingly polarized between the extreme left and extreme right, and the fate of the regime and the nation came to depend on the restoration of full employment and business prosperity. The result was a series of emergency decrees, to the point where, in the words of Brady, Germany could be taken as the closest approximation to the Marxian theoretical state outside of the U.S.S.R.[2]

The characterization would seem exaggerated, but not by much. The financial crisis of 1931 led the government, as we have seen, to acquire a substantial interest in most of Berlin's great banks and to establish institutional controls over the activities of the banking sector as a whole. Given the close tie in Germany between banks and industry, these measures gave the state effective influence over all the larger

---

[1] On this point, see the important work of Gerald Feldman, *Army, Industry, and Labor in Germany, 1914–1918* (Princeton, 1966).

[2] Robert Brady, *The Rationalization Movement in German Industry* (Berkeley, 1933), p. 388.

manufacturing enterprises, the more hard-pressed of which, like the Gelsenkirchener Bergwerks A.G. and the Vereinigte Stahlwerke, it either bought up or took directly under its wing. Meanwhile, to help agriculture, strict limits were placed on imports of food, while a special fund, the Osthilfe, was established to help heavily indebted grain growers east of the Elbe. This assistance, however, was not offered gratis. The state reserved the right to take over the management of those estates that were not being properly or efficiently operated; and Chancellor Brüning prepared a decree to permit the government to divide the bankrupt domains and distribute the parts to small proprietors. But this was too much for Hindenburg, himself a Junker and the owner of an estate at Neudeck; so he refused to sign, and on 30 May 1932, Brüning resigned.

The next eight months saw a fulminating disintegration of the German polity. Popular sentiment became more and more polarized, while the regime made repeated but vain efforts to form a viable middle-of-the-road ministry. On 30 January 1933, Hitler became Chancellor: if the governing elites were going to have to choose between extreme right and extreme left, there was no question where their choice would fall.

At first the coming of National Socialism meant little change in the structure and pattern of economic activity: the great bulk of the means of production remained in private hands; the various cartels, combines, and trade associations continued to have an important role in the organizing of production and distribution; and the state already had and continued to exercise great power in a number of spheres. What was new, however, was the goals and character of the regime, and with time these inexorably altered the character of the economy.

Any effort to sum up these goals runs up against the difficulty that National Socialism had no consistent ideology at the time it seized power. Hitler's adherents were a motley lot, ranging from petty bourgeois, filled with fear that the depression, like the earlier inflation, would rob them of dignity and status as well as income, to ironmasters and financiers who thought they saw in Hitler a useful tool in the fight against Communism. Some saw in National Socialism the socialism: a system in which private profit and enterprise would be curbed in the interest of national community and well-being; in which the economy would be purged of its parasitical elements (read middlemen, Jews, bankers, speculators, etc.) and productive forces liberated; in which control of the means of production would pass from private businessmen to the workers or the people. Others saw the nationalism: the apotheosis of *Volk* and *Vaterland*, the exaltation of race, the restoration of German status and power. The potential contradiction between these two emphases was solved by Hitler within a year and a half of his accession to power: on 30 June 1934 killer squads shot to death an unknown number of alleged plotters against the regime: among them were Gregor Strasser and the rest of the radical wing of the party leadership.

In so far as one can distil a coherent ideology from the shrieks and roars of the surviving spokesmen of National Socialism, two themes seem paramount: first, the 'purification' and ordering of the economy as part of a larger effort to transform the German people into a community of disciplined 'Aryan' heroes; and second, the enhancement of German power and the achievement of that hegemony due the 'master race'. The attainment of these goals justified any and all means. In particular, the cause of National Socialism could not be made to depend on the intrigue and calculation of party politics or to suffer the restraints of obsolete legislation and judicial pettifoggery. Germany needed a leader who represented the will of the people and could act for that will.

In the period before Hitler's assumption of power—and to some extent even after that time—there were many who simply refused to believe that he meant what he said. He couldn't mean it. Those virulent promises and threats were electoral propaganda—bombast to quicken the pulse of the German voter. Once Hitler took office, it was argued, the responsibilities of power would tame him. This, it must be conceded, is the usual effect of responsibility, at least on rational persons. The only trouble was that National Socialism had an irrational component that was far greater than many appreciated and that grew with power until it passed the point of madness.

In the event, careful though the Nazis were to cloak their seizure of power with the appearance of a legal transfer of government, their regime knew in fact no law but the will of the leader and his minions, enforced when necessary at the point of a gun. In the space of a few months Germany passed from a *Rechtsstaat* to a *Machtstaat*.

The impact of this combination of visionary goals and unlimited power was felt in every aspect of German life, not least in the economy. In accordance with the goal of 'purification', the regime expelled the Jewish component from the business system by confiscation and terror, waging war with particular ferocity on enterprises in retail trade, brokerage, and banking—branches it was inclined to look upon as intrinsically parasitical.[1] And in accordance with the larger goal of community and discipline the traditional labour movement was suppressed

---

[1] On the profitable business of anti-Semitism, see Helmut Genschel, *Die Verdrängung der Juden aus der Wirtschaft im Dritten Reich* (Göttingen, 1966).

and all producers, employers and employed, were enrolled in the German Labour Front. Class conflict became a dirty word, a device invented by Jewish Marxists to dissolve the fabric of German society. How could there be conflict when all productive citizens were 'soldiers of work'? Within the enterprise, relations between employer and employed were governed by a law of 20 January 1934 (*Gesetz zur Ordnung der Nationalen Arbeit*), which provided for the institution of the 'enterprise community' (*Betriebsgemeinschaft*) and assumed away the possibility of divergent interests. The law did make paternalistic provision for disagreements. In particular, it relied heavily on state-appointed Trustees of Labour 'to secure the maintenance of industrial peace' by supervising the conditions of work and terms of employment within the individual enterprise. This tutelage was supplemented by a characteristic Nazi innovation, the Honour courts, which were empowered to try either employers or employed for violations of the regulations or spirit of the 'enterprise community'.[1]

The enrolment of employer and employed in a community of enterprise did not eliminate the hierarchy of authority within the business unit or the power of organized business within the economy as a whole. Within the *Betriebsgemeinschaft*, the employer was the leader and the workers were followers; and the worker was not left in doubt as to his subordination. In the words of the Leader of all: 'There is only one right in this community, the right that results from the observance of duties which are assigned to every individual.'[2] On the level of the economy, the Nazi regime strengthened and simplified the traditional interlocking structure of cartels and trade associations, extended their jurisdiction over entire industries, established them where they had never existed.

This reinforcement of the combinative apparatus has been diversely interpreted. Marxists in particular have been inclined to see here evidence of the equivalence of fascism and monopoly capitalism. Yet it seems clear that the regime, in strengthening the hand of organized business vis-à-vis labour or the individual enterprise, had no intention of sanctioning a state within the state. The same laws that formalized the new compulsory cartel arrangements (the *Gesetz über Aenderung der Kartellverordnung* and the *Gesetz über die Errichtung von Zwangskartellen*, both of 15 July 1933) gave the state the power to invalidate existing

---

[1] On Nazi labour policy, see Otto Nathan, *The Nazi Economic System: Germany's Mobilization for War* (Durham, N.C. 1944), ch. vii. Nathan notes, p. 177, n. 10, that few suits were brought against workers (there were presumably quicker, more effective means of dealing with labour intransigence), but that penalties against employers were generally mild.

[2] *Ibid.*, p. 172.

agreements and dictate future cartel policy, in particular, to prohibit any increase of productive capacity, whether in the form of new units or the expansion of old.

To be sure, the meaning of any such ambivalent reform depends on its application. To the extent that entrepreneurs could now take monopolistic organization for granted, they found business less uncertain, more stable, and generally more profitable. In the first years of the new regime, when the Nazi elite was still a little intimidated by the exercise of power and anxious to retain the support of the entrepreneurial establishment, the hand of big business was probably strengthened. With time, however, the state intruded more and more into the economy, and its potential domination of organized business was translated into working control. The transition was implicit in the second major goal of National Socialism: the enhancement of German power.

From the beginning, the Third Reich anticipated the possibility of war and was determined to avoid the mistakes of World War I. In all domains, the state bent its efforts to promote national self-sufficiency, and where this was impossible, to draw its supply from those nations that it could hope to maintain ties with in time of war. Domestic resources like iron ore were exploited beyond the limits of commercial profitability, if necessary by state enterprises created for the purpose; and a substantial portion of national research went toward the discovery or invention of substitutes (*Ersatz*) for imports like petroleum, rubber, and cotton. Needless to say, this policy entailed direct intervention in industrial production, both to compel or persuade businessmen to invest in costly and risky technologies, and to force manufacturers to choose plentiful as against scarce, domestic as against foreign, artificial as against natural raw materials, even at the expense of quality. In 1934, when the state decided to push the manufacture of synthetic gasoline, it drew up a list of lignite producers to finance, build, and operate plants for the purpose: all were compelled to contribute to the Braunkohlen Benzin A.G. (*Brabag*), a *Pflichtgemeinschaft* or obligatory corporation established in October of that year to exploit the lignite hydrogenation process. A year later the regime created another *Pflichtgemeinschaft*, the Ruhr Benzin A.G., to produce synthetic oil by the Fischer–Trapsch technique; this time it was the coal mines of the Ruhr which subscribed the original funds, which were augmented by long-term bank credits guaranteed by the state. And in February of 1936 a third such corporation was created to produce Diesel oil by the low-temperature carbonization process; again the Ruhr coal mines were the 'volunteer' entrepreneurs. By dint of a similar combination of compulsion and incentive, the government got the textile industry to take up the manufacture of staple wool, the paper industry to produce cellulose, the vegetable oil refiners to try their hand at whaling.[1]

In general, the state pressed for the expansion of those enterprises it thought of as contributing to the national strength: it limited cash dividends and then compelled reinvestment of undistributed profits, sweetening the obligation with subsidies when necessary; and it permitted business firms to make certain investments—in workers' housing, for example—only on condition that they make others. Whenever possible, the regime preferred to get entrepreneurs to carry out these policies voluntarily. A much used technique was to obtain a corporate commitment from the firms in a given branch, so that there was strong group pressure for conformity. But the state always had incontrovertible 'arguments' in reserve: control of key raw materials, including electric power, and of the supply of labour and credit; and the ultimate possibility of recourse to force.[2]

The other side of the coin was the restriction of production and investment in nonessential branches. Thus the textile decree of 19 July 1934 sharply curtailed the output of the industry by reducing the work week while forbidding increase of the labour force, and made any expansion of old plant or creation of new contingent on official approval. Similar controls were placed on certain lead-using trades and all branches working or dealing in rubber, including motor car tyre manufacture.

None of this constituted a planned economy. For all the unity of command in the person of Hitler, there was no centralized control of production and distribution, no overall year-to-year calculus of ends and means. But while improvization and incoherence were tolerable in these early years, when the regime was more concerned to consolidate its power than to provoke the hostility of neighbouring states by bellicose gestures, they were incompatible with an aggressive foreign policy and an ambitious rearmament programme. In 1933/34 and 1934/35, German military expenditures were of the order of 1·9 billion marks, respectively 24 and 18 per cent of total government outlay. This represented 4·1 and 3·6 per cent of national income, roughly half the French or Japanese level. Then on 16 March 1935, Hitler denounced the clauses of the Versailles treaty prohibiting German rearmament, and in 1935/36 military spending more than doubled to 4 billions—31 per cent of government outlays and 6·7 per cent of national income. From then on, the figure mounted every year, until by 1938/39, expenditures were 18·4 milliard marks—32 per cent of government outlays and 22·5 per cent of national income.

[1] Nathan, *Nazi Economic System*, pp. 166–9; L. Hamburger, *How Nazi Germany Has Controlled Business* (Washington, D.C. 1943), pp. 22–4.
[2] *Ibid.*, pp. 77–9.

This heavy military effort inevitably led to increased state intervention in the economy. In October of 1936 the Nazis established the Office of the Four Year Plan under the direction of Hermann Goering, to serve as a kind of superagency with authority over the rest of the heterogeneous and unco-ordinated apparatus of government control. The aims of the plan were four: (1) increased self-sufficiency; (2) the relocation of strategic industry away from the frontiers, in particular the development of a new centre of steel and chemical manufacture in central Germany; (3) the expansion of the capacity of strategic branches; and (4) the rationalization of industrial organization and technique.

In all of these areas, the regime achieved considerable success. Industrial investment rose by 71 per cent in two years (1936-8), while almost doubling in the producers' goods branches. Output per head rose 14 per cent—a gain that is not unknown in the post-World War II period, but one that was unheard of in the 1930's.[1] In the meantime, output of armaments soared:

Table 29. *Germany: Index of Armaments Output (1943 = 100)*

1933	2	1937	9
1934	2	1938	20
1935	4	1939	25
1936	6	1940	44

SOURCE: *Die deutsche Industrie im Kriege*, p. 23.

Rapid expansion made scarce items scarcer. The effort to reserve raw materials for strategic branches of production entailed close control over investment in industrial plant; hence decrees like that of 16 September 1937, which ordered the Wirtschaftsamt to pass on all new capacity in the iron and steel industry. This surveillance was extended to all metal-using industries, to the point where 'the establishment of new enterprises, the resumption of operations in previously idle enterprises, the erection of a new production line, the switching of production to a different class of metals, and virtually every change in the production programme' were dependent on state authorization.[2] By March of 1938, special permits were required for all construction projects using more than two tons of steel. Behind all this lay a system of priorities: armaments first, Four Year Plan second, industrial replacement third, agriculture fourth.

Labour, particularly skilled labour, also began to be a scarce resource. As early as June 1935 the law required all men and women between the

[1] *Die deutsche Industrie im Kriege* (Berlin: Deutsches Institut für Wirtschaftsforschung, 1954), pp. 20–1.
[2] Nathan, *The Nazi Economic System*, p. 161.

ages of 19 and 25 to perform some work essential to the public interest. This was quasi-military service, and the manpower so levied was used in emergencies—to fight fire or flood or relieve the victims of natural disaster; or to supplement the regular work force in situations of peak demand—the harvest, for example. More directly aimed at fitting the labour supply to economic and military requirements were a series of decrees to protect the work force of strategic branches, limit turnover, and if necessary, conscript the manpower needed. By decree of 29 December 1934, skilled metal workers could be hired only with the written permission of the employment office; and in November 1936, this rule was extended to all metal workers, regardless of skill. Similar shortages developed in the building industry from 1936 on and were met in the same fashion. These interferences with the market inevitably stimulated a certain amount of sophisticated evasion—if one is to judge from further decrees issued to close the loopholes. Thus on 7 November 1936, the Office of the Four Year Plan prohibited cipher want ads for metal and building trades workers. Another order of the same date instructed industrial employers to notify the authorities whenever they used workers for more than two weeks in occupations for which they had not been trained. This may have been an effort to control the flow of labour skills; but more likely, it was aimed at preventing labour hoarding.

One of the sectors to suffer a chronic shortage of manpower was agriculture, largely because workers could earn more in industry and because towns and cities were more interesting places than the countryside. Here the answer was found at first in regulations designed to fix the labourer to the soil. By the law and decree of 15 and 17 May 1934, persons employed in agriculture on the date of the decree or for a total period of a year in the three years preceding could not be hired for nonagricultural work without the permission of the authorities. But this was not enough, and the government was compelled to find ways to bring ex-agricultural workers back to the land. A law of 26 February 1935 gave the Reichsamt the power to compel dismissal of any person who had once worked in agriculture and was now otherwise employed; and a month later the state took advantage of this power to order certain workers back to the farm. But now the great industrial effort was getting under way, and this forced reversal of the flow of manpower had to be abandoned. Instead, the regime had recourse to subsidies, loans, propaganda, and the like—the carrot instead of the stick. And in so far as it continued to use force, it applied it to those marginal elements who might otherwise have been lost to the work force altogether: thus it was decided in 1938 to stop relief payments to unemployed who could make a living in agriculture but refused the opportunity; and most radical of all, a decree of 15 February 1938 conscripted all women for one year's work on farms.[1]

From conscription of agricultural labour to general conscription of civilian labour was a short step, and one that was the logical consequence of the whole programme of economic and military aggrandizement. By decrees of 22 June 1938 and 13 February 1939, the employment offices were authorized to conscript any employable resident of Germany for critical work. The state's discretion in this matter was almost unlimited: workers could be assigned to their jobs for an indefinite period of time; could be used for any kind of work, regardless of skill or experience; and could be placed anywhere, even if it meant change of residence or separation from family. In sum, the free labour market was abolished—in principle. How much use the state made of these powers is hard to say, but such statistical evidence as we have would seem to indicate either that conscription was not practised or that, such as it was, it was not effective. Thus from 1939 to 1940, the number of men employed fell from 8,194,000 to 7,331,000, which is just what one would expect in view of the substantial growth of the armed forces. But in the same period, the number of women employed also fell, from 2,767,000 to 2,682,000, and it was not until 1941 that this figure rose to the 1939 level.

Interference of this kind in the allocation of resources and conditions of production was bound to perturb the market. Here the Nazis had learned from the experience of the First World War, when price controls had been applied piecemeal and serious anomalies and distortions had resulted. To avoid these difficulties and gain time for a systematic review of the entire price structure, the Nazis made use of an ingenious device: the price stop. By decree of 26 November 1936, the Price Commissioner ruled that all prices were to be set at the level prevailing on the previous 17 October. This avoided all manner of dislocations and facilitated enormously the task of the authorities. In subsequent years, of course, these prices had to be adjusted repeatedly to take into account changes in supply and demand—to say nothing of the introduction of new commodities; Nathan speaks of seven thousand special rulings in less than four years. The end result, however, was a remarkably stable price level.

[1] Nathan, *The Nazi Economic System*, p. 203–4. This was later modified (23 December 1938) to provide that unmarried women under 25 who had not been employed before were not to be hired by private or public enterprises unless they could show they had spent at least one year in agricultural or domestic work. Needless to say, this requirement aroused little enthusiasm, and there is good evidence that the rules were often circumvented; hence an order of 11 November 1940 that women who spent their year on the farm taking courses in typing and shorthand would not be considered to have satisfied the requirement.

Table 30. *Germany: Prices under National Socialism* (1913 = 100)

	Agricultural prices	Industrial raw materials	Finished manufactures	
			Producers' goods	Consumers' goods
1933 (aver.)	86·4	88·4	114·2	111·7
1936 (aver.)	107·5	94·0	113·0	127·3
1937 (aver.)	106·0	96·2	113·2	133·3
1938 (aver.)	105·9	94·1	113·0	135·4
1939 (August)	108·8	94·9	112·8	136·1

SOURCE: Ch. Bettelheim, *L'économie allemande sous le Nazisme: un aspect de la décadence du capitalisme* (Paris, 1946), p. 211.

This review of the Nazi attempt to militarize and organize the German economy while retaining the forms and much of the substance of a private-enterprise system is necessarily incomplete. It does not deal, for example, with the multiple controls on banking, the money and capital markets, dividends, and profits. Nor does it treat what for many foreign observers was the area of most radical innovation—foreign trade and exchange. In both these spheres the logic of mobilization and the distortions produced by intervention in other sectors made strict management indispensable and inevitable. The curious reader has at his disposal a library of work on the subject.

Marxist observers of the economy of the Third Reich interpreted it as an expression of monopoly capitalism. Their first inclination was to see the regime as the creation and instrument of big business, and even after it became obvious that Hitler was no one's straw man, they clung to the conviction that, as Bettelheim put it, 'the Nazis were in no way able to dominate the contradictions inherent in monopoly capitalism, for the very reason that they were the auxiliaries of finance capitalism'.[1] It is these contradictions, the argument goes, that give such an economy its regressive character, which would ordinarily be expressed in a contraction of capacity (or output) and a fall in productivity. To be sure, nothing of the kind occurred in Nazi Germany, although one can cite instances of official impediments to technological advance or plant expansion. (Bettelheim mistakes rationing of resources for symptoms of technological regression.) Yet this is only because the armaments programme concealed these inner ills under a hectic flush of health; and even so, Bettelheim sees evidence of the malady in what he calls 'the relative slowness and the *partial character* of the progress effected in the strategic sectors of the economy'.

[1] Bettelheim, *L'économie allemande*, p. 277.

Table 31. *German economic indices 1928–38*

	Gross national product current RM (billions)	Gross national product 1928 RM (billions)	Index of industrial production (1928 = 100)	Labour Force Employed (millions)	Unemployed (millions)
1928	90	91	100	18·4	1·4
1929	90	89	101	18·4	1·9
1932	58	72	59	12·9	5·6
1933	5c	75	66	13·4	4·8
1934	67	84	83	15·5	2·7
1935	74	92	96	16·4	2·2
1936	83	101	107	17·6	1·6
1937	93	114	117	18·9	0·9
1938	105	126	122	20·1	0·4

SOURCE: Burton H. Klein, *Germany's Economic Preparations for War* (Cambridge, Mass., 1959), p. 10.

It is hazardous to appraise and characterize something so complex as an economy on the basis of a few years' experience, especially when these were years of mobilization for war. One hesitates, for example, to extrapolate and to speculate about what would have happened had Germany not gone to war and the Third Reich had continued. It may well be that these alleged contradictions would have made themselves felt, that growth would have slowed, that technology would have stagnated or retrogressed. But this we cannot know. What we do know is that in spite of a cumbersome and sometimes disharmonious control apparatus, in spite of inadequate theoretical conceptions and tools, the German regime did effect important economic gains—in output, employment, technique, and income.

As Table 31 shows, a gain of 68 per cent in gross national product was achieved from 1933 to 1938 with a labour force only 50 per cent larger; the system, in other words, was clearly capable of a general advance in productivity. Without attempting to impute weights, one can ascribe this principally to four factors: (1) The earlier trend to elimination of inefficient smaller units continued. (2) The working day grew longer and the pace of work faster, especially in the capital goods' industries. This intensification led to a substantial rise in the number of work accidents, which more than doubled from 1932 to 1937.[1] (3) New investment inevitably entailed the installation of more

[1] See Jürgen Kuczynski, *Germany: Economic and Labour Conditions under Fascism* (New York, 1945), pp. 117–26. The accident rate per person employed rose somewhat more slowly—67 per cent over the same period.

efficient equipment. Thus the index of machine construction (1928 = 100) rose from 40·7 in 1932 to 147·7 in 1938.[1] (4) Significant technological advances occurred in a number of industries. The chemical manufacture, as always, was the bellwether: the need to find substitutes for costly and strategic imports led to the development of a whole array of synthetic substitutes based on the hydrogenation of coal and the processing of cellulose from wood, straw, and other natural organic matter. In the same way, the Germans found new uses for light metals like aluminium and invented new alloys, while innovating in the substitution of glass and plastics for iron and steel. In ferrous metallurgy, they learned to process low-grade ores; began using oxygen in the blast furnaces at the Hermann Goering Werke just before the War; and were the first in Europe to build a wide continuous strip mill, at Dinslaken in 1937 (see below, p. 479). In general there was a strong effort to reorganize plants, among other things, by greater use of the assembly line, and to standardize products.

Most of these changes took place in those branches of production linked directly or indirectly to rearmament and preparedness. From this it is easy to conclude that technological advance under Nazism was an artificial by-product of a militaristic regime. Yet this is only partially true. The effort of the State to prepare for war inevitably shaped the direction of technological advance, if only because strategic branches and enterprises were given prior access to labour and capital, to say nothing of permission to build and orders to innovate. But as Gurland points out, the roots of 'technological reconstruction' were 'deeply imbedded in the entire economic and technological set-up of production in pre-Nazi Germany.'[2] Change, in other words, was built into the system, and the engineers and technicians kept working so long as their employers paid them and furnished the means. British observers were much impressed after the War, for example, to see what the steel plants in the Ruhr had been able to do with 'patching' and 'urgent improvization' when the Nazi regime starved them of capital for the benefit of safer plants in the interior.[3]

Whether these gains were greater or less than they would have been in a different political and economic system is perhaps more to the point, though also a matter of speculation. One test of performance may perhaps be relevant here. One of the primary economic objectives of the regime, as we have seen, was mobilization for war. In a

[1] A. R. L. Gurland, 'Technological Trends and Economic Structure under National Socialism', *Studies in Philosophy and Social Science*, IX (1941), 236, n. 2.

[2] *Ibid.*, pp. 239f.

[3] Duncan Burn, *The Steel Industry 1939–1959: A Study in Competition and Planning* (Cambridge, 1961), p. 197.

secret memorandum to Goering in October 1936, at the time of his appointment as chief of the Four Year Plan, Hitler made the categorical observation that war was inevitable, declaring that it was 'Germany's task to defend Europe against Bolshevism' and that 'a final solution of the food problem can only come through an expansion of living space [*Lebensraum*]'. The document went on to denounce Schacht's Ministry of Economics for sabotaging the rearmament programme and concluded by giving Goering two general orders: to get the army ready for war in four years; and to get the economy ready for war in four years.[1]

It is generally believed that the German economy was ready for war in 1939/40—certainly more ready than those of its opponents. Yet the experience of the war itself and information captured during the conflict or become available since have made it clear that Germany's advantage was far less than her adversaries supposed and feared. Thus military expenditures in 1939 were not much larger in proportion to gross national product than in Britain. Output of combat planes was running about 500 a month, about 60 per cent of the rate credited by British Intelligence; and in the last three months of 1939, when the war had already begun, Germany turned out only 247 tanks, some 45 per cent of the Intelligence estimate. As for the supply of critical raw materials, which the regime and the economy had spent so much money and effort to assure, stocks were in many instances sufficient for only a few months of combat.[2]

What is more, even after the war was under way, Germany mismanaged her economic effort. It was only after the defeat at Stalingrad, when it was too late to win, that the regime faced up to the need for total resource mobilization and began to make effective use of its powers to plan and direct industrial activity. The comparison with the far freer economies of the supposedly decadent democracies is not favourable to Germany:

Both Britain and the United States moved much faster in developing efficient techniques for determining military production objectives and for assuring that the objectives were reasonably met. It was not until the third year of the war that the Germans finally managed to work out a realistic picture of materials requirements, and not until then that a partially effective materials rationing system was substituted for an unworkable priorities scheme.

The improvements in the economy brought about by Speer and his associates during the last two years of the war were very impressive (the gain in

[1] Klein, *Germany's Economic Preparations for War*, p. 18.
[2] See the table in *Die deutsche Industrie im Kriege*, p. 18, which exaggerates if anything the size of the stocks by assuming the continuation of peacetime rates of consumption.

military output far outweighed the loss through the use of additional resources) but mainly by comparison with the previous state of affairs. Many of Speer's 'revolutionary' measures were revolutionary only to Germany. For example, his great drive to rationalize fighter aircraft production in 1944 consisted essentially of adopting practices that were common in the United States and Britain.[1]

How is one to account for this failure? The answer, as usual, comprises several elements. First, the regime was long paralysed in its efforts by fiscal conservatism. Hjalmar Schacht, Minister of Economics, President of the Reichsbank, and from May 1935 Plenipotentiary-General for War Economy, was the spoilsport here. In the early years of the regime Schacht performed marvels of monetary and financial manipulation to pay for the early, secret stages of rearmament; and on the occasion of his sixtieth birthday, the Army journal *Militär-Wochenblatt* lauded him as 'the man who made the reconstruction of the Wehrmacht economically possible'.[2] But Schacht, for all his ingenuity and lack of scruples, had an abiding fear of inflation, a fear shared to some extent by even the most fanatical members of the regime; so that when, in 1935-6, military preparations began to pose the danger of public deficits, Schacht put on the brakes. When Goering asked, for example, at a meeting of the Council of Ministers in May 1936, what objections there might be to a programme for developing substitutes for imported raw materials, Schacht replied that there were no objections in principle, that indeed self-sufficiency was indispensable, but that there would be serious financial difficulties:

Providing money by taxing capital is impossible. Circulation of money cannot be increased beyond a certain amount. Previous measures were executed correctly and without danger to monetary value. Further increase seems precarious; a matter of confidence.[3]

By this time Hitler, Goering, and the other party leaders were losing patience with Schacht, who was replaced by Goering as economic director of the military effort in 1936 and dismissed as Minister of Economics in August 1937. Nevertheless he continued as head of the Reichsbank until 1939, holding to the end to monetary orthodoxy.

This disagreement between the fiscal conservatives and the zealots of the the-means-will-take-care-of-themselves school was only one of several major divisions of interest or opinion that worked to slow the rearmament programme. Thus even if one rejected the technique of

---

[1] Klein, *Germany's Economic Preparations*, p. 236.
[2] William L. Shirer, *The Rise and Fall of the Third Reich: A History of Nazi Germany* (New York, 1960), p. 260.
[3] As cited in Klein, *Germany's Economic Preparations*, p. 23.

deficit financing, the state still had the possibility of diverting funds from nonmilitary to military use. In the years 1935-8, of total public expenditures of 34 billion RM, only 18 billion went for armament. Not until 1938 did the latter category account for over half, and even then, 'nonessential' projects continued to compete for scarce resources. But vested interests within the regime, in particular, the nonmilitary elements of the party hierarchy, made any abrupt shift of resources difficult if not impossible. Hence the exasperation of Goering in October 1938:

He [Goering] is going to make barbaric use of his plenipotentiary power which was given to him by the Fuehrer.

All the wishes and plans of the state, party and other agencies which are not entirely in this line have to be rejected without pity...

He warns all agencies, particularly the labour front, price controller, etc., [against] interfering with these proposals in any way. He is going to proceed ruthlessly against every interference on the part of the labour front. The labour front would not receive raw materials and workers for its tasks any more. Similarly all other party requirements have to be set aside without consideration. Foreign workers can continue being employed except in the particularly secret sections of the enterprise. At the present time the plants should not be burdened with unnecessary demands, such as athletic fields, casinos or similar desires of the labour front.[1]

To these impediments should be added several others: the preference of many industrialists for business-as-usual, and for those industrialists engaged in the production of strategic materials, for military contracts *cum* business-as-usual; the backwardness of Germany's economics, both theoretical and applied; and the optimistic assumption that war, if it did come, would be short and sweet. Here Hitler was repeating the error made by all the belligerents of World War I. They, of course, made their inferences from the brief episodes of the Austro-Prussian War of 1866 and the Franco-Prussian War of 1870; but he drew his conclusions from several years of piecemeal aggrandizement in the face of pusillanimous appeasement, and who is to blame him for extrapolating?

Yet is was more, or less, than a rational extrapolation, for Hitler was moved—and increasingly—at least as much by fantasy as by reason. One can understand the complacency of the first eight months—the *drôle de guerre*—when Hitler and Stalin were allowed to swallow Poland without effective reprisal; or the jubilation of May and June 1940, when everything looked just as easy as Hitler had promised it would be. But how can one explain that on 25 January 1943, when the German army at Stalingrad was on the point of surrender and the losses of material in

[1] In a speech before the Air Ministry, cited *ibid.* p. 25.

Russia and the Mediterranean compelled a substantial increase in armaments manufacture, Hitler was anxious above all not to lose time in building a stadium at Nürnberg that would provide a suitable scene for celebrating the conquest of Russia? Klein argues that it was only the succession of major setbacks on the battlefronts and the destructive raids on German cities that finally forced the adoption and acceptance of a total war effort; and he offers the paradoxical suggestion that if these crises had come earlier, the Germans would have faced up to reality much sooner and the ultimate Allied victory would have been much slower and costlier.

In terms of the regime's objectives, therefore, the Nazi economy was not very efficient. But could one not argue that, from the standpoint of the system *qua* system, these objectives were secondary, that the 'command economy', as Franz Neumann described it, was subordinate to the 'monopolistic economy'?[1] And here the criteria of success were presumably different: profits, stability, elimination of competition, concentration.

In all these respects, the system certainly performed to the satisfaction of its adherents—not so much the small entrepreneur, however, but the big businessman. The ranks of the former had supplied some of the strongest supporters of National Socialism in the years before Hitler's seizure of power; and they derived initially considerable material benefit from the elimination of Jewish competitors and the increased official demand for handicraft production. But the state had little patience for swarming inefficiency and moved to assist the normal course of competition in purging the economy of its marginal units; so that the number of handicraft enterprises fell from 1,734,000 in 1934 to 1,471,000 on 1 April 1939.[2] As the Reichskommissar für den Mittelstand put it, National Socialism had improved enormously the condition of the artisan and skilled craftsman; but these benefits were reserved only to the diligent. The struggle for survival would never cease.[3]

The main beneficiaries of the system were those who could operate efficiently in both the economic and political spheres. These were prosperous years for men of resources and connections, not only because economic growth generated a 'natural' increase in the demand for goods and services, but because political and social upheaval inevitably created windfalls and furnished tremendous opportunities for personal enrichment. Aryanization, for example, made it possible for some of Germany's wealthiest industrialists to pick up valuable properties at

[1] Franz Neumann, *Behemoth: The Structure and Practice of National Socialism 1933–43* (2nd ed.; New York, 1944; reprinted 1963), part II.

[2] *Ibid.*, p. 283.

[3] H. Rolf Fritzsche, ed., *Jahrbuch der deutschen Wirtschaft 1937* (Leipzig, 1937), p. 113.

fictitious prices, to the point where the government even contemplated some kind of retroactive tax to recover some of the loot in 'special cases of an especially aggravating kind'. The rearmament programme was another vein of profits, the more so as the state was prepared to furnish the capital required to build strategic plants in safe areas and to exploit the new chemical technology. So remunerative were these arrangements that German industry became addicted to them. 'The endless clamour for Reich guarantees,' complained Reichswirtschafts-minister Funk in 1941, 'is a downright *testimonium paupertatis* to private initiative and to private business' willingness to bear responsibilities.'[1]

The war itself promised the biggest rewards of all: wherever the German army went, the jackals of enterprise followed. Everywhere there was more Jewish property to be seized; and what could not be seized—the non-Jewish property—could be 'acquired'. Representatives of heavy industry, oil refining, the big banks, in conjunction with party officials and military personnel, formed the Continental Oil Corporation to manage German oil interests outside Germany—in Roumania, for example, where French and Belgian shareholders would be 'persuaded' to sell their interests. In Lorraine, the French iron and steel combines were allotted to the great German combines: Stumm, Flick, Röchling, Klöckner, and the Göring works. Some of these companies had played a similar role in occupied French Lorraine during World War I. But Flick was a new giant, one of a number of industrial *condottieri* (to use Neumann's term) who managed to put together business empires in a matter of years.

The economy, then, was essentially one of private enterprise based on profit and material gain. It had an important nonrational element in the form of political interference for ideological as well as material ends; but those who possessed the requisite talent and connections could turn these intrusions to advantage. This they did, up to the point where the costs of totalitarianism and aggression far exceeded the rewards. In view of the eventual débâcle, one may be inclined to argue that from the standpoint of profit as well as of military preparedness, the system was a failure. Yet this is a meaningless judgment, for it cannot be verified. The German defeat was by no means a foregone conclusion, especially if one is ready to entertain the possibility of a less than all-or-nothing effort. Or is there something in the ideology of total personal power that makes sweet reasonableness impossible and carries its own nemesis? One thinks of Napoleon, who could have had almost everything if he had been ready to settle for less than everything.

Yet these are the *if*'s of history. To return to the fact of the disaster,

[1] Gurland, 'Technological Trends', p. 232, n. 3.

those who view the Nazi regime as the creation and creature of business interests would not accept the ultimate bankruptcy of the venture as disproof of their interpretation. History is full of unanticipated consequences; and besides, this is just what one would expect of so desperate an effort to shore up a rotten structure in the last stages of decay. Indeed, they would go beyond the German experience and assert a general link between monopoly capitalism and national socialism (or fascism), arguing that the one necessarily entails the other.[1] If that is correct, then what happened in Germany is presumably a prodrome of the fate of other capitalist nations. Thus Bettelheim: '...present-day capitalism contains in latent form an economic structure analogous to that of Nazi Germany. Which means that the definitive exclusion of an aggressive revival of Nazism, no doubt under another name, with another political coloration and possibly in another country than Germany, presupposes fundamental changes in the economic and social structure of the economically advanced countries.'[2]

The trouble is that one can not disprove this proposition; for even if Nazism does not reappear, who is to say that it will not? All one can say at this point is that it has not appeared in the advanced capitalist countries, even under conditions that one might think favourable to the development of dictatorship. In the light of the historical evidence, moreover, there does not seem to be a simple one-way relationship between a highly cartelized or concentrated economy and authoritarian or totalitarian government.

What the record does show is a whole array of special circumstances that conjoined in Germany to produce a monster. Some of these circumstances had deep roots in the German past; some were the aftermath, in part adventitious, of World War I. This was a sick society thrown into convulsion by a trauma. Some kind of authoritarian solution was highly probable; and the balance could have gone either way—toward Fascism or Communism.

Once the choice was made, there was a chain of circumstances that progressively reduced the options and increased the probability of a violent dénouement. But if one is to see an element of determinism in this course to disaster, it comes more from the political than from the economic side. The danger lay not in the rational power of money but in the power of irrational men.

There is no stronger testimony than the 'Thousand Year Reich' (which fortunately lasted only twelve years) to the significance of the

---

[1] Thus Neumann, *Behemoth*, p. 354: '...in a monopolistic system profits cannot be made and retained without totalitarian political power, and that is the distinctive feature of National Socialism'.

[2] *L'Economie allemande*, p. 279.

War as watershed. Monetary instability, new barriers to trade, and increased government intervention constituted together a major change in the economic environment—even though they were in part continuations of prewar trends. Yet important as they were, they drew their force and virulence from the collapse of the old political order. From the economic standpoint, the gravest consequence of these four years of death and ruin was their legacy of hatred, violence, and generalized egoism. In this sense World War I was only the beginning of an age of troubles—what Fritz Stern has aptly called the second Thirty Years' War.

TECHNOLOGICAL CHANGE IN NEW INDUSTRIES AND OLD

We have seen how, in spite of war, postwar maladjustment, and depression, the economies of western Europe grew during these years—not only absolutely but in real income per head. To be sure, they grew more slowly than they had even in the 'long depression' of the late nineteenth century. Thus real income rose in the U.K. and Germany by barely 1 per cent per annum from 1913 to 1937/38, while French gains were smaller still.[1] Yet the point is that they did grow, and this is testimony to the power of continued technological change to stimulate investment and raise productivity in the most adverse circumstances. The system was far from healthy; but change was built into it and more than outweighed the deleterious effects of uncertainty, periodic crises, and harmful medication.

The data on changes in productivity call for careful scrutiny. Ideally, the best statistical measure of productivity would be output per unit of labour input, and we do have estimates of this ratio (see Table 32).

It is important, however, not to read the wrong meaning into these figures. They do not reflect simply advances in technology—the introduction of new and perhaps better equipment and processes—but also shifts in employment from sectors, branches, or enterprises of lower productivity to those of higher. The most important of these shifts was that from agriculture, which traditionally retained a large force of semi-employed, into industry and services. The movement was slowed in

[1] These are based on Svennilson, *Growth and Stagnation*, pp. 28–9, 233. For the U.K., see also C. H. Feinstein, 'Income and Investment in the United Kingdom, 1856–1914', *E.J.* (June 1961), and A. R. Prest, 'National Income of the United Kingdom, 1870–1946', *ibid.* (1948). (The tables are reprinted in B. R. Mitchell and Phyllis Deane, *Abstract of British Historical Statistics* [Cambridge, 1962], pp. 367–8.) Feinstein's figures show an increase in net national income (in 1900 prices) of 2·3 per cent per year from 1870 to 1913; in income per head, of 1·4 per cent per year. (Note that Svennilson, for reasons that are unclear, has seriously underestimated the British gains in income per head—20, instead of 30, per cent from 1913 to 1938.)

Table 32. *Output per Man-hour in all Sectors of
the Economy (1913 = 100)*

	1870	1913	Average annual rate of growth, 1870–1913 (in per cent)	1938	Average annual rate of growth, 1913–1938 (in per cent)
United Kingdom	52·3	100	1·5	167·9	2·1
France	46·3	100	1·8	178·5	2·35
Germany	42·3	100	2·1	137·1	1·3
Belgium	42·1	100	2·0	144·2	1·5
Switzerland	—	100	—	183·1	2·45
United States	37·3	100	2·4	208·8	3·0

SOURCE: Angus Maddison, *Economic Growth in the West* (New York, 1964), pp. 232–3 (the figures are based on Table H-2).

the interwar period by the persistence of a high rate of industrial un-employment; even so, the number of male workers in agriculture de-clined in the major industrial nations—the United Kingdom (including Ireland), Germany, and France—by about 15 per cent from 1920 to 1940, while output rose everywhere except in France. Some of this transfer was the consequence of mechanization or similar labour-saving improvements; but much was simply an extrusion of underemployed labour by falling farm income. As a result, productivity gains in agri-culture are biased upward and are a poor indicator of technological advance. (This statistical distortion becomes more serious in the post-World War II period.) Some of the older staple manufactures went through a similar catharsis—cotton is the best example—and here too the productivity figures are not a sign of health and growth, but of a drastic loss of fat.

Still, any effort to separate the influence of reallocation from that of technology is artificial; it may be useful for purposes of analysis, but it does violence to reality. For one thing, the shift of labour from agri-culture or declining staple trades was only partly the result of changing patterns of demand. It was also a response to differences in productivity, hence wages; and these differences were at bottom technological. It was the more progressive, more innovative branches that grew fastest and drew redundant labour from lagging sectors. For another, this movement of workers conduced to higher wages for those who remained, so that it paid to substitute capital for labour. The result was a stimulus to technological improvement in these lagging sectors, which in turn hastened the purge of inefficient enterprises and the process of reallocation. Prosperity may be the best friend of progress, if only because new investment usually entails new and better ways of doing things. But adversity can also be a stimulus. Witness the examples discussed above: coaching confronted by the railway, sail menaced by steam, the Leblanc process challenged by the Solvay technique.

In short, the advance of technology in the interwar years was as always unequal, but it continued to characterize the entire range of economic activity. As we noted in the case of Nazi Germany, change was built into the system.

If it was already impractical to pretend to full coverage of the technological changes of the latter decades of the nineteenth century, the continued ramification of innovation makes the task even more difficult as we advance in time to the present, the more so as the content of the technology becomes more esoteric. We must therefore content ourselves with a drastic condensation and simplification of a very complex reality. To this end, I shall follow the method of isolating what appear to be major general aspects of the process of development and then selecting for closer examination specific areas of change—chosen not so much for their intrinsic importance as for their illustrative value.

We may begin with a number of general observations. First, there was no major departure in the interwar period; rather these were decades of working-out, when the discoveries of the prewar generation found technological and commercial fruition. The second characteristic of the interwar technology is implicit in the first: since what we have is essentially an extrapolation of prewar trends, the division between new and old branches of industry remains and the composition of the two groups is unchanged. On the one hand we have electrical power, electrical manufacture, chemicals, the automobile; on the other, the manufacture of textiles from natural fibres, iron and steel, machine tools, shipbuilding, railway transport. The former group show rates of growth far above the average and comparable to those of prewar years. They are on the steep spine of their logistic curve, and it is their expansion that accounts for overall growth in the presence of the impediments and difficulties outlined above. By contrast, the older branches grow slowly, stand still, or even decline. It is not that their technology is ossified; but such advances as do occur offer relatively small gains and, given the state of the market, find slow application.[1]

This divergence between old and new industries was aggravated by the War. The effect of war on technological progress and economic

---

[1] On the relation of diminishing technological gains to the rate of industrial growth, see the classical statement of Simon Kuznets, 'Retardation of Industrial Growth', *Journ. Ec. and Business History*, I (1929), 534–60.

development is a moot subject, and economic historians have not found it difficult to adduce evidence in support of both the optimistic and pessimistic points of view. The explanation of these contradictory data is simple enough: the fact is that war serves both to promote and impede innovation and growth, and there is no *a priori* reason to assume that the balance will fall on one side or the other of the ledger. Nor do we have at the moment the techniques or information needed to establish a balance sheet for any given conflict; the less so, as the problem is complicated by the difficulty of disentangling war from the many other forces influencing the economic conjuncture in a given place and time. In effect, one has to conjecture what the economy might have done had peace prevailed.

The problem becomes more manageable, however, if one distinguishes the effects of war on different sectors of the economy. It is here that the new-industry, old-industry dichotomy is determining. The stimulatory effect of war takes the form of sharply increased demand for certain goods and services, a demand that presses against severe constraints of supply—shortages of labour, real capital, and raw materials. Those of the older industries producing 'nonessential' consumers' goods are often compelled, either by fiat of the state or resource bottlenecks, to curtail output and investment. Those of the older industries producing for the war effort are in a better position to profit from heightened demand; but their expansion does not necessarily entail advances in technique or improvements in equipment. On the contrary, their first recourse will be to such unemployed capacity as may have existed before the increase in demand. This may take the form of stand-by machines of somewhat lower efficiency or even obsolete equipment resurrected for the emergency; so that the war may actually promote a kind of technological retrogression. Even when new plant is required and the resources are made available, the gain in productivity may not be so great as it would ordinarily; for time is short, and the quickest solution to many problems is the tried-and-true technique. In general, expansion of output in these older branches will take the form of capital widening rather than deepening.

The real beneficiaries of war are young industries supplying goods or services to the military. In the first place, they must meet the surge in demand by building new plant, and this gives them scope for technical innovation. Secondly, the intellectual burden of precedent is light. Finally, much of the increased demand for their products is generated by new applications, many of them suggested by the unanticipated circumstances of combat. Demand, therefore, is a qualitative as well as quantitative stimulus.

In World War I, for example, military transport and communications requirements altered and proliferated as the conflict grew and the armies became familiar with the possibilities of the aeroplane, motor vehicles, the telephone, radio. Thus the development of telephone technology was much advanced by the need to handle a large flow of messages in battle; so much so, that the French saw fit as late as 1936 to build central switching stations based on techniques developed by the American Expeditionary Force. The radio was another gainer, for war enhanced enormously the importance of ship-to-ship, ship-to-shore, and air-to-ground communications; it was these years that saw the general adoption of the vacuum tube, the triumph of the Alexanderson alternator over other transmitting devices, the introduction of the superheterodyne circuit. Similarly aeronautical design made great strides after 1914. At the beginning of the war the aeroplane was not far removed from a flying tricycle; by the end, it was a much stronger, faster, more reliable vehicle.

Against this impetus from war must be set the dislocations of peace and reconversion. These tended to vary for any given branch with the gap between wartime and peacetime demand for its products. The biggest loser, undoubtedly, was aircraft manufacture. The aeroplane had become an effective fighting instrument by 1918; but it was still far from a suitable vehicle for civilian passenger or cargo transport. The first British commercial air route was opened in August 1919 between London and Paris; the small two-plane line was the first of several such enterprises to fail in the effort to make air transport pay. In the end, Britain, like all the Continental nations, was forced to adopt a policy of direct and indirect subsidies to keep her civil aviation alive. Even so, the private airlines, especially in the first postwar decade, could use only a fraction of the wartime output of the aircraft industry; after all, there is nothing like combat to accelerate depreciation and promote scrapping. So that the industry necessarily continued to depend in peacetime on military support, even in Germany, where such a tie was technically forbidden by the terms of the peace treaty. On balance, these were not particularly fruitful years for aviation technology. They passed rapidly, though, and by the late twenties the aircraft industry was growing and changing fast.

For an industry like radio, however, the demands of peace were almost as large as those of war; indeed larger in the long run. To be sure, there was a painful legal shake-out when the tolerances of the emergency ceased and it was no longer possible to 'borrow' gratis enemy or government patents for the manufacture of military equipment. This had been more than a convenience; as Edwin Armstrong put it to the U.S. Federal Trade Commission in 1923: 'It was absolutely impossible to manufacture any kind of workable apparatus without using practically all the inventions which were then known.' And Commander Loftin of the U.S. Navy in a memorandum of 1919: '. . . there was not a single company among those making radio sets for the Navy which possessed basic patents sufficient to enable them to supply, without infringement. . . a complete transmitter or receiver.'[1]

These remarks concern American producers, but in the international sphere as well, no one could manufacture or operate without trespassing on the rights of some competitor. Once this wartime laxity was over, therefore, a long and costly period of litigation was inevitable. It ended in a series of cross-licensing agreements—between RCA, General Electric, Westinghouse, and American Telephone in the United States; and between American firms and such big European producers as Marconi in Britain, Telefunken in Germany, the Compagnie Générale de Télégraphie sans Fil in France, and Philips in Holland. On the strength of these arrangements, the industry maintained its technological fecundity and changed its character radically, shifting from an almost exclusive preoccupation with direct communication to a mixture of direct and broadcast communication.

Here we are getting ahead of our story, however, and it is a story that merits more than passing attention. For one thing, radio was the first product of a new electronic technology that has since developed beyond even the dreams of its creators and continues to generate innovations of the widest economic import. Some would even view it as the precursor of a new Industrial Revolution. For another, few stories illustrate so well the salient characteristics of modern technological advance, in particular, the combination of team research and individual genius, of deliberate, organized discovery and happy serendipity.

The central problem of wireless communication is that of emitting and receiving signals at a distance without direct contact or the use of an intermediary vehicle. In principle, the apprehension of these signals could take place via any of the senses. From the start, however, it was taken for granted that the most convenient mode of perception would be auditory, and here the already developed technology of the telegraph and telephone offered ready-made solutions to the problem of converting signals into sound.

Meanwhile the theoretical basis of wireless transmission had been laid in the early 1860's by Maxwell, who postulated the existence of electro-magnetic waves and worked out their properties; and by Heinrich Hertz, who explored the nature of these waves during the decade 1884–93 and was able in the course of his experiments to transmit electro-magnetic impulses over a distance of 20 or 25 feet. So firm

[1] W. Rupert Maclaurin, *Invention and Innovation in the Radio Industry* (N.Y. 1949), pp. 99, 105.

was Hertz's allegiance to pure as against applied science that he never realized the potential value of his work for telecommunication. There were others, however, to take his place, and nothing is so indicative of the improved conditions of scientific experiment and intellectual communication as the rapidity with which the advances in this field were disseminated from one country to another. The array of scientists and technicians who shared in the early development of the wireless reads like a UNESCO committee: Oliver Lodge and J. A. Fleming in England; Edouard Branly in France; Alexander Popov in Russia; Guglielmo Marconi in Italy and then England; Ferdinand Braun, Rudolf Slaby, and Georg von Arco in Germany; Reginald Fessenden and Lee De Forest in the United States.

The principal tasks were to develop a reliable transmitter and receiver. The earlier devices employed were ingenious but primitively inefficient. Take Branly's so-called coherer. This was a tube of loose metallic filings that, when placed in an electrical circuit, responded to electromagnetic waves by aligning themselves and permitting a flow of current; but by this very alignment, the coherer lost its sensitivity and had to be jarred after each signal to make it work. This was replaced by Fessenden's electrolytic detector (1903), a fine filament dipping into a solution of nitric acid and sensitive enough to pick up the undulations of the human voice; and by the crystal receivers (1906) of General Henry Dunwoody (carborundum) and G. W. Pickard (silicon, galena, iron pyrites), almost as sensitive, easier to handle, and so cheap as to place radio within reach of an army of amateur enthusiasts.

These in turn gave way to the vacuum tube. The tube, or the valve as it is often called (because its initial and principal function is to 'rectify' an electric current, so that it can pass in only one direction), goes back to J. Ambrose Fleming's diode (two-electrode) detector of 1904 and Lee De Forest's triode with grid of 1906–7. This 'miniature gadget', writes one historian of the industry, 'was the truest "little giant" in all history, perhaps the nearest approximation to an all-powerful genie that the brain of man ever created'.[1] The assessment is less hyperbolic than it seems; the valve made possible that proliferation of inventions that constitute the multifarious electronic industry: radio, radar, recording devices, computers, automated control systems, television, and so on—in a list that continues to grow.

De Forest's triode was used from the start as rectifier, detector, and amplifier (the last function led him to call it an audion); by 1913 it was also used as a generator of high-frequency oscillations. Its performance was weak and irregular, however, so much so that De Forest never derived from it the financial benefit he hoped for and deserved. The

[1] A. F. Harlow, *Old Wires and New Waves* (New York, 1946), p. 462.

source of trouble, unsuspected for some years, was the presence of gas in the tube; and it was not until 1912–13 that Harold Arnold of American Telephone and Telegraph and Irving Langmuir of the General Electric Research Laboratories, working independently, produced the so-called 'hard valve' or vacuum tube. As often, this achievement depended not only on the intellectual conception, but on new instrumental possibilities. In particular, the Gaede molecular pump, invented in Germany in 1910, provided the means of producing at moderate cost a higher vacuum than ever before. By the middle of 1913, American Telephone had produced a valve with a laboratory life of one thousand hours—as against fifty for De Forest's triode.

The vacuum tube came to be the heart of the principal instruments of wireless communication, but each of these has its own story of research, invention, and development. There is no space here to follow in detail this complex stream of ideas and applications, which even specialists have trouble organizing along lines comprehensible to the layman. Three main categories of technological advance may be discerned: (1) the invention of continuous transmitters capable of cutting through atmospheric static (the key inventions were the high-frequency alternator, for long waves, and the valve transmitter, for medium and short waves); (2) the development of techniques of amplification that, first, would permit the human voice to modulate the strong currents of the transmitter, and second, would make it possible for small receivers to convert into audible sounds that minuscule fraction of the transmitted energy picked up by any given listener (feedback, neutrodyne, heterodyne, and superheterodyne circuits); (3) the introduction of devices to focus transmission on the one hand (directional aerials) and permit discriminatory tuning on the other.

The latter two were particularly important to the success of entertainment broadcasting, for wireless receivers could never have become a household fixture had it not been possible to build them small and simple. Before the invention of the feedback circuit (1912), aerials had to be inconveniently large; those employed for long-distance communication were as much as a mile long (not in a straight line, of course), 400 to 850 feet high, and had to be placed on the seashore well away from cities to minimize interference. Afterwards, one could pick up transatlantic signals in the heart of the city with comparatively low aerials. Similarly, the earliest home receiving sets were delicate and discouragingly fickle; it took an expert to tune them and keep them tuned. Worse yet, there was no way to get the same station regularly by turning the dials to some set position. Finally, these manipulations would often cause the tubes to oscillate. This turned the receiver into a transmitter and made the other sets in the vicinity squeal and howl. It was L. A. Hazeltine's neutrodyne circuit (introduced commercially in 1923) that overcame most of these difficulties and made the radio a household necessity; and this in turn was quickly rendered obsolete by a succession of innovations in Britain, Holland, Germany, and the United States: H. J. Round's screen grid valve, or tetrode (1926); the Philips company's pentode, with suppressor grid (1927-28); Loewe's multi-electrode valves (1926 on); and the whole array of heterodyne and superheterodyne valves.[1]

Regular broadcasting of programmes for entertainment began in the United States and Holland in 1920, in Britain in 1922. In spite of the relatively high cost of a receiver, plus a licence fee in Britain, sales rose spectacularly fast. In the United States, the 100,000 sets of 1922 became 550,000 in 1923, 1,500,000 in 1924, to reach a first peak of 2 million in 1925.[2] In Great Britain, we have to count licences:[3]

end of 1922	36,000
end of 1924	1,130,000
end of 1926	2,178,000
end of 1929	almost 3 million

In Germany also, our statistics are of licences; here the start of broadcasting was delayed by an interdiction of radio reception imposed by the victorious Allies (lifted 11 April 1923):[4]

1 January 1924	1,500
1 January 1926	1,022,000
1 January 1928	2,009,842
1 January 1930	3,066,682

These figures, spectacular as they are, probably underestimate the rate of growth of the industry. For Britain, to be sure, they are swelled somewhat by sets of foreign manufacture.[5] But this is more than compensated by evasion of the registration requirement and by an extraordinarily high rate of obsolescence. In these early years of rapid technological change, wireless sets went out of date even faster than

[1] On the history of the valve and its manufacture, see S. G. Sturmey, *The Economic Development of Radio* (London, 1958), ch. II, in addition to the sources already cited. The above, very incomplete, list of innovations makes no mention of French work; I suspect that a French history of the subject would tell a different story.

[2] Maclaurin, *Invention and Innovation*, p. 139.

[3] Pollard, *The Development of the British Economy*, pp. 160-1.

[4] Gustav Lucae, *40 Jahre Rundfunkwirtschaft in Deutschland 1923-1963* (Düsseldorf, n.d.), p. 24. I have not been able to find figures for French output or sales of radio receivers for these years. The official statistics begin in 1933, when the law required that all radio sets be declared.

[5] Both Britain and Germany exported sets in quantity, but the former seems to have imported even more: net retained imports in 1934 amounted to 82,000 sets. Alfred Plummer, *New British Industries in the Twentieth Century* (London, 1937) p. 45, n. 1.

out of order, and the statistics on licences take no account of this turnover.

By the end of broadcasting's first decade, the manufacture and servicing of wireless equipment had changed from a promising but minor capital goods specialty to a major branch of industrial production. In Britain, annual turnover increased from £7,800,000 in 1926 to almost £30 million in 1931;[1] by comparison, the value of output of new motor vehicles (excluding motor-cycles) was about half again as high;[2] while total expenditure for household durables in that year is estimated at £218 million.[3]

What was more important, the radio was an excellent example of what might be called a counter-income or counter-status luxury, that is, a product whose utility varies inversely with income and which therefore is taken up by the poor faster than by the rich. (Television is perhaps an even better example.) For those whose resources opened to them a wide range of recreation and distraction, the radio was just one more source of entertainment, however important. For those with less means, radio rapidly became the principal diversion, and listening to certain programmes assumed almost a ritual character. As a result, demand was almost impervious to cyclical contraction and was more a function of electrification and the radius of broadcasts than of income (see Table 33).

Even these impressive figures of output and licences do not convey the full significance of the radio to the economies of western Europe. More than most other hard goods, the wireless generated a lively demand for replacement parts and services; sales outlets and repair shops proliferated. This in turn was part of a larger process attendant on the multiplication of consumers' durables. The bicycle and the motor car gave birth to their thousands of garages and show rooms. The box camera and its more advanced avatars spawned hundreds of photography shops. The growing variety of electrical appliances had similar consequences. All of this was in sharp contradiction to the allegedly inevitable proletarianization of small enterprise and polarization of society.

In addition to radio's substantive economic significance, its story is of interest to the historian because of the light it sheds on the character of

[1] *Ibid.*, p. 45.
[2] Calculated by multiplying the number of new passenger cars and commercial vehicles by their respective average export prices. London, Society of Motor Manufacturers and Traders, *The Motor Industry of Great Britain 1939* (London, n.d.), pp. 45, 106.
[3] Mitchell and Deane, *Abstract of British Historical Statistics*, p. 370. Again by way of comparison, expenditures for alcoholic beverages totalled some £282 m.; for tobacco, £140 m. Together they exceeded the outlays for rent—£410 m.

Table 33. *Radio Sets in Selected Countries, 1930–39 (in thousands)*

	U.K. Licences[a]	Output	Germany Licences[b]	France Sets declared
1930		506	3,510	—
1931	4,300	850	3,981	—
1932		1,000	4,308	—
1933	6,000	1,281	5,053	1,308
1934		1,757	6,143	1,756
1935	7,400	1,850	7,137[c]	2,626
1936		1,910	8,168	3,219
1937	8,500	1,918	9,087	4,164
1938		1,434	11,503	4,706
1939	8,900	—	13,711	4,992

[a] As of 31 December.   [b] As of 1 January of the following year.
[c] Without the Saar. With the Saar the number was 7,193,000. From 1937 on, the Saar is included.

SOURCES: For the U.K., Sturmey, *Economic Development*, p. 177; Duncan Burn, ed., *The Structure of British Industry: A Symposium* (2 vols.; Cambridge, 1958), II, 137. For Germany, Lucae, *40 Jahre Rundfunkwirtschaft*, p. 24. For France, *Annuaire statistique*, LVII (1946), résumé rétrospectif, p. 120*.

modern technological progress. Few devices, indeed, illustrate so well the nature of the process: the multiple contributions, coming from several countries and often simultaneously; the flow of ideas from science to engineering to business; the role of subsidized group research; the high yield of technological fall-out. The radio was testimony to the existence of one world of knowledge, sharing a common stock of ideas, data, and methods, a world, moreover, in which the improvement of communications and the professionalization of science and engineering had enormously speeded the diffusion of each new idea and each successive advance. Listen to Lee De Forest describe the beginnings of the research that led to the invention of the triode valve:[1]

October 1 [1899]...I have begun a systematic search through *Science Abstracts*, Wiedemann's *Annalen*, etc., for some hint or suggestion of an idea for a new form of detector for wireless signals...

November 5, 1899. Finally, in the April number of Wiedemann's *Annalen* in an article by Aschkinass, I found a brief description of a phenomenon newly discovered which promised to be the solution to my problem.

Ironically enough, this very universality makes it hard to write a balanced, 'fair' history of the radio and its industry, for each country

[1] From MacLaurin's classic *Invention and Innovation in the Radio Industry*, p. 71. MacLaurin got permission to reprint these and other extracts of De Forest's diary from De Forest himself.

can and does have its own version of the story. Almost every advance of importance has been credited to two or more people: the alternator to Fessenden, Ernst Alexanderson (General Electric), and Rudolph Goldschmidt (Allgemeine Elektrizitäts-Gesellschaft); the triode valve as amplifier (1911) to von Lieben (Germany) and Edwin Armstrong (U.S.); the feed-back circuit (1912) to Armstrong, Meissner (Telefunken), De Forest, Irving Langmuir (General Electric), and C. S. Franklin and H. J. Round (English Marconi); the valve as generator of high-frequency oscillations (1913) to Meissner (Germany), Armstrong, Franklin and Round.[1]

As this list makes clear, the effectiveness of subsidized group experimentation had not yet eliminated the gifted individual inventor: the history of wireless communication is brightened by the achievements of independents like Guglielmo Marconi, Lee De Forest, Reginald Fessenden and Edwin H. Armstrong. These were, however, a new breed of tinkerers, far better trained in science than their predecessors of the eighteenth and nineteenth centuries; electronics was too esoteric to admit of innocent empiricism. The weakest in this respect was Marconi, though he made up for his cognitive deficiencies by native ingenuity and an invincible optimism: it was he who persisted in seeking a way to transmit sound over long distances in the face of stern scientific opinion that radio waves would simply follow a straight line out through the atmosphere away from Earth. Once established as an entrepreneur, moreover, he never hesitated to hire the scientific competence he needed. Fessenden was trained in mathematics and physics and taught as a professor of electrical engineering from 1892 to 1900. Like Marconi, he was a man of creative stubbornness: at a time when all the experts were content with the intermittent performance of the coherer, Fessenden insisted that a good receiver should work continuously. De Forest did a Ph.D. thesis at Yale on wireless telegraphy. And Armstrong, who studied physics under Pupin at Columbia, was professor there from 1934 to 1954. Like Marconi and Fessenden, Armstrong had his own genial obstinacy, which armed him against the indifference and hostility of business rather than the despair of science. His invention of frequency modulation in 1933 was turned down by the Radio Corporation of America and opposed by the large broadcasting companies. Thanks to a sympathetic friend, however, it did get a hearing on the small Yankee Network of New England, and consumer preference did the rest.

★   ★   ★   ★

[1] John Jewkes, Sawers and Stillerman, *The Sources of Invention*, p. 352.

Few industries, if any, grew so fast in these years as radio, which profited, as we have seen, from a peculiarly favourable demand and a rapid flow of technological improvement. By comparison, even so buoyant a branch as electric power seems sluggish. Yet consumption of electricity increased fourfold in the interwar years (1920–39). This continuation of the prewar surge reflected in part the still incomplete substitution of the new form of power transmission for the traditional steam engine and shafting; and of the electric light for older forms of illumination. (Compare the boost that cheap steel got from the need to replace the existing stock of wrought iron rails.) Increasingly, however, it was the new applications, among them radio, that pushed up demand.

This substantial growth in power consumption was not a smooth process. In the twenties, European output of current rose from 52·8 billion (10^9) kilowatt-hours to 114 billion, a gain of 116 per cent; from 1930 to 1939, the rise was slower—to 199 billion kilowatt-hours, an advance of 74 per cent. That this slowing was the effect of the depression and not of a definitive movement to a lower trend is shown by the experience of the postwar period. Once the initial confusion was overcome and damaged plant restored, the growth of consumption resumed the pace of the twenties: in the OEEC area (which excludes socialist Europe and Finland, but includes Turkey), output of electric current rose from 199·5 billion kilowatt-hours in 1948 to 434 billion in 1958, or 117 per cent.[1]

Here a word of caution is in order. This impressive increase does not reflect the general pattern of energy consumption. This grew far more slowly, from $4,415 \times 10^{15}$ to $5,340 \times 10^{15}$ Calories in the quarter-century from 1913 to 1937.[2] Indeed, for the most advanced industrial nations of Europe, input of energy was standing still, if not actually shrinking, in our period, as Table 34 indicates.

In order to understand this levelling-off of energy consumption in a growing economy, one must distinguish first between input of energy into the system of converters and output of energy by the system; the ratio between these two amounts is the measure of efficiency of the system.[3] It is thus possible, by improving the converters (steam engines,

[1] The effect of the depression was even more severe in the United States. There output of current went from 56·6 billion in 1920 to 116·7 in 1929 (thus keeping pace with Europe), to only 161·3 billion in 1939. The growth of the thirties was thus 38 per cent, about half the European. Svennilson, *Growth and Stagnation*, p. 256, Table A. 26; OEEC, Energy Advisory Commission, *Towards a New Energy Pattern in Europe* (Paris, 1960), p. 119; OECD, *The Electricity Supply Industry in Europe*, 12th Enquiry (Paris, 1962), Table 1.   [2] *Ibid.*, p. 104, Table 23.

[3] One should properly distinguish between technical and economic efficiency. The former is the ratio of the energy output of a converter (the heat equivalent, for ex-

Table 34. *Inputs to the Energy Systems of Major European Countries* $(Btu \times 10^{12})$, *1865–1939*

Germany		France		United Kingdom	
1876	1,280	1885	930	1865	2,911
1890	2,574	1895	1,176	1881	4,578
1907	5,641	1905	1,453	1890	4,495
1913	6,800	1911	1,805	1913	5,657
1929	7,583	1928	2,170	1929	5,691
1937	6,682	1938	2,368	1939	5,952

SOURCE: Palmer C. Putnam, *Energy in the Future* (Toronto, New York, London, 1953), pp. 447–9.

water turbines, or other), to increase actual output of energy considerably while holding consumption down; by the same token one can, by moving the energy better and by improving the quality of the machines and tools driven by it, make such output go farther. Thus production of energy rose substantially in the interwar years in each of the 'big three', with the exception of France in the 1930's:

Table 35. *Outputs from the Energy Systems of the Major European Countries* $(Btu \times 10^{12})$, *1865–1939*

Germany		United Kingdom		France	
1867	132	1865	236	1885	107
1890	271	1881	389	1895	147
1907	654	1890	413	1905	191
1913	843	1913	731	1911	221
1929	1,240	1929	994	1928	360
1937	1,270	1939	1,274	1938	344

SOURCE: Putnam, *Energy in the Future*, pp. 447–9. These estimates are not based on an aggregation of direct measures of energy output. Rather, they were calculated by multiplying the estimates of energy inputs by estimates of efficiency.

The decline in French output in the thirties is the more striking in view of the concomitant increase of energy input. The paradox assumes

ample, of the electricity produced by a generator) and the energy put in (the heat equivalent of the coal used to drive the generator). But energy is consumed in bringing fuel to the converter—to mine the coal, for example, and deliver it to the power plant or engine; and from the economic point of view, these costs are an integral part of the calculation of efficiency and should be added to the denominator. Economic efficiency is thus invariably lower than technical efficiency. Since data on economic efficiency are few and far between, however, all statistics in the text are of technical efficiency.

a significant decline in efficiency—from 16·6 to 14·5 per cent. Unfortunately, these estimates of efficiencies are based only in part on direct measurements; as Putnam puts it: 'The slope in the curve of French efficiency was determined after considering the growth rates of over-all technical progress, technical progress in specific industries, and national income...' There is good ground, however, for such an inferential calculation. The stagnation of French industrial production in the 1930's presumably imposed cutbacks in the use of existing energy converters; and since such engines, as we have seen, operate most efficiently at or near capacity, the ratio of output to input must have declined.

The gain in overall efficiency in energy conversion during the interwar period was part of a long-term trend going back as far as our statistics permit us to go. The trend was the result of improvements in the techniques used to produce both comfort heat (the shift from open fireplaces to stoves, and eventually to central heating) and work (shift from water wheels to turbines, savings in steam engine fuel consumption, introduction of the steam turbine). But it was actually slowed down by the steady increase in the share of energy devoted to work as against comfort heat, for the efficiency of all but the most rudimentary systems of domestic heating has always been far greater than that of engines and motors.

Table 36. *Estimated Aggregate Efficiency of Energy Output in Selected Countries, 1860 and 1950 (in per cent)*

	1860	1950
Russia[a]	35	23
Germany	10	20
United Kingdom	8	24
United States	8	30
France	12 (1885)	20

[a] Apparently includes Asiatic Russia (Putnam uses the designation U.S.S.R.). The high Russian figure in 1860 reflects on the one hand the relative efficiency of the typical domestic heating device, a closed stove, and on the other, the very low proportion of energy devoted to work.

SOURCE: Putnam, *Energy in the Future*, p. 90.

It is here that electricity made one of its most important contributions. The gap in efficiency between the two classes of energy converters, which has narrowed with time, has shrunk especially fast since the turn of the century. The timing is not coincidental. It was those years that saw the beginning of the industrial application of electric power. Electric generation, as noted above, was a more efficient source of work energy than the usual steam engine to begin with;[1] and this margin increased with time as power lines ramified, thereby diversifying demand and improving the load factor, and as the technique of generation advanced. Here the major gain was the substitution of the steam turbine for the piston steam engine in the production of thermal electricity. Hydro-electric generation was always relatively efficient.

It is not easy to find statistics on the overall efficiency of electricity generation, but disparate occasional data are suggestive. Thus the efficiency of generation by steam rose in Germany from 10–11 per cent in 1913 to 15–19 per cent in 1929.[2] And Putnam has the aggregate efficiency of electricity generation in the United States (including hydroelectricity) rising from something less than 4 per cent in 1890 to 20 per cent in 1940.[3] Finally, we have the indirect test of the real cost of electrical power in terms of the cost of coal. (Here economies in the extraction and distribution of coal are inextricably mixed with gains in the efficiency of electrical generation and distribution, and the relation-ship is further confused by commercial as well as political and other nontechnological influences on the prices of the two commodities.) In the United Kingdom, one could buy 51 kWh of electricity for house-hold use in 1925 for the price of a ton of coal; in 1938, 123; the respective figures for industrial electricity were 194 and 301. In France, the gain for all uses was fourfold from 1913 to 1938, from 41 to 162 kWh.[4]

Britain offers a particularly good example of the transformation. In the early decades of electric power, she was notorious for the diversity of her system of generation and the smallness of her central stations. Voltage varied from town to town and even street to street; those sys-tems that furnished alternating current did so at different cycles; the

---

[1] The reference here is to the steam engine when used to drive working machines and tools. The steam engine was also used, of course, to drive electric generators; indeed for all the major industrial countries of Europe, except those like Norway and Switzerland that were exceptionally endowed with water power, the steam engine has remained to the present the principal prime mover in the generation of electricity. The combination of steam engine and generator tended to be more efficient from the start than the steam engine alone.

[2] Bruno Benkert, *Grundlagen zur Berechnung der Selbstkosten elektrischer Energie* (Erlangen-Bruck, 1935), p. 31. Brady, *Rationalization Movement*, p. 209, nn. 42 and 43, offers another measure of this gain: the amount of coal required to produce one kilo-watt fell about half from 1913 to 1926/27—from 1·05–1·15 kg. to 0·58 kg. By com-parison, a gas motor of the early twenties had an efficiency of 20–25 per cent; and a Diesel motor, up to 35 per cent for large units and 20–25 per cent for small.

[3] According to the U.S. Federal Power Commission, *National Power Survey* (Washington, D.C. 1964), p. 64, the thermal efficiency of steam-electric power generation rose from 5 per cent in 1900 to 30 per cent in 1940.

[4] Svennilson, *Growth and Stagnation*, p. 113.

effect on the electrical goods industry may easily be imagined. As late as 1925 there were 438 stations in operation, the 28 largest of which accounted for half the output of power while the 322 smallest shared only 11 per cent among them.[1]

At this point, the state stepped in to encourage nationalization and amalgamation. A Central Electricity Board was created (1926) with the right to monopolize all wholesaling of electricity and the power to borrow money to buy up and close down the inefficient units. By 1935 the Board had succeeded in concentrating output in some 144 base load stations and 'super' centrals, tied together in a national grid that made possible a far more even distribution of load. At the same time, the industry moved to standardize its product. Whereas in 1929, the most widely used pressure, 230 V, furnished less than a fifth of domestic current, ten years later the figure was up to 50 per cent.[2] The result was lower rates, and these not only further improved load and diversity factors, but in conjunction with continued investment in power lines, brought electricity within reach of a rapidly growing body of consumers: 730,000 in 1920, 2,844,000 in 1929, 8,920,000 in 1939.[3] Output rose from 12·7 billion kWh in 1926 to 35·8 in 1939 (see Table 40, below) —a gain all the more impressive because most of it took place in the 1930's.[4]

As might be expected from Germany's precocious competence in electrical engineering and the technological rationality of her large-scale industrial enterprise, she was quicker than comparable countries to supplant traditional forms of power by electricity. In Europe, it was only the coal-poor, hydro-power-rich countries like Norway, Switzerland, and Sweden that surpassed her by a significant margin in consumption of current per head; compact Belgium was slightly ahead; the United Kingdom and France, well behind. In 1925 her industries were

[1] H. H. Ballin, *The Organisation of Electricity Supply in Great Britain* (London, 1946), p. 185. P.E.P., *The British Fuel and Power Industries* (London, 1947), p. 158, gives a higher figure: 491 authorized stations in 1926.

[2] Ballin, *Organisation*, p. 242. Even so, there were in 1936 forty-three different voltages in use between 100 and 480 V.

[3] Price of electric power in the United Kingdom (pence per kWh):

	Household use	Industrial use
1925	3·815	0·995
1929	2·862	0·817
1935	1·921	0·659
1938	1·598	0·655

SOURCE: Svennilson, *Growth and Stagnation*, p. 255.

[4] The above discussion owes much to Pollard, *The Development of the British Economy*, p. 100.

getting two thirds of their power in this form; Britain's industries were getting barely half in 1924.

It is interesting to compare the power patterns of the two countries in greater detail. In the newer industries, there was little to choose between them: in machine building and motor car manufacture, for example, Germany was slightly ahead in the mid-twenties, but the differences were measured in a few percentage points. But in older trades the German advance was considerable: 74 as against 42 per cent in iron and steel; 72 as against 52 in chemicals—one more evidence of retardation in those branches that had once been the foundation of British industrial superiority.[1]

For Germany, in contrast to Britain, diversity of current characteristics was not an acute problem; at least this is what one infers from the silence of the sources on the subject. Instead, the main effort toward rationalization took the form of wider distribution systems, with consequent gains in load factor, and of larger generating plants, with concomitant improvements in the technique of energy conversion.

It is not easy to impute to each of these changes its own share in Germany's overall advance in power technology. The biggest single factor was probably the increased efficiency of thermal generating plants, which almost doubled, as we have seen, from 1913 to the late twenties. Economies of scale were less important: if all technical and efficiency factors were held constant, the saving in fuel consumption per output of current in going from a plant of 10,000 kW capacity to one of 100,000 kW was of the order of 10 per cent; to this must be added a saving of about a third in capital costs per unit of output—2·3 as against 3·4 pfennigs per kilowatt. The point is, however, that all these changes were interdependent: bigger networks made possible larger generating plants, and bigger plants permitted the installation of new and better equipment.

All in turn were dependent on changes in the structure of enterprise in the power industry. To begin with, there was a shift from private generating plants, serving the needs of an individual user, to public centrals. The technical advantages of central as against private stations are obvious: a diversified clientele makes for a better load factor; and as Table 37 makes clear, central stations were substantially larger, with attendant economies of scale.

At the same time, there was a progressive concentration of enterprise. Of the 1,488 central stations producing 16·4 billion kWh in 1929, the six largest delivered 8·8 billions.[2] The two biggest German electric

[1] Brady, *The Rationalization Movement*, p. 199.
[2] Delivery is not the same as production, since some of these enterprises had a deficit on current account (if I may be permitted a pun), that is, they bought more

Table 37. *Germany: Output of Electric Power by Type of Plant*

		Number	Output (million kW)	Share of total output (%)
Public works	1925	1,370	9·915	48·8
	1929	1,488	16·391	53·4
Private works	1925	6,122	10·413	51·2
	1929	5,622	14·269	46·6

SOURCE: Brady, *Rationalization Movement*, p. 197. N.B.: Public centrals are not to be confused with publicly owned power plants.

utilities, the Rheinisch-Westfälisches Elektrizitätswerk and the Elektro-werke were the largest in Europe, surpassed only by the three biggest American enterprises. The former was founded in Essen in 1898 by the Elektrizitätswerke A.G. (formerly W. Lahmeyer and Co.). With the support of Stinnes, Thyssen, and other magnates of the steel industry, it grew rapidly from a municipal power source to supplier to the great industrial complex of western Germany: of the two billion (10^9) kWh it produced in 1928/29, only 135 million went for domestic use; the rest went to industry. The RWE produced most of its power in its own central stations, the biggest of which was the 500,000 kW Goldenberg-werk near Cologne, fuelled by brown coal; but it drew additional current from the industrial plants in the area, many of which generated surplus power in the course of normal operations. As it grew, the RWE also contracted with other distributors to exchange current as needed, and by 1925 a *Dachgesellschaft* called the Westdeutsche Elektrizitäts-Wirtschaft A.G. united it with the other major producers of western Germany, making possible by the early 1930s a single distribution system from the Rhine to the Elbe and from the North Sea to the Alps.

In central and eastern Germany, the publicly owned Elektrowerke, the Preussische Elektrizitäts A.G., and the Bayernwerke founded in 1928 a similar joint venture, the A.G. für Deutsche Elektrizitätswirt-schaft, to explore the possibilities of a unified network.[1] Here too the main connections were completed by the early 1930's, and western and eastern systems were partially joined by an agreement for exchange of current between the Rheinisch-Westfälisches Elektrizitätswerk and the Bayernwerke. So that when in 1930, O. von Miller prepared his plan

current from other producers than they sold, in order to satisfy peak demands exceed-ing their capacity. Even so, other estimates indicate a higher degree of concentration, imputing two thirds of output and delivery to the seven largest concerns. *Ibid.* pp. 212 f.

[1] The most important member of the Westdeutsche Elektrizitäts-Wirtschaft, the Rheinisch-Westfälisches Elektrizitätswerk, was mostly privately owned. But cities and communes owned about one third of the common stock, the Prussian state 6·83 per cent, and the central government (indirectly) something less than 2 per cent.

for a national network for the Wirtschaftsministerium, some of his proposals were already out of date by the time of publication.

The experience of the French electric power industry during these years was in many respects parallel to that of the British and German industries. Here, too, the greatest obstacle to rationalization was the multiplicity of enterprises, with consequent inefficiencies of scale and impediments to the standardization of electrical products. These difficulties were aggravated in the French case by the hostility of vested interests to hydroelectric development, which, far more efficient than thermal generation, would have permitted lower rates and encouraged consumption. Whereas Italy, which has almost no coal, had developed about two fifths of her potential supply of hydropower by 1939, France was exploiting only a fifth of her potential at that date.[1]

What is more, the weaknesses on the side of supply were compounded by those of demand, particularly among domestic consumers. It took a long time for the French householder to accustom himself to the desirability, even the necessity, of domestic appliances. In our period, he used his current only for lighting, plus usually a radio (though less frequently than in other countries), and often but not always, an iron.[2] The more costly appliances—refrigerators, stoves, water heaters, vacuum cleaners, and the like—were viewed as bourgeois luxuries, and even the bourgeoisie seems to have adopted them with reluctance. One can hear even today Frenchmen who contend that the taste of refrigerated food is necessarily altered for the worse; or that while an electric oven may be suitable for making pastry, only a gas stove will do for meats and vegetables, and that one should really use a coal or wood stove for certain other culinary operations. Such fastidiousness is no doubt justified for gourmets; though one may be permitted to wonder how many of those who cherish such finesses have the palate to go with them. (One is reminded of the American passion for high-fidelity recording and play-back apparatus with capacities that exceed the range of the human ear.) In any event, the non-electric way of life is in itself tied to a given pattern of social action and relationships. Refrigeration is unnecessary if one shops every day, or even several times a day, and up till now—or at least very recently—daily shopping has not only pro-

[1] Svennilson, *Growth and Stagnation*, p. 116. Svennilson suggests a series of further reasons for this delay: the concentration of industries and population in the Paris area and the North, in proximity to the coal fields; the high cost of capital; the French investor's avoidance of long-term risks; the special character of private property in waterfalls.

[2] Radio sets per thousand inhabitants in 1950: Sweden, 307; United Kingdom, 244; Switzerland, 221; Netherlands, 195; West Germany, 184; Belgium, 179; France, 165. Arnold B. Barach, *The New Europe and Its Economic Future* (New York, 1964), p. 132. (See also Table 38.)

vided the French household with fresh food but has afforded the French housewife, or her maid, one of her most agreeable distractions. Similarly, only the availability of cheap domestic help made it possible for otherwise elegant people to do without hot running water in the kitchen; so that one can find some of the finest apartments in Paris with hot water piped into bedrooms and baths only.

Yet when all is said and done, the great majority of French housewives have always had to do their own housework (though for an American, it is always striking to note how far down in the social and economic scale the institution of regular domestic service extends). Their long reluctance to make use of electric appliances was due largely to lack of means; and this lack reflected in turn the high cost of these devices. In 1933, for example, a Swiss could buy a variety of electric stoves at a price of 740 French francs; a Frenchman would have had to pay 1,200 to 1,400 francs, in itself a sharp fall from the 1,800–2,000 francs of 1931.[1] The difficulty was aggravated, moreover, by the inadequacy of domestic wiring. For reasons of economy, the capacity of most entry services was extremely low—as small as two or three amperes for modest apartments even after the Second World War, perhaps ten amperes for a bourgeois flat in Paris. The addition of even one or two devices, therefore, often imposed the further expense of a new service (related costs again!).

The statistics bear eloquent witness to these impediments:

Table 38. *Electrical Appliances in Use in Selected Countries c. 1932 (per 10,000 people)*

	U.S.	Switzerland	France
Irons	1,580	1,750	850
Percolators, kettles	490	520	200
Heaters, radiators	280	340	85
Stoves	180	460	8
Water heaters	—	360	7
Vacuum cleaners	740	—	120

SOURCE: Lejay, *L'utilisation domestique*, p. 90. Lejay does not give a date for these figures, and I have had to infer one from the text. Lejay also warns that these figures 'cannot be considered as strictly exact'.

All of this necessarily meant a lower consumption of electric power for domestic use (see Table 39).

As a result, the output of electricity in France, though rising steadily, increased somewhat less rapidly than in the other major European countries. The gap was not so large as is sometimes stated, however,

[1] André Lejay, *L'utilisation domestique de l'électricité* (Paris, 1933), p. 53.

Table 39. *Consumption of Electricity* per capita
in *Selected Countries* (in *kilowatt-hours*)

	Consumption outside industry and transport per head of total population		Consumption for domestic use per connected household
	1929	1938	1932
Canada	—	—	1,380
Norway	547	747	1,300
Sweden	—	—	800
U.S.A.	—	—	600
Switzerland	249	317	500
Germany	—	—	360
Great Britain[a]	58	187	340
France	31	57	200
Belgium[b]	56	69	180

[a] For Column 3, England. But in view of the French imprecision about the designations of the sundry political units of the British Isles, either the United Kingdom or Great Britain is probably intended.

[b] For Columns 1 and 2, Belgium–Luxembourg.

SOURCES: Columns 1 and 2 from Svennilson, *Growth and Stagnation*, p. 118; Column 3 from Lejay, *L'utilisation domestique*, p. 147.

and was confined largely to the 1930's, when French production rose 30 per cent, as against 100 per cent in the U.K. and Germany.

★   ★   ★   ★   ★

One more young and expansive industry is worth examining, partly as an example of the kind of concentration and rationalization that characterized the electric power industry, even more as a critical factor in the overall process of economic growth. This is the motor car manufacture. Like electricity, it was born and took its first steps before the War; the first motor vehicles date from the 1890's. But for the first decade at least, especially in Europe, the motor car was an expensive toy. It was difficult to operate and was made to order for those wealthy few who could afford, not only the initial outlay, but the high cost of operation and maintenance—including the salary of the almost indispensable professional driver or *chauffeur*. Motor cars were constantly breaking down, not only because of engine failure, but because the tyres could not stand up to the strain of poor suspension and wretched roads. It was not uncommon to take along three or four spares on any trip beyond a radius of five or ten miles; even so, the patch kit was an

Table 40. *Europe: Production of Electrical Energy, 1920–39*
(in billions [10⁹] of kWh)

	Germanyª	U.K.	France	Sweden	Switzer-landᵇ	Belgium	Italy
1920	(14·5)	(8·5)	(5·8)	2·6	2·8	(1·3)	4·7
1921	(15·7)	(8·4)	(6·5)	2·2	2·7	(1·4)	4·5
1922	(17·0)	(9·3)	(7·3)	2·7	3·0	(1·5)	4·7
1923	18·3	(10·3)	8·2	3·0	3·3	(1·7)	5·6
1924	19·8	(11·3)	10·0	3·5	3·7	(1·9)	6·5
1925	20·3	(12·1)	11·1	3·7	4·0	2·3	7·3
1926	21·2	(12·7)	12·4	4·0	4·4	(2·8)	8·4
1927	25·1	(14·5)	12·6	4·4	4·7	3·2	8·7
1928	27·9	(15·6)	14·3	4·4	5·0	3·7	9·6
1929	30·7	(17·0)	15·6	5·0	5·3	4·0	10·4
1930	29·1	(17·7)	16·9	5·1	5·2	4·4	10·7
1931	25·8	(18·2)	15·7	5·1	5·0	4·2	10·5
1932	23·5	(19·5)	15·0	4·9	4·8	3·9	10·6
1933	25·7	(21·2)	16·4	5·3	4·9	3·9	11·6
1934	30·7	(23·4)	16·7	6·0	5·3	4·0	12·6
1935	35·7	(25·9)	17·5	6·9	5·7	4·5	13·8
1936	41·3	(28·9)	18·5	7·4	6·1	4·9	13·6
1937	47·7	(31·9)	20·1	8·0	6·8	5·5	15·4
1938	54·0	(33·8)	20·8	8·2	7·0	5·3	15·5
1939	60·2	(35·8)	22·1	9·1	7·1	5·6	18·4

ª Boundaries of 1937, excluding the Saar.
ᵇ Twelve months ending September 30 of the year stated.

SOURCE: OEEC, *Basic Statistics of Industrial Production, 1913–1952*, p. 39. Figures in parentheses are estimates.

indispensable accessory. The task of the motorist was aggravated by the lack of repair facilities: garages were few; the supply of parts, thready; and motorists were obliged to seek their cans of petrol from food shops and hardware stores, which sold it like the kerosene for lamps. The oil companies themselves took the precaution of delivering their product to retailers in horse-drawn wagons.[1] In short, motoring was an expensive adventure.

Even so, the motor car offered two advantages that more than compensated for the high cost and inconvenience: the thrill of speed and freedom of movement; so that by 1913 over 400,000 motor vehicles were registered in the United Kingdom, France, and Germany, the vast majority of them passenger cars. In that year alone, over one hundred

[1] On the conditions of distribution of petrol in the prewar period, see Donald Dixon, 'Petrol Distribution in the United Kingdom, 1900–1950', *Business History*, VI (1963–4), 1–19.

manufacturers in Britain produced 34,000 units. Some of these firms were very small and hopelessly inefficient; the largest, however— Daimler, Wolseley, Humber, Sunbeam—employed thousands and were comparable to the great engineering companies; while the industry as a whole employed over a hundred thousand.[1]

The great expansion of the industry was just beginning, however. The path of growth was foreshadowed by developments in the United States, where the introduction of precision manufacture, interchangeable parts, and the assembly line brought the motor car within reach even of the workers who made it. The Model T dates from 1908 and cost $1000 at first; sixteen years later, in 1924, the price had fallen to less than $300, and by 1926 Henry Ford had sold 15 million of his motorized buggies. They can have any colour they want, he said, so long as it's black. As a result, the United States had about three times as many cars registered by 1913 as the three major western European countries together; by 1921, owing to the war, the ratio had risen to 13 to 1, and to 10 to 1 for Europe as a whole.

European industry made big strides, however, in the interwar years. To be sure, in absolute terms, output still fell far short of the American: some 10 million motor vehicles for the four leading European producers (U.K., Germany, France, Italy) from 1923 to 1938 against 57 million for the United States. But the European rate of growth was faster: an increase in output of 300 per cent as against at best 20 per cent. (Actually American production in 1938 was 38·5 per cent less than in 1923! Only twice in the 1930's did output exceed that of 1923; while annual production 1923–29 [4,200,000 vehicles] ran 38 per cent higher than in the years 1930–8 [3,050,000 vehicles].) At the end of our period, the number of registrations in Europe was up to about two-sevenths that in the United States.

It would be hard to exaggerate the significance of this growth for the

Table 41. *Registered Motor Vehicles in Selected European Countries and in the United States, 1905–38 (in thousands)*

	1905	1913	1930	1938
U.K.	32	208	1,524	2,422
Germany	27	93	679	1,816
France	22	125	1,460	2,251
Italy	—	—	293	469
All Europe	—	—	5,182	8,381
U.S.A.	79	1,258	26,532	29,443

SOURCE: Svennilson, *Growth and Stagnation*, p. 147.

[1] On the early history of the motor car: S. B. Saul, 'The Motor Industry in Britain to 1914', *Business History*, V (1962–3), 22–44.

overall expansion of the European economies. The motor car industry was beginning to play at this point a role analogous to that of the railroad in the mid-nineteenth century: it was a huge consumer of semi-finished and finished intermediate products (sheet steel, timber, glass, and paint) and components (tyres, lamps, generators, etc.); it had an insatiable appetite for fuel and other petroleum products; it required a small army of mechanics and service men to keep it going; and it gave a powerful impetus to investments in social overhead capital (roads, bridges, tunnels). At the same time, it posed new technical problems in metallurgy, organic chemicals, and electrical engineering, eliciting solutions that had important consequences for other industries as well. In the language of development economics, no other product yielded so rich a harvest of forward and backward linkages.

One would like to be able to quantify the contribution of the motor vehicle industry to the general development of the European economies; but the authors of the few histories of the industry seem to have studiously avoided this aspect of the subject. For the United States, there are the figures of the Automobile Manufacturers Association:

Table 42. *United States: Share of Automotive Consumption in Total Consumption of Selected Products* (%)

	1929	1938
Strip steel	60·4	51
Bar steel	28·7	34
Sheet steel	29·2	41
Alloy steel	—	54
Steel, all forms	18[a]	17
Malleable iron	52[a]	53
Plate glass	73[a]	69
Rubber	84·2	80
Aluminium	37·4[a]	10·6
Copper	15·7[a]	12·1
Tin	23·6[b]	9·2
Lead	31·2[c]	35·1
Zinc	5·5[c]	10·3
Nickel	26	29
Mohair	—	36·6

[a] Share of U.S. output, not consumption. The source is not clear, but it is probable that this applies also to the various types of steel for 1929.
[b] Share of total deliveries in U.S.
[c] Share of production from domestic ores.

SOURCE: National Automobile Chamber of Commerce, *Facts and Figures of the Automobile Industry*, 1930; pp. 82–3; Automobile Manufacturers Association, *Automobile Facts and Figures*, 1939, pp. 38–9.

For the European industry, we have data only for Britain, and then in a form that makes the estimation of percentages hazardous. The Statistical Department of the Society of Motor Manufacturers and Traders furnished in its annual survey, *The Motor Industry of Great Britain*, the amounts of the materials consumed by the industry. (The last of these lists appeared in 1937 for the year 1936 and was reprinted in the PEP report on *Motor Vehicles* of 1950.) Unfortunately, the S.M.M.T. made no attempt to reckon the share of the motor industry's consumption in total consumption, and much of the information required to do this is no longer easily obtainable, if at all. Still, a few of the more standardized materials lend themselves to this calculation (see Table 43 below). As might be expected, the place of the motor industry in the British economy was much smaller than in the American economy. But it was substantial in many areas and dominant in a few—rubber, petroleum derivatives, sheet steel. It was the largest consumer of machine tools, and no other branch of manufacture offered so rapidly growing a market to heavy industry. Thus consumption of finished steel by 'Motors, cycles, and aircraft'—of which the motor industry presumably constituted by far the most important component—increased by more than five times in the quarter-century from 1924 to 1949, from 187,000 to 1,045,000 tons. The only group to show a comparable rate of increase (actually very slightly higher) was electrical engineering, whose consumption of steel rose from 100,000 to 565,000 tons over the same years. By comparison the next most rapid gain, that of mechanical engineering, was of the order of one to two.[1]

Table 43. *Great Britain: Materials Consumed in the Manufacture and Repair of Motor Vehicles in 1936*

	Quantity	Share of total production or consumption
Iron and steel	900,000 tons	8·2
Brass and copper	13,400 tons	—
Lead and lead oxide	8,100 tons	9·6
Tin	1,400 tons	6·3
Aluminium and bronze	450 tons	—
Glass	8,830,000 sq. ft. ⎫ 5,000 tons ⎭	—
Paints	2,350,000 gals. ⎫ 10,490 tons ⎭	—
Rubber	63,000 tons	—
Timber	111,000,000 board feet	—

SOURCE: S.M.M.T., *The Motor Industry of Great Britain*, 1937 (London, 1938).

[1] P. W. S. Andrews and Elizabeth Brunner, *Capital Development in Steel: A Study of the United Steel Companies Ltd.* (Oxford, 1952), p. 96. The figures are based on data

The growth in output of motor cars was accompanied, both as cause and effect, by significant gains in technology. The American example was there to be followed; what was needed was capital and imagination. The adoption of what the Germans liked to call *der Fordismus* entailed a heavy investment in fixed plant and special-purpose machinery, while yielding large economies of scale. It was thus beyond the means of all but the biggest producers. Here the fragmentation of the European industry was a serious handicap. In contrast to the United States, where Ford had managed to win more than half the market by 1921 and Chevrolet (General Motors) was beginning the spectacular climb that was to take it past Ford by 1927, Europe had no giants on the morrow of the war. There were 96 motor car factories in Britain in 1922, 150 in France in 1921, more than 200 in Germany in 1925.

The requirements of the new technology, however, in combination with the intensified competition of the 1930's, inexorably winnowed this plethora of producers. In both Britain and Germany, moreover, the process was hastened by the establishment of American-owned assembly-line plants in the 1920's. By 1938, the 'Big Six' British companies were making 90 per cent of the passenger cars and 81 per cent of the commercial vehicles.[1] Even so, production was far less mechanized than in the United States: according to one estimate, the ratio of horse-power to operatives was four to five times higher in America than in Britain in the 1930's. The difference was reflected in productivity: in 1935 the American manufacturers turned out three times as many cars per worker—and larger cars at that—as their British competitors.[2]

Concentration proceeded even faster in Germany. By 1937, the three largest German producers accounted for 74 per cent of total output; the five largest, almost 90 per cent.[3] Yet here too technique fell well short of

compiled by the Iron and Steel Federation. In making comparisons of this kind, questions of definition and hence aggregation are obviously decisive. Thus the data show that 'Motors, cycles, and aircraft' took 3·8 per cent of the finished steel in 1924, as against 19·0 per cent for 'Shipbuilding and Marine engineering' and 16·0 per cent for 'Mechanical engineering'. But whereas shipbuilding is a relatively homogeneous activity, mechanical engineering is a congeries of diverse branches, and its share in consumption would be much diminished if it were redefined into some of its major components. By the same token, 'Motors, cycles, and aircraft' is a composite group, and although the motor industry was by far its biggest component, it would nevertheless have been preferable to separate it from the others.

[1] P.E.P. (Political and Economic Planning), *Motor Vehicles* [PEP Engineering Reports, II] (London, 1950), p. 26, Table 14. The 'Big Six' were Nuffield, Ford, Austin, Vauxhall (a subsidiary of General Motors), Rootes, and Standard.

[2] George Maxcy and Aubrey Silberston, *The Motor Industry* (London, 1959), pp. 210–11.

[3] Svennilson, *Growth and Stagnation*, p. 151, citing R. Stisser, *Standort and Planung der deutschen Kraft-Fahrzeugindustrie* (Bremen-Horn, 1950). The three largest producers

American standards. Observers after the War were struck by the diversity of types of passenger cars offered in Germany; mass production was 'almost completely lacking', and manufacturers were apparently ready to 'try anything'. The result was good product innovation, but slow diffusion of novelty and a widespread persistence of older manufacturing techniques. Special-purpose equipment seems to have been the exception, and there was insufficient collaboration between parts suppliers and vehicle producers. Best practice, however, as exemplified in the new Volkswagen plant (which had barely begun manufacture before the war), was very good indeed, and the motorcycle industry was particularly progressive in its technology.[1]

By comparison with Britain and Germany, France was not very hospitable to foreign enterprise. But she did not lack for aggressive entrepreneurs, who did the job of concentration just as fast: by 1928 three firms (Renault, Citroën, Peugeot) had 68 per cent of total sales; by 1938 their share had risen to 75 per cent.[2]

The two men most responsible for this development were very different types. First there was Louis Renault (1877–1944), the son of a cloth merchant and button-maker, who showed a gift for tinkering and mechanics at an early age and disappointed his mother by dropping out of the traditional bourgeois educational curriculum, giving up his preparation for the Ecole Centrale to study industrial design at the modestly vocational Ecole Diderot. (Louis's father had died in 1889, already troubled by his son's preference for shop work over studies.) Louis began his working career in the design department of Delaunay-Belleville, at the time a producer of steam boilers, though it was later to go into motor car manufacture. But in 1898 we find him building on his own his first car, a small vehicle of 350 kg. that incorporated, for the first time in France, direct rather than chain drive. He never went back to Delaunay-Belleville. In March of 1899 he and his brothers founded the Société Renault, capital 60,000 francs, and in the next four months turned out 80 cars.

In the following years Louis won fame for himself and sales for his cars by his successful participation in the hazardous, madcap road races

in 1938 were Adam Opel (a subsidiary of General Motors), making 40 per cent of the pleasure cars and 30 per cent of the light commercial vehicles; Ford, making 10 per cent of the cars and 20 per cent of the commercial vehicles; and Auto-Union, 25 per cent of the cars. P.E.P., *Motor Vehicles*, p. 116. The output of the Auto-Union is described for some reason as 25 per cent of home sales.

[1] Maurice Olley, *The Motor Car Industry in Germany during the Period 1939–1945* [British Intelligence Objectives Sub-Committee Overall Report No. 21] (London, 1949).

[2] Svennilson, *Growth and Stagnation*, p. 151, citing R. Hoenicke, *Die amerikanische Automobilindustrie in Europa* (Berlin, 1933); P.E.P., *Motor Vehicles*, p. 120.

that stimulated the rise of the infant motor industry. (His brother Marcel died in the Paris–Madrid race of 1903, which was marked by so many accidents that the French government cut it short.) In 1906 he got his first chance at mass production when the Société des Automobiles de Place ordered 1,500 taxicabs at 3,800 francs ($760) each. By 1914 the 9,600 square metres of 1902 at Billancourt, on the outskirts of Paris, had become 150,000; Renault stood at the head of what was perhaps the best equipped plant in the French auto industry.

This growth continued during the war. Some of the equipment was converted to the manufacture of artillery shells. At the same time Renault developed a light combat tank, far more manoeuvrable than the first British models, which made its debut defending against the Ludendorff push of March 1918; by the end of the war, there were four thousand of these in service.

The coming of peace did not interrupt this expansion. Renault moved into all branches of vehicle and motor manufacture, including aviation and marine engines. But the motor car remained the heart of the enterprise, and the plant at Billancourt became the largest in Europe: 30,000 workers, 15,000 machines. In addition, Renault integrated backwards and forwards, built new plants in the Paris area and the provinces, took a large share in what had been Thyssen's iron works at Hagondange in order to free himself from the yoke of the Comité des Forges, and set up assembly plants in a half-dozen foreign countries, including Britain and Germany.

For all this, the Renault enterprise was not in the forefront of technological progess. Billancourt, like so many successful business enterprises, had grown like Topsy—here a foundry, there a shop, the pieces fitted together as well as improvisation and space would allow. Only the installations on the Isle of Seguin, built around 1931 and linked to Billancourt by a bridge, represented best practice. Besides, Louis Renault had all the strengths and weaknesses of the naturally gifted mechanic. He was capable of brilliant solutions to problems of detail, but was often hostile to the ideas of others; and although he was invariably inspired and stimulated by his visits to the United States, which revealed to him another industrial world, he was not prepared to undertake the massive transformation needed to bring him into this promised land. He made no radical model changes; in the words of his biographer: 'No permanent revolution, as at Citroën [of whom more below], but a slow evolution that tirelessly reconsiders the models of the year before and improves them, rejecting the while any adventures.'[1]

[1] Saint Loup, *Renault de Billancourt* (Paris, 1956), p. 219. The author is a novelist and writes his biography as a kind of fictional reconstruction. He avers, however, that 'each sentence of the book, whose romanticized form should not give rise to illusions,

In so far as Renault did undertake major investments in the inter-war years, he was moved as much by self-esteem—Citroën was right across the river—as by a rational drive to maximize profit. Besides, Louis Renault had an invincible distaste for credit and bankers. Though he had not adopted the social aspirations and educational values of his parents, he had inherited the conservative financial principles of the French bourgeoisie. He paid cash for everything he bought or built and got a 3 per cent discount from his suppliers. As a result, the Société Renault was just about depression-proof.

André Citroën was not a born mechanic. As a car manufacturer, he was never a production man. The son of a diamond merchant who died while André was still a child, André was the very model of a good student, did brilliantly at the Lycée Condorcet, and went on to the Ecole Polytechnique. He began his business career, not as a worker, but as an entrepreneur: he manufactured a system of gears that he discovered on a trip to Poland. The enterprise prospered and provided him with the capital and the confidence to enter and reorganize in 1908 the Société d'Electricité et d'Automobiles Mors, a small, inefficient producer—four cars a day, every one different. Like many firms in those early years of the industry, Mors had come to motor cars by a most indirect route—via artificial flowers, electric bells, railway signalling devices, and light electric equipment. Citroën really knew nothing about motor cars when he took over the direction at Mors, and it is not surprising to find the company still a small producer in 1914. But Citroën had nerve and unlimited ambition; so that when the war came and created an unprecedented demand for ammunition, André offered to make one million shells in a factory that did not yet exist. In spite of considerable scepticism in some quarters, the government took the gamble and gave him the order. With contract in hand, André borrowed from every friend and connection, put in every cent the Citroën family could raise. This was the start of the great plant on the Quai de Javel. By the end of the war, it covered some 37 acres of precious Paris real estate, employed 13,000 workers.

Then came the peace. It is not clear whether Citroën intended from the start to go from artillery shells to motor cars. Some say (the biographies of all tycoons contain a generous mixture of myth and speculation) that he wanted to go into the manufacture of sewing machines. Be that as it may, Javel began to make motor cars, bringing

rests on the testimony of a living person or on a document left behind by someone deceased'. *Ibid.*, back cover. One interesting aspect: the author reverts repeatedly to Citroën and his Jewish origins, which he seems to treat at times as an explanation of entrepreneurial characteristics and performance. In this, however, he may simply be reflecting faithfully the prejudices and reasoning of his subject.

out in the spring of 1919 France's first popular motor car, the A-1, a light vehicle, easy to maintain, cheap to repair, and selling fully equipped at 6,950 francs (about 1,850 prewar gold francs). This system of pricing was in itself a major innovation. French motor producers, aiming at a small, rich market, had always billed their cars as French hotel keepers their rooms: everything but chassis and body was an extra. The profit was in the surprises.[1]

After the A-1 came the Torpedo, type A; then a number of models of a new type, type B, with self-starter, in a wide variety of bodies. And then, in 1922, came the French analogue of the Model T, the 5 CV (the five [fiscal] horsepower), priced at 10,000 francs (approximately 2,750 prewar gold francs).[2]

Citroën's formula was a success from the start. Orders poured in; the shops at Javel multiplied and grew; the cadence increased from 100 vehicles a day in 1919, to 200 in 1924, to more than 400 in 1927. Technologically, Citroën was in the forefront of the industry. He had no head for the details of manufacture; but he had a sense of general principles, and these he took from the most advanced American practice: interchangeable parts, extreme division of labour, moving assembly lines, concentration on long runs of popular models. All of this cost money, and André Citroën was not a man to stint. His munificence is evident in his advertising. In a country that tended to look on publicity as the last refuge of charlatans, he wrote the name of Citroën in the sky and flaunted it on banners towed by aeroplanes above the

[1] This practice was introduced in England in 1912 by Rover and Morris. The Morris Oxford included for a price of £175 all 'accessories' except the tyre for the spare wheel. Dudley Noble and G. M. Junner, *Vital to the Life of the Nation: A Historical Survey of the Progress of Britain's Motor Industry from 1896 to 1946* (London, 1946), p. 38. In this, as in other aspects of automobile technology and marketing, however, America led the way. Ford was selling the Model T both 'equipped' and 'unequipped' in 1909. Equipment included brass windshield, two gas headlights with generator, two oil side lamps, one tail lamp, and horn. Charles E. Sorensen, *My Forty Years with Ford* (New York: Collier paperback, 1962), p. 121.

[2] The price index (wholesale) for home products averaged 362 in the last quarter of 1922. If one uses the index for industrial raw materials, which averaged 411, one arrives at an equivalence of 2,500 gold francs. Even at this price, this was not a car for the masses. In 1922 a carpenter, plumber, or locksmith in the Paris area earned about 3·50–3·60 frs per hour (equals about 8,500 frs for a working year of 300 8-hour days); a specialized worker in the Paris metal trades (perhaps the best-paid industrial workers in France) earned 2·35 frs per hour (equals 5,640 frs per year). In other words, even a well-paid worker would have to work more than a year (fourteen and twenty months respectively for the two cases examined here) to earn the price of a 5 CV. Compare the workers at Ford, who could earn the price of a Model T in less than ten six-day weeks. The French wages are taken from the *Annuaire statistique*, LVII (1946), résumé rétrospectif, pp. 222*–226*. For the building trades, 1922 wages are estimated by interpolating between 1921 and 1924.

cities and resort beaches; in his greatest coup, he leased the Eiffel Tower and inscribed his name in lights on Paris's first monument. (The authorities have since seen to it that such a 'desecration' not be repeated.)

He never stuck at paying the price for what he wanted. He hired the best men at what were for the time princely salaries, took away from Billancourt some of Renault's top technicians. When, in the depths of the depression, Citroën decided to retool, he did what Carnegie had done at Homestead a half-century before: he threw the whole works down and built anew. When he wanted someone else's innovation, he paid for it without haggling. Renault preferred to evade the patent and fight the matter in court if necessary; even if he had no case, he might be able to beat his adversary down to a lower royalty rate. Renault never borrowed; Citroën is pictured by his biographers as fighting, always fighting, to stay afloat in a sea of bonds, notes, and other instruments of indebtedness; he closed each business day by signing paper.

Business is cruel to spenders and dreamers. They may escape the consequences of their mistakes and follies in time of prosperity; but debit and credit have their revenge in depression. When the contraction of the thirties came, Citroën found it harder and harder to walk the tightrope of solvency. Already in the twenties the enterprise had fallen for a time under the control of the Banque Lazard, but Citroën had retrieved it. Now all he needed was a little time to perfect and bring out his new model, the revolutionary *traction-avant*, a front-wheel-drive sedan with floating motor that was a decade or more ahead of its contemporaries. His creditors were insistent. Citroën rushed the first copies of the new car through the line and on to the market. They broke down. He asked for three more months. Only ninety days. His creditors were adamant. And this time there was no second chance.

The firm came into the hands of the Michelin tyre company, a solid, bourgeois enterprise like Renault, swimming in cash and careful to make even its publicity pay for itself. The takeover meant the end of Citroën's insouciant management; the Michelins ran a tight ship. It also meant the end of André Citroën, who died of cancer in July 1935, six months after his firm was declared in liquidation. The Michelins took over with the plant a huge short-term debt that had been converted by consent of the creditors into thirty-year obligations; Michelin had no trouble buying the claims in at a fraction of their nominal value. More important, they also took over the new model that André Citroën had counted on to save the day: the *traction-avant*, now free of the 'bugs' that had plagued the first hasty version. The 'black swallow' was an unbelievable success. French gangsters would use nothing else for their getaways. For over twenty years it ruled the highways, France's fastest, best-performing car in mass production. Only the Model T and Volkswagen can show a similar record of longevity.

★   ★   ★   ★   ★

Having looked at some of the best performers in the interwar array of industries, it is time to turn to the laggards. The most important of these was undoubtedly the textile manufacture, and particularly cotton. The industry that had triggered the first Industrial Revolution was the sick man of the second.

To be sure, cotton was not sick everywhere. In some of the smaller countries—Holland especially, but also Belgium–Luxembourg—output grew substantially in these years. In the Netherlands, for example, it rose to more than triple the prewar level. And in the world as a whole, production of cotton piece goods in 1936–8 was up 30 per cent over the 1910–13 figure. But output was actually falling sharply in the United Kingdom and Germany, the two largest European producers; while France, in third place, barely sustained her prewar performance.

Table 44. *Raw Cotton Consumption in Selected Countries (thousand tons), 1900–50*

	1909/13	1925	1938	Change 1909/13–1938 (%)	1950
U.K.	898·3	738·3	569·0	− 36·7	453·5
Germany	393·5	261·2	232·0	− 41·0	215·3[a]
France	224·0	249·1	249·0	+ 11·2	243·9
Italy	184·9	213·0	152·0	− 17·8	202·9
Belgium–Luxembourg	48·8	60·9	79·0	+ 62·0	86·9
Netherlands	18·2	28·5	56·0	+207·5	60·5
Switzerland	23·8	27·8	28·0	+ 17·7	30·4
Sweden	22·1	18·0	26·4	+ 19·4	28·2

[a] Includes East Germany.

SOURCE: Svennilson, *Growth and Stagnation*, p. 143.

The reasons for this stagnation or decline vary with the country. The hardest hit was Britain, which had always disposed of most of her output abroad, and now found itself driven from these markets by cheaper Japanese or Indian goods, or by protected indigenous manufactures. Everywhere, would-be industrial nations turned first to cotton—following the British pattern and often using British machines. The loss of the Indian market was particularly costly. In 1913 India took over three billion yards of British cotton cloth, which amounted to 43 per cent of total exports in that year and 38 per cent of total output in 1912.[1] By 1924 sales to India had dropped by almost half, to 1,553 million yards, down to 33·5 per cent of exports and 28·5 per cent of output. And that was only the beginning: the depression brought further measures to protect the Indian home market, and by 1938, imports from Britain were less than one tenth of prewar purchases (258 million yards), equal to about 3 per cent of the output of 1912. The disappearance of this one outlet, therefore, blasted one third of the industry.

The same story was repeated on a lesser scale throughout the world. Brazil is a good example: higher duties cut imports of British piece goods from an average of 63·5 million square yards in 1925–7 to less than 3 million in 1932. Even the more advanced industrial nations had recourse to prohibitive tariffs, and British exports to the United States plunged from 163 million square yards in 1924 to 11 million in 1931.[2] As a result, net exports of piece goods fell to 2,100 million square yards in 1935/37 (from over 8,000 million linear yards in 1912); and whereas these represented over five sixths of total output in the earlier period, they constituted slightly more than half at the latter date. A slight gain in domestic sales offered little offset to this catastrophic drop.

The reaction of the industry was to retrench, disinvest, and regroup. There was some effort to modernize equipment in the twenties, but the nature of British cloth output did not seem to lend itself to the best of the new techniques. Thus the automatic loom made little headway, and manufacturers argued that while it might be all right for long runs of standard cheap goods, it was less suited for the high-quality specialties of Britain. By the same token, the mule gave ground only slowly to the ring frame, which worked faster and turned out a tougher, tighter yarn; it was alleged that ring yarn would not do for cloth where 'feel' was important. In any event, the Great Depression put an end to these velleities, and the thirties witnessed a panic of scrapping. Spindlage, which was still slightly higher in 1930 than prewar, fell by one third in the next eight years; and the number of looms, already down about 11 per cent, fell 35 per cent further.

These impersonal numbers conceal, needless to say, a long record of human hardship and tragedy. As the Working Party Report of 1946 put it, in a metaphor typical of our mechanical age: '...throughout all the shocks which have struck the Lancashire industry, the main shock-

---

[1] In 1912 exports accounted for 86 per cent of the total output of cloth. Statistics are from Committee on Industry and Trade, *Survey of Textile Industries*, pp. 51, 54–7. There does not seem to be a figure for total output in 1913.

[2] Great Britain, Board of Trade, *Working Party Reports: Cotton* (London, 1946), p. 5.

absorber has been the great army of operatives' (p. 7). The number of workers who looked to the cotton industry for jobs held up well in the 1920's—572,400 in 1924 and 564,100 in 1930—in the face of heavy and growing unemployment. But the Great Depression broke this resistance. Where there had been 73,000 jobless at the earlier date, the number stood at three times that in 1930, and in the following years a substantial portion of the labour force either left the industry or retired. By 1938 the work force was down to 393,000, a drop of almost a third, and unemployment had been halved to 105,200. The war, which provided an abundance of alternative job opportunites, then completed the process: in 1945, the work force stood at 209,000, slightly over a third of what it had been in the early twenties, and unemployment was negligible. In the course of these changes the average age of those employed had risen considerably, for younger people saw little future in cotton. Supply and demand had balanced, and one of England's richest regions had walked its *via dolorosa* (see Table 45, p. 454).[1]

The cotton industries of the Continent stood up better than Britain's to the vicissitudes and pressures of the interwar period. For one thing, they could and did cut down their imports of cotton fabrics; the British were the heavy losers here. For another, they had always put more of their effort into the less standardized, more differentiated fabrics, and these did not have to meet the competition of the newer, cheaper producers. In this race for cover, the French were especially favoured, for they could build fences not only around themselves but also around their empire; and they did not have to fear the competition of growing colonial manufactures as the British that of India. As a result, export of cottons to the so-called *pays d'outremer* rose from 28,000 tons in 1913 to 41,000 in 1929; then, after a dip in the early and mid-thirties, to

---

[1] Even this was not an equilibrium position. There was some increase in output immediately after the war to meet the demand of a market long starved for consumers' goods. But then the contraction resumed:

Data on the British Cotton Spinning, Doubling, and Weaving Industries

	No. of firms	Mule spindles (millions)	Ring spindles (millions)	Looms ('000)	Labour ('000)
1948	—	19	—	—	—
1951	—	—	—	380	—
1954	—	—	11	—	300
1961[a]	469	—	—	167	—
1962	—	—	—	—	160
1963[b]	—	1·1	5·3	129	—

[a] March 1961.　　[b] End of 1963.

SOURCE: W. T. Cowling, 'The History of Textiles', *The Journal of Industrial Archaeology*, 1 (1964), 137.

Table 45. *Changes in the British Cotton Industry, 1912–38*[2]

Year	Output Yarn (million lb.)	Cloth (million sq. yd.)	Exports piece goods (million sq. yd.)	Machinery Spindles (millions)	Looms ('000)	Labour ('000)
1912	1,963	8,050[b]	6,913[b]	61·4	786	621·5[c]
1924	1,395	6,046	4,444	63·3	792	572·4[d]
1930	1,048	3,500	2,472	63·2	700	564·1[e]
1938	1,070	3,126	1,449	42·1	495	393·0[e]

[a] The table tends to understate the decline of the traditional cotton industry by including such processing of artificial fibres as was done by the old trade. Thus yarn output includes cotton waste and spun rayon yarns; while both cloth output and exports comprise rayon piece goods and mixtures woven by the trade. The spindlage figures are also adjusted upwards to take account of the increasing use of ring spindles, each of which is reckoned as equivalent to 1–1½ mule spindles. The Report warns that spindlage data for 1912–30 are only approximate and are not strictly comparable with the 1938 figure.

[b] Linear yards.

[c] Number actually employed.

[d] Number of insured workers, age 16 and over.

[e] Number of insured workers, ages 16–64.

SOURCE: Gt Britain, Board of Trade, *Working Party Reports: Cotton*, p. 6.

44,000 in 1938.[1] By contrast, exports to foreign countries fell from 26,000 tons in 1929 to 3,200 in 1935, with a slight recovery in the years following, to 4,100 tons in 1938.

Exports were an important element in the health of the French cotton industry, accounting for a third of output in 1929. They were far less significant in Germany, where exports of yarn had been negligible before the war and sales of piece goods abroad, averaging 40,000 tons in 1910–13, constituted about a tenth of total output.[2] In Germany, the threat to the cotton manufacture came from another direction: the output of man-made fibres.

We have already had occasion to note the beginning of the manufacture of cellulose fibre and rayon fabrics in the years before the First World War. At that time, world production of artificial silk (as it was called originally) amounted to about 20 million pounds a year and was increasing rapidly; output of rayon and mixed cloth averaged (1910–13) perhaps 50 million square yards. The numbers seem big, but they were tiny compared to the huge outpouring of cotton yarn and cloth in the

[1] Francois Capronnier, *La crise de l'industrie cotonnière française* (Paris, [1959]), p. 263. For a discussion of protectionist policies in the colonies, see pp. 53 f.

[2] Imports of yarn had averaged 28,000 tons in 1910/13, 80 per cent of which came from the U.K. Gt Britain, Committee on Industry and Trade, *Survey of Textile Industries* [being part III of a Survey of Industries] (London, 1928), p. 87.

same period: thus the United Kingdom alone consumed over 1,600 million pounds of cotton yarn per year from 1909 to 1913. Here, as in radio, prewar growth was an exercise, a technological and commercial preparation for maturity.

The industry went back, as we have seen, to Hilaire de Chardonnet's nitro-cellulose process (patent 1884; commercial production 1890). This was followed by the viscose process of C. F. Cross and E. J. Bevan (patent 1892; commercial exploitation 1901 in France, 1905 in the U.K.); the cuprammonium technique (patent 1890; commercial production 1898); and Napper's zinc-in-spinning-bath technique (1912), to maintain the plasticity of the filaments in the coagulating bath of the viscose process. And to these should be added a multitude of mechanical as well as lesser chemical advances—to effect the extrusion of uniform fibres, to increase the rate of extrusion, to stretch the filaments without excessive loss of strength, to collect and store them during a long succession of chemical treatments, and to twist and spin them into yarn of pleasing feel and appearance that would maintain its tenacity wet as well as dry. All the major industrial nations contributed to these advances, though as we shall see, the output of the industry was by no means so evenly distributed as the technological inputs. As always, small anonymous improvements accounted for much of the gain between laboratory invention and commercial realization. One aspect of the whole process was relatively new, however, though it was foreshadowed in the development of such complex equipment as the steam turbine and the motor car: we are obviously entering here upon a technology whose scientific and intellectual requirements lie well outside the realm of on-the-job empiricism—not only in its chemical aspects but in its mechanical ones as well.

Before the War (1909), roughly half the rayon output was being made by the Chardonnet nitrate process and a third by the cuprammonium technique, with viscose accounting for the rest. But the last was clearly the cheapest (the usual raw material was wood or cotton pulp), and the proportions began to shift markedly even before the War. By 1924, the nitrate and cuprammonium processes accounted for only 8 and 1 per cent of total output respectively.

Technological advance continued during and after the War and undoubtedly goes far to explain the sustention for a period of decades of spectacular exponential rates of growth. Yet the most rapid increase occurred in the period 1920-5—about 45 per cent per annum—when improvements took the form of perfecting the existing technology. The key impetus at this point was demand, much stimulated by changes in price on the one hand, in fashion on the other. Thus whereas the cost of silk ranged from about $9·50 to $6·50 per pound in these years, that of viscose rayon fell steadily from almost $5 to about $2. At the same time, women had now given up for the first time in history the full-length skirt, and the leg—and hence the stocking that encased it—became a focus of interest and concern. Already by 1913, 40 per cent of rayon output in the United Kingdom went to hosiery; and the figure was even higher in the United States—50 per cent in 1913, 70 per cent in 1915.

To this demand was added that for knitted underwear. The early success of rayon in knitwear was no accident. The yarn was not strong enough in these early years for weaving and could be used only in combination with other fibres. Not until 1924 was the technique of sizing improved to the point where a satisfactory warp yarn could be produced; compare the analogous difficulties of the early cotton industry. The task was aggravated by the consumer demand for ever finer, softer yarn: in 1919 there were 12 to 14 filaments in a standard 15-denier yarn; by 1931 there were 40, and by 1939, 150 to 225; as a result, it was possible to use ever-lower deniers without sacrificing strength.

The great innovations of the interwar years were:

(1) The staple technique, which instead of extruding filament yarn directly, produced an intermediary 'tow' (a large bundle of filaments), which could then be cut and 'crimped' for spinning into yarn of the thickness desired. As a result, one could make do with viscose of lesser quality; control requirements were lower; and spinning and stretching machines could be simplified. (There is perhaps a technological analogy here with the contribution of the blast furnace to iron manufacture.) Staple, indeed, opened to cellulosic fibres an entirely new market. It was cheaper than filament in the heavy counts and indeed could compete in price with cotton; as a result, it found quick adoption in coarser or mixed fabrics. On the eve of the Second World War, staple already accounted for about 40 per cent of world output of cellulosic filament; by the early 1950's, the share had risen to 57 per cent. Staple proved particularly popular in Germany, Italy, and Japan—economies aiming at self-sufficiency, hence seeking *Ersatz* for natural fibres that had to be imported. As a result these countries raised their share of world rayon production from 10 per cent in 1929 to 60 per cent in 1939; by that date, their share of staple output was 80 per cent.

(2) The acetate process, which made possible a substantial reduction in the cost of the finer yarns. The technique was invented by Cross and Bevan before the War, but was not adapted to the manufacture of textile fibres until the early twenties. By 1930 it accounted for 7 per cent of world rayon output; by 1939, 17 per cent. At that point its share began to level off, presumably because of increased competition in the finer deniers from synthetic fibres.

The first of these synthetics to achieve commercial success, and still the most important, was nylon. But although Du Pont was making it in a pilot plant in 1938, nylon is in fact a post-World War II product. More than rayon, which is not so strong as cotton, nylon benefited from wartime demand: it has high tensile strength and was used extensively in the manufacture of parachutes, cord, and other military equipment—to the point where it was almost unavailable for civilian use. In the meantime its reputation as a superior fibre for thin, 'gossamer' fabrics was nourished by its prewar performance. The United States knew during these years a black market in nylon stockings, a black market that American expeditionary forces took with them wherever they went. When peace came, consumers everywhere were awaiting their chance to buy nylons, which thus enjoyed a pent-up demand almost without comparison. Years of deprivation had even given rise to myths about the indestructibility of nylon stockings that were bound to be disappointed; to the point where Du Pont had to soothe outraged women who insisted that nylon stockings were deliberately being made weaker, to shorten their life and increase sales. Protestations that prewar nylons had been coarser and that the new stockings were shorter-lived because made of finer-denier yarn fell on deaf ears; women remained convinced that they were the victims of a new kind of planned obsolescence. But none of this really mattered. Nylon stockings, sturdy or not, were thinner and more flattering than silk or rayon, and that was all that counted. After all, if sturdiness was the goal, there was always cotton to go back to. No one went back.

Within the general framework of spectacular expansion—world output of rayon yarn shot from 12,000 tons in 1913 to 536,000 in 1937, while the make of staple fibre (*fibranne*) ran the same course in a decade, from 3,000 tons in 1929 to 490,000 in 1939—growth varied considerably from one European nation to another.[1] The major determinant of this variation would seem to have been commercial policy. Germany and Italy, as we have seen, arming for war and striving for self-sufficiency, took eagerly to a technology that freed them from the need to import raw material from overseas and pay for it with scarce foreign exchange. By contrast, Britain and France left the new industry to make its own way; and although it did well, it was not able, as in the Fascist countries, to displace a substantial fraction of the pre-existent cotton manufacture while generating a net increase in the demand for cheap textiles. Thus the British home market for domestic cotton fabrics fell some 26 per cent in the interwar years, from 393,300 tons to 289,500; and this loss of over 100,000 tons was not balanced by an increase of

[1] OEEC, *Basic Statistics of Industrial Production, 1913–1952* (Paris, n.d.), pp. 72–3.

some 75,000 tons in the production of man-made fibres. In France, home consumption of French-made cotton fabrics actually rose slightly in these years, so that the growth of the artificial silk industry (a modest 29–30,000 tons) was all gain. In Germany, however, output of rayon and staple yarn leaped from almost nothing to over 270,000 tons, far outbalancing a drop of 134,000 tons in consumption of domestic cotton cloth; while in Italy, the 45,000 tons lost on cotton were only a third of the 140,000 tons added to the make of rayon.[1]

As the above analysis makes clear, any discussion of the growth or decline of an industry is dependent on the labels employed. Viewed by itself, the cotton industry of these years was sickly and technologically stagnant. Thanks to artificial fibres, however, the textile manufacture as a whole was changing and growing rapidly. The need to compete with a cheap material like cotton—as against the more costly early rival, silk —created a strong pressure for technological improvement; while the economics of large-scale manufacture, which allowed a few progressive firms to dominate the industry, not only enabled them to hold prices down but impelled them to do so, for profits in excess of the 'normal' rate immediately attracted competitors into the trade and encouraged expansion by smaller producers.

The economic stimuli to rapid technological change have been the more effective because of the close tie between science and technique in the creation and manufacture of synthetics. There is a heady freedom about explorations in this field: the searcher is not constrained by the characteristics of raw material won from nature; rather, he makes his own stuff, and in the long run his possibilities are limitless. The result is a boundless faith in ever-retreating horizons, a faith that communicates itself from the laboratory to the plant, the business office, and the boardroom. It is no accident that Professor D. C. Hague, writing of the man-made fibres trade in Britain, should refer to the 'missionary spirit' of the industry. As an economist, he introduces the notion apologetically: 'It may seem somewhat fanciful to give such prominence to what is after all a purely psychological factor'; but he sticks to his guns: 'that prominence is fully deserved.'[2]

★   ★   ★   ★   ★

[1] Cotton consumption from Svennilson, *Growth and Stagnation*, p. 143, Table 37; output of artificial yarns from OEEC, *Basic Statistics...1913–1952*, pp. 72–3. It would be desirable for purposes of comparison to have statistics on the prewar output of rayon fabrics. But these do not seem to be available.

[2] D. C. Hague, 'The Man-Made Fibres Industry', in D. L. Burn, ed., *The Structure of British Industry: A Symposium* [The National Institute of Economic and Social Research, 'Economic and Social Studies', vol. xv] (2 vols.; Cambridge, 1958), II, 289.

The traditional textile industry thus presents an almost unrelievedly dark picture during the interwar years—unless one takes into consideration the spectacular progress of substitute fibres. By comparison, the poor performance of the iron and steel industry in this same period is in no way compensated by the admittedly rapid rise of competitive materials—aluminium and reinforced or pre-stressed concrete. These innovations had a great future; but in 1939 it was still almost all future, and the output of aluminium was being measured in thousands of tons, instead of millions for iron and steel. To be sure, nowhere did the ferrous metals industry contract like the British cotton manufacture; indeed in most European countries output rose over our period (see Table 46). But the rise was slow and uneven and profits small or nonexistent; and no industry offers a better example of the vicious circle of inadequate growth and technological torpor.

Table 46. *Output of Crude Steel in Western Europe, 1913–39*
(millions of tons)

	1913	1929	1939
United Kingdom	7·8	9·8	13·4
Germany[a]	14·3	18·4	22·5
France[b]	7·0	9·7	7·9[c]
Belgium–Luxembourg	3·9	6·8	4·9
Total of four largest European producers	33·0	44·7	48·7

[a] 1937 boundaries, including the Saar.
[b] 1919 boundaries, including Lorraine.
[c] Corrected to conform to the official figure.

SOURCE: OEEC, *Basis Statistics of Industrial Production 1913–52*, p. 47.

The most striking aspect of this deceleration is its abruptness. The contrast with the prewar vigour of the industry is brutal. Cotton shows nothing like this: it was already in trouble by the end of the nineteenth century, and Lancashire in particular was hard pressed to meet the competition of new, non-European centres of production. But iron and steel had boomed—outside of Britain, to be sure—right up to the eve of the war. From 1880/82 to 1911/13, the make of pig of the four leading European producers (Germany, U.K., France, Belgium–Luxembourg) rose on the average by 3 per cent a year; that of steel, by 7·5 per cent. If one excludes Britain from this calculation, the growth rates were even more impressive: 10 per cent per year for German steel; and 8·75 per cent for France and 9·5 per cent for Belgium–Luxembourg once the newly discovered Briey minette ores became available around 1895. Indeed, one of the difficulties of the postwar industry was the persistence of expectations inherited from a more prosperous era.

The prewar expansion had been the result of an unusually favourable conjuncture. In the first place, the demand for ferrous metal grew with industrialization: iron and then steel ships replaced wooden vessels; Europe was still building fifty thousand miles of new railroad track in the 1880's and then was relayed by Russia and continents overseas;[1] the steam engine first came into its own in the follower countries in the third quarter of the century, and even in the earlier industrializers, the volume of power plant added in the second half of the century far exceeded that installed in the first half. Secondly, the steel branch benefited specially from the changing pattern of demand: whereas in the 1860's output of wrought iron far exceeded that of steel, the positions were reversed by 1880, and by 1913 the old staple accounted for less than 10 per cent of European output; in the 1870's and 1880's, all of Europe's railroad track was converted from wrought iron to steel. Both these factors depended in part on a third—the technological creativity of the industry, as expressed in the Bessemer converter, the Siemens–Martin open hearth, the Thomas–Gilchrist process, the electric furnace. Nothing like it had been seen since the eighteenth-century cluster of coke smelting, Cort's puddling-rolling combination, and the steam-powered blast. As a result, iron and steel was the only one of the branches that had made the Industrial Revolution to have a second youth. Finally, the response of output to demand was greatly facilitated by the opening of important sources of raw materials: the *minette* of German Lorraine, the ores of northern Sweden, and then the deeper beds around Briey—this last to the consternation of those German engineers who thought they had taken all the iron in north-eastern France when they drew the new boundaries of 1871. This factor, too, was not entirely autonomous, for the use of these ores in steelmaking was possible, as we have seen, only after the invention of the Thomas–Gilchrist basic process.

All of these stimulants lost their force in the interwar period. The substitution of steel for wrought iron had been accomplished, and demand was now primarily a function of the cyclical conjuncture, in particular of investment in plant and equipment. (So close is this dependence of steel on investment that Svennilson uses long-term changes in domestic steel consumption 'as a general indicator of the corresponding trends in the volume of investment' [p. 209].)[2] But this, as we

---

[1] New railway mileage in the world amounted to 239,189 km. in the first decade of this century—just about as many as in the peak decade of the eighties (244,856 km.). Wl. Woytinsky, *Die Welt in Zahlen* (7 vols.; Berlin, 1927), v, 29.

[2] For our purposes, of course, such an indicator of investment would be tautological. We need a direct measure rather than a surrogate. The difficulty is that most purportedly direct measures are built up by the aggregation of sales of producers' goods and include steel consumption.

have seen, was far less robust in the interwar years than in the prewar decade. For Britain, the ratio of net capital formation to net national product fell from 13·0 per cent in the years 1905/14 (it had been 10 per cent or higher from the 1860's on) to 5·5 per cent in the twenties and 2·6 per cent in the thirties; and Britain, remember, had an unusually rapid recovery from the depression of 1929.[1] For Germany, the figures are not complete; but we have an estimate of 10 per cent in 1928, at the top of the postwar boom, as against 15·9 per cent in the period 1901–13. Then the depression brought new investment almost to a standstill (0·8 per cent in 1929–33), and even the rearmament programme of the Third Reich could not lift the ratio to the prewar level (11·2 per cent in 1934–8).[2]

As a result, the amount of steel consumed by each of the major west-European producers was at best slightly higher in this period than before the war:

Table 47. *Apparent Annual Consumption of Steel in Western Europe (millions of tons)*

	U.K.	Germany[a]	France	Belgium–Luxembourg	All four countries
1913	6·3	11·9	4·8	1·1	24·1
1922–9	6·5	11·3	5·7	1·4	24·9
1930–8	8·3	11·8	5·5	1·1	26·7

[a] For 1913, Luxembourg is included with Germany.

SOURCE: Svennilson, *Growth and Stagnation*, p. 310. Consumption in 1913 has been corrected to correspond to interwar boundaries. (This can be done easily enough for production; but how this was done for consumption is not clear.)

This levelling off, after decades of euphoric expansion, was the more painful in that the major producers expanded capacity considerably during the war and in the years immediately following. The French, for example, who saw their most important metallurgical centres occupied within weeks of the start of hostilities, invested heavily in replacement plant behind the lines. Thus they built twelve blast furnaces, with an aggregate capacity of some 600,000 tons a year—slightly larger, therefore, than the average prewar unit, which made about 40,000 tons in 1913. Smelting, however, is very closely bound by the nature of the

[1] Simon Kuznets, 'Quantitative Aspects of the Economic Growth of Nations: VI. Long-Term Trends in Capital Formation Proportions', *Economic Development and Cultural Change*, IX, no. 4, part 2 (July 1961), p. 58. The effect of this drop in investment on the demand for steel was mitigated in the twenties by the rising share of machinery and equipment in such capital formation as occurred: 55·9 per cent in 1921–9, as against 39·2 per cent in 1905–14. But in the thirties, this was down again to 38·2 per cent. *Ibid.*, p. 63.

[2] *Ibid.*, pp. 64–65.

technology to the site of raw materials; so that the French properly made their big wartime effort in steelmaking. New open-hearth capacity alone was half again as large as the total steel output of Lorraine in 1920—1,560,000 as against 1,120,000 tons; and the margin is even greater if one adds new Bessemer converters totalling about a quarter of a million tons.[1] Then came victory, and the French acquired the iron and steel plants of reannexed Lorraine—some of the biggest and most modern installations in Germany. Victory in turn was followed by reconstruction: the French government furnished funds to those enterprises whose plants had been damaged or destroyed during the fighting, to enable them to rebuild bigger and better than before. As a result of these changes, the capacity of the industry in 1927 was about twice what it had been in 1914.[2]

The iron and steel industry that was probably hardest hit by the War was Belgium's. It was almost wiped out: at the armistice pig iron capacity had fallen to 6·3 per cent of prewar. For the ironmasters, this holocaust was a blessing in disguise. As in France, they received reparations and loans to build anew, and these, combined with the boom profits of the first postwar years and an inflation that eroded much of their debt, gave them a modern plant on extremely favourable conditions. Output of pig passed the 1913 mark by 1924, and the subsequent years saw a continued modernization of blast furnace plant, which was probably the most advanced in western Europe.[3] If one may assume that output in 1913 ran about 100 per cent of capacity, then capacity was up about 50 per cent above the prewar level by 1927.[4]

In the meantime, Germany, which had lost by the Treaty of Versailles some 43·5 per cent of her pig iron output and 38·3 per cent of her steel (see Table 48), and whose own treatment of France in 1870 had given her some experience of the rewards and penalties of industrial plunder, was determined not to allow herself to sink to the rank of a second-class power. The government therefore compensated the enterprises of the transferred territories and stipulated that the funds be employed for the improvement of existing, or the creation of new,

[1] J. W. Schwenker, *Die Absatzfrage der eisenschaffenden Industrie Frankreichs in der Nachkriegszeit* (n.p., 1934), p. 8.

[2] Great Britain, Committee on Industry and Trade, *Survey of Metal Industries* [being part IV of a Survey of Industries] (London, 1928), p. 95. Svennilson, *Growth and Stagnation*, p. 125, gives a gain of 23 per cent for pig iron, 42 per cent for steel over 1913 output. But his figures for prewar production are adjusted upward to include output of the area acquired at the peace.

[3] C. Reuss, Koutny, and Tychon, *Le progrès économique en sidérurgie*, pp. 95–6. Average output of German furnaces matched that of the Belgian only in 1936. British and French producers lagged behind.

[4] Great Britain, Committee on Industry and Trade, *Survey of Metal Industries*, p. 98.

facilities. This investment in new plant was the easier because nowhere in western Europe was money depreciating so fast and the burden of debt so light; and even after 1923, one could always borrow from the United States. By 1927, iron capacity was up to 90 per cent of that of the prewar area (less Luxembourg); the figure for steel was 97 per cent.[1]

Table 48. *Germany: Output of Iron and Steel in 1913 (thousand tons)*

	Pig iron	Steel
Germany (postwar frontiers)	10,904	12,182
Upper Silesia[a]	625	1,050
Lorraine	3,864	2,286
Saar[b]	1,371	2,080
Luxembourg[c]	2,548	1,336
Total	19,312	17,598

[a] Partitioned by the League of Nations in 1922.
[b] Placed under international administration for a period of fifteen years.
[c] Then part of the German Zollverein.

SOURCE: Frederic Benham, *The Iron and Steel Industry of Germany, France, Belgium, Luxembourg, and the Saar* (London, 1934), p. 18.

In Britain, the circumstances were different, but the effect was the same: already during the war the swollen demand for iron and steel in all forms had called forth a certain amount of new plant (some of it paid for by the government) and encouraged plans for further expansion. This momentum carried into the postwar period, the more so as the pent-up civilian and foreign demand, combined with all manner of market dislocations, gave rise to temporary scarcities and drove prices sharply upward. Some of the work undertaken in this period was suspended in 1921 and 1922, when bottlenecks eased and prices fell; but this was only a pause, and investment resumed in 1926 and 1927, when conditions once again seemed favourable. By the latter date, British capacity was half again as large as in 1913—a gain that corresponded more or less to that of the European steel industry as a whole.

As a consequence, the European iron and steel industry operated throughout the interwar period—even in the most prosperous years—at a level well below capacity. Much of the unemployed capacity was obsolescent and should normally have been purged by competition. But imperfections in the market, both on the side of producers, who joined in cartels to avoid price competition, and on that of buyers, who irrationally clung to old channels of supply and disregarded the potential savings of alternative sources, kept these marginally efficient units

[1] Again the assumption is that output in 1913 was substantially equal to capacity. *Ibid.*, p. 89.

working. What we may call mummification was particularly marked in Britain, where the obsolescent enterprises were long nourished by financial resources accumulated in more prosperous years; meanwhile those enterprises that might have effected a salutary concentration and rationalization were handicapped by the difficulty of raising fresh capital for an industry whose profits were depressed by the very disease that new investment might have cured.

Financial conditions on the Continent were more favourable to a reorganization of the industry. In France and Belgium, not only were government funds available for reconstruction and expansion, but the sharp decline in the value of the franc made borrowing so profitable that even those entrepreneurs imbued with the traditional abhorrence of credit learned to sacrifice commercial morality to pecuniary advantage. In Germany, the runaway inflation of 1923 had similar consequences, leading directly to the creation in 1926 of the Vereinigte Stahlwerke, which put together the debris of four of the largest producers in the Ruhr to make the largest iron and steel concern in Europe. Its size, both absolute and relative, may be judged by the following comparison with the biggest producer in the world, United States Steel, in that year:

Table 49. *A Comparison of the Outputs of United States Steel and the Vereinigte Stahlwerke in 1926*

| | United States Steel | | Vereinigte Stahlwerke | |
	Output (million tons)	Share of national output (per cent)	Output (million tons)	Share of national output (per cent)
Coal	27	4·5	30	20·6[a]
Pig iron	13	31·9	4·8	50·0
Steel	17	34·6	5·0	40·7

SOURCE: *Die Wirtschaftskurve*, IV (1926), 448, cited in Brady, *The Rationalization Movement in German Industry*, p. 109, n. 10.

The Vereinigte Stahlwerke was far ahead of any other iron and steel enterprise in Germany; but it was followed at a distance by four giants, any one of which was bigger than the biggest in Britain. Together these five accounted for 73 per cent of the German make of pig iron in 1929, 67 per cent of the output of crude steel.[1]

It is less easy to follow and measure the process of concentration in

[1] These figures differ somewhat from those of Brady, *Rationalization Movement*, p. 108. They are based on the output data given *ibid.*, n. 9, and the statistics of national output in OEEC, *Basic Statistics of Industrial Production*, pp. 46–7. See also Benham, *Iron and Steel Industry*, p. 25, for data on the concentration of capacity, as against output.

Belgium–Luxembourg and France, in part because complex financial arrangements mask the pattern of ownership. The general trend, however is clear. In Belgium, there was a wave of amalgamation from 1927 on: merger of Angleur et Charbonnages Belges with Athus–Grivegnée to make Angleur–Athus (1927); absorption of the Usines de Châtelineau by Sambre-et-Moselle (1927); of Alliance–Monceau by Ougrée–Marihaye (1931); of the Charbonnage des Liégeois by Cockerill (1930). On France, Frederic Benham, writing in 1934, speaks of 'numerous amalgamations and poolings of financial claims or interests'. But then he goes on to say: 'There is so much "interpenetration" between the leading groups through "participations", exchanges of shares, companies owned jointly by several groups, and so on, that it is impossible to state briefly the real distribution of ownership.'[1] This complex interweaving of interests continues to characterize the French industry to this day.

In all these countries amalgamation was accompanied by an increase in the scale of production and a substantial rationalization of the technological process. Thus the Vereinigte Stahlwerke systematically closed down its less efficient plants, reducing by 1934 the number of its iron and steel works from 145 to 66, its blast furnace systems from 23 to 9, its rolling mills from 17 to 10. Rail production, once undertaken in nine different plants, was concentrated in one; output of semis (bars, billets, slabs, and the like), in two or three. Every effort was made to make the most of locational advantages and minimize the disadvantages inherited with certain plants acquired in the original merger. Thus the manufacture of heavy crude products was confined to those works situated on the Rhine or other navigable waterways; whereas the plants in the interior specialized in highly fabricated commodities. As a result, the company was able to achieve major gains in labour productivity: in smelting, daily output per worker rose from 1·17 to 1·60 tons from September 1925 to August 1926; in steelmaking, the corresponding figures were 1·25 and 1·77 tons.[2]

In all of this, the Vereinigte Stahlwerke was the bellwether for the industry as a whole: the average weekly make of a German blast furnace rose from 1,127 tons in 1913, to 1,655 tons in 1924, to 2,567 tons in 1929—a gain of 128 per cent. Average converter capacity rose from 20–25 tons before the war to about 40 tons; and output per converter from 87,700 tons a year to 108,700. The comparable figures for open hearths were 16,900 and 22,900 tons.[3]

Larger equipment was in itself conducive to fuel economy; but this

[1] *Ibid.*, p. 34.
[2] Gt Britain, Committee on Industry and Trade, *Survey of Metal Industries*, p. 92.
[3] Benham, *Iron and Steel*, p. 23; Brady, *Rationalization Movement*, pp. 114, 116.

was further promoted by a systematic pursuit of what came to be known as the science of *Wärmewirtschaft*. To this end, the iron and steel industry established in 1919 a *Wärmestelle*. This was not so much a research bureau as a centre for the exchange of information and the dissemination of propaganda. The result was a rapid diffusion of best practice. This in turn advanced rapidly thanks to the vertical integration of the leading iron and steel firms, which made it possible to effect and cumulate savings of energy at each stage of the production process: by standardizing, cleaning, and concentrating the raw materials before introducing them into the furnace; by moving the pig iron directly to the converters or open hearths (no more cooling, soaking, and reheating); by allowing the crude steel to harden only enough to permit reheating to a uniform temperature before insertion in the rolling mill. According to Brady, the German steel industry achieved a reduction in fuel consumed per ton of product from 15 million BTU in 1900 to about 6 millions in 1930—a saving of some 14·4 million tons of coke in the latter year. For the postwar period, the British *Survey of Metal Industries* cites a claim of a reduction of about 15 per cent in fuel consumption in 'the heavy branches of the industry' from 1919 to 1927. By comparison with the Brady figure, this would indicate a distinct slowing of gains in this area; but this is precisely the kind of asymptotic performance one would expect of an industry that had been in the technological vanguard for half a century.[1]

It may not always be easy to trace the combinations and affiliations of the French iron and steel industry and hence to calculate the degree of financial concentration, but the trend to increasing scale of production is quite clear. Burn offers data on this point, with comparable figures for Britain (see Table 50). The contrast is instructive.

For Belgium–Luxembourg we have similar figures on the scale of smelting (see Table 51).

As in Germany, the increase in scale that marked the decade of the twenties made possible and promoted gains in efficiency. The newer, larger iron- and steelmaking units were in a better position, for example, to make the most of by-product gas to drive their own machines and even to sell their surplus to outsiders either directly or in the form of electricity. The gains here, when they did come, were rapid: in 1928 French iron and steel works sold 250 million kilowatt-hours of current; two years later, they sold more than three times as much. Still, the data would seem to indicate that many of these mergers were motivated more by financial considerations and potential administrative economies

[1] Brady, *Rationalization Movement*, p. 111, citing Hans J. Schneider, *Der Wiederaufbau der Grosseisenindustrie an Rhein und Ruhr* (Berlin, 1930), p. 67; Gt Britain, Committee on Industry and Trade, *Survey of Metal Industries*, p. 92.

Table 50. *The Scale of Steelmaking Plants in France and Britain ('ooo tons of ingots)*

	France		Britain	
Plants producing	1913[a]	1929	1900	1929
Over 600	3	3	—	—
500–600	—	2	—	—
400–500	—	6	—	3
300–400	6	2	—	2
250–300	1	5	2	3
200–250	1	—	2	5
150–200	2	—	5	14
100–150	2	2	8	15
50–100	—	—	22	9
Under 50	—	—	21	5

[a] Postwar boundaries. The three prewar giants, plus others of the larger units, were all in German Lorraine.

SOURCE: D. L. Burn, *The Economic History of Steelmaking*, p. 433. The French figures for 1913 cover almost 75 per cent of output; those for 1929, 80 per cent. The British figures for 1900 include all makers of steel ingots for rolling; those for 1929 omit the highly specialized Sheffield firms. According to Burn, figures for 1913 would come much closer to those of 1929 than to those of 1900.

Table 51. *Iron Smelting: Scale of Production in Belgium and Luxembourg ('ooo tons)*

	Belgium		Luxembourg
	Per blast furnace[a]	Per plant	Per furnace[b]
1920	42·9	79·7	53
1929	71·0	252·6	82
1930	71·6	210·3	87
1939	76·5	235·3	83[c]

[a] The interwar peak was 86,900 tons per furnace in 1934.
[b] The interwar peak was 103,000 tons in 1937.
[c] 1938.

SOURCE: C. Reuss, Koutny and Tychon, *Le progrès économique en sidérurgie*, pp. 386, 426.

than by technological opportunity. Thus the productivity gains of Belgian industry in these years came before the wave of amalgamations, as Table 51 makes clear.

Up to now we have said very little about Britain, not because the British iron industry did not move in the direction of increased scale and improved techniques, but because its performance in these regards was distinctly inferior to that of its Continental competitors and calls

Table 52. *Belgium: Productivity in Iron and Steel 1913–39*
(in tons per man per year)

	Smelting	Crude and Semi-finished steel
1913	470	—
1920	258	—
1921	244	—
1922	360	205
1923	435	237
1924	534	274
1925	429	150
1926	547	311
1927	525	336
1928	543	334
1929	525	329
1930	471	291
1931	562	359
1932	568	418
1933	622	424
1934	716	477
1935	756	463
1936	757	415
1937	754	404
1938	520	258
1939	592	354

SOURCE: Reuss, Koutney, and Tychon, *Le progrès économique*, pp. 386, 370–1, 391. Productivity in steelmaking has been obtained by dividing output of crude and semi-finished steel by the number employed in that branch of the industry.

for detailed consideration. This inferiority of the British industry—and no other word will do—was not entirely a new phenomenon. As we have had occasion to discuss, the British iron- and steelmakers began to fall behind their German rivals in the last decades of the nineteenth century; and by 1914 the gap had widened to the point of national embarrassment and danger. What was new about the interwar period is that Britain now fell behind her lesser rivals, even France, a pillar of metallurgical conservatism in the nineteenth century.

She fell behind in organization. Her iron and steel industry, like those of the Continent, had been moving toward concentration of ownership and management even before 1914, and the bottlenecks of the war years had encouraged the more aggressive enterprises to buy up the plant of unco-operative suppliers or of competitors slower to meet the irregular surges of wartime demand. It was a series of *ad hoc* amalgamations of this kind that led to the establishment of the United Steel Companies Ltd in March of 1918. Yet the trend toward consolidation was slower than on the Continent: a calculation based on the Stock

Exchange Year Book for 1927 shows twelve of the largest combines with 47 per cent of the smelting and 60 per cent of the steelmaking capacity—a far cry from the German or French proportions. What is more, British entrepreneurs were slow to use mergers as a means of purging the industry of inefficient units. Sometimes, as in the United Steel combine, they permitted the pre-existing companies to continue as autonomous units (the 'Companies' in the title was not a coincidence) with their own legal identities. The result, at least at first, seems to have been a complication rather than a simplification of the structure of the industry. The Committee on Industry and Trade noted circumspectly in 1928 that 'it had been suggested' that amalgamation had given rise to an excessive number of executive posts, which is just what one would expect to happen when various companies join without giving up their separate managements; but this, the Committee noted, was disputed. One thing was clear: many of these mergers had been financed by new stocks or bonds that may not have been excessive at time of issue, but were to prove a heavy burden subsequently when competition became keener and prices fell. So that when the Committee looked at the merger movement, they did so, not with the optimism and confidence of their German counterparts, but with considerable reserve: 'The effect of the formation of these large concerns upon the competitive efficiency of the industry cannot yet be judged...Much depends upon the efficiency of management.'[1]

What is more, for reasons that are not entirely clear, the best British plants were unable or unwilling to use their superior efficiency to force their weaker rivals from the field. Much of this reflected imperfections in the market on the side of both buyer and seller: an excessive differentiation of finished products, the preference of buyers for customary sources of supply, sporadically effective price agreements among producers. But the last are really an expression of noncompetitiveness; they do not explain it. The reluctance of steelmakers to push their rivals hard was, as always, composed of rational and nonrational elements: anxiety lest price competition bring on costly reprisals; economy of effort; a fear of the financial implications of vigorous competition (expansion costs money and may entail borrowing or dilution of capital); an avoidance of ungentlemanly behaviour.

The question inevitably arises why, in the absence of a protective tariff, more efficient foreign producers did not force a purge of domestic industry. United Kingdom imports of iron and steel did in fact increase sharply in the twenties, from an average of 1,476,000 tons for the quinquennium 1920–24 to 3,176,000 tons during 1927–31, the last five years

---

[1] *Survey of Metal Industries*, pp. 33 f.

of free trade. Yet British domestic prices remained high, well above the level in international trade. Once again some of this reflects imperfections in the market: international cartel agreements; prescriptive use of British steel for national or municipal projects, including shipbuilding subsidized by the state; codes that discriminated against the use of Thomas steel (basic Bessemer), which was the strongest product of the Continental works. In addition, British steelmakers were prepared to give special prices to regular customers; so that the index of nominal prices is not strictly accurate.[1]

In fact, however, foreign competition was squeezing the British industry. Output more or less levelled off from 1923 on, while exports fell steadily. Yet it was not the smaller, more old-fashioned enterprises that suffered most in this conjuncture. Many of these had long since amortized all or most of their equipment, whereas some of Britain's most modern plants had been built or enlarged in the costly postwar years and carried a heavy burden of fixed financial obligations. Moreover the older plants were in a much better position to handle the small, almost custom orders of a thin market. The chairman of United Steel Companies had occasion to explain this paradoxical superiority of seemingly less efficient installations to his shareholders: 'Unless [modern] plants can operate at full capacity, they are inefficient on the ground of lost time, idle plant and idle capital, and plants less elaborate and less modern, but which can operate more regularly, may really be more efficient.' And he noted that at Steel, Peech & Tozer (a branch of United Steel), the old hand-rolling mills had kept busy, while the new mills, which should have replaced them, had not got the large uniform orders they needed to work at low cost.[2]

The question remains, of course, whether a more systematic rationalization of production, along with stronger price incentives to the use of standardized shapes and qualities, would not have given the newer plants the runs they needed. This is just what United Steel and similar companies set out to do, somewhat belatedly to be sure, with the onset of the Great Depression.

In any event, the result was the survival of small units and, with them, older methods of manufacture. We have already seen something of the first in the tabular comparison of British and French plants (see above, Table 50). The latter deserves detailed consideration.

Duncan Burn, in his classic *Economic History of Steelmaking*, points out that British technique did not stand still during what he calls the 'Black Decade' of the twenties. Producers sought new ways to save

[1] On all this, cf. Svennilson, *Growth and Stagnation*, p. 128 and n. 1.
[2] P. W. S. Andrews and Elizabeth Brunner, *Capital Development in Steel: a Study of the United Steel Companies Ltd.* (Oxford, 1962), pp. 168 f. Also pp. 94, 137.

fuel and succeeded in reducing coke consumption in smelting from 28·4 cwt in 1920 (about the same as in 1913) to 25 cwt in 1929. In post-smelting processes, the gains were even more impressive: the Iron and Steel Federation claimed a drop from 1·55 tons of coal per ton of finished product in 1920 to 1·13 tons in 1929 (although Burn argues that much of this improvement was due to the change in the product mix—the increased proportion of import 'semis' that needed only re-rolling to be finished, and the diminishing share of wrought iron and other fuel-hungry items).[1]

Yet with all this improvement, British practice was far behind that of the Continental countries. Against 25 cwt per ton of pig should be set the German *mise au mille* of 19·6 cwt. Against a post-smelting figure of 22·5 cwt should be placed a Belgian average of 4·9 cwt; and the German figure was undoubtedly lower. What is more disturbing, the British figure did not simply reflect the performance of unintegrated plants, although these were far too common. Even the big combines that were able to process their metal hot from refining through finishing used their fuel far too wastefully.

Why this poor performance? On one level, one can speak of under-investment. Annual expenditure on capital account ran to one or two million pounds a year at the height of the boom in the late twenties, a mere 1 or 2 per cent of the value of plant. To be sure, profits did not warrant more and the financial situation of most firms did not permit it. Indeed, given the persistent burden of excess capacity, one might even look upon such expenditure as did occur as overinvestment. And that it was, so long as the new plant did not yield gains in productivity that could be translated into competitive advantage; or so long as the investing firms did not use their equipment to that effect.

Unfortunately, the calculations of the potential profitability of new investment were unduly conservative, especially in the years preceding the introduction of protective duties, and rested on the assumption of modest growth and a relatively traditional market. Few steelmen enter-tained the possibility of developing demand (which was in the aggre-gate inelastic, though not necessarily so for the individual firm) or of influencing the location of steel-using industries.[2] Moreover, such in-

---

[1] Burn, *Economic History*, p. 435, n. 1.

[2] Thus Andrews and Brunner, *Capital Development in Steel*, p. 82, note that a difference of 5s. a ton on an Association price of 175s. was sufficient to gain the United Steel plate mills at Appleby a good market. And yet see the critique by the same authors, *ibid*. pp. 97–8, of D. L. Burn's analysis of the should-have-beens of the in-dustry and his recipe for improvement. The essence of their argument is that there were rational reasons for the persistence of Britain's traditional locational pattern: that cold-metal steelmaking (as against the hot-metal technique in which smelting and refining are integrated and the hot metal goes without cooling from the blast furnace

vestment as did occur was almost invariably piecemeal and surprisingly often mismanaged. Much of it consisted in additions to existing plant, where layout and previous equipment imposed severe constraints on technological possibilities; the result was patchwork improvement that never yielded optimal returns. More serious, even brand new plant was poorly conceived and located. This was an old story. Burn notes that the only two combined works built in Britain before the War— Lysaght's at Normanby Park and the Partington Iron Works near Warrington—were both small compared to new German plants. Of the new installations built during the war, only a few represented best practice, and these remained more curiosities than models to be imitated, perhaps because even best practice was not what it might and should have been. Thus a continuous billet mill built by Steel, Peech, and Tozer near Sheffield had prime costs from 6s. to 10s. a ton below those of other mills; but their lead was not followed, perhaps because, as Burn notes (p. 367), 'since the mill was handicapped by its site, it was an imperfect advertisement'. In several cases, the equipment for the different processes was not matched to permit continuous, efficient flow at capacity output: the cooling banks were too small, railway facilities exiguous, space for further expansion inadequate.

This kind of investment in obsolescence continued to characterize the high-cost construction of the postwar years. When the Consett Iron Company decided in 1923 to use its large accumulation of cash to re-build its steel plant, it unhappily chose to do so on the old site, which no longer enjoyed the advantage of cheap local ore and coal. The old melting plant had consisted of 39 small acid open hearths, 20 to 35 tons capacity, dispersed in three locations. Now some nine 75-ton furnaces were concentrated in one works; but these were half, or even a third, as large as the most advanced tilting furnaces of the prewar decade; and the installation of soaking pits and reheating furnaces makes it clear that there was to be no maximization of fuel economy.[1] The company long got little or no return on its investment: the ordinary dividend of

to the open hearths or converters) can make good sense where a high percentage of scrap is employed; and that cold metal plants may well be better off closer to the market for the finished product than to the ore fields, since it is these markets that furnish the scrap and the savings on transport of scrap and finished products may more than compensate for the cost of moving such pig iron as is employed and remelting it. The trouble with this kind of argument is that it always assumes the immutability of the status quo and sees the industry in question as a passive respondent to the economic environment. The result is that whatever is, always turns out to be for the best. As a result it leaves no room for those innovations that fly in the face of the prevailing pattern and succeed in altering it.

[1] Burn, *Economic History*, p. 432; Carr and Taplin, *History of the British Steel Industry*, p. 381.

December 1924 proved to be the last in over a decade. In all fairness, though, it should be noted that other, more efficient enterprises were also in trouble.

Yet it was only in radical reconstruction of this kind that lay the hope of the British iron and steel industry. Piecemeal improvement of existing plant was expensive and messy; as Sir Francis Samuelson put it in his presidential address to the Iron and Steel Institute:

If we increase our engine power, we have not enough stove power: we may add new stoves if we have room, which often we have not: we may raise the height of old ones, if they are strong enough—even then they are probably not strong enough for the new pressure. If we surmount the stove difficulty, we find our mains and connections are not large enough to take the increased volume of air. If by partial scrapping we get over all these difficulties, we are apt to find that our yard is not equal to the increase of traffic....[1]

Small wonder that average output per furnace ran to about 40 per cent of the German level in 1925 (41,000 against 96,000 tons per year). To quote Sir Francis again: 'There seemed to be no halfway house between leaving moderately-well alone and complete scrapping.'[2]

The depression that began in 1929 forced the industry to choose between Sir Francis's alternatives, and a number of enterprises opted for the more drastic solution. A new wave of mergers occurred, and this time, there were numerous casualties: Cammell Laird's works at Grimesthorpe and Penistone were shut down towards the end of 1929 in the amalgamation with Vickers and Vickers-Armstrong to form the English Steel Corporation; in February 1930, David Colville and Sons took over the good will of the plate, section, and rail branches of Wm Beardmore & Co., and Beardmore's Parkhead rolling mills stopped (their Mossend works had been closed since the summer of 1928); Ebbw Vale, the old Welsh giant, closed down its iron and steel department in October 1929; the nearby works at Dowlais, even older and once the largest in the world (see above, pp. 121, 180), put out its fires a year later.[3] All in all, 135 blast furnaces were dismantled from 1932 to 1939.

This catharsis was facilitated, and in some instances imposed, by institutional forces. For one thing, the government was now aroused by the obsolescence of the industry and its mounting financial troubles; it was like a festering boil sending poisons through a grievously weakened system. Starting with the traditional committee of inquiry, which told the authorities what they already knew, the government moved to promote concentration, rationalization, and modernizing in-

[1] *Journ. of the Iron and Steel Institute*, 1922, I, p. 36, cited in Burn, *Economic History*, p. 366, n. 5.

[2] Brady, *Rationalization Movement*, p. 115; Burn, *Economic History*, p. 366.

[3] Carr and Taplin, *History of the British Steel Industry*, pp. 443, 446, 450, 447.

vestment. It was much assisted in this effort by the leading London banks, which held a fortune in notes, bonds, and overdrafts of iron and steel companies and were concerned not only to protect their money, but also to prevent the injection of political considerations into problems they wanted decided on economic and financial grounds. (In this they were only moderately successful, as we shall see.) The key figure here was Montagu Norman, Governor of the Bank of England; his chief collaborator, Charles Bruce Gardner, managing director of the Shelton Iron, Steel and Coal Co., whom Norman named to head the newly founded Securities Management Trust and the Bankers' Industrial Development Co. The former was formed in November 1929 to develop plans for the rationalization of whole industries and find men to execute them; the latter, in April 1930, to bring together the leading public and private banks of the City in furtherance of this objective. In her hour of trial, Britain was turning away from the classical banking formula to something much closer to the German model.

Active intervention by banks undoubtedly shaped the pace and character of amalgamation in the iron and steel industry. In at least one instance, the absorption of Bolckow, Vaughan by Dorman Long in 1929, the bank decided the issue: Barclays simply refused to renew Bolckow's overdraft of £1 million unless it went through with the merger. In Lancashire, the Bank of England helped finance and fixed the terms of a succession of reorganizations and consolidations, beginning with the formation of Vickers–Armstrong in 1927, continuing with the above-mentioned creation of the English Steel Corporation and the Wigan Coal Corporation in 1930, the last two specifically conceived by the Securities Management Trust and the Bankers' Industrial Development Company as part of a scheme of regional rationalization.

The other major institutional change, more decisive perhaps for new investment as against amalgamation and rationalization of existing units, was the coming of protection. The government took this step reluctantly. It was convinced that modernization should come first, and that only if that proved insufficient should it step in and interfere with the free play of the market. Besides, in an industry in which vertical integration was far from a commonplace, there were a large number of enterprises processing semifinished shapes that stood to lose if the price of imports rose. But the pressure built up inexorably, both on the side of the producers and the workers, many of whom were unemployed. At the end of 1930, the steel industry was working at 30 per cent of capacity and imports were exceeding exports for the first time since the eighteenth century.[1]

---

[1] Excepting 1927, which reflected the special circumstances of the great coal strike of 1926.

There is no question that the institution of protective duties (temporary in April 1932; indefinite in May 1934) was the signal for a substantial amount of new investment that otherwise probably would not have taken place. Thus the British Iron and Steel Co. (an amalgamation of Baldwins and Guest, Keen & Nettlefold) had had new works at Cardiff on the drawing board since 1930 but had deferred action so long as commercial policy remained uncertain; they began construction as soon as the time limit was lifted and were able to roll their first ingots in 1936. The modernization of Dorman Long, which entailed demolition of Lowthian Bell's old smelting plant at Clarence on the Tees, also dates from 1934. And it was in November 1932 that Stewart & Lloyd decided to go ahead with what was probably the most important iron and steel undertaking of the interwar period: the establishment of an integrated plant at Corby, to smelt the long-neglected ores of Northamptonshire, refine them by the long-abandoned basic Bessemer process, and shape them in semi-continuous and continuous tube, strip and pipe mills.

Yet it would be a mistake to view the growing influence of government and commercial policy as uniformly favourable to growth and rational investment. The construction of Britain's first continuous wide strip mill comes to mind here. The wide strip mill was the most important single advance in iron and steel technology in the interwar period. Starting with the thick, coarse ingot of crude steel, it moved the metal through a series of graduated rollers, compressing and stretching it until what began as a slab bumping sluggishly between massive cylinders became a long, undulating strip racing through the final yards at up to sixty miles an hour. The sheet that resulted was smoother and more uniform in thickness than that produced by the discontinuous process, hence better able to withstand the stresses of a stamping press and to take a glossy paint finish. It also came off the mill in convenient coils or neatly cut pieces, ready for further shaping by automatic or semi-automatic machines. As a result, it was far better suited than ordinary sheet to the manufacture of consumers' hard goods—motor cars in particular, but also refrigerators, washing machines, space heaters, and similar devices. What is more, the continuous mill did all this faster and with a fraction of the manpower required by the traditional technique, with its multiple passes and dangerous manipulation of hot metal. It therefore constituted from the start an unbeatable competitor.

The first continuous wide strip mill was developed in the United States by Armco (the American Rolling Mill Co.) in 1928, and the British had contemplated importing the technique from the start. A committee had gone over to the States to see the new mill in action and had returned with the kind of mixed report that had characterized the British steel industry in the late nineteenth century: most of its members argued that the Welsh tinplate industry was not so far behind after all; the more progressive insisted that Britain would have to go over to the continuous strip mill sooner or later. The greatest impediment to the introduction of the American technique was its scale of working, which was at minimum so large that the new mill would necessarily displace many of the characteristically small units in the trade, the more so as there was already considerable excess capacity. A committee was set up to examine the possibility of some kind of co-operative arrangement to ease the pain of this invasion; but its chairman died in 1929, and with the coming of the depression, the scheme was dropped. When Richard Thomas & Co., under the chairmanship of Sir William Firth, revived the project in 1932, its first step, significantly enough, was to buy up as many tinplate mills as possible, thereby decimating the enemy ranks.

Firth's first thought was to put the new mill in Lincolnshire, on top of England's largest and cheapest beds of iron ore; this would make possible the substantial economies of an integrated operation. But the government thought differently. Wales was already suffering from severe unemployment as a result of closings and cutbacks in the old and tired coal and iron trades; the prospect of a hecatomb of tinplate mills was politically intolerable. Among the most distressed areas was Ebbw Vale, where, as the reader will recall, the iron and steel works had been shut down since October 1929. By a judicious mixture of carrot and stick, the authorities persuaded Sir William to change his mind and opt for Ebbw Vale. He did so with misgivings, though he presented the brightest, most sanguine face to his shareholders and the investing public.

As a result, the works cost more to build and operate than it should have. The initial objective had been an output of 300–350,000 tons of steel strip a year at an investment of about £4·5 million. The technology of the continuous mill was very young, however, and still changing rapidly, so that plans were revised in the course of development; by the time construction got under way in 1936, the aim was over 600,000 tons of strip at a cost of £6 to 6·5 million. On this scale, the site at Ebbw Vale soon proved more difficult than anticipated, and by the end of 1937, estimates had risen to £8·5 million, and more realistic observers were predicting that the cost would go much higher yet. They were right. By 1938 Richard Thomas & Co. was in serious trouble, and only the intervention of the Bank of England saved the day. But this too had its price. Norman would not move without the advice of the Iron and Steel Federation, and the Federation, which was prepared to view the projected works as an undertaking of national importance, recommended assistance only on condition that the mill accept production quotas compatible with the well-being of the rest of the industry. In the end, Firth was compelled to accept the surveillance of a committee of control composed in good part of his own competitors. Once again, he put the best face he could on a *pis aller;* but he clearly found it disagreeable to have to subordinate his own judgment to team decisions. In April 1940 he retired. Carr and Taplin quote the eulogistic opinion of the *Iron and Coal Trades Review*: '...his name will go down to posterity as the one who introduced and laid down the first plant in Great Britain for the continuous rolling of sheet strip'. He had done the job; but because of official intervention, he had not been able to do it as he would have and should have.[1]

For all this distortion of the investment pattern, however, the British iron and steel industry did grow and modernize considerably in the thirties, after fifteen years of marking time. Average output per blast furnace rose to 73,700 tons by 1939, and the new furnaces coming into blast had an average capacity of perhaps 125,000 tons. Thus Britain, which had been in the ruck of major European producers in the early twenties, passed the level of French performance (69,000 tons) by a small margin and almost caught up with the Belgian (76,500 tons). We do not have comparable figures for steelmaking, but here too the average size of furnace increased substantially. The new fixed open hearths ran to 90 tons and more; the new tilting furnaces, to 250 and 300 tons. As a result of these and other improvements, the amount of coal used to make a ton of finished steel fell from 50·7 cwt in 1929 to 40·7 in 1938. Even so, some of the old weak spots remained. Thus, although the tonnage of hot metal used in basic steelmaking increased substantially, the proportion to total pig iron used fell from 66 per cent in 1935 to 62 in 1940. The British steel industry continued to suffer from inadequate integration.[2]

On the Continent, the course of development was reversed. Here it was the decade of the twenties that was the era of growth and rationalization. The depression of the thirties struck very hard at producers whose capacity now far exceeded demand, the more so as inflation now gave way to deflation and the old stimulus to investment was gone. When the French had occasion to survey their plant in 1943, they found that all their mills, with the exception of those built in the reconstruc-

---

[1] *History of the British Steel Industry*, p. 548, citing the *Iron and Coal Trades Review* of 11 August 1939. The above account relies primarily on Carr and Taplin, pp. 542-8, and Burn, *Economic History*, pp. 459-61.

[2] The data in the preceding paragraph are drawn from Carr and Taplin, *History of the British Steel Industry*, p. 557.

tion programme of the early twenties, dated back to the War and earlier. She had no furnaces of more than 500 tons capacity, although the optimal size was at least that, and only a handful between 400 and 500 tons.[1] Similarly, no French converter was more than 30 tons, although the Germans were building units of 50 tons; and open hearths of 100 tons were extremely rare. A more precise idea of the size distribution of this equipment may be had from the following table:

Table 53. *Sizes of Installations in the French Iron and Steel Industry in 1943 (in tons of capacity)*

Blast furnaces		Thomas converters		Open hearths	
Size	Proportion[a]	Size	Proportion[a]	Size	Proportion[a]
Under 125	17	10–15	22	10–20	20
125–250	31	15–20	21	20–30	22
250–300	24	20–25	18	30–50	35
300–400	21	25–30	39	50–100	23
400–500	7	—	—	—	—

[a] The source does not make clear whether this proportion is share of units or of aggregate capacity. It is presumably the latter.

SOURCE: Inst. Nat. de la Statistique et des Etudes Economiques, *Etudes et conjoncture*, VIII (1953), special number: 'L'industrie française', p. 14.

No wonder the authors of the above-cited study of I.N.S.E.E. could write that on the eve of the war, 'French metallurgical plant was in a state of profound obsolescence'.

The effects of this increasing obsolescence show clearly in the statistics of productivity and fuel performance. The output of iron and steel per worker rose sharply in the twenties, to a level roughly twice as high as before the War. These gains peaked out, however, in 1931, and from then on productivity declined steadily, with the exception of a small, short-lived recovery in 1933. The slide became a sharp retreat in 1937–38, probably more for reasons of labour unrest than of technological inadequacy, which would not itself suffice to explain a drop in output per man of 18 per cent in a single year. The same sharp downturn occurs in fuel efficiency, which stood up better on the whole than productivity. In any event, the French iron and steel industry was not performing much better on the eve of the War than it had some fifteen years before.

By the same token, German producers also marked time in the thirties. Even the armaments programme of the Third Reich did little to promote technological advance. Most producers found it easier and

[1] These are daily capacities. Working seven days a week and forty to forty-five weeks a year, such a furnace would make 140,000 to 150,000 tons of pig a year.

Table 54. *Productivity and Fuel Efficiency in the French Iron and Steel Industry, 1905–38*

	Output per worker per year[a] (in tons)	Output per ton of coal consumed[b] (in tons)
1905	35·1	345
1906	36·4	356
1907	34·3	331
1908	34·8	359
1909	36·0	377
1910	36·2	377
1911	39·8	393
1912	41·6	414
1913	38·5	383
1920	27·3	323
1921	30·2	378
1922	43·2	436
1923	44·5	443
1924	53·1	423
1925	58·5	446
1926	66·4	450
1927	64·6	439
1928	64·5	474
1929	64·6	438
1930	74·1	490
1931	79·4	493
1932	64·4	533
1933	68·8	536
1934	66·4	517
1935	64·8	530
1936	62·3	516
1937	58·4	482
1938	48	470

[a] All iron and steel products, less output of semis sold as such.
[b] Coke converted to coal equivalent by factor of 1·3.
SOURCE: France, Service National des Statistiques, Institut de Conjoncture, Etude spécial No. 3: *Le Progrès technique en France depuis 100 ans* (Paris, 1944), p. 99.

more profitable to put unused capacity back into production than to innovate. As a result, of 418 rolling mills at work in 1938, 300 dated from before the World War, 100 from the war years and the twenties, and only 18 had been built in the thirties. To be sure, one of these was a continuous wide strip mill, completed in 1937 to furnish sheet for the projected people's motor car (*Volkswagen*).[1] Similarly, average yearly

[1] German data from Svennilson, *Growth and Stagnation*, p. 131.

output per blast furnace, which had risen by 130 per cent from 1913 to 1929 (58,000 to 134,000 tons), more or less levelled off, reaching 154,000 in 1936, 147,000 in 1937. Even so, this was double the Belgian, British, or French performance.[1]

In general, the interwar years were a period of travail for all the major European producers. Their difficulties were reflected in the pattern of trade as well as in that of investment. The overall tendency was once more the selfish retreat: closure of the home market against outside competitors and fencing of foreign preserves by bilateral agreements. In the meantime, however, their foreign customers were playing the same game—building up their own steel industries and closing their doors to European products. Thus steel output in all 'overseas' (non-European) countries, excluding the United States and the U.S.S.R., rose from 1·2 million tons in 1913 to 9·6 million in 1936/37; the gain was substantially larger than the 6 million tons that these countries had imported from Europe and the United States in 1912/13.[2] So that although world consumption of steel grew some 75 per cent from 1912/13 to 1936/37, exports from the four major European producers to outside countries actually fell slightly, after an initial period of gains in the 1920's. Here again the biggest loser was Britain, for some of her favourite imperial customers (Canada, Australia, South Africa) were now in the full flush of their own industrial revolutions. But Belgium and Luxembourg, both heavily dependent on export markets, were also hard hit.

★　　★　　★　　★　　★　　★

Every generation has its own intellectual problems. In view of the unhappy conjuncture of the 1930's, it is no surprise that the economists of that day concerned themselves primarily with the problem of the business cycle. The great theoretical innovation was Keynes's *General Theory*, which offered the first plausible explanation for persistent unemployment and, so doing, made a major breach in the classical model of general equilibrium. In the years that followed, economists chose sides, pro- and anti-Keynes, and devoted themselves to the elaboration of the Keynesian model or its disproof. The core problem continued to be the nature and determinants of systemic equilibrium.

In so far as some economists moved out beyond the short run and

---

[1] Svennilson, *Growth and Stagnation*, p. 265. Svennilson's figures for France and Belgium, which are based on the bulletins of the Comité des Forges, differ somewhat from those given in the *Annuaire statistique* or in Reuss, Koutny, and Tychon, *Le progrès économique en sidérurgie*. Svennilson does not give a figure for German blast furnaces or average output in 1938.

[2] Svennilson, *Growth and Stagnation*, p. 137.

concerned themselves with growth rather than with cyclical fluctuations, they focused on the question of stagnation: What light did the Keynesian model throw on the manifest slowing of growth, with attendant unemployment, in the most advanced industrial nations? This way of posing the issue rested on assumptions that we today, with the advantage of hindsight, can recognize as erroneous; they had a certain plausibility, however, in the thirties and forties. Even the adversaries of the stagnationists met them on their chosen ground; that is, they accepted the tacit limitation of the determinants of growth to endogenous (intrasystemic) variables. In particular, they tended to look on investment as a function of savings and demand; and to the extent that anyone postulated the possibility of exogenous stimuli to investment, he thought in terms of government intervention or similar acts of fiat. What we today would look upon as the most powerful incentive to investment and hence determinant of growth—technological change—was largely ignored. The most important theoretical model of those years, that proposed by Roy Harrod in his famous article of 1939, assumed set capital-labour ratios and no technical progress.[1]

One could extend this observation to a wider range of commentators: the popularizers and nonacademic economists as well as the university scholars were preoccupied by questions of stability and organization rather than growth; and to the extent that they turned their attention to growth, they gave little thought to the implications of continued technological change.

In this intellectual context, a series of articles published by *Fortune* Magazine beginning in October 1939 on 'The U.S. Frontier' stand out by their perception and imagination. One expects a certain optimism from a journal catering to the community of business executives; but these articles are far more than a mere expression of confidence in the future. They are an effort to see into the future, or rather to extrapolate the future from the character of American economic performance in those years; and they base this extrapolation, not on the record of unemployment and prolonged depression, but on the swelling tide of what we now call R & D—research and development.

The editors who wrote these articles did not lack for discouraging data

[1] R. F. Harrod, 'An Essay in Dynamic Theory,' *Economic Journal*, XLIX (1939). The article appeared years ahead of its time. The issue of growth was not really taken up by the profession until after the War.

The only major exception to this rule was Schumpeter, with his model of a system dependent on successive pushes from sporadic technological advance *cum* entrepreneurial innovation; and even he, asking in 1942 whether capitalism could survive, pushed technological innovation under the rug, as it were, by assuming its reduction to a routine stream of predictable improvements. J. A. Schumpeter, *Capitalism, Socialism and Democracy* (New York, 1942; 3rd ed., 1950), p. 132.

and advice. In the very issue in which the first piece in the series appeared, they also published the minutes of a round table on full employment that included among the participants Harvard's Alvin Hansen, a major spokesman of the stagnationist school. Hansen had serious reservations about the future. In the past, he noted, American economic growth had rested in roughly equal proportions on increasing population and improving techniques. Now population growth was slowing down, and if the rate of investment was to be maintained, some offset would have to be found on the side of invention. Yet technology, argued Hansen, would not necessarily take up the slack: 'Research and invention in an advanced industrial society may frequently prove to be capital saving and thereby reduce the demand for capital.' As a result, income would fall, employment would contract, and the gap between full and realized employment would widen. The gap could of course be closed by 'appropriate price and other policies'; but there was no assurance that it would be.[1]

The editors of *Fortune* were prepared to accept the necessity and desirability of some such policies, but they had misgivings about the assumptions they were based on and the purposes they were directed to:

> If they are directed toward a static economy, upon the assumption that there is no more frontier, they are inacceptable. For the evidences of a frontier are overwhelming. It is a different kind of frontier from that which governed the expansion of the nineteenth century, but it is just as surely there. FORTUNE has been sending out reconnoitering parties for the last six months, and the preliminary reports indicate the existence of a new world that is virtually immeasurable... This frontier is technological in character, complex, difficult for the layman or even the businessman to comprehend. It is not charted or mapped; even the technicians, though familiar with their special areas, know little about it as a whole. But it is only by virtue of the narrowest sort of definition, together with a thorough ignorance of American industrial science, that anyone can deny it exists.

The article went on to take a classical Schumpeterian position: the two 'prime movers of the frontier' were the 'inventor, who creates it, and the entrepreneur (whether corporate or individual), who develops it.' The link between the two was industrial research, which had been growing much faster than industry itself. Before World War I, the editors noted, such research was the exception—'a kind of big-business luxury.' As late as 1920 it employed only 8,000 persons. By 1927, however, according to the National Research Council, the number was up to 17,000, and by 1938 to 42,000. The number of industrial laboratories showed a parallel rise: from 350 in 1920 to some 1,000 in 1927, to about 1,800 in 1933.

[1] *Fortune*, xx (October 1939), 113.

With this record behind it, and with the pace still accelerating, American industrial science is in the process of creating the greatest frontier ever known to man. And if the second step can be taken, if corporations and individuals can be induced to develop these areas as entrepreneurs, a new world will emerge. For it is a fair preliminary guess that the development of this frontier would have the same long-term effects upon the economy as the development of the old frontier. On the one hand, labor shortages would be created, especially in the skilled categories, with a consequent increase in wages; and, on the other hand, the prices of consumers' goods now rated as luxuries or semiluxuries would be cut—relatively—to a fraction of their present level. These results would have the combined effect of raising the standard of living beyond anything so far dreamed, and of increasing manyfold the opportunities available to the individual.[1]

Fortune was sinning no doubt on the side of overoptimism. Even assuming the exploitation of the technological frontier, one could not simply infer therefrom a general improvement in the standard of living. There is a large, complex intermediary system of distribution between producer and consumer through which the gains of technology are channelled, and one must specify the conditions of this distribution before one can evaluate the ultimate consequences of invention. The decades that have passed since this confident prognosis of 1939 have seen the standard of living of the average American rise considerably; yet large areas of poverty remain, and it seems clear that even the most progressive system of production is compatible with selective deprivation. Moreover, *Fortune* said nothing about the negative aspects of technological change: the displacement of older techniques and those dependent on them; the swelling tide of waste; the poisonous by-products of a modern economy; the loss of the amenities of a slower, smaller society.

Even if one makes allowance for these omissions, however, which are not surprising in a publication aimed at a business constituency, one has to give the authors of the article some kind of award for prescience. They saw clearer than their contemporaries, and their vision is still more impressive when compared with European writings on the subject. In Britain, which had suffered far less in the depression of the thirties than the United States, even the business community was resigned to a static, defensive future. In 1942 the Federation of British Industries, the Association of British Chambers of Commerce, and the London Chamber of Commerce all issued reports on the problems and opportunities of the postwar economy to come. The reports made obeisance to the large prospects of a new world and exhorted their readers to make their own future with 'new methods and a positive policy': 'Such methods will require a fresh outlook, a mutual readiness to face sacrifices, and the determination on the part of all to develop their maximum effort.' Yet the substance of these reports contradic ս their rhetoric, and the British journal *Nature* compared them unfavourably with a contemporary memorandum on 'Relations with Britain' by the editors of *Time*, *Life* and *Fortune*. It chided the British authors for their negative, defensive approach, their failure to see demand as something to be made as well as submitted to, their inability to recognize the opportunities offered by fuller international co-operation, both among advanced industrial nations and between the advanced countries and 'the backward regions of Asia, Africa and America'. As to the significance of technological advance:

> The value of research in agriculture is recognized, but as to industry, the Federation of British Industries report alone has a stray reference to the necessity of a most active policy of research to develop new types of exports and to obtain maximum efficiency. Our assets of scientific and technical knowledge and ability are silently discounted. Apart from a wise reminder that it will only be possible to preserve a reasonable standard of life by hard work, and by attaching as much importance to our obligations towards the community as to the rights we claim from it, there is scarcely a reference to the need for great technical efficiency, for more output per head and the development of new techniques and industries.[1]

One could give other illustrations of this short-sightedness. Roy Glenday—to choose the example of a man who was economic adviser to the Federation of British Industries—wrote in 1944 that the economy was peaking out. The impetus provided by the Industrial Revolution was exhausted. The latest cluster of innovations, associated with electricity and motor transport, had given the system a final push, but only thanks to hire-purchase, that is, by buying prosperity today at the expense of a slump tomorrow. The familiar S-curve of growth, as exemplified by the experience of particular branches, applied, he argued, to the economy as a whole. In the Introduction to his volume, Glenday harked back to an earlier work on the *Economic Consequences of Progress*: 'The method of analysis employed in that earlier book, written nearly ten years ago, has been so far justified that it has been unnecessary substantially to alter the forecasts and recommendations then made. There has been an acceleration of the pace of change; that is all.'[2]

The line between obstinacy and the courage of one's convictions is very thin.

Yet as the analysis of economic change between the wars shows, the

---

[1] *Nature*, CL (11 July 1942), 33–4.

[2] Roy Glenday, *The Future of Economic Society: A Study in Group Organisation* (London, 1944), p. 3.

pessimists and stagnationists had good reason to be discouraged. They were the realists. The signs of dislocation, contraction, egoism, and failure were everywhere, and even such recovery as had taken place seemed to rest on the pathological foundation of war and preparations for war. The optimists were visionaries; their confidence flew in the face of the 'facts'. All of which would seem to show that sensitivity to the ills of today can be a poor guide to tomorrow. It is too easy to hear the loud noises and miss the silent, steady work beneath.

CHAPTER 7

Reconstruction and Growth Since 1945

If it is difficult to write the economic history of the interwar years, it is even harder to write that of the period after World War II. The one is confused and often murky; the other is current, and one's interpretation of the course of development is subject to the vagaries of change. Fifteen years ago, in the early 1950's, a number of observers, myself included, were offering careful analyses of France's economic retardation; and the fact was that France, after the stagnation of the thirties and the dislocation of the forties, did not seem to be pulling herself out of a morass of persistent inflation, technological conservatism, and social discontent. Ten years ago, the tune had changed as a result of rapid and sustained growth; a new wind was blowing in the land. A few years later, after the economy had shown intermittent signs of slowing, the assumption of a new era of ceaseless expansion gave way to a more cautious but still confident assessment. And today, with the slowdown of the mid-sixties behind us, the tone of the observer is once again hopeful, though the riots and strikes of 1968 have served to remind us of the primacy of politics and the fragility of man's plans and expectations.

This is the hazard of contemporary history: every opinion is a speculation on the future as well as a judgment of the past. Nevertheless, a full generation has elapsed since the start of the Second World War, a generation marked by substantial economic development that is the more important for its contrast with what preceded it. It is desirable, therefore, that we give some attention to these postwar years, if only by way of epilogue.

Like the First World War, the Second was enormously destructive of persons and things. In Europe, the pattern of conflict was drastically different from what it had been in 1914–18. Except on the Russian front and in Italy, battles tended to be short and decisions swift; and nowhere was there anything approaching the stalemate of trench warfare. As a result, there was nothing like the pulverization that certain areas of France and Belgium had known in the first war. On the other hand, the more mobile armies of the second war spread ruin more widely; and the advances in the technology of destruction, in particular, the development of air bombardment, made possible the devastation of civilian areas far behind the lines of battle. Also, vandals though the Germans were in 1918, when they systematically laid waste the area they abandoned in their final retreat (to the point of cutting the bark of trees so that they should no longer bear fruit), they were as nothing to their children, who chose to treat Jews and Gypsies as non-human, Slavs as sub-human, and utilized technology to create and rationalize a new industry of murder.

As a result, the losses of men and capital were substantially greater in the second war than in the first. There were, to begin with, the actual casualties: some 4·2 million dead in Germany (including civilians killed by bombing); 1·5 among Germany's allies (Austria, Italy, Rumania, Hungary); 1·5 million in Japan; almost 1 million among the Western powers (France, Great Britain, the United States); perhaps 25 million in Soviet Russia (again including civilians killed during the occupation or, to a much smaller degree, by Russian purges). These figures, moreover, are only a partial measure of the net loss, which includes (in addition to the maimed and stunted) those not born as a result of the excess mortality, hardship, separation, and disease of these war years. Thus the population of the areas that were to become the scene of war (including Southeast Asia) stood at 728 million in 1940. If numbers had continued to grow at the rate of 1920–40 (a fairly low rate in Europe), population would have stood at about 806 million in 1950. Instead, it stood at 751 million, a deficit of 55 million—of which 15 million in Europe and 31 million in the U.S.S.R.—this, mind, after some five years of recuperation.[1]

These figures of population loss are approximate; but they are far better than any direct estimates one can offer on the value of capital destroyed or damaged. Instead, a better measure of the material cost is furnished by a comparison of output immediately before and after the war.

As Table 55 shows, the only gainers during World War II were those countries that participated in the conflict but did not suffer occupation or direct attack; and of the European neutrals, Sweden. The greatest increase in output—indeed, the only substantial increase—took place in the overseas belligerents: the United States, but also Canada and, to a lesser degree, Australia and South Africa. Most of this increase, however, went to war production; so that in the United States, for example, output *per capita* net of government expenditures was actually lower in 1945 than in 1939. The European neutrals, surprisingly enough, grew slowly or barely held their own; and this in itself is a measure of the degree to which the disruption of international trade and business hampered even those well placed to take advantage of swollen wartime demand.

[1] The above figures are taken from Simon Kuznets, *Postwar Economic Growth: Four Lectures* (Cambridge, Mass., 1964), pp. 72–6.

Table 55. *Impact of World War II on Total Product, Population, and Product per Head. (Levels in 1945 as proportion of those prevailing in year indicated in left-hand column)*

	Product	Population	Product per head
United Kingdom, national income, 1937	115	104	111
France, national income, 1937	54	95	57
Netherlands, national income, 1937	52	108	48
Denmark, total available supply, 1939	84	106	79
Norway, gross domestic product, 1939	103[a]	106	97
West Germany, net domestic product, 1936	94[b]	121	78
Italy, national income, 1939	49	104	47
Austria, gross national product, 1938	85[b]	104	83
Greece, net domestic product, 1938	31	104	30
Switzerland, net national product, 1938	96	106	90
Sweden, gross domestic product, 1939	120	105	114
U.S.S.R., gross national product, 1940	82[c]	90	91
U.S.A., gross national product, 1939	172	107	161

[a] 1946.   [b] 1948.   [c] 1944.

SOURCE: S. Kuznets, *Postwar Economic Growth*, pp. 91–5.

All the others saw output and productivity plummet. (The West German index number of 78 for output per head is deceptive, since it reflects the results of three years of reconstruction and is based on a comparison with 1936; Kuznets estimates that it was about 47 in 1945.)[1] Usually the drop came late in the war; indeed the mobilization of resources for the conflict often produced a rise in output in the early years —a rise that showed surprising resistance to sabotage and bombing damage. But with time, the tempo of bombardment picked up, and the invasion of the Continent brought with it further destruction and disruption. When peace came in 1945, much of Europe was momentarily prostrate.

As in 1918, so in 1945 the recuperation of Europe's economies depended on the political decisions of the victorious allies. And as in 1918, these decisions were a mixture of wisdom and folly, vengefulness and forbearance, generosity and selfishness. These conflicting impulses were to be seen at work in both the relations of the victors to one another and in their treatment of the defeated Axis powers; and the decisions taken in the one sphere were determining of those taken in the other.

Within the Allied camp, there were, as we have seen, the fat and the

[1] According to M. M. Postan, *An Economic History of Western Europe, 1945–1964* (London, 1967), p. 12, German national income and output in 1946 were under one third, probably as low as 29 per cent, of 1938 levels. And they were no higher than 40 per cent in 1947.

lean—those powers that had suffered little and grown much, in particular, the United States; and those that had suffered much and shrunk, in particular, the countries that had been fought over and occupied. As in the First World War, the former had furnished the latter with money and material; so that by the end of the war, all the European victors had been compelled to liquidate their assets in the creditor countries and had accumulated enormous debts, and this at a time when further assistance would be needed for reconstruction. The economic recovery of Europe depended, then, on the disposition of these debts; on the availability of additional credit; and—along with this credit or as a substitute for it—on the ability of the victors to extract resources from the vanquished.

The solution of 1918, remember, was a return to financial normalcy. The creditors, principally the United States, expected to be repaid: 'They hired the money, didn't they?' rhetorically asked Calvin Coolidge. And the victorious debtors expected to get both the money to repay and reparation for their losses from the defeated enemy. These expectations, as we have seen, were disappointed—because Germany could not pay all that was demanded of her; because she would not pay what she could; and because the Allies insisted on linking their reimbursement of Uncle Sam ('Uncle Shylock') to the effectiveness of their own collections. These disappointments gave rise in turn to frustration and acrimony and did much to sour the international relations of the interwar decades.

This disagreeable experience should have served as a lesson; and it did. The only trouble is that the lessons of history vary with the student. The Americans learned to be more generous the second time: unlike the loans of World War I, the lend-lease programme of World War II called for assistance free of charge for the duration of the conflict. On the other hand, the disputes of the interwar years had sensitized the American people and their legislators to the whole question of debts and debtors: newspapers, for example, never failed to laud little, honest Finland for punctually meeting her engagements. So strings were attached to lend-lease that, however reasonable, vexed the recipients and tempered their gratitude; and the whole programme was abruptly halted upon the surrender of Japan, which left a bad taste in everyone's mouth.

Moreover, creditors are never beloved of those who owe them; or even helpers, of those who are beholden to them. There is usually no way to make an obligation palatable, because it is an expression of inequality. Hence the need of the recipient to view the loan or aid as a remuneration—for services rendered or sacrifices endured. This is often myth: every man, every nation has its dignity and believes what it has to. Yet the myth almost always has a part, even a sizable part, of truth, because nations rarely help or lend for purely altruistic reasons: if the United States helped Great Britain even before Pearl Harbor, it was essentially because the American government was convinced that Britain was fighting America's war.

Still, there is no assurance that a country will know its interests, and this intelligent awareness of interest is what most sharply distinguishes the United States of 1945 from that of 1918. In the year following the cessation of lend–lease, the debts of the Allies were largely cancelled and America initiated a new programme of foreign credit and aid. Thus by agreement of 6 December 1945, Great Britain was asked to pay only $650 million of the almost $25,000 million she had received (net of reverse lend–lease); and of that sum, $532 millions represented unused stocks, delivered or in the 'pipeline'. At the same time, the United States lent Britain the $650 million, while opening a line of credit of $3,750 million, with interest at 2 per cent payable in fifty years beginning in 1951. To be sure, this was considerably less than the 6 billion dollars that Britain had requested, and it was a loan at interest, rather than a grant or interest-free loan, as the British would have liked. Moreover, there were strings attached. In particular, Britain was to restore the pound sterling to convertibility by 1947, rather than within five years of ratification of the Bretton Woods agreement (1944), as originally provided; and this was to prove impossible. Nevertheless, the loan did tide the British over some difficult years, more difficult, indeed, than anyone could have anticipated.[1] The original intention was to make the credit last until 1951; but 1947 alone saw a deficit on balance of payments with the dollar area of $2,300 million.[2] The next year, however, saw a substantial improvement; and although Britain was to have another payments crisis in 1949, by that time the Marshall Plan was furnishing substantial assistance and the worst was over.

The same kind of ambiguous lesson was drawn from the history of reparations in the interwar years. On the one hand, it was clear that there was no point in asking for some outlandish amount far exceeding Germany's capacity to pay in the reasonably near future; so that the sum due was fixed at Potsdam at 20 billion dollars, as against the 137 billion gold marks (equal some 34 billion dollars) of 1921. On the

---

[1] Although the British accepted the terms of the loan—with some reluctance— within two weeks of the conclusion of the negotiations in December 1945, the American Congress did not give its approval until July 1946. In the meantime, the British had recourse to a loan of $1·25 billion made by Canada in March 1946. On the whole question of lend-lease and the financial arrangements of the immediate postwar period, an excellent source is William A. Brown, Jr., and Redvers Opie, *American Foreign Assistance* (Washington, D.C., 1953), ch. iv.

[2] Pollard, *Development of the British Economy*, p. 360.

other, the victors had also learned the old adage about a bird in the hand. They moved quickly to seize whatever real assets they could lay their hands on; and the Russians especially, who had suffered most from the war and had the best reasons for keeping Germany down, sought to confiscate whatever modern industrial equipment had escaped destruction. The Allies also imposed a ferocious territorial penalty. The Germany of Versailles had suffered some painful losses: Alsace-Lorraine, the Polish Corridor, the Saar (until 1935), and by the partition scheme of 1922, a part of Upper Silesia. Some of these were of considerable industrial importance. Yet they were as nothing to the drastic amputations inflicted on the Third Reich. Aside from the return of areas annexed during the war, like Alsace-Lorraine, all the land east of the line of the Oder and Neisse rivers was given to Poland as an offset to Polish territory annexed by Soviet Russia; and the border of the U.S.S.R. was advanced in a westward salient to take in the old German city of Koenigsberg, renamed Kaliningrad, thereby restoring to the Slavs, after the better part of a millennium, the old stamping ground of the Teutonic knights. In addition, Austria was once again established as a separate state. Meanwhile, what was left of Germany was divided into four zones of military occupation; the old regime was dissolved; business organizations and civil service were purged of those most blatantly linked to National Socialism; and the occupying powers, each in its own way, went about the task of building a democratic, peaceful nation.

The initial assumption of the victorious allies was that the best assurance of a peaceful Germany was a weak Germany. No one was prepared to follow the Morgenthau proposal and pastoralize the country; but in March 1946, the Allied Control Council agreed to limit German industrial output to half the 1938 level and hold steel capacity to 7·5 million tons (37·5 per cent of 1938). On the other hand, the occupation authorities, that is, those charged with the direct administration of the country, developed a conflicting concern for the restoration of the economy and the improvement of the conditions of existence. They were particularly anxious to re-establish communications and increase the supply of food, both to diminish the cost of occupation and to assist in the maintenance of public order. Almost from the start, therefore, the Allies were giving with one hand what they were taking with the other; and these cross purposes did much to mire the economy in a mass of inflation, mistrust, hoarding, and either sullen inertness or illicit enterprise. In a country rich in coal, food and manpower, dignified, middle-aged men could be seen, in coat, tie, and the other trappings of middle-class respectability, picking up horse dung in the streets to fuel their stoves or fertilize their vegetable gardens. By 1947 the system was on the verge of a complete breakdown. Official prices and wages were still only 20 per cent above pre-war levels, while the volume of money had soared fantastically and production stagnated. The real currency was no longer banknotes, but ration coupons and cigarettes, and a substantial portion of commercial transactions took the form of barter.[1]

Here, however, a new consideration intervened. In the First World War, the Allied powers had had their differences, but these differences were essentially external; that is, they concerned the conduct of the war and the treatment of the enemy and did not arise from any fundamental conflict within the Allied camp. The French, British, and later the Americans did not always agree; but they were held together by bonds of sympathy and by common political and social values.

This harmony of heart as well as of interest was missing in World War II. The Allied armies co-ordinated their efforts with considerable success; and the Western powers, in particular the United States, gave generously of money and supplies to their 'gallant' Russian allies. There was even a surge of public admiration for the Cossack cavalry, and for a while the moving strains of *Meadowland* could be heard on the 'hit parade' of popular tunes. Yet the Western powers never forgot the Russo–German pact of 1938 or lost their fear of Communist revolutionary ambitions; while the Russians, sensitized by two decades of hostility and quarantine, remained equally mistrustful of their wartime comrades, set strict bounds to their military co-operation, and did their best to maintain the curtain of secrecy that had long thwarted the curiosity of outsiders about Russia and of Russians about the rest of the world. Long before the war was won, both sides were anticipating the possibility of a postwar divorce and manoeuvering to secure guarantees and advantages for the future, and peace only widened the rift. At the very time when the peoples of the world were meeting in San Francisco to establish an organization to promote international co-operation, the Soviet manipulation of ostensibly representative (coalition) regimes in eastern Europe made it clear that while world parliaments were fine, power remained the gage of security. In the following years, Poland, Bulgaria, Rumania, Hungary, Yugoslavia, and Albania all became 'popular democracies' under varying degrees of Soviet control; while Greece was torn by a civil war that was liquidated only when Yugoslavia's break with the Soviet Union deprived the rebels of asylum. When Winston Churchill spoke in March 1946 of an iron curtain that had descended on Europe 'from Stettin in the Baltic to Trieste in the Adriatic', he gave to many the impression of premature and unfortunate pessimism. Instead, he was only giving an eloquent name to the facts of international relations.

[1] Cf. Robert Triffin, *Europe and the Money Muddle: From Bilateralism to Near-Convertibility, 1947–1956* (New Haven, 1957), p. 57.

All of this had a decisive influence on American policy toward Europe and toward her West European allies in particular; and on Allied policy toward Germany. In contrast to her behaviour after the First World War, the United States now recognized that the frontier of her security lay far from her shores and that she had a direct political interest in the economic recovery of Europe. Hence the Marshall Plan, proposed in June of 1947, eagerly accepted by the nations of western Europe, and put into effect on an interim basis before the year was out. In the next five years (to June 1952), the United States furnished foreign countries with some 22·5 billion dollars—more than half the net amount provided on lend–lease during the War itself; and of this amount, seven eighths (19·7 billion) took the form of outright gifts.[1] The emphasis on gifts rather than loans was a major reversal of policy; of 15·5 billion dollars in American aid from 1945 to 1948, more than half (8·7 billion) had taken the form of loans. The other major innovation was the provision of substantial assistance to the former enemy, Germany—1·3 billion dollars, or 9·5 per cent of the total. Only Britain and France got more.[2]

This, more than anything, was a touchstone of the transition from war to peace—or hot war to cold war, if one prefers. The western Allies, and the United States in particular, had simply reversed themselves on the issue of Germany. In March of 1946, as we have seen, the Allied Control Council voted to limit Germany's industrial production to one half the level of 1938. One year later, at the Moscow conference of the foreign ministers of the 'Big Four', the Russians and the western powers divided on the issue of German reparations, the Russians holding

[1] The Marshall Plan gave rise from the start to considerable controversy. Many Europeans, unwilling to concede to the Americans qualities of altruism and generosity that were foreign to their own character (*Honi soit qui mal y pense!*), were convinced that the whole thing was simply a scheme to fuel an American economy that was running out of steam now that the immediate postwar demand had been satisfied. The fact that such an interpretation ran counter to the conditions of the programme and the principles of economic theory did little to weaken these convictions. At the other extreme were those Europeans who saw the Plan essentially as a noble gesture of comradeship and responsibility. It was certainly that to a degree—here the experience of the interwar debacle had left its mark; but it was, more than anything else, a political act. Under-Secretary of State Acheson's statement of May 1947, anticipating by one month George Marshall's Harvard speech and pointing to 'the facts of international life' that linked the well-being of the United States to that of Europe, conveys as well as anything the fundamental motivation. For a well-written analysis of some of these issues, see Bertrand de Jouvenel, *L'Amérique en Europe: le Plan Marshall et la coopération intercontinentale* (Paris, 1948), which advances the responsibility argument.

[2] C. Ambrosi and M. Tacel, *Histoire économique des grandes puissances à l'époque contemporaine 1850–1964* (2nd ed.; Paris, 1963), pp. 683–9.

out for the ten billion dollars promised them at Potsdam, the Western powers insisting on plausible pecuniary grounds that Germany had to become self-supporting again. From that point on, the two camps went their separate ways. The western occupying powers refused to permit further dismantling of industrial plant in their zones; and in August of 1947, they drafted a new plan for German industry setting the 1936 level of production as an ultimate goal. The break became definitive in June of 1948, when the western Allies, who had long since stopped the use of common military scrip to prevent the Soviet occupation forces from printing and spending money at American expense, now moved similarly to separate the currency of western Germany from that of the Russian zone by introducing a new monetary unit, the Deutsche Mark, to replace the much inflated Reichsmark at a ratio of 1 to 10. This currency reform is generally recognized as the generating impulse of Germany's economic recovery and growth. The brutal deflation forced speculators and hoarders to sell their stocks, and shelves and shop windows that had been bare for years were suddenly filled. Farmers were more willing to bring their crops to market. The sudden increase in the supply of consumables did wonders for workers' morale and, indirectly, for productivity;[1] while manufacturing enterprise found it more profitable to make and sell finished goods than to hoard raw materials. If the statistics are to be believed, industrial output rose by nearly 50 per cent in the last six months of the year.

Nowhere was the transition from postwar paralysis to recovery so abrupt as in Germany; but in most of western Europe, 1948 was a year of passage from illness to health, discouragement to confidence, emergency to normalcy. In Britain, the winter of 1946–7 had been a disaster, a cruel trick of fate that consumed the nation's fuel supply (stocks were less than half of normal in the autumn of 1946), crippled production and trade, and cost some £200 million in exports. France and the Low Countries had not been spared; and in France particularly, the effect of shortages and social conflict had been to accelerate an inflation more rapid than the one that had followed the First World War. Between Liberation and the end of 1948, prices increased seven or eight times;[2] and so ingrained was the habit of inflation that an increasing proportion of security issues tied their returns in one way or another

[1] At the same time, employers were less willing to hold on to redundant labour, now that money was once again valuable; and this too increased productivity. United Nations, *Economic Survey of Europe since the War: A Reappraisal of Problems and Prospects* (Geneva, 1953), p. 73.

[2] The index of retail prices (1938 = 100) went from 300 to 2000; that of wholesale prices, from 250 to more than 2,000. André Piatier, 'Business Cycles in Post-War France', in Erik Lundberg, ed., *The Business Cycle in the Post-War World* (London, 1955), p. 108.

to the cost of living.[1] 'Two full years after hostilities had ceased,' writes Triffin, 'Europe found itself on the verge of a financial bankruptcy whose economic consequences threatened to topple over a political and social structure already weakened by ten years of depression followed by the most destructive war in history.'[2]

At this point Marshall Plan aid played a decisive role in shifting the economies of Europe from a rut of dislocation and crisis to that path of independently sustained growth they have followed ever since. The character of the transition varied with the country, each using the funds at its disposal to meet its own difficulties and objectives. The biggest beneficiary was Great Britain, which received almost a quarter of the total and utilized the 'counterpart funds', in the proportion of 95 per cent, for the redemption of her short-term debt.[3] Britain's critical problem in these years was her deficit on the balance of payments, with each gain in industrial output pushing up the demand for imports and putting heavy pressure on the pound. The Marshall Plan gave her a badly needed 'breather', removed many of the most serious shortages of goods, and made possible the lifting of a large array of price, import, and investment controls by 1950. At the same time, the effort to shift from the old and long-declining staples to newer, more expansive lines of manufacture bore fruit, so that by 1952-3 almost two thirds of Britain's exports fell in the latter category (65 per cent, as against 53·6 per cent for world exports as a whole); while the value of exports, which still was lower in 1947 than it had been in 1938, jumped 61 per cent in the next three years.[4] Even so, the pound was subject to recurrent difficulty, and in September 1949 Great Britain devalued from $4·03 to $2·80. The cut was more drastic than comparative prices re-

---

[1] As the United Nations *Economic Survey of Europe since the War* (1953) pointed out, p. 80, n. 7, 'This practice implies a defeatist belief in the everlasting continuance of inflation. By providing *rentiers* with a hedge against inflation, it removed the one real merit that inflation has always had—that it reduces the burden of past debt on active capitalists and consumers'.

[2] *Europe and the Money Muddle*, p. 31. In that year, in order to maintain 'minimal levels' of imports, consumption, and investment, Europe absorbed $9 billion in loans, grants, and foreign assets. 'In the absence of foreign aid', notes Triffin, 'such a deficit would have just about wiped out the total gold and dollar holdings of Europe'.

[3] Counterpart funds were the proceeds in local currency from the sale to public and private enterprises of the physical goods purchased with Marshall Plan funds by the recipient governments. These proceeds were to be set aside to promote economic recovery and development. As the name suggests, counterpart funds did not represent a net addition to Marshall Plan aid. They were the equivalent thereof and served as the channel by which American assistance flowed into the recipient economy. Cf. Henry C. Wallich, *Mainsprings of the German Revival* (New Haven, 1955), pp. 364-5.

[4] Pollard, *Development of the British Economy*, p. 363; U.N., *Economic Survey of Europe* (1953), p. 255.

quired and ended for the moment the speculative attacks on sterling. Gold and dollar reserves rose in less than a year from $1,425 million to $2,422 million; and in December 1950 Britain was able to give up further Marshall Plan aid. She was now 'home free', and even the severe deficit on balance of payments of 1951—a product of the Korean War—could not reverse her upward course.

France followed a different path. For her the major task was to provide the technological basis for economic growth. The stagnation of the thirties had cost her dearly; and what was already an obsolescent industrial plant in 1939 was that much more out of date after six years of war and occupation. In the meantime, the responsibility of the state for economic prosperity and growth had increased sharply as a result of the nationalizations of 1944–5: coal mining, gas and electric power, air transport, the large insurance companies, the Bank of France, the major commercial banks, the Renault motor firm, and sundry lesser enterprises. It is in this context that Jean Monnet and his collaborators worked out the first *plan de modernisation et d'équipement*, which called for heavy expenditures on the 'infrastructure' of the economy—energy and transport—and aimed at a national product equal to that of 1929 by mid-1948, and 25 per cent higher by 1950. If one remembers that when this plan was drawn up, French output was only a fraction of what it had been in 1938, and that 1938 was well below 1929, the daring of Monnet's conception is evident.

In France, as in Britain, economic expansion called for massive imports at a time when there was still little to export by way of return. Hence a large and cumulating deficit on balance of payments, which was covered in the first postwar years by American loans, from 1947 on by Marshall Plan aid. In the same way, the instability of the franc was a serious deterrent to private investment; so that contrary to expectations, the greater part (over 60 per cent) of the cost of reconstruction and new equipment in these years (1947–50) had to be borne by the state. Much of the money required was raised by increasing the note issue and borrowing; but most of the marginal outlays required for new investment came in the last analysis from foreign aid. Thus in 1948, the first full year of the Plan, the Fonds de Modernisation spent 155 milliard francs; while the counterpart funds made available to the French treasury amounted to 130 milliards.[1] In the course of the period 1947–52, France received some five billion dollars from the United States: 22 per cent of that went to Electricité de France; 13 per cent to Charbonnages

---

[1] France, Commissariat Général du Plan, *Deux ans d'exécution du plan de modernisation et d'équipement, 1947–1948* (Paris, 1949), pp. 174–7. Of these 130 milliards, only 95 were actually assigned to the Fonds de Modernisation; but this was a question of bookkeeping.

de France; 11 per cent to the Société Nationale des Chemins de Fer. In spite of these efforts, economic growth was not quite so fast as Monnet had envisaged: the 1929 level was not reached in 1948, but two years later. Still, American assistance made it possible to extend the life of the first plan to 1952, by which time French output stood 8 per cent above 1929, the trade deficit had been more or less wiped out, and the recovery-reconversion phase had been substantially completed.

Table 56. *Compound Rate of Growth of Gross Domestic Product in Selected Countries, 1949–63 (in percentages)*[a]

	1949–54	1954–59	1948–63
Western Germany	8·4	6·6	7·6
Austria	5·7	5·7	5·8
Italy	4·8	5·6	6·0
Spain	6·4	5·7	—
Switzerland	5·7	4·6	5·1
Netherlands	4·9	4·1	4·7
France	4·8	4·1	4·6
Portugal	4·2	4·0	—
Norway	4·2	2·7	3·5
Sweden	3·5	3·2	3·4
Denmark	3·7	3·4	3·6
Belgium	3·7	2·5	3·2
United Kingdom	2·7	2·3	2·5
United States	3·6	3·3	—
Canada	4·2	4·4	—

[a] Gross domestic product at 1954 factor-cost prices, except for Spain and the Netherlands (1953 prices).

SOURCES: Columns 1 and 2 from United Nations, Economic Commission for Europe, *Economic Survey of Europe in 1961*, Part 2: *Some Factors in Economic Growth in Europe during the 1950s* (Geneva, 1964), ch. ii, p. 20; column 3 from M. M. Postan, *Economic History*, Table 1, who bases his calculations on the previous source.

The end of the Marshall Plan did not see the end of American aid to Europe; but from about 1952, the emphasis shifted from economic to military assistance, while the very process of growth cured the dollar shortage and freed the European economies from the need for outside support. It was this sustained and powerful expansion of the 1950's that made the deepest impression on contemporaries and has continued to dominate our image of postwar economic history. Not that rates of growth were higher in this period than before; indeed, the contrary was true. But what had happened before was recovery, with all its precariousness and dependency, and one could argue that Europe was simply making up for lost time; whereas now Europe was moving ahead on its own, and every year brought a new record output. Between

1938 and 1963 the aggregate gross national product of western Europe, measured at constant prices, increased more than two and a half times.

From about the mid-1950's, when observers became aware that Europe was no longer a convalescent, this unexampled surge became a favourite subject of economic analysis. Not only was it more rapid than anything these countries had known before—more rapid, indeed, than the growth of the American economy over the same period—but with the passage of years, it proved to be remarkably sustained, extending almost without a pause well beyond the time period of an ordinary cyclical upswing. The European economies seemed to have learned the secret of eternal growth and prosperity.

How can one account for this achievement? The answer to that question depends on what one is trying to explain; and that in turn depends on where one stands to view the record. One can, for example, look at this extraordinary boom as the beginning of a long-term trend, a new path of growth with parameters quite distinct from those of the interwar or even pre-World War I economy. Or one can view the boom as a particularly strong cyclical upswing—unprecedentedly prolonged to be sure, but like all such upswings, transitory.

The former position looked better in 1958 than it does now (1968), after spotty years of slower growth and even recession in those countries that have been the leaders of the European parade. First France, then Italy ran into trouble; and beginning in late 1965, even the Germany of the 'economic miracle' began to see its climbing indexes turn downward. Still, both France and Italy have since started back and show signs of resuming the same high rates of growth as before; and there is no reason to believe that Germany will not follow suit; so that the new-trend interpretation, though shaken, is by no means ruled out.

If one adopts the cyclical-upswing position, the explanation is usually in terms of demand. In this view, the economies of western Europe benefited after the war from an accumulation of unsatisfied wants—first thwarted by the depression, then by years of conflict and destruction. There was, to begin with, the demand for necessities—the meat and fats and sweets that people had almost forgotten, the clothing that had to be replaced after years of patching, the houses that had to be repaired and built, the public services that had to be restored and expanded. And then, after about 1948, there were the luxuries: the scooters and motor cars; the radios and television sets; the vacuum cleaners, refrigerators, and washing machines. In this view, all that was needed after the war was to clear away the clutter and debris of physical destruction and market constraints and provide sufficient money and credit; the rest would, and did, take care of itself.

Associated with this view is the explanation, on the supply side, in

Table 56a. *Estimates of Gross Domestic Product of Selected European Countries, 1957–66*
(at fixed prices, in billions [10⁹] of national monetary units)

	1957	1958	1959	1960	1961	1962	1963	1964	1965	1966
Austria (1954)[a]	115	120	123	134	140	143	150	160	164	171
Belgium (1963)[a]	556	552	567	598	628	661	690	739	764	786
France (1959)[a]	253	260	267	288	301	321	337	357	372	390
West Germany (1954)[a]	200	207	221	255[b]	269	280	290	309	325	333
Italy (1963)[a]	20,989	22,015	23,419	24,907	26,844	28,498	30,072	30,891	31,924	33,656
Netherlands (1963)[a]	41·7	41·2	43·2	47·1	48·5	50·6	52·2	56·9	59·7	61·4
Sweden (1959)[a]	55·8	56·7	59·9	66·0	65·4	66·9	71·0	76·4	79·1	81·1
Switzerland (1958)[a]	31·8	31·2	33·3	35·2	37·8	39·7	41·6	43·7	45·3	46·4
United Kingdom (1958)[a]	22·7	22·8	23·7	24·9	25·8	26·0	27·2	28·8	29·4	29·9

[a] Base year for prices in parentheses.
[b] Data not strictly comparable to those of previous years.

SOURCE: United Nations, *Monthly Bulletin of Statistics*, XXII (April 1968), 188–9.

terms of manpower: postwar Europe was the beneficiary of something approaching Arthur Lewis's 'unlimited supplies' of labour. Those who take this position point to rising activity rates, that is, an increased tendency of those of working-class age to enter the labour market; to the movement of persons out of agriculture and small enterprise into large-scale manufacturing and services; and not least, to the large flow of immigrant labour to the industrial centres of western Europe. This flow was in part a direct consequence of the war; Germany in particular was called upon to absorb millions of refugees, first from those areas given or restored to her Slavic neighbours and from old areas of Germanic settlement in eastern Europe, then from the German Democratic Republic. (The latter were an especially valuable addition to the labour force, since they included some of the most enterprising and best-trained people in the Eastern Zone.) But it was also a mass response by the people of the poorer, more backward countries to the higher wages of northern and western Europe. In this way Britain was able to draw in a steady stream of immigrants from Ireland (about 25,000 a year), the West Indies, India and Pakistan, and Africa. France drew the larger part of her foreign work force from Algeria, at first in the persons of indigenous Algerians, then, after the revolution and the recognition of Algerian independence, in a flood of almost a million refugee *colons*, afraid or unwilling to live under Algerian rule. But France also attracted immigrants from Italy, Spain, and Portugal, who were prepared to slip in illegally if necessary to have a chance at French minimum wages and shanty housing—to the point where a well-organized industry developed to smuggle in contraband workers. The countries most dependent on these reinforcements, however, were Switzerland and Luxembourg, where one third of the manual labour came to be foreign. Here what had started as a convenient supplement became a substantial and vital fraction of the work force, posing serious problems of assimilation. Swiss authorities, fearing for the character of the society as a whole, enforced an array of defensive regulations: immigrant workers were prohibited from bringing their families with them; newcomers were confined to the status of temporary residents, with the right to engage only in that occupation for which entry had been granted; and starting in 1964, limitations were imposed on the right of private enterprise to recruit foreign labour.[1]

---

[1] The last of these constraints was imposed at a time when public concern over the threat of ethnic adulteration reached an emotional peak—this, in spite of the fact that the increase in the number of foreign workers had been tapering off. Later that year the Swiss government tried to institute a special convention with Italy liberalizing the regulations concerning the immigration of wives and dependents and shortening the waiting period for permanent residency from ten to five years. The agreement failed

This flow of cheap manpower unquestionably contributed mightily to European expansion. First, under conditions of full employment, each additional pair of hands added to output. Secondly, and more important, quasi-unlimited supplies of cheap labour removed what could have been a most serious constraint on investment. They insured that wages would lag behind prices and that costs would remain competitive in the world market; and this was vital to a continent that had to export to live. Thirdly, these newcomers to the labour force, whether from within or without the society, were relatively mobile and could be hired specifically for jobs in the more rapidly expanding branches. To the extent, moreover, that housing shortages were an impediment to geographical movement, the newcomers were often content with or resigned to less space and comfort than older workers. This was particularly true of the immigrants from poorer lands, who came from hovels at home and were prepared to live in hovels again in order to save as much as possible for the family left behind. The result was a situation reminiscent, in the small, of the industrial slums of the early nineteenth century. The *bidonvilles* were a blot on the landscape and the social conscience; they did, however, facilitate economic expansion by permitting the deferral of outlays for capital-intensive housing and ancillary facilities. (These savings were partially offset, in turn, by the related costs of poverty *cum* segregation: higher disease and crime rates, and social and political alienation.)

To be sure, most of these new industrial workers—again, from within and without the society—lacked the education and skills needed for modern technology. The immigrants were particularly weak in this regard, if only because they generally did not even speak the language of the host country. So one must not think of this increment to the supply of labour as homogeneous and interchangeable with the existing supply. In 1964 there were almost a million jobs open in Germany, but only 45,000 requests for foreign workers.[1]

On the other hand, one of the salient characteristics of modern technology is the division and simplification of complex tasks, so that work that once called for a high degree of skill can be performed by the unskilled. Moreover business enterprise has learned to replace or supplement slow and costly methods of man-to-man apprenticeship by group training programmes, so that raw men, fresh in from the country, can be turned into semiskilled workers in a matter of weeks to months. Some enterprises even prefer such new men to experienced workers on the ground that, while they have more to learn, they have less to unlearn.

to pass the Swiss legislature. Charles P. Kindleberger, *Europe's Postwar Growth: The Role of Labor Supply* (Cambridge, Mass., 1967), pp. 46–7, 193 n. 54.

[1] *Ibid.*, p. 189.

Besides, it takes more than skills to expand production, and one must not underestimate the significance of an increased supply of labour for menial tasks. For one thing, some growth industries need and can use just this kind of personnel: hotels are a good example, of particular importance in a country like Switzerland that relies heavily on tourism for foreign exchange. For another, the assumption by unskilled newcomers of the hardest, least attractive jobs in the economy releases manpower for higher posts. The technically advanced operations of modern industry are not performed in a vacuum. Every highly trained worker is supported by others less trained, both within the manufacturing enterprise and outside it. Someone has to move goods, drive the men to work, clean the mills, the shops and the streets. If Europe had not been able to draw on an abundant supply of raw manual labour, the price of skilled labour would have gone up even faster than it did.

This is the case for a labour interpretation of the postwar boom. It has been argued most cogently and subtly by Professor Kindleberger; but the evidence offered is less than convincing. Thus the correlations among labour supply, mobility, wages, and rates of growth leave much to be desired. Kindleberger himself admits that France and Austria do not fit his model, and some people would add Sweden to the list of deviants.[1]

Yet even if the correlations were perfect, the task would still remain of assessing the nature and importance of the labour factor; after all, correlations in themselves show only connection and not causation, much less the direction of causation. Here Kindleberger gives the cue: excess labour, he says, is permissive rather than initiating; and he adverts on a number of occasions to the importance of demand as an engine of growth.[2] To be sure, there are some instances in which an abundance of cheap labour has served as a prime mover of industrial expansion, in which manpower has attracted capital and enterprise. One thinks, for example, of the German industrialists who have established factories in Ireland. But such cases are exceptional and the results have been less than satisfactory, even when, as in the Italian Mezzogiorno, the state offers substantial incentives to the entrepreneur.

More typical is the record of a country like Germany, for which we have good statistics. Here one can see clearly the way in which the economy succeeded in prolonging the postwar boom by shifting from one source of manpower to another as supply conditions changed. Throughout most of the fifties, the major source of foreign labour was the population of refugees—first those who had fled west during and immediately after the war, who show up in the statistics as decreases in

[1] For a sceptical analysis of the labour thesis, see Postan, *Economic History*, ch. iii.
[2] Kindleberger, *Europe's Postwar Growth*, pp. 14, 154–5.

unemployment; and then expatriates from East Germany. Only at the very end of the decade did the immigration of non-Germans pick up, and then abruptly; and when the largest component of this group, the Italians, dwindled in number because there were jobs enough in home industry, German employers turned to Spain, Greece, and Turkey. In sum, it is industrial development that calls up labour, not the reverse.

Analogous to the stimulus afforded by a peculiarly elastic supply of labour was that provided by an unusually high productivity of capital: both were temporary postwar phenomena, and both made their effects felt on the supply side. On the other hand, the high return to capital was much more a primary stimulus to investment and growth. Here one must begin by distinguishing the recovery of the immediate postwar years from the new growth that began in the early fifties. In the former period, a number of European countries inherited a capital plant that had been much damaged by war and crippled by gaps in the chain of production and transport, but that, for this very reason, could often be restored to full operation by a relatively small investment in repairs and replacement. Germany is the best example of this, and indeed it has been argued that it is precisely this latent capacity that accounts for the prodigious gains she made after 1947. Thus the researches of the Institut für Wirtschaftsforschung show that Germany was investing at an extraordinary rate between 1940 and mid-1945—3·36 billion DM (at 1950 prices) per year, as against 0·89 billion from 1935 to 1939 and 1·86 from 1924 through 1929; so that, in spite of extensive bombing and postwar dismantling, fixed assets in industry in 1946 were about equal to those of 1939. Yet output in 1946 was less than a third of what it had been in 1939.[1]

Even after recovery was more or less complete, however, there was a reason why the latent productivity of capital should still be very high. This was the technological lag—already serious before the war but much aggravated, particularly in 'nonessential' industries, by the years of emergency and dislocation. The weakness lay not in the area of knowledge—on the contrary—or even necessarily in best practice, but in average practice. Much of Europe's capital plant was old and tired, while all kinds of far more efficient techniques and equipment lay at her disposal; hence rates of saving and investment without precedent.[2] Here one word of caution is required: it should not be inferred from the above analysis that this technological gap was the sole source of these high returns. Obviously, those factors already discussed—

[1] Postan, *Economic History*, pp. 23–4.

[2] Cf. Simon Kuznets, 'Quantitative Aspects of the Economic Growth of Nations: Long-Term Trends in Capital Formation Proportions', *Economic Development and Cultural Change*, IX, no. 4, part II (July 1961), pp. 10–11.

strong demand and cheap labour—contributed mightily to this result. The point is simply that because of exogenous interruption of the normal process of technological diffusion, the marginal gain in efficiency and quality afforded by new techniques was exceptionally large—larger perhaps than at any time since the early nineteenth century. With time, the gap tended to narrow; and it is this that may account for what seems to be a tendency for incremental capital-output ratios to rise in the course of the fifties.

One more development that is often cited as contributing to the buoyancy of the postwar expansion is the trend toward economic co-operation and integration. Once again we have a marked contrast with the interwar period. Then, as we have seen, the European economies took the legacy of regulations and constraints bequeathed them by the war and, after some well-intentioned moves in the direction of liberalization, reinforced it. The tendency to rugged individualism in matters of international exchange was already marked in the twenties but it was substantially aggravated in the depression, when commercial and monetary policy reduced itself to a *sauve qui peut* and trade languished in a jungle of duties, quotas, barter arrangements, currency and exchange controls, special accounts, bilateral treaties, and similar products of official ingenuity.

The situation was even worse in 1945. For one thing, the bureaucrats of the Second World War were that much more experienced in these matters than their predecessors. For another, European reserves of foreign exchange, especially dollars, had fallen so low that only the most stringent controls and quotas could contain the pent-up demand for imports within manageable proportions. This time, however, the Allied governments, inspired in part by a small but influential group of economists-turned-civil-servants, were determined not to repeat the mistakes of an earlier generation. Beginning in 1943, that is, well before the battle was won, the economic technicians of the Allied powers and interested neutral countries began meeting to frame the rules and devise the institutions of a free international economy. The most important of these early, but not premature, consultations was the Bretton Woods conference of July 1944, which proposed the creation of what became the International Monetary Fund and the International Bank for Reconstruction and Development, worked out explicit arrangements for the stabilization of exchange rates and a rapid return to monetary convertibility, and offered recommendations for the reduction of trade barriers and the maintenance of a high level of employment. (The linking of international economic stability to national levels of employment was in itself a policy innovation and a measure of the influence of the newer economic doctrine.)

Once the war was won, efforts toward international co-operation and integration multiplied. The Americans kept pushing in this direction, partly because they feared that they would be the principal victims of a return to autarky, partly because they were convinced that this was the only way to put Europe back on its own feet. And there was a whole school of internationalist Europeans, led by men like Jean Monnet, which sought to achieve economic integration not only for itself, but as a means to political unification and a guarantee of peace. (The chain of reasoning is very similar to that offered by Cobden and the other advocates of free trade in the mid-nineteenth century.)

These efforts bore fruit in a wide variety of international organizations and agreements, too numerous to list and describe here. The most important, however, should be noted in passing. First there was the Organization for European Economic Co-operation, created in April 1948 at American behest to serve as an international clearing house for Marshall Plan aid.[1] Over and beyond this instrumental role, however, the OEEC was conceived by the Americans and their European collaborators as a school for economic expansion and independence. To this end, the Council of the Organization called for the gradual elimination of trade quotas (as opposed to tariffs), beginning with an initial liberation of 50 per cent of imports in 1949 and aiming at 75 per cent by February of 1951, 90 per cent by October of 1955. Most members met these deadlines. The major exception was France, which resorted repeatedly to the clauses of 'derogation', on the ground that its commercial deficit left it no choice, while profiting from its partners' more liberal policies. The French were not able to attain the 75 per cent level until 1955, and not until December 1958, when they devalued the franc to bring its exchange rate into closer accord with its purchasing power, were they ready to align their commercial regime with that of the other members of the Organization. Overall, the proportion of effective liberalization within the OEEC rose from 56 per cent in 1950 to 65 in 1951, 84 in 1955, 91 in 1960, and 94 in 1961. By comparison the lifting of restrictions on dollar purchases was necessarily slower, although the discrepancy narrowed rapidly as the European economies passed from convalescence to growth: from 11 per cent in 1953, the proportion of quota-free imports from the dollar area rose to 44 per cent in September 1954, 54 per cent in early 1956, 89 per cent in May 1961.[2]

---

[1] Membership consisted originally of the sixteen European recipients of Marshall Plan aid, with West Germany and Spain joining later. In 1960 the United States, Canada, and Japan joined the group, and the name was changed to the Organization for Economic Co-operation and Development (OECD).

[2] Edward F. Denison, *Why Growth Rates Differ: Postwar Experience in Nine Western Countries* (Washington, D.C., 1967), p. 259.

A major factor in the success of this campaign for the progressive liberalization of international trade was the European Payments Union (1950), a clearing house for financial claims between the member countries that made it possible to carry debtor nations over periods of difficulty without forcing them to apply for loans or resort to discriminatory bilateral agreements. When it was liquidated in 1958, the largest debit to be settled was $1·6 billion, and balances cleared over the eight years of its existence had totalled $46·4 billion. By that time, European gold and dollar reserves were up to $20 billion, and convertibility could be instituted without imperilling the course of economic expansion.

Almost contemporary with EPU was the European Coal and Steel Community, first proposed in May 1950 by Robert Schumann, then French Minister of Foreign Affairs. The aim here was primarily political —to bring German heavy industry into an international organization controlling all western European coal and steel production and thereby block any move to economic nationalism and renewed militarism. The means proposed were drastic: the creation of a supranational High Authority with effectively sovereign powers over public and private enterprises in the member nations; and it was this condition that led the British to refuse the opportunity to join. Looking back from the perspective of the Fifth Republic, this contrast of British isolationism and French internationalism seems strange. Yet destinies were then in different hands; the memory of the war was still fresh; and Britain misread completely the needs and opportunities of the postwar economy. Her face was resolutely turned backwards; her efforts, directed towards the restoration of the *status quo ante*: the primacy of the pound sterling, the special commercial ties of the Empire and Commonwealth, the protection of British workers from painful competition. The record of British negotiations in the forties and fifties is a litany of timorous clichés covering the rejection of promising but hazardous opportunities. This is the sin of anachronism—for a nation, there is none more deadly—and the penance is far more painful than the options originally rejected.

The guiding principle for the Community was the establishment of a single European market for coal and steel—no more tariffs or quotas, no discrimination on prices or freight charges, no special privileges or subsidies. To this end, the agreement called for an end to cartel arrangements in restraint of trade, substituting in effect the one gigantic cartel of the Community itself. Unlike private cartels, however, this one aimed, not at maintaining the status quo and preserving the members from the pains of competition, but at expanding and rationalizing the industry. This required the closing of marginally inefficient enterprises and a substantial re-allocation of resources—measures necessarily painful to those persons and countries adversely affected. The Belgian coal industry, for example, was no longer competitive; neither were the iron and steel works of central France. Eventually even those branches and areas that seemed most strongly placed—the coal mines of the Ruhr, the iron mines and smelting plants of Lorraine—would be similarly threatened.

To deal with these problems without offending the governments concerned was not an easy task. Yet somehow the Community had to come to terms with political reality, for its supranational status would be meaningless without the co-operation of the member states. The answer was found in a tactic of gentle expediency today for the sake of economic principle tomorrow. Thus the French government was temporarily permitted to maintain various subsidies designed to facilitate competition with Germany, on condition that it co-operate in closing the high-cost mines of the Centre. The Community offered similar concessions to Italy and Belgium, always on a terminal basis, while contributing its own resources to the indemnification of those displaced or unemployed by the process of rationalization. By February of 1958, the last of these breaches of free competition disappeared, except for the special status accorded the Belgian coal mines. There the purge required was too big, the political implications too serious for an unconditional application of the principles of economic rationality; in 1960 the Community had to admit temporary defeat and segregate the Belgian mines from the rest of the West European market.

In the years since the establishment of the Community in 1952, the iron and steel industry of its members has flourished. Between 1951 and 1963, output of crude steel more than doubled (35·2 to 72·5 million tons), while labour inputs remained the same.[1] How much of this was due to the intervention of the Community is hard to say. It is worth noting, however, that steel prices in the member countries rose far more slowly than in Great Britain or the United States—a disparity the more impressive because it is at variance with general price trends;[2] and this would seem to be evidence, even if indirect, of an exceptional improvement in the effectiveness of competition and the allocation of resources.

Actually economists are by no means agreed on the consequences of integration, and nowhere is this discord more obvious than in the

[1] Man-hours in the steel industry of the Community remained at about one billion (10^9) per year over the period 1952–62. Richard Mayne, 'Economic Integration in the New Europe: A Statistical Approach,' *Daedalus*, Winter 1964, p. 120.

[2] According to Ambrosi and Tacel, *Histoire économique*, p. 700, the rise was 3 per cent in the Community, as against 16 per cent in Britain and 25 per cent in the United States.

assessments of the fourth, and last, postwar international creation to be discussed here. This was the European Economic Community, or Common Market (Treaty of Rome, signed 25 March 1957, to take effect 1 January 1958), which grew out of the same concerns that had led to the establishment of the Coal and Steel Community and comprised the same membership. Its purpose was to extend to the whole range of commodities the same freedom of trade already secured for coal, ore, and iron and steel.[1] Since the stakes were now far greater and the potential social consequences more serious, the Treaty called for a gradual diminution of customs barriers within the Market, to the point of complete abolition in a minimum of twelve years, a maximum of fifteen. Like the Community, the Common Market was not to permit agreements in restraint of trade, discriminatory practices, or state subsidies; but exceptions were permitted for so-called underdeveloped areas (e.g., the Italian Mezzogiorno), and a safety clause permitted the signatories to institute import quotas in the event of severe crisis or deficit on the balance of payments. Finally an explicit exception was made for agriculture, habituated to a regimen of protection and subvention, hence ill-prepared in most of the member countries to stand up to competition; besides, the farmers had a lot of votes.[2]

In the very first years of the Common Market, customs duties were reduced almost twice as fast as had been provided by the Treaty of Rome. By 1 January 1961, tariffs on manufactures were down 30 per cent

[1] It should be noted that this was not the first attempt to promote trade by the reduction of import duties. Organized efforts along these lines go back to establishment in 1947 of the worldwide General Agreement on Tariffs and Trade (GATT), under whose auspices a series of reductions were negotiated in 1947–9 and 1951. But for Europe at least, these were of minor significance so long as quotas constituted the critical barrier. By 1956–7, however, the volume of trade jumped sharply when Germany cut tariffs on industrial products by more than half. Denison, *Why Growth Rates Differ*, p. 259.

[2] The United Kingdom had the opportunity to join the European Economic Community at the time of its creation but looked upon the proposed arrangements as incompatible with her responsibilities to the Commonwealth and her freedom of political action. She also clearly underestimated the economic significance of the projected union. Later, in 1958, she proposed a wider free trade area for industrial products, but when this suggestion encountered French opposition, she joined in May 1960 with the Scandinavian countries, Austria, Switzerland, and Portugal in a peripheral European Free Trade Assn. (EFTA), which made no provision for the creation of supranational advisory bodies like those of the Common Market and left its members free to determine their own tariff policies toward the outside world. It would seem that the founders of EFTA looked upon it as a transitional organization —a stepping stone to a union with the EEC. But here political considerations—in particular, France's unwillingness to alter the balance of power within the Common Market—have proved to be overriding, and the split between the two groups has turned out to be more durable than anyone expected.

(instead of 15 per cent) below their 1957 levels; one year later they were cut another 10 per cent, and by that time all quotas had disappeared.[1] This liberalization—on top of that of the preceding decade—presumably promoted a more rational allocation of resources within the Community and, with that, higher output per head. It did this, in principle, in one or both of two ways: first, by inducing each country to specialize in those branches of production where it was comparatively advantaged; and secondly, by fostering within each country the elimination of marginally inefficient enterprises and concentrating production in those units large enough to adopt the latest techniques and realize economies of scale.

I say 'presumably' and 'in principle' because a number of economists have called into question the alleged contribution of freer trade to European growth. For one thing, the statistical data are at best ambiguous. Take the growth figures: the members of the Common Market prospered very unequally during the years following its establishment. At the extremes, Italy's gross national product rose 58 per cent in the quinquennium 1958–63; Luxembourg's and Belgium's, only about 15 per cent. Germany and the Netherlands, with 35 and 34 per cent respectively, and France with 29 per cent came in between. By contrast a country like Austria was able to increase its industrial output by some 70 per cent from 1953 to 1960, outside the framework of an international trading community. Trade is obviously not the be-all and end-all of economic growth.[2] In the same way, an attempt to calculate the apparent impact of the relaxation of commercial restrictions shows negligible gains to national income—on the order of less than 0·2 per cent per year.[3]

For another thing, the theoretical arguments for free trade, however plausible in general, do not seem to some analysts to be applicable to the European context. Take the classical Smithian thesis on the size of the market and specialization: the question has been raised whether the human resources and material endowments of the various European countries are in fact sufficiently different to give much opportunity for an international division of labour. This position received considerable

---

[1] *10ᵉ rapport général de la C.E.E.*, Avril 1967, provisional edition. I owe this information to Prof. Max Peyrard.

[2] Mayne, *Economic Integration*, p. 119. Walter Hallstein, the chairman of the Council of the Common Market, had this to say about these data: 'It may be objected that these growth figures are no index of the success of the Common Market; but my reply would be that they certainly show that it has not failed.'

[3] Denison, *Why Growth Rates Differ*, pp. 260–2. For a survey of similar efforts to calculate the 'welfare loss' resulting from misallocation of resources due to restraint of trade, see Harvey Leibenstein, 'Allocative Efficiency vs. "X-Efficiency"', *Amer. Econ. Rev.*, LVI (June 1966), 392–5.

attention at the time when Britain was debating the advantage of joining the Common Market, when it was music to the ears of the isola-
tionists of the extreme right and the extreme left. (Economics, which
prides itself on being the most rigorous—the 'hardest'—of the social
sciences, nevertheless bears the taint of the whole field: that truth is as
much a function of sympathy as of evidence.)

As for what we may call the cathartic effect of the Common Market,
much depends on one's view of the *status quo ante*. Those who feel
that European economic development has long been impeded by agreements in restraint of trade and artificial protection for small, inefficient
producers are inclined to give heavy weight to the effect of international
competition. Others, like Angus Maddison, feel that the noncompeti-
tive predilections of European business before liberalization have been
much exaggerated. In particular, they are not prepared to credit the
argument that the European businessman is somehow less competitive
than, say, his American counterpart; that he prefers his own little comfortable niche to the perils of commercial warfare; or, if he is a strong
producer, that he is only too happy to let his weaker competitors survive while he enjoys a larger profit margin.[1] Maddison also argues that
'in spite of barriers, intra-European trade has always been very large'
(p. 71), implying that it was sufficient to perform the competifacient
functions assigned it by classical theory. To this, other economists would
reply that market competition is never so effective in fact as it is in
theory; that it is never strong enough to compel all enterprises to purchase and use all inputs efficiently; and therefore, that there is between
actual and optimum practice a substantial gap that can and will contract
under additional pressure. The potential gains here, notes Harvey
Leibenstein, are of an entirely different order from those imputed to
improvements in the allocation of resources. Instead of fractions of
1 per cent, we are talking—on the level of the individual enterprise—
of labour and capital savings of between 10 and 50 per cent, sometimes
much more. At least these are the gains achieved in both advanced and
less developed countries by firms that have significantly reordered their
production process (without addition of labour or capital) or offered
new incentives to their employees. What these performances imply for
an economy as a whole is not entirely clear. These firms, for example,
may be exceptional; the average enterprise might do much less well,
possibly because it had less slack to take up, possibly because it lacked
the knowledge and drive to respond effectively to market pressure.
Yet it stands to reason that some would react vigorously; and Leiben-

[1] Cf. Maddison, *Economic Growth in the West* (New York, 1964), pp. 71–3. Maddison is apparently prepared to make an exception for France, 'which in this, as in other
respects, is *sui generis*' (p. 73).

stein has argued that it is precisely the gains achieved by this kind of response that constitute a good part of the so-called 'residual'—that part of the growth of national product that cannot be accounted for by inputs of land, labour, and capital. Since this residual amounts to some 50 to 80 per cent of the recorded growth of advanced industrial nations, we may well have here a far more important element of expansion than is conveyed by the conventional measures of the impact of freer trade. After all, intra-European exchanges more than tripled from 1950 to 1961, rising from 41 to 53 per cent of a rapidly growing world total. It is hard to believe that a change of this magnitude did not add considerably to the effectiveness of competition—as French manufacturers of refrigerators, cameras, and television sets will testify.

One way in which it made this contribution is presumably by enabling the better located, more efficient enterprises to take advantage of previously unavailable economies of scale. This is a commonplace of economic theory, and Europe, divided as it is among more than a dozen small and middling nations, would seem to furnish an abundance of examples of the cost of market fragmentation. Some economists, to be sure, have expressed doubts in this regard, pointing out that the small countries of Europe have always been able to produce certain articles competitively far in excess of their own needs; and this would indicate that opportunities for specialization have not been lacking. Yet aside from the fact that what may be true of some articles need not be true of others, such an observation is not really to the point. The question is not whether specialization and economies of scale were impossible before the liberalization of the fifties, but whether new economies became possible thereafter. In this connection, one must not forget that the technological determinants of economies of scale are always changing. (Here, as much as anywhere, the hazards of contemporary history are evident.) Postan notes that the first polymer plant built by Imperial Chemical Industries after the War was built every bit as large as the economies of production required. Its successor plant, erected in the fifties, was eight times as big; while its grandchild will be twice as big again. For a polymer plant of this scale, the British market, or even the sterling market, is simply not enough.[1]

One thing almost everyone is prepared to agree on is the contribution of increased trade (extra-European as well as intra-European) to demand and, indirectly, to productivity. Here the contrast with the interwar period, or even the halcyon days before 1914, is too sharp to be ignored: there was clearly a major shift in the conditions of international trade sometime around the late forties.

[2] *Economic History*, p. 110.

Table 57. *Volume of Exports, 1890–1960:*
Compound Annual Rates of Growth (in percentages)

	1890–1913	1913–50	1950–60
Belgium	3·5	0·2	7·7
France	2·8	1·1	7·2
Germany	5·1	−2·5	15·8
Italy	—	1·4	11·8
Netherlands	4·6	1·2	10·0
Sweden	3·8[a]	1·9	5·5
Switzerland	—	0·3	7·8[b]
United Kingdom	2·1	0·2	1·9
Western Europe	3·2	0·1	7·0
Canada	6·5	3·3	3·8
United States	3·8	2·3	5·0
World	3·5	1·3	6·4

[a] 1893–1913.   [b] 1950–9.

SOURCE: A. Maddison, *Economic Growth in the West*, p. 166.

This increase in foreign sales made itself felt in several ways. First, it raised personal incomes and the level of demand at home, while paying for the imports drawn by this higher purchasing power. It thereby shielded national currencies from what could have been a disastrous drain. Britain, for example, would certainly have been spared her balance-of-payments crises, had her exports grown faster; she would also have been spared the deflationary responses to these crises, which have acted as so many braking actions on the economy. Secondly, because trade provided security against deflationary shocks of external origin, it contributed to the inculcation of a new code of co-operative international behaviour and dulled the retaliatory instinct nourished over the preceding two or three generations. Otherwise, how to account for the patience of other countries for France's recourse to commercial restrictions long after everyone else had abandoned them? Or for her go-it-alone behaviour in the councils of the Common Market? Finally, increased trade encouraged a shift of resources to the exporting industries—electronics, optics, chemicals, engineering—and these were the most dynamic branches of the economy.[1]

By this time, the reader who has tried conscientiously to follow the pros and cons of the argument may be ready to give up the struggle. How, indeed, is one to balance macrostatistical calculations that attri-

[1] For general discussions of the economic implications of integration, see especially Tibor Scitovsky, *Economic Theory and Western European Integration* (Stanford, 1958); and Bela Balassa, *Trade Liberalization among Industrial Countries: Objectives and Alternatives* (New York, 1967).

bute only a slight effect to freer trade against what could easily be a myriad of individual examples of keener competition and lower prices? How is one to choose between cogent arguments that start from different assumptions about the *status quo ante*? Most important, how is one to assess the correlation between increasing trade on the one hand and growing product on the other? One could as easily argue, for example, that it was the general economic expansion that made possible the relaxation of commercial restrictions and generated a larger volume of exchange, rather than the reverse; and clearly, we are dealing at the very least with something that is effect as well as cause. (Compare the generalization of the gold standard and the reduction of tariff barriers in the mid-nineteenth century.) The problem is complicated by the obvious complexity of the forces shaping European growth: how can one segregate trade from other stimuli?

One solution is to fall back on faith. Richard Mayne, an economist on the staff of Jean Monnet, wrote in 1964:[1]

The European Community...is still young. Economists will probably always differ as to how much the integration of Europe's economies can be proved to have accelerated these processes of modernization. For my own part, I believe that its true impact is likely to increase. Ultimately, however, it must always remain unmeasurable, because it is psychological and political, not statistical. But for 'unmeasurable' I personally prefer to read 'immeasurable.' Nicholas of Cusa [who said 'knowledge is always measurement'] was not always right.

★ ★ ★ ★ ★ ★

As the preceding discussion makes clear, history typically abhors simple cause and effect. Certainly in the economic sphere, significant changes are almost invariably the resultant of a mutually sustaining conjuncture of factors, so most variables are at once both cause *and* effect, independent and dependent. This is equally true of the sources of expansion that remain to be considered: those institutional and material arrangements on the one hand and those human elements on the other that generate and apply technological change. Yet here we come as close as anywhere to the economist's will-o'-the-wisp: the autonomous first cause or prime mover. Ironically, there was a time, not very long ago, when few economists would concede so much importance to technology, worker skills, management, and entrepreneurship. Only when the data of national accounts, fitted to various production functions, showed that the conventional inputs could account for only a fraction of economic growth, was the old indifference to what had been

---

[1] *Economic Integration*, p. 129.

defined as extraneous considerations shaken. Even so, many have found the new revelation hard to accept, partly for fear of the unknown, partly because these elements are not easy to apprehend by the traditional techniques of analysis or to integrate into the corpus of established theory. The best of the economists, however, have moved eagerly into this new area of inquiry, trying to domesticate (I use the word advisedly) for purposes of systematic analysis a whole array of recalcitrant qualitative factors, ranging from the educational and scientific sources of new knowledge, through the translation of this knowledge into economic applications, to the quality of the actors involved (what is sometimes described as 'human capital') and the organizational arrangements and entrepreneurial decisions that govern their actions.

In the postwar world, the most prominent of these elements has been the cognitive one—the growth of scientific knowledge and its translation into a stunning array of new products and techniques. Any of us can draw up a list of these innovations, many of which have changed in the space of a generation from curiosities to staples of twentieth-century life and work—from the miniature portable radio that the hypnotized teenager holds to his ear as he walks along the street, to the tape recorder of the music lover or anthropologist, to the huge multi-million-dollar computers of I.B.M.'s 360 series. Television was one of the wonders of the New York World's Fair of 1939; and even after the War, the first sets were so costly and few, that to buy one was to expose oneself to a daily invasion of friends and neighbours. Today large sets with screens ten times as large as those of twenty years ago cost one third as much, and even the poor—especially the poor—look upon television as a necessity rather than a luxury.

Like the electronic industry, the chemical manufacture is a large and consistently creative family—too large and too creative to do justice to in a few paragraphs. The best known innovations here lie in two areas: the invention of new materials for the production of consumers' goods—artificial fibres, leather substitutes, plastics, protective coatings (silicones), and the like; and new drugs—the antibiotics, antihistamines, tranquillizers, above all perhaps, the Pill. Here again, one had a foretaste of things to come in the interwar years: nylon, the first all-synthetic fibre and still one of the greatest, was invented in 1935 and entered commercial production in 1939, and the sulfonamides, discovered in 1935, were being used clinically the following year.[1] But the growth of these

---

[1] Until then, the known array of antibacterial agents had proved too toxic for internal use. Two isolated exceptions were Ehrlich's use of salvarsan against syphilis (although the spirochete of syphilis is not a true bacterium); and the use of atabrine in the treatment of malaria from 1930 (again, the malarial parasite is not a bacterium, but a protozoön).

branches of chemistry into major industries is postwar, with some products (magnetic tapes, penicillin) getting their initial push from the War itself.

These were the areas of spectacular advance. It would be a mistake, however, to assume that other branches of the chemical industry have lagged or made a lesser contribution to postwar growth. The field of heavy chemicals, for example, long based essentially on the transformation and production of inorganic materials (salts, acids, alkalis) has been changed out of recognition by the technology of heavy organics.[1] The large and growing family of detergents is the best-known example of innovation in this area. (Again the research and the first commercial applications go back to the interwar period; but the rise of a detergent industry is postwar.) Even more important in its consequences has been the extraction of key inorganic compounds like ammonia from the great organic storehouse—coal, natural gas, petroleum—and their use in the synthesis of more complex substances, both inorganic and organic. It is this technique that has yielded a wide array of fertilizers, pesticides (D.D.T.), and weed killers, which have in turn made possible extraordinary gains in land productivity, sometimes of the order of several hundred times. The social and political significance of this is obvious. The rapid, exponential growth of population is pressing heavily on food supply in much, if not most, of the world; and if these poorer nations succeed in holding off the Malthusian apocalypse until they can effect their demographic transition and adjust their birth rates to the low death rate made possible by modern medicine and hygiene, it will be largely because of these man-made substitutes for land.

Here again postwar gains have their roots in prewar advances. Indeed, one can take the story back to the middle of the last century, when Solvay learned to make alkali with by-product ammonia. He was drawn to his method, the reader will recall, by an accident of parentage: his uncle was the director of a gas works, where ammonia in large quantities was being thrown away as waste. The Solvay process, however, was a spur off the main line of technological development. The main antecedents of today's heavy organics branch are to be found in petroleum refining, which goes back to the rudimentary cracking techniques of the 1850's, and in coal distillation, which, in combination with hydrogenation and polymerization techniques, made possible the synthetic fuel and rubber of the interwar period.

The greatest advances in this field were made in Germany, where petroleum was costly and brown coal cheap; and where economic considerations were strongly reinforced in the thirties by Hitler's military

---

[1] The term 'heavy' is used to connote large volume of output (measured in tons rather than pounds or ounces) and low price per volume.

ambitions and the concomitant campaign for autarky. In 1933 the output of synthetic fuels and oils from German raw materials was already 0·83 million tons; by 1938 it had tripled, to 2·7 million tons. And while our figures for the production of *Buna* (synthetic rubber) are less reliable, one source of early 1939 speaks of a target production in that year equal to one quarter or one third of total rubber requirements. This would make an output of 33,000 or 50,000 metric tons. By comparison, Britain's prewar effort in this field was extremely modest: one pilot plant for the manufacture of synthetic fuels, with an output in 1938 of about 140,000 tons; and nothing in synthetic rubber.[1]

The fact was that these early *ersatz* materials left something to be desired from the standpoint of both quality and price; so that the more favoured countries were inclined to look at the whole field as essentially experimental, with commercial applications in the distant future. But the war brought shortages to all, especially of rubber, and condescension changed rapidly to interest, the more so as the German synthetics were clearly doing a good job. Then the return of peace made possible the diffusion of German technology in these branches, complementing the progress already made in other countries. The result was a rapid proliferation of products on a wider entrepreneurial and resource base.

These two aspects—the entrepreneurial and material—were closely related and together supplied an important stimulus to technological improvement and the growth of the industry. The older European chemical industries had built their production of heavy synthetics on coal. Now, however, the great international oil companies moved into the market—Shell, British Petroleum, Standard; and by the late 1950's, when petroleum became the cheaper raw material, even a giant like Imperial Chemical Industries was fighting for its life. In the meantime, both the United States and France were making comparable advances in the utilization of natural gas, which took on new importance in Europe with the discovery of a giant Dutch field in 1959 and even larger North Sea deposits shortly after. At the moment, the governments concerned are doing their best to ease this new supply of fuel and raw material into the market gently; and they are the more insistent in their efforts because of their own investments in other fuels. Even so, it is one more stimulus to the proliferation of enterprise in this area, where

[1] On German output, A. R. L. Gurland, 'Technological Trends and Economic Structure under National Socialism', *Studies in Philosophy and Social Science*, IX (1941), 235, nn. 2 and 3; on the British industry, H. Frank Heath and A. L. Hetherington, *Industrial Research and Development in the United Kingdom* (London, 1946), pp. 36–7; Gilbert T. Morgan and David D. Pratt, *British Chemical Industry, Its Rise and Development* (London, 1938), pp. 228–30.

the old boundaries within the chemical industry and between the chemical and other industries are losing their meaning.

Alongside these newer areas of innovation, the older industries have not stood still. Iron and steel technology, which had not seen a major change since the introduction of the Thomas process, was transformed by the use of oxygen for both smelting and refining, the continuous casting of steel, the diffusion of the continuous strip mill. Here too, one can see prodromes before the war: the continuous strip mill, for example, dates in the United States from the twenties and made its first appearance in Europe on the very eve of the War. But its general adoption came after and was closely linked to the growing demand for high-quality thin sheets used in the manufacture of consumers' durables. At the same time, the iron and steel industry profited from advances in outside fields: it would be impossible, for example, to operate the continuous strip mill at speeds of up to sixty miles an hour without automatic quality controls; and indeed, the whole technique of automatic control has become an industry in itself.

One could go on in this way at great length—through optics, air transport, photography (the polaroid camera), xerography, and light metals to nuclear power. The harvest of both product and process innovations is extraordinarily varied and rich. The question is: is this flow of change any faster than that of earlier periods?

A great number of people have argued just that; and some would even say that technological change is getting more rapid all the time. These are not the same assertion, however, and the evidence that supports the one will not necessarily demonstrate the other.

The argument is usually based on two kinds of evidence: data on the sources of technological change; and data on the speed of the change itself. The first takes the form of statistics, of various degrees of precision, on the human and material inputs to scientific and technical knowledge.[1] It has been asserted, for example, that there are more scientists alive today than have lived in all previous generations together. This may be true, although one suspects that the assertion rests on a particular definition of science and scientists. But even if hyperbole, the statement conveys a truth, that the number of such persons has been increasing at an incredibly fast, even exponential rate. Thus Gilfillan has calculated indexes of 'inventive inputs' for the United States during the period 1880–1955, including among other things the number of members of scientific and technical societies, of graduates from engineering schools, and of professional personnel in organized research, and

---

[1] In strict logic, data on inputs would not necessarily prove anything about output. Yet in fact most writers on the subject adduce these, explicitly or implicitly, as evidence of the growing volume and speed of invention and innovation.

finds a 226-fold increase; the curves, on a logarithmic scale, are almost linear.[1] The same, *mutatis mutandis*, is unquestionably true of other advanced countries. By the same token, expenditures on research and development (R & D) have risen sharply everywhere, outstripping in the 1950's even the large gains in national product.[2]

As for the speed of technological change, the evidence usually takes the form of comparisons of the development time of yesterday's inventions and innovations with today's. The steam engine, for example, took more than a century to evolve from the paper sketches of the seventeenth century to Watt's low-pressure condenser device and the more compact high-pressure engines of Trevithick and Evans; whereas nuclear power went in less than a generation from the theoretical equations to commercial stations.

Even the newer industries seem to tell the same story. It was 1884 when Edison patented his 'electrical indicator', a device embodying the so-called Edison effect. The indicator was of no commercial consequence, but it is unmistakably the distant ancestor of the valve or tube, which made its appearance in 1904 with Fleming's diode. It was almost another decade before Arnold and Langmuir brought out the hard valve, or vacuum tube; and one has to wait for 1920 to see quantity production of valves for the general public.[3] By contrast, Bell Telephone announced the invention of the transistor in 1948. The first point-contact transistors were noisy, could not handle high voltages, and found limited applicability; but within a matter of years the introduction of the junction transistor and the substitution of silicon for germanium eliminated these defects and made possible the use of transistors in equipment of high frequency and power. As a result, it was possible to reduce substantially the size of complicated electronic machines (to say nothing of cutting power requirements and heat waste) and use them under conditions that would have been unthinkable in the age of the vacuum tube. The radar installation in a modern aeroplane, for example, would occupy the whole fuselage and more if it had to be built with valves.

Yet this is only the beginning of the story. The effort to squeeze more and more electronic gear into ever smaller packages led by 1958, that is, in a decade, to the development of the integrated circuit, a complete electronic unit placed on a chip of silicon smaller and lighter than a soap flake. The first prototypes had many of the disadvantages of the early transistors: they could not handle high power, and the components within the circuit could not be built to close tolerances. They were also ex-

[1] National Bureau of Economic Research, *The Rate and Direction of Inventive Activity* (Princeton, 1962), pp. 83–4.
[2] See E. G. Mesthene, ed., *Ministers Talk about Science* (OECD., 1965), p. 112.
[3] Maclaurin, *Invention and Innovation*, pp. 46–8, 91.

tremely expensive, selling for $720 each; it was not until 1961 that the unit price fell below $100. Here, however, the same conceptual ingenuity that had devised the integrated circuit found the means to mass-produce it: each circuit was first designed on a large-scale sheet (perhaps three feet square), reduced to a photo negative one five-hundredth the size, and then projected on to photo-sensitive silicone wafers, which could then be tested mechanically. By 1964 Fairchild Camera was selling integrated circuits for as little as $2·55. The effect of less than two decades of extraordinarily rapid innovation may be measured by the experience of one company. A 1952 vacuum-tube model of I.B.M.'s first generation of computers contained about 2,000 components per cubic foot; the new (1967) System/360 model 75, using hybrid microcircuits, has about 30,000 components per cubic foot.[1] Where the former performed about 2,500 multiplications a second, the latter is designed to do about 375,000; and where the cost of doing 100,000 computations on the first-generation machine was $1·38, the cost on the new one will be $3\frac{1}{2}$ cents.[2]

These are, to be sure, particular instances, chosen for their saliency. Yet larger samples, for what they are worth, confirm this thesis of accelerated development. Thus Frank Lynn did a study for the United States Commission on Technology, Automation, and Economic Progress on the rate of maturation of twenty major American innovations of the period 1880–1955; the results show an average span of 37 years from conception to commercialization during the period 1885–1919; 24 years during the post-World War I era; and 14 years since the Second World War. Moreover, by far the greater part of these gains seems to have occurred in the cognitive phase, that is, in the interval between basic discovery and the start of commercial development.[3] Lynn's study is based on the American experience. But there is no reason to believe that European data would yield different results.[4]

[1] Actually the hybrid circuit is not so compact as the monolithic integrated circuit discussed above and represents an obsolescent technology.

[2] On the history of microcircuitry, see the excellent article by Philip Sieckman, 'In Electronics, the Big Stakes Ride on Tiny Chips', *Fortune*, LXXIII (June 1966), 120 *et seq.* On I.B.M., see T. A. Wise, 'I.B.M.'s $5,000,000,000 Gamble', *ibid.*, LXXIV (September 1966), 118 *et seq.*

[3] U.S., National Commission on Technology, Automation, and Economic Progress, *Technology and the American Economy*, vol. 1 (February 1966), pp. 3–4.

[4] Cf. the table of decreasing lead time between discovery and application in Robert Gilpin, *France in the Age of the Scientific State* (Princeton, 1968), p. 24. It should be noted that not all the evidence on this point is so pronounced as that advanced by Lynn. The same Report of the National Commission on Technology etc. cites a study by Edwin Mansfield of the diffusion of twelve major innovations in the period 1890–1958. Mansfield 'found only a slight and unclear tendency for innovations to spread more rapidly than in the past' (*ibid.*, pp. 4–5). But Mansfield's sample

Granted that the rate of technological innovation is faster than ever before, what have been the economic consequences? Can one, in fact, link this cognitive acceleration with the rate of economic growth?

The question is really two. The first concerns the apparent break represented by the higher growth rates of the postwar period. What is there in the course of technological development to account for such a break? The answer would seem to be: little, if anything. To be sure, one has no difficulty enumerating as above an array of new products and processes. But most of these date back to the interwar years, and however much expenditures for research and development have grown since 1945, it is not clear that they have grown significantly faster than in the preceding generation or two. Moreover, in so far as the technological advances of the postwar years rest on a scientific base, it is a chemical and electrical base that goes back a century or more.

One way to reconcile these apparently contradictory data is to postulate that the new science-based technology did indeed shift the long-term rate of economic growth upward, but not in the 1940's. *Rather the break took place, as one would expect, about the time the seminal innovations in science and technology took effect, that is, at the turn of the century.* Seen in this light, the expansion of the years preceding the First World War was in fact the beginning of a trend rather than an intercyclical upswing after the long depression of 1873–96; and it was only the exogenous influence of war and a restless peace, with all the dislocation and mismanagement that they entailed, that dampened the effects of the new technology and thereby concealed it. If this interpretation is correct—and there is much to be said for it—then the so-called 'second industrial revolution' well deserves its name.

A second aspect of the question concerns the postwar period proper. What hard evidence is there of a link during these years between science at one end and economic expansion on the other? The answer is, not much, and that spotty. About the best one can do is point to a correlation between expenditures on R & D and the rates of growth of different industries. Thus American and British data on research expenditures in 1958 and growth of output from 1949 to 1959 show the heaviest spending in aircraft manufacture, telecommunications, precision engineering, and chemicals, all of which were among the fastest-growing branches, and the lowest spending in fields like food processing, textiles, and ferrous metallurgy.[1] The qualitative data are actually more reassuring.

includes none of the science-intensive innovations of the electronics, chemical, and similar industries; and more to the point, he is concerned with the post-cognitive aspect of development, that is, the period from commercial introduction to general adoption.

[1] U.N., Economic Commission for Europe, *Some Factors in Economic Growth in Europe during the 1950s*, ch. v, p. 9. The data leave much to be desired. No figures are

Thus in 1962–64 P.E.P. (Political and Economic Planning) in England did a study of attitudes in industrial management that turned up sharp differences between branches in regard to R & D. In a slow-growing industry like the wool manufacture, one respondent after another lamented the inadequacy of research, both within the industry and among suppliers. Several complained, for example, of the machinery offered; and one man, who had bought some equipment in Italy, offered the following explanation:

We can't get it in England. I always say that we need a new awareness on the part of textile machine manufacture of the need for semi-automation in this industry rather than going on with machines of a design and a principle that have been accepted for the last hundred years or so.

In contrast, the director of an electronics company—a small one at that —spoke of R & D as a way of life:

I would say simply that, of all the money that was available, the first call on every money being spent that one can afford to spend is always in technical development. It is the prime function, as I see it, of an industrial company to spend every possible penny it can afford on technical development.[1]

Even if one accepts, however, the principle that R & D make for increased productivity in given branches, it is not easy to find empirical evidence for the assertion that the increase in R & D accounts for the general expansion of the postwar period. The proposition makes sense *a priori*; but when one attempts to correlate the inputs into R & D with national growth rates, no pattern emerges. The European country that spent the most on R & D in the 1950's was Britain, whereas Germany and France ranked near the bottom; and the only reason France made even the modest showing it did was because of heavy military outlays linked to the creation of a nuclear 'deterrent'—the so-called *force de frappe*. If one deducts such military expenditures from the R & D budgets of the two countries, one finds Britain spending £541 million in 1961–2, as against 1,959 million francs for France in 1961—a ratio of almost four to one.[2]

given for growth of output in the four heavy-spending branches cited, and one is obliged to assume, perhaps not unreasonably, that they did in fact grow faster than the average. Similarly, it is always hazardous to base inferences of this kind on one year's experience, in this case, 1958. Most serious is the choice of a year that falls almost at the end of the period covered: one could easily argue that growth produces R & D, rather than the reverse.

[1] P.E.P., *Thrusters and Sleepers* (London, 1965), pp. 126, 136.

[2] These data are derived from the tables in the above-cited study by the Economic Commission for Europe, *Some Factors in Economic Growth in Europe during the 1950s*, ch. iv, pp. 4–11.

One can easily suggest, of course, a number of reasons why there is this discrepancy between cognitive inputs and economic outputs. For one thing, the fruits of advancing science and technology tend rapidly to become common property. Scientists as a group are opposed to secrecy; on the contrary, they are avid for publication, which is the key to fame and immortality, and their findings now appear in over one hundred thousand professional journals. These in turn are indexed, excerpted, summarized, and translated, so that no serious researcher need be ignorant of work done in other countries and languages. As for technical applications, these are, to be sure, often patented or kept secret; but patents can usually be rented, especially by one country from another, and it is not easy to keep a product or process secret once it has been marketed. As a result, an industry or economy can flourish on the strength of outside research. The Japanese furnish the classical example of profitable imitation, but Germany and France in the post-war period show similar deficits in their technology accounts. The principal exporter of knowledge and techniques has been the United States, which took in some $175 million in royalties from the nations of western Europe in the period 1957–61, while paying out about $41 million. From the standpoint of the recipient, this dependency, if economically convenient, has not always been comfortable politically, and the French in particular have tended to view it as an impairment of national sovereignty.[1]

Secondly, one must not forget that much research expenditure contributes only indirectly to economic growth, and then marginally. Not everyone would go so far as Denison, who argues that, 'aside from any slight indirect effect on the quantity or quality of labour input', the growth rate would have been the same whether or not antibiotics had been developed.[2] It is, however, clear that a large share of outlays on R & D has been devoted to armament, moon races, and similar projects, which, however justifiable on political or spiritual grounds (Man must go to the moon because, like Everest, it is there), do little if anything for

[1] They have found this dependency particularly vexatious in a field like computer technology, which has obvious military implications. Here their national pride has been wounded twice: first by the difficulties of the indigenous computer firm, Bull, which had to be refloated by the American firm, General Electric; and secondly, by the refusal of the American government to allow I.B.M. to sell France two of the large new Series 360 computers for use in military nuclear research. Hence the Plan Calcul (Operation *Computer*) and the recent creation of a state-subsidized Compagnie Internationale d'Informatique. *New York Times*, 14 April, 1967, p. 55. On this whole question, the best study is Gilpin, *France in the Age of the Scientific State*.

On the flow of international technical knowledge, see OECD, *Science, Economic Growth, and Public Policy* (February 1964).
[2] Denison, *Why Growth Rates Differ*, p. 288.

economic development that more prosaic investments could not do better. All of these programmes yield a certain amount of technological 'fall-out', as their corporate beneficiaries are wont to emphasize. Yet they yield even more fall-out of a different kind—in the sense of wasted resources and opportunities.

A third, and equally important, explanation for the discrepancy lies in the character of the economic process. The effective utilization of scientific and technical knowledge requires a whole sequence of decisions and actions in the world of production and distribution. Pioneering entrepreneurs and managers must be prepared to risk money on the translation of ideas into commercially feasible techniques and then invest in those techniques; while others must be incited by the prospect of gain, or compelled by fear of loss, to follow suit. The course of this adoption and diffusion, moreover, will depend considerably on the quality of performance of all concerned—management, technical staff, labour force—and the means and tastes of the consumer. As a result, scientific creativity is by no means an assurance of growth and economic success: there are too many slips between the idea and the profits.

The experience of Imperial Chemical Industries, the world's second-largest chemical company, is a case in point. Here was a firm run in a way that one would have thought admirably suited to the needs of a scientific age: the top management consisted largely of scientists, and the company spent generously on research. As a result, I.C.I. was always in the forefront of chemical technology, with notable achievements in inorganics (synthesis of ammonia) and in plastics and artificial fibres (methyl methacrylate [introduced in the United States as lucite], polyvinyl acetate, polyethylene, terylene [invented by Calico Printers' Association, which I.C.I. acquired in 1947]); and I.C.I.'s patent and process agreement with Du Pont, concluded in 1929, was a highly profitable two-way street.[1]

Yet I.C.I. had been born of a desire for security from competition and had rested its growth on the principle of restraint of trade. It was founded in 1926 by an amalgamation of four major manufacturers of explosives, alkalis, and dye-stuffs, who saw in combination a way of stabilizing the market and meeting the challenge of such big foreign rivals as I.G. Farben and Du Pont. (The reader will recall that this was the procedure resorted to by the moribund British Leblanc soda industry in an effort to stave off its demise.) One of the first things I.C.I.'s management did was join with Farben, Solvay, Du Pont, and

[1] Cf. Willard F. Mueller, 'The Origins of the Basic Inventions Underlying Du Pont's Major Product and Process Innovations', in National Bureau of Economic Research, *The Rate and Direction of Inventive Activity*, pp. 323–46.

others to carve the world into spheres of influence, pool patents, combine forces in new markets, and generally keep the industry on an even keel. As one officer of I.C.I. put it: 'We were in every cartel going.'

All of this worked well enough in the Malthusian climate of the thirties or in the guaranteed wartime market; but I.C.I. began running into trouble in the fifties, when the American courts annulled the partnership with Du Pont and changing technology brought new, giant competitors into the industry. Now the entrepreneurial weaknesses of management were a serious handicap: the scientists in charge were strong on research, but weak on organization and marketing; in the words of one officer: 'We had scientists running the company who happened, secondarily, to be directors.' Even research, which was generously financed, suffered from lack of co-ordination and purpose. As the cost curves of coal and petroleum crossed, the company reacted much too slowly, so that by 1960 its competitive position was seriously eroded. Indeed by 1960, writes one reporter, 'nothing short of full-scale industrial revolution...could have saved I.C.I.—new leadership, new plants, new markets, but most of all new vision.'[1] In subsequent years, the company found all of these, moved aggressively into petrochemicals, enlarged considerably the integrated complexes at Wilton and Billingham on the river Tees, built one of the world's most modern polyethylene and artificial fibre plants in Rotterdam to penetrate the Common Market, and put some of its money into prospecting the North Sea gas field. All of this has called for heavy investments—about two billion dollars from 1964 through 1967—but it has given I.C.I. a much stronger competitive position.[2]

That is growth: a marriage of knowledge and action. It is not something produced by impersonal forces of supply and demand, or something that follows automatically from new knowledge and ideas; and economists who resort to mechanisms like 'the general momentum of the economy' to explain differences in entrepreneurial behaviour are like the poor playwright who calls in a *deus ex machina* to resolve a complicated plot.

Yet laying down a principle of this kind is one thing; giving it explanatory content is another. Can one, for example, link the pattern and course of economic growth in the postwar period to the quality of entrepreneurial performance?

[1] Murray J. Gart, 'The British Company that Found a Way Out', *Fortune*, LXXIV (August 1966), 104. This discussion is based largely on the Gart article.
[2] Whether this investment will pay off in increasing profits remains to be seen. The chemical industry is caught at the moment on a treadmill of increasing scale: each unit must grow fast if it is to meet its competitors' prices; and aggregate capacity seems for the while to have outstripped demand.

Here we shall follow the same procedure already used in the analysis of the cognitive factor; and we shall encounter some of the same difficulties. There, the reader will recall, we found a fairly good correlation between expenditures on R & D and growth rates by branch of production; and the same link would seem to exist between entrepreneurial attitudes and performance by branch or firm. There, however, as with all correlations, one could not take cause-and-effect for granted; and the same problem arises here.

Perhaps the most extensive study of entrepreneurial attitudes for any European country is the above-cited inquiry by P.E.P., which examined forty-seven firms in a representative sample of industries—wool textiles, machine tools, shipbuilding, electronics, domestic appliances, and earthmoving equipment. Personal interviews with company officers provided a basis for a classification of management into three groups: the 'thrusters', who were oriented to change and growth, disrespectful of the traditional rules of the game, open-minded in matters of hiring and promotion, sensitive to objective criteria of performance, and so on; the 'sleepers', who were not 'growth-conscious', preferred not to 'rock the boat', 'did not make use of modern techniques of cost accounting, would not hire good men away from competitors, were indifferent to R & D, and so on'; and those who fell somewhere in between the ideal types. The results were then compared with the financial performance of the companies surveyed, in so far as it could be ascertained, and showed not only a good correlation between attitudes and record by industrial branch, but what is more to the point perhaps, between attitudes and the record of companies within the same branch. Thus the most thrusting branch was electronics; and shipbuilding, the least; and within each of the industries, the thrusting firms generally had the best record of growth of capital and the highest earnings on their capital.

Now it is not hard to find fault with this kind of inquiry: the attitudes of the respondents constitute 'soft' data by comparison with the 'hard' figures on capital and earnings; and even the 'hard' numbers, for all their appearance of homogeneity, are not necessarily comparable. Capital may have a distinct meaning for economic theory; but it is a protean concept for entrepreneurs and bookkeepers, and depending on financing and accounting procedures, the same company could show very different rates of growth or return. Even so, the correlation found by the survey is unambiguous and probably reliable, the more so as it is supported by similar inquiries in other contexts.

The import of the correlation is less clear. One might well argue that it is growing, profitable industries and companies that produce thrusting management, rather than the reverse; this is Professor Habakkuk's position, for example, in his comparison of British and German industrial performance in the late nineteenth century,[1] and Mr Maddison's in his study of postwar economic growth. Yet it is here that the variation of performance within a given branch would seem to be relevant: if growth, that is, demand, were the decisive and autonomous determinant, one would expect greater uniformity of entrepreneurial attitudes within a given industry. Moreover, in terms of the criteria used by P.E.P., that is, growth of book capital and rate of earnings on book capital, the most conservative firms within an industry might well be expected to show the best performance, since these are the ones that tend to nurse equipment as long as possible, write down assets rapidly, and accumulate reserves rather than distribute profits.[2] Given this bias, the superior results of the 'thrusting' firms are the more impressive. One thing, at least, is clear: enterprises perform differently under the same conditions of demand and technological opportunity. It is reasonable to attribute part of this variation to the quality of entrepreneurship and management.

The link becomes more problematical, however, when we move from interfirm and interbranch to international comparisons. To what extent, for example, can one account for Germany's 'economic miracle' by the relative superiority of German management; or Britain's lag, by the shortcomings of British entrepreneurship?

One cannot give a simple answer to this kind of question. National differences in entrepreneurship seem to be real enough. One finds for example, in the structure and behaviour of business firms, a significant contrast between Britain and France during the period of the Industrial Revolution; or among Britain, France, and Germany in the late nineteenth century. An observer like David Granick concludes, on the basis of studies of both socialist and capitalist business practice and of extensive personal contact with managerial personnel, that 'if the basic criterion [of entrepreneurship] is that of risk-taking, then both the American businessman and the Soviet industrial manager are "entrepreneurs" in a sense quite foreign to the British, the French, and the Belgian.' He then goes on to specify the difference:

In all three of the above West European countries...the main tendency in business is to play the game for safety. Both in England and France I have met top managers who were highly annoyed at the fact that the stock prices of their companies had skyrocketed. Such public recognition of their own personal managerial success, and confidence in it for the future, was regarded

[1] See the discussion above, pp. 355–7.
[2] On the other hand, the conservative firm would also not be likely to borrow and thereby expand faster than its own resources would permit; and this lack of leverage would tend to lower the rate of return on book capital.

principally as a major threat rather than as a profitable compliment. Due to the higher stock market prices, management would be forced to distribute higher dividends—and this would likely lead to pressure toward bolder market and investment strategies. This future pressure was resented in advance not because it would lead to more work for the top managers—in both my interview cases, the men involved appeared to be hard workers—but because it would push them toward taking risks. Having talked at length with these top policy makers, I felt considerable confidence in their ability to resist such pressure.[1]

As for the one major European industrial power not included in the above comparison, Granick offers the following anecdote:

Several years ago in Boston, an American executive bemoaned his difficulties in doing business in Europe. The attitudes of European businessmen were utterly foreign to his stateside experience.

Only Germany made him feel at home. When he made short trips to Europe to talk with suppliers, Germany was the one nation where he could conduct business on Saturday afternoon and Sunday. In the other countries, top managers were more interested in their weekend than in their product.

To an American, the present-day German management world often appears positively un-European.[2]

Anecdote is not argument. To be sure, Granick buttresses his initial illustration with an explicit analysis of those aspects of German business enterprise that are conducive to effective performance and rapid growth. Yet he himself admits that 'with much the same antipathy toward risk in Britain, Belgium, and France, radically different patterns of industrial growth have resulted' (pp. 127 f.); and he calls particular attention to the case of France, 'which has done almost as well as Germany during the 1950's, although with a completely different approach to entrepreneurship and to management generally' (p. 174).

The trouble is that entrepreneurship is a difficult factor to specify and assess. Its characteristics do not lend themselves to quantification (hence the economist's almost instinctive distaste for the whole subject); and they are so overlaid by other considerations that it is almost impossible to segregate their influence. It may well be, for example, that the more effective or aggressive entrepreneurial performance of a given economy is a consequence, not of autonomous social values and attitudes, but of the proportion of 'new' to 'old' industries, or of the age of the capital stock.

What is more, entrepreneurship is not homogeneous: the entrepreneurs, that is, the decision-makers of the economy, include not only

[1] David Granick, *The European Executive* (London, 1962), p. 127.
[2] *Ibid.*, p. 157.

the traditional owner-operators and the newer class of pure managers, but a growing number of government bureaucrats and technicians, some of them assigned to the actual direction of productive enterprises, others acting through their influence on economic policy and planning. This mixture varies in space and time and no doubt goes far to explain national and temporal differences in performance. The third group in particular—the state managers and technocrats—has flourished since World War II and must be reckoned with in any attempt to assess the contribution of entrepreneurship to postwar growth.

The interplay of all these considerations may best be followed in the case of an economy like the French, where the quality of enterprise has always been a significant determinant of the course and pace of development. We need not repeat here the detailed analysis given elsewhere of the nature and influence of French entrepreneurship. Suffice it to note that before the war the modal enterprise was family-owned and operated, security-oriented rather than risk-taking, technologically conservative and economically inefficient. There were, especially in the younger, more capital-intensive industries, a number of progressive, efficient enterprises, usually organized as joint-stock corporations and reasonably universalistic in their recruitment of personnel.[1] But these were only too happy to set their prices high enough to preserve the swarm of inefficient family firms about them; so that technological change and growth of output were less rapid than they would have been under more effective competition. Both big and small enterprises were abetted in this comfortable stalemate by the state and society, which took stagnation for granted, looked on most forms of competition as *déloyale*, and preferred the social criterion of contribution-by-work to the market criterion of contribution-by-efficiency.

It is only against this background that one can assess the changes in-introduced since the War. These changes have occurred in the realms of both the spirit and the flesh—in the ideas and attitudes that have set the tone of French enterprise and in the personnel that have made the economic decisions.

Let us look at ideas and attitudes first. At the risk of oversimplification, one can discern two major currents of fresh air that have, over the last two decades, transformed the economic climate of opinion. The first is the rebirth in the 1920's of the technocratic tradition of the Old Regime on the basis of a new cult of science, technology, and rational organization. Some of the leading proponents of the new faith were private businessmen or consultants: Henri Fayol, the prophet of a gallicized Taylorism; Ernest Mercier, managing director of the Union

[1] Universalistic in the sociological sense of recruitment on the basis of ability rather than personal origin and connections.

d'Electricité and one of the founders of the national electric grid;[1] and Eugène Mathon, self-made textile manufacturer and proponent of a corporatist solution to the social conflicts of his day.[2] These so-called neo-Saint-Simonians were often men of good technical education—many were graduates of the Ecole Polytechnique—and they formed, together with their classmates in government service, a kind of technocratic freemasonry that enjoyed tremendous influence in the highest business and political circles.[3] Many of them were conservative, and some even had fascistic leanings; for they despised the inefficiency of the Third Republic and feared or resented the rising power of the radical parties. And while their political efforts in the interwar years found little echo among the population at large (these were not the kind of men who have a popular touch), they found new opportunity and hope in the Vichy regime. It is no coincidence that the first historical survey of French productivity appeared in 1944: in those unhappy years of enforced domestication, the technical cadres of the French civil service could console themselves with visions of a more efficient, hence more effective nation.[4]

The second current of fresh ideas came from the progressive side of the political spectrum. This was a combination of Keynesian theory and national income accounting and offered the possibility of a productive reconciliation between mercantilist management of the economy and free enterprise. Its advocates were more often economists than engineers, graduates of the Science and Law faculties (where Economics is taught in France), rather than of such *grandes écoles* as the Polytechnique. Many of them spent the war in exile, working with de Gaulle or the Allied governments, and made close and valuable contacts with British and American economists. And like the technocrats of Vichy, they too dreamed of the day when France would be free and they would have an opportunity to put their ideas into practice.

[1] See the recent biography by Richard J. Kuisel, *Ernest Mercier, French Technocrat* (Berkeley and Los Angeles, 1967).
[2] See H. L. Dubly, *Vers un ordre économique et social: Eugène Mathon, 1860–1935* (Paris, 1946).
[3] The disciples of the Comte Claude-Henri de Saint-Simon split after his death (1825) into two groups: the cultists, who stressed the more 'idealistic' aspects of the doctrine and scandalized contemporaries by what was looked upon at the time as loose, immoral behaviour; and the technicians, many of them professional engineers, who had been attracted by the vision of a rational, production-oriented society run by workers rather than drones. The latter preferred positions in business to the utopia of the communal retreat and played a major role in the construction of the French railway system and the introduction of corporate investment banking. (The Pereire brothers of the Crédit Mobilier were both Saint-Simonians.)
[4] France, Service National des Statistiques, Institut de Conjoncture, Etude spéciale No. 3: *Le progrès technique en France depuis 100 ans* (Paris, 1944).

These two schools of thought, the one stressing productivity, the other, growth, found expression after the war in the Plan de Modernisation et d'Equipement, the creation of Jean Monnet, a *grand commis* in the best tradition of the Old Regime. It began operations, as we have seen, in 1947, concentrating at first on a few selected sectors of economic activity, then widening its purview as the economy grew and improving national accounts furnished a wider and stronger basis for forecasts and planning. Expansion was the primary aim, but not without gains in productivity; as Monnet put it in his preface to the fourth semi-annual report of the Commissariat du Plan:[1]

To develop productivity at the same time as production is the only way of raising the French standard of living, as well as of eliminating the risk of insufficient demand by increasing the real purchasing power of the mass of consumers.

To this end, the Commissariat established *commissions de modernisation*, combining representatives of both industry and government, to examine the technology of a given branch, propose needs and opportunities for improvement, and assist and urge the component enterprises in the right direction.

This combination of representatives of the private and public realms is very typical of the Plan. It is not, like its analogue in socialist countries, a kind of national budget, with strong normative and even compulsory connotations. Rather it is a set of goals and priorities, which indicate the directions in which the economy should and hopefully will go. The achievement of these goals is left to the free play of enterprise, whether private, nationalized, or mixed; hence the name 'indicative planning'.

The effectiveness of the Plan has been the subject of considerable controversy. One economist has said that the French have accomplished their postwar growth in spite of the plan; and another has argued that indicative planning is nothing more than a kind of revival meeting, in which the planners cheer on the industrialists and hope for the best. Most observers, however, are of another opinion. For one thing, the revival aspect, however trivial it may seem, has undoubtedly been extremely important in a country long mired in a slough of Malthusian despond. The exhortations of the planners have taken hold, and while one must always make allowance for rhetoric, the statements of business leaders make it clear that they now accept growth as a goal and see their own gains as part of a larger national achievement.

For another, one must not mistake the indicative technique of the Commissariat for weakness. There is a strong suspicion and dislike of

[1] *Deux ans d'exécution du plan de modernisation*, p. 15.

dirigisme in France; so that the staff of the Commissariat have taken pains to put their hortatory role in the softest light possible. In fact, they have had strong weapons at their disposal and have used them freely to move industry in the desired direction. Thus especially in the early years of Marshall Plan aid, the Commissariat controlled substantial funds, which could be invested in those enterprises that furthered the goals of the Plan; and its approval has been required for almost any bank loan of importance. As a result, the planners have been able to hold out a juicy carrot to those firms that are prepared to co-operate; and they have had a big stick to keep the recalcitrants in line. Needless to say, this kind of steering is only approximate, since it touches directly only those enterprises that want help. When the Plan thought in the early 1960's, for example, that the automobile industry was growing too fast, it tried to get Renault, France's biggest producer and a nationalized enterprise, to cut back on investments; but since Renault had its own funds to work with, there was no way to stop it. In general, the Plan has been able to influence most those industries in which production is concentrated in the hands of a few large firms; and has been least effective with branches like textiles, where not only is production dispersed but most firms are still family-run, self-financed, and less susceptible to the exhortations or blandishments of civil servants.

No other west European country has placed so much reliance on planning, even indicative planning, as the French. Yet almost all have adopted some kind of national plan, if only in the form of forecasts, and all have committed themselves to some degree of management of the economic system. This management has sometimes been confined more or less to anticyclical fiscal and monetary policy, but even this is a substantial gain over the neutrality or, worse yet, economic conservatism of the interwar period. If, as some economists argue, the long-term trend is nothing more than the sum of the short cycles, with their upswings and contractions, then the elimination of severe, periodic depressions is in itself a major contribution to a higher rate of growth.

In most of the western European countries, however, economic management has meant more than this. Even a country like Germany, where the government has cherished an almost doctrinaire faith in the virtues of *laissez-faire*, has found it advisable on occasion to intervene systematically in the allocation of resources. This was particularly true in the crucial years of recovery after 1948, when the state disposed of billions of dollars in counterpart funds. To distribute these to worthy recipients, it established the KW, the Kreditanstalt für Wiederaufbau [Reconstruction Loan Corporation], a bank of banks that sifted out from the recommendations of the private financial institutions those that fitted the national programme. The amounts furnished in this way constituted an important fraction of the 'free funds' available for industrial investment; thus from 1948 to 1953, the KW issued loans totalling 5·5 billion DM, as against 7 billion in new issues of stocks and bonds; and as late as 1955, these loans amounted to almost a billion DM, against 5·25 billion in fresh securities.[1]

The organization and procedure of the KW reflected the commitment of the German government to free enterprise and its determination not to poach on the territory of the private financial institutions. The Kreditanstalt was prohibited from competing with the existing banks and was normally required to bring these in as intermediaries in granting loans; the law further provided that the head of the KW and his deputy be commercial bankers, not bureaucrats. In the course of the 1950's, therefore, as the private banks grew in resources and power, the KW stepped aside and turned over to the private sector its strategic role of supplier of credit to large-scale industry. In the process the KW did not disappear; it was converted in the late fifties from a temporary to a permanent institution. But it looked around for areas of the economy ill-served by the regular banking system and capital market and found them chiefly among the small and medium firms. This was not, it should be noted, an act of public charity or social engineering: the KW has continued to earn a good profit on its operations.

This transfer of responsibility from the public to the private sector did not entail any real sacrifice of centralized direction. Owing to the preponderant position of a handful of banks in the major industrial firms, a few men have not found it difficult to push whole industries in the direction of concentration, rationalization, and measured growth.[2] To be sure, this influence is not a one-way street. The large industrial enterprises have their own views, which they contribute to what amounts to a kind of give-and-take; or they may go their own way and let the rest of the economy take care of itself. Shonfield cites Krupp—'still a private company and therefore without the supervision of outsiders on an *Aufsichtsrat*'—as this kind of maverick.[3] Yet Krupp is

---

[1] Andrew Shonfield, *Modern Capitalism: The Changing Balance of Public and Private Power* (London, 1965), p. 277 and n. 33.

[2] An official inquiry of 1960 showed that in a sample of corporations whose aggregate share capital represented three quarters of the nominal value of all shares quoted on the exchanges, 70 per cent of the capital was controlled by banks. This reflects only in small part actual bank ownership of shares; most of this power comes from shares entrusted by depositors to the banks and voted by them. This voting power, moreover, is highly concentrated. The same inquiry showed that, thanks to the practice of *Stimmenleihe* (lending of votes), 70 per cent of proxies cast by the banks were controlled by the Big Three—the Deutsche Bank, Dresdner Bank and Commerzbank. *Ibid.*, pp. 249–50.

[3] *Ibid.*, p. 261.

the exception that proves the rule. By 1967, its hasty expansion in foreign markets had led it to run up large debts, and the banks agreed to keep it afloat only on condition that it abandon just that family character that had made it an independent, unco-operative enterprise: Alfred Krupp (since deceased) and his son would have to give up control to a supervisory board [*Aufsichtsrat*] consisting of two bankers, an industrialist, a union chief, and two economists.[1]

All of this has taken place under an elaborate camouflage of *laissez-faire*. Both the German government and German business have been at great pains to avoid even the appearance of the *Wirtschaftslenkung* (economic steering) of the Nazi period, partly out of concern for the good will of the occupying powers, partly out of a sincere revulsion from 'the arbitrary procedures, the cartel-mongering, the compulsory price agreements, and the general atmosphere of bullying by the big of the small.'[2] In 1952, for example, when the state levied on all of German industry what amounted to a forced loan to cover the costs of expansion of selected basic sectors, it presented the operation as a stock issue, with the individual contributors receiving shares in beneficiaries that they had not chosen. One billion marks were invested in this way in iron and steel, electric power, coal, gas supply, and a variety of lesser public utilities; and this was a small consideration compared to the quiet but substantial effect of discriminatory tax benefits to these same branches in these years.

The question still remains, as in the case of France, whether these elements of centralized control have in fact promoted growth; or to put the matter contrafactually, would growth have been any slower in their absence? It is not hard, for example, to point to some aspects of German economic policy that have probably retarded expansion: the Ministry of Finance in particular was dogmatically conservative in the years immediately following the monetary reform, and its emphasis on 'orderly housekeeping' aggravated the cyclical fluctuations of the early fifties. Moreover, one may be permitted some doubt about the consequences of bank dominance for the course of technological change and industrial output. Banks favour high productivity and growth; but they also like stability, security, and order; and the German banks have, on more occasions surely than we know about, discouraged the ambitions of their clients and blocked what seemed to be unwise investments. No doubt they have often been right in doing this; but they have undoubtedly also been wrong, and there is no way of knowing the net results.

[1] *New York Times*, 2 April 1967, p. 22; James Bell, 'The Fall of the House of Krupp', *Fortune*, LXXVI (August 1967), 72 ff.

[2] Shonfield, *Modern Capitalism*, p. 244.

One thing is clear, that the significance of this 'planning' factor—if we subsume under that head this whole complex of prediction, information, co-ordination, goal-setting, and steering—has varied considerably in both time and space. In all the west European countries, it seems to have been more important in the critical years of recovery and first new growth (the late forties and early fifties), when private enterprise lacked for resources and the state had substantial free funds at its disposal. Once the economy was on its feet and business was feeling its oats, the pressure grew for a retreat from intervention. In France, for example, the tendency in the sixties has been to rely more on monetary and fiscal measures and less on investment controls; and the state has been more concerned on balance with limiting inflation and protecting the franc than in pushing for growth. The same trend to withdrawal started even earlier in Germany. To be sure, there are signs of a contrary tendency among those countries, such as Britain and Belgium, that were initially opposed to centralized management and forced feeding and, for this or other reasons, have grown more slowly than their neighbours. Rightly or wrongly, they want to try some of the potent medicine that seems to have done the others so much good. Meanwhile everywhere, even in those countries that have retreated from neo-mercantilism, the improvement of statistical and economic knowledge has substantially increased the effectiveness of such growth-promoting arrangements as are in force.

In similar fashion, the planning factor has clearly benefited some economies more than others. It was undoubtedly of special importance in France, where, as we have seen, there was a heavy legacy of Malthusianism and technological conservatism to overcome. If the hortative element has been so prominent in France, it is because exhortation has been needed. Listen to the predicatory prose of the Productivity Group of the Commissariat du Plan:[1]

Productivity is above all a state of mind. It is the spirit of progress, of the constant improvement of what is. It is the certainty of being able to do better today than yesterday, less well today than tomorrow. It is the determination not to be satisfied with the status quo, however good it may seem and however good it may be in reality. It is the perpetual adaptation to the new conditions of economic and social life; it is the continual effort to apply new techniques and new methods; it is faith in human progress.

By contrast, planning was relatively less important in Germany because the Germans needed it less. As Shonfield puts it:[2]

---

[1] France, Commissariat Général du Plan, Groupe de Travail de la Productivité, *Programme français pour l'accroissement de la productivité* (mimeographed; February 1949), p. 17.
[2] Shonfield, *Modern Capitalism*, p. 275.

It is, indeed, not at all apparent that there was any great difference in practice between the special effort made by the German authorities to refurbish their basic industries at the beginning of the 1950's and the early phases of the Monnet Plan in France. If the Germans did not use the apparatus of a plan, as the French did—though it should be observed that the French apparatus of planning had at this stage a very primitive, ad hoc character—the difference could be accounted for, in large part, by the much greater self-reliance of large-scale German industry. The industrialists did not have to be told where to go. Once given their opportunity, in the form of high profits, a plentiful, skilled and low-cost labour supply, and the backing of a series of generous tax concessions on certain kinds of investment, they went ahead very fast in the required direction. In a sense, it was unnecessary for the German authorities to plan the growth of the country's productive capacity as a formal exercise in prediction, in the French manner, because what had to be done was essentially to reconstruct something which had existed before. The guide-lines were provided by the past; there was no need for a German Monnet to invent them.

*   *   *   *   *   *

As we have seen, this variation in influence of the planning factor—variation in time and space—is true of all the determinants of technological change and industrial growth. The postwar expansion of each country has been the product of a changing mix of factors, some permissive, some stimulative; and this mix has reflected the peculiar needs, opportunities, and traditions of the particular economy and society. There has been no one path to wealth.

This conclusion will disappoint some economists, who have a strong predilection for the one ultimate or fundamental cause that makes everything else go. This preference is built into the technique of economic analysis, which relies heavily on the construction of simple explanatory models; but it also reflects a mental stance: as one economist likes to put it, 'One good reason is enough'.

The historian's instincts all tend in the other direction. He seeks, in principle at least, the wholeness of reality, however complex it may be; and nothing rouses his suspicions faster than the monistic explanation—what we may call 'the analytical fix'. This concern with complexity—with multiple, interacting forces of varying potency—is sometimes a refuge for obscurantism or equivocation. (The historian is the master of the on-the-one-hand, on-the-other.) But it represents in the last analysis an effort to see things as they are, not as manifestations of idealistic models (in the technical, philosophical sense).

If one had to select from the various national experiences those elements that come closest to being 'prime movers', the major elements shared in common (we are concerned here with those enduring factors that would account for what appears to be a new long-term trend), four would undoubtedly stand out. The first, and perhaps most important, has been the increase in knowledge, both scientific and technical. The second would be the new spirit of international co-operation. It has been far from perfect; but it marks an incalculable advance over the egoism of the interwar decades. The third has been the increase in economic knowledge. Again, this still leaves much to be desired, and further, its application has fallen short of its possibilities. Even so, it marks a sharp break with the conventional, counterproductive wisdom that the interwar generation clung to.

Finally, and closely linked to the others, we have the postwar commitment to change and growth. Here, too, the contrast with the earlier Malthusian assumptions is striking. European businessmen of the fifties were learning to look upon change as normal, even good, where they had once feared it and worked to dampen its effects. The European governments that had, as a result of the depression of the thirties, assumed with some reluctance the obligation to maintain employment, now accepted the much more far-reaching obligation to sustain and foster growth. And the people of Europe—from the wealthy capitalist whose primary concern had been to preserve his wealth against inflation and disaster, to the poor workman, perhaps unemployed, whose misery went back generations and seemed to stretch ahead into the indefinite future—the people of Europe came to look at expansion and improvement as normal, even indispensable.

This was in a way the greatest change of all—a revolution of expectations and values. The expectations were not new; they were a return, rather, to the high hopes of the dawn of industrialization, to the buoyant optimism of those first generations of English innovators. Yet never before had they been so widespread; and never before had they been so strikingly confirmed by the facts.

Whether the facts will continue to bear them out, remains to be seen. Certainly the fruits of modern economic growth are unevenly distributed, and many, even in the wealthiest countries, remain poor. Great expectations can become, indeed are becoming, great frustrations. Yet the promise is there, where once many had given up the fight; and it is this very promise that makes the difference between frustration and despair. In 1943, Joseph Schumpeter began an essay on 'Capitalism in the Postwar World' with the statement, 'It is a commonplace that capitalist society is, and for some time has been, in a state of decay.' This is the background against which one must assess the significance of what Max Ways calls 'the great rediscovery of the postwar period', that 'capitalism as a whole is *not* subject to a ceiling of diminishing returns; innovation is *not* a self-exhausting process; the era of radical change we now experience is *not* headed toward a new "point of rest"; all the buffalo on the plains of progress have *not* been shot—indeed, they are breeding faster and faster'.[1]

This is an expression of faith, wrapped up as a prediction. But it is this kind of faith that helps make predictions come true.

[1] Max Ways, 'The Postwar Advance of the Five Hundred Million', *Fortune*, LXX (August 1964), 108.

CHAPTER 8

Conclusion

Economic history has always been in part the story of international competition for wealth; witness the literature and politics of mercantilism—or the title of Adam Smith's classic study. The Industrial Revolution gave this competition a new focus—wealth through industrialization—and turned it into a chase. There was one leader, Britain, and all the rest were pursuers. The lead has since changed hands, but the pursuit goes on in what has become a race without a finishing line. To be sure, there are only a few contestants sufficiently endowed to vie for the palm. The rest can at best follow along and make the most of their capacities. But even these are far better off than those who are not running. No one wants to stand still; most are convinced that they dare not.

The laggards have good reason to be concerned: the race is getting faster all the time, and the rich get richer while the poor have children. It took man hundreds of thousands of years to learn to grow crops and domesticate livestock and, in so doing, to raise himself above the level of subsistence of a beast of prey, however efficient. The increased food supply that this neolithic revolution provided made possible a substantial growth of population and a new pattern of concentrated settlement with specialization of labour that had the most fertile consequences for man's intellectual development.

It took another ten thousand years or so to make the next advance of comparable magnitude: the industrial breakthrough that we call the Industrial Revolution and its accompanying improvements in agricultural production. Once again the results have been a huge increase in numbers, more and bigger agglomerations of people, greater specialization of labour, and rapid intellectual progress, at least in the domain of science and technology.

Thanks to this progress it has taken man less than two hundred years to leap to atomic power and automation; and in the course of this time, the pace of change has speeded in every domain: compare the centuries of development of the steam-engine with the decades of internal-combustion engines, jet propulsion, and rocket motors. The point, as we have noted, is that man can now order technological and scientific advance as one orders a commodity. This acceleration has produced such interesting anomalies as newly graduated engineers who are paid almost as much as men with decades of experience. It was once thought that this preferential treatment of beginners reflected a temporary maladjustment of the market, a lag in the response of supply to increased demand. There is good reason to believe, however, that this imbalance will persist and even increase, and that it is due in large part to the superior knowledge of men who have received the latest instruction, who have been trained in schools whose curriculum depreciates and is transformed faster than the human products it turns out. Even more must teachers of scientists and engineers labour under the threat of accelerated obsolescence: a man who does not retool constantly is unfit to teach graduate students after ten years, advanced undergraduates after twenty.[1]

The historical experience of western and central Europe provides us with some of our best insights into the nature of this race after wealth and the power that goes with it: into the sources and dynamics of industrial development; stimulants and deterrents; the implications of precedence and backwardness; the effect of non-economic values and institutions on economic performance. Nowhere else is the course so long: one can see the runners coast as well as sprint, follow them from youthful ardour to maturity, observe the working out of at least two technological revolutions. And within this course, one can see such a variety of institutional forms as facilitates the kind of comparison and contrast that is the historian's strongest asset in disentangling and appraising the determinants of complex phenomena.

Needless to say, it is impossible in the present state of our knowledge to evaluate the parameters of economic development. Even the European experience, the one we have studied longest and presumably know best, is still in many areas *terra incognita*. It is perhaps premature, therefore, to proffer generalizations. Yet an end calls for conclusions, and this may serve to exculpate my temerity.

It will help to begin by defining the methodological context of these remarks. The interest of economic theorists and historians in growth has led to the invention of a large number of schemas designed to conceptualize and elucidate this process. Some of these schemas are true models, that is, they take a group of interacting variables and trace a cause-and-effect sequence of changes in these variables to an end result. Others are essentially taxonomies, that is, they classify the stages that an economy or some aspect of an economy passes through on the path of development and growth, without analysing the

[1] Thomas Stelson, 'Education for Oblivion; or, Change: Grow, or Perish', *Carnegie Alumnus* (April 1961), summarized in 'What the Colleges Are Doing', *Ginn and Co. Newsletter*, no. 119 (Autumn 1961), p. 2.

mechanism of passage from one stage to another. Others combine both of these features.

Some of these conceptions pretend to universal application: they may be essentially imaginary constructions, tied to historical experience only by the most diffuse common sense; or inductive derivations from a sample of historical experience. Other schemas are what Robert Merton has called middle-range hypotheses, that is, generalizations about a closely specified phenomenon or relationship based on a given body of empirical data; as such, they are essentially explanatory or descriptive, though they may have predictive implications. Some of these, such as Professor Gerschenkron's model of the conquest of backwardness, we have encountered at various points in the discussion. Others, like the 'staples theory' of growth, are relevant to patterns of development other than those described by the nations of western Europe.

For obvious reasons, historians are more sympathetic to these limited inductive analyses than to the more ambitious universal abstractions. In this they are mistaken, for the two approaches perform different functions and both are indispensable. A model is not worthless or anathema because it is not empirically anchored. If well constructed, it offers the scholar an analytical pattern against which to hold the experiences of history and appreciate their elements of uniqueness and uniformity. The value of such a model is thus heuristic rather than informative: it does not *tell* what happened but helps one to find and understand what happened.

There is no question here of attempting to catalogue this multiplicity, indeed this plethora, of schemas and evaluate them *seriatim* in the light of the evidence. At most I have space for a small number of middle-range conclusions of my own that modify some widely accepted generalizations. The reader will note that the tone of these remarks is fundamentally negative; in view of our ignorance, it is often easier to say no, or maybe, than yes.

1. It has often been asserted that backward economies develop faster than their predecessors, that given what one writer has called the tension between their existing state and their potentialities, their industrialization takes the form of an eruption.[1] There is some truth in this. The retarded nation, once it has overcome those social and institutional forces that have held it back, can move ahead more quickly for the experience and advances of others. If it has the means, it can make use of the latest equipment, teach the newest techniques; it can even attract the capital and talent of richer economies in proportion to the opportunities it offers.

[1] Thus Gerschenkron, *Economic Backwardness in Historical Perspective*, pp. 5–30.

On the other hand, the assumption on which this thesis is based—like most such assumptions—tends to beg the question. Once retardative forces are overcome...but that is a long and difficult job, and that is why the backward economy was backward to begin with. German industrial growth looks extremely rapid if one dates it from 1850. It is much slower, slower at first than the British for example, if 1815 is the starting-point. Too often it is assumed that non-economic obstacles simply melt in the face of economic opportunity.[1] In fact, they are extraordinarily resistant, and it is the tension building up behind this resistance that accounts in large measure for the rapidity of development once the spring is released. As a result there is an initial spurt of growth, a making-up of lost time. But there is no reason to assume, as some do, that this pace can be maintained indefinitely.[2] Follower countries also have their fluctuations in rate of growth. And they too mature.

2. It is sometimes asserted that follower countries, unlike Britain, base their breakthrough to industrialization on heavy rather than light manufactures—on iron and steel, mining, chemicals. The Belgian, German, American, and Russian examples all seem to justify the generalization. The argument is twice wrong. First, it confuses the increasing importance of heavy industry in the economy—any economy —and the specific characteristics of backwardness. In western Europe the critical period of expansion and development was the second third of the nineteenth century. These were also the years of what Schumpeter called 'railroadization', and the economies of Germany, Belgium and France showed it in the place assumed by metallurgy and engineering; but then so did that of Britain in this period. And second, the argument ignores the historical validity of the law of comparative advantage. Heavy industry, for example, was far more important in Belgium and Germany than in France and Switzerland—or, for that matter, Japan. And a country like Denmark developed by rationalizing her agriculture. As for subsequent experience—that of the under-developed countries of the twentieth century—it goes without saying that their obsession with heavy industry has only a coincidental connection with economic vocation. The historian should never make the mistake of taking political choice for material necessity.

[1] Cf. *ibid.*, pp. 68–9.

[2] Cf. Surendra J. Patel, 'Rates of Industrial Growth in the Last Century, 1860–1958', *Economic Development and Cultural Change*, IX (April 1961), 316–60. This is essentially a declaration of faith in the power of compound interest. But Patel remarks, p. 330: 'A more appropriate strategy of growth for these [newly industrializing] countries would be to attain very high rates of growth in the earlier phase and cumulate the enlarged mass of output at somewhat lower rates.'

3. One frequently assumes that follower countries will adopt the most advanced techniques and equipment available. Sometimes this assumption is based on a deceptive kind of common sense: if one is going to buy machinery, one might as well buy the best. Sometimes it is based on the more subtle argument that, while there may be an apparent superabundance of labour in the backward country and relative factor costs seem to militate against capital-intensive techniques, skilled workers are in fact scarce and labour-saving devices more necessary even than in advanced economies.

Here, too, the historical facts will not support so simple a generalization. As we have seen, continental industry of the first half of the nineteenth century developed largely with equipment that was already obsolete across the Channel. Two considerations were determining here: first, for all the scarcity of certain kinds of skills, relative factor costs in the follower countries favoured labour-intensive techniques; and secondly, the choice of production functions was not always governed by the rational calculations of theory. Habit, social prejudice, and entrepreneurial caution all conduced to a relatively conservative investment policy.

In the second half of the century this pattern changed, though the shift to ultra-modernity was by no means so extensive as the customary discussion would lead one to believe. It was most marked in heavy industry and in the younger, more scientific branches of manufacture. Even there, however, there were important differences between countries. French and Belgian enterprise adhered in large measure to earlier policies of labour-intensive production and prolonged obsolescence. Cost of production and consequent limitations on the size of the market clearly played a role: hence the modest equipment installed in the infant Dutch steel industry on the eve of the First World War.[1] On the other hand, Germany took the lead in European technology, though both skilled and unskilled labour were cheaper than in Britain and often even France; and Russia, wretchedly poor in domestic capital and rich in manpower, was building its iron and steel industry by the turn of the century on some of the largest blast furnaces in Europe.[2]

---

[1] R. M. Westebbe, 'The Iron Age in the Netherlands', *Explorations in Entrepreneurial History*, IX (1956–7), 172–7.

[2] The modernity and gigantism of the Russian iron and steel industry has been somewhat exaggerated. The old iron manufacture of the Urals was notoriously backward, and the first efforts of an outsider to build a modern plant in the Donetz basin (John Hughes in the 1870's) rested on techniques that, while superior to anything yet seen in Russia, were far behind those employed in western Europe. Methods and equipment improved markedly in the 1890's when there was a massive infusion

This late nineteenth-century pattern of mottled modernity can be explained only partially in terms of relative factor costs. Heavy weight must be given, as we have seen, to non-economic considerations, in particular the technological rationality of engineers, who could hardly be expected to deviate from best practice as they had learned it. Germany here represents almost an ideal type. She had no shortage of skilled hands. Her wages and salaries for equivalent work were distinctly lower than those of her competitors. To be sure, capital for investment in heavy industry was relatively abundant thanks to the banking system and an interested capital market. Yet it was not so cheap as in Britain, and in the last analysis the decisive consideration was one of attitudes and values.[1]

It should be noted, however, that modernity is often meretricious, and that even in technologically oriented industries, the law of relative factor costs was operative—either in the positive sense of determining ratios of factor inputs, or in the negative one of punishing deviations from the rational. The best evidence of the former is to be found, first, in the relatively high labour intensity of processes utilizing modern equipment: the Russian iron plants, for example, used more men per furnace or per ton than German or British enterprises with comparable equipment; just as German cotton manufacturers employed far more men per thousand spindles than the British.[2] It is also to be found in the generous use of labour in auxiliary processes, particularly in the handling and movement of materials and finished goods. The evidence for the latter—the penalization of irrationality—is less clear because of the difficulty of separating out the causes of poor performance. Yet it is worth noting that with the exception of German industry, where

of Belgian and French money and enterprise. Even so, the scale of production was well behind that of even the more conservative producers in the West. M. Goldman, 'The Relocation and Growth of the Pre-Revolutionary Russian Ferrous Metal Industry', *Explorations in Entrepreneurial History*, IX (1956-7), 19-36; L. Beck, *Geschichte des Eisens*, V, 1223-24.

[1] The ratio of factor costs would seem to have had more influence on Russian development; perhaps not so much on the ground usually adduced, that skilled industrial labour was scarce, as for the opposite reason, that risk capital was in fact abundant—in certain sectors. Thus the foreign entrepreneurs of the Donetz basin were generally iron and steel men from older centres in the West. They had funds to invest and had no intention of turning banker and placing their money in perhaps more remunerative but also less familiar and, inferentially, riskier operations. Had the new Russian iron industry confined itself substantially to domestic capital, the technological pattern might have been drastically different. Yet even in the Russian case non-economic considerations, in particular the predilections of imported entrepreneurs and technicians, played a significant role.

[2] Cf. G. von Schulze-Gaevernitz, *The Cotton Trade in England and on the Continent* (London and Manchester, 1895), pp. 97f.

technological and pecuniary rationality coincided in the long run, the output of capital-intensive industry in labour-rich underdeveloped countries tended to be well below theoretical capacity. Much of this was due, no doubt, to inefficient organization and lack of skills; but much also reflected demand limited by high prices due to the poor combination of factors.[1]

The extent and cost of such deviations from the rational has tended to increase over time, as ever more backward economies have been drawn into the stream of industrialization. On the one hand, these newer candidates have been poorer in capital and richer in manpower than their European predecessors. On the other, they have been more dependent on imported technical expertise, hence more subject to the influence of technological rationality. Moreover, they have been slower to develop a machine-construction industry of their own to fabricate equipment suitable to their circumstances; or what amounts to the same thing, they have been far quicker to develop certain machine-using branches than the producers' goods industries to supply them. They have therefore been compelled to import their equipment and have had little choice but to purchase the models made and used in more advanced countries.[2] It is this combination of material and non-material considerations that accounts for such apparent anomalies as more modern spinning machinery in India, Japan, and parts of Latin America than in Britain, in spite of factor-cost ratios far more favourable to labour-intensive techniques.[3]

If there is some general conclusion to be drawn from all this, it is the complexity of economic development. This is a process that, particularly when it takes the form of industrialization, affects all aspects of social life and is affected in turn by them. The remark may seem an empty truism, a typical flight of the historian into the refuge of multiple

[1] The allusion is specifically to heavy industry: cf. the gap between capacity and output in Russian iron manufacture, which accounts in part for the contradiction between its reputation for gigantism and the statistical evidence of performance. The same discrepancy characterized Dutch iron production between the wars, although much of the difficulty there lay in the inadequate absorptive capacity of the home market.

In light industry, on the other hand, one is often struck by use of equipment beyond rated capacity, aggravating wear and tear and increasing maintenance costs substantially.

[2] This element of compulsion is apparent in the tendency to keep this modern equipment in use an inordinately long time—up to and beyond the point that cheap labour (for maintenance and repair of damage caused by worn machinery) makes advisable.

[3] On much of the above, see V. V. Bhatt, 'Capital Intensity of Industries: a Comparative Study of Certain Countries', *Bull. Oxford University Institute of Statistics*, XVIII (1956), 179–94; also United Nations, Dept. of Economic Affairs, *Labour Productivity of the Cotton Textile Industry in Five Latin-American Countries* (1951), p. 9.

interrelationship. Yet it has content, as the denial of a sociologist like Herbert Blumer makes clear.[1] And the serious empirical basis of this denial, as well as the weighty implications of such a relationship between industrialization and the social order, were it to be proved, justifies, indeed calls for, some serious consideration of the subject.

Economic theory has traditionally been interested in one half of the problem—the determinants of economic change—rather than its non-economic effects; and it long vitiated that half by holding non-economic variables constant, for reasons that, as we have seen, often have little to do with the empirical evidence. Professor Blumer has come to his conclusions from the other direction. Rather than deny or affirm *a priori*, whether for analytical convenience or out of logical conviction, the influence of the non-economic on the economic (and vice versa), he has looked at the wide variety of human experience in this regard and induced therefrom that the relationship is so diverse and free in its working and that so much of what is often derived from economic development, population growth for example, is in fact autonomous, that one is not justified in speaking of uniform causal ties or influences. Indeed he goes beyond this purely negative position to argue that economic development and even industrialization are 'neutral' and have no specific or necessary effect on social institutions.

It seems to me that such an affirmation overdoes a salutary reaction to the abstractions of sociological system makers. Clearly there are no rigid compulsory relationships between a modern industrial economy and the entirety of its complex, multifaceted environment. Rather there is a wide range of links, direct and indirect, tight and loose, exclusive and partial, and each industrializing society develops its own combination of elements to fit its traditions, possibilities, and circumstances. The fact that there is this play of structure, however, does not mean that there is no structure; by the same token, the fact that many of the non-economic institutions of a society are of autonomous origin does not mean that their subsequent development is unrelated to economic change.

Let us try briefly to consider the European experience in the light of these remarks, looking first for the proximate concomitants of industrialization and proceeding by degrees to institutions less tightly confined by the logic or requirements of economic growth. The former, by implication, will have a kind of universal application, transcending time and place. By the same token, the latter will be distinctively European, or British or continental, as the case may be, and will in

[1] H. Blumer, 'Early Industrialization and the Laboring Class', *The Sociological Quarterly*, 1 (1960), 5–14; *Idem*, 'Industrialization as Agent of Social Change' (MS.), *passim*.

effect represent one society's or one area's choice of the range of possibilities offered.

When all the complicating circumstances are stripped away—changing technology, shifting ratios of factor costs, diverse market structures in diverse economic and political systems—two things remain and characterize any modern industrial system: rationality, which is the spirit of the institution, and change, which is rationality's logical corollary, for the appropriation of means to ends that is the essence of rationality implies a process of continuous adaptation. These fundamental characteristics have had in turn explicit consequences for the values and structure of the economy and society, consequences that centre in the principle of selection by achievement.

The significance of this principle is obvious: just as the industrial system tries to combine non-human factors of production efficiently, so it will seek to maximize its return from wages and salaries by putting the right man in the right place. This 'universalistic' standard of selection contrasts sharply with the so-called 'particularistic' criteria of the pre-industrial society, dominated by agriculture, landed property, and an Establishment resting on interlaced family ties and hereditary privileges. Men are chosen, not for who they are or whom they know, but for what they can do.

The logical concomitant of such selection is mobility: otherwise, how make the choice effective? A competitive industrial system—whether the competition takes place internally, between productive units, or externally, with rival systems, or both—will therefore place a premium on easy movement of labour power, technical skills, and managerial talent. It will encourage geographical mobility, separating men and women from their ancestral homes and families, to work in strange places; and it will increase social mobility, raising the gifted, ambitious, and lucky, and lowering the inept, lazy, and ill-fortuned. This is the kind of thing one sees in eighteenth- and nineteenth-century Germany, dissolving the bonds of serfdom and the privileges of guilds so as to create a free market for labour and a free field for enterprise; or in nineteenth- and twentieth-century Japan, making extensive use of adoption as a device to recruit talent into the tight familial framework of enterprise: or in France, where the so-called *politique des gendres* has much the same motivation; or in the India of today, striving to break down the once inexorable boundaries of caste. Industrialization is, in short, a universal solvent, and its effects are the more drastic the greater the contrast between the old order and the new.

At this point, the reader impatient with this somewhat theoretical discussion may protest. How much, he may ask, have objective principles of selection really governed the assignment of position and responsibility in societies like England, where higher education has been the prerogative of a favoured few and where personal connections have been an open sesame to success, in business as well as in social intercourse and politics? And how effective have geographical and social mobility been in the industrializing nations of Europe—or of the world, for that matter? The existence, throughout the Industrial Revolution, of chronically depressed areas and trades is eloquent testimony to the reluctance of people to move, even in the face of necessity.

The answer is that no economic and social system, at least historically, has ever been pushed to its extreme logical consequences. No one will pretend that the Industrial Revolution gave rise, even momentarily, to perfect mobility or created a paradise of universal opportunity. Man is too perverse a creature to admit of absolute systematization, even that of absolutely rugged individualism. Fortunately. And vested interests, especially in a free society, have ways and means to preserve something of their advantages.

The point made here is an entirely different one. It says, first, that industrialization promoted certain social consequences; and there is no blinking the fermentation produced by this drastic economic change in traditionalistic, sluggish agrarian societies. But second and more important, it says that in so far as different countries effected these related social adjustments, they advanced the process of industrialization; and conversely, that in so far as they failed to adjust, their economic growth was retarded. The analogy is complete with the role of rationality in economic theory. Just as all enterprises fall short of absolute rationality yet survive and even flourish thanks to the imperfections of the market place, so societies live and even prosper in spite of the contradictions of their structure. By the same token, however, just as deviations from rationality have their price and if pushed too far can result in elimination of the enterprise, so deviations from economic and social logic entail costs, and if pushed too far can have analogous consequences for an entire nation.

Less universal only by comparison are the social stigmata of backwardness-in-emulation, for this after all is a category that embraces all industrializing nations but the first. One of these we have already considered in detail: the development of a system of general education, whose function is partly to provide training in the skills and sciences required by industry, but even more, as we have seen, to facilitate the selection and recruitment of talent. But I have said little or nothing about two other frequent concomitants of emulation: government intervention and ideological exaltation—for the simple reason that these have been characteristic, not so much of the early industrializers of western and central Europe, as of the rushing laggards like Japan and Russia.

Each of these deserves a moment's attention here. First, political structure: even a cursory consideration of the comparative government of industrialized and industrializing nations makes it clear that a wide variety of institutional arrangements have been compatible with this course of development. Britain has been a parliamentary democracy; the United States, a presidential democracy; France has lived under a diversity of regimes; Russia has passed from autocracy to totalitarianism; Japan effected her industrial revolution under the rule of an alliance of military and plutocrats, whose closest parallel was the Junker-industrialist oligarchy of the German empire. Moreover, there has been only a loose correlation between the degrees of political and economic freedom. There was as much intervention in the economy in parliamentary Belgium as in imperial Austria; more intervention in France under the *monarchie censitaire* than under the Second Empire; and more everywhere in the twentieth century than in the nineteenth.

One can, of course, speak of minimal political requisites: security, first, in the widest sense that transcends mere physical safety of persons and possessions and implies the ability to assume the working out of economic decisions without arbitrary non-economic interference—no security, no prediction; and second, effective management of the affairs of government. The latter is the kind of thing that European nations have more or less taken for granted since the city- and nation-states of the late Middle Ages developed bureaucracies and, drawing in part on the Church, a corps of professional civil servants. But as anyone who has tried to get something done in the underdeveloped countries of the twentieth century can testify, administrative competence is not easily acquired and is adequately appreciated only in its absence.

The critical importance of effective government in the twentieth century is due to the increased responsibility for economic development assumed by or devolving upon the State. Here the argument of Gerschenkron is persuasive: the more backward a country—the bigger the gap between its economic performance and possibilities—the more necessary the intervention of authority in promoting growth. One of the ironies of history is that the nations of western and central Europe, with their long experience of centralized government and mercantilistic policy, largely eschewed economic management. It was not only that it was not required, that these societies were ready and able to mobilize voluntarily the resources required and utilize them on the basis of free choice. The fact was that, given Europe's limited experience with industrialization in the nineteenth century and the shortcomings of the economic science of the time, no superior authority could have effected an industrial revolution so rapidly and efficiently as the impersonal market. Under the best of circumstances, the governments of the day were ignorant; in addition, they were usually perverse in their judgments and inconsistent in their actions. As we have seen, such efforts as authoritarian regimes were ready to make to develop their economies were liable to promote misallocation of resources or lose their force in the face of contradictory measures in support of the *status quo*. It is no coincidence that the areas of most rapid industrial growth in the eighteenth and nineteenth centuries were those free of supervision and constraints—the textile centres of the Rhineland, for example, rather than the hothouse factories of Frederick II.

The apparently perverse reliance on planning and management by the industrializing nations of the twentieth century, who lack even the rudiments of administrative competence, is explained only in part by the even more serious scarcity of private capital and enterprise. The heart of the choice is ambition, a hunger for growth (which is assumed to mean industrialization) and the fruits of growth that chafes at delay, has no patience for the workings of the free market, and sees in authority a means of forcing the gates of time. To a degree the calculation is correct: in so far as the attitudes and values of the society are such that its members will not respond creatively or rationally to opportunity, direction and stimulation from above are indispensable. Yet to an even greater degree the calculation is ideological, based on value judgments about the contrast between stereotypes of capitalism—exploitive, unjust, enriching a few at the expense of the many—and socialism—egalitarian, placing the resources of the society in the hands of the representatives of the society, for the benefit of all.

There is neither point nor space here to examine the merits of this value judgment. Suffice it to point out that that is what it is, and that as such, its empirical justification is necessarily adventitious. Moreover, the choice of the authoritarian way in no wise exempts an economy from the iron laws of growth: that one never gets anything for nothing and must save first in order to enjoy more later on; and that growth is most rapid when resources are allocated to the area of highest return. The former is inviolable, except in so far as an economy can obtain gifts or loans from outside; and the pain of saving is even more severe in economies that are in a hurry than in those that depend on voluntary abstinence. All the sufferings endured by the English and European working classes during their decades of incipient industrialization bulk little alongside the hardships, insecurity, and death imposed on the proletariats and peasantries of Soviet Russia and Communist China in the name of 'singing tomorrows'. The second law is violated all the time—always at a price—though generally more in authoritarian societies than in free. For where deviations from rationality in market economies generally reflect the aberrations of tradition or prejudice and are penalized to the degree that the market is free and competition effective, they are often the result of deliberate choice in the planned economy, where they are sanctioned and sustained by the exigencies of ideology.

The role of ideology, like that of government, tends to increase with degree of backwardness; and indeed the two go hand in hand. Here, too, there is a functional justification: some kind of psychological reassurance and inspiration is necessary to comfort the members of a society in their years of privation and stimulate them to labour for better times to come; and they are the more necessary, the more difficult the effort, the more ambitious the goal, the greater the sacrifices demanded.

But ideology has roots of its own, and the economy is as much its servant as its master. The great religion of today is nationalism, with its companions of pride (which starts as self-respect) and ambition (which starts as hope). It is nationalism, working through authoritarian government, that directs the economic planning of the under-developed countries of today and has dictated the choice of industrialization as the path to wealth and power; and it is nationalism that justifies this decision and the sacrifices it entails to the people who bear them.

One cannot generalize about the consequences of nationalist ideology for economic growth. Admittedly it can inspire to labour, but its influence may or may not be well directed. It tends to encourage a preference for industry rather than agriculture, for heavy rather than light industry, for monuments rather than utilitarian investments. The price of such a bias will vary with the endowment and vocation of an economy; often it will far surpass the compensating gain of stimulation received.

For the industrializing nations of western and central Europe, ideology, whether nationalist or otherwise, played a less obvious, more subtle role than it does today. It was of modest significance in Britain, though even there, a certain precocious chauvinism, linked to a long history of naval exploits and successful imperial conquests, contributed to the confidence and drive of British trade. It had even less influence in small countries like Belgium, Holland, and Switzerland, where the realities of power precluded patriotic fancies; on the other hand, the ready acceptance by the small countries of a commercial-industrial vocation and their relative immunity to the temptations of what we may call the politics of *gloire* was in itself an aid to effective enterprise. It is no coincidence, for example, that the Belgian aristocracy, more than any other on the Continent, was intensely venal, alert to business opportunity, and ready, like the British gentry, to shift its capital wherever most remunerative.[1]

The reverse is apparent in a country like France, victim in a way of past glories and too much inclined to cherish the predilections and prejudices of the pre-industrial society. The France of Louis XIV and then again of Napoleon had dominated Europe, awed the rest of the world by her pomp and circumstance, scintillated by her artistic and intellectual achievements. She had developed in the process, especially at the upper levels of society, a highly integrated set of values, suffused with a sense of satisfaction and superiority. As is characteristic in such cases of identification between way of life and values on the one hand and self-esteem on the other, her reaction to those areas of activity in which she could not achieve pre-eminence was simply to reject them as unworthy. Britain was more successful commercially? What else could one expect from a nation of shopkeepers?

The successive military and naval defeats by Britain, from Blenheim and Ramillies through Plassey and Quebec to Trafalgar and Waterloo, did not shake this conviction of superior virtue. On the contrary, they reinforced Britain's position as France's traditional rival and enemy and confirmed the French in their hostility to what was viewed as a competitive way of life. Especially after 1815 there was a tendency—alongside a powerful current of cultural and intellectual Anglophilia—to seek comfort for defeat by noting the evils that industrialism had brought to England: the periodic crises, the hordes of blanched children slaving in the mills, the excrescent slums. Along with this went a tacit surrender of economic aspirations: France would never be able to compete with Britain in an industrial world based on coal and iron; hence the need for high protection and even prohibition to preserve a different kind of economy—a more humane economy based on family units of enterprise, a market place free of cannibalistic competition, a healthful balance between agriculture and industry. The consequences of this rejection of the new industrial civilization for both public policy and entrepreneurial behaviour are not easy to measure, if only because this factor blends in with many others. It was nevertheless extremely important in fixing dispositions and justifying them; for it was this value judgment that furnished the moral sanction for economic retardation.

Finally there was Germany, which faced the rest of Europe at the start of the nineteenth century enfeebled by division and still impoverished by the wars of the seventeenth century. The low point was

---

[1] See the fascinating study of G. Jacquemyns, *Langrand-Dumonceau, promoteur d'une puissance financière catholique* (5 vols.; Brussels, 1960–5); also any of the literature dealing with Leopold II and his entourage, especially with their appropriation of the Congo.

reached in 1805, when, after the battle of Jena, the largest and most powerful north German state, Prussia, was threatened with dissolution. At that point there was nothing to look backward to; only the present, which offered a last chance to remake the society and bolster the polity, and the future to build toward. The increasingly close identification of this future, envisioned as one of national rehabilitation, international power and, with time, of a united Germany, on the one hand, and economic growth, on the other, was a powerful support for the new industry, especially for those branches of manufacture that were directly or indirectly linked to power: coal, iron, engineering, eventually chemicals and electricity. The chimney aristocracy could claim a prestige based not only on wealth—for new wealth is always resented—but on their contribution to national aggrandizement. At the same time, German enterprise in general became imbued with a chauvinism that found expression, first, in confidence in its ability to overtake its British precursor and, later on, in an aggressive determination to establish its supremacy throughout the world. The tone was sharply different from that prevailing in France, and while it is easy to point out that the discouragement of the one and assurance of the other were simply based on the realities of economic life, the fact remains—as any athlete will testify—that attitude is an important element, win or lose, of any performance.[1]

Ideology is only one of many non-economic factors autonomous in origin but closely connected both as cause and effect with the Industrial Revolution. We could not possibly try to resume all of these here, but two—demographic change and urbanization—are worthy of special notice, not only for their intrinsic interest, but also for the light they throw on the general problem of analysing complex historical inter-relationships.

Look again at the growth of population in the eighteenth and nineteenth centuries. It is clear that its source was in large measure independent of the Industrial Revolution, as Ireland alone suffices to demonstrate. The key factor was a more abundant, regular food supply, which led to a lower death rate, principally by mitigating the periodic winnows of famine and disease.[2] As a result, by the end of the eighteenth

[1] On the link between Prussian political requirements and ambitions on the one hand, and industrialization on the other, see D. S. Landes, 'Japan and Europe: Contrasts in Industrialization', in William W. Lockwood, ed., *The State and Economic Enterprise in Japan* (Princeton, 1965), pp. 93–182.

[2] The elimination of what have been called 'dismal peaks' of mortality was probably of least importance in England where, even before the eighteenth century, the supply of food to local areas seems to have been more regular and responsive to demand than in other countries. Indeed, the increase of population there may have been due more to a higher birth rate, the result of earlier age of marriage, than to a

century population was already beginning to exert severe pressure on resources in certain parts of western Europe, which was threatened in principle with the kind of general fall in the standard of living that has attended similar discrepancies between growth of numbers and growth of social product in other areas of the world. That such a disaster did not occur was the work partly of major improvements in agricultural productivity but even more of the industrialization of western Europe and the creation of a surplus of manufactures that could be traded for nourishment from outside.[1] What is more, by creating opportunities for employment, industrial growth almost surely encouraged the long persistence of a high birth rate, which might otherwise have been expected to adjust fairly rapidly to a higher rate of survival (as it did in fact in France), and thereby turned an increase in numbers into an explosion.

The same combination of autonomous origins, at least in part, and subsequent interaction may be seen in the case of urbanization. There is nothing in industrialization itself that will account for the growth of the giant capitals of Europe, which have remained essentially administrative, financial, commercial, and 'cultural' in character. Cities like London, Paris, and Berlin had and have their industry, often based on the availability of cheap labour (crowded immigrants in sweatshops) or highly skilled labour (the woodworking artisans of the Faubourg St-Antoine or the imaginative craftsmen who make *articles de Paris*), or on the preferences of technicians and management who want to live and work in the centre of intellectual, economic, and political activity. Yet their manufactures are rarely the stuff industrial revolutions are made of; and if they engage in the heavier, more capital-intensive branches, they are compelled with time to expel them—to the outskirts or farther, where land costs are commensurate with industrial use.

But industrialization does tend to the development of another type of city, based on locational advantages and the external economies of proximity in interdependence. Just as the craftsmen of the Middle Ages found it convenient and profitable to work in the company of their trade—their very concentration was a form of advertising that drew the customers to their place of work—so the modern factory often gains by working alongside competitors, not only because the site may be convenient, but also because the presence of a number of producers makes possible the existence of accessory specialists who are indispens-

lower death rate; and population growth may well have been a response to the opportunities created by expanding industry. But the data are most uncertain, and the matter is still a subject of controversy.

[1] On the expansion of western Europe's food supply by the opening of new areas of specialized cultivation trading with the industrial zone, there is an excellent essay by Karl Helleiner (ed.), in his introduction to his *Readings in European Economic History* (Toronto, 1946), pp. 24-37.

able to the efficient working of the branch as a whole. It is this combined process of growth by expansion and diversification that accounts for the massive localization of the textile industry in Lancashire and of metalworking trades in the Ruhr and the Birmingham area.

These centres of factory manufacture may be small or large, depending on size of market, vocation of the area, and technology. The last factor merits a moment's special attention. We have seen that so long as industry was compelled or well advised to rely on water for power, the development of manufacture led, not to urbanization, but to a new kind of rural settlement. The coming of the rotary steam-engine changed this; but the subsequent invention of electric power and the development of cheap local transport (tramways and automobiles) altered once again the technological basis of location and made possible competitive dispersed production. It even gave, as we have seen, a new vitality to craft and domestic manufacture. Nevertheless, the external economies of localization are such that although the advantages of site have diminished and the ecological pattern of the manufacturing city has changed, with industry moving more and more to the suburbs, the tie between factory production and urban concentration has never been broken and is not likely to be.

The convolution of the above discussion may discourage the reader, the more so because it gives at best an incomplete and oversimplified picture of a complex phenomenon. How much more agreeable it would be to reduce everything to a handful of aspects and explain these by a handful of causes! And how comforting it would be to be able to draw unambiguous lessons from this rich tapestry of human experience and present them for the guidance of the industrializers of today, that they may avoid the mistakes of their predecessors. History, after all, is a sacrifice on the altar of hope—hope that man will one day know more about man and be able to master himself as he now masters nature.

In the meantime, the industrialization of the world proceeds, for better or worse. This world, which has never before been ready to accept universally any of the universal faiths offered for its salvation, is apparently prepared to embrace the religion of science and technology without reservation. There are some in the more advanced industrial countries who have qualms about this worship of material achievement; but they are wealthy and can afford this critical posture. The overwhelming majority of the inhabitants of this world, especially the great mass of the hungry and unwashed, take it for granted that food, clothing, and other creature comforts are not only good for both body and soul but lie within reach.

The reason for this optimism is the assumption that man's capacity to know and do is infinite; we have here the age-old heresy of man's worship of himself. Now we are come full circle to the place where we started—to the *hubris* that has been a recurrent motif of Western thought and mythology, going back to the Judaic story of the Fall in the Garden and the Greek legends of Prometheus and Daedalus. The West, at the very time when it is losing some of its own faith, when some of the most successful or favoured of its children are looking to new cults and idols for salvation, is transferring its most profound and original heresy to others. It is a dangerous export, for aspirations and pretensions are not enough—indeed are worse than nothing if not accompanied by the values and ways of thought that promote effective performance.

Yet *hubris* is a start. The first time I cited the stories of Eve and Prometheus and Daedalus as evidence of the age and continuity of the spirit of striving and mastery in Western culture, an audience of sceptical colleagues objected that the legends proved rather the hostility of Western tradition to such insolent aspirations: Were not Adam and Eve evicted from Paradise? Was Prometheus not chained to the rock, his liver daily consumed by an eagle? Did not Daedalus lose his son Icarus, that 'prideful soarer', and spend his declining years in mournful exile? Is not the point of all these stories that man will be punished for his presumption?

The answer, of course, is yes; but only part of the answer. Adam and Eve lost Paradise for having eaten of the fruit of the Tree of Knowledge; but they retained the knowledge. Prometheus was punished, and indeed all of mankind, for Zeus sent Pandora with her box of evils to compensate the advantages of fire; but Zeus never took back the fire. Daedalus lost his son, but he was the founder of a school of sculptors and craftsmen and passed much of his cunning on to posterity. In sum, the myths warn us that the wresting and exploitation of knowledge are perilous acts, but that man must and will know, and once knowing, will not forget.

One can hardly rest a serious prognosis on symbol and legend. Still, there is a certain wisdom in these old tales that has not been disproved by the experience of the last two centuries. The Industrial Revolution and the subsequent marriage of science and technology are the climax of millennia of intellectual advance. They have also been an enormous force for good and evil, and there have been moments when the evil has far outweighed the good. Still, the march of knowledge and technique continues, and with it the social and moral travail. No one can be sure that mankind will survive this painful course, especially in an age when man's knowledge of nature has far outstripped his knowledge of himself. Yet we can be sure that man will take this road and not forsake it; for although he has his fears, he also has eternal hope. This, it will be remembered, was the last item in Pandora's box of gifts.

INDEX

Aachen, 134, 137, 141, 171–2, 196
Afghans, 34
Africa, 29, 38, 53, 145, 241, 392, 487; emigrants, 500
Africa, South: wool, 202; gold, 232, 235; imperial, 239, 480
agriculture, 5–6, 8, 115, 119, 129, 155, 187–90, 242, 330, 367, 370, 391–2, 402, 419–20, 500, 538, 550; revolution, 69, 76–7; *see also separate countries*
aircraft, 423
Aix, 51
Albania: 'popular democracy', 492
Albion Mills, 72
alchemy, 26–7
Alexanderson, Ernst, 423, 430
Algeria, 164, 500
alkalis, 110–11, 202, 270–3; United Alkali Co., 247; *see also* ammonia, soda
Allgemeines Deutsche Handelsgesetzbuch, 199
Alliance-Monceau, 465
Allied Control Council, 491, 493–4
Alsace: cotton, 160–1, 163, 168–9, 213, 275
Alsace-Lorraine, 383, 491
aluminium, 287, 325
America, colonial, 22, 35–6, 83–4; Latin, 239, 544; South, 146, 202, 328, 392; *see also* United States of America
American Rolling Mill Co. (Armco), 475
Amiens, 149
ammonia, 196, 268
Amsterdam, 142
Anatolia, 34
Angleur-Athus, 465
Angleur et Charbonnages Belge, 465
animism, 24
Anti-Semitism, 403–4, 416–17, 487
Antwerp, 127, 205, 283
Appalachians, 99
Arago, Dominique, 285
Arco, Georg von, 425
Argentina, 367
aristocracy, 8, 48–9, 550–1
Arkwright, Sir Richard, 85, 140, 345
armaments, 135, 308, 374, 522
Armstrong, Edwin, 423, 430
Arnold, Harold, 426, 518
Arras, 51
artificial fibres, 276, 421, 454–8, 514, 523
assembly line, 305, 307, 442, 449
Aston, Francis, 27, 32–3
Athus, Grivegnée, 465
atomic power, 323
Aufsichtsamt, 380
Augsbrug, 172
Australia: wool, 202; gold, 235; wheat, 367; *also* 328, 480, 487

Austria: industrial development, 135–6, 497, 499, 509; cotton, 148, 215; iron, 148; banks, 155, 207, 375; currency, 200; steam power, 221; price rise, 362; German Customs Union, 374; Great Depression, 375–80; unemployment, 398; Austro-Prussian War, 415; population, 488; World War II, 491; E.F.T.A., 508 n., *also* 8, 245–6, 360, 548
automation, 323
Automobile Manufacturers Association (U.S.A.), 443

Baden, 99, 167
Badevel, 253
Badische Anilin, 275
Baeyer, Adolf von, 274
Baildon, John, 140
Baines, Edward, 211
bakelite, 276
Baku, 281
Baldwins & Guest, 475
Balkans, 33
ball-bearings, 299
Baltic, 200, 360
Ban-Hilāl, 29
Bankers' Industrial Development Co., 474
bankruptcies, 372
banks and banking, 74–5, 155–6, 198, 204–8, 349, 372–4, 381, 389; *see also* Great Depression
Banque, Adam, 382
Banque d'Alsace-Lorraine, 382; de Belgique, 156, 176; Commerciale Africaine, 283; Charpenay, 383; Courvoisier, 383; de France, 206, 377, 381–2, 384–7, 496; Lazard, 450; Nationale de Crédit, 383; Nationale pour le Commerce et l'Industrie, 383; Privée Lyon-Marseille, 383; Syndicale de Paris, 383; de l'Union Parisienne, 383–4; de la Vallée du Rhône, 382
Barclay's Bank, 474
Barker, Charles, 312
Barmer Bankverein, 379
Barrow Haematite Steel Co., 223
Barrow-in-Furness, 228
barter, 392
Basle, 168, 378
Bauwens, 141, 144
Bayernwerke, 437
Beardmore (William) & Co., 473
Bedford, Duke of, 71
Belgium: coal, 139, 156, 216–17, 292–3, 507; economic growth, 141–2, 158, 193–4, 222–3, 236, 497, 499; population, 152, 187; railroads, 153, 196; iron and steel, 156, 176–7, 180, 258–9, 352, 459, 461–7, 477, 480, 541;